ANIMAL KINGDOM

Sandcastle Books

The red fox occurs in many distinct color forms. Below, the vivid, flame-red coloring of most high-latitude red foxes (1); the silver form (2); the "cross fox," with a cross shape on its shoulders (3).

Project Director: Graham Bateman
Project Manager: Derek Hall
Art Editor and Designer: Tony Truscott
Cartographic Editor: Tim Williams
Picture Researcher: Clare Newman
Managing Editor: Tim Harris
Design Manager: Lynne Ross
Production: Alastair Gourlay
Editorial Director: Lindsey Lowe

The Brown Reference Group plc
First Floor
9-17 St. Albans Place
London
N1 0NX
www.brownreference.com

ISBN 978-1-906020-20-0

This edition published by Sandcastle Books Ltd
The Stables
Sheriffs Lench Court
Sheriffs Lenchs
Worcs WR11 4SN
UK

Printed in Thailand

Front cover: Polar Bear.

The acknowledgments on p. 448 form part of this copyright page.

Contributors
David Alderton *(Reptiles)*; Amy-Jane Beer *(Mammals and Invertebrates)*; Andrew Campbell *(Invertebrates)*; David Chandler *(Birds)*; Dominic Couzens *(Birds)*; Valerie Davies *(Reptiles)*; Euan Dunn *(Birds)*; Jonathan Elphick *(Birds)*; Rob Hume *(Birds)*; Mick Loates *(Fish)*; Chris Mattison *(Amphibians and Reptiles)*; Pat Morris *(Mammals)*; Colin Newman *(Fish)*; Derek Niemann *(Birds)*; Denys Ovendon *(Fish)*; Ken Preston-Mafham *(Invertebrates)*; Rod Preston-Mafham *(Invertebrates)*; Tony Whitehead *(Birds)*; John Woodward *(Birds)*

Artists
Graham Allen, Norman Arlott, Priscilla Barrett with Michael Long, Trevor Boyer, Ad Cameron, Robert Gillmor, Peter Harrison, Malcolm McGregor, Sean Milne, Denys Ovenden, Ian Willis

About this book

The living world is divided into five kingdoms, one of which (kingdom Animalia) is the main subject of *Animal Kingdom*. Kingdom Animalia is divided into numerous major groups called phyla, but only one them (Chordata) contains those animals that have a backbone. Chordates, or vertebrates, include all the animals familiar to us and those most studied by scientists—mammals, birds, amphibians, reptiles, and fish. There are about 38,000 species of vertebrates, the most interesting and familiar of which are covered in *Animal Kingdom*. The phyla that contain animals without backbones (so-called invertebrates, such as insects and spiders) include at least 1 million species, probably many more. Some of the most fascinating groups of invertebrates are also featured in this book. Each animal entry has an information panel giving the most important facts and figures about that group or species. Consult the contents section on the following pages to find the animal that you are looking for.

Contents

The female mocker swallowtail of the family Papilionidae (top) bears a remarkable resemblance to the common tiger butterfly, Danaus chrysippus *(family Danaidae), its mimicry model.*

MAMMALS

Giant River Otter	6
Meerkat	8
Lion	14
Tiger	20
Cheetah	26
Gray Wolf	30
Red Fox	34
Polar Bear	38
Giant Panda	44
Spotted Hyena	48
West Indian Manatee	50
Orca (Killer Whale)	54
Blue Whale	58
Mountain Gorilla	62
Chimpanzee	68
Vervet Monkey	74
Golden Lion Tamarin	78
African Elephant	82
Plains Zebra	88
Brazilian Tapir	94
Dromedary Camel	96
American Bison	102
Impala	108
American Beaver	110
Brown Rat	114
African Porcupine	118
Capybara	122
European Rabbit	126
Giant Anteater	132
Nine-banded Armadillo	136
Vampire Bat	140
Red Kangaroo	144
Duck-billed Platypus	150

BIRDS

Ostrich	154
Emperor Penguin	160

The long reach of the secretary bird's strong, well-protected legs allow it to deal with the most dangerous of all prey—venomous snakes. By punching down with its small, sharp-clawed feet, it can trample them to death.

Three of the four living species of tapir: Baird's tapir with young (1); mountain tapir (2); Malayan tapir (3). Along with the Brazilian tapir, these three species are the only surviving members of an ancient family that evolved about 55 million years ago after the extinction of the dinosaurs. Tapirs are more ancient than the horse and rhino families, and were once widespread in Asia, Africa, and the Americas. Fossils and other remains show that today's animals are the sole survivors of what was once a large and successful family group.

Wandering Albatross	**166**
Brown Pelican	**172**
Arctic Tern	**176**
Common Loon	**180**
American Bittern	**186**
Greater Flamingo	**188**
Wood Duck	**194**
Belted Kingfisher	**196**
Osprey	**200**
Bald Eagle	**204**
Tawny Owl	**210**
Barn Swallow	**212**
Mourning Dove	**216**
Budgerigar	**218**
Ruby-throated Hummingbird	**224**
Hawfinch	**228**
Black-capped Chickadee	**230**
Pileated Woodpecker	**236**
Bohemian Waxwing	**242**
Blue Jay	**246**
Scarlet Macaw	**252**
Great Indian Hornbill	**258**
Raggiana Bird of Paradise	**262**
Secretary Bird	**264**
Greater Roadrunner	**270**
AMPHIBIANS	
Axolotl	**276**
Midwife Toad	**280**
Red-eyed Leaf Frogs	**282**
American Bullfrog	**288**

REPTILES

Marine Iguana 294
Gila Monster 300
Komodo Dragon 304
Leatherback Turtle 308
Galápagos Giant Tortoise 312
American Alligator 318
Emerald Tree Boa 324
Sidewinder 328

FISH

Hammerhead Shark 330
Great White Shark 336
Common Stingray 342
Rudd and Roach 344
Marine Hatchetfish 348
Sea Horses 350
Flounders 360
Sunfish 364

INVERTEBRATES

Sponges 368
Jellyfish 374
Sea Anemones 380
Corals 386
Millipedes 392
Dragonflies 398
Earwigs 408
Swallowtail Butterflies 412
Ants 418
Honeybees 436

PICTURE CREDITS 448

After feeding, mountain gorilla groups—like the one above—gather around the silverback to rest in the middle of the day. Females with infants (1) move closest to the silverback (2), while females without young stay farther in the background (3). The juveniles will play close to the silverback under his protective gaze (4), but subadult males are merely tolerated (5).

Giant River Otter

Pteronura brasiliensis

Common name Giant river otter

Scientific name *Pteronura brasiliensis*

Family Mustelidae

Order Carnivora

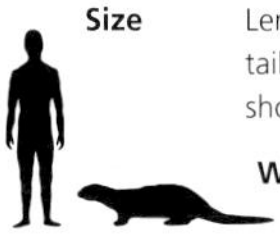

Size Length head/body: 34–55 in (86–140 cm); tail length: 13–39 in (33–100 cm); height at shoulder: 16 in (40 cm)

Weight Male 57–75 lb (26–34 kg); female 48–57 lb (22–26 kg)

Key features Large otter with short, glossy brown fur that looks black when wet; often white or creamy nose and throat; webbed feet; tail tapers and is flattened with a flange along each edge

Habits Lives in family groups, mostly in the water

Breeding Up to 5 young born in a single litter each year after gestation period of 65–70 days. Weaned at 3–4 months; sexually mature at 2 years. May live over 14 years in captivity, possibly similar in the wild

Voice Loud yelps, barks, and whistles; very vocal

Diet Mainly fish, but also freshwater crabs and occasional mammals

Habitat Slow-moving rivers, creeks, and swamps, especially within forested areas

Distribution Once over much of tropical South America south to Argentina; now rare and patchy

Status Population: perhaps fewer than 2,000 left in the wild; IUCN Endangered; CITES I

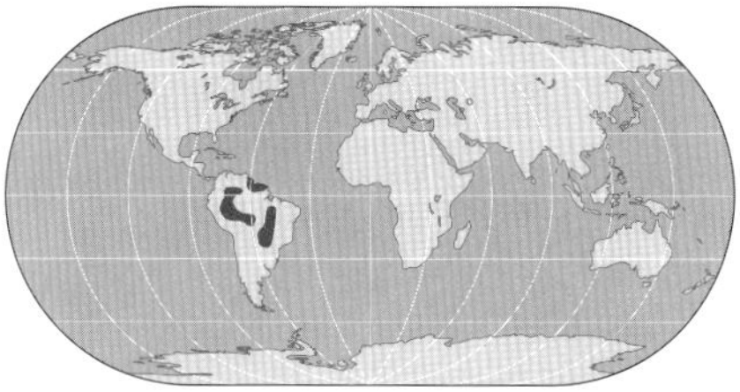

The giant river otters of South America have been severely reduced in numbers as a result of hunting for their fur. They also suffer from habitat damage, but fortunately, small populations survive in protected areas.

GIANT RIVER OTTERS LIVE IN family groups of six to eight animals, although sometimes there can be as many as 20 individuals living together. Groups usually consist of a mated pair, along with their young born that year and often a few animals from the previous year as well. Giant otters are the most sociable of all the world's otter species. They stay close together, often calling loudly to each other or indulging in play. The adult male and female often share the same den, a habit that is not seen in the more familiar river otters of the Northern Hemisphere. Giant otters are also believed to help each other by driving shoals of fish into shallow water where they can be caught more easily. They usually feed on slow-moving species, such as catfish, which are easy to catch. Some such fish can be over 2 feet (60 cm) long.

Coveted Fur

The giant river otter is the largest of the freshwater otter species, and has a distinctive flattened tail. As with other types of otter, the fur is dense and helps protect the animal from getting cold when in the water. However, the giant otter's fur is very distinctive, being short and glossy, like velvet. It became particularly sought after in the 1960s when wearing furs was very fashionable. Native hunters could earn more money by selling a single giant otter skin than they would get in their pay packets for working hard as laborers for two or three months. The same skin would be worth five

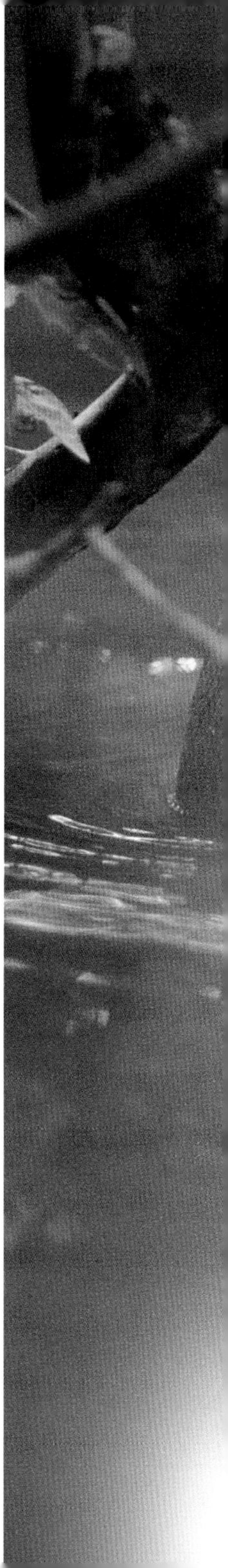

↑ *The giant river otter of South America is the most sociable of all the otter species—a characteristic that has sadly helped decimate populations. Nowadays it is a rare sight.*

times as much in the fur trade after processing. Financial rewards provided a major incentive for hunters to kill otters, and in the 1950s over a thousand giant otter skins were exported each year from Peru alone. Since otters reproduce slowly, with only a single litter each year, breeding rates were not enough to keep up with such high levels of loss.

Giant otters are mainly active during the daytime and so expose themselves to many dangers, particularly from humans with spears or guns. Giant otters are also very vocal, frequently calling to each other using a wide range of squeals, barks, and whistles. Their noise draws attention to them and makes it easier for hunters to locate and kill whole family groups. Another fatal characteristic is that giant otters are very curious animals: They often swim around with their heads held high out of the water to keep an eye on their surroundings—a habit that makes them easy to shoot. They will often swim toward intruders and potentially dangerous situations to investigate more closely—again making it easier to shoot them and to kill others of the group that stay around to see what has happened.

A Host of Threats

As huge areas of the South American forests were opened up for logging, new roads and tracks made it much easier to reach places that had otherwise been remote retreats for the giant otter. Gold mining has been a problem, too: Large amounts of cyanide and other poisonous pollutants have been released into the rivers where the otters live. Dredging for gold also makes rivers very muddy, which severely reduces the fish populations needed by the otters. People fish the rivers, too, removing still more of the otter's food supply.

It is little wonder that giant otter populations collapsed, and soon the species seemed to be heading for early extinction. Trade was banned in 1970, but there was considerable black market activity, and skins were smuggled through countries where law enforcement was slack. Nowadays otter skins are not fashionable, so the market no longer richly rewards hunters for killing the animals. Fortunately, giant otters are still fairly numerous in the Pantanal (bordering Brazil and Paraguay) and in parts of Peru. Some of the best habitats are relatively secure in national parks, and today the giant river otter enjoys full legal protection.

Meerkat

Suricata suricatta

A meerkat sentry is a familiar sight on the southern African savanna, demonstrating the selfless and cooperative behavior of this plucky mongoose species toward members of its own pack.

Common name Meerkat (suricate, gray meerkat, slender-tailed meerkat)

Scientific name *Suricata suricatta*

Family Herpestidae

Order Carnivora

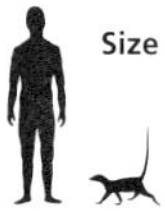

Size Length head/body: 12–18 in (30–45 cm); tail length: 6–12 in (15–30 cm); height at shoulder: 4 in (10 cm)

Weight 3.3–5 lb (1.5–2.3 kg)

Key features Slender, short-legged animal; tan to gray with broken brown bands on back and sides; black eye rings, ears, and tail tip

Habits Social: lives in colonies of up to 30, but usually 10–15, animals; sentries posted to watch for predators while colony is foraging

Breeding Two to 5 young born after gestation period of 75 days. Weaned at 9–10 weeks; sexually mature at about 12 months. May live 13 years in captivity, up to 10 in the wild, but more commonly 6

Voice A variety of chirrups, trills, growls, and barks

Diet Insects, scorpions, and grubs; occasionally lizards, small snakes, birds, and mice

Habitat Dry savanna, open plains, and scrubland

Distribution Southern Africa in Angola, Namibia, South Africa, and southern Botswana

Status Population: abundant. Not threatened, but numbers have fallen in some areas

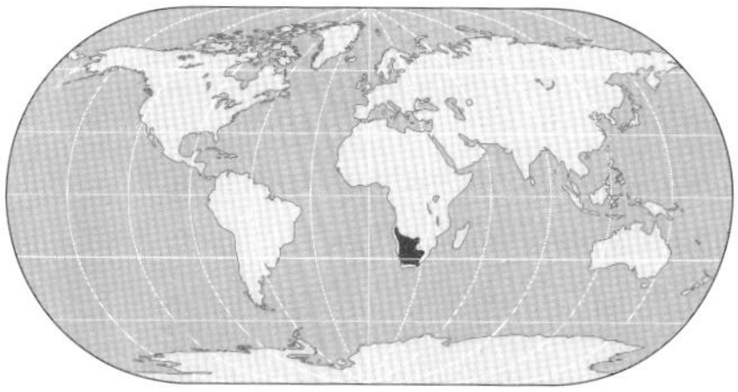

MEERKATS ARE THE MOST SOCIABLE members of the mongoose family. They live in packs, which may include several breeding pairs. The female of a breeding pair may be larger than the male and may dominate him. However, no distinct hierarchies have been observed in meerkat packs, and group members are rarely aggressive toward each other. All group members take part in the various tasks involved in pack life, such as baby-sitting, tunnel maintenance, and sentry duty. Both females and males without young of their own will help guard and provide food for other meerkats' young. Some females will produce milk even if they have not been pregnant and will suckle other females' babies.

Juvenile Followers

Meerkats breed throughout the year, but most births occur during the warmer, wetter months. Young meerkats begin to take adult food when they are about three to four weeks old. Toward the end of weaning the young begin to follow the rest of the group. While adult meerkats are reluctant to share food with each other, they will often give food to juvenile members of the group, even if they are not their own offspring. Each youngster will associate itself with a particular adult and follow it around, begging food from it. The adult will pass on its best-quality prey to its follower, who will not only be fed, but will also learn how to behave as a meerkat. When the young start following, the juvenile meerkats from earlier litters may get confused between begging for food from adults and giving food to the new arrivals: Adolescent meerkats have been seen to beg food from an adult only to pass it onto young from the next litter, or to give food to a youngster, then steal

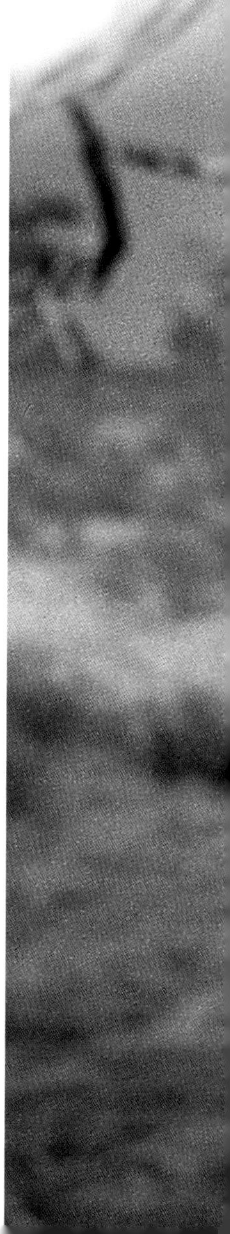

it back again. Meerkat life is complicated, but also highly social.

Meerkats have strong, muscular forelimbs with large claws, which make them excellent diggers. Their long, slender, short-legged bodies are perfect for traveling inside underground tunnels. Although they are quite capable of digging their own burrows (or warrens), meerkats often share dens with African ground squirrels or yellow mongooses. In such cases the dens are usually dug by the ground squirrels, and the meerkats move in later. Neither species appears to object to the presence of the other—in fact, the meerkats ignore the ground squirrels altogether.

Underground Refuge

Meerkat warrens typically cover an area about 16 feet (5 m) across and, depending on ground conditions, may have up to three levels, with the deepest tunnels about 10 feet (3 m) below the surface. The largest warrens may have up to 90 entrances, but about 15 entrance holes are more usual. Within the warren a series of tunnels connects chambers of about 12 inches (30 cm) across. Meerkats usually stay within easy reach of a warren, which is their main refuge from predators. The temperature in deeper tunnels may vary by only a degree or two, making the warrens important shelters from the extreme desert temperatures above ground. Meerkats spend nighttime within their warrens—the coldest parts of winter days and the hottest parts of summer days are spent inside too. The territory of a meerkat group may be up to 6 square miles (15 sq. km) and will contain five or six warrens, occupied in rotation. Meerkats spend from a few days to several months around one warren, moving on when the surrounding food supply has been used up.

A meerkat pack is very protective of its territory. Marking of territories using scent from

A male meerkat on guard duty in the Kalahari Desert, southern Africa. Sentries are posted in high places to watch out for predators while the group is foraging.

Dicing with Death

Meerkats will take on venomous snakes much larger than themselves—either as a potential source of food or in order to rid their den sites of lurking predators. Members of the mongoose family in general have a higher resistance to snake venom than humans, and meerkats are no exception. However, it is the speed and skill of their attack that usually prevents the animals from getting bitten. Meerkats are also particularly fond of scorpions and can withstand stings strong enough to kill a human being.

the anal glands is generally performed by the males. If a rival pack is spotted entering the territory, it will first be approached in a threatening manner. If the threat does not discourage the trespassing group, the two packs may end up in a fight, often led by the largest male. All members of the pack except the young will take part. Once the fight is won or lost, the two packs separate. Low-ranking males from the winning side may take the opportunity to improve their breeding status by chasing off the losing males and taking over both their territory and their females.

Takeover Bids

All meerkats reaching maturity within a group have the problem of establishing themselves as breeding animals. Some males may form bachelor groups that roam around without a territory, sometimes attacking established packs in an attempt to drive out the resident males and take over their females.

Young female meerkats may also group together to leave their parent pack, often meeting up with bachelor male groups and forming packs of their own. Dominant females may try to stop the young females from leaving, since they do not want to lose their helpful baby-sitters. Females may also try to join an established group, although it may take a long time to be accepted. One lone female followed a pack for two weeks until an established female gave birth, and the lone female was taken on as a baby-sitter. She was forced to continue her role for several weeks, with little time for foraging, before attacks on her became less severe, and she was fully accepted into the pack.

Safety in Numbers

Meerkats take a different foraging route every day. They usually allow about a week before returning to an area to enable their food sources to be replenished. The clawed muscular front arms are used to dig out prey and to hold larger animals, such as lizards and mice. Like other social mongooses, meerkats feed as a group, but spread out to forage and do not cooperate in looking for food. The group provides protection against predators; but since the meerkats' own prey is small, there is no point in hunting together in order to bring down large animals. There are some exceptions, however. For example, if a meerkat gets the scent of a large gecko, it will accept the help of another animal to dig the lizard out of its burrow. Although it may take half an hour to uncover the gecko, the effort is worthwhile,

Meerkats take part in the communal digging of a den. Although meerkats are quite capable of digging their own dens, they often move into dens dug by African ground squirrels. Neither animal seems to mind the communal living arrangement.

since geckoes are big and often live in pairs. The meerkats will cooperate in this situation since each is guaranteed a good meal.

Foraging in a group reduces the danger of any one meerkat being caught by a predator, since it is more likely an attacker will be spotted by a group of meerkats than by a single animal. Safety is further improved since guards are posted in high places to keep watch over the foraging group. When it spots a predator, the sentry gives an alarm call that tells the rest of the pack to run for cover. Meerkats cannot concentrate on foraging and watch for predators at the same time. Therefore the more time a meerkat spends looking out for predators, the less time will be available for feeding. By foraging in a group, individual animals can find more food and will be healthier than animals foraging alone.

Sentry Duty

By performing guard duty, a sentry meerkat is sacrificing valuable feeding time. Its position on high points, such as rocks or bushes, also exposes it to danger from predators and heat stroke. Being a sentry is a job done on behalf of the group, but the animals take turns and share the risk. Meerkats that remain behind baby-sitting young at the den will not leave to feed themselves. Since many members of the meerkat team perform such "selfless" tasks, it could encourage an individual to take advantage of the help given by others. However, such behavior is not tolerated in a meerkat pack. For example, it was observed that during a fight with a rival pack a female member of a meerkat group was seen lazing in the shade rather than helping her companions. After the pack had chased off the intruders, they turned on the idle female—seemingly as a punishment for her selfish behavior.

As well as foraging in a group and having sentries, meerkats have other antipredator defenses. Like the banded mongoose, meerkats make mob attacks against animals that are potential threats—such as snakes and jackals. In encounters with predators or other meerkat gangs individuals make themselves look more imposing by raising their tails vertically, arching their backs, making their hair stand on end, and growling and spitting like a cat. If the meerkat's tactics do not work and it is threatened by a predator, it will take up the classic mongoose defense position: It will throw itself on its back, so protecting the sensitive nape of the neck, with teeth and claws facing the predator. The

(↑) A meerkat "helper" acts as a baby-sitter for young animals. Meerkats are the most social of the mongooses, and members of the pack will take turns performing group duties such as baby-sitting and tunnel maintenance.

bushy tail with hairs standing up may be placed over the belly and head. An attack from the sky by an eagle or hawk causes the meerkats to run for cover. If a pack is attacked in the open, away from their warren, the adults will throw themselves over the juvenile members of the pack to protect them. Like banded mongooses, if a member of the pack is captured, the others will launch a rescue attempt.

Nursing Care

If a member of the pack is left injured after an attack, it may be nursed back to health by the other members. A female meerkat that had been caught and injured by an eagle was observed being surrounded by her pack and helped back to the warren. The female had produced a litter of kittens a few days earlier and was left with them in the burrow while the rest of the pack went to forage. She was fed with grubs by the other members of her pack and was also helped to stand upright during the morning sunbathing session. Thanks to the support of the group both the female and her litter survived. Invalid care is only performed for adult meerkats, since the loss of a baby is less damaging to the group than that of an adult.

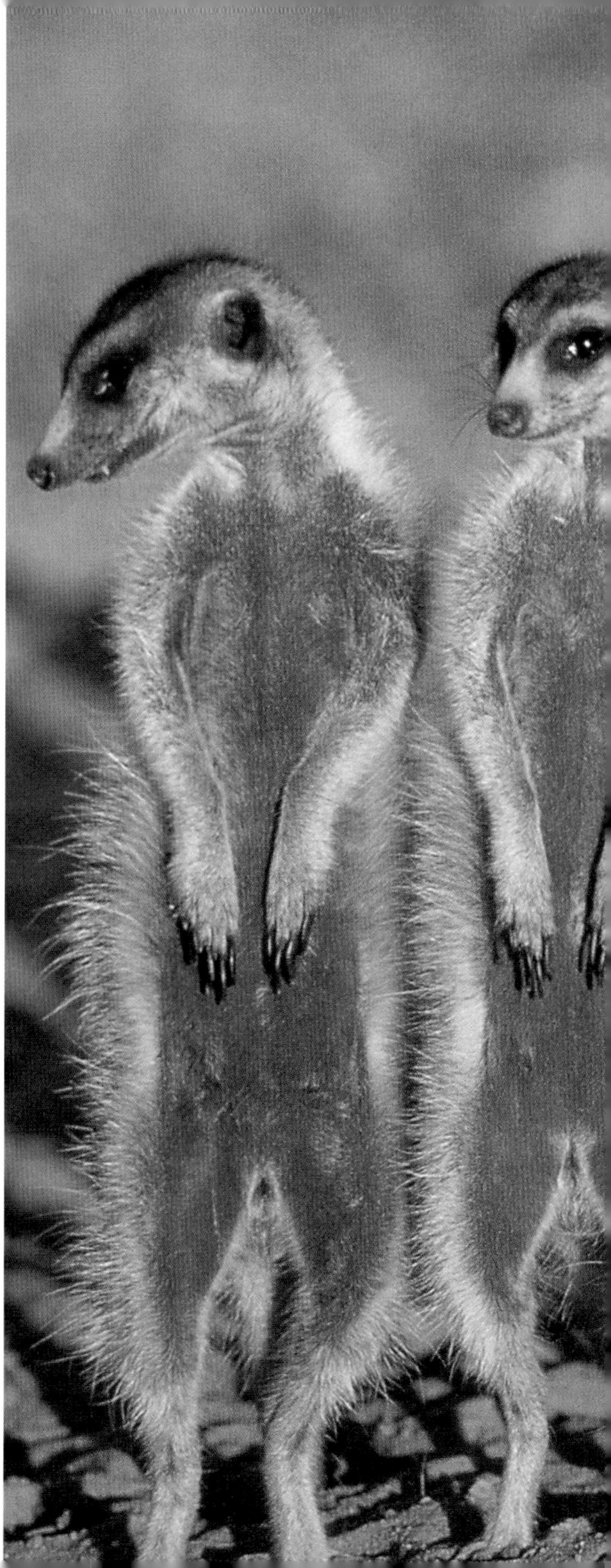

A meerkat group basks in the morning sunshine. Meerkats need to sunbathe each day to keep themselves at the correct body temperature.

Sun Worshipping

Along with underground dens and group nesting, sunbathing plays an important part in keeping meerkats at their correct body temperature. When they leave the burrow, members sit or stand in an upright position with their stomachs facing the sun. They may then lie down and bask on their backs or spread themselves over rocks to absorb heat. During the hottest part of the day, however, they retreat to the coolness of their underground burrows or lie over damp patches of shady ground.

Lion

Panthera leo

Common name Lion

Scientific name *Panthera leo*

Family Felidae

Order Carnivora

Size Length head/body: 5–8 ft (1.4–2.5 m); tail length: 27.5–41 in (70–105 cm); height at shoulder: 42–48 in (107–123 cm). Male 20–50% bigger than female

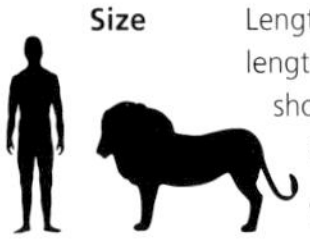

Weight 265–550 lb (120–250 kg)

Key features Huge, muscular cat with long, thin tail tipped with black tuft; body light buff to tawny brown; male develops thick mane of dark fur; head large with powerful, crushing jaws; eyes yellowish-brown

Habits Lives in prides; hunts alone and cooperatively; most active between dusk and dawn; rests up to 21 hours per day

Breeding One to 6 cubs (average 3–4) born after gestation period of 100–119 days. Weaned at 6–7 months; sexually mature at 3–4 years. May live up to 30 years in captivity, rarely more than 13 in the wild

Voice Variety of puffs, grunts, snarls, and roars

Diet Large mammal prey, including antelope, giraffe, zebra, hogs, and buffalo; also carrion

Habitat Savanna grasslands, open woodlands, desert margins, and scrub

Distribution Scattered populations in sub-Saharan Africa; population in Gir Forest, northwestern India

Status Population: several thousand; IUCN Vulnerable; CITES II. Asian lions fewer than 300; IUCN Endangered; CITES I. Declining outside protected areas

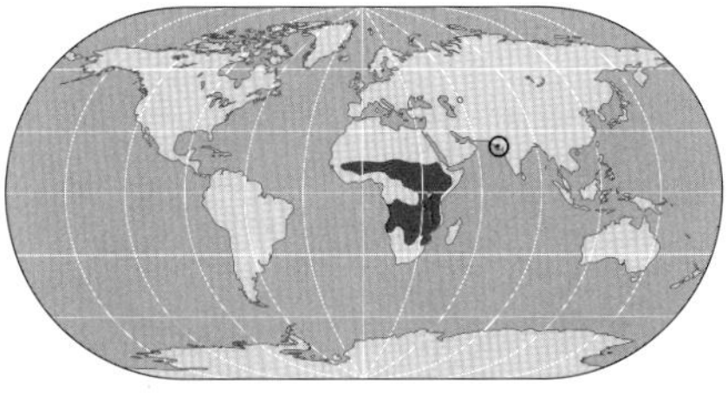

Lions are by far the most social of the cats, breeding and hunting in large family groups. The male, with his magnificent mane, is much larger than the female, but lionesses are the superior hunters.

The lion has always been regarded with awe. It is enshrined in the myths and legends of many cultures, and its popular image as the King of Beasts goes back to ancient times.

Widespread

Fossil evidence and cave paintings show that lions were once among the world's most widespread land-dwelling animals, second only to humans. During the Pleistocene era (2 million to 10,000 years ago) there were lions not only in Africa but throughout Eurasia and the Americas. The American and northern European varieties went extinct after the last ice age as forests grew up and human hunters advanced, depleting stocks of the lion's main prey. In southern Europe and the Middle East lions lasted a lot longer. The Greek scholar and philosopher Aristotle wrote about lions in 300 BC, and the Romans made grisly sport of pitting the animals against Christians condemned to death. Such lions were captured in North Africa, but the species is now extinct there. Lions were relatively common in the Middle East 500 years ago, and some survived there until as recently as the early 1900s.

Lions have been killed for a variety of reasons, including sport and self-defense. They are not instinctive man-eaters, but they will resort to attacking livestock and people if the availability of natural prey such as deer or antelope is reduced. Lions can become a serious threat to people involved in farming or other activities that bring humans into lion country. One pair of lions reportedly killed and ate 124 people in Uganda in 1925. The victims were

*(↑) **Lionesses and cubs keep a close watch on a resting rhinoceros. A rhinoceros can defend itself with the use of its deadly horns, and the lionesses are cautious of approaching.***

Asian Lions

The only wild lions living outside Africa today survive in the Gir Forest, a tiny pocket of protected land in northwestern India. They belong to a distinctive and highly threatened subspecies, *Panthera leo persica*, known as the Asian lion.

Asian lions differ from their African cousins in that the males have a much shorter mane, which does not cover the ears or chest. Both sexes have a fold of skin running lengthwise along the belly.

The decline of the Asian lion was largely a result of persecution by humans. In the days of the British Raj shooting lions was a popular pastime. Marksmen showed their hunting prowess by making hundreds of kills. The population dropped to an all-time low of fewer than 100 animals at the start of the 20th century, by which time the Asian lion had been declared a protected animal.

An Asian lion and lioness. Asian lions belong to a separate subspecies from African lions.

There are currently 120 or so Asian lions living in captivity around the world. While there may be enough to prevent their extinction, the future of Asian lions in the wild is far from secure. The Gir Forest Reserve is now too small for the 250 or so lions that live there. In times of prey shortage they resort to attacking livestock; some have even become man-eaters. Between 1988 and 1991 Gir lions killed 20 people. It is not surprising that suggestions to release some to other reserves in India have met with stiff opposition.

working on the construction of a new railway, a project that eventually had to be abandoned. Today in Africa humans and lions get along much better because most lions now live in large conservation areas such as the great national parks of Kenya, Tanzania, and southern Africa. Here they have the space and prey they need to survive without attacking people, and they contribute to the local economy by attracting fee-paying tourists.

About 20 percent of African lions are nomadic. They live in small groups, the members of which come and go. They wander over a huge area, following migratory herds of antelope and zebra. Nomadic lions are nonterritorial, and most encounters are nonaggressive. However, most lions live in resident prides, jealously guarding the same territory for generations.

Boundary Patrol

Defense of the territory is usually done by the males, but the whole pride helps define the boundaries by roaring, scent marking with urine, and regular patrolling. The size of a pride's home range varies considerably, depending on the number of animals in the pride and the local abundance of prey. If food is scarce for part of the year, a pride will range over a much larger area. The ranges of neighboring prides may overlap to an extent, but individual lions usually take care to avoid each other. An intruder in the core part of a pride's range will be driven off ferociously.

The need to defend a territory is the main reason why male lions are so much larger than females, up to half as big again in some cases. They need to be big to chase off rivals. Two competing males will size each other up before fighting, and the inferior male will usually back down and go away without a fight. This reduces the risk of these big and well-equipped

The roar of a lion can be heard over distances of up to 5 miles (8 km) and is used to define boundaries and warn off rivals. Lions also roar after devouring a kill.

Vocal Communication

Lions have a varied repertoire of vocalizations. The various sounds are distinctive and are usually accompanied by body language that makes their meaning obvious, even to humans. Members of a pride use a gentle huffing sound to greet and reassure each other, while purring communicates contentment (for example, when being groomed). Mewing sounds are used mostly by cubs and vary from short squeaks of excitement to yowls of distress. Growls and snarls are warning sounds, while charging lions often give a gruff coughing sound. A "woofing" grunt signifies surprise and is often followed by a sharp hissing or spitting to show displeasure. The best-known lion vocalization is, of course, the roar. Males start roaring from the age of one year, females slightly later. A full-blown roar can easily be heard up to 5 miles (8 km) away, and the sound is used to define territorial boundaries and to intimidate rivals. Roaring in chorus enhances the bonds between pride members. Most roaring happens at night.

animals fatally wounding each other. However, there is a definite home advantage; the resident males are more confident and quicker to launch an attack, so they usually win any contest.

The mane is an important factor in male aggression. For a start, a male with a huge mane may be able to fool opponents into believing that he is more powerful than he actually is. If the bluff does not work and a fight ensues, the mane helps protect the vulnerable area around the neck and throat from slashing claws and teeth. The now extinct Barbary lion, a subspecies that lived in North Africa until 1920, had a huge mane that extended well down its back and under its belly.

Female Hunters

The adult male members of a pride do little hunting. Males are capable of catching their own food, but they are rarely as good at it as the females. A large male with a bulky mane will find it difficult to remain inconspicuous, while a slim lioness can creep forward with her body pressed flat to the ground, making use of even very sparse cover. The chances of making

A lioness with her cubs. The boisterous rough-and-tumble games of the cubs are tolerated by all members of the pride, since everybody is closely related. Cubs are even allowed to suckle from any female in the group. At less than a year the young cubs will join the lionesses in the hunt, but they are usually more of a hindrance than a help!

Social Creatures

Lions are by far the most social of the cats. While some individuals live alone, a solitary lifestyle is the exception rather than the rule and loners are usually old males that have been ousted from a pride. Such animals rarely live long.

Lion prides are based on a group of related females, including sisters, daughters, mothers, and grandmothers, most of whom stay with the pride throughout their lives. Females will only be required to leave if the pride gets too big. In such cases small groups splinter off and try to start their own pride. The adult males of the pride are not permanent. In fact, they rarely last more than three or four years before they are displaced by younger, stronger animals. Young males are forced to leave the pride in which they were born at about the time they reach puberty (two to three years of age).

Males often team up to defend a pride. Such coalitions almost always consist of related males (brothers or cousins). On taking over a pride, by killing or driving out the previous males, the first priority is getting the females pregnant. Because female lions cannot breed while they are still suckling young cubs, the males usually kill any cubs younger than about 24 months. Older cubs (especially females approaching breeding age) may escape with their lives, but young males are rarely permitted to remain. The pride females are more inclined to defend older cubs in which they have invested a great deal of care; but on the whole they seem to accept the loss of their cubs and a new boss, and get on with raising a new family.

A receptive female may mate 50 or more times in 24 hours, usually, but not always, with the same male. When the cubs arrive three or four months later, they are usually allowed to suckle from any female, and their boisterous games are tolerated and even encouraged by all members of the pride. This extraordinary benevolence stems from the fact that the members of the pride are closely related. An adult male cannot be sure that the cubs are his offspring, but most will carry his genes and be worth nurturing.

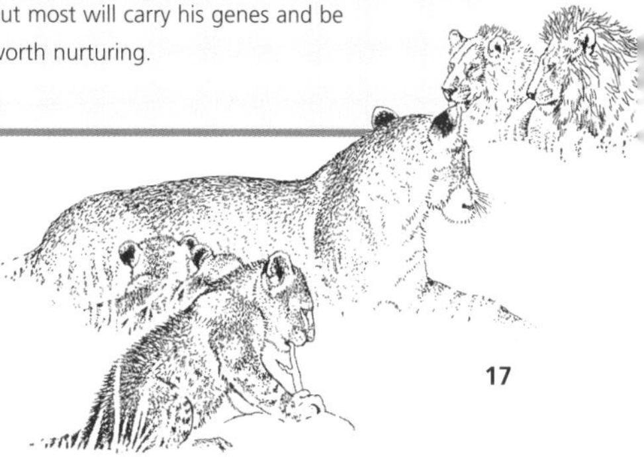

a kill increase when lionesses hunt together. They are highly organized, with different lionesses taking on specialized roles. One female usually takes the lead, selecting the target and signaling the start of the hunt. The fastest females do the chasing, while others ambush and disable the prey. Sometimes the whole pride will join in, fanning out and surrounding the victim. Excitable young cubs are often of little help, but by the age of one year they can make a useful contribution.

Surprise Attack

The lion's hunting technique is all about stealth and surprise. It can run up to 38 miles per hour (60 km/h), but only for short distances. To catch a fleet-footed target such as an impala or zebra, lions need to be within 50 yards (46 m) before launching an attack. They do not usually jump on top of their prey. Instead, they try to knock it off balance with a mighty swipe of the front feet aimed at the prey's flank or rump. Once the prey has been pulled down, the lion clamps its mouth over the throat or muzzle, killing by strangulation or suffocation. The lion can breathe deeply through its nose, so it can keep a tight hold of the prey for as long as necessary, even after a hard chase.

Scavengers

Only about a quarter of hunts are successful, and lions also feed by scavenging. In fact, for some prides four out of five meals are stolen from hyenas, a statistic that contradicts the long-held belief that hyenas routinely harass lions and scavenge their kills. It is actually the opportunist lions that use their superior size and strength to drive the hyenas away.

If the carcass is large, the pride will share the food fairly amicably. On smaller kills there is a definite order of seniority. The males feed first, and young cubs go last. If food is scarce, the cubs are the first to starve.

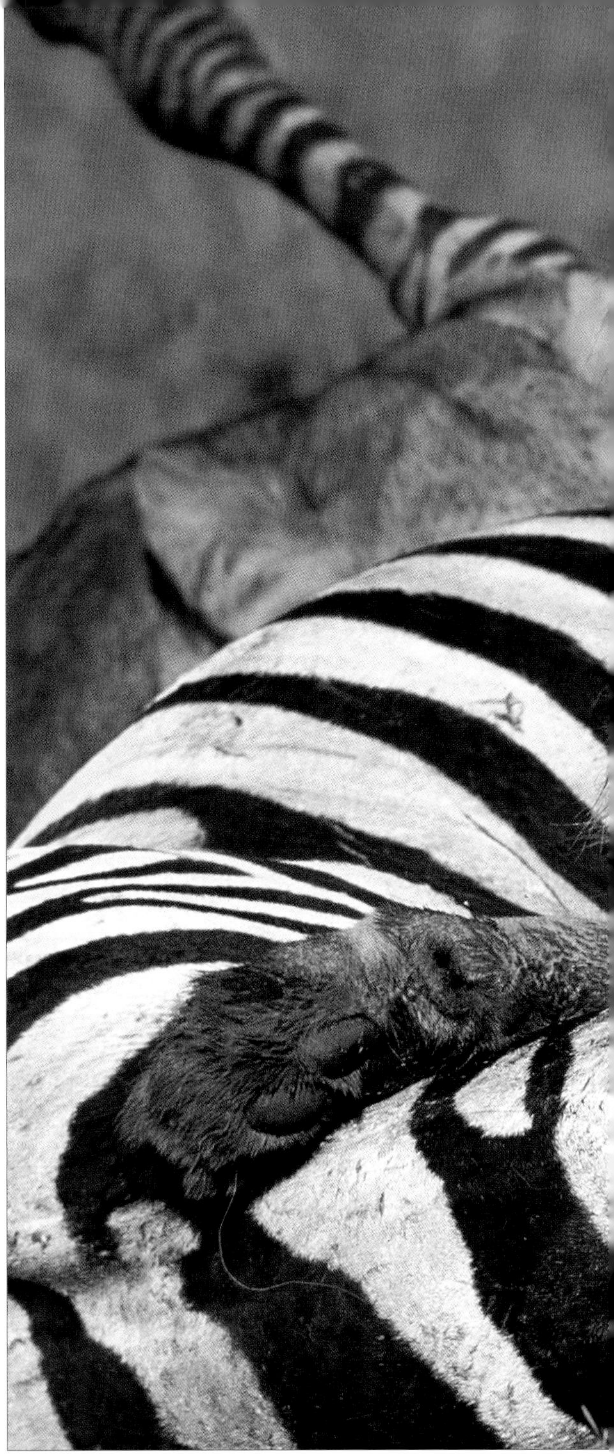

An adult lion needs to eat an average of 11 to 15 pounds (5 to 7 kg) of meat a day. Males get a good share of a kill, even if they have not participated in the hunt.

Tiger

Panthera tigris

The tiger, with its black-and-orange striped coat, is one of the most distinctive of all mammals. It is feared the world over, but nowadays the species is severely reduced in numbers.

Common name Tiger

Scientific name *Panthera tigris*

Family Felidae

Order Carnivora

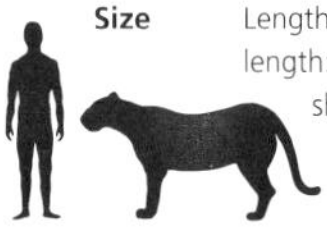

Size Length head/body: 4.6–9 ft (1.4–2.7 m); tail length: 23–43 in (60–110 cm); height at shoulder: 31–43 in (80–110 cm)

Weight Male 200–660 lb (90–300 kg); female 143–364 lb (65–165 kg)

Key features Huge, highly muscular cat with large head and long tail; unmistakable orange coat with dark stripes; underside white

Habits Solitary and highly territorial; active mostly at night; climbs and swims well

Breeding Litters of 1–6 (usually 2 or 3) cubs born at any time of year after gestation period of 95–110 days. Weaned at 3–6 months; females sexually mature at 3–4 years, males at 4–5 years. May live up to 26 years in captivity, rarely more than 10 in the wild

Voice Purrs, grunts, and blood-curdling roars

Diet Mainly large, hooved mammals, including deer, buffalo, antelope, and gaur

Habitat Tropical forests and swamps; grasslands with good vegetation cover and water nearby

Distribution India, Bhutan, Bangladesh, Nepal; China; southeastern Siberia; Myanmar (Burma), Vietnam, Laos, Thailand, and Sumatra

Status Population: 5,000–7,500; IUCN Endangered; CITES I. Previously hunted for fur and body parts, and to protect people and livestock

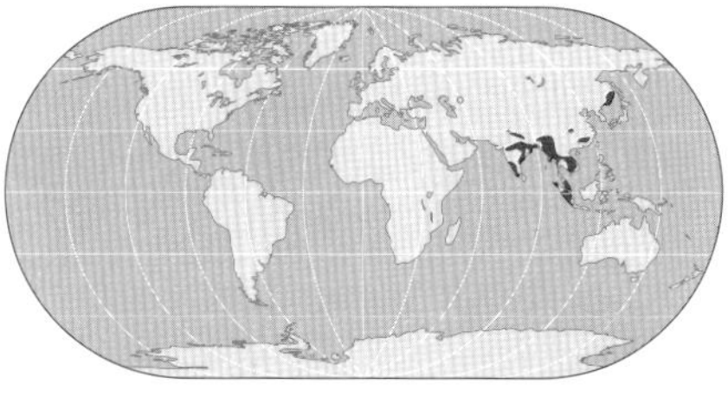

IN MANY WAYS THE TIGER IS MORE deserving of the title King of Beasts than its close cousin, the lion. It is the largest of all the cats, and its range once extended from the fringes of Europe eastward to Russia's Sea of Okhotsk and south to the Indonesian islands of Java and Bali. Tigers from different parts of this vast range differ considerably, so the species has been divided into eight subspecies. They are named after the region in which they occur, but most can also be distinguished by their appearance. For example, Siberian tigers are consistently bigger than other subspecies, with males weighing up to 660 pounds (300 kg). This almost certainly makes them the biggest cats ever to have lived, including huge extinct species such as the saber-toothed tiger and the cave lion.

⊖ A Bengal tiger wades through water. Tigers are proficient swimmers and can cross rivers that are 4 to 5 miles (7 to 8 km) wide without difficulty.

Different Adaptations

The smallest tigers came from Bali and rarely exceeded 220 pounds (100 kg) in weight. They are now probably extinct. As a general rule, body size relates to the climate and the type of prey available in different parts of the tiger's range. Siberian tigers need to cope with intensely cold and snowy winters, and specialize in catching large prey such as cattle and deer. In contrast, tigers in Indonesia inhabit tropical jungle where overheating is a serious problem for large animals, and the favored prey includes pigs and small deer. The Chinese tiger is thought to be the ancestor of the other types. Fossils show that tigers first appeared in China about 2 million years ago, and they spread north, south, and west from there. Modern Chinese tigers have several traits that zoologists consider rather primitive, including a shortened skull and relatively close-set eyes.

⊕ Juvenile tigers are fond of play fighting, like the two below.

Subtle differences aside, all tigers have the same adaptations to a predatory way of life. They have long hind limbs that enable them to cover up to 30 feet (10 m) in a single bound. Their forelegs are immensely powerful and armed with long claws that can be retracted when the tiger is walking. The tiger uses this combination to deadly effect when hunting. It usually rushes prey from behind, either knocking it to the ground with the force of its charge or hooking its claws into the rump or flank and dragging the animal over. Smaller prey is dispatched with a bite to the neck. The tiger's canine teeth are long, sharp, and slightly

The Disappearing Tiger

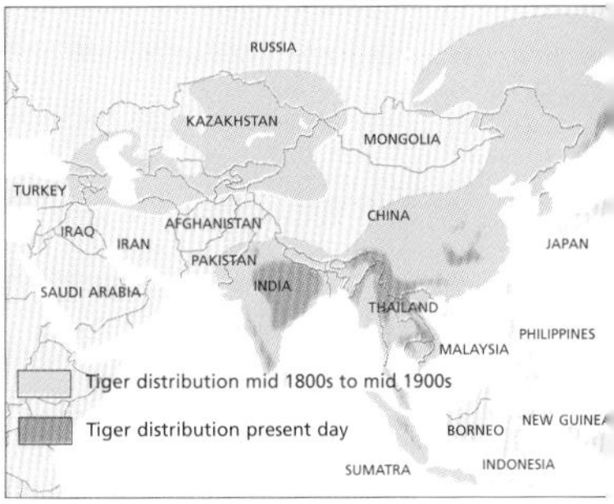

The decline in range and numbers of the magnificent tiger is well documented. Logging and the expansion of agriculture have removed huge areas of tiger habitat. Hunting has also reduced tiger numbers substantially. Of the eight recognized subspecies of tiger the Caspian, Bali, and Javan tigers have become extinct in the last 50 years. Siberian and Chinese tigers are listed by the IUCN as Critically Endangered, and the Sumatran, Indochinese, and Bengal tigers are listed as Endangered.

All tigers are supposed to be protected by international law, but even in some national parks and reserves illegal hunting continues. The biggest threat is the demand for tiger body parts for use in traditional Asian medicine. In the past the main culprits were the Chinese, who have hunted their own wild tigers to virtual extinction. Today tigers are hunted by poachers everywhere. Body parts are then smuggled into China, where they are turned into pills and potions, many of which are exported and sold on the black market for vast sums. Some, such as ground bone to treat rheumatism, can be bought in Asian communities the world over. Demand remains high, despite the lack of scientific evidence that they actually do any good.

Man-Eaters

Tigers are among the few animals known to frequently prey on people. Some tigers even seem to prefer human flesh over that of other species. Sometimes tiger predation has taken a huge toll on human life. For example, over 1,000 people a year were killed in Singapore in the 1940s, 1,000 a year in India in the 1970s, and even now about 100 a year in the Sundarbans mangrove forest near Calcutta. However, these alarming statistics actually relate to comparatively few tigers. Tigers are not born man-eaters; but it seems that once they have made a kill (perhaps after an accidental encounter), some realize the potential of the alternative food source and then exploit it. After all, an unarmed human cannot run fast and is relatively easy to kill. However, most tigers are wary of people and under normal circumstances will avoid any contact. Problem tigers are most common in places where human activity has encroached on their habitat, reducing the availability of natural prey and introducing alternatives such as domestic animals and people themselves.

flattened, and can separate the bones in a victim's spine with ease. A larger animal is more of a challenge; but once it is on the ground, a tiger kills it with a long, suffocating bite around the throat. Even when mortally wounded, a large animal like a gaur could kill a tiger with its flailing hooves, so the tiger maintains the throat bite long after the animal stops struggling, just to be sure it is really dead. It then drags the carcass under some kind of cover before feeding. An adult tiger can eat over 90 pounds (40 kg) of meat in one meal, but with a large kill the tiger is more likely to eat smaller quantities at intervals over the next few days. Sometimes several tigers are seen feeding from one carcass, but they are usually members of the same family.

Necessary Requirements

Although the tiger can live in a variety of habitats, it is restricted to environments that meet three vital requirements: There must be plenty of suitable prey, enough dense cover to allow the tiger to approach prey, and a reliable source of water. Areas of suitable habitat must also be large if they are to support a viable population of tigers. As a general rule tigers live alone, and animals of the same sex tend not to occupy the same range. The size of home ranges varies greatly from place to place, with males in Nepal typically claiming 8 to 40 square miles (20 to 100 sq. km). Male Siberian tigers, on the other hand, may range over 1,600 square miles (4,000 sq. km). Females occupy

A leaping Bengal tiger. Tigers have long hind limbs that enable them to leap up to 30 feet (10 m) in a single bound, helping them bring down prey.

A tiger needs to attack prey from quite close range. It usually rushes a victim from behind, aiming its claws for the shoulder, back, or neck.

much smaller ranges; typically three or four females live within the range of one male, and he can mate with them all.

Tigers tend not to defend territories fiercely, and fights over land are unusual. Nonresident animals seem to respect the owner's rights. Although they may pass through each other's ranges, they do not stay long and keep out of the way. Resident tigers, especially males, visit all parts of their range regularly, leaving scent marks on trees and other landmarks. The marks not only let other tigers know the area is occupied, they also carry information about the individual that made them, such as its sex and reproductive condition. Scent marks fade; and if they are not replaced within three or four weeks, another tiger may attempt to move in. In the case of males this usually means the original resident has died, although females may lose distant parts of their range while they are confined to a small area by the birth of their cubs.

A white Bengal tiger. All white tigers in captivity are descendants of a white male captured in India in 1951.

White Tigers

There is a rare variety of tiger that lacks the pigment which gives other tigers their characteristic orange coat. The dark stripes are still there, but the coat is otherwise creamy-white. Likewise, the tiger's eyes lack brown pigments and are pale blue. Not surprisingly, such animals have always been considered very special, so much so that they have apparently been eliminated from the wild by hunters and collectors. The last record of a wild white tiger was in 1958. Since then, however, many white specimens have been bred in captivity, and there are currently about 40 in zoos around the world.

Fighting is rare among tigers, but those spats that do occur are more often than not between females with cubs and unfamiliar males. Rearing cubs is the sole responsibility of the females, who are ferocious in defense of their young; a spirited attack may be enough to drive even a large male away. When a male takes over a new range, he will often attempt to kill any young cubs in the area. This is so that the females come into breeding condition sooner, and he can begin fathering offspring of his own. Young tigers are vulnerable for a long time: Fewer than half of all cubs live to more than two years of age, and infanticide (killing of young by adults) is by far the most significant cause of death. Once a male is established in an area and can be confident that all cubs are his own, his murderous tendencies subside, and he rarely makes any attempt to approach families.

Playful Cubs

A female tiger will choose a secure den, such as a cave or dense thicket, to give birth. The young stay there for up to two months while their mother leaves them for short periods in order to feed. After that the cubs emerge from the den; but they do not wander far, and their mother still returns at regular intervals to suckle them. Most of their waking lives are spent playing, building up the strength, agility, and coordination they will later use to deadly effect. By the age of five or six months the family begins to accompany their mother to hunt. By 11 months they are capable of catching and killing smaller prey items. Even so, they will still depend on their mother for at least part of their food until they are 18 months old and often remain under her protection for a further year. After that they move on, usually joining the ranks of nonbreeding, largely nomadic tigers that occupy marginal habitats on the fringes of occupied ranges, awaiting an opportunity to claim a range of their own.

Licking cubs with the tiger's rough, hairy tongue helps keep them clean. Young tigers leave their mother, or may be pushed out, at the time her next litter is due.

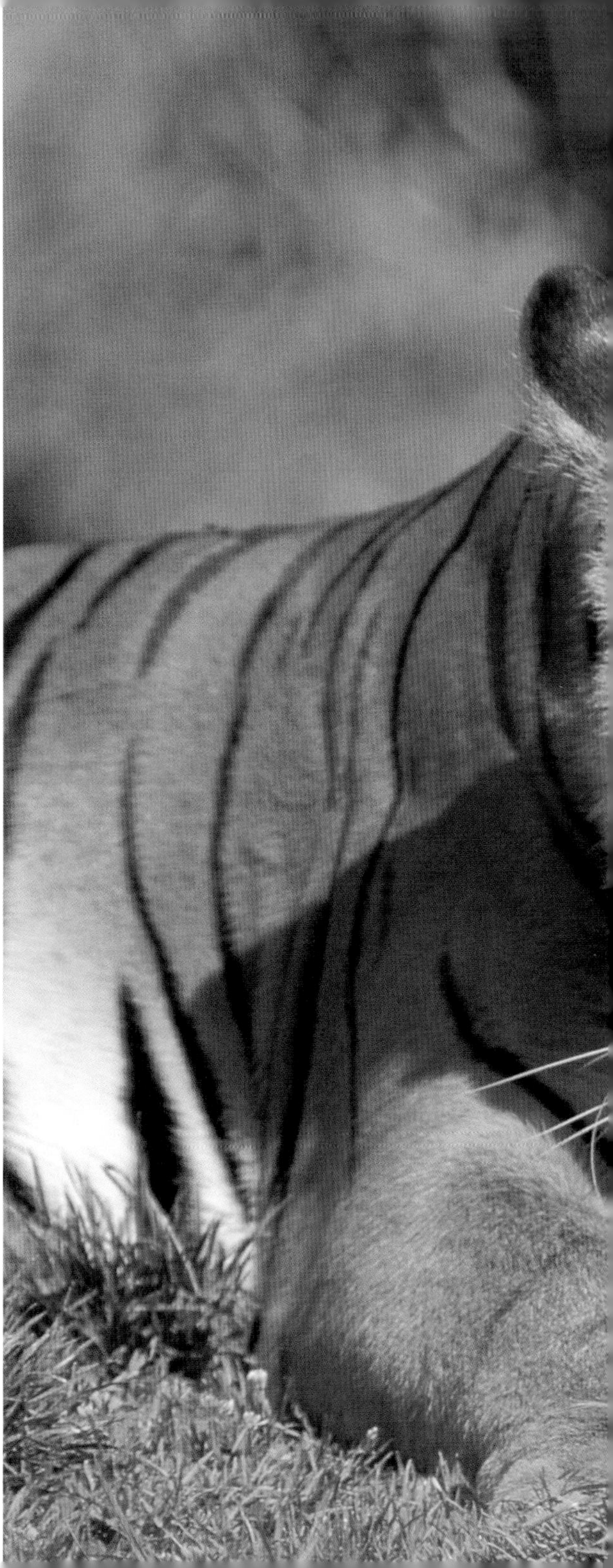

Common name Cheetah

Scientific name *Acinonyx jubatus*

Family Felidae

Order Carnivora

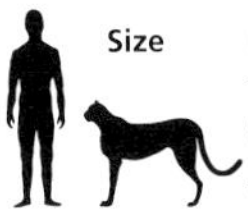

Size Length head/body: 44–59 in (112–150 cm); tail length: 24–31 in (60–80 cm); height at shoulder: 26–37 in (67–94 cm)

Weight 46–159 lb (21–72 kg)

Key features Very slender, long-limbed cat with small head, rounded ears, and long tail held in low sweep; fur pale gold to tawny, paler on belly with black spots; end of tail has dark bands

Habits Diurnal; can be solitary and nomadic or live in small groups

Breeding Litters of 1–8 (usually 3–5) cubs born at any time of year after gestation period of 90–95 days. Weaned at 3–6 months; sexually mature at 18 months but rarely breeds before 2 years. May live up to 19 years in captivity, up to 14 in the wild, but usually many fewer

Voice Purrs, yelps, moans, and snarls; also a high-pitched churring; females use birdlike chirping to reassure young

Diet Mostly gazelles and impalas; other hoofed animals depending on opportunity

Habitat Savanna grassland, scrub, and semidesert

Distribution Widespread but scattered populations throughout sub-Saharan Africa, excluding the Congo Basin. Small population in Iran

Status Population: fewer than 15,000; IUCN Vulnerable; CITES I. Range and population greatly reduced, now protected in most of its range

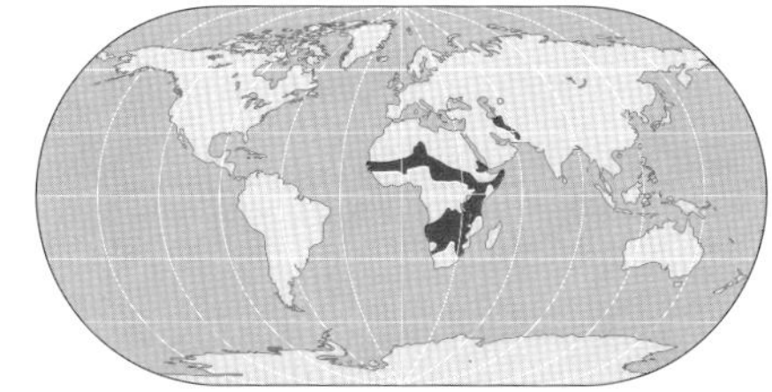

Cheetah

Built for speed, the cheetah is the world's fastest land animal. However, its extraordinary sprinting ability is no defense against habitat loss and other pressures that threaten its existence.

THE CHEETAH IS THE FASTEST animal on four legs. Over even ground it can reach speeds of p to 65 miles per hour (105 km/h), and it has powers of acceleration that rival many modern sports cars. Its body is long and lean, like that of a greyhound, and its spine is remarkably flexible, allowing it to take huge strides that carry it forward up to 26 feet (8 m) in one bound.

Unrivaled Sprinter

The cheetah's legs are long but very slender, the lightness of the bones reducing the need for huge muscles. The paws are small but hard, with blunt, nonretractile claws that help it turn very fast. No other mammal has such extreme adaptations to speed, and none comes close to the cheetah in terms of sprinting ability. The fastest greyhounds, honed by centuries of selective breeding, reach about 40 miles per hour (65 km/h) over short distances. The American pronghorn antelope can run fast for longer distances, but cannot match the cheetah for acceleration and sprints.

The cheetah has made sacrifices for its supreme speed. Compared with other big cats, it has little stamina. In spite of the enlarged lungs and heart that keep oxygen circulating as fast as possible to the cheetah's muscles, it cannot keep up a full pursuit for more than about a minute. Three in every four hunts fail because the cheetah cannot get close enough to the prey before launching an attack.

The cheetah is not particularly powerful, and its relatively small teeth and claws do not make good weapons. The teeth have to be small in order to make room for the

A cheetah's power of acceleration and sprinting ability are unmatched by any other mammal. However, it begins to tire after 30 seconds and after a minute has virtually no chance of making a kill.

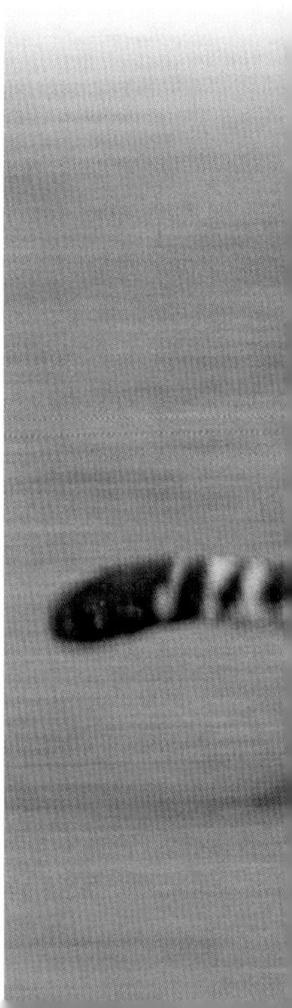

enlarged nostrils that enable the animal to breathe efficiently when running and when strangling its prey with a vicelike throat hold. But once the prey is dead, the cheetah has to spend a few minutes getting its breath back before dragging the prey to a secure place as fast as possible. If a scavenger spots the carcass, the cheetah's efforts may have been for nothing, since it will rarely defend a kill against lions or hyenas. Cheetahs can sometimes even be scared off by vultures, although this may have more to do with the fact that vultures attract other, larger scavengers than a fear of the birds themselves.

An adult cheetah stands among tall savanna grasses in Zimbabwe, southern-central Africa. Scattered cheetah populations are found throughout sub-Saharan Africa.

Wasted Energy

If forced to abandon its hard-earned meal, the cheetah has to chase and kill again, using up yet more energy to feed itself. Being disturbed and driven off its food is a constant threat. Even in national parks where they are safe from other dangers, cheetahs are often forced by tourist buses to abandon their prey to scavengers.

Cheetahs do not seem to target old, young, or sick prey like other large carnivores, nor do they try to approach downwind. They simply select the animal that is nearest them or one that is separate from the main herd and then try to outrun it. Mothers with cubs have a particularly hard time. They need to kill a gazelle or impala almost every day to keep their families

A cheetah suffocates a gazelle in Kenya. The animal's enlarged nostrils allow it to breathe efficiently while keeping a vicelike hold on its victim's throat.

well fed (compared with the need for one every two to five days when there are no cubs). Before they reach the age of three months, when they begin to gain some hunting sense of their own, the cubs can be a serious hindrance.

Female cheetahs are generally solitary. Unusually among cats, they have much larger home ranges than males, anything from 20 to 580 square miles (50 to 1,500 sq. km). They cannot hope to defend an area this size, and the ranges of several females usually overlap, although they rarely meet.

Males, by contrast, are highly territorial, but unlike females they rarely live alone. Territories are in such demand that the males have to team up in order to defend one. Such teams are known as coalitions and often contain two or three males, usually brothers. By working together, they can keep other males off their patch and win access to any females that might pass through. Cheetahs are not generally aggressive animals, but males from different coalitions have been known to fight to the death over females and defense of their territory. Fights within a coalition are generally very rare.

Cheetah Cubs

A pair of cheetahs may mate several times over a couple of days, but then they go their separate ways. The female gives birth in a secluded spot, usually in dense vegetation. The cubs are blind and helpless at birth, and the mother goes to great lengths to keep them hidden from view. She will move them one by one to a new hiding place if she suspects they have been spotted. After five weeks, however, they are able to follow her around.

For the first three months of their life young cheetahs have a cape of long gray fur that covers the back of the head, the shoulders, and back. It helps to disguise their outline in long grass. Despite their natural camouflage and the mother cheetah's best efforts to protect them, the great majority of cheetah cubs do not survive to independence. The estimates of infant and juvenile mortality vary from 70 to 95 percent. A great many are killed by lions and hyenas, while many others starve or succumb to disease or congenital birth defects.

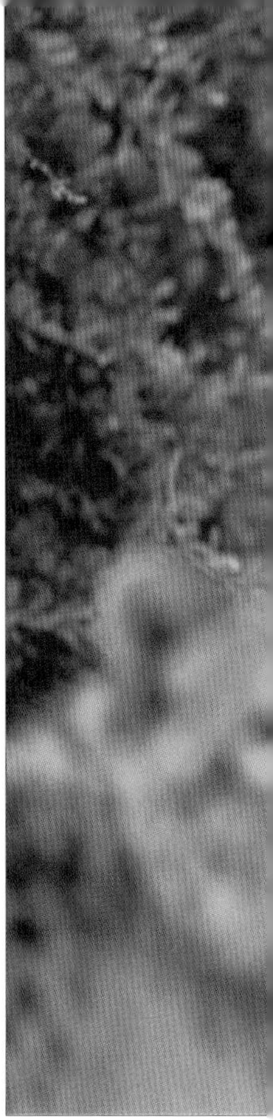

The unusual markings of a king cheetah. The coat pattern is blotchier than that of the majority of cheetahs and is due to a rare gene, like that found in albinos.

A typical family of three cubs. The youngsters will remain with their mother for up to six months before becoming fully independent.

Threatened Existence

Cheetahs need open country with patches of tall grass or other vegetation, which they can use as cover when ambushing prey. However, over the years much of this type of habitat has been given over to agriculture, depriving cheetahs of places to live. Hunting also took a grave toll on cheetah numbers in the past and remains a serious problem in some places.

Cheetah populations have undergone a worrying decline in recent years, despite the fact that there is legal protection for the species almost everywhere. At one time the species was widespread throughout Africa, the Middle East, and southern Asia. Now there is only one population left outside Africa. It consists of a mere 250 animals in northern Iran. In Africa the cheetah's distrib-

King Cheetahs

In 1927 zoologists studying cheetahs in Zimbabwe came to the conclusion that there were in fact two species in the area. The second, which they called *Acinonyx rex*, the king cheetah, was distinguished by a much blotchier coat pattern and a "mane" of longer hair around its shoulders. King cheetahs have always been rare, and until recently it was thought that they only occurred in Zimbabwe. However, a wild specimen has since been found on the edge of the Sahara in Burkina Faso, and a number of animals with king cheetah markings have been born in captivity. We now know that king cheetahs are not a separate species or even subspecies of cheetah. They are simply a rare genetic form of *A. jubatus* that turn up in the population, like albinos in other animals. King cheetahs can be born to normal-looking parents and have normal-looking siblings.

Common name Gray wolf (timber wolf)

Scientific name *Canis lupus*

Family Canidae

Order Carnivora

Size Length head/body: 35–56 in (89–142 cm); tail length: 12–20 in (30–51 cm); height at shoulder: 23–28 in (58–77 cm)

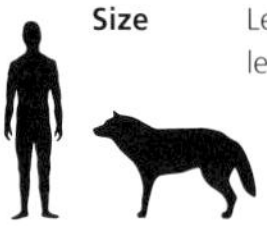

Weight 22–175 lb (10–80 kg). Male larger than female

Key features Large, long-legged dog with thick fur and bushy tail; fur usually gray, although color varies with distribution

Habits Social, although sometimes solitary; more or less nocturnal; hunts communally to bring down prey up to 10 times its own weight

Breeding One to 11 (average 6) pups born in a den after gestation period of 63 days. Weaned at 5 weeks; sexually mature at 2 years. May live up to 16 years in captivity, rarely more than 13 in the wild

Voice Growls, barks, whines, and howls

Diet Mainly large mammal prey, including deer, moose, muskox, mountain sheep, bison, beavers, and hares

Habitat Almost anywhere from tundra to scrub, grassland, mountains, and forest

Distribution Northern Hemisphere

Status Population: many thousands; IUCN Vulnerable; CITES I (India, Pakistan, Nepal, Bhutan); elsewhere CITES II. Now more stable following centuries of persecution

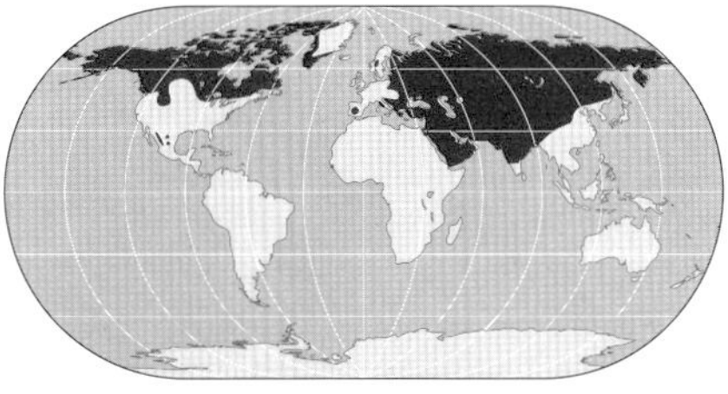

Gray Wolf

Wolves are intelligent and adaptable creatures, often living in close-knit family groups. Human attitudes to wolves range from deep respect to outright hostility, fueled by chilling folk tales of their wickedness.

The gray wolf is the largest species of dog. It once lived throughout the Northern Hemisphere in all but the most extreme tropical and desert habitats. There is only one other mammal that has a greater natural range or lives in a wider variety of habitats—our own species. Persecution by humans led to a dramatic decline in wolf numbers worldwide over the last 300 years, and the species has become extinct over much of its former range. The wolf is now associated only with areas of wilderness. Wolves disappeared altogether from Britain in the 18th century and from Japan and much of western Europe during the following 200 years.

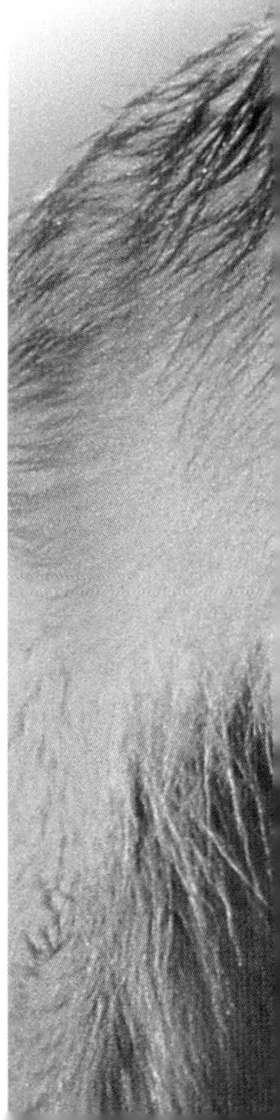

Gray wolves from different geographical areas may vary in size and appearance. Those living in arctic and mountainous regions, for example, are much larger than their relatives in the hot, dry scrublands of Arabia.

Eradication Program

In North America the gray wolf was the chief target of a prolonged campaign of predator eradication that began not long after the arrival of European settlers. Wolves were shot and trapped in such numbers that by 1940 there were none left in the western United States, and numbers elsewhere were in serious decline. More recent methods of control include poisoning and sport hunting from aircraft. Similar eradication programs in the former Soviet Union have reduced wolf numbers there by about 70 percent. In other parts of Asia the wolf is now extremely rare. The Mexican wolf is officially listed by the IUCN as Extinct in the Wild, with only about 140 remaining in captivity.

More recently, however, studies of wolf populations have convinced biologists that far from being a scourge of the land, wolves

Folklore: Who's Afraid of the Big, Bad Wolf?

Wolves have long been the subject of myths and legends. Stories such as *Little Red Riding Hood* and *The Three Little Pigs* cast wolves as cold-blooded killers of men and also domestic animals. On the other hand, the legend of Romulus and Remus — the babies raised by wolves—and the *Jungle Book* stories by Kipling portray wolves as wise and devoted parents. In reality the wolf is all these things and more.

are in fact an important stabilizing influence on wilderness ecosystems. Such discoveries, along with a growing sense of responsibility toward wildlife in general, have prompted several wolf conservation projects around the world. Several European populations have now been saved from extinction, and the range of the wolf in North America is increasing slowly. In most places where man and wolf still live side by side there is now an uneasy truce enforced by laws protecting the wolf from direct persecution, but giving livestock owners some rights to protect their property. Nevertheless, many people living in the country are not happy to share their land with wolves and want them shot or trapped. Efforts to reintroduce wolves to Yellowstone National Park have also run into difficulties with hostile residents in surrounding areas.

Geographical Differences

Not surprisingly for such a widespread species, wolves from different geographical areas vary considerably in size, appearance, and behavior. The biggest wolves live in large packs in the tundra regions of Canada, Alaska, and Russia. Their relatives in the hot, dry scrublands of Arabia are smaller and more likely to live alone or in small groups.

The size of a wolf pack is controlled largely by the size of its most regular prey. Lone wolves do well where most of their food comes from small prey, carrion, or raiding human refuse. Where deer are the main prey, packs of five to seven animals are usual.

However, pack sizes may be larger still where wolves feed on very big prey. In the Isle Royale National Park in Lake Superior, for example, where the animals feed almost exclusively on moose, packs may include more than 20 animals.

Selective Predation

Wolves will normally hunt either old, young, weak, or disabled prey and soon give up on an attack if the animal is able to defend itself or make a quick getaway. In fact, only about 8 percent of all wolf hunts end successfully in a kill, which is why it is highly unlikely that wolf predation does any real harm to prey populations as was once feared.

A large wolf needs to eat an average of 5.5 pounds (2.5 kg) of meat every day, but will often go for several days without food. However, when a kill is made, it can make up for any such lean periods by "wolfing" up to 20 pounds (9 kg) of meat in a single meal. A large prey animal may keep a pack well fed for several days. During the time they are not actively feeding, the wolves may rest near the carcass to defend it from scavengers.

Wolf attacks on humans are fortunately rare. In North America, for example, there are no fully documented cases of unprovoked attacks on people by healthy wolves. However, wolves can and do attack livestock. Sheep and cattle are, after all, close relatives of the wolf's natural prey and yet they are far easier to catch and kill because generations of domestication have made them virtually incapable of defending themselves. They are large, meaty, and prone to panic, and are often penned in with no hope of escape. Even so, it would rarely take more than the sight of a human to cause the wolves to abandon the hunt and run away.

The size of a wolf pack is usually determined by the size of available prey. For example, when deer are the main food source, packs of five to seven are common. Wolves preying on larger animals, such as moose, often belong to packs of 20 or more.

Reintroduction

In 1995, after many years of careful planning and much controversy, 31 Canadian-born gray wolves were successfully released into Yellowstone National Park. The park contains over 17 million acres (7 million ha) of prime wolf habitat and also supports large herds of elk. The relocated wolves have thrived since their introduction, as have those released in other locations in Montana and Idaho. The interests of local ranchers are protected in that they are compensated for wolf attacks on their livestock. In addition, farmers now have permission to shoot wolves on their own land. In the first four years of the program nine wolves were shot legally.

The success of the Yellowstone National Park project has encouraged conservationists to consider reintroducing the wolf elsewhere. One highly controversial plan is to release captive-bred wolves in Scotland, a country that has not seen wild wolves for 300 years. The problem with the idea is that islands where wolves could be out of the way of humans are usually too small to support a viable population. Yet on the mainland there are too many people and sheep for the wolves to live without causing trouble.

A gray wolf pup at the entrance to its den. On average, a litter contains about six pups.

Sibling Care

A wolf pack is made up of a single breeding pair and their offspring of the previous one or two years. The nonbreeding members of the pack are usually young animals. They are prevented from breeding by the dominant pair, but help care for their young siblings. In areas where good wolf habitat is plentiful, young wolves may leave their parents' pack as early as 12 months of age. Some stay with the family for a further season; but by the time they are fully mature at around 22 months, they will move on. Dispersing animals may live on the edge of their parents' territory until a suitable mate comes along. Other young wolves scatter widely in search of a mate and territory of their own.

Territorial Howling

The pack occupies a territory of anything from 8 to 5,200 square miles (20 to 13,000 sq. km), the exact size varying according to the number of wolves and the quality of habitat. All members of the pack help defend the territory, and they will travel to every part of it at least once a month, moving in single file along regular routes. They mark their territory with scents, scratches, and long sessions of howling. In open country wolf howls can be heard up to 10 miles (16 km) away, even by human ears. When wolves from neighboring packs do meet, the encounters often lead to serious fights in which one or more of the animals may be fatally wounded. In order to minimize the risk of such incidents, the wolves usually leave a kind of buffer zone of land that they seldom visit around the edge of their territory. Such areas can also serve as a kind of reservoir for prey, which is only exploited in times of food shortage.

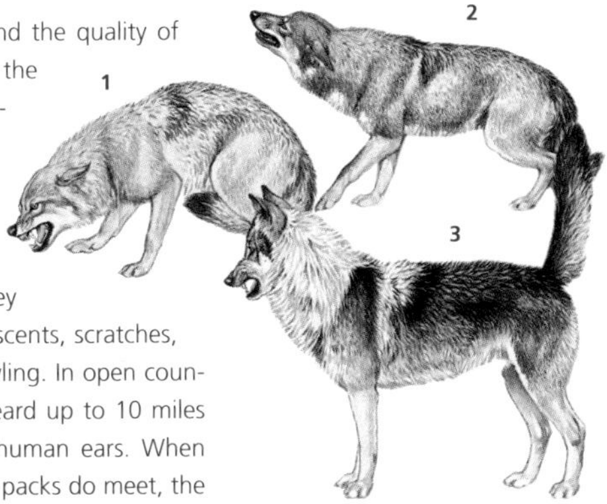

Ⓘ ***Wolves communicate using body language and facial expressions. Above, a defensive threatening posture (1); a submissive greeting (2); and an offensive threatening pose (3).***

Red Fox

Vulpes vulpes

Common name Red fox

Scientific name *Vulpes vulpes*

Family Canidae

Order Carnivora

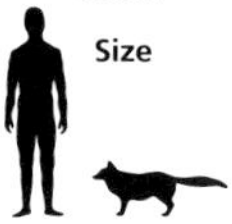

Size Length head/body: 18–35.5 in (45–90 cm); tail length: 12–21.5 in (30–55 cm); height at shoulder: up to 14 in (36 cm)

Weight 7–31 lb (3–14 kg)

Key features Typical fox with long, narrow body ending in thick, brushy tail; pointed muzzle and ears; neat legs and feet; fur typically red, but varies from deep gold to dark brown, fading to white on muzzle, chest, and belly; often darker on legs; black and pale variants known

Habits Mostly nocturnal; sometimes lives in family groups, but usually hunts alone; nonbreeding males are solitary

Breeding Litters of 1–12 (usually 3–7) cubs born in spring after gestation period of 51–53 days. Weaned at 8–10 weeks; sexually mature at 10 months. May live up to 12 years in captivity, rarely more than 5 in the wild

Voice Barks, whines, yelps, screams, excited "gekkering" when playing

Diet Omnivorous; rodents and other small mammals; also insects, worms, and fruit

Habitat Diverse; includes farmland, forest, grassland, moorland, tundra, and urban areas

Distribution Europe and North America; also parts of Africa and Asia; introduced to Australia

Status Population: abundant. Persecuted as vermin; also hunted for sport

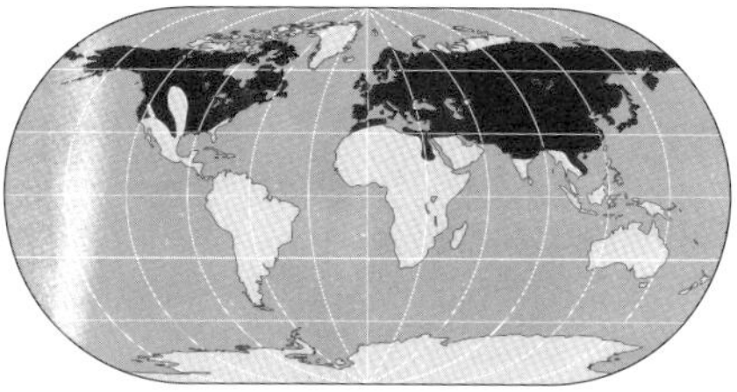

The red fox is one of the most widespread, and certainly one of the most adaptable, members of the dog family. It even rivals the gray wolf in terms of global distribution.

RED FOXES LIVE WILD IN NORTH America, Europe, Asia, and Africa, and have become widespread in Australia and on many islands to which they have been introduced. There is considerable variation in size and appearance throughout the range, with the largest foxes occurring in Europe. The typical red fox coat is a deep red-brown, with white on the muzzle, chest, belly, and tail tip, and black on the legs. In North America, however, there are many distinct color varieties, with up to 20 percent of red foxes being black or silver. Other varieties include so-called "cross foxes," which are basically red with a cross-shaped mark of darker fur on the shoulders. "Samson foxes" have coats that lack the normal long guard hairs and therefore look somewhat fluffier than usual.

Misrepresented

Throughout their huge geographical range foxes are loved and loathed in almost equal measure. It is difficult not to admire an animal so smart and adaptable that it is able to live almost anywhere that people can. The fox features frequently in folk tales and fairy stories, and its glorious pelt is valued as an expensive fashion accessory. However, the animal is traditionally detested by farmers and is persecuted throughout much of its range because of its predatory habits and the risk of transmitting rabies. Foxes are trapped, shot, and hunted almost everywhere they occur, and yet they still manage to thrive.

Foxes' diets and their hunting and foraging techniques vary as much as their habitat. In temperate climates in late summer many foxes exist almost entirely on sugary fruits, such as blackberries and apples. On warm, humid

⊕ A red fox holds an Arctic ground squirrel firmly in its jaws. The fox's sharp features and smart nature contribute to its reputation as a wanton predator. But contrary to popular opinion, foxes rarely kill more than they need.

evenings in summer when earthworms come to the surface on open grassland and pasture, a fox can eat enough in an hour to keep it going for the whole day. At other times hunting is more intensive, and foxes will stalk, chase, and pounce on prey, including voles, rabbits, frogs, and birds. Ever the opportunist, a fox will also take advantage of roadkills and refuse. Excess food is usually stored—bones and bits of meat are buried in the ground to be dug up and eaten later, maggots and all. Rotten meat does not appear to do foxes any harm.

Chicken Runs

Foxes are messy eaters, and food remains are often scattered widely, but little is actually wasted. Contrary to popular opinion, foxes are not wanton killers and will rarely kill more than they need. Stories of foxes running amok in chicken runs and killing dozens of birds at a time have more to do with the unnatural conditions in which chickens are kept than the fox's killer instincts. In a run where chickens live at high density and have no way of escaping, a fox cannot simply make a kill and slink away to eat in peace. A flock of panicking birds causing mayhem all around sends the fox into a frenzy. As long as the chicken farmer ensures his enclosures are fox-proof, the problem does not arise.

↑ The red fox occurs in many distinct color forms. Above, the vivid, flame-red coloring of most high-latitude red foxes (1); the silver form (2); the "cross fox," with a cross shape on its shoulders (3).

Bakewell
Tart

Communal Lifestyle

Until recently foxes were thought to be solitary animals. They are certainly territorial and tend to hunt alone. However, in the privacy of their breeding dens the story can be quite different. A single communal territory can be home to as many as six adult foxes: one dominant male (the dog-fox) and up to five vixens (females). The vixens are apparently always related, each one either a sister, mother, or daughter to the others. The male usually mates with just one of the vixens, occasionally two if the habitat is productive enough to support an extra litter.

Breeding vixens are dominant over all the others. Status within a group is often established when the vixens are very young, long before they reach breeding age, and is reinforced continually. The dominant vixen is sometimes aggressive, sometimes friendly and reassuring, but her mood can change in an instant. Her subordinates are always ready to adopt cowering, submissive postures and to make themselves scarce when she chooses to remind them who is boss. Subordinate females seem to take great pride in caring for the dominant vixen's litter and compete for the privilege of baby-sitting.

Red Fox Cubs

Baby foxes are born in litters of one to 12, the average number varying according to the quality of habitat. The cubs are born blind but furry, and each weighs between 2 and 6 ounces (57 and 170 g). To begin with, their fur is dark chocolate brown, and their eyes, which open after two weeks, are blue. By the time the youngsters are one month old and ready to leave the safety of the breeding den for the first time, they have already begun to look more like foxes. Their fur lightens, their eyes turn brown, and their muzzles are longer and more pointed.

← Urban foxes make a good living feeding on refuse and bird-feeder leftovers, and by killing rats, pigeons, and other town-dwelling wildlife. Often the pickings are so rich that foxes in towns and cities live at much higher densities than they ever manage in the countryside.

A young fox's first taste of meat is usually in the form of partially digested scraps coughed up by its mother. Later the cub's milk teeth drop out and are replaced by the adult dentition. The jaws and teeth are strengthened by chewing on bones, sticks, and other objects, and the cub's coordination and hunting skills are developed by hour on hour of boisterous play with its siblings. Adult foxes retain a playful streak, and games can involve the whole family in a noisy rough-and-tumble.

↑ A female red fox with a cub. The cubs are ready to leave the safety of the breeding den at about one month. They can fend for themselves at six months and breed at 10 months.

Habitat Requirements

Young females may stay with the family group, but males always disperse, traveling about 30 miles (48 km) or sometimes farther, to establish their own territory. The size of a fox's territory depends on the quality of the habitat and especially on the availability of food. Ideal fox habitat has a selection of different habitat types: Areas of woodland and pasture crisscrossed with hedgerows and the odd garden are ideal. Sometimes a fox can find all it needs in a territory of about 25 acres (10 ha). In less hospitable habitats, such as the Canadian tundra, a fox may require a hundred times as much space to supply its needs. Territories are diligently marked with urine and droppings.

Deadly Virus

One of the most serious and widespread threats to foxes other than human persecution is the rabies virus. Rabies is found in much of the world's fox population, except in Britain, whose strict quarantine laws have kept the disease from becoming established. In continental Europe rabies has been largely eliminated from the fox population in several countries by using special vaccines distributed in baits, which the wild foxes eat. Vaccination programs reduce the threat of rabies because the disease dies out when there are enough foxes in the population that are immune to it. The method is expensive but humane and can be very effective as long as enough baits are distributed.

Polar Bear

Ursus maritimus

The polar bear is the world's largest land carnivore and is superbly adapted to life in one of the harshest regions on earth.

Common name Polar bear

Scientific name *Ursus maritimus*

Family Ursidae

Order Carnivora

Size Length head/body: 6.6–8.2 ft (2–2.5 m); tail length: 3–5 in (7–13 cm); height at shoulder: up to 5.2 ft (1.6 m)

Weight Male 660–1,760 lb (300–800 kg); female 330–660 lb (50–300 kg)

Key features Huge bear with thick, off-white coat; head relatively small; feet large and furry

Habits Solitary; migratory and partially nomadic; pregnant females hibernate in winter; excellent swimmer

Breeding Litters of 1–4 tiny cubs born in midwinter after gestation period of 195–265 days (includes variable period of delayed implantation). Weaned from 6 months; sexually mature at 5–6 years. May live up to 45 years in captivity, 30 in the wild

Voice Grunts and growls

Diet Carnivorous: mainly seals but occasionally other animals such as reindeer; also fish, seabirds, carrion, and plant material in summer

Habitat Sea ice, ice cap, and tundra; equally at home in water and on land

Distribution Arctic Circle; parts of Canada, Alaska, Russia, Scandinavia, and Greenland

Status Population: 20,000–30,000; IUCN Lower Risk: conservation dependent; CITES II. Main threat is from human exploitation of Arctic habitats

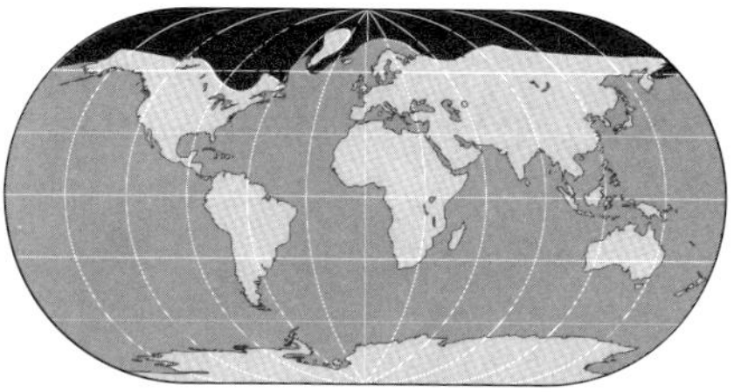

Polar bears and brown bears are more closely related than their appearance and different lifestyles suggest. Until about 100,000 years ago they were the same species, and even today individuals in captivity are able to interbreed. The special features that allow polar bears to survive life in and out of the water in one of the bleakest, most inhospitable parts of the world are all fairly recent adaptations, providing a good example of how evolution can proceed quickly under extreme conditions.

Cold Weather Protection

The most striking polar bear characteristic is, of course, its color. But there is more to the coat than meets the eye. Not only are the hairs very long, trapping a deep layer of warm air against the skin, but (under a microscope) the individual hairs can be seen to be hollow. Each has air spaces running along its length, which help make the coat extra warm because air trapped inside the hairs improves the insulation effect. It is the hollowness of the hairs and the lack of pigment that makes the fur appear white. The dense coat is also surprisingly light. Late in the season, before the fur is molted, it begins to look rather yellow, owing to a combination of accumulated dirt and the oxidizing effect of sunlight. Zoo polar bears sometimes get algae from their pool into the coat hairs, turning them temporarily green, but this does not happen in the wild!

The other obvious feature of polar bears is their size. Fully grown males are the world's largest terrestrial predators, measuring about 8 feet (2.5 m) long on all fours and weighing as much as 10 large men. Females are less than half this size, but still number among the world's most powerful animals. Large body size

is another adaptation to the cold, because larger animals are more efficient at preventing loss of body heat. Being big also allows polar bears to tackle large prey—for much of the year seals are the only other animals around, and a polar bear can scoop one out of the water using just a single paw. Another special adaptation is the huge furry feet, which help spread the polar bear's weight so effectively that a bear weighing half a ton (508 kg) can walk carefully across ice too thin to support a human. The soles are also furry, protecting the pads from frostbite and giving the bear extra grip on the ice: They also help reduce the tendency to sink into soft snow. The bears are

Polar bears test their strength in bouts of play wrestling. Fully grown males are the world's largest terrestrial predators and can weigh as much as 10 large men.

nimble for their size and can gallop at speeds of up to 30 miles per hour (50 km/h) for relatively short periods.

Long-Distance Traveler

Polar bears have never actually been recorded at the North Pole. Here the sea ice is thick and continuous, with no access to open water for the bears or for the seals on which they feed. However, they do occur almost everywhere else within the Arctic Circle, concentrating their activity around the thin, cracked edges of the pack ice where seals haul out. In winter, when the sea ice reaches its maximum extent, the bears venture as far south as Newfoundland, southern Greenland, and the Bering Sea.

Polar bears wander widely, but they are not true nomads as was once believed. Recent studies show that bears from different parts of the Arctic form distinct populations, with individual bears using ranges of up to 200,000 square miles (500,000 sq. km) over the course of a few years. There is a resident population of polar bears around the Hudson and James Bays, members of which do not need to travel so far. They spend their summers on land, venturing up to 120 miles (200 km) inland, and move out onto the vast expanse of ice when the bays freeze over in winter.

A female polar bear with her cubs. Polar bear cubs stay with their mother for about two and a half years, only leaving when she is ready to breed again.

Delayed Implantation

Most polar bears are solitary and wander over vast areas. Males and females rarely meet, so they are ready to mate whenever the opportunity occurs between March and June. Whatever the time of mating, the cubs are nearly always born in midwinter. It is the best time of year for births because it allows the maximum period for growth and development after the babies have left the den. A polar bear's pregnancy can therefore be anything from six and a half to almost nine months. Soon after fertilization of the mother's eggs the tiny embryos go into a state of suspended animation. It is the fact that the embryos do not begin to develop immediately that makes the variable gestation period possible. Pregnancy and rearing cubs over the winter put a huge strain on the female's body and can be fatal if she is not in good health. Delaying the development of the embryos until the female has put on enough weight to survive the pregnancy and provide milk for the cubs through the winter guards against starvation of the entire family. If the female is not in top condition by the late fall, the embryos are spontaneously aborted.

Smash and Grab

Ringed seals are the most important prey species, and polar bears show considerable flexibility in the techniques used to hunt them. In late spring female ringed seals give birth to their young in well-hidden dens. The dens have openings to the sea below but are invisible from above, being roofed over with snow. However, polar bears have an acute sense of smell and can detect the pups lying quietly below. They break into the den using brute force, rearing up on their hind legs and pounding the roof with their front feet. They then seize the seal pup inside. Hunting adult seals, on the other hand, is all about stealth and patience. Bears wait silently by a breathing hole for a seal to emerge, then grab it and heave the animal onto the ice. Sometimes the bears sneak up on a seal resting on the ice, using snow ridges and ice blocks as cover. They creep forward in a low crouch, keeping still every time the seal looks around. Not every hunt is successful, but the bears often kill enough to feed not only themselves but an entourage of scavenging Arctic foxes as well.

Varied Diet

Individual bears have distinctly different hunting techniques, which they develop according to their own experience. Other items that may appear on the polar bear's menu include harp and bearded seals, young beluga whales, walrus, reindeer, fish, seabirds, dead animals, and occasionally plant material. Bears arriving on land in the summer may spend hours browsing on leaves and berries, which, although not especially nutritious, contain some vitamins and minerals otherwise completely lacking in the bear's diet. For many bears summer is a time of hunger because the lack of sea ice means they cannot hunt seals. The Hudson Bay bears may go for months without eating, living only on their fat reserves and staying as inactive as possible to save energy and to avoid overheating in the weak sunshine.

The Sea Bear

The polar bear could just as correctly be called the sea bear (indeed, its scientific name means precisely that). It is a superb swimmer and is just as comfortable in the icy water of the Arctic Ocean as on land or pack ice. Polar bears can float effortlessly in seawater and do not sink even when dead. The hollow hairs in their coat are much more buoyant than normal fur. The fur is also slightly greasy and repels water. After a swim the bear only needs one quick shake to remove most of the moisture from its coat, so there is little danger of ice forming in the fur. The toes of the bear's enormous paddle-shaped feet are slightly webbed, making them more effective for swimming. The bear's neck is long, and it swims with its head held high above the water so that it has a good view over the waves.

Polar bears can swim for hours, using a steady dog paddle. They have even been known to swim up to 40 miles (65 km) across open water. They can dive under ice and climb out through seal breathing holes or leap 7 feet (2 m) onto ice cliffs. Hitching a ride on a passing ice floe is a favorite way of getting around, and the bears seem quite happy to plunge in and out of the cold water dozens of times a day.

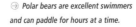

Polar bears are excellent swimmers and can paddle for hours at a time.

Breeding Dens

Most polar bears remain active throughout the winter, only seeking shelter in temporary snow holes during the worst storms. They do not normally need to hibernate because there is no shortage of food at this time of year. Pregnant females, however, build substantial dens in which to spend the winter. The dens, which are dug into a bank of snow, usually consist of a tunnel up to 10 feet (3 m) long and a large oval chamber. Some are rather more elaborate and may have several interconnected rooms. The female sleeps in the den throughout the winter, during which time the cubs are born. They are very small and need protecting from the harsh climate for the first few months of life. The newborn young make their own way to their mother's teats, and she suckles them without appearing to wake up. This long sleep is not true hibernation because although the female's heart rate and breathing slow down, her body temperature only drops by a few degrees. As a result, the den remains cozy, and she can wake up quickly if need be. By the time spring comes, the cubs have increased in weight from just over 1 pound (500 g) to between 25 and 30 pounds (11 and 14 kg) apiece. The mother is half-starved, having used up most of her fat to produce milk. Her first priority is to find food, but that is not easy with up to three lively cubs romping by her side.

Bear Attacks

Polar bears are aggressive. They can and do kill humans; but since little of their range is populated, the number of fatalities is low. People who live and work within the polar bear's range are generally well informed when it comes to bears, and visitors are given plenty of advice on how to avoid danger. Bear attacks are most frequent in the Hudson Bay area, especially around the town of Churchill, where several people have been attacked in the last 40 years. The bears pass by the town on their regular migrations and are attracted to the municipal waste dumps where they are liable to attack anyone who disturbs them.

Polar bears wander widely, with individuals using ranges of up to 200,000 square miles (500,000 sq. km) over the course of a few years.

Polar Bears and Humans

Polar bears have been known to the Inuit people from the time they settled in the North American Arctic about 4,000 years ago. The bears figure prominently in native folklore and spirituality. They were traditionally hunted for meat, fur, and other body parts. More recently polar bears were also hunted commercially, but the practice ceased in 1976 as the result of an agreement between the five "Polar Bear Nations"—the United States, Canada, Norway, Russia, and Denmark. Conservation laws now include controls on commercial hunting: Most of the bears hunted today are killed as part of the traditional Inuit hunt. However, hunting is not the only threat, and polar bears currently face problems associated with pollution and the exploitation of the Arctic for mining and oil extraction.

Common name Giant panda (panda, panda bear)

Scientific name *Ailuropoda melanoleuca*

Family Ursidae

Order Carnivora

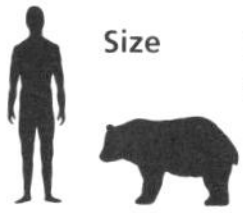

Size Length head/body: 47–59 in (120–150 cm); tail length: 5 in (13 cm); height at shoulder: up to 27.5–31 in (70–80 cm)

Weight 165–350 lb (75–160 kg)

Key features Unmistakable large, furry bear with black legs, shoulder band, eye patches, and ears; rest of body is off-white

Habits Solitary; nonterritorial; active between dusk and dawn; climbs well

Breeding One or 2 cubs born August–September after gestation period of 97–163 days (includes variable period of delayed implantation). Weaned at 8–9 months; sexually mature at 6–7 years. May live up to 34 years in captivity, fewer in the wild

Voice Varied sounds, including growls, moans, barks, squeaks, and bleats

Diet Omnivorous, but mostly bamboo and some other plant material; occasionally small animals

Habitat Mountainside forests with bamboo thickets at altitudes of 3,300–13,000 ft (1,000–3,900 m)

Distribution Small remaining range in central China

Status Population: about 1,000; IUCN Endangered; CITES I. Has declined greatly in range and population due to hunting, habitat loss, and specialized lifestyle

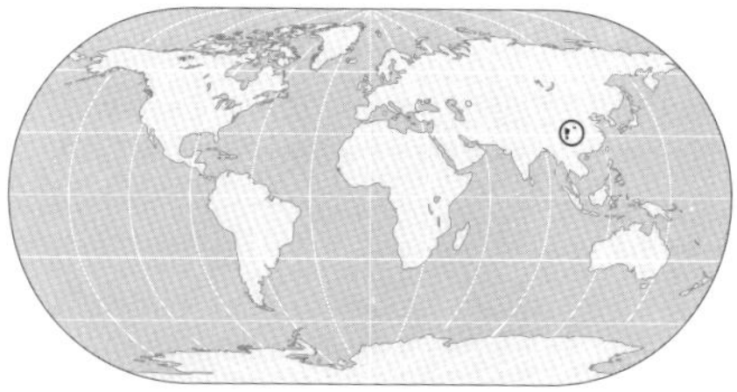

Giant Panda

One of the world's most easily recognizable animals, the panda has rarely been seen alive outside China and is now in serious decline. Its distinctive appearance has become the symbol for all animals threatened with extinction.

DESPITE BEING NATURALLY RARE and elusive, the giant panda is one of the world's most widely known and best-loved animals. Chinese writings from as long as 3,000 years ago refer to the panda, but the species was unknown to the outside world until 1869, when a skin was sent to the Museum of Natural History in Paris by a French missionary. The species was then formally described, but it was a long time before western scientists were able to see a live one. Even today fewer than 100 pandas have been seen alive in zoos outside China. The name panda is Nepalese, while its former species name, Ursus melanoleuca, meant simply "black-and-white bear." Ailuropoda, its more recent scientific name, refers to the claws and feet.

Vegetarian Diet

Pandas are almost exclusively vegetarian. However, they evolved from carnivorous ancestors and still have the digestive system of a meat-eater. It includes a short intestine, which is not the best arrangement for digesting the plant material on which pandas mainly feed. Muchof the goodness in the panda's diet is never absorbed because meals simply do not spend enough time in the short gut to be properly digested. In order to obtain enough nourishment to survive, the panda has to spend 10 to 12 of its 15 waking hours

feeding and eat between 22 and 40 pounds (10 and 18 kg) of bamboo every day. During the bamboo's new growth phase, when the stems are more succulent, such a requirement can almost double, since much of what the pandas consume at that time is just water in the juicy plant stems. However, the panda is not completely unsuited to its diet, and has evolved some physical characteristics that make feeding a little easier. For example, its cheek teeth are unlike those of other bears, being bigger and flatter and well adapted for grinding and crushing rather than slicing. An extra molar helps make chewing more efficient. Not surprisingly for an animal that chews almost allday long, thepanda has well-developed jaw muscles. The cheekbones are enlarged, which makes the panda's face appear very wide and round. The jaws are powerful enough to crunch bamboo stems up to 1.5

Pandas once inhabited the subtropical lowlands of China, but now can be found only in high-altitude areas where farming and logging have not yet encroached.

A Bear or Not a Bear?

The panda's relationship to other bears is one of the longest-running puzzles in animal classification. At first sight the animal certainly looks like a bear, and 19th-century zoologists had no hesitation in classifying it in the bear family, Ursidae. However, there is another species of panda, the red or lesser panda *(Ailurus fulgens)*, which looks rather like a raccoon. Certain aspects of giant panda physiology are also raccoonlike, and for a while both pandas were placed in the raccoon family, Procyonidae.

Other experts placed them in a family by themselves, the Ailuridae. Modern science has clarified the situation a little. It has revealed that the giant panda's DNA (genetic molecular structure) is more like that of a bear than a raccoon. As a result, the merry-go-round has turned full circle, with most zoologists now agreeing that the giant panda is a rather special kind of bear, or at least an offshoot of the bear family.

Thumbs Up!

The panda's most extraordinary feeding adaptation has nothing to do with its jaws, teeth, or gut. One of the reasons people find the panda so appealing is the way it sits up to eat, clasping a bamboo stem in its paws, much as a human would, rather than browsing off the ground or the growing plant as other herbivores (plant-eating animals) do or lying down and using its mouth to pull its meal to pieces like most carnivores. Bears and their relatives have five digits on each foot, but the thumbs do not oppose the other digits, so they cannot be used to grasp objects the way humans and apes do. The only way most carnivores can hold objects is to clamp them awkwardly between two paws. In order to clasp bamboo shoots the way it does, the panda has developed a new "thumb." It is actually an extension of a bone from its wrist (the radial sesamoid), which grows into a lobe off the main pad on each forefoot. This new thumb is not mobile like a true thumb, but it provides a support against which the panda can press its first two fingers and thereby grip the bamboo stems.

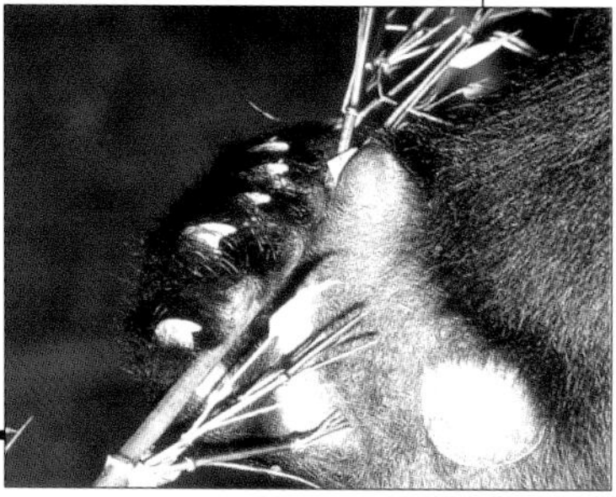

The panda's extra "thumb" helps it grasp bamboo more easily when feeding. Its habit of picking up food in its paws endears the animal to people.

Giant pandas feed almost entirely on bamboo. When plants die back, the animals must find new sources, but that is becoming increasingly difficult.

inches (4 cm) in diameter, although the panda prefers thinner shoots. Dry bamboo tends to splinter when it breaks, so the panda's mouth, esophagus, and stomach have an extra thick, leathery lining to prevent injury.

Pandas live alone, but their home ranges often overlap a good deal. They leave scent marks and other signs to indicate their presence, but they take pains not to meettheir neighbors. It may be that the panda's striking black-and-white markings actually help them spot each other at a distance and so avoid getting too close. Keeping spaced out helps ensure they do not compete for the same food supplies. The average panda uses a home range of between 1.5 and 2 square miles (4–6 sq. km) a year, but it rarely moves more than 650 yards (600 m) during the course of a day. Larger movements tend to be seasonal (pandas descend to lower altitudes in winter) or enforced by the cycles of bamboo die-off and regrowth. A stand of bamboo might grow for as long as 100 years before it suddenly flowers, sets seed, and dies back completely. When that happens, the pandas have to move on, unless they are to starve. They are unable to hibernate assome other bears do in times of food shortage because their poor diet does not allow them to build up the necessary fat reserves to sustain them over long periods of inactivity.

Disappearing Habitats

The unpredictable growth cycles of bamboo are not a problem for pandas as long as they are able to move to a new area where there is younger bamboo. But the development of human settlement and agriculture makes doing so very difficult. In the 1970s hundreds of pandas are thought to have starved to death when their bamboos died off, and encroaching farmland meant they had nowhere else to go.

Another serious problem the panda faced in the past was hunting. The skins of pandas were highly prized for their unusual markings, and various body parts were said to have special medicinal properties. By the late 20th century there were fewer than 1,000 pandas left alive in the wild. Today the remaining populations are restricted to three small areas in the central Chinese provinces of Shaanxi, Sichuan, and Gansu. They are protected by some of the strictest conservation laws in the world: In the late 1980s the Chinese government sentenced 16 people to life imprisonment and three to death for hunting pandas.

There are currently just over 100 pandas living in captivity, mostly in China. Captive-breeding success is low, partly because pandas naturally reproduce very slowly (usually

Common name Spotted hyena

Scientific name *Crocuta crocuta*

Family Hyaenidae

Order Carnivora

Size Length head/body: 39–71 in (100–180 cm); tail length: 10–14 in (25–36 cm); height at shoulder: 28–35 in (70–90 cm)

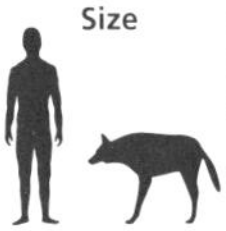

Weight 88–200 lb (40–91 kg); female generally about 12% heavier than male

Key features Doglike, powerfully built animal with short tail and sloping back; pale sandy gray coat with dark, irregular blotches

Habits Usually nocturnal, but will venture out during the daytime; lives in clans

Breeding Usually 2, but up to 4 cubs born after gestation period of 4 months. Weaned at 8–18 months; sexually mature at 2 years. May live to over 40 years in captivity, probably fewer in the wild

Voice Loud whooping noises; crazy-sounding giggle

Diet Meat from carcasses killed by other predators; slow animals like waterbuck; also tortoises, fish, insects, and garbage

Habitat Acacia savannas; urban fringes

Distribution Africa south of Sahara, except for areas of thick forest; absent from most of South Africa

Status Population: several thousand; IUCN Lower Risk: conservation dependent. Widespread and fairly common, but disappearing from many places being unpopular with farmers

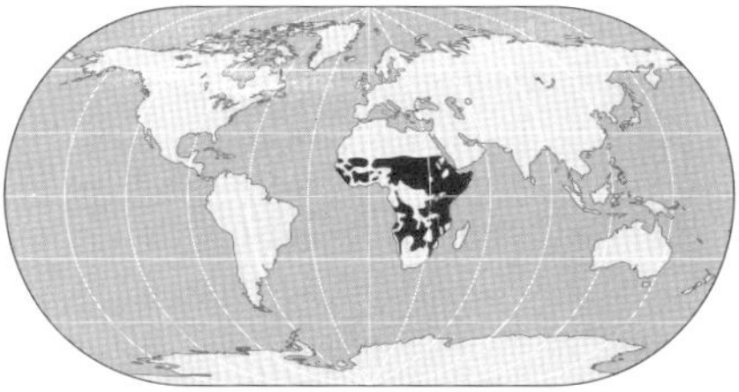

Spotted Hyena *Crocuta crocuta*

The spotted hyena has few friends. It is rapidly disappearing from large parts of Africa as a result of its reputation as a killer and undesirable neighbor.

SPOTTED HYENAS LIVE IN SOCIAL groups called clans, which defend a shared territory against rival groups. The clan territory—which may be very large—is staked out with scent marks on logs and boulders. Clans may divide into smaller subgroups and live in a series of burrows that they dig for themselves. Bigger groups occupy a large communal den, often among rocks. Some dens have been used by generations of hyenas over hundreds of years. Although a clan may number over 40 animals, its members seem able to recognize each other, mainly by smell.

Big-Game Hunt

Hyenas are active mainly in the evening and early part of the night. A clan may gang together to kill large mammals such as a wildebeest or zebra. During a chase hyenas are known to manage speeds of 35 miles per hour (60 km/h) or more, but they soon tire and usually give up after less than a mile or so. Only about one-third of such hunts are successful.

Large victims are torn apart, with each hyena greedily swallowing as much as possible in a short time, often as much as 30 pounds (14 kg) of meat. Hyenas will take advantage of sick and injured animals and also pick at carcasses left by lions and other predators. Occasionally, larger groups of hyenas manage to force lions to abandon their fresh kills. Spotted hyenas are also known to exploit the large numbers of young wild antelope and zebra available during the calving season. They may even follow wildebeest herds to pester the females while they are giving birth.

However, most spotted hyenas live in small groups and prefer to forage alone. They may cover up to 50 miles (80 km) in a night, searching for whatever can be picked up with

the least effort. Nowadays that often means garbage scavenged from around the edges of towns and villages, but hyenas will also eat reptiles, eggs, and even large beetles.

Breeding can occur at any time of the year, although only some females have offspring. In a communal den one female is dominant, but others in the same den may be allowed to breed. Young spotted hyenas are born blind and helpless, but develop fast. Only their mother feeds them, providing milk for up to 18 months. She does not normally carry food back to the den, and unlike some hyenas, other females in the clan do not assist in rearing the family. The dominant female is an overbearing individual, and others in the clan will allow her to eat as much as she wants unchallenged. The general behavior of clan members centers around appeasing the dominant female. She will signal her aggressive mood by raising her tail and sometimes snarling. Unlike all other mammals, her sexual organs look almost exactly like those of a male.

Young hyenas are independent at about 12 to 16 months, and they are sexually mature at two years old. The females generally stay with the clan into which they were born, while the males disperse and join another clan, remaining there for a few years before moving on again. This ensures that the clans do not become inbred. There is no permanent bond between males and females.

Spotted hyenas are especially good at crunching up fresh bones using their massive jaws and teeth. The shearing teeth are extremely effective and can slice up tough sinews and thick mammal skin better than most knives.

Refuse Collectors

Formerly a successful and widespread species, the spotted hyena is still one of the most abundant large African carnivores. However, it has an uneasy relationship with people. Many believe that its weird laughing giggles and manic whoops are associated with evil spirits. Its cringing behavior and habit of scavenging around latrines and garbage dumps make the animal seem unclean. It is also known to attack and eat domestic stock. The spotted hyena has been shot and poisoned wherever land is taken for farming and has become quite rare over large parts of its former range. It is now only really abundant in protected areas such as national parks. Yet it has an important role to play, cleaning up after other animals. By scavenging, ripping apart carcasses, and crunching up bones, the hyena actually helps speed up decomposition.

West Indian Manatee

Trichechus manatus

Common name West Indian manatee (Caribbean manatee)

Scientific name *Trichechus manatus*

Family Trichechidae

Order Sirenia

Size Length: 12–15 ft (3.7–4.6 m)

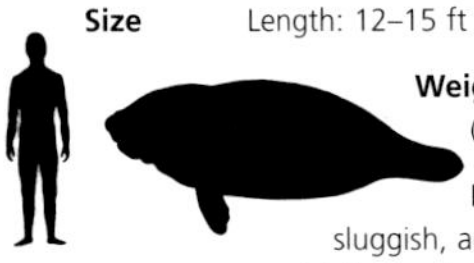

Weight up to 1.4 tons (1.2 tonnes)

Key features Large, sluggish, and slow-moving creature; grayish-brown in color, with paddle-shaped tail and no hind limbs; skin naked with patches of green algae and a few scattered, bristly hairs; blunt-ended head with thick, fleshy lips and small, piggy eyes

Habits Moves slowly, floating and diving in shallow water; often found in small family groups

Breeding Single young born after gestation period of about 1 year, with long intervals between births. Weaned at 2 years; sexually mature at 8 years. May live at least 28 years, probably considerably longer

Voice Normally silent

Diet Aquatic plants, floating and submerged; also grass and other vegetation overhanging from riverbanks

Habitat Estuaries, large rivers, and shallow seas

Distribution Florida, Caribbean, and coastal waters of South America as far as Brazil

Status Population: probably about 10,000 12,000; IUCN Vulnerable; CITES I

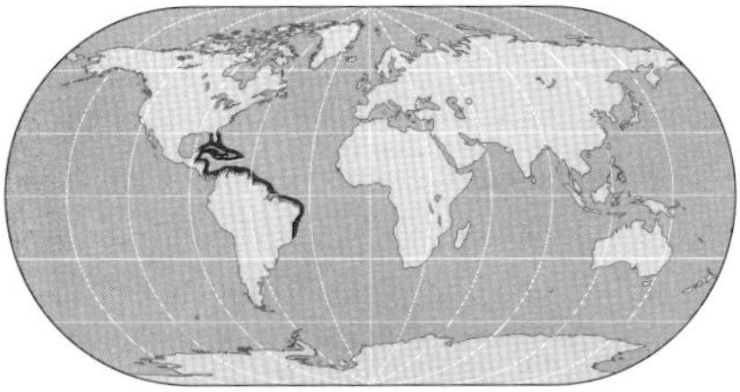

Manatees float gently in shallow waters, munching on floating and submerged vegetation. These large but harmless creatures do a useful job keeping waterways free of weeds, but their reward is to be the frequent victims of collisions with motor boats.

West Indian manatees occur around the coastal waters and large rivers of Florida, the West Indies, and the coasts of northern South America. They are sometimes regarded as forming a northern and southern subspecies. The former, based around Florida, probably numbers about 2,000 to 3,000 animals. The southern subspecies—up to 10,000 or so—are spread over the rest of the Caribbean and along the coast of South America as far as Brazil. The animals generally live alone, but sometimes gather in groups of six or more. While they tolerate each other, manatees do not form a true social structure with dominant and subordinate individuals. In fact, the animals may casually join and leave the groups whenever they like. They are probably drawn together by an attractive resource, such as a plentiful supply of food or stretches of unusually warm water.

Signs of Affection

Apart from the close association between mothers and their offspring, there are few interactions between manatees. Nevertheless, they show signs of affection and may indulge in gentle "kissing." There is also evidence that manatees may leave scent marks on logs and submerged rocks. The scent cannot be detected underwater, but may be tasted instead. Such a form of chemical communication is common among land mammals, of course, but unusual in the water. It may indicate that manatees make some sort of social arrangements after all. But there is no sign of territorial behavior, and aggressive interactions of any kind are rare.

A Diet of Greens

Manatees cannot come onto land to forage, since they have no hind limbs. Instead, they dive underwater to feed. As they breathe out, they become less buoyant and sink below the surface. Here they gently paddle around seeking food. They may stay underwater for up to half an hour without needing to breathe. Sometimes they may even take a rest lying on the bottom, apparently asleep. Manatees eat mainly aquatic vegetation, both submerged and floating; in coastal areas they may include mangrove shoots in their diet. Feeding off the bottom is made easier by the West Indian manatee's downwardly directed snout, which enables it to browse underwater beds of sea grass and waterweeds. Altogether, more than 50 plant species have been recorded in the manatee's diet. The animals seem able to consume large amounts of floating water hyacinth, a plant that few other creatures will eat. Water hyacinths are a major pest in tropical rivers, where they clog the waterways and prevent the passage of boats. The manatees' liking for the plant is therefore beneficial to humans, helping maintain open water. Manatees sometimes raise their head well above water to crop overhanging vegetation or nibble at grass along river banks.

Most of the time manatees just float motionlessly at the surface like large logs in the water. With only the top of their back visible, they are difficult to spot and cannot see much themselves. Such behavior is dangerous where

West Indian manatees move slowly through shallow waters, often traveling in small family groups. As they swim, they feed on aquatic plants that float on the surface or grow under the water.

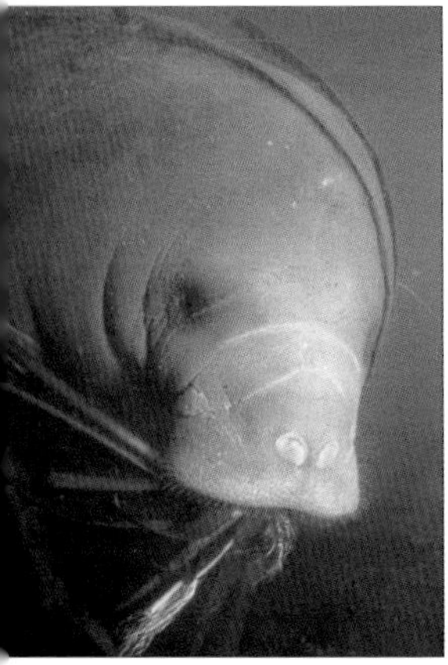

A West Indian manatee munches on aquatic plants. As the downward-pointing snout suggests, the species feeds mostly on the seabed.

large numbers of fast launches and other boats skim the water. In the coastal waters of Florida and parts of the Caribbean many people have waterside houses and use their boats for fishing and for visiting stores and neighbors. Other boats may be ferrying passengers, towing water skiers, or making local deliveries. Collisions with manatees are frequent and often result in nasty wounds or even death as propellers cut deep into their body. Outside United States waters hunting for their tasty meat is probably the main threat to manatees, but many also drown after getting tangled in big fishing nets.

Breeding Patterns

Breeding can occur at any time of the year. In cooler waters, however, manatees tend to be seasonal breeders, and the calves are mostly born during the summer. A female may mate with several males, not forming a permanent bond with any of them. Pregnancy lasts for about a year, after which a single calf is born. It stays with its mother for up to two years, sucking milk from one or the other of her two teats, which are located in her "armpits." Within a few weeks of birth the calf also begins to eat plants. By keeping close to its mother, it learns where to find food—a vital skill, especially when seasonal changes in water temperatures may make certain feeding areas unsuitable and force the animals to move on. It will be at least two years before the mother has another offspring. Meanwhile, the calf grows slowly and may not reach breeding condition until it is up to eight years old.

Such a slow rate of reproduction reflects the fact that manatees have few natural enemies and do not need to breed rapidly. Indeed, they might well run out of food sources if they did. However, various unnatural dangers now threaten the animal's placid and stable existence—beside the particular problem of collisions with motorboats. In 1996 over 150 dead and dying manatees were found in Florida waters, apparently poisoned as a result of an unusual bloom of toxic algae. Again, pollution may have been responsible for the huge increase in algal production.

The slow-breeding manatees cannot quickly make good extra losses to their populations, however they are caused. If natural mortality is increased by only a few percent, manatees may easily die out. As a result of injuries and general disturbance, manatees have already declined along the coasts, especially in Florida. They are

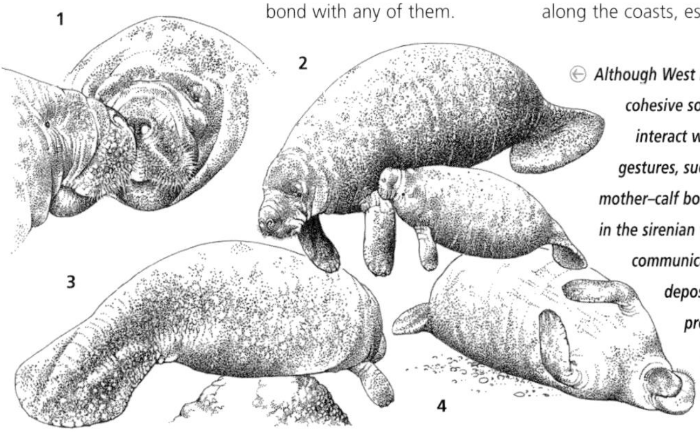

Although West Indian manatees lack any cohesive social organization, they will interact with each other using simple gestures, such as "kissing" (1). The mother–calf bond (2), however, is the strongest in the sirenian world. Manatees also communicate via "rubbing posts" (3). They deposit tastes and odors onto prominent objects, where they can be detected by others. Sometimes, manatees relax on their backs on the seabed (4).

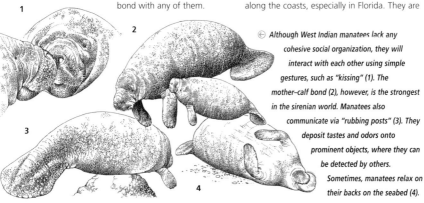

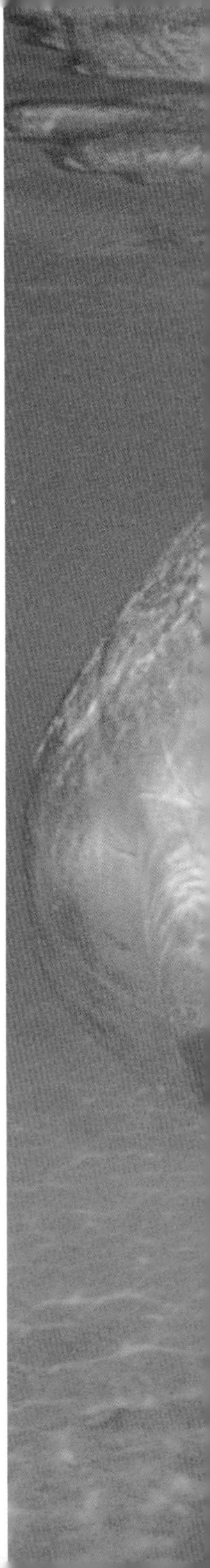

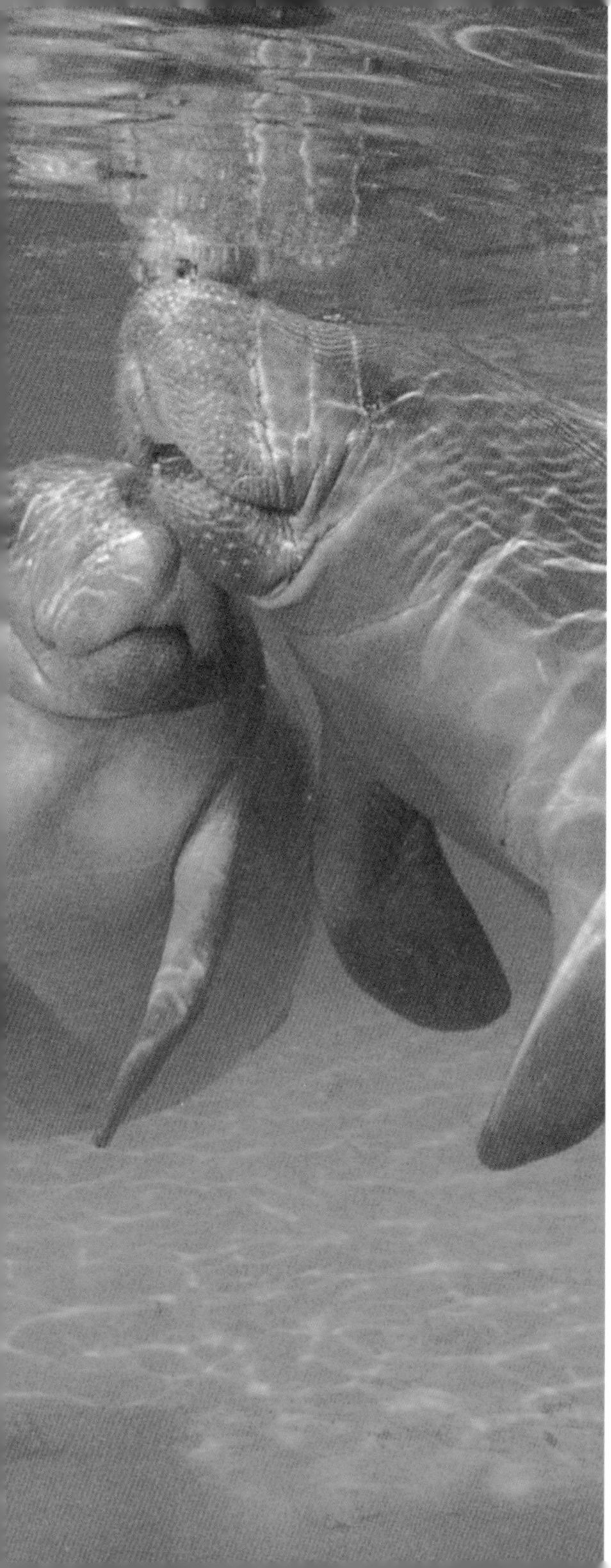

now quite rare in places and may disappear altogether if the activities that cause manatee deaths are not controlled. If the present losses could be reduced, even by a small amount, the manatee population would enjoy a small but steady growth. Boat-free zones and lower speed limits might help protect populations.

Tourist Attraction

Manatees are a popular tourist attraction, especially where they are easily visible drifting in the clear waters fed by springs from the limestone below. However, too many visitors approaching too close may not be beneficial. Local legislation in Florida aims to control the problem. The United States Fish and Wildlife Service has created a special sanctuary at Three Sisters Springs in the Crystal River, where more than 250 manatees spend the winter because the water there is pleasantly warm. Disturbance had been driving them away, but the area will now be off-limits to visitors and boats between November and March.

A mother and calf. In the 12 to 18 months after birth the young manatee stays close to its mother, learning about feeding areas and annual migration routes.

A Warm Welcome

Manatees do not like water that is cooler than about 68°F (20°C). In summer Florida's manatees disperse widely along coasts and rivers. In cooler periods, particularly in winter, they make local migrations and often gather together in places where power plants discharge warm water into the sea, such as at Cape Canaveral, Fort Myers, and in Tampa Bay. Farther south in the Caribbean the water remains warm most of the time. Here manatees tend to move around less according to season, congregating to feed rather than to enjoy warm water.

Killer Whale/ Orca

Orcinus orca

The largest member of the dolphin family, the killer whale (or orca) is the top sea predator. Hunting in groups, orcas will even attack giant blue whales.

Common name Killer whale (orca)

Scientific name *Orcinus orca*

Family Delphinidae

Order Cetacea

Size Length: male 17–29.5 ft (5.2–9 m); female 15–25.5 ft (4.5–7.7 m)

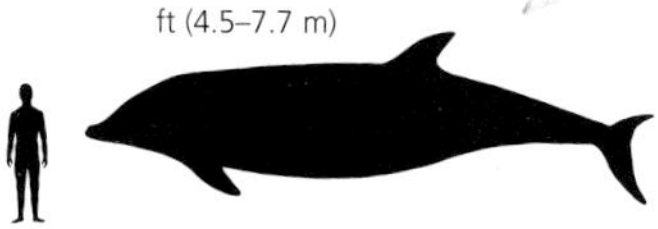

Weight 3–10 tons (2.5–9 tonnes)

Key features Striking black-and-white markings; body mainly black with white patch behind eye, white cheeks and belly, and gray saddle patch; head rounded with no obvious snout; tall, triangular dorsal fin, up to 6 ft (1.8 m) high in male; broad, rounded flippers; tail black on top, white on underside

Habits Social, living in a tight-knit family group or "pod"; fast, active swimmer; acrobatic at the surface, will breach, spy-hop, and tail slap

Breeding Single calf born about every 8 years after gestation period of 17 months. Weaned at 14–18 months; sexually mature at 12–16 years. Males may live 35–60 years, females up to 90 years in the wild; rarely survives more than a few years in captivity

Voice Varied, including complex, often pulsed, calls

Diet Ssmall fish and squid to seals, turtles, seabirds, and even other whales

Habitat Open sea to coastal waters; estuaries; often around ice floes in polar waters

Distribution Every ocean in the world, from polar regions to equator

Status Population: 100,000, IUCN Lower Risk: conservation dependent; CITES II. Widespread and quite numerous

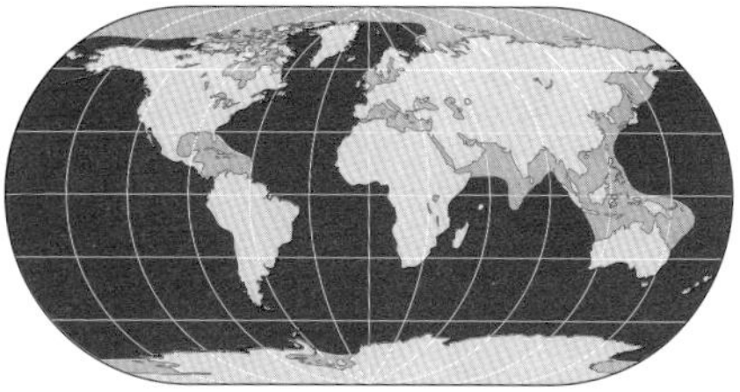

KILLER WHALES ARE ONE OF the most recognizable cetaceans, familiar from their antics in captivity and in the *Free Willy* movies. They are very large, heavily built dolphins with characteristic black-and-white markings. Their muscular bodies make them the fastest mammal in the sea, with sprints recorded at 35 miles per hour (56 km/h)—almost as fast as a racehorse.

From a distance the most recognizable feature of a killer whale is the tall, triangular dorsal fin. In a mature male it can be up to 6 feet (1.8 m) tall—the height of a man. In females the dorsal fin is only half as tall and has a more curved shape. The flippers are also large, especially in males. Killer whales have 20 to 26 sharp teeth in both the top and bottom jaws. The teeth are pointed, conical, and each is up to 2 inches (5 cm) long. When the jaws close, they interlock perfectly, clamping fish and other prey in a vicelike grip.

Not So Deadly

Killer whales are formidable hunters and gained their name from 18th-century whalers who saw them attack other whales and believed that they would also eat humans. This belief lasted until the 1960s, when people began to study whales more closely. Despite their reputation, there are no records of humans ever being killed by a killer whale, so some people prefer the more kindly name of "orca."

Killer whales are one of the most widely distributed animals in the world. They live in every ocean and have adapted to both the icy conditions of the Antarctic and the warm, equatorial seas. However, individuals do not appear to migrate between them as some

↑ *Killer whales are the top sea predators. They will catch and eat almost any type of prey—from seals and turtles to other whales. However, they tend to feed on locally abundant resources and this can affect hunting techniques and even body size in different parts of their range.*

species of whale do. They are more common in cold, polar waters. One of the best places to see orcas in the wild is the waters of the Juan de Fuca Strait and San Juan Islands between Washington State and Vancouver Island, British Columbia, Canada.

Killer whales live in social groups known as "pods." These consist of up to 50 animals, usually one mature male, several mature females, and young of both sexes. They are stable, tightly knit groups, with animals staying with the same pod for their whole life.

Group Dialects

Animals in a pod communicate with complex calls, some of which may serve to identify the group to other pods. Each pod has a distinct dialect, using a characteristic pattern of repetitive sounds. The dialects are so distinctive that by listening to the calls, even a human researcher can tell which pod an animal is from.

Three types of killer whale have been identified, each with different social habits. There are residents, transients (or wanderers), and offshore animals. Residents stay in large family pods, usually of five to 25 animals, and have a relatively small home range. They tend to be very noisy, communicating to each other with frequent calls. They hunt using echolocation and feed mainly on fish and squid. Transient orcas live in smaller pods with one to seven animals. They roam over a wide area and are quieter, using stealth to hunt sea mammals such as seals, sea lions, and other dolphins. Offshore orcas spend most of their time in the open sea, much farther away from the coast, and probably eat mainly fish. They seem to stay in large groups of 25 or more, communicating with each other frequently and noisily.

Killer whales will catch and eat almost any type of prey. They have been recorded eating over 100 species of animal, more than any other cetacean. As well as fish and squid, they will eat seals, dugongs, turtles, penguins, gulls, and even other whales more than 10 times their size. When they attack large whales, they tend to bite pieces off their lips and tongue.

They hunt cooperatively in a team, like a wolf pack, and use different techniques to catch different prey. They will herd salmon by making noisy calls and slapping their flippers on the surface, trapping the fish in a tight, frightened bunch before lunging in to eat them. Seals and sea lions are one of the killer whale's favorite foods, and the whales go to great lengths to catch them. Prey animals are not even safe out of the water: In parts of Argentina and on the Crozier Islands in the Indian Ocean killer whales launch themselves onto the beach to seize baby sea lions resting there. Then, using their front flippers, they wriggle back into the sea to eat their victim. Killer whales in antarctic waters have been known to hunt seals by tipping them off ice floes. A researcher watched a group of whales, their heads poking out of the water, scanning the ice for seals. When they spotted one, they watched it carefully for a few minutes. First, the whole group swam rapidly toward it, then all together dived under the ice. Their dive caused a big wave to wash over the loose ice floe, tipping it at such a sharp angle that the seal slid off into the sea where the whales could catch it. Such an example of cooperative behavior suggests that killer whales are very intelligent creatures, capable of problem solving and coordinating their actions as a group for the benefit of all.

A killer whale off the coast of Patagonia, Argentina, snatches a sea lion for its meal.

Killer whales are social animals that live in tightly knit groups known as "pods."

A killer whale pod surfacing in Canada. Often the whales will work together to hunt prey, such as salmon, trapping shoals between the pod and the shore.

Killer whales have no natural predators; but as with many other species of whale, human interference causes many deaths. Some killer whales are hunted, although less so now than in the past. In the years between 1938 and 1981 Japanese, Norwegian, and Russian whalers killed 5,537 killer whales. A few orcas have also been caught for exhibition in major aquaria—over 150 since the 1960s. Once in captivity, most killer whales only live for a few years, but offer a fascinating and educational spectacle for millions of visitors each year.

Salmon Stealing

Killer whales also come into conflict with fishermen, who will sometimes kill them if they believe that they are taking valuable fish. In Alaska killer whales have learned to steal salmon directly from fishing hooks. Fish farms can also cause problems. Intensively farmed fish are a source of diseases, and pesticides used to control fish lice can get into the food chain.

Studying Killer Whales

Orcas in the waters around Vancouver Island in British Columbia, Canada, have been studied for many years. Individual animals can be identified by the different shapes and sizes of their dorsal fins. Some have distinctive nicks and scars on their bodies. The shape of the gray saddle marking often varies, enabling individuals to be recognized. By following particular animals from birth, recording their family histories, habits, and interactions with other orcas, researchers are learning more and more about the complex lives of these previously misunderstood creatures.

Other threats include boat traffic and underwater noise from engines. The killer whale is also particularly vulnerable to pollution, which affects its prey and can lead to the accumulation of dangerous substances in the whales' own body tissues.

Blue Whale

Balaenoptera musculus

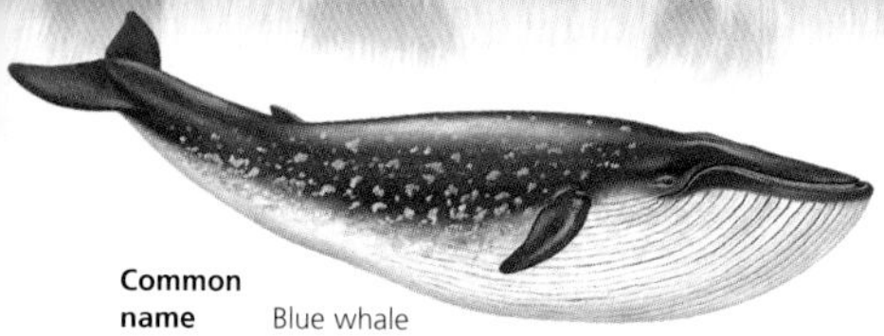

Common name Blue whale

Scientific name *Balaenoptera musculus*

Family Balaenopteridae

Order Cetacea

Size Length: 80–100 ft (24–30 m). Female generally larger than male

Weight 114–136 tons (100–120 tonnes), occasionally up to 216 tons (190 tonnes)

Key features Long, streamlined rorqual whale—largest animal on earth; blue-gray with pale mottling; ridge runs along top of flat, "U"-shaped head; 2 blowholes with fleshy splashguard; tapered flippers up to one-seventh of body length; small, stubby dorsal fin; tail flukes broad and triangular

Habits Shy and wary; mother and calf travel together, otherwise tends to be solitary; sometimes larger numbers found close together feeding or migrating; may associate with fin whales

Breeding Single calf born after gestation period of 10–11 months. Weaned at 7–8 months; sexually mature at 5 years in females and just under 5 years in males. May live 80–100 years

Voice Loud, low rumbling calls that travel long distances underwater

Diet Principally krill, but also other small crustaceans and fish

Habitat Mainly open ocean, but will come closer to shore to feed or breed; migrates between polar feeding grounds and warmer subtropical and tropical breeding grounds

Distribution Found in all oceans of the world

Status Population: 3,500; IUCN Endangered; CITES I

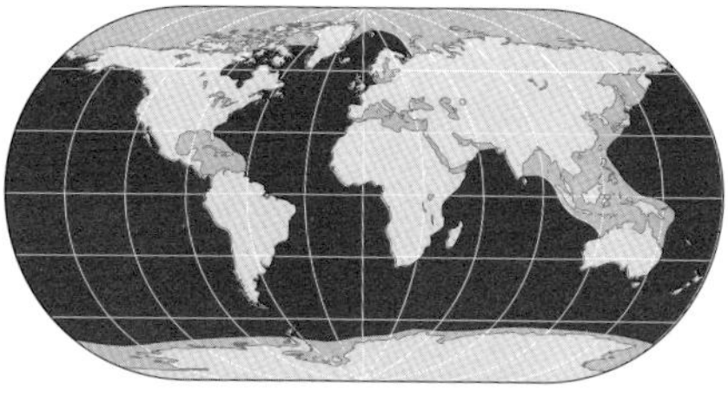

Bigger than any of the dinosaurs, the blue whale is the largest creature ever known to have lived on the earth.

Weighing more than 20 African elephants, the blue whale is gigantic—the biggest animal on earth. The largest known dinosaur, *Argentinosaurus huinculensis*, was about 100 feet (30 m) long and weighed a massive 89 tons (81 tonnes), but the blue whale has been known to attain lengths of 108 feet (33 m) and weigh nearly 180 tons (163 tonnes). A heart the size of a small car pumps roughly 6 tons (5.4 tonnes) of blood around the body. The main artery, the dorsal aorta, is large enough for a human to crawl through it. The mouth of the blue whale is so big that an entire football team could stand inside on the tongue. In fact, the tongue alone weighs nearly 4 tons (3.6 tonnes), as much as a school bus.

Abundant Food Supplies

Blue whales have been able to grow to such incredible sizes by making use of the plentiful supply of food present at their fertile polar feeding grounds. Their size is possible because their body is supported by water, and so they do not require the large, heavy, and impractical bones that a land animal of equivalent size would need. Furthermore, support from the water is spread out evenly over the whole of the whale's underside, not concentrated on the bones of the hips and shoulders.

The blue whale has a slim, streamlined shape with a girth that is less than that of an adult right whale. But when it feeds the 80 to 100 throat grooves, which run from the chin to the navel, expand and increase the whale's volume as it takes in 36 to 45 tons (33 to

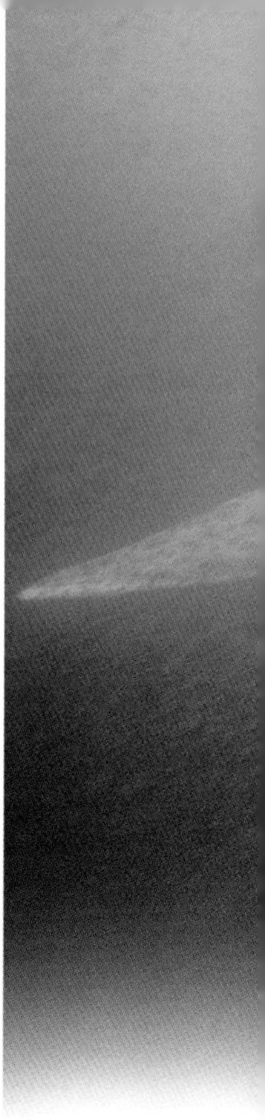

↑ ***An underwater view of a blue whale feeding. The throat grooves can expand to increase the whale's volume, enabling it to take in immense quantities of water and krill—its main food.***

41 tonnes) of food and water. Surprisingly, the largest creature in the ocean feeds on one of the smallest—krill. These tiny crustaceans are only a couple of inches (about 5 cm) long, but they are the main energy source of blues. The krill are filtered out from huge mouthfuls of water by the whale's baleen plates.

Nickname

The blue whale takes its name from the slate-blue color of its skin, which is mottled with gray and white blotches. Algae sometimes attach themselves to the stomach of the whales, giving them a yellowish tinge. The algae are actually responsible for the animal's nickname of "sulfur bottom." Blue whales have a small dorsal fin about three-quarters of the way along the back. It is tiny in relation to the rest of the body, only about 15 inches (38 cm) high. It also varies in form from triangular to sickle shaped. The tail flukes are broad—about as wide as the wingspan of a small aircraft. The flippers are slender and tapered. A single, raised longitudinal ridge runs along the top of the broad, "U"-shaped head from the tip of the snout to the two distinct blowholes. The blowholes are surrounded by a prominent fleshy splashguard, which helps keep water out of the whale's nostrils.

As well as being the largest animal, the blue whale is also the loudest. Its calls are emitted at a very low frequency and at a volume of 188 decibels. As a comparison, a human shout is only 70 decibels, and a jet engine at full blast is barely 140 decibels. Since decibels increase by factors of 10, the whale's call is thousands of times louder than that of a human. The loudness enables the sounds to travel for many miles underwater. The calls are highly structured, with long sequences of varied sounds, like our sentences. It is thought that the "songs" are used to communicate with other whales, especially during the breeding season. Effective communication is important because blue whales are thinly spread across the world's seas, with each one having hundreds of cubic miles of ocean to itself. Meeting to mate would be a very chancy affair were it not for the ability of the whales to tell each other where they are. Because the intensely loud calls travel for thousands of miles in deep water, there is the possibility that blue whales could even communicate across whole oceans. In addition to communication the blue whale may use sound to navigate, bouncing echoes off the seabed.

Ⓣ ***An aerial view of a blue whale and two calves off the Pacific coast of Mexico.***

Solitary

Blues seem to be fairly solitary whales. There is a strong bond between a mother and her calf, but otherwise they are found alone or in small groups of two or three individuals. Larger groups sometimes form at good feeding places. However, we need to be cautious when looking at the social behavior of these creatures because our perception of "solitary" may not be the same as that of the blue whale itself. Being such large animals, they require a great deal of space. Therefore, what we may think of as a lonely blue whale may actually, from its own perception, be in "company" with other whales that are only a few miles away. From time to time blue whales are found in association with fin whales, probably drawn together by a shared interest in abundant food.

In winter blue whales migrate from their polar feeding grounds to warmer waters to breed and calve. Little is known about mating in blue whales, since they are shy creatures and hard to locate in the open seas. Pregnancy is unusually short for such a large animal, only 10 to 11 months. When the calves are born, they are about 18 to 20 feet (5.5 to 6 m) long and weigh 1.8 to 3.6 tons (1.6 to 3.2 tonnes). The mother produces over 450 pounds (200 l) of milk every day to nourish her calf. Her milk is rich and creamy, containing 35 to 50 percent fat, and the young calf will gain more than 200 pounds (90 kg) a day. The mother and calf stay close together, since blue whale calves are occasionally the target of a pack of killer whales. After only seven or eight months the calf is weaned, weighing at least nine times its birth weight and having doubled in length. The weaning of the calves coincides with migration back to the cold waters of the feeding grounds.

Most blues are migratory, but in some areas—such as the Pacific waters off Costa Rica (known as the "Costa Rican Dome") and off Baja California—blue whales are seen all year round. That could be because some whales do not embark on the full migration every year and stay behind. Otherwise, the population is perhaps permanently resident there. It could also be due to the seasonal overlap of populations: When the Northern Hemisphere whales migrate north to their feeding grounds, the Southern Hemisphere population replaces them at the breeding grounds. Blue whales have been observed feeding on krill off Baja California. It is unusual for the warm breeding waters to support large enough quantities of krill and this may explain why some whales

seem to remain all year round: Since food is available, they do not need to undertake the exhausting journey to the polar feeding grounds, hence saving precious energy reserves.

Despite their size, blue whales are fast swimmers: When alarmed, they can reach speeds of over 30 miles per hour (48 km/h). Their streamlined bodies allow them to move quickly through the water, faster than most ships. But they rarely leap out of the water, unlike many of their smaller relatives. They are also timid, which, combined with their swiftness, makes them hard to approach. It is also surprisingly hard to locate them, since they tend to stay submerged for long periods, only surfacing for a few minutes to breathe, then diving for up to 45 minutes. As a result, little is known about the everyday life of blues.

Favored Catch

Before the mid-1800s the blue's enormous size and speed were to its advantage. Whalers were unable to catch it, so the species was spared the massive exploitation suffered by other whales. However, the introduction of faster boats, improved whaling techniques, and the depleted stocks of more traditional catches led to the blue whale becoming the favored target. In fact, the animal's large size now provided a strong motive to hunt it. Whalers could extract about 120 barrels of oil from a single blue whale; and being so valuable, they soon made up almost 90 percent of the whaling industry's total catch. The slaughter peaked in 1931, when more than 30,000 blue whales fell victim to the whaling industry. The International Whaling Commission banned hunting of blue whales in 1966, when numbers had declined so much that the species was close to extinction. However, there are now concerns about the influence of other human activities on blue whales, such as pollution, habitat degradation, and increased levels of acoustic disturbance. Some people fear that numbers have fallen too low for a recovery to happen. It would certainly be a tragedy if this phenomenal animal were to become extinct because of human exploitation.

Big Appetites!

The gigantic blue whale requires huge amounts of energy to sustain its large body. It gorges itself at its polar feeding grounds, taking advantage of the plentiful supply of krill. At the fertile polar waters the whales eat an estimated 3 to 3.6 tons (2.7 to 3.2 tonnes) every day, the equivalent of about 40 million krill. Some blue whale populations fast once they leave the feeding grounds because there is not such a plentiful supply of food in the warmer waters where they breed. Also, they must dedicate their time to mating. Instead of feeding, they obtain energy from their vast store of blubber (fat) that may weigh 54 tons (49 tonnes) per animal.

Blue whales usually stay underwater for 10 to 20 minutes at a time before surfacing to take a dozen or so breaths. With each exhalation they spray a jet of water as high as 30 feet (9 m).

Common name Mountain gorilla (eastern gorilla)

Scientific name *Gorilla beringei beringei*

Family Hominidae

Order Primates

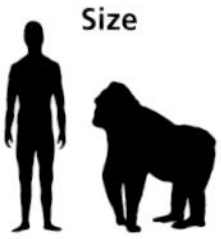

Size Height (standing upright): male 4.6–5.9 ft (1.4–1.8 m); female 4.3–5 ft (1.3–1.5 m); arm span: 7.5 ft (2.3 m)

Weight Male up to 400 lb (181 kg); female up to 200 lb (90 kg)

Key features Large, bulky ape with barrel-shaped body; muscular arms longer than legs; coat blue-black, turning gray with age, males with silver patch on back; hair short on back, long elsewhere; broad face and massive jaws

Habits Social groups of 5–30 animals centered around 1 (or occasionally 2) dominant "silverback" male; docile, spends most time feeding or resting; males display their strength by chest-beating and plant-thrashing

Breeding Usually 1 infant born every 4 years after gestation period of 250–270 days. Weaned at 2.5–3 years; females sexually mature at 8–10 years, males at 10 years. May live 35 years

Voice Howling, roaring, grunting, and snarling

Diet Leaves, stems, berries, roots, pulp, and bark

Habitat Montane rain forest and subalpine scrub at altitudes of 5,400–12,400 ft (1,645–3,780 m)

Distribution Borders of Democratic Republic of Congo, Rwanda, and Uganda

Status Population: about 320; IUCN Critically Endangered; CITES I. Most threatened gorilla species

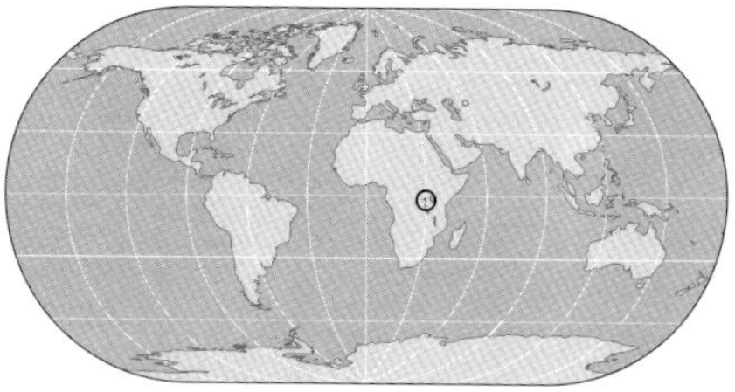

Mountain Gorilla

Gorilla beringei beringei

Mountain gorillas are gentle giants. They live in peaceful groups with a single dominant male. Of the five subspecies of gorilla, the mountain gorilla is the most studied and perhaps the most threatened.

MOUNTAIN GORILLAS LIVE IN a small area of the volcanic Virunga mountain range on the borders of Rwanda, Uganda, and Democratic Republic of Congo. High in the mountains the rain forest is almost always cloudy and cold, even though it is near the equator. Occasionally, the gorillas venture even higher into the alpine meadows at 13,100 feet (4,000 m), where temperatures fall well below freezing at night.

Dominating Presence

Gorillas are huge. Females weigh around twice as much as an average person, and the males weigh twice as much as the females. The only other animals that gorillas could be confused with are chimpanzees, but gorillas are much bigger and bulkier than chimps.

Mountain gorillas have long black fur to keep them warm in the cold, wet mountains. The hair on the back of a mature male gorilla is gray, hence the name of "silverback." Mountain gorillas have a broad, hairless face, small ears, nostrils banded by a wide ridge that extends to the upper lip, and massive jaws. They need big jaw muscles to chew the tough plant material that they eat. There is a ridge on the skull that the jaw muscles are attached to. In males the ridge and the jaw muscles are huge and give the head a characteristic bulge. Males also have long and robust canine teeth. Gorillas, especially the males, need to spend a lot of time eating to maintain their huge bulk. They eat a wide range of plants, including wild celery, nettles, wild cherry, bamboo, and thistles. As well as leaves, they will also crunch up bark, coarse stems, roots, and vines. In the

A female mountain gorilla eating spiny leaves: These gentle giants are exclusively vegetarian. A mountain gorilla's diet is mainly made up of leaves, stems, roots, and other types of vegetation, but rarely fruit.

mountains where they live, there is not much fruit, but they love to eat berries when they are available. They will eat fungi and some insects such as ants, but such small items are hardly worth the bother. They use their hands when they eat to pick plants and strip bark from stems to reach the succulent pith inside.

Laid-back Lifestyle

Gorillas are very docile animals. They are active during the day and spend about a third of the daytime resting, when the group gathers around the silverback male. They sleep or peacefully groom each other while the youngsters play.

They usually move slowly and spend most of their time on the ground. They mostly walk on all fours, with their hands curled into fists so they walk on their knuckles. They are able to climb trees, but the huge males are too heavy for all except the largest lower branches to support their weight. Only the young animals are light and agile enough to swing through the thinner branches high up.

Every night each animal builds a nest to sleep in by bending branches to make a comfortable, springy platform.

Gorilla Groupings—Species and Subspecies

Gorillas live only in equatorial Africa. There are two species, the western gorilla (*Gorilla gorilla*) and eastern gorilla (*Gorilla beringei*). They are divided into five subspecies.

There are three subspecies of eastern gorilla: the mountain gorilla (*G. beringei beringei*), which lives on the borders of Democratic Republic of Congo (DRC), Uganda, and Rwanda; the eastern lowland gorilla (*G. b. diehli*), which lives in the eastern central region of DRC; and another (unnamed) subspecies from the Bwindi Impenetrable Forest in Uganda.

Of the western gorillas the most common is the western lowland gorilla (*G. gorilla gorilla*). The Cross River gorilla (*G. g. diehli*), which lives along the border of Nigeria and Cameroon, has recently been classed as a separate subspecies and is Critically Endangered.

The nests are either in trees, on steep slopes, or on the ground. Since each gorilla makes its own nest, researchers can count the nests to ascertain how many animals are in a group even after they have left the area.

Despite their fierce reputation from films such as *King Kong*, gorillas have a quiet temperament and are very gentle unless they are threatened. They will let people get close to them as long as they sit quietly and do not stare. Staring is seen as a threat in gorilla society. If threatened, a male will protect his group, first with a display of strength and then by attacking fiercely.

Gorilla Society

Because mountain gorillas feed mainly on leaves, which are plentiful and available all year round, they can live in large groups without taking the risk of running out of food. The same animals stay with the group for months or years. There are usually between five and 10 animals in a group, but there can be up to 30 or 40. Groups are not territorial: Their feeding ranges often overlap, but their loud calls let other groups know where they are, so they avoid direct contact.

A large silverback male leads each group. He decides where the group will feed each day, protects them from danger, and usually fathers all the offspring. If the leading male dies, a younger male will quickly take over. As well as the silverback, there will usually be one or two subadult "blackback" males, several adult females, and up to 10 infants in one group.

Females nearly always leave their mother's group when they become sexually mature. This is unusual in primates, but prevents inbreeding. If a female stayed in the group, she would mate with the dominant male. He would be her father, or if he had died, a cousin, since one of his sons usually takes over. The offspring of such matings are usually not as healthy as those from matings between unrelated animals.

A female leaving a group will head straight to a nearby solitary male, but she does not necessarily stay with him. She probably chooses

↓ ***After feeding, mountain gorilla groups—like the one above—gather around the silverback to rest in the middle of the day. Females with infants (1) move closest to the silverback (2), while females without young stay farther in the background (3). The juveniles will play close to the silverback under his protective gaze (4), but subadult males are merely tolerated (5).***

a male according to the quality of the habitat in his home range and his fighting ability. Such matters are important if he is to protect her and her offspring from predators and other males.

Although groups are stable, it is each female's contact with the leading male, rather than with each other, that keeps them together. Bonds between the dominant male and the females, and females and their offspring, are maintained by mutual grooming. However, it is rare to see social grooming between mature females that are not close relatives.

When young males mature, at 11 to 13 years old, around half leave the group that they were born in. A male may choose to stay with the group if there are too many mature females for the dominant male to mate with alone or if the dominant male is old. If they leave, young males spend time on their own or with a small group of other bachelor males before starting their own harem, usually by luring females away from an established group.

If the leader of a group is threatened by a solitary male, he asserts his dominance with a show of strength. He roars loudly, draws himself up to his full height, and beats his chest with his hands. Then he rushes toward the intruder, tearing up bushes and small trees. Such behavior is a big bluff, designed to intimidate a rival and avoid a fight. Fights between males are rare; but when they do happen, they can be extremely fierce. The animals' long canine teeth can cause serious wounds and sometimes even death.

Competition between males is one reason why they are so large compared with the females and have much bigger canine teeth. Bigger males are more likely to succeed in scaring away rivals with their displays or to win a fight. A successful male gorilla may father 10 to 20 offspring over a 50-year life span. Unsuccessful males may never mate at all.

Studying Mountain Gorillas

The mountain gorillas have been studied very closely for many years. Dian Fossey was one famous researcher who lived with the gorillas. Researchers allow the gorillas to get used to their presence by spending a lot of time just hanging out with them. The process is called "habituation." Once the gorillas are used to people, they behave normally, and the researchers can study them without causing disturbance.

↑ ***Despite their size, mountain gorillas are really gentle giants. They will tolerate people as long as they do not stare, which the gorilla's regard as a threat.***

Caring for Young

Female gorillas become sexually mature at about six to eight years old, but they will not have their first baby until they have joined a stable group, usually around the age of 10. Gorillas will mate at any time of the year. Gestation lasts for about eight and a half months, after which a single baby is born. Twins are very rare; and because they are so difficult to look after, one of them usually dies.

At birth, a baby gorilla is almost bald and weighs about 4 pounds (1.8 kg), around half the weight of a human baby. At first it is carried by its mother, who holds it to her tummy. After a few weeks it can hang onto its mother's long chest fur by itself. Older babies ride on their mother's back. They start to eat solid food at around three years; but they will stay with their mother, sleep in her nest, and drink her milk until the age of four to five years.

Many baby gorillas die young, so a mother may only rear one offspring to reproductive age every eight years. The slow reproduction rate means that gorilla populations take a long time to recover from losses.

Future Threats

Mountain gorillas are Critically Endangered animals. There are only about 300 of them left, and these remaining few are under pressure from hunting and a shrinking habitat. Although most of the area where the gorillas live is protected as a national park, people trespass on their habitat, chop down the trees, and build houses right up to and even inside the park boundary. Gorillas are also threatened by poachers (illegal hunters), who use guns or snares to kill the animals. Most snares are made of a wire loop connected to a rope tied to a bent bamboo pole. When an animal steps into the wire loop, the bamboo springs back and pulls the wire tight around its leg or neck, trapping it painfully. Snares are particularly dangerous to baby gorillas because they are inquisitive and will investigate anything new.

Male mountain gorillas are twice the size of females. Their huge bulk and the low nutritional content of their food mean they must spend much of their time feeding.

Gorillas and Guerillas

In recent years the countries where the mountain gorillas live have been in conflict. During war saving gorillas is not the highest priority for local people, and their governments are too poor to protect the animals. There are not enough park wardens, and it is a dangerous job because guerillas (members of unofficial armies) use the forest to hide in. Some gorillas have been shot accidentally, and the guerillas also kill the animals to eat.

Chimpanzee

Pan troglodytes

Common name Chimpanzee

Scientific name *Pan troglodytes*

Family Hominidae

Order Primates

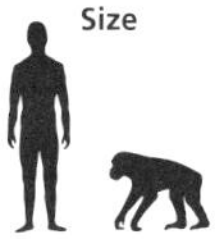

Size Length head/body: male 27.5–35 in (70–89 cm); female 25–33 in (63–84 cm); height: 39–66 in (99–168 cm)

Weight Male 75–154 lb (34–70 kg); female 57–110 lb (26–50 kg)

Key features Coat brownish or black, graying with age; face bare and brownish pink

Habits Active during the day, nights spent in platform nests in trees; usually seen in groups; generally travels on ground, sometimes walks upright, but usually on all fours using knuckles of hands

Breeding Single young born every 5 or 6 years after gestation period of about 230 days. Weaned at 3.5–4.5 years; sexually mature at around 7 years, but females do not breed until aged 14–15, males at 15–16 years. May live up to 60 years in captivity, similar in the wild

Voice Wide range of calls, including hoots, barks, grunts, and screams

Diet Varied; includes fruit, flowers, seeds, bark, insects, birds' eggs, and meat

Habitat Deciduous, montane, and tropical rain forests; also patchy savanna woodland

Distribution Western and central Africa

Status Population: 150–230,000; IUCN Vulnerable; CITES I. Threatened due to deforestation

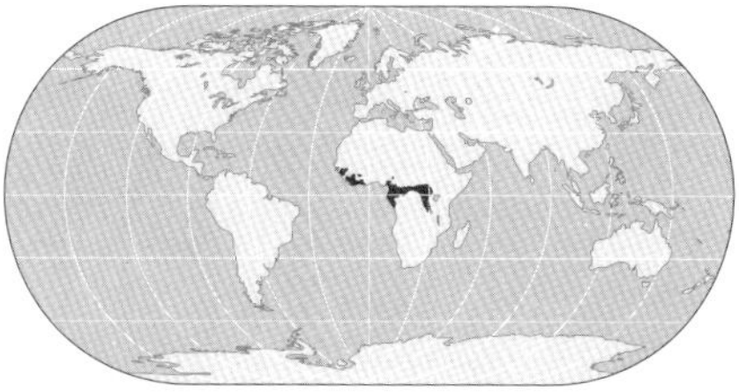

Chimps are close relatives of humans. They are intelligent and adaptable, and learn quickly how to exploit new situations. The animals lead complex social lives, with each individual having its own distinct personality.

CHIMPS LIVE IN LARGE GROUPS known as communities. A community can have up to 120 animals, but they are rarely all together at once. They spend time on their own or in small groups. One day they might be hunting with a large gang, the next foraging in a smaller group with different individuals, and the next sneaking off with a partner. Females tend to spend more time on their own or with their offspring, while the males are more sociable.

Knowing Your Place

Hierarchy is very important in chimp society. The dominant male often has three high-ranking males as aides, with other males forming a constantly shifting power network among the subordinate animals. A hierarchy exists among females too, but it is less important and less vigorously fought over. In chimp communities rank is not inherited as in many other primate societies, but has to be earned and maintained by constant effort. Hierarchy positions can change with an animal's health, strength, and the influence of his friends.

Bonds between animals are very important. The strongest are between a mother and her offspring, and may last for the mother's lifetime. Males make strong friendships with each other. Having friends that will back them up in fights is a good way of defending their position within the hierarchy. While a male on his own may not be strong enough to challenge a higher-ranking male, together two males may be more successful. Close alliances can be more important than strength and bullying tactics in chimpanzee society.

Chimps as Doctors

Chimps sometimes eat soil to aid the digestion of plants that contain toxins. They also eat plants for medicinal purposes: Chimps occasionally eat *Aspilia*—a plant with very rough leaves. They usually eat it first thing in the morning and in a very different way than normal food. They choose each leaf carefully, holding the leaves between their lips and rejecting some but eating others. They do not chew the leaves, but roll them around in their mouth before swallowing. Some African people also use *Aspilia* for stomach complaints, and it has antibiotic and antiparasitic properties. It is thought that chimps use *Aspilia* to remove intestinal worms.

↑ A male chimpanzee eating harungana berries in the Mahale Mountains, Tanzania. Chimpanzees eat a huge range of foods, although around 60 percent of their diet consists of fruit. They also consume meat and will kill monkeys and other mammals.

Friendships are maintained by grooming, hugging, kissing, and patting on the back. Hugging and kissing are seen more often between male chimps than between females. Animals spend many hours grooming each other, removing dirt and parasites from the fur, and cleaning wounds. As well as being physically beneficial, grooming has an important social function: It is used to strengthen friendships, patch up quarrels, confirm dominance, and to exchange favors.

Females do not tend to make such close friendships as males. The most important thing for them is to secure a good area in which to live. They tend to rely on their family members to support them, rather than on friends. A female's rank is therefore highly dependent on how many offspring she has.

Home Ranges

Each community of chimpanzees has its own home range. The size depends on the number of animals in the group and the quality of the habitat (especially the amount of food available in it). In a good rain forest with lots of fruiting trees the area a group uses will vary from 2 to 15.5 square miles (5 to 40 sq. km), averaging about 5 square miles (13 sq. km). In open savanna country, where good fruit and nesting trees are scarce, chimps need a larger range. In one savanna community in Senegal 30 chimps ranged over an area of 129 square miles (334 sq. km).

Animals know their home range well and have a "mental map" of the network of paths within it. They remember where to find fruiting trees, and when the fruit is likely to be ripe. When they go foraging, they do not move randomly, but use their knowledge of the area

⇧ *The chimpanzee has a more varied repertoire of facial expressions than any other mammal except humans. The play face (1) is characterized by an open mouth and concealed teeth; threat display face used during an attack (2); pout used for begging for food (3); full grin, showing intense fear or excitement (4); submissive pout (5); and fear grin, used to approach a higher-ranking animal (6).*

to search in likely places. Each day is planned so that not only are they more likely to come across food, but they will also not be too far away from nesting trees at night or from places to drink. Remembering where streams are is particularly important in the dry season.

Females, particularly those with young, do not travel as far as the males. They stick to their own "core ranges" and may only travel 1 or 2 miles (1.6 to 3 km) per day. Males can easily trek 4 miles (6.4 km) in a day and may explore the whole of their home range. In doing so, they overlap with the ranges of several females.

Tribal Warfare

Chimpanzees are territorial and protect their home ranges from other chimp communities using noisy threat displays and physical assaults. Groups of males patrol the borders of their range and use loud calls to announce their presence. When two groups from different communities meet, there is usually a display of strength that only rarely ends in actual fighting. Occasionally, males will mount deliberate invasions of another group's range. They have been known to carry out raids, repeatedly entering another group's territory, hunting and killing individual members until the entire group is wiped out. Such behavior is strikingly similar to tribal warfare in humans and is not known in any other type of animal.

Communication between group members is vital if they are to maintain social bonds, reaffirm positions in the social hierarchy, announce food discoveries, and alert others to leopards and other threats. Communication is both vocal and visual. Chimps use a wide variety of calls, including barks, contented "hooing" and lip-smacking, sociable grunts, loud "pant-hoots," and also piercing screams. Sound is an important way of staying in contact when groups are in dense forest and cannot see each other. When animals are within sight, sounds are usually

⇩ *A chimpanzee group in Tanzania. Groups are territorial and protect their home ranges with loud calls, threats, and even physical violence.*

accompanied by postures and facial expressions. Their naked faces and large, muscular lips give chimpanzees very expressive faces on which emotions and messages can be easily read. A wide-open mouth with the lips covering the teeth is a "play face." Chimps use the expression during play or to encourage a game. In contrast, an open mouth with lips pulled back to expose the teeth and gums is a "fear grin," showing anxiety and distress.

Posturing is important in communicating rank and acceptance. A dominant male maintains his position by his behavior, using displays of strength in which he charges around screaming and throwing branches. With his fur standing on end he makes himself look even larger. A subordinate, lower-ranking animal will behave submissively to him. With fur laid flat he darts to and fro in front of the dominant male, panting and screaming, then turns his back and crouches or bobs up and down. The dominant male acknowledges the submissive male with a hand on his back to reassure him.

Drum Beating

Vocal noises will also be supplemented by beating trees like a drum. The large, flat buttress roots of many tropical forest trees reverberate when hit with the fists: Male chimps often use the trees to send throbbing signals echoing through the forest to other members of their group.

Chimpanzees eat an enormous range of foods. At least 60 percent of their diet is ripe fruit. They also eat leaves, seeds, and other plant parts. Insects, especially termites, are an important source of protein and so are birds' eggs. Chimps also like to steal honey from bees and will eat over 20 different types of insects. Their identification skills are better than most human naturalists', and they select food from among 150 to 200 different plants, recognizing the edible ones from the many other poisonous or inedible species in the forest.

Chimps also eat meat. Males will go on organized hunting expeditions. They will hunt and kill monkeys, baboons, pigs, and even small antelope. A group of animals works together to ambush or chase prey. Chases can be very noisy and last up to two hours. When a victim is caught, the chimps go into a frenzy of excitement and tear it apart.

Tool Users

The use of tools to help perform additional tasks that cannot be completed with bare hands used to be considered one of the key differences between humans and all other species of animals. However, it is now known that several nonhuman species often use tools—chimpanzees foremost among them. Chimps show a great deal of intelligence in their choice, preparation, and use of tools. They strip leaves off long, thin sticks to poke around in termite nests, and use bent sticks to pull down fruit-laden branches that are otherwise out of reach. Sticks are also used as weapons, levers, and even to clean teeth. They use leaves to wipe themselves clean or to pick up sticky food. Leaves are also used to collect drinking water from tree holes. Spongy leaves are chewed first to make them more absorbent. Some chimps use stones to crack open hard nuts. They use a "hammer and anvil" technique, choosing a rock or exposed tree root as an anvil and a large, carefully selected stone as a hammer. Hammer stones can weigh up to 20 pounds (9 kg) and need to be held at just the right angle and used with enough force to crack the nut without spoiling the edible kernel

↑ ***A chimpanzee in Liberia cracks a nut with a stone, using a tree trunk as an anvil. Chimps show a great deal of intelligence in their use of objects, such as sticks and stones, as both tools and weapons.***

Chimp Culture

Chimps show cultural traditions that are learned and passed on in the group. One example is in tool use. Some chimpanzee communities use stones as hammers to crack nuts, while other groups have never learned the trick. In one part of Africa chimps crack oil palm nuts. Another community farther away uses heavier stones to break open harder nuts, and the animals ignore the easier oil palms. Yet another group of chimpanzees uses branches as wooden clubs, but few others are known to do so.

inside. Good hammer stones are hard to find in the forest, so chimps use the same one time and time again, remembering where they left it and carrying it from one place to another.

Playful as a Chimp

Young chimpanzees are born very small and helpless. The mother carries her baby under her belly until it is old enough to hang onto her chest hair. After five or six months the baby rides sitting upright on its mother's back.

Young chimps are extremely curious and playful. They will examine anything they can reach, including any other chimps that the mother will allow near. Other chimps are always very curious about new babies. They have to earn the right to come close to the baby, usually by giving the mother grooming sessions.

Weaning begins when the baby is at least three years old. The young chimp learns which foods are good to eat by exploring everything its mother has, often chewing the other end of whatever she eats. Mothers encourage their young to eat certain plants by dropping them in their path and discourage them from poisonous ones by taking them out of their hands.

Young chimps are taught by their mother, but also learn by experimentation or through watching others. Learning how to groom, recognizing group members, and learning the rules of social behavior are vital if a chimp is to get on in a community. Many lessons are learned during play: Hours are spent in rough-and-tumble and play-fighting games.

By the age of five a young chimp may be physically independent of its mother, but still very close to her emotionally. As they get older, juvenile chimps spend less time with their mother, and males increasingly venture out with gangs of other young males. Many females, however, stay with their mothers for the rest of their lives. However, some young females leave their birth group and join another. It is a risky venture, and it may be many years before they are fully integrated into the new community.

A female chimpanzee is receptive for 10 of the 36 days of her estrus cycle and advertises the fact with a pink swelling at her rear. During that time she is irresistible to males and may mate often. The top male in the group tries to monopolize mating opportunities by keeping close by, grooming her, and fending off other males. A lower-ranking male may be able to gain her favor, but has to attract her attention without the rest of the group noticing. Sometimes these illicit couples leave the group and disappear into the forest together for the duration of her fertile phase or even longer. The male then has a guarantee of being the father of the offspring, but both animals risk finding it difficult to rejoin the group or losing their rank in the social hierarchy.

Threats to Survival

Huge areas of African forests have been cut down for timber or to grow cash crops. What is left is very fragmented, with small pockets of trees that can only support a few isolated animals. Chimps are also killed to supply the bushmeat trade and were captured for zoos, the entertainment industry, and for biomedical research. The only way to catch a live baby chimp is to kill its mother, and many other members of the group may be killed or injured in the process.

Chimps in the Rain

Chimpanzees detest the rain, since their fur is not waterproof. They are normally up at dawn, but are reluctant to get out of bed if it is raining and shelter under trees or sit hunched up waiting for it to stop. However, a rainstorm sometimes encourages a male to perform a bizarre rain dance. First he rocks gently, then he stamps his feet, waves his arms, and throws branches around as though he is having a temper tantrum at the weather.

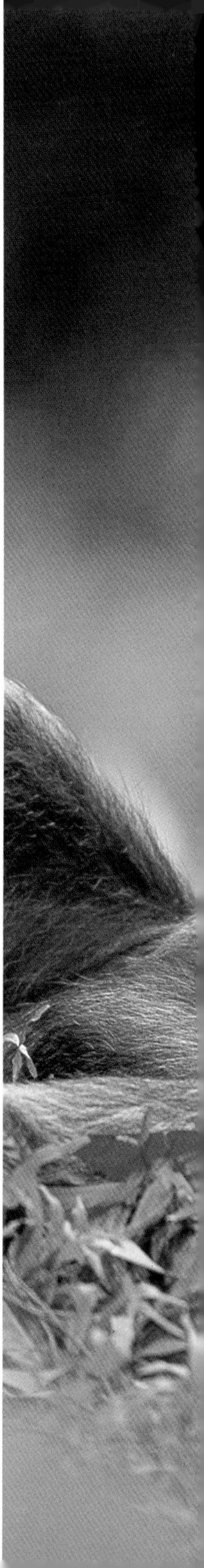

A juvenile chimp plays with an adult. Young chimps are extremely curious about their new environment, but adults are also interested in new additions to the group.

Vervet Monkey

Cercopithecus aethiops

Common name Vervet monkey (savanna guenon, grivet, or green monkey)

Scientific name *Cercopithecus aethiops*

Family Cercopithecidae

Order Primates

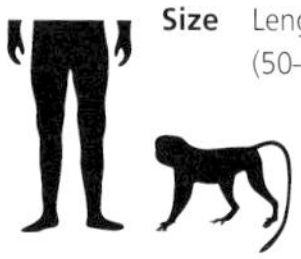

Size Length head/body: male 20–26 in (50–65 cm); female 15–24 in (38–62 cm); tail length: 19–30 in (48–75 cm)

Weight Male 9–18 lb (4–8 kg); female 8–11 lb (4–5 kg)

Key features Back and outer limbs grizzled gray or olive, underparts white; dark hands, feet, and tip of tail; face is bare and black, with white cheek tufts and eyebrows; eyelids white; scrotum bright blue, penis red

Habits Alert, lively, sociable monkey; active during the day; spends time on the ground as well as in trees

Breeding Single young usually born in favorable season after gestation period of 7 months. Weaned at 8–9 months; females sexually mature at 2 years, males at 3 years. May live up to about 30 years in captivity, 10 in the wild

Voice Includes barks, grunts, and screams

Diet Mainly fruit; also leaves, flowers, and crops; occasionally insects, eggs, nestlings, and small animals

Habitat Savanna and woodland edges near water

Distribution Most of Africa: Senegal east to Somalia and south to South Africa

Status Population: abundant, many thousands. Common and widespread

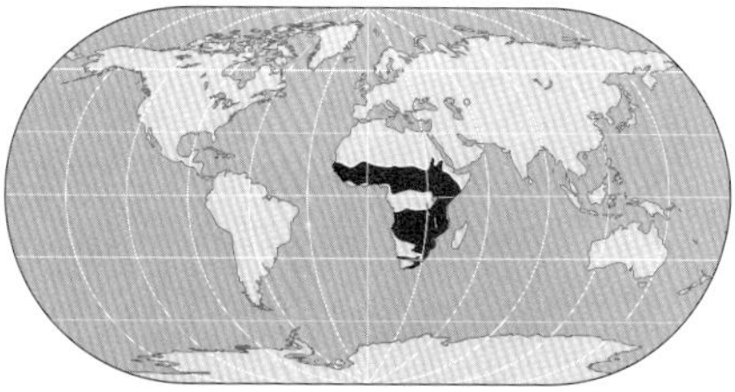

Vervets are successful, adaptable monkeys, living throughout a large part of Africa in many different habitats. They thrive almost anywhere where there is water and fruiting trees.

THE VERVET IS ONE OF THE GUENONS, a group of small- to medium-sized monkeys that have a long tail, grizzled fur, and dramatic face patterns. All guenons live in Africa. Vervets are the most widespread of the group, living across a large swath of the continent north and south of the equator and at altitudes of up to 10,000 feet (3,000 m). There are around 16 local variants throughout Africa, each differing slightly in appearance, but able to interbreed where their regions overlap.

Striking Looks

Vervets have a striking appearance, with their black face framed by white eyebrows and long, white cheek fur. The males have a turquoise blue scrotum and a red penis. The back, crown, and outer limbs are grizzled, gray, olive, or brownish, depending on the region in which the animal lives. In the eastern parts of southern Africa they are gray, becoming more olive green in the west. From the Indian Ocean to the great lakes of the Rift Valley they are an olive-fawn color; on the Atlantic side of Africa they are olive-gray with a blotched face; and in Somalia they are brownish. The underside is white; the hands and feet are dark. The long tail has a dark tip and red tufts at its base, but it cannot be used for gripping branches, as in many American monkeys.

Unlike other guenons, which tend to be forest dwelling, vervets prefer more open areas. They live mainly on the savanna and in lightly

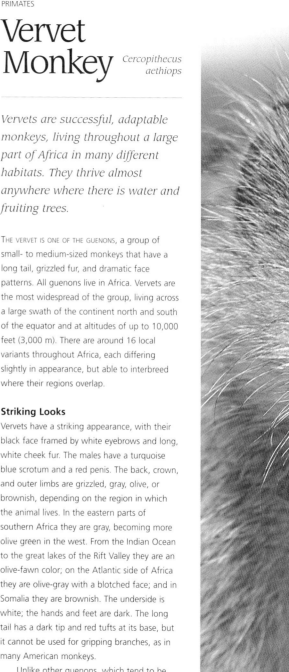

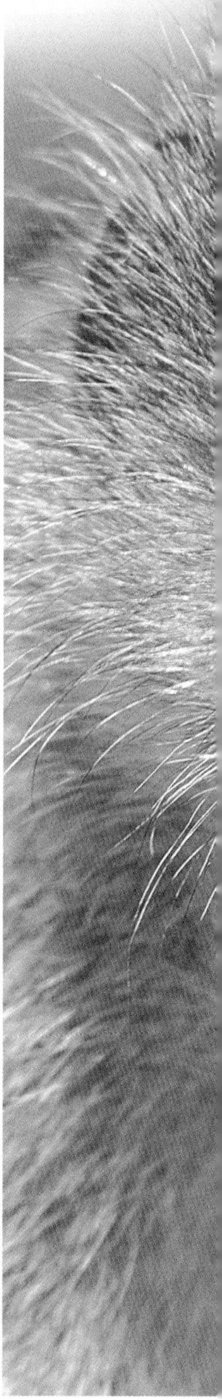

wooded areas. Their favorite habitat is in the acacia trees that line riverbanks, but they are very flexible about the types of habitat that they occupy. They are also found along the edges of rain forest, in mangrove swamps, and even on agricultural land. In fact, they seem able to live anywhere there is water and enough trees to supply fruit, shade, and somewhere to sleep.

The vervet monkey's diet consists mainly of fruit, particularly figs. Outside the fruiting season, when such food is not available, they will eat flowers, buds, and leaves. Acacia trees are also an important source of food, providing seeds, flowers, fruit, and gum. Vervets often raid crops and can become a pest in coffee plantations. They will also eat some animal food, such as invertebrates, especially insects, eggs, and small lizards and mice. However, their tiny thumbs mean that they are not very good at catching and handling live insects or other small, active sorts of prey.

When foraging for food, vervets are equally happy on the ground as in the trees. However, they may spend a lot of time out of the trees, particularly when there is no fruit available. But they will always try to keep close enough to trees to allow a swift escape off the ground if danger threatens. Vervets always sleep in trees. They are good climbers, but only rarely leap from tree to tree. They come down from the trees head first. When on the ground, they walk or use a fast, bounding gallop on all four limbs. In tall grass they will run on their hind legs to get a better view. They can also swim, but do so only occasionally.

Inherited Rank

Vervets are sociable animals. They live in groups (called troops) of about two dozen animals, but sometimes as many as 70 or as few as five. Troops usually include several males, and both

Vervet monkeys look very striking. Their black faces are framed by white eyebrows and white cheek fur. Their body fur can be a gray, fawn, or olive shade.

the males and females adopt a hierarchy of dominance. High-ranking individuals have priority when there is competition for food, and high-ranking males also perform most of the matings. Rank within females is inherited, so a daughter born to a high-ranking mother automatically has a high rank herself. Rank also depends on age. If more than one female in the group is ready to breed, the males will tend to prefer the older one. Similarly, females tend to prefer older males. The males are usually dominant over the females, but females will often band together to prevent males from attacking their young.

Although a troop will forage and sleep close together, the animals tend to interact mainly with close family members. Such practices are especially common among females. Individuals within a family form close bonds and will sit together and groom each other. They will also defend each other in fights. Juveniles tend to form close bonds among themselves, and young males will carry and care for younger relatives. However, adult males show no interest in infants. Mothers will allow other females to hold their babies, and the young of high-ranking females seem to be preferred for such "fondling."

Daughters stay with their mothers in the same social group as long as they live, while sons usually leave the troop when they become sexually mature. They will go to join a neighboring troop, losing their inherited rank.

Vervets are alert monkeys. High-ranking males are especially cautious and are constantly looking out for trouble, whether in the form of a predator or a gang of rival males. Vervets are at risk from many predators, including eagles, leopards, and pythons, which often wait in ambush at the base of trees.

Troop Signals

Living in a group demands a certain amount of coordination and communication. Vervets have a wide range of calls that they use to communicate warnings, threats, submission, or pleas for help. When defending territories, they will use a loud bark. Both males and females use a "chutter" of low staccato barks as an aggressive threat and to call for support from the rest of the group. If two vervets within the troop are fighting, others will use a low bark to encourage them to stop. A deep, guttural "woof" or exhaled "wa" sound shows submission by a lower-ranking male to a more dominant animal. Females and juveniles let out a high-pitched, piercing scream or squeal if they feel threatened and want assistance. Members of the troop give a nasal grunt when they are about to move off to a new area.

Vervets have a complex system of alarm calls, with different calls for different predators. For example, they give a short, sharp "chirp" call for mammalian predators, such as leopards, and a short, rough "rraup" for birds of prey. The different calls allow the others in the troop to take appropriate action. On a "leopard" call the group runs into the trees. On an alarm call for an "eagle" the animals look up and run into the bushes, while a "snake" alarm call causes them to stand up on their hind legs and peer into the grass around them.

As well as their extensive range of calls, vervets also use visual and tactile signals to communicate. When a vervet is standing on all fours, the position of the tail is a good clue to the animal's mood. When feeling confident, a vervet holds his tail high, arched over the body.

Defending Territory with Red, White, and Blue

Vervets are highly territorial and will defend their home range against other troops. Although females are territorial, the males are most active in defense of their home area. When two troops meet, they use aggressive calls and body language to intimidate their rivals. The males use a threat display known as "red, white, and blue" in which they walk back and forth or stand upright, each displaying its bright-red penis and blue scrotum to the intruders.

↑ ***A troop of vervet monkeys perches in the lower branches of a tree in the Moremi Reserve, Botswana. Troops can number anything from five to 70 individuals. Dominance hierarchies operate within the troop, with rank being inherited from parents.***

If fearful, the animal will hold his tail lower, parallel to the ground. Staring with raised eyebrows and head bobbing are both threat displays, while rapid glancing toward and away from an aggressor indicates submission. When two vervets meet, they touch muzzles together in a nose-to-nose greeting. It is usually followed by play or grooming, which is an important way of maintaining social bonds.

Flexible Breeding

One of the reasons for the vervets' success is their flexible breeding rate. Females can breed at any time of year, but numbers of births tend to peak during the seasons when food is most abundant. During times of drought or famine they are less likely to reproduce; but when good times return, they quickly resume breeding.

When a female is receptive, she will present herself to the male to encourage mating. A single infant is subsequently born, although occasionally there are twins. A mother will nurse her young until the next infant is born, which will usually be the following year.

Young vervet monkeys mature quickly: Females are able to reproduce in two years and males in three. However, females do not reach full adult size until they are four years old, and males take five years to reach maturity.

Two vervets in the Kruger National Park, South Africa, take turns in mutual grooming. As in other primates, grooming is an important way of maintaining social bonds.

Common name Golden lion tamarin

Scientific name *Leontopithecus rosalia*

Family Callitrichidae

Order Primates

Size Length head/body: 8–13 in (20–31 cm); tail length: 12.5–16 in (32–40 cm)

Weight 21–28 oz (600–800 g)

Key features Small, lively monkey with a long, silky golden coat; long hair on crown, cheeks, and sides of neck forms mane; long tail; bare, flattened face with widely spaced nostrils

Habits Social animal that lives in small groups of 3–7 individuals; active during the day, spending most of the time in the dense middle layers of the forest; rests at night in tree holes

Breeding Young (most commonly twins) born September–March after gestation period of 128 days. Weaned at 12 weeks; sexually mature at 2–3 years. May live 28 years in captivity, many fewer in the wild

Voice A variety of calls, including trills, clucks, and whines

Diet Mostly fruit and insects; small animals such as frogs and lizards; also birds' eggs

Habitat Lowland tropical forests from sea level to about 3,000 ft (1,000 m)

Distribution Rio de Janeiro state, southeastern Brazil

Status Population: fewer than 1,000; IUCN Critically Endangered; CITES I. Destruction of lowland forest is greatest threat to survival

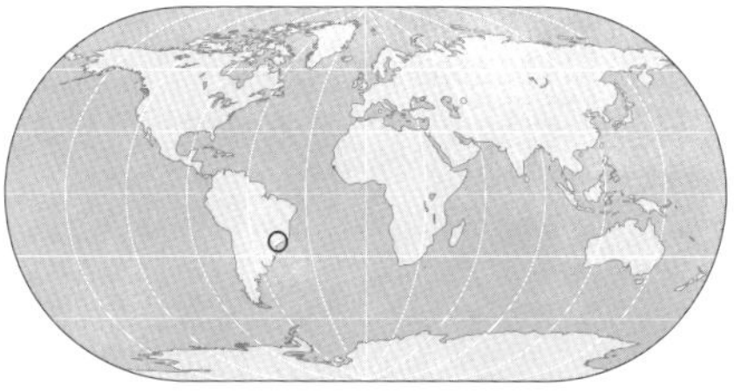

Golden Lion Tamarin

Leontopithecus rosalia

The golden lion tamarin is one of the most threatened mammals in the world. It has been rescued from the brink of extinction by successful reintroduction of captive-bred animals to their natural habitat.

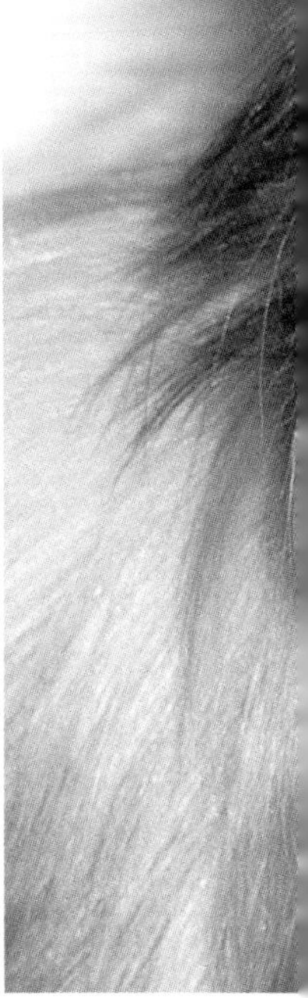

Lion tamarins are only the size of squirrels, but they are still the largest members of the callitrichid family. There are four types of lion tamarin, all of which are threatened in the wild. The four species have a golden coloration, but only the golden lion tamarin is golden over its entire body. The others are the black-faced lion tamarin (*Leontopithecus caissara*), golden-headed lion tamarin (*L. chrysomelas*), and black lion tamarin (*L. chrysopygus*).

Golden Fur

The golden lion tamarin is almost uniformly a golden-red color, with the occasional splash of orange, brown, or black on the tail and hands. It has soft, silky fur and a thick golden mane of long hairs on the top of the head, cheeks, throat, and neck. Its stunning color is one of the reasons that the animal is now so close to extinction. Demand for the golden lion tamarin as a pet and zoo animal has meant that many have been taken from the wild. However, by far the largest threat has been the destruction of the lowland forests in which it lives.

Like other tamarins, golden lions are diurnal. At night they sleep in tree holes or occasionally among vines or dense creepers that grow on tree branches. Tree holes provide a warm, safe shelter for the night. They must be at least 4 inches (10 cm) in diameter, but not so large that predators can get in.

Tamarins spend most of their time in trees at a height of 10 to 33 feet (3 to 10 m). Here the dense canopy of leaves protects them from the sharp eyes of hawks and other raptors. The tangle of vines and branches provide easy

↑ The golden lion tamarin's magnificent coat made it one of the most highly sought after animals in zoos and by private owners. It is now illegal to take specimens from the wild.

pathways between trees, so the animals rarely have to use the ground for getting from one to another. Golden lion tamarins are very agile and leap from branch to branch with ease, using all four limbs. They dart around quickly and nervously, constantly on the move.

Golden lion tamarins are mainly killed by hawks and other raptors, as well as cats and large snakes. Recently a weasel-like animal called the tayra has learned to dig tamarins from their nest holes and is wiping out whole groups in some areas. Tamarins use alarm calls when they feel threatened. They have a specific type of call for large birds flying overhead: When other tamarins hear it, they head for the shelter of the tree trunks or sometimes just drop to the ground.

Family Groups

Golden lion tamarins are social animals, living in groups of between two and 11 animals, although five or six is most common. The group usually consists of a mating pair of adults, plus the juvenile offspring from one or two recent litters. Sometimes extended family members are included. Some groups contain two adult males. However, only the dominant one will father the female's offspring, by monopolizing her at the time when she is likely to conceive. Groups with more than one adult female are infrequent; but when it happens, it is usually only the dominant female that breeds. Her aggression prevents subordinate females from mating, but in times of plenty the second female may also breed. Unlike most other tamarins and marmosets, the dominant female does not seem to exert any pheromone control (chemical signals) over her subordinates to prevent them from breeding.

Groups can travel 0.8 to 1.6 miles (1.3 to 2.6 km) a day when foraging. They occupy home ranges of up to 500 acres (200 ha), although the average is nearer 100 acres (40 ha). Golden lion tamarins are territorial and will defend the core of their home range against other groups. They use scent markings from the neck and genital region, and threat calls and postures. Aggressive postures include staring with an open mouth and arching their back. Chases sometimes end in fights.

The lion tamarin's diet consists mostly of fruit and insects, but it also eats spiders, snails, frogs, small lizards, and birds. It consumes eggs, plant gums, and nectar when available. It uses its long, slender hands and fingers to probe for prey in the crevices of tree bark, rotting wood, piles of dead leaves, or dense foliage.

A Family Affair

Rearing young is a family effort. All members cooperate, but the father does most of the work. The female gives birth in the warmest and wettest period of the year, between September and March. In captivity seasonality of birth can be broken so that a female can have two litters per year. Unlike most other primates, lion tamarins usually have twins rather than a single young. The babies are born fully furred, and their eyes can open immediately. For the first few weeks they cling tightly to their mother, but the father soon takes over in carrying the young around. By the third week he spends more time with them than the mother. Other members of the group also help with rearing. It is a valuable learning experience for juveniles who may have their own young in a year or two's time.

At about five weeks the young get more adventurous, leaving the safety of their parent's fur to explore their surroundings. They are weaned at around 90 days. Sometimes groups share food by offering it to the young family members. At other times the juveniles playfully steal it, which is tolerated by their elders. Young animals will often make a rasping noise as they try to take food from another animal.

Females reach sexual maturity at 18 months and males at 24 months. Unlike most other primates, it is the young females that are likely to leave their family group first. When they become mature, young females are chased away by their mother. They often have a hard time finding a new territory and are chased aggressively by members of established groups until they find an unoccupied area.

Disappearing Forest

The golden lion tamarin lives in the narrow strip of Atlantic coastal forest in eastern Brazil. It was the first part of Brazil to be colonized by Europeans and is now the most heavily populated region in the country. The lowland forest is easy to get to and easy to clear. For well over two centuries trees have been felled for timber and to make charcoal or cleared to make way for plantations, rice fields, cattle pasture, buildings, and roads. At one time the habitat in which the tamarins lived covered an area about the size of Texas. Now only 2 percent remains as forest. Even worse, much of the area is divided into tiny fragments of forest separated by open ground, so groups of animals cannot mix. As a result, inbreeding is a problem among the remaining tamarins.

A coordinated captive-breeding program began in 1973, involving zoos in many countries. At that time golden lion tamarins were on the brink of extinction. There were only about 200 animals left in the wild and 70 in zoos. Within 10 years the numbers of captive animals had increased to 600, providing enough to start reintroducing them to the Brazilian forest.

Zoo-bred animals were released into a nature reserve near Rio de Janeiro. At first many of the released animals died. Some were killed by predators, partly because they spent more time on the ground than the more wary wild

Tamarins and Bromeliads

Bromeliads are a common sight in the humid forests where the tamarins live. They are plants that grow high on the branches of other trees without ever touching the soil.

Many of the insects on which the tamarins feed hide in the bromeliads' leaves. In the center of each bromeliad plant is a hollow that collects rainwater. The wells are useful sources of drinking water for tamarins, and they also harbor another of the tamarin's favorite foods—small frogs.

Golden lion tamarins tend to inhabit the dense branches and vines that grow at heights of 10 to 33 feet (3 to 10 m) in the forest canopy. Here they are safe from the sharp eyes of hawks and other birds of prey.

↑ *The golden-headed lion tamarin is one of four species of lion tamarin, all of which are threatened. Its home in the Una Biological Reserve in Brazil is being stripped of trees by landless squatters.*

animals normally do. Also, they were not used to finding their own food, so they relied on handouts. As scientists and zookeepers became better at preparing captive-bred animals for life in the wild, survival levels increased. Now reintroduced animals have a better breeding rate than those kept in zoos.

Because each family group needs an area of about 100 acres (40 ha), patches of forest that are any smaller will not be enough to support the lion tamarins and allow their offspring to spread. An important part of the conservation program has been to plant more trees in deforested areas in order to create corridors that link small patches of habitat. A huge tree-planting program to improve the area for lion tamarins has also benefited many other forest animals. Another vital aspect of the conservation program has been educating local people. By encouraging people, especially ranch owners, to value the animals, it is more likely that they will want to protect the forest. Brazilians are now proud of their tamarins.

Common name African elephant

Scientific name *Loxodonta africana*

Family Elephantidae

Order Proboscidea

Size Length head/body (including trunk): 20–25 ft (6–7.5 m); tail length: 40–60 in (100–150 cm); height at shoulder: male 10.8 ft (3.3 m); female 8.9 ft (2.7 m). Female generally smaller than male

Weight Male up to 6.8 tons (6 tonnes); female up to 3.4 tons (3 tonnes)

Breeding Usually 1 calf born every 3–4 years in wet season after gestation period of 656 days. Weaned at 6 years; females sexually mature at 10 years, males at 25–30 years. May live more than 70 years in captivity, 60 in the wild

Key features Gray body with large head and ears; long ivory tusks; flexible trunk; skin with sparsely scattered black, bristly hairs; flat forehead and back; 4 toes on front feet, 3 on hind feet

Habits Females live in family groups of typically 2 or 3 sisters, plus offspring

Voice "Trumpeting," rumbles or "purring," roars, snorts, squeals, screams, and low growls

Diet Grasses, tree leaves and fruit, bark

Habitat Mainly savanna grassland

Distribution Eastern and central Africa south of the Sahara Desert

Status Population: fewer than 600,000; IUCN Endangered; CITES I in most countries, II in Botswana, Namibia, and Zimbabwe. Declining species

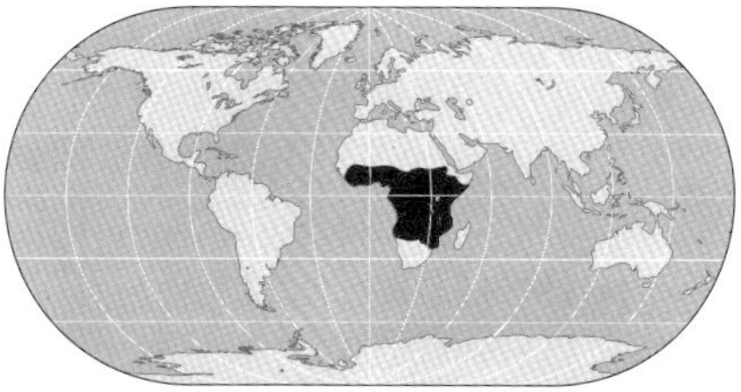

African Elephant

Loxodonta africana

African elephants are the largest living land animals. They have the biggest brains in the animal kingdom, live as long as humans, and have excellent memories.

THE LARGEST MAMMALS ON THE planet, African elephants are easily recognizable by their long trunk, large ears, and pillarlike legs. Their skin varies from black to pale gray or brown in color and in places is up to 1.5 inches (4 cm) thick.

Skin Care

Despite its thickness, the skin is sensitive and requires frequent bathing, massaging, and powdering with dust to keep it in good condition. Skin color is often modified according to the soil type of their habitat, since elephants spend a lot of time wallowing in mud until it cakes their body or blowing dust over themselves through the trunk. Newborn elephants are often very hairy, but lose this covering as they get older. They keep a few short bristly hairs on the trunk and chin, and a sparse scattering of hairs over the rest of the body. The huge ears can grow as large as 6.6 feet (2 m) high and 5 feet (1.5 m) wide.

The African elephant is bigger than the Asian species, with the largest recorded individual weighing 11.3 tons (10 tonnes) and standing 13.1 feet (4 m) tall. African elephants have 21 ribs, one more pair than in Asian elephants. Their back dips downward slightly in the middle, unlike the Asian species, which has a slightly humped back. The large, flat forehead is often used as a ramming device to push over whole trees and gain easier access to the leaves.

Elephants have round feet with toes embedded in a soft mass of fibrous tissue. The sole of the foot is smooth, with the skin cracked into individually recognizable patterns.

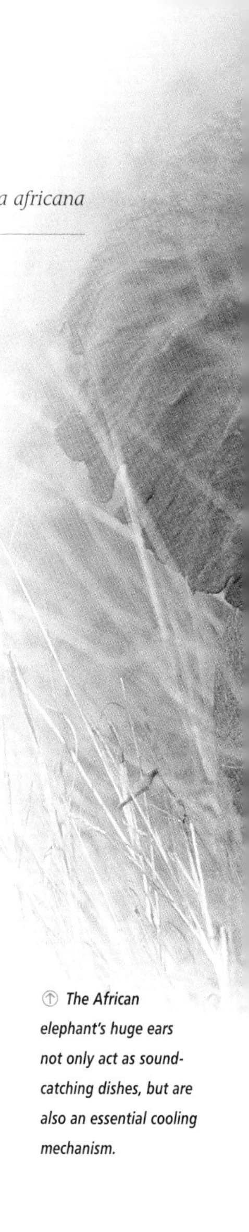

The African elephant's huge ears not only act as sound-catching dishes, but are also an essential cooling mechanism.

Tusks are present in both sexes. They are formed from one elongated upper incisor tooth on each side of the mouth. They are generally thicker and more forward pointing than in the other species. Tusks are used for fighting, digging, and feeding. The tusks of the bull (male) elephants grow in length and bulk throughout life, while cow (female) elephants grow more slender tusks at a slower rate.

The foot is so spread out that an elephant presses on the ground with about the same force per square inch as a person. So, despite their huge weight, elephants hardly leave any tracks except on soft ground. Their soft feet allow silent movement, despite their size.

The trunk of the African elephant bears two fingerlike projections ("lips") at the tip, which are very sensitive and skillfully used to pick up food or other articles and manipulate objects. Although strong enough to rip up trees, the trunk is also a sensitive organ of touch and smell, as well as being used for drinking, communication, threatening, and increasing the volume of vocalizations. It may also be used to rub an itchy eye or to pick up a stick and scratch the skin.

Big Ears!

A distinctive characteristic of the African elephant is its extremely large ears. Besides their important use in hearing, the ears serve as radiators to prevent overheating, similar to those of the fennec fox in Volume 2. They provide a large surface area through which runs an extensive network of blood vessels. When the animal is hot, the blood vessels expand and rise above the skin, so that blood running through them is more exposed to the air. Spreading of the ears and ear-flapping are characteristically seen when elephants stand in the shade on hot days. The action increases the air currents over the blood vessels so blood is cooled more efficiently, helping reduce the body temperature.

The African elephant ranges throughout Africa south of the Sahara in almost all habitats from forests to open savannas, swamps to deserts, and seashores to high mountains. Its requirements are water, food—in the form of grasses or trees—and shade. To find such conditions, elephants may have to make long annual migrations. If food, water, and shade remain available, elephants will not venture far, although a general pattern of migration follows the seasons. Elephants tend to migrate from permanent water sources at the start of the rainy season, then return again to such sites when the rains end and waterholes dry up. In the dry season they may dig holes in dry riverbeds with their trunk, tusks, and forefeet to find water. They will also travel long distances to find salty soils, which they eat. Sometimes they will even go underground into caves to scrape salt from the walls.

Elephants are active both by day and night, although activity drops during the hottest hours of the day, when they seek shade. They sleep in the afternoon or after midnight, usually standing up. Sometimes they will lean against one another or against a tree.

African elephants seek water regularly and need to drink 20 to 40 gallons (90 to 180 l) every day. They drink by sucking water up into their trunk, then squirting it into their mouth. To cool down, bathe, or wallow, they throw water over their back. Occasionally they submerge themselves completely, using their trunk as a snorkel, with only the tip appearing above the water. In that manner they are able to walk or swim underwater for considerable distances. On land elephants usually amble slowly, but walking speeds can increase to about 2 to 2.5 miles per hour (3 to 4 km/h). Their maximum speed can reach 25 miles per hour (40 km/h) when charging or fleeing. Many a big game hunter has been shocked at just how fast these ponderous creatures can charge!

Space Requirements

The space needed by elephants varies enormously. Some herds living in forests can manage with as little as 4 square miles (10 sq. km). On the other hand, those living in desert areas, where there is less to eat and drink, may need to range over more than 7,000 square miles (18,000 sq. km). After the rains have ended, elephants feed on woody materials, ripping out whole trees with their

The African elephant's dexterous trunk serves many purposes, including plucking succulent leaves and shoots from high branches.

A herd of African elephants migrating. Deforestation, along with expansion of roads, farmland, and towns, leaves less space for elephants. Migration routes are sometimes cut off, preventing access to vital food and water.

trunk and stripping them of leaves and bark. They will also eat fruit and flowers when available, and dig for roots once the first rains have softened the soil. The elephant's main diet during the wet season consists of savanna grasses, plus small amounts of leaves and bark. The skull, jaws, and teeth are designed to crush plant material that is often too coarse for other mammals, helping the elephants avoid competition for food. But their teeth cannot effectively grind coarse material. Nor do elephants have the efficient rumen system of antelope and cattle, in which microorganisms assist in digesting plant material. As a result, large amounts of bulky food need to be taken in, and much of it passes through without being digested. Consequently, the elephant's droppings contain big pieces of undigested plant material and many seeds that can still germinate in the surrounding dung. Adult elephants need to consume a huge 165 to 330 pounds (75 to 150 kg) of food a day. They therefore spend three-quarters of their time searching for food.

When excited, surprised, playing, upset, or about to attack, elephants produce distinctive "trumpeting" sounds, amplified by the trunk. Aggression is shown by raising the head and trunk, holding the ears out from the body, kicking dust, swaying the head, and making either a mock or serious charge. But the most common sounds produced in communication are rarely heard by the human ear and are a form of tummy rumbling. Visual signals are also important in elephant communication and include changes in the position of the head, ears, trunk, and tail. Smell plays a significant part in social contact within a herd and in detecting danger. A herd of elephants may lift their trunks high in the air to gain advance warning of distant threats by their smell. Elephants are highly affectionate to their family members and, like humans who kiss in greeting, will touch each other's mouths with the tip of the trunk.

Male Reproductive Cycle

When male African elephants near maturity, at 25 to 30 years of age, they enter a sexual condition each year known as musth. It is characterized by an increase in aggressive behavior and association with female groups. Bulls in musth produce secretions from facial glands behind the eyes, and a continuous dribble of urine is leaked, which contains hormones to attract females. Their posture also changes as they lift their heads up and hold out their ears. It is accompanied by a distinctive "musth rumble," a growling noise that sounds similar to a diesel engine. Musth occurs mainly just after the rainy season and lasts for two to three months. When in musth, a bull becomes dominant and may win contests with other males that are not in musth, even if they are the larger animal. It is unusual among mammals for breeding to be driven by cycles in the male—usually it is the female's hormonal cycles that are most important.

When a female is ready to mate, she will emit low-frequency calls to attract a partner, often from far away. The bull will then guard her from other males that may try to mate with her. Sadly, this selective form of mating is in decline, since the oldest bulls with the largest tusks are the first to be hunted for their ivory, and the females have to make do with relatively young and inferior mates.

Females become sexually receptive at about 10 years of age, for two to four days every four months. Mating therefore takes place at different times of the year, and births can occur in different seasons. But most calves are born just before the height of the rainy season, when cool temperatures prevail, and there is plenty of vegetation for cover. The increased nutritional value of plants in the rainy season also provides mothers with the necessary food supply to produce milk for their offspring.

Twins are rare, occurring in only 1 to 2 percent of births. Newborn calves can stand within half an hour of birth, although it takes a couple of days before they have the strength to roam with the herd. The calf suckles from its mother with its mouth (not trunk) and rapidly gains weight. By the time it is six years old, it may already weigh nearly a ton. Weaning takes places after six to 18 months, although a mother may continue to produce milk for four years and occasionally nurses an offspring for six years or more.

When the young bulls reach maturity, the older females drive them out of the family group. They may form small bachelor herds or live on their own. Old bull elephants are always solitary. Female society is essentially matriarchal. One female is dominant (usually the oldest), with the group being composed of a few closely related adult cows and their young in a stable family unit. When female calves reach maturity at 10 years, they stay with the family herd to have their young. The dominant female usually maintains her position until death, when her eldest daughter takes her place. As the size of the herd increases, a few of the young adult cows leave to form a subgroup, causing the family to split up. However, the small herds often become reunited, since they travel together in associations known as kinship groups.

Only an hour old, an elephant calf pulls itself to its feet and takes its first tentative steps.

Most struggles for dominance between bulls involve pushing and light battle with the tusks. In a serious fight the tusks are used in earnest and can inflict fatal wounds.

Family Ties

The social bonds between family members are strong. In times of danger the group will form a defensive circle, moving all calves to the center, with the adults facing outward. The group leader will move outside the circle to check out the threat and may spread her ears, trumpeting and growling in an attempt to deter an intruder. Because of the bravery displayed by the matriarch she becomes vulnerable and so is often the first to fall prey to poachers, against whom her methods of defense are useless.

The African elephant was formerly distributed south of the Sahara wherever water and trees occurred, but its range and numbers have shrunk as development, the human population, and poaching have increased. As recently as the early 1980s there were an estimated 1.3 million elephants in Africa, but numbers have fallen sharply. The price of ivory rose dramatically in the early 1970s and triggered an upsurge of elephant killing. By 1989 the population had plummeted to 609,000, suggesting that over half of Africa's elephant population had fallen prey to ivory poaching in less than a decade.

In the late 1980s a ban was imposed on trade in elephant products. Monitoring plans were set up, and by the 1990s numbers had begun to stabilize. However, despite protection, numbers have fallen dramatically in almost all elephant populations. Even though hunting may have been reduced, deforestation continues, accompanied by the expansion of roads, farmland, and towns—a consequence of the ever-expanding human population.

Who's Afraid of Mice?

There is an ancient belief that elephants are afraid of mice. The notion may have been reinforced by stories of a zoo elephant that was found dead from a hemorrhage with a mouse jammed inside its trunk. Since then experiments have been carried out in which mice and rats have been put into elephant enclosures and in their hay. In each case the elephants showed no response to the mice, even if the rodents climbed onto their trunk.

Common name Plains zebra (common zebra, Burchell's zebra)

Scientific name *Equus burchelli*

Family Equidae

Order Perissodactyla

Size Length head/body: 7.2–8.2 ft (2.2–2.5 m); tail length: 18.5–22 in (47–56 cm); height at shoulder: up to 43–57 in (110–145 cm)

Weight 385–710 lb (175–322 kg)

Key features Deep-bodied, short-legged zebra; mane erect and thick; black stripes broader than in other species, especially on rump, and do not always extend onto belly and legs; stripes sometimes interspersed with pale-brown lines

Habits Social: lives in nonterritorial, single-male harems or bachelor groups; active day and night; feeds almost constantly when awake

Breeding Single young born after gestation period of 360–396 days. Weaned at 7–11 months; females sexually mature at 16–22 months, males from 4 years. May live up to 40 years in captivity, usually many fewer in the wild

Voice Typical equid calls, including snorts, gasps, and squeals; males give short bark

Diet Mostly grass; some shrubs and flowering plants; shoots, twigs, and leaves of trees

Habitat Savanna and lightly wooded or scrubby grassland

Distribution Southern and eastern Africa outside forested and developed land

Status Population: 750,000; IUCN Data Deficient. Declining; protected in several national parks

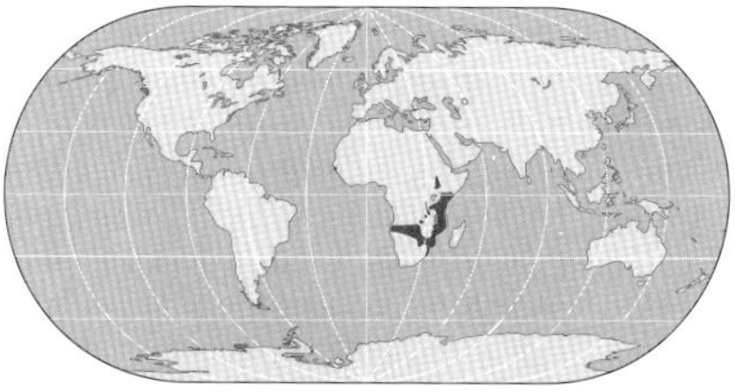

Plains Zebra

Equus burchelli

The plains zebra currently occupies the largest natural range of any equid and is the only wild member of the family not threatened with extinction. The species has a large but patchy distribution across much of eastern Africa and is a major safari attraction.

As their common name suggests, plains zebras favor open land, where they feed mostly on grasses. However, they are not particularly fussy grazers and will venture into rank grassland and even lightly wooded terrain. In doing so they

prepare pastures for other more selective species, such as gazelles and wildebeest, by grazing down the taller grasses and other vegetation and stimulating a regrowth of tender young shoots. The main natural restriction on zebra distribution is the availability of drinking water. Individuals are almost never found more than about 20 miles (30 km) from water, and they usually stay much closer so that they can make daily visits. Water is especially important to mothers, who have to satisfy the milk requirements of their foals.

Establishing a Harem

Like horses, plains zebras operate a harem system whereby a single male collects and tries to hold onto a group of up to six females with whom he claims exclusive mating rights. The arrangement results in a lot of "spare" males, mostly youngsters that are not yet strong enough to defend a harem of their own and elderly or weakened stallions that have lost their females. The excess males form bachelor groups of up to 15 individuals. Without the responsibilities of females and dependent young bachelor males appear to have more than their fair share of fun—bouts of playfighting and chasing games are commonplace. Such spirited contests prepare the young males for defending a harem of their own in future. To do so, they must find a young filly in breeding condition and steal her away from the herd in which she was born. That is easier said than done, since every other eligible stallion in the area will have similar ideas. Once he has a female, a stallion will mate with her every time she comes into estrous (once a month for about five days). However, if she is young, it may be a year before she conceives a foal. Only when that has happened will the female form any kind of attachment to the stallion, giving him enough peace of mind to go and find

Plains zebras spend between 60 and 80 percent of each day feeding. As well as grazing on grass, they browse the tender shoots, twigs, and leaves of trees.

a second filly to expand his harem. The process can continue for several years, with a maximum of about six females joining the harem. At first, each new female is persecuted by the existing members of the harem, but with the stallion's protection newcomers are eventually accepted.

Heading for a Fight

The abduction of females is the main cause of violence between stallions. Under most other circumstances males interact peacefully. Bachelors in the same herd are generally on friendly terms, and harem stallions perform ritualized greeting ceremonies to confirm mutual respect. Even the ousting of an elderly or unfit harem stallion often happens without a fight. Inadequate males are apparently well aware of their shortcomings and will relinquish ownership over a period of a few days if an obviously fitter male has attached himself to the group. But stealing a mare from a stallion in full control of his harem is another matter: Fighting males attempt to strike each other with flailing front hooves and move in tight circles, trying to bite each other's legs. The hock joint is especially vulnerable, and sometimes both animals end up on the ground, having gained a grip on their adversary.

Female plains zebras are capable of producing one foal a year, but in reality they only do so under very favorable conditions. There is usually about a two-year gap between births. Foals can be born at any time of year. However, there is a peak during the early wet season, when there is plenty of fresh grass to sustain the mare as she produces milk for her young. At about one week old zebras take their first taste of grass, but they will not be fully weaned off their mother's milk for another year.

↑ Two male plains zebras sparring. A kick with the hind legs is the zebra's most powerful weapon, but is generally a last resort, since it requires the animal to turn away from its rival.

The Quagga

The quagga (*Equus quagga*) of southern Africa was the first kind of zebra to be discovered and described by modern zoologists. Quaggas were hunted to extinction in the wild by the mid-19th century, and the last captive specimen died in the Amsterdam Zoo in 1883. The quagga lacked stripes on most of its body, except for the neck and shoulders, but in every other way it was much the same as the plains zebra. The ranges of the two types were, in fact, continuous.

There is a strong case for suggesting that the quagga and plains zebra were one and the same species. Modern plains zebras show a clear trend toward reduced striping from the north of their range to the south, and the quagga would have been a continuation of that trend. Such a probability creates an interesting situation for people who classify animals and plants because the rules of classification say that the earliest name given to a species is the correct one. That would mean that today's plains zebras are in fact subspecies of quagga, not the other way around. Because they are closely related, it should also be possible to recreate quaggalike animals by selectively breeding southern plains zebras, favoring those with fewer stripes. The procedure is now being attempted.

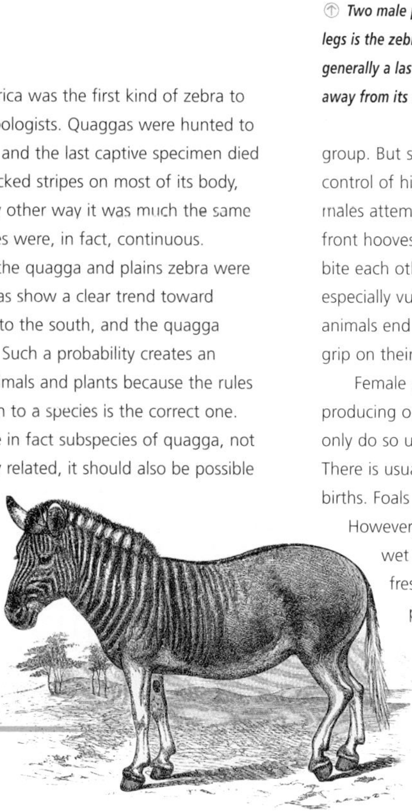

In the quagga the striping that characterizes all zebras was confined to the head, neck, and forequarters.

Zebra Language

Zebras communicate using a broad range of vocalizations, tactile signals, facial expressions, and other body language. There are about half a dozen distinct zebra "calls," most of which are similar to those made by other equids. A sudden snort or "ee-aah!" is an alarm signal. Short squeals are used in greeting and play, while long squeals signal distress, pain, or anger. Loose-lipped "brrrrrr" sounds are made by relaxed, contented animals. The harsh bark given by plains zebra stallions is unique to the species and is used to summon attention and keep the group together.

Tactile signals are used in greetings and friendly interactions. Nose-to-nose followed by nose-to-genital touching is used when strangers meet or when two animals have been apart for some time. Standing head to tail or resting heads on another zebra's back is not only companionable, but it means both animals can take advantage of the other's flicking tail to avoid flies. Also, between them the pair have 360-degree vision.

Mutual grooming is an important means of reinforcing social bonds and can happen between any two animals in a group regardless of rank. Grooming involves nibbling and scraping the fur of the neck, back, and shoulders with the teeth. The same mouth movements (known as chewing or champing) are used as an appeasement signal, especially by low-status animals when challenged by a superior. Other signs of submission are flattened ears and, in males, adopting a head-down posture with the hind legs planted firmly apart. This is an imitation of the female estrous display and helps pacify an aggressor. Dominant animals stand erect and step confidently, tossing their head. If provoked, they flatten their ears, bring their head down, and weave it from side to side in a snakelike threat display.

Early on, the foal learns to recognize its mother by her smell, voice, and unique pattern of stripes. During the first few days of its life the mother keeps other members of the group away from the foal to avoid confusing it.

Eating and Sleeping

Groups of plains zebras spend the night in special bedding areas, which tend to be on relatively high ground with short grass and a good view of the surrounding area. The zebras alternate between two- to three-hour bouts of grazing and sleeping, which they usually do lying on the ground with their legs tucked under them to one side. They appear to sleep quite deeply, but at least one member of the herd remains on its feet, scanning the plains with eyes and ears alert for predators. In the morning the herd commutes to grazing pastures where the serious business of feeding begins. In rich habitats groups may be fairly sedentary, using an annual home range of fewer than 80 square miles (200 sq. km). In the Ngorongoro Crater in Tanzania there are herds that live for years within a range as small as 12 square miles (30 sq. km). Population densities in such an incredibly productive locality are up to 10 times those found elsewhere, with up to 50 zebras per square mile (20 per sq. km). In the nearby Serengeti National Park herds make seasonal migrations of up to 90 miles (150 km) in search of richer grazing land, so increasing their home range over the course of a year to between 120 and 240 square miles (300 and 600 sq. km). Plains zebras are nonterritorial, and the home ranges of several groups will overlap. Groups often come together to form huge herds, especially when migrating, when there is safety to be had in numbers.

When traveling, a group usually moves in single file along well-used trails, with the highest-ranking animal leading the way. The status of a female in a harem group is determined by the length of time she has been a member. The longest-serving mare is the highest ranking, and her offspring

Foals are incredibly well developed at birth. They are often on their feet within 15 minutes, walking steadily after half an hour, and running gently before they are an hour old.

will inherit her status until they join a new group. Then the youngsters have to begin at the bottom of the social ladder. Males leave of their own accord to join bachelor groups, and fillies are taken by a stallion to join a harem elsewhere. Once breeding, mares will stay with a group throughout their lives. The whole harem helps protect young foals. At the first sign of danger the youngster and its mother are surrounded by adult females, and the herd moves off together, leaving the stallion to bring up the rear or turn and face the threat. Stallions will face most predators, and their potentially lethal hooves are enough to deter all but the most determined hyenas, lions, and leopards.

Plains zebras run through water. Zebras are always found within 20 miles (30 km) of a water source and make daily visits to drink.

How the Zebra Got Its Stripes

Conventional wisdom once had it that the zebra's stripes were a means of camouflage to help it blend into long grass, or that they served to confuse predators. Neither theory really stands up to much scrutiny, however, because zebras do not hide from predators in long grass, and lions are no more successful at catching zebras with fewer stripes.

It seems certain that the unique pattern of stripes on each zebra helps with individual recognition. Current opinion also favors the idea that stripes act as a kind of social stimulus (zebras are attracted to stripes) and a target for grooming. All zebras, even partially striped subspecies like the quagga, have similar patterns of stripes around the main grooming area (the neck and shoulders). The question of why stripes should prompt grooming is less easy to answer, but it seems that zebras like stripes because they have always been stripey! The ancestor of all living equids was probably striped, since stripes appear occasionally on all other species in the horse family (on the legs of asses and wild horses, for example).

Brazilian Tapir

Tapirus terrestris

Common name Brazilian tapir (South American tapir)

Scientific name *Tapirus terrestris*

Family Tapiridae

Order Perissodactyla

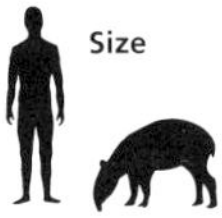

Size Length head/body: up to 7.2 ft (2.2 m); tail length: 3 in (8 cm); height at shoulder: 30–42 in (77–108 cm)

Weight Up to 550 lb (250 kg)

Key features Bulky animal with narrow front end, rounded rump, slender legs, and short tail; head tapers to short snout; ears oval and erect, eyes small; coat sparse with narrow mane; 4 toes on front feet, 3 on hind feet

Habits Mainly nocturnal; solitary and aggressive to other tapirs, but nonterritorial; swims and dives well; wallows in mud

Breeding Single young (occasionally twins) born after gestation period of 13 months. Weaned at about 12 months; sexually mature at 2–3 years. May live up to 35 years in captivity, probably many fewer in the wild

Voice Loud squeals and low-frequency clicks and whistling sounds

Diet Mainly grass, leaves, and shoots of terrestrial and aquatic plants; also twigs, bark, and fruit; sometimes raids crops such as rice and corn

Habitat Humid forest with dense vegetation and permanent water

Distribution Northern and central South America east of Andes

Status Population: probably several thousand; IUCN Lower Risk: near threatened; CITES II. Declining due to habitat loss and hunting

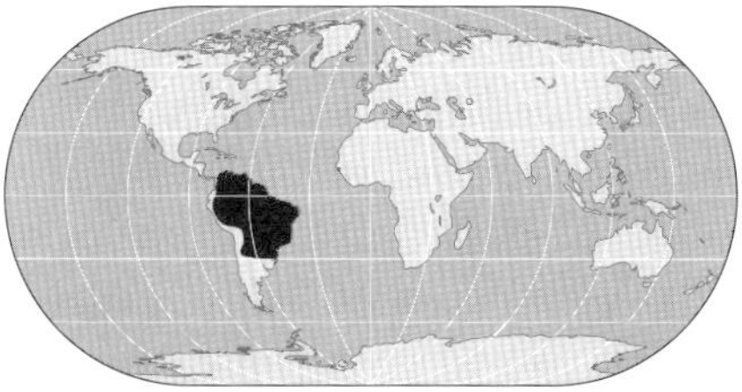

A surprisingly nimble and sure-footed resident of the Amazon region, the Brazilian tapir is at home on land or in water. But its survival is threatened by habitat loss and illegal hunting.

THE BRAZILIAN TAPIR IS THE MOST piglike member of the genus *Tapirus*. It has a short, fleshy nose and a coat of sparse reddish-buff or blackish hair that barely covers its thin skin. The hairs of the cheeks, throat, and ears are lighter than elsewhere on the body.

Brazilian tapirs live alone in the humid forests of the Amazon Basin, favoring dense vegetation close to the water's edge. They are semiaquatic and can hold their breath for many minutes, swimming underwater or walking hippolike on the riverbed. Much of their food comes from water plants. The animals retreat to rivers in order to escape predation, cool down, and rid themselves of flies. Cool mud serves a similar antiparasite function, and tapirs seem to enjoy wallowing in it.

On land Brazilian tapirs move quickly and nimbly, using regular tracks through the dense undergrowth. They generally emerge around dusk to begin foraging for fresh leaves, shoots, and other vegetable matter.

Heavy-Duty Teeth

The tapir's tough diet requires heavy-duty teeth, and the animal has three molars and three premolars on each side of its upper and lower jaw. Each of the molars has sharp ridges and crests. The powerful jaw muscles are attached to a pronounced ridge of bone along the top of the skull. It is this bone that gives the tapir's face its distinctive convex-curved profile or "roman" nose. Fruit forms an important part of their diet, and tapirs perform a valuable service

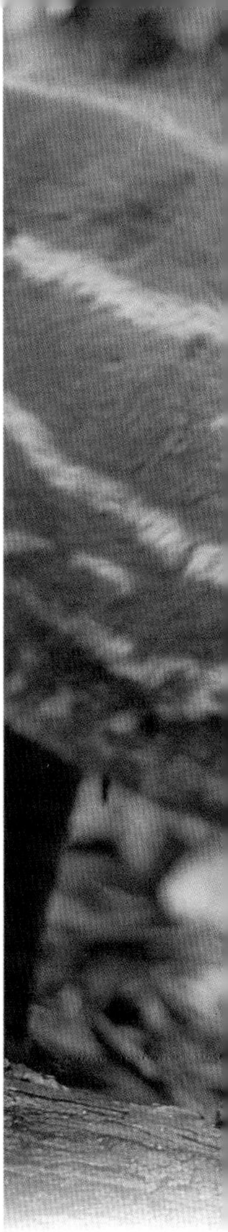

Young Brazilian tapirs are born with a distinctive striped coat. The stripes are not present in the adult coat, which is brownish-gray. In adults a narrow mane runs from the head to between the shoulders.

to many rain-forest plants by distributing their seeds over wide areas in their feces. Some of the seeds do not germinate unless they have passed through the gut of an animal like a tapir, so the relationship between plant and mammal is mutually important.

It takes practice for a human to learn to recognize tapir droppings, but to other tapirs they are completely unmistakable. A small heap of dung carries all kinds of information about the individual that left it, and tapirs use their droppings and urine to mark out their own personal territory.

Breeding Signals

Male tapirs use a special organ—the vomeronasal or Jacobson's organ—in the roof of the mouth to sample female scents. Like many other ungulates, tapirs pull their lips back in a distinctive "flehmen" expression when they scent a sexually receptive female. Females come into breeding condition once every couple of months throughout the year, except, of course, when they are pregnant. Males converge on the territory of the receptive female and will fight with each other, biting and jostling for the right to mate.

Courtship and mating are brief—the female will not tolerate any intruder on her territory for long—and the male plays no further part in rearing his offspring.

The young tapir, when it arrives after about 400 days, is covered in brown fur with white speckles and longitudinal stripes. It weighs about 10 pounds (4.5 kg). To begin with, the mother suckles it in a safe hideout among dense undergrowth, but after a week or so the youngster will emerge to follow her on nightly excursions. It molts into its adult coat at about six months of age. Captive tapirs grow faster than those in the wild and can be ready to breed in just two years. In the wild development usually takes longer: Tapirs may not reach full size until they are four years old.

Tapirs are widely hunted by local people, but their low rate of reproduction means that their population cannot sustain heavy exploitation. As a result, tapir numbers are in decline. People pose an indirect threat, too, because of their damaging effects on the tapir's forest habitat. Even where trees are not cleared, people often heavily exploit forest palms for their fruit. Taking away the fruit removes a vital source of nourishment for the tapirs.

Dromedary Camel

Camelus dromedarius

The dromedary is the largest camel; and thanks to its usefulness as a domestic animal, especially as a beast of burden, it is also by far the most common.

Common name Dromedary camel (Arabian camel, one-humped camel)

Scientific name *Camelus dromedarius*

Family Camelidae

Order Artiodactyla

Size Length head/body: 7.5–11.4 ft (2.3–3.5 m); tail length: 14–21 in (35–55 cm); height to top of hump: 5.9–7.5 ft (1.8–2.3 m)

Weight 660–1,540 lb (300–698 kg)

Key features Tall; long neck and legs; single large dorsal hump; tail thin and hairy; head small, with small, furry ears, large, thickly lashed eyes, closable nostrils, and split upper lip; fur short and woolly, pale beige to dark brown

Habits Active during the day in small herds; not territorial and generally nonaggressive

Breeding Single calf (twins rare) born every other year at most at any time of year after gestation period of 15 months (births peak in the rainy season). Weaned at 12–18 months; females sexually mature at 3 years; males take 6 years to reach size at which they can defend mates. May live up to 50 years in captivity, similar in the wild

Voice Rumbling moans and grunts

Diet Any desert plant, including those with high salt content

Habitat Deserts

Distribution Originally from Arabian Peninsula; feral and semiwild populations also in North Africa, Asia, and central Australia

Status Population: may exceed 19 million; IUCN Extinct in the Wild. Domesticated

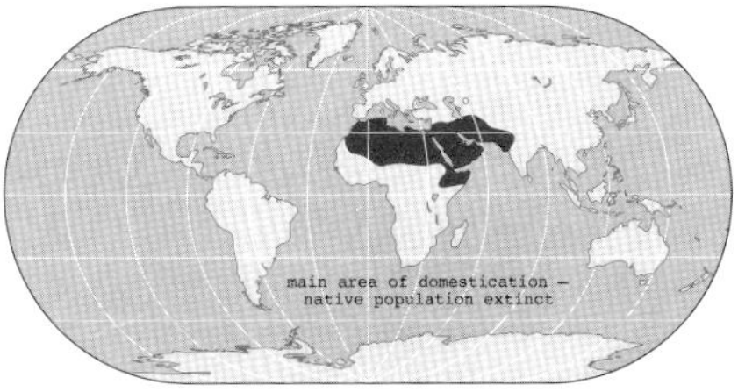

THERE IS NO SUCH THING as a truly wild dromedary camel. The species *Camelus dromedarius* has been technically extinct in the wild for hundreds of years, probably since biblical times. However, dromedaries are far from threatened—recent estimates put the world population at close to 19 million animals. Of them, the vast majority are under domestication. However, a few hundred thousand have gone wild in places as far apart as the Sahara and central Australia, where they are classed as feral animals.

The dromedary's ability to withstand drought is legendary. Some reports suggest that a camel in prime condition can survive months without drinking. Certainly, working camels are

often required to walk for a week or two between watering holes. In the wild not needing to drink often would have given camels a huge ecological advantage, allowing them to exploit a habitat that would quickly kill other large animals.

Desert Adaptations

The two main problems for animals that live in hot deserts are overheating and dehydration. Most mammals sweat and pant to help regulate their body temperatures, since water evaporating from damp skin takes heat with it. In most animals, sweating or panting begins as soon as the body temperature increases above the normal level. In a desert, however, animals cannot afford to sweat away their precious reserves of water. They must find alternative ways to keep cool. Camels are already at an advantage over other desert animals because of their large size. It takes a lot more energy to heat up a large object with a relatively small surface area than a small one whose surface area is large in relation to its volume. The camel can reduce the body surface available to absorb heat by lying down with its legs folded underneath. The thick woolly fur on the camel's back serves as a layer of insulation, slowing down the rate of heat absorption still further. Even if the camel starts to overheat, it can tolerate a temperature increase of several degrees before it begins sweating; the animals appear untroubled by a rise in body temperature that would

A dromedary camel in front of the pyramids, Egypt. It is thought that people may have first taken domesticated camels to Africa around 4,000 years ago.

seem like a fever to us. At night camels allow their body temperature to drop very low, so that in the heat of the following morning it takes longer to reach a temperature at which it becomes necessary to sweat to cool down. A dehydrated camel will allow its temperature to drop to 93°F (34°C) overnight and increase to 108°F (42°C) the next day before it begins to sweat. Such fluctuations of temperature would be fatal in most other mammals.

Water Reabsorption

Mammals lose water from their bodies in many other ways, including excretion, exhalation, shedding tears, bleeding, drooling, spitting, and vomiting. In warm, dry environments there is inevitably also a certain amount of evaporation from moist surfaces such as the mouth, eyes, and nose. Evolution has provided camels with ways of reducing all such excretions. The high salt content of the camel's diet helps its body effectively retain water. Its urine is extremely concentrated because a lot of water is absorbed back into the body by the kidneys. The structure of the camel's nostrils means that water vapor from its lungs condenses on the inside of the nose rather than being breathed out. The nostrils can also be closed at will to keep out sand and dust during storms. Any dribbles of moisture from the camel's nose are channeled straight into the mouth via grooves in the upper lip. A double row of extralong eyelashes protects the eyes from windblown sand, so that less water is needed to wash them with tears. Of course, it is

Multipurpose Camel

Dromedaries are phenomenally useful animals. They provide meat and milk, also wool, hide, and sinew for clothing and construction. Their dung makes good fuel, and their milk can be fermented to make an alcoholic drink called kumiss. Fully laden, they can carry heavy loads over baking-hot, barren sand. They can maintain a steady 2.5 miles per hour (4 km/h) for 12 to 14 hours a day if their human companions are prepared to travel in the cool of the night and early morning. Camels can also gallop faster than most horses, but this kind of exertion will cause them to overheat very quickly. Although it is extremely difficult to ride a galloping camel, racing them is a popular sport in some parts of the world. The jockeys (often small boys) need to be securely tied down to prevent them from being bounced off.

A dromedary camel running with its Rajasthani rider, India. In some parts of the world camel racing is a popular sport.

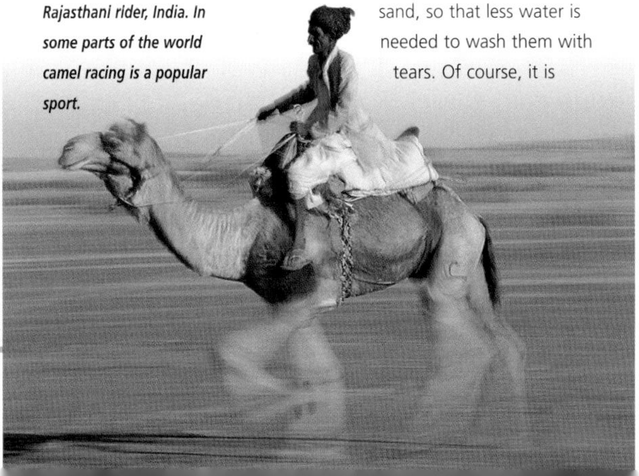

Camels in Australia

The interior of Australia is one of the hottest, driest deserts in the world. Countless early European expeditions to the region failed, since horses died of heat and thirst. Domesticated camels were imported throughout the second half of the 19th century to assist in exploring the inhospitable landscape. They proved invaluable to explorers and settlers alike. Inevitably, some animals escaped or were allowed to wander, and these individuals formed the basis of a feral camel population that now numbers over 40,000 animals.

Domestic camels are still bred in Australia, where their uses include a limited market in meat, hides, and wool. They also provide an entertaining alternative to four-wheel drive vehicles for tourists exploring the Outback. Australian-bred camels have such a reputation for toughness that some are now being exported back to Arabia and Africa to boost the breeding stock there.

A camel safari in the Northern Territory, Australia. Camel trips are popular tourist excursions.

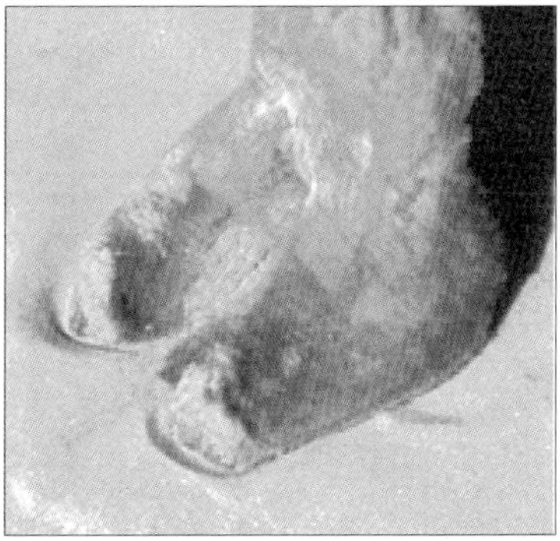

Camels' feet are broad with a fleshy sole. They are able to easily walk on sand without sinking because their weight is spread over a large area.

impossible to prevent water loss completely. Camels must urinate; and when hot enough, they will sweat. A camel can survive losing 40 percent of its body weight in water—a human losing more than 15 percent will certainly die.

Therefore, a well-fed and hydrated camel can go without drinking for many weeks, even months if not expected to work hard. Left to their own devices, camels have been known to survive 10 months without water. Once they find water, they can rehydrate amazingly quickly, drinking 26 gallons (118 l) or more in the space of a few minutes. Dromedaries can also go for long periods without eating. The hump, once thought to store water, is actually a large fat reserve. In a well-fed camel the hump is fat and firm. Undernourished camels live off the fat in their hump, which gradually shrinks and eventually becomes thin and flabby.

Chewing It Over

Camels will eat almost any kind of desert plant. They actually favor those that no other herbivore will touch because of their high salt content. In most mammals the excess salt has to be flushed from the body with urine, while the dromedary uses it to keeps its own salt levels high in order to help retain water. The dromedary also has tough lips to cope with the vicious spines of many desert plants. Although they are fundamentally vegetarian, starving camels will eat just about anything, including the flesh, skin, and bones of dead animals.

Tough vegetation is not easy to digest, and camels spend a lot of time chewing and rechewing their food, which helps break the tough material down into something the digestive juices can work on. Leaves are plucked using two upper and six lower incisor teeth, then ground to a pulp with 22 cheek teeth. The camel's stomach has three chambers, and food can be regurgitated for a second bout of chewing, as with cattle. Food in the stomach is digested with the help of bacteria before passing to the gut.

A dromedary camel's feet are broad, with an undivided fleshy sole. Although padded, the sole does not provide much grip and is easily cut and damaged by sharp stones. Dromedaries are therefore at a disadvantage on rough or slippery ground. On sand, however, they are in their element. They do not sink because their weight is spread over a large area. The two toes on each foot do not have true hooves, just large nails on their upper surface.

Feral Populations

Since there are no truly wild dromedary camels, most of what is known about the species' natural behavior patterns is based on studies of feral populations. The animals tend to form three main groups: The family group or harem contains a single dominant male, up to 30 breeding females, and their older offspring. Bachelor groups are usually made up of young adult males and older individuals that often have not been able to gather or defend a harem of their own. The third kind—the nursery group—consists of females and their newborn calves, and tends to occur during the seasonal peak in births. Females that breed at other times may stay with the harem, but remain a little aloof until their youngster has learned to recognize its mother's smell and voice.

Groups of camels move in single file, with females taking turns to lead and the male bringing up the rear. They seek out company and often huddle together in the heat of the day to reduce water lost to evaporation. A family might use a home range of several thousand square miles in one year. It will concentrate on a small area of about 20 to 60 square miles (50 to 150 sq. km) before moving on every few months. In Australia the ranges of families overlap, and feral groups may join up to form herds of up to 500 animals. Despite the scarcity of food, camels do not strip large areas of vegetation. They feed selectively, browsing a few leaves at a time from a single plant.

Fighting Tactics

Dromedaries appear to be nonterritorial, but that is not to say they are never aggressive. Male camels compete for females, and harem males will drive rivals away with threat displays and violence. The displays include standing tall, making rumbling calls, tail-slapping, defecation, and spitting stomach contents in the face of a rival. Fighting camels attempt to shove each other over, striking out with their forelegs. They will also try to bite each other's legs and head.

Breeding in free-living populations happens at different times of year in different parts of the world. However, it is clearly timed so that births coincide with the wet season, when there is plenty of food to support the mothers' production of milk. Young camels are able to walk and run within hours. Calves in captivity put on weight at a rate of up to 4.5 pounds (2 kg) a week. Adult size and sexual maturity is attained in three to six years. Female camels give birth to one youngster every two years at most and may breed for 20 years or more.

History of Domestication

The ancestors of the modern dromedary arrived in the Middle East about 5 million years ago, toward the end of the Pliocene epoch. To early humans wild camels were an important source of meat long before they were used for riding or carrying goods. The earliest evidence of domestication dates back 4,000 years, and people may have been responsible for taking camels to Africa at about that time. For a while there were dromedaries living both wild and captive. However, it seems that around 2,000 years ago the last wild dromedaries were captured or killed, leaving the Bactrian camel of Central Asia as the only camel species living a truly wild existence. The dromedary is less docile and more difficult to ride than the Bactrian, but its longer legs allow it to move somewhat faster. It is therefore useful for traveling rapidly in hot deserts.

A dromedary camel market in Rajasthan, India. It is believed that dromedaries were first domesticated as long as 4,000 years ago.

American Bison

Bison bison

The fate of the American bison demonstrates one of the worst examples of ruthless exploitation, which reduced the animal to the point of extinction. Conversely, it is also one of the best examples of successful conservation management.

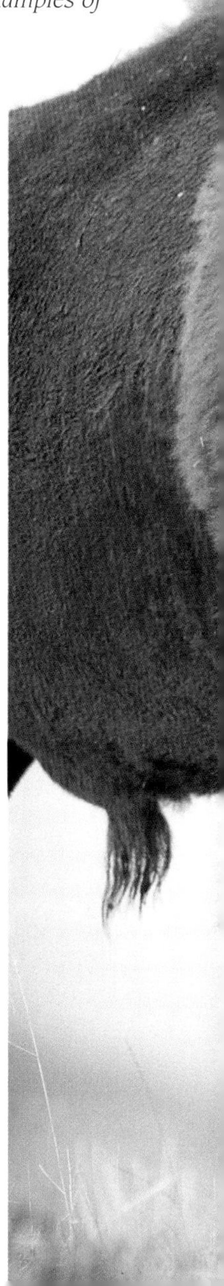

THE BISON IS THE BIGGEST ANIMAL to have roamed the North American continent in historic times. Scientists know it by this name, but to most Americans it is more familiar as the buffalo. The two names apply to the same animal, and confusion arises as an accident of history. A similar problem applies to the use of the word "Indian" in reference to the native people of North America. Logically, Indians come from India, not America, but European explorers meeting these people for the first time called them Indians to differentiate them from white men like themselves. Similarly, when the bison was first discovered by European explorers, they sometimes called it "buffalo" because it reminded them of the water buffalo—a species that was domesticated in Asia hundreds of years ago. It was also rather similar to the African buffalo. They were the nearest familiar creatures to the newfound bison of North America. The terms "Indian" and "buffalo" have continued to be widely used to this day.

Dangers from Humans

Huge herds of bison used to roam the open plains and lightly wooded areas of central North America. It is claimed that the total population may have numbered up to 50 million animals, but they were slaughtered mercilessly by the spreading human population. As a result of such actions, the bison had already become extinct east of the Mississippi River by the early 19th century. As ranching and settlement steadily expanded westward in the United States, the bison's decline may also have been hastened by diseases caught from domestic

Common name American bison (buffalo)

Scientific name *Bison bison*

Family Bovidae

Order Artiodactyla

Size Length head/body: male 10–12 ft (3–3.8 m); female 7–10 ft (2.1–3.2 m); tail length: 17–35 in (43–90 cm); height at shoulder: up to 6.2 ft (1.9 m)

Weight Male 1,000–2,000 lb (454–907 kg); female 790–1,200 lb (358–544 kg)

Key features Large, oxlike animal with head held low and large hump over the shoulders; forelegs, neck, and shoulders covered in long, dark-brown hair; horns present in both sexes

Habits Lives in large herds that migrate across open grasslands; feeds mostly early and late in day

Breeding Single calf born May–August after gestation period of 9–10 months. Weaned at about 6 months; sexually mature at 2–3 years. May live up to 40 years in captivity, up to 25 in the wild

Voice Snorts, grunts, and cowlike noises; bulls bellow and roar during the rut

Diet Mostly grass; also sedges, wild flowers, and shrubs such as willow, birch, and sagebrush; lichens and mosses in winter

Habitat Prairies, sagebrush, and open wooded areas

Distribution Midwestern U.S. and Canada

Status Population: 200,000–500,000; IUCN Lower Risk: conservation dependent; Endangered (subspecies *B. b. athabascae*); CITES II

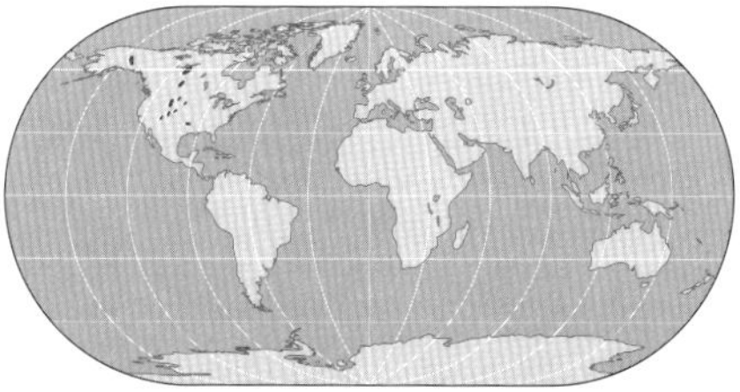

cattle, to which the wild species was not resistant. In the Midwest commercial hunting for hides and meat resulted in massive slaughter. The coming of the railroads not only created a market for meat, but also made it possible to export meat, hides, and bones to distant buyers, increasing the pressure on the herds.

Wasteful Executions

Professional hunters like "Buffalo Bill" Cody were engaged to supply railway workers with food, and many of them killed several thousand buffalo each year. The hunting was exceedingly wasteful, since often only the skins were taken. Sometimes just the tongues were collected, the rest of the meat being left on the prairie to rot, since it was not valuable enough to warrant the cost of transporting it elsewhere. Some animals were shot from moving trains for target practice and never used at all. For every bison skin that actually reached the market, at least three other animals were often wasted. An English traveler in 1873 counted 67 carcasses at one spot where hunters had shot buffalo coming to drink along the Arkansas River. An army colonel counted 112 bodies within a 200-yard (183-m) radius, all shot by one man from the same spot in 45 minutes.

← The American bison is an unpredictable animal. It can sometimes be approached closely, but at other times will stampede at the least provocation.

Railroad Casualties

The transcontinental railroad also split the bison herd in two, making two smaller populations and also making it easier to gain access to the animals. As late as 1870 there were still 4 to 5 million buffalo to the north and plenty more to the south. Today it is difficult to believe that so many large animals ever roamed the American plains, and people assume stories told about "millions of buffalo" must surely be exaggerations. However, there is documentary evidence proving that there were indeed enormous numbers killed. For example, fur company records show more than 35,000 bison skins being shipped from Fort Benton in 1857 alone. The Santa Fe Railroad carried over 1.3 million hides in just three years (1872 to 1874). In the north the manager of the Northern Pacific Railroad reported that his company had transported 30,000 to 40,000 skins each year in the late 1870s from Bismarck, North Dakota. In 1881 the quantities reached over 75,000. But within 10 years the trade had virtually collapsed, reflecting the almost total extermination of the bison.

Bison Census

A census in 1887 found only 541 bison left on the prairies. Conservation efforts, led by W. T. Hornaday, established captive herds in Montana and Oklahoma, and the bison has not looked back since. Today bison roam widely on the American prairies and in the sagebrush country of Wyoming. There are also large herds in South Dakota and on many private ranches. The only place where a wild population has always remained is Yellowstone National Park. About 1,500 animals live there, but sometimes range outside the park, where they damage crops and perhaps also spread disease to cattle.

A herd of bison graze in Yellowstone National Park—the only place where wild herds have lived continually.

Protected from hunters and predators, bison numbers have steadily increased, and by 1995 the total population was about 150,000—almost 90 percent of them on privately owned ranches. The herds now need to be culled annually to avoid the animals becoming too numerous for their food supply to support. Bison meat has high market value, being tasty and low in fat, and many cattle ranchers keep bison as a commercial venture.

European Bison

The European bison *(Bison bonasus)* is Europe's largest land animal and looks like its American cousin, but is taller and more slender in appearance. It is bigger than an ox, with a short, thick, hairy neck. The humped shoulders are less pronounced than in the American species, and the head is held higher. European bison are forest-edge inhabitants, coming out to graze in the open, where they eat about 65 pounds (30 kg) of grass per day. They also eat leaves and bark. In winter they are often given additional food to help their survival. The bison live in small herds of up to 20 animals. Their rutting season extends from August until October, and a single calf is born between May and July. Calves are fed by their mother for up to a year, and they can live to be more than 25 years old.

The species used to occur widely in the forests of Europe, but was brought to the brink of extinction by habitat loss and excessive hunting. By the 19th century only two populations remained, one in Poland and the other in the Caucasus Mountains of southeastern Europe. Both were wiped out early in the 20th century as a result of poaching. About 50 bison remained in various parks and zoos. Enough animals were bred from them to support reintroductions to the wild. The total number of European bison now exceeds 3,000, distributed among more than 20 wild populations and over 200 parks and zoos.

Slow Grazers

Bison are essentially grazing animals, living in large herds on the short-grass prairies, but also in lightly wooded areas. They are active during the day and also at night. They generally spend their time moving slowly, grazing as they go. They cover a mile or two (about 3 km) each day. In the past they would migrate long distances to fresh feeding areas, but that is rarely possible now, since almost all the modern herds live within enclosed areas.

Nevertheless, where there is room to do so (in Yellowstone National Park, for example), the bison still move seasonally from the high ground where they spend the summers to richer pastures on lower ground in the fall. Bison normally spend much of their time resting, but they also like to wallow in dust or mud and rub themselves against fence posts, boulders, and trees. They have acute senses of hearing and smell. Despite their large size and rather ungainly appearance, they can run at speeds of nearly 40 miles per hour (64 km/h)—at least for short distances. They are also capable of swimming across large rivers. Bison herds are normally composed of a few dozen animals, although in the past many thousands might occur in the same area. Mature males travel alone or in small groups for most of the year and join with the females for the summer breeding season.

During the rut, in July and August, dominant males fight fiercely by butting each other head to head. They make a lot of noise at that time of year, bellowing and roaring to establish status—sounds that can sometimes be heard miles away. Successful males stay close to receptive females for several days until they are able to mate with them, meanwhile keeping rival males away. A single calf is born after about 10 months—twins are very rare. The young animals become capable of breeding

↑ Two European bison bulls sparring. The rutting season in European bison is from August to October, with one calf born between May and July. These bison are Europe's largest land animals—taller and more slender than their American cousins.

from the age of about two years, but there seems to be a geographical variation in breeding success. In Oklahoma about two-thirds of the adult females may be found breeding each year, but more than three-quarters of females do so in Montana. Females can produce a calf every year but sometimes miss a year, allowing time to build up their body reserves before becoming pregnant again.

Little to Fear

Newborn calves weigh about 35 to 70 pounds (16 to 32 kg). They can run after three hours and are weaned by the time they are one year old. The mother guards her calf jealously and will chase away predators and other intruders. Wild bison have little to fear these days now that wolves and other large predators are scarce. They are the biggest land mammals in the Western Hemisphere, and many will live to be 20 years old unless they are culled by herd managers or licensed hunters.

A smaller type of bison known as the wood bison (*Bison bison athabascae*) occurs in wooded areas of southwestern Canada. It is often treated as though it were a different species, and it has been listed as Endangered by the United States government. However, DNA (genetic molecular structure) analysis suggests that the wood bison is in fact not a separate species, merely a smaller northern race.

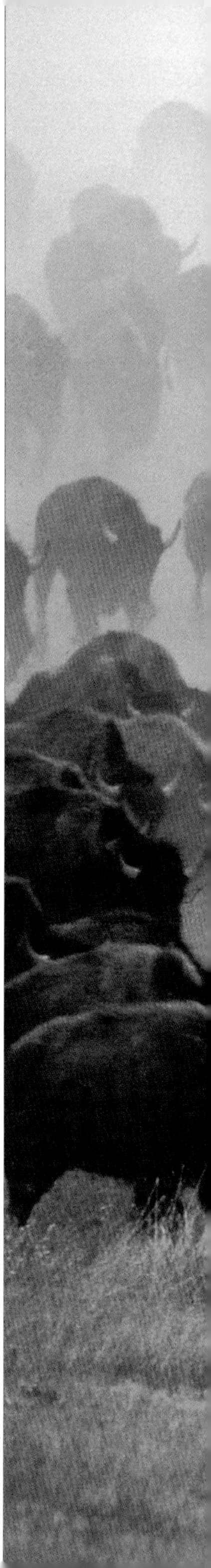

A herd of bison stampeding across the prairies is an awe-inspiring sight. The bison were once found in vast numbers, but hunting brought them to the brink of extinction. Now they are no longer threatened.

A Keystone Species

The bison was once the dominant factor in the ecology of the North American continent. Its grazing helped maintain short-grass prairies in a condition that was suitable for many plains species of birds, reptiles, and plants that were unable to thrive where the grass grew taller. Bison are among the natural prey of cougars and wolves. The remains of their carcasses fed scavengers, and their molted fur was eagerly collected by nesting birds. Some Native American people depended heavily on the bison herds for meat, hides, and many other useful products. The skins were used to make weatherproof tents and clothing sewn with lengths of bison sinew. Hair was used for bedding, and bones were carved into ornaments and tools. The bison supported a whole community of plants and animals within which it lived. Removing these vital creatures from the scene disrupts the whole ecosystem, just as removing the keystone from the center of the arch of a bridge will cause it to collapse. For a while it was even official policy to remove bison in an effort to undermine Native American communities during the westward colonization of North America.

Two elderly Native American women photographed in the 1950s clad in buffalo-skin capes. Some Native Americans were heavily dependent on the buffalo.

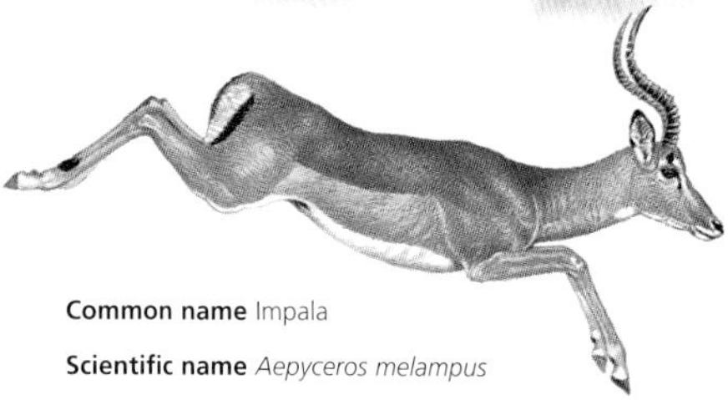

Common name Impala

Scientific name *Aepyceros melampus*

Family Bovidae

Order Artiodactyla

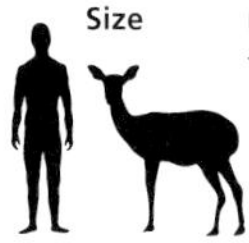

Size Length head/body: 47–63 in (120–160 cm); tail length: 12–18 in (30–45 cm); height at shoulder: 30–37 in (75–95 cm)

Weight Male 99–176 lb (45–80 kg); female 88–132 lb (40–60 kg)

Key features Medium-sized, sleek, and lightly built antelope; long, slender legs; characteristic tuft of black hair on lower and rear edge of hind legs; upper body bright reddish-brown, sides fawn, and underparts white; black-tipped ears, white eyebrows; male bears slender, ridged horns

Habits Gregarious; acute senses: explosion of activity when disturbed; social structure differs with season; mostly active during day, although avoids midday sun; some nocturnal activity

Breeding Generally single calf born each year after gestation period of 6.5 months. Weaned at 5–7 months; females sexually mature at 18 months, males at 12–13 months. May live about 15 years in captivity, similar in the wild

Voice High-pitched bark and snorts when alarmed; males roar, snort, and growl during rut

Diet Grass; also leaves and shoots, fruit and seeds of trees and bushes

Habitat Open woodlands and grasslands

Distribution Central and southeastern Africa from Kenya to South Africa; small population in southwestern Africa around southern Angola

Status Population: many thousands; IUCN Lower Risk: conservation dependent

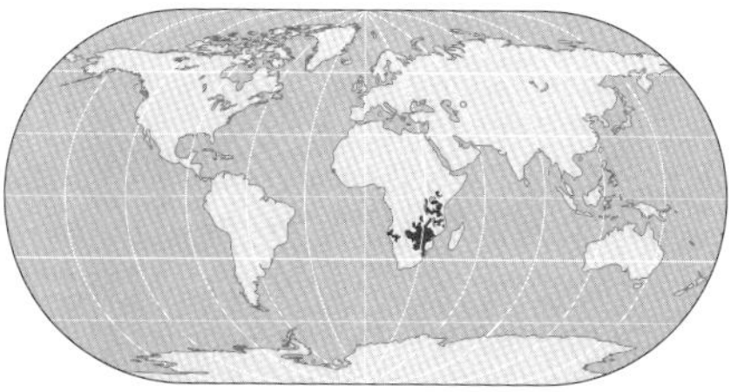

Impala

Aepyceros melampus

With a lightly built frame and long, slender legs, the impala is an elegant antelope that is famous for its agility, grace, and beauty.

While some species of antelope prefer to live in open grasslands and others in deep forest, the impala is typically found in open woodland and areas where the trees blend into grassland.

Inhabitant of "Ecotones"

During the wet season, when the plains are green with the fresh growth brought on by the rains, impala can be found grazing on the new, lush grasses. When the rains end, the grasses dry out, and the adaptable antelope move toward woodland areas. There they find nourishment from the leaves, shoots, fruit, and seeds of trees and bushes. Consequently, impala prefer to inhabit so-called "ecotones," the transition zones between open grasslands and woodlands, where they can use the varying food resources available with the seasons. Being able to switch their feeding habits means that impala need not undertake lengthy migrations. However, because they need a highly specific habitat (including cover, moisture, and year-round nourishment), the animals will either be found in large numbers or not at all.

Impala are adapted to living at high densities, making them a frequent target of many of the larger predators, including lions, cheetahs, leopards, wild dogs, and hyenas. However, the sprightly antelope can be a difficult meal to catch. The benefit of living in large groups is that there are always numerous eyes and ears on the lookout for danger. If an impala becomes aware of danger, it barks an alarm call to the rest of the herd. As the predator moves closer, more alarm calls are sounded; if it attempts to attack, impalas take flight in an explosion of activity. The lightly built antelope are extremely fleet of foot. They leap

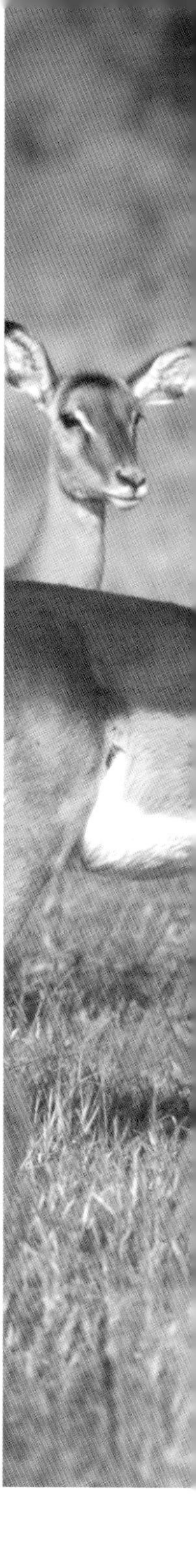

↑ ***A group of impala in Lake Nakuru National Park, Kenya. Impala live in highly specific habitats with year-round nourishment and therefore do not need to undertake migrations.***

wildly in all directions, confusing the predator as they vanish into nearby bushes. Impressive athletes, they make astounding jumps that carry them over distances of up to 40 feet (12 m). With apparently little effort they appear to float gracefully through the air, clearing obstacles up to 8 feet (2.5 m) high. Speeding into dense vegetation, the impala can also weave through narrow gaps in the trees without hesitation. When fleeing from danger, it kicks out its hind feet, releasing scent from the black tufted ankle glands. The scent trail helps the individuals regroup after the chase, especially if they have fled into dense cover.

Social Organization

Impala organize themselves into bachelor, breeding, and nursery herds. Bachelor herds include adult males that are potential territory holders and juvenile males. Breeding herds contain adult and juvenile females, juvenile males, and at times other than the rut, a number of adult males. Sometimes nursery herds of juveniles occur, but they are only temporary groups that will later disperse and become part of the breeding herds. In some areas males are territorial throughout the year, but in southern parts males establish their territory just for the period of the rut. They will defend their territory aggressively, using vocalizations and displays including head-bobbing, horn-clashing, and head-pushing. Bouts of serious fighting may occur. The horns are vital weapons and indicators of status, used for head-to-head wrestling. Only present in males, they are distinctive structures that sweep upward, out, and backward in a lyre shape. The sharp horns can cause serious injuries or even death. They may grow up to 31 inches (80 cm) long, but the average is about 20 inches (50 cm).

The impala is an important member of its ecosystem. Its grazing habits help shape the landscape, and it is a valuable prey item for many predators. There is also an important relationship between impala, termites, and acacia trees. During the dry season when grass is scarce, impala feed on the ripe pods of the acacia. The seeds pass through the gut unharmed and are dispersed in the impala's droppings. Termites also use the acacia as a source of food, and in some areas the dead thorn trees are an important part of their diet. Star grass, attractive nourishment for impalas, often grows on the side of deserted termite mounds. While feeding on it, the impala nourishes the soil with its droppings.

Common name American beaver (Canadian beaver)

Scientific name *Castor canadensis*

Family Castoridae

Order Rodentia

Size Length head/body: 31–47 in (80–120 cm); tail length: 10–20 in (25–50 cm)

Weight 24–66 lb (11–30 kg)

Key features Robust body with short legs and large, webbed hind feet; tail scaly, flattened, and paddlelike; small eyes and ears; coat dense and waterproof, light to rich dark brown

Habits Lives in small territorial colonies of related animals; semiaquatic; fells small trees to build lodges and dams that are of great importance to wetland ecosystem; largely nocturnal

Breeding Single litter of 1–9 (usually 2–4) young born in spring after gestation period of 100–110 days. Weaned at 3 months; sexually mature at 18–24 months. May live over 24 years in captivity, up to 24 in the wild

Voice Hisses and grunts; also announces presence by slapping tail on water surface

Diet Aquatic plants such as water lilies and leaves; also bark, twigs, roots, and other woody tissues of waterside trees and shrubs

Habitat Lakes and streams among light woodland

Distribution Canada, Alaska, and much of contiguous U.S.; introduced to parts of Finland

Status Population: 6–12 million. Abundant—recovered well after serious decline due to excessive fur trapping in 18th and 19th centuries; regulated hunting still takes place

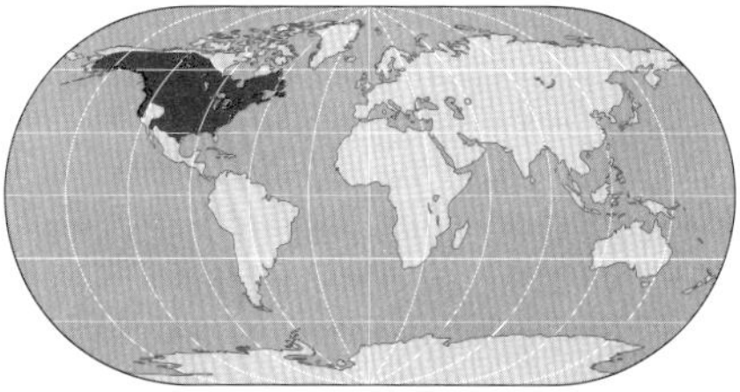

American Beaver

Castor canadensis

The industrious American beaver has helped shape the economic and ecological history of North America. Prodigious construction skills, a cooperative family life, and usefulness as a fur-bearing animal have given the rodent huge significance throughout its range.

AMERICAN BEAVERS ARE NATURALLY widespread, occurring from Alaska to northern Mexico. There are also thriving populations in Europe, especially in Finland, where the species was introduced following the decline of the native Eurasian beaver. Good beaver habitat consists of lightly wooded country dominated by species such as aspen, willow, and alder, all of which grow best in wet conditions. Water is vital to the beaver, which has a semiaquatic lifestyle.

Happy Families

Beaver colonies usually consist of one breeding pair along with their offspring of the past year or two. Beavers usually pair for life, and all members of the family help with chores such as maintaining the home (a lodge built of timber), watching over the babies, and gathering food. This kind of arrangement is close to the idealized human family, and it is one reason why beavers are regarded with affection by most people. Beaver family life is not without its trials, however, and young adults that have outstayed their welcome will eventually be driven out by their parents. Interactions with neighboring colonies are not necessarily amicable either: Members use scented heaps of dirt, twigs, and dung to mark out their territory and indulge in tail-slapping displays in the water to warn off intruders.

Where a beaver territory includes a suitable sheltered waterside bank, the family may set up home in a specially dug burrow. But if there is no natural site available, the resourceful beavers build one. First, they dam up a stream, creating

a large pool in which they can construct an island of timber and silt. Within the mound is a spacious living chamber, the entrance to which is underwater. These "lodges" are excellent places to bring up young beavers, since they are protected from most predators by the surrounding moat of cold water.

Construction Workers

Among the mammals the architectural and construction skills of beavers are second only to those of humans. Beaver dams and lodges are large structures, made mostly of timber—branches, logs, and sometimes whole trees up to 40 inches (100 cm) in diameter! That is unusual, however, and most trees felled are less than 10 inches (25 cm) thick. They are felled close to the water's edge by the beaver's huge gnawing teeth, then towed through the water and wedged firmly into place with dexterous front paws. Lodges, dams, and burrows are not the beaver's only feats of engineering. In order to transport enough timber for building, the beavers often have to excavate substantial canals through areas that are either too shallow or weed-choked to accommodate large floating branches without snagging.

← The North American beaver is perfectly adapted to its semiaquatic lifestyle. Its fur is warm and waterproof, and it can close its ears and nose while diving underwater.

Once built, beaver dams require constant maintenance and repair, especially during

Beaver Scent

The scents used by beavers to mark out their territory are produced in glands connected to the urinary tract. One of these scents is a substance unique to beavers and is known as castoreum. In the past castoreum was used to treat medical conditions including stomach cramps, ulcers, and various other aches and pains. The active ingredient that made these treatments effective is almost certainly salicin, a compound produced by willow trees. Salicin is the compound from which the common painkiller aspirin is derived. Beavers feeding on willow accumulate salicin in their body and use it in the production of scent. In recent times castoreum has become more commonly used as a base for perfumes.

spring, when many timbers are dislodged by fast-flowing melt water. A well-maintained dam will serve many generations of beavers, but they do not last indefinitely. Sooner or later the pool behind the dam becomes silted up, and the water will find an alternative route around the site, leaving the lodge high and dry. The resident beavers must then move on and begin again from scratch. The silted-up pools created in such a way eventually become willow thickets and lush meadows, replacing the woodland that once grew there. That offers opportunities for many species of insects, birds, and plants to live in an area where they would otherwise be absent. The beaver acts as a landscape architect, transforming the habitat. It is a good example of a keystone species on which many others depend for their survival.

Beavers do not hibernate, but in the north of their range they are seldom seen during winter. There is often a thick layer of ice and snow covering the pool, which effectively seals the beavers in. The silt in the thick lodge walls freezes solid, so that even if predators such as wolves and bears cross the ice, they are rarely able to break in. The beavers, however, can still come and go from the lodge by underwater entrances. During winter, when food is scarce, they can survive on plant material (mainly shoots and woody material) stored in special "caches" during the summer. The animals also have a reserve of fat stored in the tail, which helps them survive if spring comes late and food stocks run low.

During their winter confinement beavers live for several months without seeing true daylight. As result, their daily cycles of rest and activity are regulated by their own body clocks, rather than by the rising and setting of the sun. During these times they appear to

The beavers' home is a large pile of mud and branches sited on a riverbank or in the middle of a lake. It contains different rooms, with a living chamber above the water level and sometimes a dining area nearer the water.

switch from a regular 24-hour cycle to a longer one, something between 26 and 29 hours. Interestingly, the same happens with humans. People such as prisoners or experimental volunteers who live without natural light or artificial aids to telling the time develop a similar extended daily cycle and therefore often miscalculate the number of days they have been shut away.

Beaver Wars

The beaver's lustrous fur is soft, warm, and waterproof—qualities that are also greatly valued by humans. In the early colonial history of North America beaver trapping was so profitable that wars were fought over ownership of large areas of beaver habitat. Access to beaver skins was a major incentive to the exploration and opening up of the continent. Later, the fashion for felt top hats made from beaver fur encouraged still more trapping. Beavers were killed by the hundreds of thousands each year, and not surprisingly the population dwindled rapidly. Beavers are easy to find and are also easily trapped. By the early 20th century beavers had disappeared from much of their former range, and the species was in real danger of extinction. The loss of the beavers had enormous carry-over effects on entire wetland ecosystems. Without the beavers to build dams water drained rapidly from areas where it had formerly remained as pools. While excess water from heavy rainfall and spring thaws once spread gently over a wide area, in the absence of beavers it created raging torrents and flash floods.

Thankfully the danger was recognized in the nick of time, and legislation was put in place to preserve the remaining beaver stocks. Careful management has enabled numbers to recover, while allowing controlled trapping to continue. Beavers returned to much of their former range through recolonization, and other populations have been restocked artificially by bringing in beavers from elsewhere.

The reappearance of beavers is not always welcome, and there is an ongoing conflict between conservationists, trappers, and people who want to use the land for other purposes. Arable farmers claim that beaver activity harms their interests by flooding crop fields. Floods can also damage roads and other human infrastructure—one example of a situation in which commercial interests are at odds with ecological considerations. Establishing a compromise is one of the toughest challenges facing policymakers now and in the future.

↑ *Beavers only produce one small litter of kits each year. All members of the colony, which includes young of previous years, share tasks such as baby-sitting and providing the kits with solid food.*

← *An American beaver building a dam. Although sometimes considered a nuisance by humans, dams in fact provide a natural filtration system that removes harmful impurities from the water. The large areas of wetlands that dams create also encourage greater biodiversity.*

Brown Rat

Rattus norvegicus

Common name Brown rat (common rat, Norway rat)

Scientific name *Rattus norvegicus*

Family Muridae

Order Rodentia

Size Length head/body: 9–11 in (22–29 cm); tail length: 7–9 in (17–23 cm)

Weight 9–28 oz (255–790 g)

Key features Typical rat with short legs, longish fingers and toes, and pointed face; ears pink and prominent; scaly tail noticeably shorter than head and body; fur dull grayish-brown, fading to white or pale gray on belly

Habits Generally nocturnal; social; cautious at first but can become bold; climbs and swims well

Breeding Up to 12 litters of 1–22 (usually 8 or 9) young born at any time of year (but mostly in spring and summer) after gestation period of 21–26 days. Weaned at 3 weeks; sexually mature at 2–3 months. May live up to 6 years in captivity, 3 in the wild

Voice Loud squeaks when frightened or angry

Diet Anything edible, including fruit, grain, meat, eggs, wax, and soap; will catch and kill other small animals

Habitat Almost anywhere food can be found

Distribution Worldwide in association with humans; not normally in more sparsely populated areas of the world

Status Population: several billion

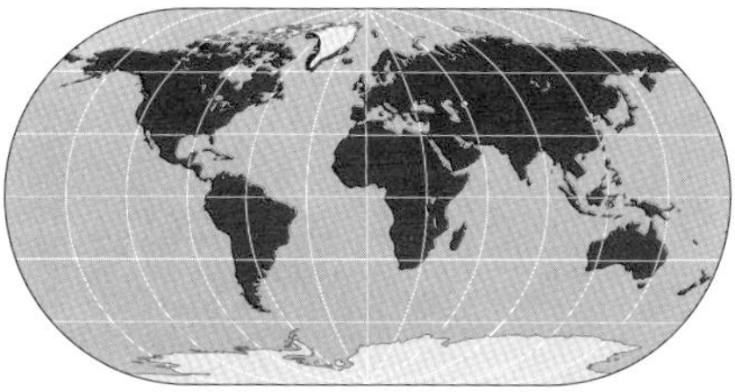

The brown rat is one of the most successful mammals on the planet. It rivals humans in terms of distribution and number, and continues to exploit us successfully despite our best efforts to exterminate it.

THE BROWN RAT IS PERHAPS the most reviled of all mammals. Even the word "rat" has all kinds of meanings, every one of them negative. Someone in a bad mood is described as "ratty," we detect wrongdoing when we "smell a rat," and telling tales to get someone else into trouble is "ratting."

Rats have few friends in spite of the fact that the vast majority of species are totally harmless. The brown rat is one the largest of 56 species in the genus *Rattus*, most of which live completely wild and never trouble people at all. But such is the strength of the brown rat's bad reputation worldwide that virtually all rats and ratlike rodents are treated as vermin.

Eastern Origins

Despite the misleading alternative name of Norway rat, the brown rat is thought to have originated in India or northern China. It spread to Europe and the Americas less quickly than its more inquisitive cousin, the ship rat, but today it is the dominant commensal rat species in most temperate parts of the world. In many places it has displaced the ship rat altogether. Brown rats prefer to live on the ground rather than in trees, and their liking for wet places suggests that their natural habitat may once have been stream banks. Brown rats swim well and are often associated with canals, sewers, and irrigation systems. They are expert at catching fish. They are also proficient diggers, and in the wild they create extensive burrow systems with many entrances and chambers.

The diet of brown rats can be extraordinarily diverse. They even manage to survive on the debris of seashores. Given a choice, however, they seem to prefer eating

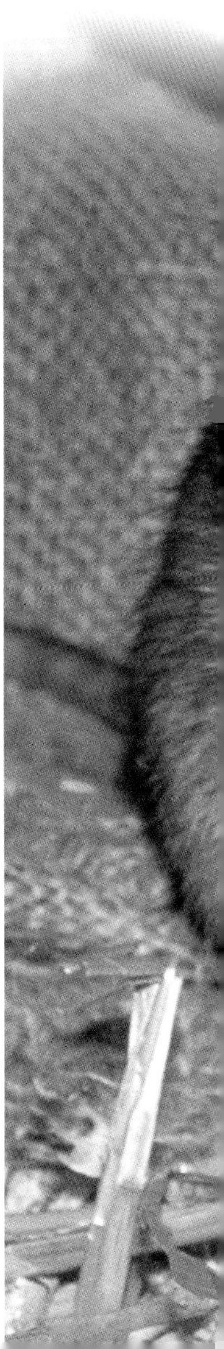

Brown rats can feed on a wide variety of foods. They are a versatile species and can make their living almost anywhere there is human habitation.

meat and animal matter to fruit and grains. Their teeth are relatively unspecialized: They use their incisors for gnawing and their molars for grinding fragments of food. In association with humans rats will eat almost anything, including soap, wax, leather, and paper. They thrive in cities, where drains provide them with shelter and food. Litter and overflowing trashcans offer all kinds of high-energy fatty foods loved by humans and rats alike. Food is often so abundant that an urban brown rat can spend its entire adult life in a home range as little as 80 to 500 feet (24 to 150 m) across.

The social structure of brown rats is rather variable, with the level of organization depending on the density of the local population. At low densities dominant males defend territories within which several females will collectively and cooperatively rear his offspring. If all available territories are taken, the excess rats form large gangs within which many males try to mate with every estrous female. Aggression is rife, there is no fixed dominance structure, and the stresses of life mean that reproductive success is low compared with that in the well-organized world of the territory-holding rats.

Rapid Breeders

Under good conditions brown rats can breed prolifically. A single pair can, in theory, multiply to over 15,000 animals in the space of a year. Rapid increases in population cannot be sustained for long, however, and brown rat numbers tend to fluctuate considerably. Overcrowding either leads to population crashes caused by starvation or disease, or to sudden mass dispersions, with thousands of rats suddenly on the move.

Brown rats will fight fiercely for their lives and will attack dogs, cats, and even people if cornered. There are even reports of brown rats killing babies and helpless humans by biting them continuously until they bleed to death. Of course, such incidents are extremely rare, but they add to the rat's evil reputation.

It surprises most people to discover that brown rats are actually quite clean animals. Wherever possible they take pains to groom themselves using their tongue, teeth, and claws to wash and scrape dirt from their fur. They cover their palms in saliva to wipe their face and whiskers clean. However, such is the filth in some of the man-made environments they frequent, it is virtually impossible for some rats to ever get fully clean. It is true that rats carry many diseases that can infect people. Rabies, typhus, Weil's disease, rat-bite fever, and food poisoning (*Salmonella*) are just a few of the more serious infections known to be spread by brown rats.

Pest Control

The battle to control rats has been running for centuries. People have been employed as rat catchers since the Middle Ages, and there were dogs trained specifically for the task. The legend of the Pied Piper of Hamelin tells how the mysterious piper led the town rats to their deaths in the local river, having bewitched them with his music. When the townspeople refused to pay him, the piper took revenge by piping away all their children, who were never seen again. The rats in the story were probably ship rats rather than brown rats, but either way it normally takes more than music to rid a town of rat infestations. However, rats are vulnerable to poisoning. They cannot vomit; so even if they realize something is making them ill, they cannot void it from their stomach. One of the earliest rat poisons

The fairytale of the Pied Piper of Hamelin tells of a piper who charmed the rats away from the German town with his mysterious music.

A brown rat carries an infant. The young are born blind and naked but are quick developers—after just three weeks they are ready to leave the nest.

Even Rats Have Their Uses

Albino brown rats are naturally more docile than their full-color relatives. After generations of selective breeding they have become exceedingly tame and are widely used in medical and scientific research. Twenty million white rats are used in United States labs every year. Some are bred with specific weaknesses so that medical researchers can assess the efficacy of various new therapies. Others are used in experiments on physiology, neurology, genetics, behavior, and psychology. Brown rats have even been into space. In 1960 two lab rats spent time in orbit aboard a Russian satellite and returned to earth apparently none the worse for their adventure.

was derived from a plant called Mediterranean squill. Eaten by a human or a dog, it causes severe nausea and vomiting, but in rats it causes paralysis and death. However, rats are smart, and once one rat has been poisoned by something, others in the colony will avoid eating the same thing. Also, rats will not eat anything that has made them feel ill before, so slow-acting or cumulative poisons are no use. Brown rats are also naturally suspicious of anything new. Ship rats are less cautious, which is one reason why poisoning campaigns have been more effective with that species.

Death Sentence

A breakthrough in rodenticide technology came in 1950 with the development of a poison called warfarin. Warfarin contains dicoumarol, a small dose of which causes massive internal bleeding and death. Most importantly, the rats are unable to detect warfarin in foods and so do not learn to avoid it. Nor do they learn from others' mistakes, because death occurs some time after the poison is eaten. Yet as early as 1958 there were examples of rats that were apparently unharmed by dicoumarol, and the percentage of resistant rats is growing. The development of new poisons continues.

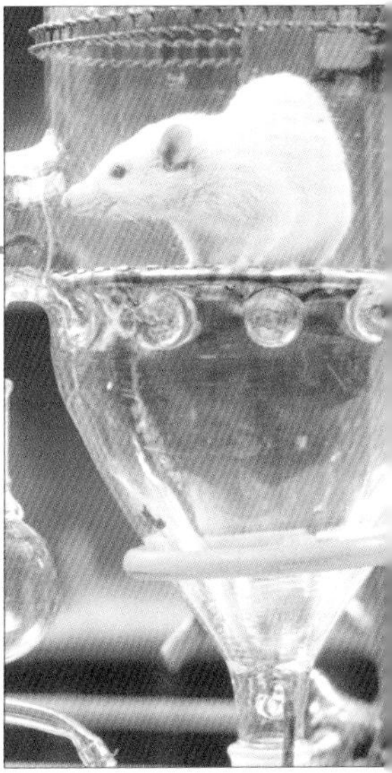

An albino brown rat in a piece of laboratory equipment being used in a toxicology test.

African Porcupine

Hystrix cristata

Common name African porcupine (crested porcupine, North African porcupine)

Scientific name *Hystrix cristata*

Family Hystricidae

Order Rodentia

Size Length head/body: 23.5–39.5 in (60–100 cm); tail length: 3–6.5 in (8–17 cm)

Weight 26.5–60 lb (12–27 kg)

Key features Large rodent with dark-brown to black fur; long black-and-white spines on back and rump; crest of stiff hairs from head to mid-back; legs sturdy, feet have powerful claws; blunt snout, medium-sized ears, small eyes

Habits Nocturnal; lives in burrows in groups but forages alone; rattles quills when threatened

Breeding One, sometimes 2, litters of 1–4 (usually 1 or 2) young born at any time of year after gestation period of 3.5 months. Weaned at 6–7 weeks; sexually mature at about 1 year. May live up to 20 years in captivity, about 14 in the wild

Voice Grunts, growls, and "peeps"; also shakes hollow quills on rump to make rattling sound

Diet Roots, tubers, fruit, and tree bark; carrion and bones; crops such as yams and corn

Habitat Savanna, woodland, and rocky steppe, especially on hilly ground

Distribution Throughout northern Africa (except Sahara Desert) south to Democratic Republic of Congo and Tanzania; also Italy, including Sicily

Status Population: abundant. Persecuted as an agricultural pest in many areas

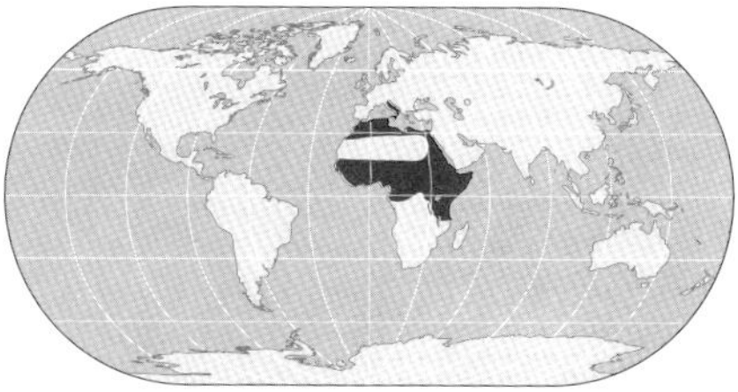

With its spectacular crest of spines raised in display the African porcupine is an intimidating sight. However, beneath its spiky armor the timid rodent usually lacks the will to do battle.

THE AFRICAN PORCUPINE IS a mild-mannered, sociable rodent that lives in amicable family groups. It comes out at night to forage for food, selecting mostly plant material. It is also known to take the occasional bone back to the burrow to gnaw. Bones provide valuable calcium, and the gnawing helps keep the porcupine's constantly growing incisor teeth sharp and healthy. Porcupines walk on the flat soles of their feet with a shambling gait, rather like a bear. When moving fast, they adopt a bounding gallop, but cannot keep it up for long. They can swim well if necessary.

Rattle Quills

Like the other seven members of the genus *Hystrix*, the crested porcupine sports a bunch of rattle quills at the end of its tail. Other Old World porcupines, such as the long-tailed and brush-tailed porcupines, do not have rattles. The rattle quills are short and stout; and instead of ending in a sharp point, their tips are expanded and hollow. When the porcupine quivers its tail, the quills rattle together, producing a sudden, whirring "pshhh," not unlike the sound made by a rattlesnake.

Porcupines use the sounds for display and communication. There is a lot of quill rattling during courtship, especially just before mating. Loud rattling is also used to deter predators, drawing attention to the sharp spines that could become embedded in their face if they do not back off. If an attack continues, the porcupine turns its back and stamps its feet,

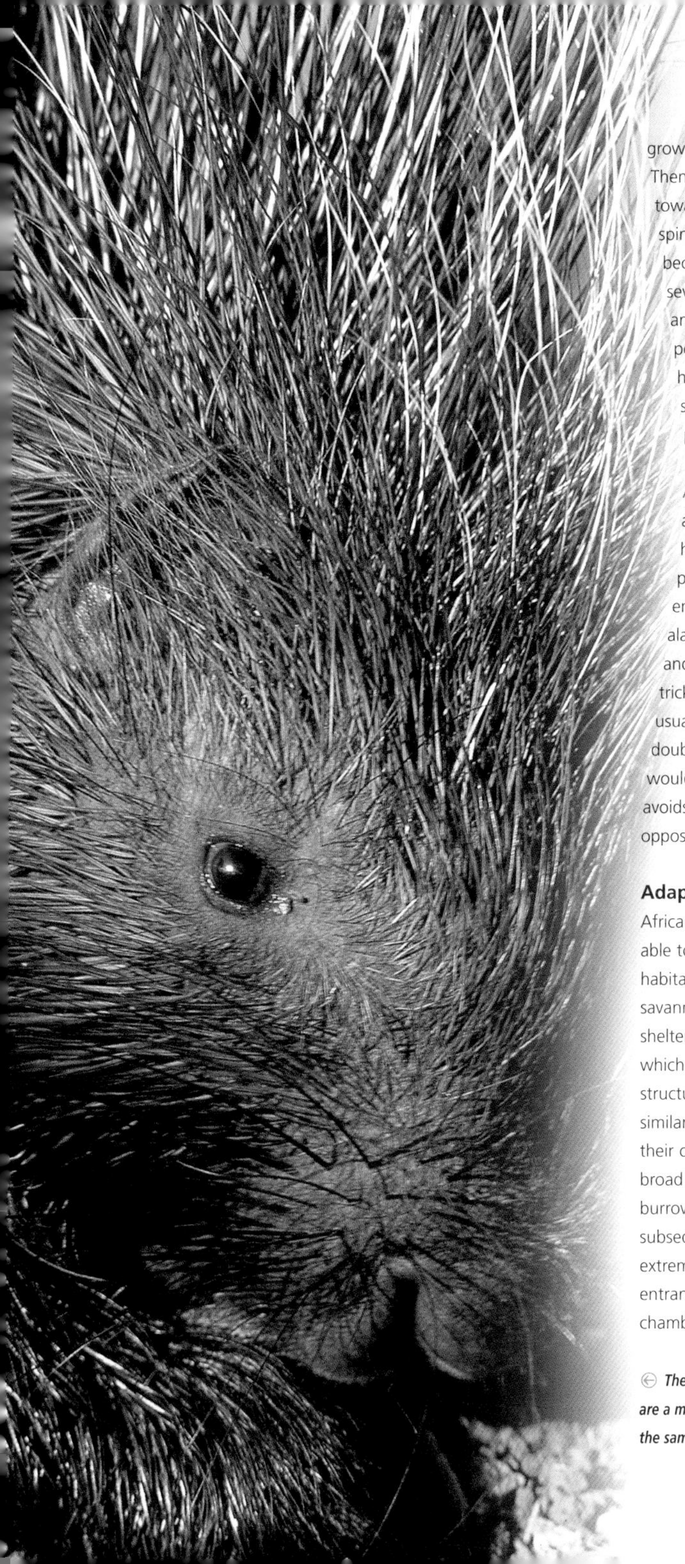

growling and continuing to rattle its quills. Then it charges backward and shoves its rump toward its would-be assailant's face. The spines, which are tipped with tiny barbs, become embedded in the flesh and cause severe pain and often infection. Even large animals like lions and hyenas can die of porcupine quill injuries. More often, however, they are left with an extremely sore and long-lasting reminder that porcupines are best left alone.

Despite their impressive weaponry, African porcupines are nervous creatures, almost to the point of paranoia. Even harmless animals or birds are treated as a potential threat, and the slightest sound is enough to startle a porcupine. When alarmed, it raises its quills from head to tail and stands tall on its four legs. That simple trick makes the porcupine look over twice its usual size and leaves the other animals in no doubt that it is well armed. But the porcupine would much rather flee than fight and usually avoids confrontation by shambling in the opposite direction or retreating to a safe place.

Adaptable Homemakers

African porcupines are adaptable creatures and able to make a good living in a wide variety of habitats from plantation forest to open savanna. They take full advantage of natural shelters, such as rock crevices or hollow logs, in which to build dens. In the absence of such structures they will "borrow" the burrows of similar-sized animals such as aardvarks or dig their own. They are effective diggers, having broad feet and long, strong claws. Once a burrow has been dug, it is often extended in subsequent years, eventually becoming extremely large, with several alternative entrances and sleeping chambers. The main chamber is lined with grass and is quite cozy. It

The African porcupine's long black-and-white spines are a modified form of hair. They are made of keratin, the same substance as human hair and fingernails.

↑ *Lions in Botswana stare in fascination at two African porcupines. Although lions have been known to eat porcupines, they find it difficult to penetrate the armory of needle-sharp quills.*

is large enough for the whole family to sleep in, with the parents lying on either side of their precious litter to keep them warm.

Young porcupines are born well developed, but remain within the safe confines of the den for several weeks. It takes a week or two for their soft baby spines to harden enough to be useful. The young begin feeding themselves before they are two months old. However, it takes a full year before they reach adult size and are ready to leave the home burrow, just in time to make room for a new litter.

Much of the African porcupine's food is unearthed from the ground, and roots, bulbs, and tubers feature strongly in the daily diet. Foraging happens at night and is usually a solitary activity, except for females with young. The infants begin to accompany their mother on her nocturnal forays before they are two months old. By watching and copying her they learn how to find food for themselves. In parts of the species' range where crops are grown, porcupines can be a menace to farmers. They enter fields at night and help themselves to

Porcupines in Europe

There is a significant population of crested porcupines in Italy, but opinion is divided on exactly how they got there. Some people think they were introduced by the Romans, while others are convinced that the porcupines are true natives of Europe and have always lived there. Certainly there were porcupines in Europe before the last ice age, since their fossils have been found throughout southern and central areas. The question is, did these early populations die out before Roman times? If so, the current population must either have recolonized naturally via the Middle East, Turkey, and the Balkans or been reintroduced by humans. The current distribution of crested porcupines is not much help, since it provides some support for both ideas. In Italy the porcupines appear to have spread north from possible release points in the south and in Sicily. However, it seems that porcupines have only recently disappeared from places such as Greece, Albania, the former Yugoslavia, and Turkey. Those countries are along the potential recolonization route between North Africa and Italy. Other species of porcupine have also been found living wild in Europe, notably in England. Such individuals were all the result of zoo escapes, and they died out after a few years. Nevertheless, the fact that porcupines can survive so far from home is further evidence of their great adaptability.

pumpkins and yams, pinning the food to the ground with their front feet and gnawing at it. They also nibble the bark of plantation trees. In such places the porcupines are trapped and poisoned and have become scarce in heavily settled areas of Egypt, Kenya, and Uganda.

The crested porcupine shares the southeastern part of its range (Tanzania) with its close relative the South African porcupine. The two animals look alike except for the tail quills, which are more conspicuous in the southern species. They also share similar lifestyles.

An African porcupine enjoys an ill-gotten meal. Stealing crops gives porcupines a bad name, and they are often persecuted where they carry out such activities.

Capybara

Hydrochaeris hydrochaeris

The semiaquatic capybara is the world's largest rodent. Its scientific name means "water-pig," and gives a good idea of the animal's general appearance and habits.

Common name Capybara

Scientific name *Hydrochaeris hydrochaeris*

Family Hydrochaeridae

Order Rodentia

Size Length head/body: 42–53 in (106–135 cm)

Weight 77–145 lb (35–66 kg)

Key features Tall, barrel-bodied rodent with slender legs and sparse reddish-brown hair; no tail; front feet have 4 toes, hind feet 3; large head with rectangular profile and deep muzzle; small ears and eyes; male has lozenge-shaped gland on top of face

Habits Semiaquatic; social; colonial; usually active by day, but often nocturnal where disturbed

Breeding One (occasionally 2) litters of 1–8 (usually 3–5) young born at any time of year after gestation period of 150 days. Weaned almost immediately; sexually mature at 12 months. May live up to 12 years in captivity, 9 or 10 in the wild

Voice Whistles, grunts, purring and clicking sounds; also coughing barks

Diet Grasses and aquatic plants

Habitat Grassland and forest alongside rivers and pools

Distribution South America: south of Panama and east of Andes Mountains, including Colombia, Venezuela, Brazil, and Paraguay south as far as northeastern Argentina

Status Population: numerous, but total figure unknown; IUCN Lower Risk: conservation dependent. Declining in many areas

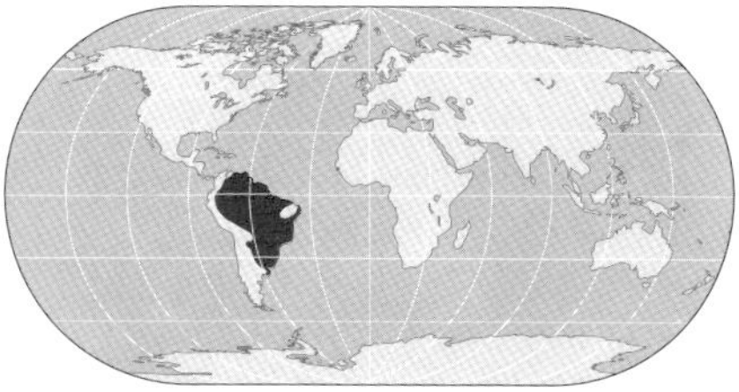

CAPYBARAS ARE THE SOLE survivors of a 10-million-year-old family of rodents. The group evolved in the late Miocene epoch, when South America was separated from other continents. For a brief period in the Pleistocene, following the joining up of North and South America, capybaras also lived in southeastern parts of what is now the United States. However, those animals appear to have gone extinct around the time of the last ice age. Some of the extinct hydrochaerids were much larger than the modern capybara—up to 6.5 feet (2 m) long—and weighed up to a staggering half a ton (450 kg).

Piglike

The body of the capybara is vaguely piglike, but the heavy, rectangular head with its blunt snout is unique. As with all rodents, the real clue to the capybara's identity is its teeth. They are big, as would be expected in an animal over 39 inches (100 cm) long. At the front there are two large, chisel-shaped incisors in each jaw. If capybaras really were pigs, the incisors would be accompanied on either side by more incisors and a pair of tusklike canine teeth. Instead, there is just a big gap, typical of rodents, which zoologists call the diastema. Farther back, behind the diastema, there are four pairs of cheek teeth (premolars and molars) in each jaw.

The eyes, ears, and nostrils are placed high up and well back on the head—a classic adaptation to a semiaquatic lifestyle (otters and hippopotamuses have a similar arrangement). It means that capybaras can swim or "hide" in water for long periods with only the top of the head above the surface. They are excellent swimmers, both at the surface and under water, where they can stay submerged for up to five

minutes at a time. Despite their competence in water, they feed mostly at the water's edge and rest in thickets of dense vegetation.

The toes of the front and back feet are partially webbed, which helps with swimming and also assists walking on soft mud by spreading the capybara's weight over a larger area. Capybaras are not particularly fast-moving animals, and they have little in the way of defensive weapons. As such they are the preferred prey of several large carnivorous animals, including jaguars, foxes, domestic and feral dogs, vultures, and caimans (small crocodilians). Young capybaras are especially vulnerable. They are also hunted by groups of bush dogs, which despite their small size are able to bring down capybaras in the water by hunting in a pack.

The capybara's coat is usually some shade of reddish-brown, although some individuals are very dark. Others appear greenish thanks to growths of algae in their hair.

Tough Diet

Capybaras are strictly vegetarian. They eat a mixture of grasses and aquatic plants such as pondweeds and water hyacinth. The flat molar teeth, which are used for grinding tough plant stems, suffer a lot of abrasion. They continue to grow throughout the capybara's life to compensate for gradual wear and tear.

In order to make the most of their tough diet, capybaras have a greatly enlarged cecum, an offshoot of the gut similar to the human appendix. The cecum contains a community of bacteria that break down cellulose, a complex form of carbohydrate that passes through most mammalian guts undigested. The bacteria turn the cellulose into smaller molecules that can be

The capybara can weigh up to 145 pounds (66 kg), 10,000 times the weight of the smallest mice. Its semiaquatic lifestyle is unusual among rodents.

Capybara Farms

Capybaras have been traditionally hunted for their meat and hides. The fat found under their skin is used as a basis for ointments, and their teeth are used in jewelry. Hunting has led to a decline in capybara numbers in many parts of the species' range and is now more closely regulated as a result. In order to meet the demand for capybara products, enterprising ranchers have begun farming them alongside cattle. The capybaras specialize in eating low-growing waterside plants, which they crop with their large incisor teeth, while the cattle graze the taller grasses that grow in drier areas. Farmers can therefore raise two different kinds of stock on the same piece of land without risk of overgrazing.

more readily absorbed into the bloodstream. The cecum is positioned near the end of the gut, so the only way the capybara can benefit from these easily absorbed sugars is to eat its own feces and let them pass through its digestive system a second time. Capybaras produce two kinds of droppings. In the morning the droppings are soft and green, having passed just once through the gut. They tend not to be seen often because the capybaras eat them immediately. The second time around the droppings are firm, dry pellets from which virtually all the goodness has been

Horsemen on a Venezuela ranch capture a capybara. Culls are allowed under license on some ranches. They take place in February, outside the main capybara breeding season.

Capybaras resting with their young of the season. A social species, capybaras live in groups averaging 10 in number or in temporary larger aggregations of up to 100 individuals.

absorbed. The efficient recycling of plant food is called coprophagy, and it occurs in several other rodents and in lagomorphs (rabbits and pikas) as well.

The basic social unit of capybaras is the family group, which usually comprises one dominant male, one or more females, and a dozen or so young. The dominant male mates with all the adult females in his band. Courtship and mating happen in the water, but the young are born on dry land, usually in dense vegetation. The young are highly precocious, able to walk almost immediately. They are reared communally, with mothers taking turns to baby-sit and suckle one another's offspring. Young capybaras start eating vegetation when they are just a few days old and are fully weaned in just a few weeks.

There may also be a small number of subordinate males associated with a family group. They help defend the group territory but are generally kept at arm's length by the top-ranking male. The subordinate males rarely get a chance to mate while the dominant male is around. Instead, they wait for the day when old age or the stress of leadership takes its toll, and the group needs a new boss. Once dominance is established, fighting is rare, and capybara colonies are generally peaceful. Both males and females help defend the territory, which can be an area of 5 to 500 acres (2 to 200 ha), depending on the quality of habitat. In the dry season, when rivers and pools begin to disappear, several capybara colonies may be forced together in herds of 100 or more animals; but as soon as the rains come, they disperse and re-form their original groups.

A male capybara marks its territory with scent from a sebaceous gland—the morrillo—on top of its snout. Members of a colony recognize each other by smell.

Smells and Sounds

Mature male capybaras have a low, hairless bump called the morrillo on the top of the snout. It contains large glands that secrete a viscous white substance. The gland is most active in dominant males. Both sexes have paired anal glands that produce personal scents unique to the individual. Scent deposited with droppings, along with urine, plays an important part in marking out the group territory.

As well as communicating by smell, capybaras use a wide variety of calls. Peaceful contentment is signaled by low clicking sounds. A steady revving purr is used as an appeasement signal, usually by subordinate animals reassuring their superiors that they pose no threat. The sound is similar to that made by young capybaras, and it seems to inhibit aggression in mature adults. When adults challenge each other, they utter gruff barks and sharp whistles and squeals. The alarm call is a sudden coughing bark repeated several times. On hearing the call, animals freeze, then make a dash for safety in the water, where relatively few predators can follow.

European Rabbit

Oryctolagus cuniculus

Common name European rabbit (Old World rabbit, domestic rabbit)

Scientific name *Oryctolagus cuniculus*

Family Leporidae

Order Lagomorpha

Size Length head/body: 14–20 in (35–50 cm); tail length: 1.5–3 in (4–8 cm)

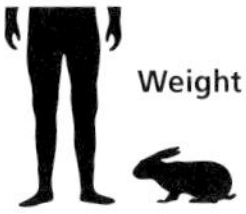

Weight 3–6.6 lb (1.3–3 kg)

Key features Stoutly built animal with powerful legs usually disguised by crouching stance; tail short and fluffy; head rounded with large, round eyes and long, erect oval ears; fur dense and soft, usually grayish-brown to black, paler on underside

Habits Mostly nocturnal but also active by day; lives in colonies in clustered burrows

Breeding Up to 7 litters of 1–9 (usually 5 or 6) young born in spring or summer after gestation period of 28–33 days. Weaned at 21 days; sexually mature at 3 months. May live up to 15 years in captivity, rarely more than 10 in the wild; most live fewer than a few months

Voice Usually silent; sharp squeals in pain or fright; drums feet to signal alarm

Diet Grass; also stems and leaves of other plants; nibbles bark in winter

Habitat Grassland

Distribution Much expanded by introductions over past 1,000 years; now occurs throughout Europe and northern Africa, also established in Australia and New Zealand

Status Population: extremely abundant, hundreds of millions. Widely persecuted as a pest

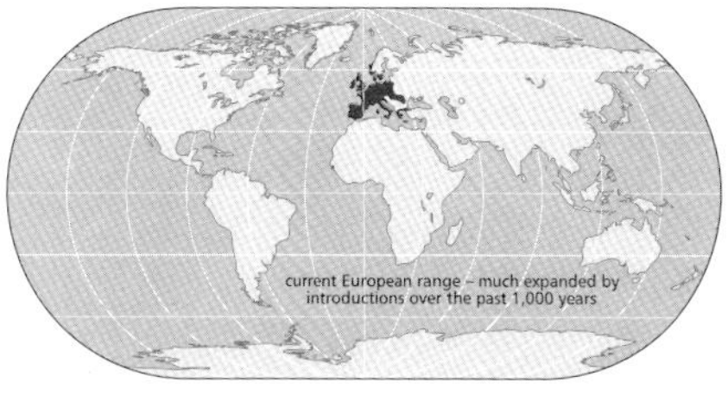

From humble beginnings the European rabbit has become the world's most widespread and abundant lagomorph. It can be a serious agricultural and environmental pest, but it is also much loved as a domestic pet and star of many folk tales.

Modern rabbits probably first appeared about 14 million years ago. Until the end of the Pleistocene epoch (10,000 years ago) the species was naturally restricted in its distribution, occurring only in the Iberian peninsula (Spain and Portugal). The country of Spain is indirectly named after the rabbits that lived there. The Roman name *Hispania* and the modern words *España* and Spain are derived from the Phoenician word *Ishaphan*, meaning "land of hyraxes." Hyraxes are small animals that look rather like rabbits. Since there is no evidence that hyraxes ever actually lived in the region, it seems almost certain that what the early explorers had seen were rabbits.

Rabbit Invasion

It was apparently the Phoenecians (from what is now Lebanon and Syria) and later the Romans who began the process of introducing rabbits to new areas outside their range about 3,000 years ago. Rabbits were taken first to North Africa and Italy, then to other parts of western Europe. The Norman conquest of England brought rabbits to that country, and they are now such an integral part of the British landscape that most people assume they are native. More recent introductions have established the rabbit in South America, Australia, and New Zealand. Rabbits were also taken to many remote oceanic islands, the idea being that self-sustaining populations would provide a food resource for sailors visiting in the future. European rabbits have also been introduced to the United States, but with less

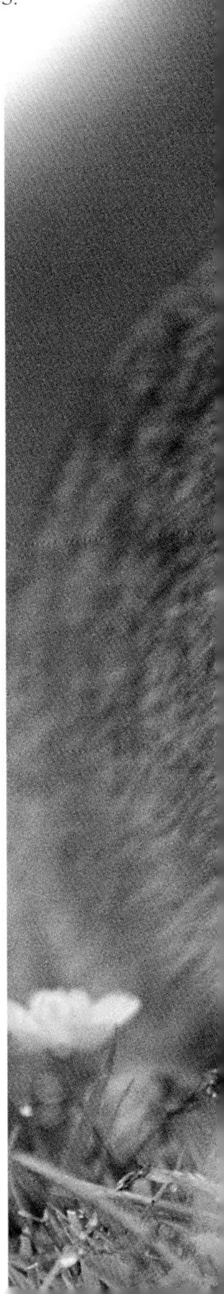

⊖ A juvenile European rabbit in Scotland outside its burrow. The young of a litter are ready to breed themselves at three months of age.

success. Their failure to get established is almost certainly because of competition with established native species such as the cottontail.

The European rabbit is a small, compact animal with short, soft, woolly, fur. It copes well with cold weather and is active all year round. Peak activity usually occurs around dawn and dusk, but rabbits can be out and about at any time of day or night. One of the key factors in the species' success is its nonselective vegetarian diet. Rabbits can eat all kinds of plant material, including grass and leaves, stems, shoots, flowers, roots, and seeds. In winter they are able to survive almost entirely on woody tissues stripped from under the bark of young trees and shrubs.

Outrunning Predators

Many of the European rabbit's most distinctive adaptations are antipredation measures. Their long legs are usually disguised by the animal's habitual crouching posture, but at the first sign of danger they are used to propel the animal at surprising speed toward safety, jinking and feinting left and right to throw a pursuer off the trail. Over short distances an alert rabbit stands a good chance of outrunning a predator such as a fox, mink, or bird of prey. The rabbit has large eyes on either side of its rounded head, providing excellent all-round vision by day or night. Its ears are likewise adapted for constant surveillance, being long and mobile. They are able to rotate in any direction to pick up the tiniest sounds of danger. Rabbits are also sensitive to low-frequency sounds carried through the earth. They use foot thumping as a way of communicating danger to other rabbits, both on the surface and underground.

The white underside of the rabbit's tail may serve as a visual warning as it runs away, but the animal rarely makes any vocal sounds except in extreme distress or pain. Silence is the best policy for avoiding the attention of predators; but once caught, the most an individual can hope for is to alert its relatives to the danger by squealing. Scent is doubly

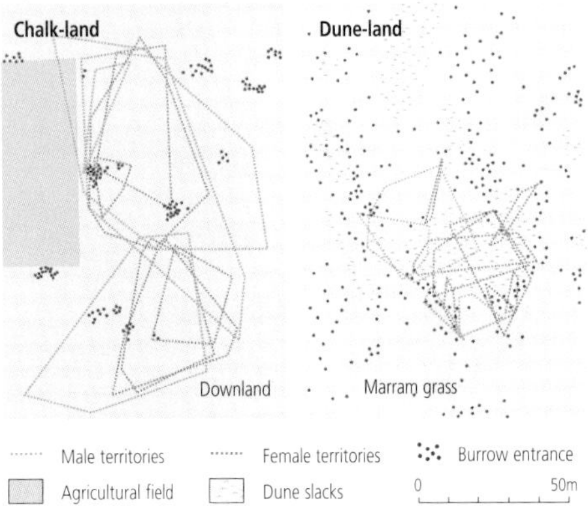

Rabbit social behavior differs in different habitats. In chalk downland rabbits have clustered burrows, and fights often break out between females. On sand dunes burrows are not clustered but randomly distributed, and there is little fighting between individuals. Home ranges overlap less among dunes than on chalk downland.

important to rabbits for recognizing danger and in social interactions. All rabbits have glands under the chin and in the groin, secretions from which are used to scent-mark parts of the home range. Dominant individuals, especially males, scent-mark more often.

Grooming between a mated pair. Females enter estrus again shortly after giving birth. With a gestation period of only 30 days or so, females can produce as many as seven litters per year.

Rabbit Warrens

Unlike most rabbit species, the European rabbit is adapted to life in open spaces. It often lives along woodland edges, but may also set up home on short turf grassland where there is not a tree or shrub in sight for cover. It would be a reckless strategy for a potential prey animal were it not for the rabbit's skill at burrowing. The European rabbit is one of few members of the hare and rabbit family to dig its own shelters. The burrows can be anything from a short tunnel with a single chamber to an extensive and interconnected labyrinth used by an entire breeding group. The communal burrow systems are known as warrens and may cover well over 2.5 acres (1 ha). They sometimes have several hundred entrances and are home to many hundreds of rabbits.

Unusually among rabbits, the European species is both social and territorial. The strict hierarchy among adult rabbits dictates which males mate with most females and which females get the best nest sites. Breeding groups usually include up to four adult males and as many as nine breeding females. The dominant male tends to achieve most matings, but DNA studies reveal that females also seek matings with other males too.

Aggression is fairly common, especially between females, who will sometimes fight hard over nest sites. The best sites are in the center of the warren. Low-ranking females may have to build their own nursery burrows on the outskirts of the group territory, where they are more accessible to predators. These simple

Breeding like Rabbits

Rabbits are famously fast breeders. Females bear large litters after a short gestation period, and the young mature rapidly so that quite soon they could be breeding too. Females that have given birth are ready to mate again almost immediately and will finish suckling one litter just in time to clear the nest for the next. Such a rapid turnover means that even though rabbits are seasonal breeders, a healthy female can rear as many as seven litters in a year. In Europe between February and August 90 percent of adult female rabbits are pregnant at any one time. Within a balanced and stable ecosystem such massive reproductive potential merely allows the rabbits to hold their own. The vast majority of young rabbits born will be picked off by predators and will never get the opportunity to breed themselves. The population rarely gets out of control because females are sensitive to food shortages, periods of bad weather, and social stress caused by overcrowding. All of these factors can cause spontaneous abortions, and over half of all rabbit pregnancies end that way. However, since most of the world's rabbits now form part of introduced "alien" populations, they are not subject to the same natural checks and balances as in their native range, and their potential for expansion can be devastating.

Six-day-old European rabbits huddle together in a nest. The mother only visits them for a short time each day to avoid alerting predators. She stops up the entrance with soil so the babies do not stray.

breeding burrows are called "stops." Male rabbits fight too, in order to achieve dominance; but once in charge, they can usually maintain order by merely threatening their subordinates. Young male rabbits disperse from the home warren as juveniles, while females do so only occasionally. Colonies therefore tend to consist of related females and immigrant males. The inclusion of new males helps maintain genetic diversity. Adult rabbits are generally sedentary, rarely wandering more than 100 yards (90 m) from their home burrow. Male ranges are usually about twice the size of a female's range.

Nurturing Young

Young rabbits are born helpless. They are naked and blind and cannot feed themselves. They must therefore be provided with warmth and food and protected from danger. However, the mother rabbit needs to find time to look after herself. She must eat enough to produce milk for the young in the nest and also to nourish the new embryos that soon develop inside her. She faces the dilemma that every visit to the breeding burrow risks attracting predators. Mother rabbits therefore try to balance adequate care with minimum attendance.

The female prepares the nest carefully, lining it with grass and fur to make it warm. Once the young are born, she visits them just once a day for only five to 10 minutes, in which time they guzzle enough rich, fatty milk to put on weight and develop.

Rabbits Down Under

The introduction of rabbits to South Australia for sport shooting in 1858 is one of the best-known mistakes of its kind. Within 60 years the species had spread across the continent to Western Australia and occupied an area of over 1.5 million square miles (4 million sq. km). Dozens of native Australian herbivores were brought to the brink of extinction by competition with rabbits, and the sheep farming industry was nearly destroyed because rabbits ate all the grass. The battle to control rabbit numbers is ongoing. Predation by introduced foxes and cats helps keep numbers in check, but also threatens native wildlife species. Fences keep rabbits out for a time but are expensive and need constant maintenance. The animals are shot for fur and meat; but the products are of low quality, and hunters rarely make much profit from rabbits alone.

In the 1950s farmers took the drastic step of introducing a nasty South American virus to the Australian rabbit population. For a while the *Myxoma* virus wrought havoc, and over 99 percent of all rabbits died. Since then, however, there has been a gradual increase in resistance, and nowadays myxomatosis epidemics rarely kill more than 30 percent of an infected population. In 1995 a new virus was unleashed on the Australian rabbits, this time from China. The resultant rabbit hemorrhagic disease has successfully reduced the population to manageable levels, but total eradication of the rabbit from Australia is still a long way off. Both diseases cause immense suffering among the rabbits, leading to ethical questions about their use as control methods. A sudden loss of rabbits also forces predators to seek other prey, with consequent threats to native fauna.

Rabbits have had such a bad press that it is easy to overlook the positive part they play in ecological systems. A sudden reduction in grazing pressure can lead to the deterioration of valuable habitats. The chalk downlands of southern England, for example, were created by the combined grazing pressure of sheep and rabbits. As sheep farming declined in Britain, most downlands became wholly dependent on rabbits to maintain their open landscapes and rich assortment of turf vegetation and insects. When myxomatosis decimated the rabbit population in the 1950s, grazing almost ceased, and large areas became overgrown with rank vegetation and scrub. Wildflowers, butterflies, and other insects adapted to living in short grazed turf were severely affected, and many species became locally extinct.

Young chocolate Dutch rabbits—a domestic breed of the European rabbit. Rabbits were initially bred for their meat and fur, but today are popular children's pets.

Domestic Rabbits

Humans have used wild rabbits as a source of food and fur for many thousands of years. However, domestication is a relatively recent development, which probably began in France about 1,000 years ago. Rabbits were kept in monasteries and bred selectively for meat and fur. Domestic breeds now include the largest rabbits. Some meat animals may tip the scales at over 15.5 pounds (7 kg), almost three times the usual maximum weight of wild individuals. More recently rabbits have become popular as pets. Today there are over 100 domestic varieties of the European rabbit, including dwarfs and giants, rabbits with lop-ears, fancy patterns, or long, silky fur. One of the most popular varieties is the white rabbit. The animal is kept as a pet by children the world over, and it often makes appearances from a magician's top hat!

Giant Anteater

Myrmecophaga tridactyla

Common name Giant anteater

Scientific name *Myrmecophaga tridactyla*

Family Myrmecophagidae

Order Xenarthra

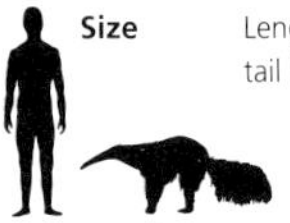

Size Length head/body: 39–51 in (100–130 cm); tail length: 25.5–35.5 in (65–90 cm)

Weight Male 53–86 lb (24–39 kg); female 48–77 lb (22–35 kg)

Key features Narrow, powerful body; small head with long, tapering snout; coat gray with black stripe from shoulders to chest and neck; hair coarse and stiff; long, bushy tail

Habits Solitary; generally diurnal; breaks into ant and termite nests

Breeding One young born in spring after gestation period of 190 days. Weaned at 6 months; sexually mature at 2 years. May live up to 26 years in captivity, unknown in the wild

Voice Generally silent

Diet Ants and termites; occasional beetle larvae and fruit

Habitat Grassland, swamp, and lowland tropical forest

Distribution Central America from southern Belize through South America to Northern Argentina

Status Population: unknown, but probably thousands; IUCN Vulnerable; CITES II

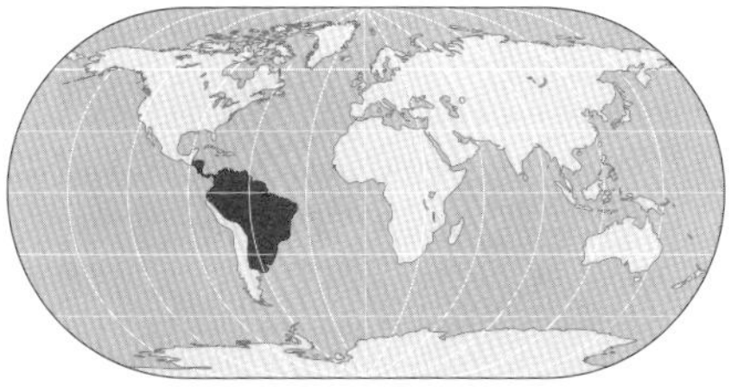

The giant anteater is the largest of the four species of anteaters and the only fully terrestrial one. Its strange body is perfectly adapted to its needs as a specialized ant- and termite-feeder.

The giant anteater has an instantly recognizable profile, with its small head tapering to a long snout, a chunky body, and long, bushy tail. Most of its physical features relate to a highly specialized mode of feeding—breaking into ant and termite nests and capturing the insects on a long, sticky tongue.

Elongated Profile

The giant anteater's braincase is small and rounded, so the tapering, tubular 12-inch (30-cm) long snout dominates the head. The long snout contains an even longer tongue. The ears and eyes are small, so the elongated profile is not interrupted. The body is narrow but muscular, with the forelimbs being particularly strong. Each ends in large, sharp claws on the second and third fingers (unlike the smaller tree-living anteaters known as tamanduas, which have three long claws). The first and fifth fingers are tiny, so it looks as though the giant anteater has only three digits, hence the scientific name *tri-*, meaning "three," and *dactyla,* meaning "fingers." The fingers are constructed so that the heavy claws can be folded against the palms when not in use.

Giant anteaters have a lumbering walk in which they keep their nose close to the ground. The fingers of the forefeet are flexed and turned inward, so the knuckles and sides of the fist touch the ground. Such an arrangement keeps the claws from being blunted. The hind feet tread in a more usual plantigrade (flat-footed) fashion. Most of the coat is a grizzled gray, with a black stripe bordered with white that runs from the shoulders to the chest and neck. The coat is coarse, with a bristly crest

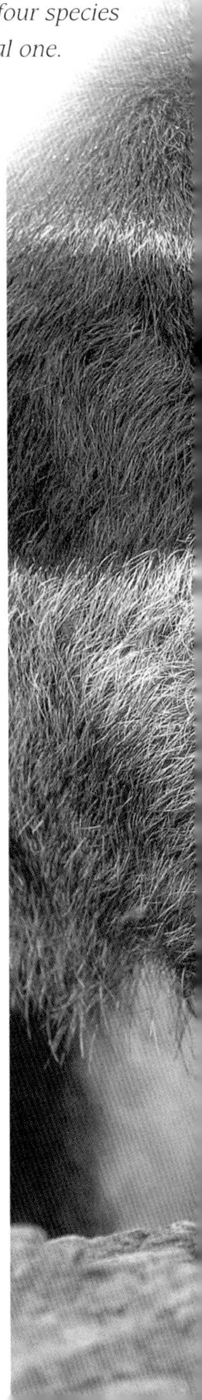

← *A giant anteater inserts its long snout into a hollow log to feed on the insects inside.*

along the back, while the body hairs are curiously flat. The tail is over half the length of the body and extremely bushy.

While all the anteaters specialize in eating ants and termites, giant anteaters tend to prefer the larger-bodied, less ferocious species such as carpenter ants. The smaller anteaters focus on smaller prey. Even though some of the termite nests are prominent, forming large mounds that stand out against the horizon, a giant anteater's eyesight is poor, so it finds food by smell. When an anteater encounters a nest, it quickly digs a hole in the side, using its huge, curved claws. As soon as the hole is large enough, it pushes in its thin snout and flicks its long, sticky tongue in and out, catching the worker ants as they run around frantically. The anteater will also eat larvae and cocoons.

Flypaper Tongue

The giant anteater's tongue is an incredibly efficient ant collector. It is covered in sticky saliva and backward-pointing spines. The spines help keep the insects firmly in place as the tongue is taken back into the mouth, rather than being dislodged and lost against the walls of the nest. The anteater can flick its tongue in and out up to 150 times a minute. With a tongue 24 inches (60 cm) long, the animal's ant-trapping capacity is equivalent to laying down 300 feet (90 m) of sticky flypaper every minute.

The giant anteater's whole eating apparatus has been honed to enable it to pull in lots of tiny insects as quickly as possible. Most mammals open their mouth by moving the jaw up and down, allowing them to chew food. Anteaters do not need to open their mouth wide, and in fact they can only open it to a small O-shape, the

Anteater Self-Defense—Claws and Forelimbs

Giant anteaters tend to avoid trouble and usually run away from potential danger at an ungainly gallop. If cornered, however, an anteater is more than a match for most predators. Rearing up on its hind legs and using the bushy tail as a prop, it slashes at attackers with its sharp claws. The claws can be up to 4 inches (10 cm) long. If the attacker comes any closer, a brutal bear hug from the anteater's strong forelimbs can be fatal. The animal's forelegs are so powerful because of the strength it builds up by demolishing concrete-hard termite nests.

width of a pencil. Nor do they need to chew, since ants are already small—so they do not have any teeth. Instead, giant anteaters have an unusual anatomical arrangement that enables them to almost hoover up ants. The jawbones are not joined at the tip, and the chewing muscles make the two halves of the jaw roll inward and outward, instead of up and down. The rolling motion helps the tongue flick in and out, and pushes any trapped insects toward the back of the mouth, where they can be swallowed in an almost continuous motion.

Giant anteaters also have an unusual tongue attachment. The tongue is even longer than the head, so it is attached in the throat—part way down the neck—to a structure called the hyoid. In most animals hyoid bones are small or fused together. However, in the giant anteater they are large and well articulated, making a supple structure that enables the tongue to move rapidly. Speed is important because ants and termites are so small and scurry around very fast. The anteater has to eat lots of ants to obtain enough nutrition. It also does not have long at each nest before the soldier ants are mustered to chase away the intruder. Although the tough skin and thick hairs provide some protection against the ants, the soldiers' fierce bites and acidic stings usually force the anteater to retreat. In the few minutes it spends at each nest an anteater will probably only eat about 150 insects. At such a slow rate it needs to visit about 200 nests per day to obtain enough nutrition.

A tough, muscular stomach grinds up the ants. Unlike in other animals, the giant anteater's stomach does not secrete hydrochloric acid, but instead relies on the ants' own formic acid to create the right chemical conditions needed for digestion.

Giant anteaters are usually active during the day; but in areas where they are disturbed by humans, they can become nocturnal. They are still

↑ ***In giant anteaters the largest claws are on digits two and three . If threatened by a jaguar or puma, anteaters will rear up on their hind legs and lash out with their claws.***

able to find food at night, relying on their sense of smell rather than eyesight. But a nocturnal lifestyle may make them more vulnerable to their only natural predators, pumas and jaguars. Giant anteaters rest for up to 15 hours a day, using shallow scrapes, hollow logs, or modified burrows of other animals rather than digging their own. In these relatively exposed sleeping spots they disguise themselves by curling up and covering their body with the huge brushlike tail. Giant anteaters are mainly solitary, except for mothers and their offspring. However, although they tend to avoid each other, males may fight. In such encounters the animals will probably just circle each other and then give chase. But if serious fighting ensues, their sharp claws can cause severe injuries.

Termites and Territory

Giant anteaters keep out of each other's way by having well-defined home ranges that are marked with pungent-smelling secretions from the anal gland. Females are less territorial than males, with home ranges that can overlap by as much as 30 percent. Those of males hardly overlap at all. The size of the home range occupied by each animal depends on the density of ant and termite nests. Each anteater needs to be able to snack on many tens or even hundreds of nests every day, but without doing lasting damage to them. In areas where there are several nests, home ranges may be as small as 0.2 square miles (0.5 sq. km). In poorer-quality habitats that support fewer ants and termites, an anteater may need 50 times as much space.

Giant anteaters mate in the fall (March to May in the Southern Hemisphere) and give birth in spring, usually to a single baby. Females give birth standing on their hind legs, using their tail as a prop. The newborns are well developed and climb on their mother's back soon after birth. Their eyes open after six days, and by about a month they are able to gallop around. However, they generally walk slowly or ride on their mother. The young are miniature versions of the adults, identical in color and markings.

Young giant anteaters are suckled for up to six months, but stay with their mother for up to two years. By that time they have reached sexual maturity. After leaving their mother, they establish a home range of their own and begin the largely solitary, food-focused life of adult giant anteaters.

A baby giant anteater rides piggyback on its mother. The stripes of the mother and young usually line up, breaking up the baby's outline and making it difficult for predators to spot.

Common name Nine-banded armadillo (long-nosed armadillo)

Scientific name *Dasypus novemcinctus*

Family Dasypodidae

Order Xenarthra

Size Length head/body: 14.5–17 in (37–43 cm); tail length: 9.5–14.5 in (24–37 cm)

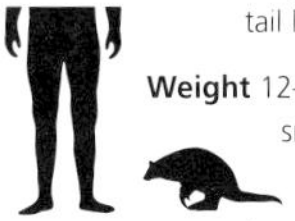

Weight 12–17 lb (5.5–7.5 kg). Female generally smaller than male

Key features Hard, shiny skin with scaly legs and tail; about 8–11 flexible bands around middle of body; long ears and snout

Habits Generally nocturnal; shuffles around seeking food; lives in shallow burrows

Breeding Four young born in spring after gestation period of 120 days (plus variable period of delayed implantation). Weaned at 4–5 months; sexually mature at about 1 year. May live at least 22 years in captivity, probably fewer in the wild

Voice Constant, quiet grunting and sniffing when out foraging; otherwise silent

Diet Mostly insects, especially termites; occasional worms, snails, birds' eggs, and frogs

Habitat Short grass, forest floor, and farmland

Distribution Southern U.S. south to Uruguay and northern Argentina and west to Peru; also Grenada and Trinidad and Tobago in the West Indies

Status Population: abundant

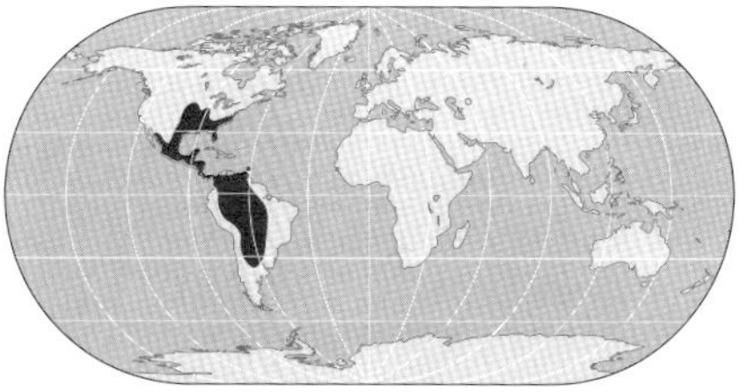

Nine-Banded Armadillo

Dasypus novemcinctus

The armored armadillo is an unmistakable creature, and the nine-banded species has been a successful colonizer of the United States.

INSTEAD OF HAVING A SOFT, FURRY skin like most other mammals, the armadillo is encased in a bony carapace that is covered with shiny plates. Around the animal's middle is a series of flexible bands that allow the creature to roll up when threatened. Usually there are about eight such bands, but armadillos living in Central America have nine or more. The tail and legs are scaly, and there are sparse yellowish hairs here and on the animal's belly. The armadillo has large, sensitive ears and a long snout. The powerful front feet each have four toes, but the hind feet have five. Despite its heavily armored body, the armadillo is a strong swimmer and can remain underwater for long periods. It can also run surprisingly fast, and the smooth and shiny body is difficult for predators to grasp.

Traveling North

The main home of armadillos is in South America. The nine-banded species is widespread there, being found as far south as Uruguay and northern Argentina. In the last 200 years it has also staged a remarkably successful invasion of North America. From the late 1800s onward the nine-banded armadillo rapidly expanded its range in northern Mexico and had reached as far north as the Rio Grande region of southern Texas by 1890. Since then it has spread steadily deeper into the United States, appearing in Tennessee by the 1970s. It is now found as far north as Nebraska and southern Missouri. Meanwhile, in the 1920s armadillos were released or escaped from captivity in Florida in several places. The animal has now become well established there and has spread north and west to colonize the southern states of the

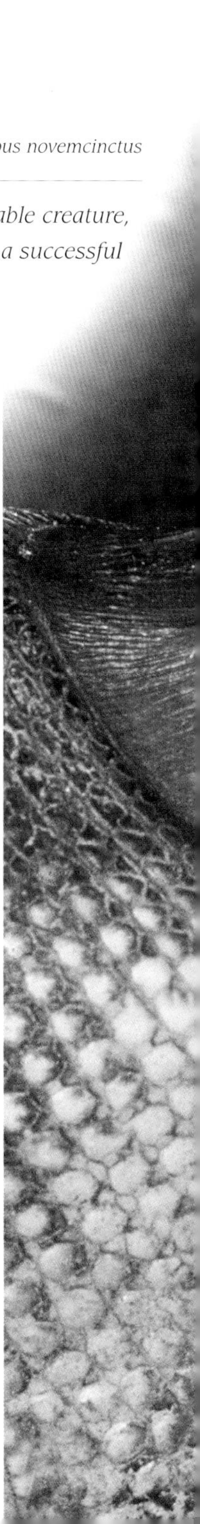

← The armadillo is an unusual-looking creature. It has large, rounded ears, a long snout, and is covered in hard, shiny armor plating.

United States, reaching Georgia and South Carolina by the 1950s. It is now sufficiently numerous in Florida to have become one of the more frequent victims of road traffic accidents.

It is not clear what has brought about the rapid extension of the armadillo's geographical range, but climatic changes might have something to do with it. More significantly perhaps, the persecution and removal of large predators such as cougars leaves the way open for the armadillo to go where it pleases, with the smaller carnivores posing little danger. Another helpful factor might be the steady expansion of ranching. Overgrazing by cattle leaves the grass short and the soil nicely warmed by the sun. Such conditions are ideal for many ground invertebrates, and the short grass enables armadillos to find them easily. Further spread to the north is now probably limited by the cold, especially in winter. In many parts of the western states the summers are also too hot and dry.

Well Protected

In the warmer parts of its range the nine-banded armadillo prefers to live in shady cover. Elsewhere, it thrives in various habitats from sea level to altitudes of more than 10,000 feet (3,000 m). The armadillo is mainly active in the late evening and at night, although it may sometimes come out during daylight on cloudy days. It shuffles around slowly, nose to the ground as it sniffs for prey. When rooting, the animal grunts almost constantly, ignoring the potential danger of drawing attention to itself. But it is well protected by its thick, bony skin. The animal can also roll up to hide its softer underbelly. Being relatively safe from predators means the armadillo can potter around confidently, even out in the open.

Periodically the armadillo will rear up on its hind legs, supported by the tail, and sniff the air. The animal has a keen sense of smell and pokes its nose into clumps of dry vegetation and leaf litter, seeking out food. It will often pause to dig something up, using the strong claws on its forefeet, and it may also rip apart rotting logs. Insects make up more than three-quarters of the diet, with termites a frequent item on the menu. Even the nests of fire ants may be attacked to get at the ant larvae within. The armadillo's thick, bony skin protects it from painful insect bites. The animal will also eat small worms, mollusks, and occasionally the eggs of ground-nesting birds.

Unimpressive Fighters

The armadillo's home range extends over about 3 to 4 acres (1.5 ha) in good habitat, but in poorer areas it may cover more than 30 acres (12 ha). The animals are tolerant of each other, and their home ranges often overlap. However, at high population densities the animals may become less accommodating, and the males will fight, scratching each other with their front feet. Armadillos are unlikely to cause serious harm and do not bite because their teeth are small and form only simple pegs. The jaws are weak too, since they are meant only for picking up small insects.

Armadillos excavate a burrow by digging with the forefeet and kicking loose dirt out of the tunnel with the hind feet. The burrow is simple and usually has only one or two entrances. The tunnels extend about 10 feet (3 m), but may be up to 25 feet (7.5 m) long. They are usually shallow, lying just below the surface, but may sometimes go down 12 feet (3.5 m) into the soil. The armadillo builds a large nest in part of its burrow. Nesting material, in the form of leaves, grass, and twigs, is gathered nearby and carried into the burrow in bundles held beneath the body. Grasping the bundle close to its belly, the armadillo shuffles backward into its burrow, often leaving a little trail of debris behind. Each armadillo has several burrows within its home range, and the same one may be used for up to four weeks before the animal moves on.

Armadillos and Leprosy

In the 1960s it was discovered that nine-banded armadillos—unlike most other mammals—could be infected with the leprosy bacillus. For the first time the disfiguring disease could be studied in the laboratory. Leprosy was later found in wild armadillo populations in Texas and Louisiana, and (less often) in Florida. There is probably little risk of humans catching the disease from these wild animals, since leprosy is an uncommon disease, and people living outside the tropics tend to be less susceptible to leprosy.

A nine-banded armadillo excavates the earth by digging with its powerful clawed forefeet. Its body is well protected by bony armored skin.

Occasionally, armadillos can be found nesting above the ground in large piles of dry vegetation.

Armadillos normally live alone, but meet to breed once a year in the summer months. (In captivity they may breed throughout the year.) They breed for the first time at about one year. Courtship is often a drawn-out affair, with the males eagerly following females and seeking an opportunity to mate. In North America the mating takes place in July and August, but implantation of the fertilized egg is delayed until November. Farther south mating may occur earlier in the summer, but implantation is then delayed for longer. Elsewhere, development of the embryos may start immediately after mating. Actual fetal development takes about 120 days. In Texas the young are born in March or April, but as early as February in Mexico. Litter sizes are small, normally four identical same-sex quadruplets derived from a single egg. Young armadillos are born fully formed with their eyes open. They weigh 1 to 2 ounces (28 to 56 g) and can walk within a few hours. They will accompany their mother on foraging expeditions within a few weeks and become fully independent at an age of four or five months.

Popular Food Source

Armadillos can become quite numerous in places and may reach densities of 130 per square mile (50 per sq. km) on the coastal prairies of Texas. In parts of South America they are a popular source of food, and catching them remains a threat to populations in many areas. The animals are also threatened by deforestation, agricultural expansion, and other forms of habitat loss. In the United States armadillos sometimes make themselves unpopular by digging in gardens and farmland. They are also accused of causing erosion and undermining buildings by their burrowing activities. However, on the whole armadillos are beneficial animals that destroy many harmful insects and are generally regarded with amusement and tolerance. Their bony skin is made into baskets, which are sold as souvenirs, and the animals are also used in various forms of medical research.

A mother and infant nine-banded armadillo in a burrow. The armadillo builds a nest from leaves, twigs, and grass in part of its burrow.

Vampire Bat

Desmodus rotundus

One of the world's most specialized and notorious mammals, the vampire bat is actually a highly sociable species and less of a threat to humans than is commonly supposed.

Common name Vampire bat

Scientific name *Desmodus rotundus*

Family Phyllostomidae

Order Chiroptera

Size Length head/body: 3–3.5 in (7–9 cm); forearm length: 2–2.5 in (5–6.3 cm); wingspan: about 20 in (50 cm)

Weight 0.5–1.8 oz (15–50 g)

Key features Dark-gray bat, paler on underside; snout flattened; vertical groove in lower lip

Habits Strictly nocturnal; usually lives in colonies of 20–100; roosts in caves, hollow trees, and old mines

Breeding Single young born once a year after gestation period of about 7 months. Weaned at 10 months; sexually mature at 1 year. May live at least 19.5 years in captivity, 15 in the wild

Voice Ultrasonic squeaks (too high-pitched for humans to hear); also aggressive squeaks if other vampires attempt to feed close by

Diet Feeds exclusively on blood, normally taken from mammals, including humans

Habitat Dry and wet areas of tropical and subtropical Central and South America

Distribution From Argentina and central Chile to northern Mexico; also Trinidad

Status Population unknown, but many thousands. Abundant, but probably declining

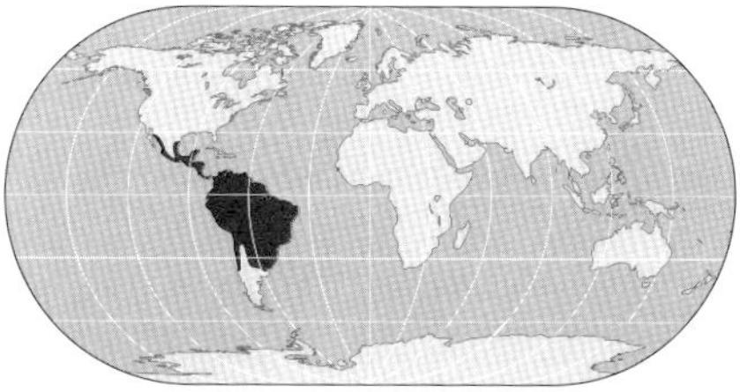

REAL-LIFE VAMPIRE BATS HAVE somehow become confused with the spine-chilling mythical fiends featured in European folklore. As a result, the species is widely known, but not because of its fascinating ecology. The vampire bat is in fact an extremely specialized animal, found only in Central and South America. Here it inhabits a wide variety of country, but especially favors forests and open grazing land.

Blood Specialist

Like its mythical counterpart, the vampire bat does indeed feed on blood and actually eats nothing else. Yet it is a mystery how such a specialized form of feeding ever evolved. Why does blood feeding occur in three species of tropical American vampires, but in none of the hundreds of other bat species that live in the rest of the world? The vampire's normal food is the blood of cattle, but horses, donkeys, and wild mammals such as peccaries and tapirs may be attacked. In coastal areas, where these animals are often scarce, vampires may even turn to sea lions for food.

Because of their specialized diet, vampires would probably be quite rare. However, the import of farm animals to the Americas, especially large cattle and horses, has provided them with more feeding opportunities than they would get from native mammals alone. Occasionally humans are bitten, but that is a rare event. In some areas vampires prey on domestic chickens and turkeys, although feeding on birds is the principal speciality of the other two species of vampire, the white-winged vampire (from Mexico to Argentina) and the hairy-legged vampire (from southern Texas and Mexico to Brazil and Bolivia).

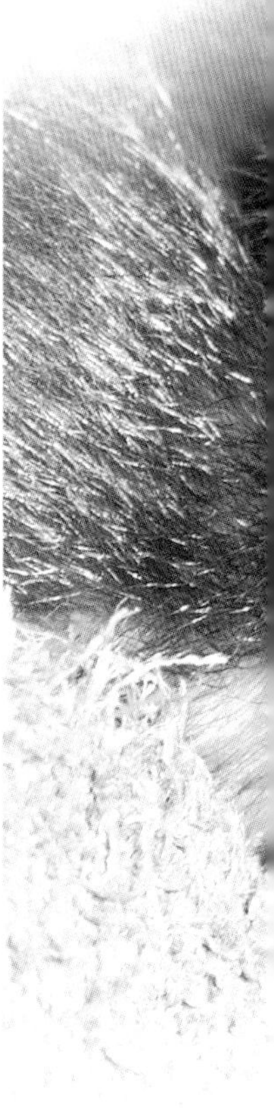

↑ *A common vampire bat. The truncated muzzle allows the bat to press its mouth close to the flesh of the animal on which it is feeding.*

Nighttime Feasts

Soon after dark a vampire bat will leave its daytime roost and fly straight and silently, close to the ground, using smell and sound to locate a suitable victim. Cattle are most commonly attacked because they are large, abundant, and tend to lie asleep out in the open. The vampire selects a suitable victim and lands nearby. It does not alight on the sleeping animal, since its weight would probably wake it up, and twitching ears or a flicking tail would prevent the vampire from going about its business. The vampire scurries toward its victim like a giant spider, with the body raised up high on its wrists and hind legs. It explores the surface of the animal, using its heat-sensitive muzzle to locate warm areas where the skin is thin and blood vessels come close to the surface. That is why cattle and horses tend to be bitten around the anus and ears, often on the neck, too, while chickens and turkeys are usually bitten around the wattles.

Having found a suitable bite site, the vampire bat licks the skin with its tongue, cuts away any obstructing hair or feathers with its teeth, and then uses its extremely sharp incisor teeth to scoop out a small piece of skin. The teeth are so sharp that this operation is almost painless; but if the victim notices, the bat may have to abandon its feeding attempt. Successful feeding takes practice, and inexperienced young vampires may frequently fail to feed. The bite is not deep, barely more than one-eighth of an inch (2 to 5 mm). The vampire presses the flat end of its snout close to the wound, but it does not actually suck blood. Instead, as the blood flows, the bat laps it up. The tongue forms a tube and is used almost like a drinking straw, slowly pumping up and down along a prominent groove in the lower lip. Blood is drawn up to

Teeth

Owing to its unique diet, the vampire bat has highly specialized dentition. There are only 20 teeth, fewer than in any other bat. Since blood does not require chewing, the teeth are small and have a greatly reduced grinding surface. The incisors and canines are big, triangular, and exceedingly sharp. They are used for cutting out the sliver of skin to initiate the bleeding process.

Ⓣ *In Trinidad a vampire bat takes blood from a resting donkey. Vampire bats feed for up to half an hour. Each bat can drink over half its body weight of blood in a single bout of feeding.*

the mouth, and at the same time, the bat dribbles saliva into the wound. The saliva contains a special anticoagulant ingredient that slows the clotting of the blood, ensuring a continued flow for longer than the bat needs to feed. Bleeding will sometimes continue for up to eight hours, so the victim loses more blood than is actually consumed by the bat. Blood consists mainly of water, which is heavy, and could impede flying after a good meal. The bat will therefore frequently urinate before it has finished feeding to rid its body of excess water. A vampire bat is known to return to the same wound on consecutive nights.

Messy Roosts

Usually vampires roost in caves, but they also use hollow trees, abandoned buildings, and old mines. A vampire roost can be easily recognized. Instead of having piles of the neat droppings that other bats produce, vampire roosts accumulate slimy masses of digested blood on the walls and floor, looking like tar but smelling strongly of ammonia.

Vampires pass the day in these dark and cool places, sleeping and grooming themselves. They are highly sociable and caring toward others of their species and will often spend long periods grooming each other's fur, just as monkeys and apes do. They will also regurgitate blood from a meal and share it with neighboring bats. Vampires are agile animals and will run around rapidly on vertical or horizontal surfaces. They are shy creatures and scurry away or retreat into protective crevices if they are disturbed in the roost. Normally the bats do not leave the roost until it is completely dark outside, and they are reluctant to emerge on nights when the moon is shining brightly. They are active until about midnight, after which those that have fed successfully may return to the roost, often long before dawn. The bats usually forage within 5 miles (8 km) of their daytime roost, but sometimes travel up to 12 miles (20 km) to feed. One colony of 100 to 150 vampires ranged over nearly 5 square miles (13 sq. km), using 1,200 head of cattle as prey.

Large vampire colonies seem to consist of sets of females with their offspring, each set belonging to a single adult male. Several other males are often close by, awaiting mating opportunities. The principal male defends his position and access to females aggressively and is thought to father about half the offspring in his group of females. He maintains his position as top bat for about two years before being displaced by a younger male. A female vampire, like other bats, normally has only a single youngster each year. It is born after a gestation lasting about seven months. The new-born young is already well developed, with its eyes open. It weighs about one-fifth of an ounce (6 g), nearly a quarter of the mother's own

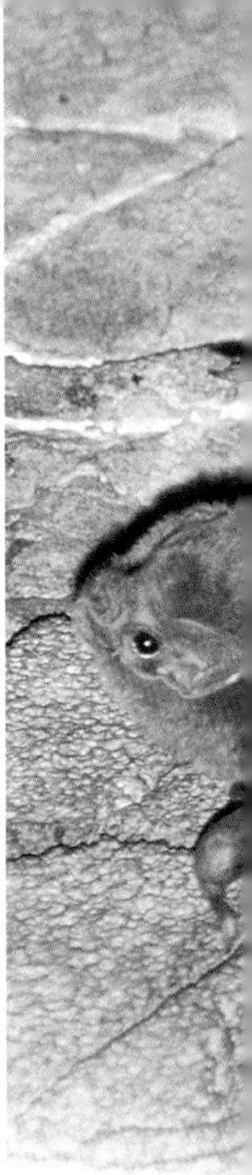

Food Sharing

Vampires will chase others away from a good feeding place, but are amazingly generous toward their friends and relatives who may have been unsuccessful in their feeding excursions. Young vampires in particular fail to get a full blood meal in about one-third of their attempts, and even the adults are not always successful in getting sufficient food—their victims may sometimes be too vigilant to permit the bats to feed freely. Disrupted feeding attempts can be serious because vampires will starve if they do not feed properly for more than three days in a row. Bats that have failed to feed successfully will return to their roost, where they will be given blood by one of their better-fed neighbors. Usually food sharing involves closely related bats and those that normally roost close together. Sharing food with each other prevents other members of the colony from starving and helps ensure a higher overall survival rate. Such unselfish behavior is extremely rare among animals and totally unexpected in a species with such a gruesome reputation.

weight. It is fed initially on milk, but is also given regurgitated blood from about two months. The young vampire grows slowly and is looked after by its mother for longer than any other bat of comparable size. It can feed itself on blood at four months old, but will not be completely weaned before about 10 months of age. Young males often disperse when they reach sexual maturity, probably driven away from the colony dominated by their father.

Rabies Risk

Vampire bats can be a serious problem, but not necessarily as a direct consequence of the blood they remove. The wounds they create often become septic, causing pain and even death to many animals. They also attract flies to lay their eggs, which then develop into larvae in the skin. Vampire bites result in extensive blood loss due to the anticoagulants produced by the bats and subsequent failure of the wound to heal. But the main problem posed by the vampire is transmission of the rabies virus. The bats pass the disease to any mammal they bite. Tens of thousands of cattle die from bat-borne rabies each year, representing a loss of nearly $50 million annually. Occasionally humans become infected and die from this particularly horrific disease. The bats die too, and vampire bat populations suffer severe losses as a result.

Attempts to eradicate rabies have often focused on removing the bats by dynamiting roosts or netting the animals as they come to feed. A more subtle form of attack is to smear a mixture of syrup and strychnine poison around vampire bites on a cow, so that a bat returning to a previously successful feeding site will get the sticky poison on its fur. When it returns to the roost, it will be groomed by other bats who will then be poisoned. In some small recompense for the problems it causes, the vampire's saliva may turn out to be valuable. A drug company has taken out a patent for producing the protein that prevents blood from clotting. Blood clots are the main cause of heart attacks and strokes in humans, so the vampire's anticoagulant protein (christened "Draculin") could help rescue the bat's dire public image.

↑ Sometimes vampires roost alone or in small groups, but normally they live in colonies of 20 to 100 bats. Occasional roosts may contain more than 2,000 vampires, and at least 20 other bat species are known to live with vampires at times.

Red Kangaroo

Macropus rufus

Common name Red kangaroo

Scientific name *Macropus rufus*

Family Macropodidae

Order Diprotodontia

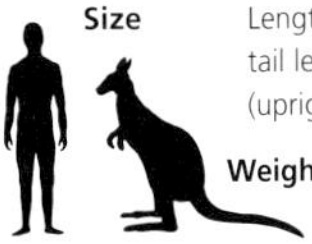

Size Length head/body: 29.5–63 in (75–160 cm); tail length: 25–47 in (64–120 cm); height: (upright) up to 6 ft (1.8 m)

Weight 37.5–198 lb (17–90 kg). Male may weigh up to twice as much as female

Key features Large kangaroo with rusty-red to blue-gray fur, paler on belly; female has 4 teats in a well-developed, forward-facing pouch

Habits Lives in loose groups; most active between dusk and dawn

Breeding Single young born at any time of year after gestation period of 33 days (plus up to 6 months delayed implantation). Incubated in pouch for 235 days. Weaned at 12 months; females sexually mature at 15–20 months, males at 20–24 months. May live more than 30 years in captivity, 27 in the wild

Voice Gruff coughing sounds

Diet Mainly grass; also leaves of other plants, including shrubs and trees

Habitat Scrub and open grassland, including arid and semiarid areas

Distribution Throughout central Australia; absent from the far north, eastern, and southeastern coasts, southwestern Australia, and Tasmania

Status Population: abundant. Remains common and widespread despite hunting and other control measures

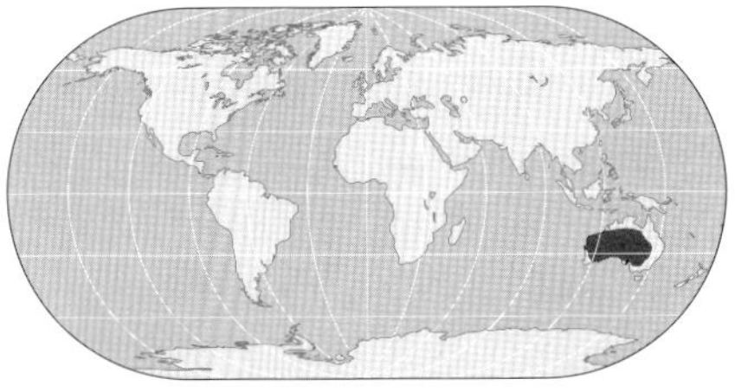

The red kangaroo is the tallest marsupial and the animal that comes to most people's minds when they think of Australian wildlife.

THE RED KANGAROO IS THE archetypal Australian mammal, sharing pride of place with the emu on the country's coat of arms, and appearing in countless other emblems and advertising logos. The red kangaroo is the only large native herbivore to have conquered the heart of the world's driest continent and as such is of great ecological importance. Today it shares much of its range with sheep, cattle, goats, and even camels—animals whose impact has been greater because of the sudden nature of their spread, following introduction by humans. But the red kangaroo is a true desert specialist, and its lifestyle and physiology are better adapted to deal with the unforgiving, unpredictable desert climate than those of any imported mammal.

Largest Marsupial

It is often said that the red kangaroo is the largest living marsupial, and in terms of height the statistic is probably true. But other large species, such as the wallaroo, can weigh more on average because of their stockier build. It is a close call. Male red kangaroos can stand over 6 feet (1.8 m) tall and weigh up to twice as much as the females. The disparity comes about because males compete physically for the right to mate and need to be large in order to succeed. Small males do not usually bother to challenge larger ones, so the genes for big, strapping males get passed on more often. Females do not need to be so big. For a start, they have to devote a good deal of their energy to rearing healthy young. In a hot climate the bigger you are, the harder it is to keep cool, so there is no advantage in large size unless you need to use it.

Apart from its size the red kangaroo differs little from its close relatives in appearance. The red fur for which it is named generally occurs in males, while the females are a soft bluish-gray, hence their nickname "blue fliers." However, red females and gray males are quite common in some places, so color alone is not a reliable way of telling the sexes apart.

Part Nomad

Red kangaroos are partially nomadic. While they will spend long periods in one area, if life should become difficult (as a result of environmental factors, such as drought or fire), or social causes (such as lack of mates or harassment from more dominant animals), they will undertake quite long journeys in search of better conditions. Individual animals have been tracked over 180 miles (290 km) before settling in a new area. Ideal red kangaroo habitat is an open grassy plain close to areas of scrub or open woodland, with a water hole nearby. Other requirements include shade from the midday sun and shelter from drying winds, but red kangaroos can make do with much less. Given a choice of fodder, they will eat mostly grass, supplemented with green leaves of other plants. They select the youngest leaves possible, since they are easier to digest. Every mouthful is chewed thoroughly so that the precious contents of plant cells are released ready for digestion. Like cattle and other ruminants, kangaroos have a large stomach containing bacteria that aid digestion.

The spread of sheep and cattle farming into central Australia has done much to improve the quality of grazing habitat. Boreholes bring drinking water to the surface for farm animals, and the grazing livestock keep down the rank vegetation, encouraging the growth of fresh new shoots. However, ranchers

A juvenile red kangaroo. Red kangaroos are desert-living specialists that can cope with the extreme dry conditions far better than most introduced mammals.

have been none too keen for kangaroos to share the newly created pastures, fearing that competition for food will disadvantage their stock. Such concerns have prompted much research into the precise feeding habits of several species of kangaroo. It appears that in favorable seasons there is no cause for concern. Livestock and kangaroos can safely graze side by side because—although both eat grass—about half the diet of each consists of very different kinds of greenery. None of the available food contains much water, and sheep and cattle have to drink regularly in order to survive. Kangaroos, on the other hand, are so well adapted to a diet of dry food that they actually lose weight if fed exclusively on lush vegetation. The water in the leaves takes up so much space that the kangaroo's relatively small stomach fills up before they have taken in enough real food.

Survival Specialists

The potential for problems between kangaroos and livestock begins during prolonged drought. At such times the leafy herbs are the first plants to disappear, and both species turn their attention to the dwindling supply of withered grass. Ranchers try to fence kangaroos out of their pastures and shoot those that do get in. In severe droughts the survival of sheep and cattle depends on whether they receive supplements of food and water from the farmer. Meanwhile, the kangaroos usually survive, making do with the tough leaves of saltbush and other desert shrubs, whose high salt content makes them toxic to other animals.

Competition with livestock is not the only way in which the interests of red kangaroos have conflicted with those of people. Many kangaroos are shot in an effort to prevent the damage they can do to rabbit fences. Rabbits are a far more serious threat to livestock than kangaroos, and special rabbit-proof fences are used to keep them out. But where kangaroos push down fences, they too are viewed as vermin and treated accordingly. Kangaroos are also hunted for their skins. Kangaroo hide makes fine leather, prized for making hats and soft sports shoes. Their meat, originally used in pet foods, is increasingly in demand as a tasty, low-fat alternative to beef.

Red kangaroos live in organized groups called mobs, usually consisting of one dominant adult male, with several females and young. Over a period of several weeks the members of

Red kangaroos take time out for a drink. Since they are superbly adapted to living in dry conditions, they actually lose weight if fed exclusively on lush vegetation. In times of severe drought they get by through eating saltbush and other desert shrubs that are toxic to most mammals.

Boxing Kangaroos

Disputes between male kangaroos are usually solved by a display of size and strength, with the two contestants standing up on their straightened back legs. If one male is obviously shorter, he will usually concede and back off, but two closely matched males may escalate the encounter to a bout of boxing or wrestling. The opponents stand face-to-face, locking arms and trying to unbalance each other. In a full-blown fight they will leap into the air, swing their hind legs forward, and aim kicks at each other's chest and abdomen.

Red kangaroos will often fight over access to females. Before a fight the two rival males may engage in a "stiff-legged walk." (1). They may also scratch and groom while standing upright on extended rear legs (2, 3). The animals then lock forearms (4), and try to push each other backward onto the ground (5).

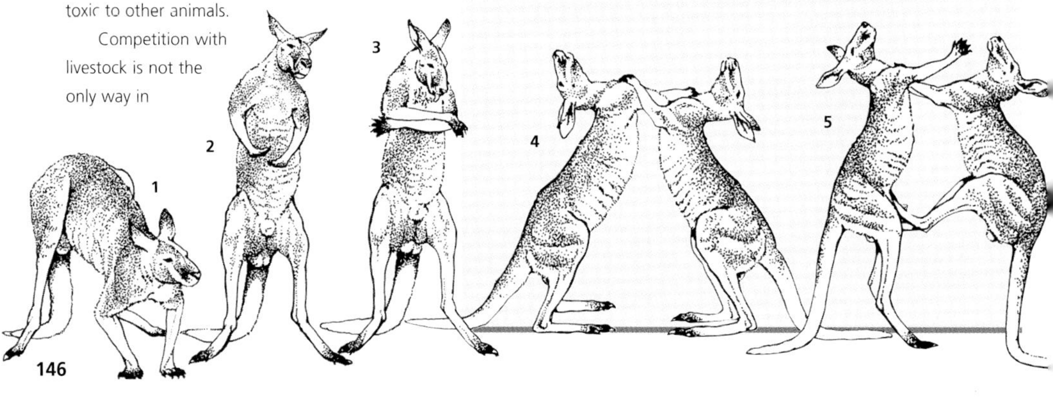

a mob may wander over an area between 600 and 1,200 acres (243 and 486 ha), but it is difficult to define a normal home range. Red kangaroos are certainly not territorial. The dominant male will do his best to ensure that he has exclusive access to the females in his group for mating purposes. The females, on the other hand, are pretty much free to come and go as they please. The male's control of the group is only ever temporary. The male may also defend good feeding areas from members of other mobs, but generally his aggression is reserved for rival males.

Continuous Reproductive Cycle

Red kangaroos are opportunistic breeders, which means they can mate and give birth at any time of year, provided the conditions are favorable for raising a youngster. Females have a 35-day reproductive (estrous) cycle during which they will be receptive for less than a day. The cycle is not interrupted by pregnancy. It takes just 33 days for the baby kangaroo to develop inside its mother, so she is ready to mate again just a day or two after having given birth. Only when she is pregnant for the second time does the estrous cycle stop temporarily. The change is triggered not by the embryo in her womb but by the newborn joey suckling on her teat. Having made its way to the pouch, the tiny morsel of a baby—the size of a jellybean and weighing less than a dime—attaches to one of four teats and stays there, growing steadily for 70 days. Meanwhile, the second embryo enters a period of suspended animation known as embryonic diapause. At this point it is no more than a ball of about 90 cells. It resumes its development precisely 33 days before the first baby (now 205 days old) is ready to leave the pouch permanently. Hence the second baby is born immediately after the pouch is vacant, and the female is ready to mate and conceive all over again.

The rather elaborate system means that a female red kangaroo can raise a baby every 240 days,

Ⓓ Red kangaroos can mate at any time of year. The female will ideally have one offspring suckling, plus a second embryo in a state of suspended development, ready to be born once the first infant has vacated the pouch.

like a factory production line, with no time wasted. More importantly, it means that if a joey should die or have to be abandoned due to a crisis (such as a fire that destroys all food or a drought), the second embryo can be immediately reactivated. The female then has another chance to raise a youngster without the need to find a mate. If there is a prolonged period of drought during which the female loses several babies in a row, her reproductive cycle comes to a complete halt, and she will not become fertile again until conditions improve.

Hop It! Kangaroo Locomotion

Kangaroos are famous for hopping. In fact, they use two very different kinds of gait depending on how fast they wish to travel. For slow movements—when grazing, for example—they use all four limbs and the tail, and progress by means of a "five-legged" lope. The kangaroo leans forward and, with the weight of the body supported on its short front legs and the thick tail, swings both hind legs forward. It then lifts its front legs and tail and rocks forward until its weight is back on the hind legs. The tail is a vital part of this maneuver. It is strong enough to carry the animal's whole weight, and without it the front legs would be useless. For traveling at speed the front legs and tail do not touch the ground. The kangaroo leaps forward, using both hind legs to propel it anything up to 30 feet (9 m). The tail is used for balance. When pressed, a large kangaroo can easily hop at over 30 miles per hour (48 km/h). At one time it was thought that kangaroos might be unable to move their hind legs one at a time. In fact, the hind legs are perfectly capable of making independent stepping movements. However, they only do so when swimming. In water the kangaroo employs a cycling "dog paddle," much like any other four-legged animal.

The red kangaroo uses its characteristic "hopping" motion to travel at speed. A large kangaroo can easily hop at over 30 miles per hour (48 km/h).

Common name Duck-billed platypus

Scientific name *Ornithorhynchus anatinus*

Family Ornithorhynchidae

Order Monotremata

Size Length head/body: 12–18 in (30–45 cm); tail length: 4–6 in (10–15 cm). Male usually larger than female

Weight 1–4.4 lb (0.5–2 kg)

Key features Flattened, torpedo-shaped animal with very short legs and large feet, each with 5 webbed toes; snout has soft, rubbery beak with nostrils on top; tail flat and paddlelike; body fur dark brown on back, paler below; male has sharp spurs on ankles

Habits Largely aquatic; most active around dusk and dawn; lives in burrows; generally solitary

Breeding One to 3 (usually 2) eggs laid after gestation period of 27 days. Young hatch 10 days later and are brooded for a further 4 months in nest burrow. Weaned at 4 months; sexually mature at 2 or 3 years. May live up to 21 years in captivity, 14 in the wild

Voice Usually silent; growls if disturbed or annoyed

Diet Small aquatic animals, especially crustaceans, insect larvae, worms, fish, and tadpoles

Habitat Freshwater streams and pools with suitable burrowing sites along their banks

Distribution Eastern Australia, including parts of Tasmania, New South Wales, Victoria, South Australia, and Queensland

Status Population: low thousands. Previously hunted for fur, now protected and doing well in most of its range, except South Australia

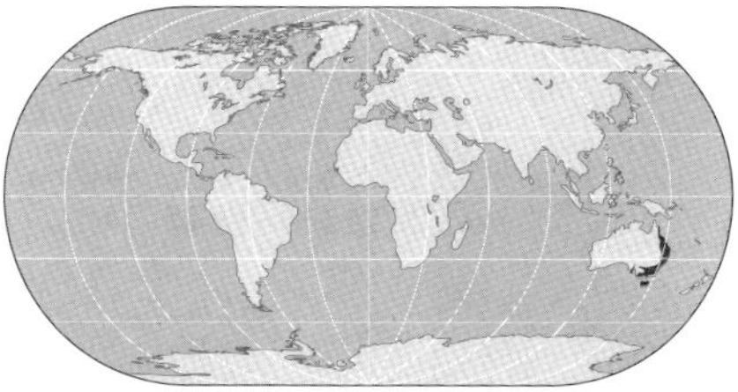

Duck-Billed Platypus

With its birdlike bill and egg-laying habits, the platypus is a strange, mixed-up creature. However, it is also extremely well adapted to its way of life.

THE DUCK-BILLED PLATYPUS is undoubtedly one of the oddest animals alive today. It is a monotreme—one of a select few mammals that reproduce by laying eggs instead of giving birth to live young. But the peculiarities do not end here. At first glance the platypus appears to be made up of spare parts taken from other animals. The combination of its robust, furry body, huge webbed feet, flat, paddle-shaped tail, and unique rubbery bill seems so unlikely that the first specimen sent back to Europe for scientific description was thought to be a hoax.

Aquatic Lifestyle

Detailed studies of the duck-billed platypus are hampered by the fact that it is a naturally shy and elusive animal. It spends much of its time hidden away in inconspicuous burrows. When it emerges to feed, usually under cover of twilight, it slips quietly into the cloudy waters of small pools, rivers, and streams and spends much of its time beneath the surface. On land the platypus gets around by waddling. Its large webbed feet, at the end of very short, stumpy legs, are not built for walking but for swimming, which the species does superbly well. Once in the water, it moves smoothly and silently, propelling itself along with its front feet and using the back ones as rudders and brakes. Underwater it moves with the speed and grace of an otter or a seal, able to accelerate rapidly and change direction in an instant. At the surface only the tip of its snout and the top of its head are visible, and it dives sud-

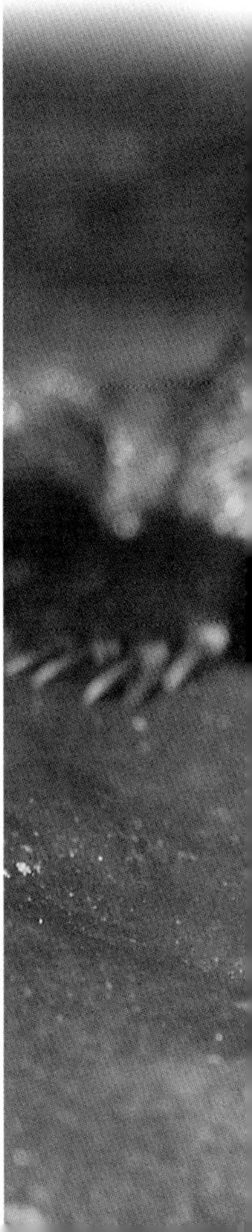

denly by rolling forward in the water without the tiniest splash. Often the only clue to the animal's presence is the rippling created in the water.

Underwater Detection

A platypus bill is not really like that of a duck at all. It is, in fact, a finely tuned prey-detection device, sensitive to touch as well as to the tiny electrical fields generated by the bodies of living animals. Unlike the hard beak of a duck, the bill of a platypus is soft, moist, and rubbery and covered in tiny pits and holes lined with highly sensitive nerve endings that carry information straight to the brain. The platypus also has quite good eyesight and hearing, but while underwater the bill provides all the information that is required—the eyes and ears are closed while the animal remains submerged. Once detected, prey animals are snapped up or sieved out of the mud using the bill.

After a successful period of foraging a platypus returns to the surface to breathe and feed. Prey items stored in large cheek pouches are brought back into the mouth, crushed and ground between horny plates that line each jaw, and swallowed. It may take several minutes to finish such a meal, during which time the platypus floats easily at the surface with all four legs spreadeagled. The animal looks relaxed, but at the slightest disturbance it will disappear once more.

Venomous Spurs

The platypus is, for the most part, a solitary animal. The home ranges of different individuals may overlap to some extent, but they apparently make an effort to avoid meeting, except during the breeding season. Early in spring male platypuses become very aggressive as they compete for the right to mate with the females living within their range.

Fighting is quite common and is a very serious business, despite the platypus's lack of conventional mammalian weapons: The

The duck-billed platypus appears to be made up of spare parts. Its anatomy seems so unlikely that the first specimen sent to Europe was thought to be a hoax.

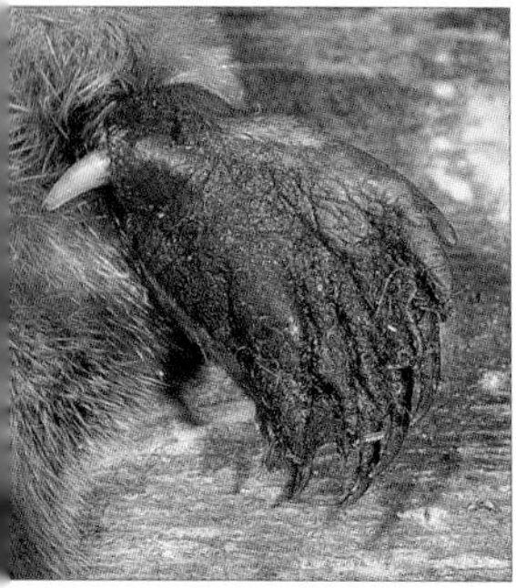

↑ ***The male platypus's poisonous spurs make it the most venomous mammal. Normally, the spurs are folded down to avoid catching on passing objects, but they are erected in a fight between two males.***

rivals have no teeth with which to bite each other, and their claws are not designed for slashing or scratching. However, each male has a pair of additional clawlike "spurs" growing from the ankles of his hind legs, which point inward and fold down when not in use. In a fight the platypus raises his spurs and tries to spike his opponent. The spurs are connected to glands in the animal's thigh that produce a potent toxin powerful enough to kill a dog and cause excruciating pain in a human. The male duck-billed platypus is the world's only seriously venomous mammal. All platypus babies have spurs, but they only develop fully in males.

Both male and female platypuses live in burrows in the banks of pools and streams. These general-purpose dens are simple oval tunnels with a sleeping chamber at the end. Breeding females also build nesting burrows, which are much more extensive. Adult platypuses have few natural predators, but the babies are highly vulnerable, so the mother goes to great lengths to build a secure home.

Humid Nests

The nest burrow may extend as far as 65 feet (20 m) into the bank. There can be several twists and turns and blind-ending offshoots. The nest itself is made of damp leaves and other vegetation, which the female collects from the water or the banks. Unlike most other mammals, which do their best to keep nesting areas snug and dry, the atmosphere inside the platypus nest must be humid to

Last in Line

The duck-billed platypus is the only surviving member of an ancient family of animals that were once much more widespread. Fossil platypuses dating from the time of the dinosaurs have been found not only in Australia but also in South America, providing strong evidence for the theory that Australia, Antarctica, and South America were once joined together as one supercontinent known as Gondwanaland. Whether or not these animals had anything like the modern platypus's ducklike bill is impossible to say because the bill is made of soft tissue, which does not fossilize. However, these ancient ancestors did have true teeth. The modern platypus only has baby teeth (milk teeth), which are replaced with flat grinding pads made of a horny substance that continues to grow throughout the animal's life. The long-extinct relatives of the duck-billed platypus probably lived mostly on land and fed on small invertebrates, much as generalist insectivores like hedgehogs and shrews do today.

prevent the eggs and their precious contents from drying out. Platypus eggs are small—0.7 inches (1.7 cm) in diameter, and rounder than those of most birds. They are sticky enough to stay put in the nest and not roll away. The mother platypus has no pouch in which to incubate her brood; instead, she tucks them safely under her tail and curls around them to keep them warm.

Once the eggs hatch, the naked, 1-inch-(2.5-cm-) long babies are cradled in much the same way. Like a newborn marsupial, a young platypus is little more than an embryo at first—barely able to drag itself along. But it is capable of finding the places on its mother's belly where milk seeps out of her mammary ducts. There are no teats that the young can latch onto, so the babies suck up

↑ ***Ideally adapted for swimming, the duck-billed platypus has a streamlined body with thick, insulating underfur that keeps the animal warm in cold water.***

Ostrich

Struthio camelus

The biggest living bird in the world, the ostrich breaks all avian records for height, weight, running speed, and power. Perhaps unsurprisingly, the ostrich also lays the largest egg of any bird.

Common name Ostrich

Scientific name *Struthio camelus*

Family Struthionidae

Order Struthioniformes

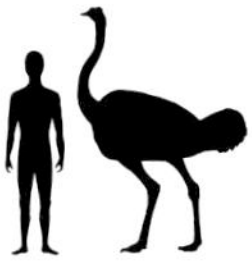

Size Height: male 83–108 in (210–275 cm), female 69–75 in (175–190 cm); weight: male 287–331 lb (130–150 kg), female 198–243 lb (90–110 kg)

Key features Bare head, neck, and legs; short, flat bill; large, dark eyes; male black with short, white wings and tail; female dull gray-brown

Habits Lives in small groups or flocks, feeding by day

Nesting Nest a scrape in the ground; usually 7 eggs; male and dominant female incubate eggs, including many laid by other females; chicks gather in large congregations, several families looked after by 1 pair of adults; young fully grown at 18 months; mature at 3–4 years; 1 brood

Voice Variety of short, hard calls, sneezing sounds, and a loud, deep, roaring or booming sound from territorial male

Diet Succulent plants, leaves, buds, seeds, fruits; rarely insects, small mammals, and reptiles

Habitat Open spaces from semiarid areas on desert edge to clearings in savanna woodland; mostly on open, grassy plains

Distribution Africa south of the Sahara Desert

Status Rare and threatened in the north and south of its range; secure in East Africa; some escaped populations from farmed stock in southern Africa

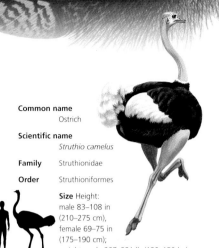

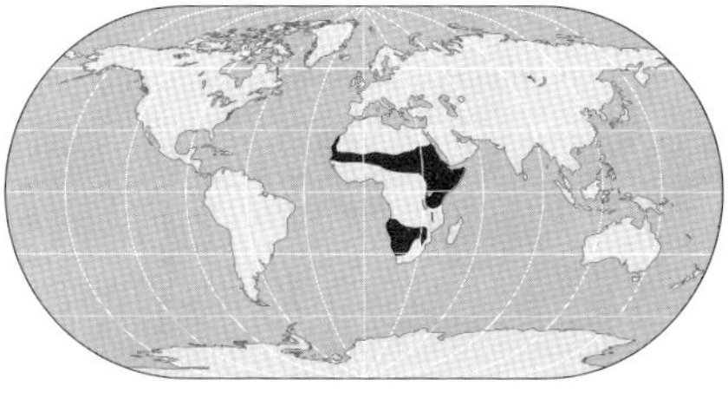

A FEMALE OSTRICH IS THE height of a tall human, while a male towers over even the tallest of humans. Old males have dense, black-and-white plumage on the body, wings, and tail. There are four races of ostrich: the Masai ostrich and North African ostrich are characterized by orange or reddish-pink skin on their necks, head, and legs, whereas in the Somali ostrich and South African ostrich the skin is blue. When breeding, blue-skinned males have vivid pink bills and shiny pink shins. Outside the breeding season the skin colors are much duller. Females, apart from being smaller, are browner and often look rather dowdy. Juveniles are drabber and much more unkempt.

Split Distribution

The present range of the ostrich is split into two areas. The northerly one stretches from the west coast of Africa across the southern edge of the Sahara Desert to Somalia and the Horn of Africa and south into East Africa in the great game parks of Kenya and Tanzania. The southern population is found in southwest Africa. Many ostriches survive in arid regions like the Sahara and the Kalahari Deserts. Others are found in much greener landscapes, with thornbush scrub and acacia woodland, provided there are grassy clearings and plenty of open spaces. Ostriches also thrive in quite hilly places, such as stony slopes with scattered bushes.

Opportunist Feeders

Ostriches eat almost anything edible they can find, but by far the greater proportion of their food is vegetable matter. They eat dry material if necessary, but prefer sweet, succulent food such as figs, juicy pods, or seeds of acacias, which are generally abundant in the less arid parts of their range. They may occasionally eat a lizard or small mouse if they can catch one, and occasionally insects such as locusts make up part of their daily diet. If a preferred source of food runs out, ostriches switch to whatever else is available, but acacias and aloes provide the staple diet almost everywhere.

Ostriches obtain all the moisture they need from the succulent plants they eat—a remarkable achievement, because they live in places that regularly reach 104° F (40° C) or more during the day. They also increase their body temperatures in hot periods, reducing the need to lose heat and thereby lose water.

Because an ostrich is so tall, it has a commanding view of the surrounding landscape. However, when it bends its neck to feed on the ground, the advantage of its high viewpoint is momentarily lost, and it can become vulnerable to predators. Therefore ostriches feed in groups, and one or two are always on the lookout while the others are feeding. They often feed close to zebras and wildebeests—extra lookouts that warn of the approach of a lion or cheetah.

A remarkable feature of the ostrich are its enormous, gleaming eyes, complete with long lashes. Their eyes are the largest of any terrestrial vertebrate and provide excellent vision.

Life on the Plains

Ostriches are social; across a wide African plain it is often possible to mistake a line of distant ostriches for a line of round-topped trees. There might be 100 or more in such elongated, extended flocks. Tighter groups usually consist of family gatherings, and outside the breeding season pairs or parties of five or six birds are the norm. The bigger flocks often include many immature birds but may consist largely of adult males and females. When

Remarkable Digestion

Ostriches eat many kinds of tough food. It is first gathered into a solid mass in the crop and is then swallowed—clearly visible as an uncomfortable-looking, descending bulge in the slender neck. Sand, grit, and stones are frequently swallowed to help grind the food in the gizzard. Like rheas, ostriches have a tendency to pick up bright or shiny objects and swallow them. In captivity they may even swallow wire, coins, nails, and other inedible items. The purpose is to help grind the food—much of it indigestible to other animals—in order to make the most of whatever the ostrich can eat in difficult conditions. The intestines of an ostrich are enormous, up to 46 feet (14 m) long, to help extract maximum nutrition from the food.

breeding, however, ostriches separate into pairs or groups consisting of single males accompanied by a few females.

It is fascinating to watch a group of ostriches going about their daily business. Older birds determine the timing of activities such as dust bathing and feeding simply by setting an example that the others follow. Occasionally there will be a short skirmish—one bird threatening another with open wings and raised head, its bare neck inflated, and its short, bushy tail cocked. The other bird will usually run from such a display or may lower its head and neck and point its tail downward, showing no willingness to contest the issue. Now and then, however, two birds will fight, using pecks or well-aimed kicks to settle the dispute.

Ostriches easily outrun predators such as lions if they spot them soon enough, but they may have to resort to more physical defense. A powerful kick from an ostrich can seriously maim a predator if it strikes a limb joint or can prove fatal if it strikes the head.

A running ostrich has a huge stride, covering 11.5 feet (3.5 m) with each step. Its feet move in a high-stepping, thrusting action that gives both great speed and endurance. An ostrich may reach 43 miles per hour (69 km/h), and it can keep up a steady 30 miles per hour (48 km/h) for 30 minutes or more.

Burying Her Head in the Sand?

When a female ostrich sits on her eggs during the day, she is at her most vulnerable—stationary, in open space, with restricted vision, and without the readiness to run that a standing ostrich enjoys. She must keep still and crouch down to avoid being seen by predators. She may even rest with her head low on the ground, probably the origin of the unlikely idea that the ostrich will bury its head in the sand. An ostrich away from the nest may also occasionally crouch as flat as it can, hoping that a nearby predator will not spot it. "Burying your head in the sand" means ignoring trouble and hoping it will go away, a fair description of this strategy. However, although the ostrich keeps its head down, it never buries it.

↑ *During courtship the male approaches the female and waves his spread wings before throwing himself to the ground and fanning his tail. He then rolls from side to side, raising his wings and swinging his head from side to side.*

Breeding Behavior

Ostriches breed in the dry season in most areas, but in some places they take advantage of the rains and breed shortly afterward, when there is a brief flush of new plant growth or an abundance of seeds. When food is scarce, as it usually is in deserts, ostriches form stable pairs. Elsewhere, when food is abundant enough to allow more ostriches to live close together, there are more complicated relationships. Usually, a mature male holds a breeding territory that includes a dominant female and several subordinate or secondary females.

The dominant male and female produce young, but the subordinate females will mate with other males and lay eggs in other nests whether they have mated with the dominant male or not. However, these eggs are not incubated and produce no chicks. Sometimes males with no territories also mate with any females they can find, but such matings do not result in the production of eggs.

The dominant male is a magnificent sight as he patrols his territory and challenges subordinate males or displays to females. The display is passionate and energetic; and if the female is not ready to mate following the performance, it is repeated with equal vigor. A territorial male has another impressive part to his repertoire: a deep, roaring "boom." It is often heard late in the day or at night.

While courting his hens, the male makes a number of shallow scrapes or pits in the ground in the center of his territory, which may be from 0.8 to 5.8 square miles (2–15 sq km) in area. Having mated, he leads the female to one of the pits, and she will lay around seven eggs, one every other day over a period of two weeks. Several other hens lay in this same nest, also on alternate days. Usually, two to five other ostriches add their eggs, but sometimes as many as 18 will add eggs to the growing clutch. Only the dominant hen will stay nearby and guard the eggs against predators, which include jackals and hyenas.

↓ *Several females may lay their eggs together, but remarkably, the dominant female is able to identify her own eggs for the purposes of incubation.*

The eggs are glossy white and measure about 6.25 inches (16 cm) in length. The shell is 0.08 inches (2 mm) thick and very strong. The complete clutch may number dozens of eggs, often more than 50, but only around 20 or 25 can be incubated properly by the sitting adult. The dominant female makes sure that her own eggs are in the middle of the nest and therefore most likely to hatch. Eggs laid by other hens are pushed to the edge and usually fail to hatch.

The female incubates the eggs by day, remaining well hidden as she sits low on the nest and relying on her dull, brown plumage to make her difficult to spot. The male, much more obvious in his striking black-and-white plumage, sits on the eggs during the night. After six weeks the eggs hatch. It is likely that while still inside the eggs, the chicks hear each others' calls and hatch out together.

It takes three months for the downy chicks to grow feathers, and this dull plumage lasts for two years before they molt into a more adult-like plumage. The chicks are not fully grown until around 18 months old. Young chicks are brooded by their parents or by other adults, and they are brave in their defense. They either use a display that feigns injury, luring predators away from vulnerable chicks, or they may choose to attack.

Sometimes, a family group consisting of a mother and her chicks may join with other, similar familes of ostriches. As many as 100 or more chicks of varying sizes may then be seen roaming the plains together with a small number of attendant adults.

Conservation Pressures

North African ostriches are endangered and rare. It was only recently that the Middle Eastern birds became exterminated by hunters. Ostriches and African people lived in harmony for hundreds of years, but the arrival of Europeans in Africa put immense pressure on most wildlife, ostriches included. They were hunted for meat, leather, and feathers, as well as for sport. Ostrich habitat has been damaged by overgrazing, forestry, and development, and it faces more pressure as Africa's human population grows rapidly. In South Africa ostriches are restricted to a tiny part of their recent range, and the presence of escaped ostriches from ostrich farms may threaten the integrity of the remaining wild populations. It is only in East Africa that ostriches still thrive, and then mainly in the national parks. But even there conservation efforts must remain strong and strictly enforced.

Barely 10 percent of ostrich eggs hatch, and despite gathering in groups for greater safety and the care taken by the adult birds, very few chicks survive to adulthood. Those that do may live for 30 or 40 years, however.

Magical Eggs

Despite their great size and strength, the eggs of ostriches still attract the attention of predators. The eggs are sometimes broken open by jackals and hyenas. Egyptian vultures (*Neophron percnopterus*) also crack them open by repeatedly tossing stones at them until the shell breaks. Ostrich eggs are also revered in certain human cultures and have been used in traditional death rites and rituals. In some places, because they were thought to have magical properties, they have been used to protect houses from fire and lightning. The ancient Egyptians used them as symbols of justice because of their perfect symmetry. Today they are still used in art, for making jewelry, and as water containers.

Emperor Penguin

Aptenodytes forsteri

The emperor penguin is the only bird able to endure the grim antarctic winter—and it actually breeds during this season. Uniquely among birds, most emperor penguins never set foot on dry land.

Common name Emperor penguin

Scientific name *Aptenodytes forsteri*

Family Spheniscidae

Order Sphenisciformes

Size Length: 43–51 in (109–130 cm); flipper length: 12–16 in (30.5–41 cm); weight: 42–101 lb (19–46 kg)

Key features Very large penguin; black head, throat, and chin; large yellow ear patch not surrounded fully by dark feathers as in king penguin

Habits Lives mainly at sea, feeding by deep diving; rests on sea ice; breeds in large colonies on ice or snow

Nesting Single egg laid onto ice and transferred to male's feet for incubation for over 60 days while females leave for open ocean to feed; young fledge after about 150 days; 1 brood

Voice Loud, trumpeting contact calls; complex, rhythmic display calls; harsh threat calls

Diet Mainly fish, small squid, and krill

Habitat Breeds on sea ice or hard snow over glaciers (except for two colonies far inland that breed on packed snow over a shingle spit and on a low, rocky headland); mostly at sea off Antarctica outside breeding season

Distribution Almost entirely Antarctic within the pack ice, usually avoiding the open sea beyond

Status Up to 200,000 pairs breed; population stable overall, with some local fluctuations

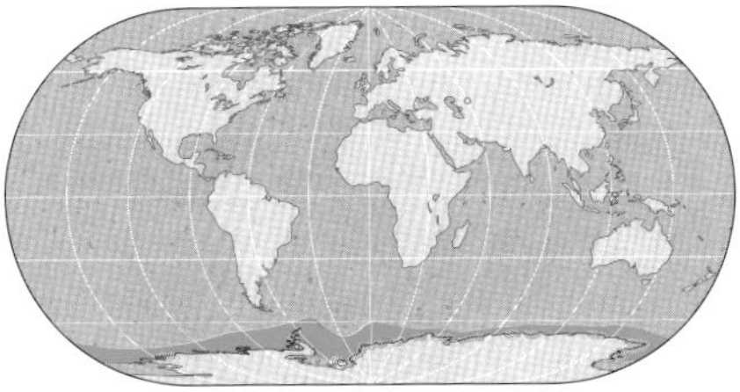

As its name suggests, the emperor is the largest of the penguins. It is also the heaviest of all seabirds; males at their heaviest can weigh as much as a small adult human. Although the emperor stands only a little taller than its close relative the king penguin (*Aptenodytes patagonicus*), it is almost twice as heavy.

Being the biggest helps the emperor survive in the coldest climate on Earth. A large body has a smaller surface area relative to volume than a small one, so it loses proportionately less heat. The emperor's exceptionally dense plumage and thick deposits of fat also help it withstand the harsh antarctic weather. Its feathers extend further onto its bill and legs than those of other penguins, to reduce heat loss from these exposed, vulnerable areas.

Like the king penguin—the only other member of the genus *Aptenodytes* (which means "wingless diver")—the emperor has a long, stout body and a relatively small head. Its upper parts are a subtle blue-gray, and the underparts are white with a pale yellow tinge. The emperor's ear patch is usually pale yellow, whereas the king penguin's is bright orange.

The emperor's bill is black with a narrow pink or lilac patch on the lower mandible, rather than the more orange patch seen on the king penguin. The bill is quite slender, slightly downcurved, and tapers to a point.

Emerging from the sea is a dangerous act for penguins, since leopard seals often lurk under the ice edge. Emperors use their swimming speed to launch themselves straight onto the ice, where they land on their bellies and rapidly toboggan to safety.

Like all penguins, a diving emperor uses its flippers to "fly" through the water, steering with its feet and tail.

Deep Divers

Emperors dive deeper than other penguins or indeed any other birds. Individual emperors have been recorded hunting at the enormous depth of 1,752 feet (534 m) below the surface and can stay under for as long as 18 minutes. Although it is exceptional, emperor penguins make an average of 100 dives during each foraging expedition, and many of these dives take them to depths of 656 feet (200 m) or more.

On land emperors do not run or hop like smaller penguins, but usually proceed by means of a stately, waddling walk. When necessary, they can go much faster by tobogganing across ice and snow on their bellies; and when they leap out of the sea, they often land on their bellies to slide across the ice.

Ocean Hunters

With their long, streamlined bodies and powerful muscles, emperor penguins are fast swimmers. They are capable of reaching a top speed of up to 9 miles per hour (14.5 km/h), although they normally travel no faster than about 6 miles per hour (9.7 km/h). Unlike many other penguins, they do not "porpoise."

Emperor penguins feed mainly on fish, supplemented by small amounts of squid and krill. Proportions vary according to local prey abundance, but generally fish account for over 90 percent of their diet. They catch the fish by diving deep into the very cold twilight zone of the ocean or even deeper into the dark zone, but they also take krill from shallow water beneath ice floes.

Huddling for Survival

Breeding during the antarctic winter means surviving some of the most harsh weather on Earth. The average temperature is only about –4° F (–20° C), but at times the windchill factor can cause temperatures to plummet to –76° F (–60° C) as blizzards driven by winds of up to 124 miles per hour (200 km/h) rage for days on end.

Emperor penguins cope with these blizzards by huddling together for warmth. Most breeding pairs of penguins are reluctant to get too close to each other; they remain at least a pecking distance apart and fiercely defend their territory. Emperors are the exception, crowding tightly together instead. Incubating males gather in dense groups, with as many as eight individuals per square yard (ten per sq m). By pooling their body heat, they save energy, and the temperature at the center of one of the huddles may be as much as 50° F (10° C) higher than that outside the group.

The males hunch in silence on the thick sea ice, slowly but steadily shuffling along, and constantly swapping places. Those that are unfortunate enough to have their backs facing the blizzard gradually edge their way forward and insinuate themselves into the warmer, central area of the group. Over the course of a two-day storm the whole huddle may move 656 feet (200 m).

Breeding on the Ice

Unlike the closely related king penguin, which breeds on subantarctic islands, the emperor breeds on the sea ice that surrounds the antarctic continent in winter. Its breeding cycle is very long, and the breeding colonies may be occupied for nine months of the year. The birds arrive at the colonies in March or April, having spent the previous few weeks engaged in concentrated feeding at sea to put on as much weight as possible. After leaving the sea, they trudge across the ice in long lines for up to 125 miles (200 km) to reach their colonies.

When they arrive, the birds quickly form pairs, displaying to the accompaniment of loud, trumpeting calls. The mutual bonding display between pairs of emperor penguins differs from that of all other penguins in that the emperors curve their necks forward so that their heads and bills point downward.

All the females in a colony lay their eggs at around the same time, usually during mid-May,

When emperor penguins are traveling across flat sea ice, they can move more rapidly by tobogganing on their bellies, propelling themselves with their flippers.

around six weeks after their return. Unlike all other penguins except the king penguin, the emperor does not build a nest of any kind. Instead, the female emperor lays her single white egg—the smallest egg of any bird in relation to its body weight—directly onto the ice between her feet. Almost immediately the male uses his bill to carefully move the precious egg onto the upper webs of his feet.

There the egg is in close contact with the brood patch: an area of the belly that becomes bare during the breeding season, so that underlying blood vessels can provide warmth to incubate the egg. Since it is laid in such extreme cold, the egg also receives extra insulation in the form of a loose fold of belly skin that covers it like a little quilt.

Hungry Work

Once the females have laid their eggs, they make their way back to the ocean to feed, leaving the males to incubate and protect the eggs until they return some 60 days later.

Meanwhile, the males must stay on the solid ice, far from open water, so they cannot eat at all. As a result, a typical male loses over 40 percent of his body weight during this period, which lasts four months or more in total. He typically ends up weighing about 48 pounds (22 kg) compared to his original weight of 84 pounds (38 kg).

The egg in the male's brood pouch often hatches shortly before his mate returns from her long feeding expedition at sea, having trudged up to 60 miles (100 km) across the pack ice in complete darkness.

The chick is almost naked when it emerges from the shell; and despite his emaciated condition, the male must feed his newly hatched offspring if it is to survive. He does so by regurgitating a rich, nourishing milklike liquid from his gullet before being relieved by his mate and leaving for a hard-earned bout of feeding at sea. He will eventually return to family duties, but not before he regains all the weight he lost during his long fast.

Both male and female emperors huddle together for warmth when brooding their

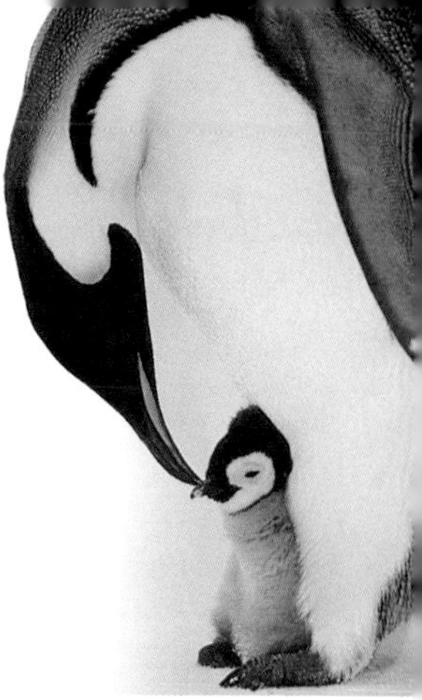

↑ A newly hatched emperor chick relies on the warmth of its parents for survival, but after about eight weeks the chicks form huddles of their own.

young chicks. When the young penguins grow larger, they exchange the comfort of their parents' embrace for the company of each other and crowd together in a crèche. They make whistling sounds that are unique to each individual chick, enabling the parent penguins to locate and recognize their own young when they come to feed them.

The Long Haul

Most emperor penguin breeding colonies are situated on expanses of sea ice that are especially firm and well anchored. They tend to be in sheltered areas of sea lying between the coast of Antarctica and small, rocky, offshore islands, reducing the chance that storms will break up the ice and destroy the eggs or young chicks. The ideal site is also close to open water where the penguins can feed; but as so often in nature, the birds usually settle for a compromise.

Many breeding sites are situated far from the open sea; and this means that even though the ice is less extensive by spring, the adults may still need to walk 60 miles (100 km) or more to keep their chicks supplied with food. They spend most of their time on these long marches, with columns of returning birds passing those setting out to fish.

As summer approaches, the young emperors acquire their first true feathers beneath their overcoats of down. Some leave with the adults on their trek back to the sea, while others fledge later and make the journey alone. It is some time before the chicks return to breed themselves. Female emperors do not become sexually mature until they are three to six years old. It may take up to nine years for males to mature, although the average is about five. They may live for 20 years or more.

The adult emperors must spend a month or more molting, standing on the ice, before

Although they are insulated against the antarctic chill by their dense coats of fluffy gray down, half-grown emperor penguin chicks still rely on their parents to bring them food—often from far away across the ice.

they can go to sea to feed again. Once at sea, a few birds—especially immatures—may wander as far north as South Georgia, southern South America, and New Zealand.

Enemies and Threats

Young emperors often fall prey to southern giant petrels (*Macronectes giganteus*). The less formidable-looking, but very wily skuas (genus *Catharacta*) work in pairs to steal eggs and chicks. The penguins' chief enemies, however, are the leopard seals and killer whales that hunt immature and adult birds in the sea.

A potential major long-term threat facing the emperor penguin is overfishing. Stocks of krill and fish in the antarctic are increasingly exploited by humans. This may be affecting some colonies already by creating food shortages during the vital periods when the birds fatten themselves up in preparation for breeding and molting.

Climatic variations can also cause problems. In cold years when the sea ice does not break up, the adults must travel much further to find food. Many of the chicks in the crèches may starve to death as a result.

It is difficult to estimate the emperor penguins' total population, particularly since new colonies are still being discovered; there may be as many as 200,000 breeding pairs.

Wandering Albatross

Diomedea exulans

Common name Wandering albatross

Scientific name *Diomedea exulans*

Family Diomedeidae

Order Procellariiformes

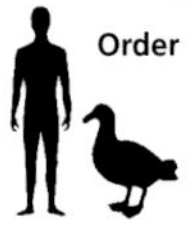

Size Length: 43–53 in (109–135 cm); wingspan: 106–136 in (269–345 cm); weight: 14–25 lb (6.4–11.3 kg)

Key features Huge, heavy-bodied seabird; very long, narrow wings; short tail; powerful hooked bill; large webbed feet; juveniles dark brown apart from white face and mainly white underwing; plumage becomes whiter with age, with broad black to wing edges

Habits Most of year lives alone in the air, traveling across oceans and feeding at sea, but forms flocks at concentrations of food; gregarious on breeding islands

Nesting Breeds once every 2 years; generally mates for life; large, cone-shaped nest of compacted grass; 1 reddish-flecked white egg; incubation 75–83 days; young fledge after 260–303 days; 1 brood every 2 years

Voice Usually silent at sea, but croaking or bleating sounds when fighting over food; loud, hoarse braying whistles during courtship displays

Diet Mainly squid and cuttlefish; also fish, carrion, offal, and jellyfish

Habitat Breeds on remote islands, often among clumps of grass; otherwise soars over oceans

Distribution Ranges the Southern Ocean; breeding adults stay near subantarctic islands

Status Classified as Vulnerable by IUCN; total world population estimated to be fewer than 8,500 breeding pairs

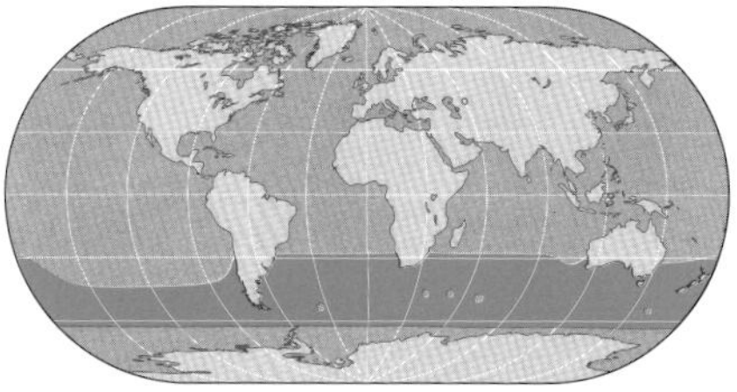

The largest and heaviest of all seabirds, the wandering albatross has the greatest wingspan of any bird—its long, narrow wings allowing it to soar immense distances across the southern oceans.

Largest of the "great albatrosses," the wandering albatross and the royal albatross (*D. epomophora*) are the mightiest of the tubenoses. The great albatross group also includes several species breeding on different islands. These include the Gough wandering albatross (*D. dabbenena*) and the Amsterdam wandering albatross (*D. amsterdamensis*).

Mature wandering albatrosses are mainly white with dark upperwings, but young birds' first feathers are almost black apart from a white face patch and mainly white underwings. Eventually, old males end up in the final "snowy stage," with only the wing edges black.

The massive bill is completely pale, with no dark line along the cutting edge, in contrast to the very similar royal albatross. The thin bill plates are translucent, like human fingernails; so when the tiny blood vessels in the skin beneath them constrict, the bill appears whitish; when they dilate, it takes on various shades of pink.

The Roaring Forties

Wandering albatrosses spend most of their lives at sea between latitudes 40° and 50° S in the belt known as the "roaring forties." There they can be assured of the strong, consistent westerly winds that enable them to soar with minimum expenditure of energy.

The birds are normally restricted to the Southern Hemisphere by the doldrums, a belt of light, unpredictable winds near the equator that prevents them from soaring. Despite this, there are several records of these spectacular seabirds appearing north of the equator. They include one seen in a field in coastal southern

California, which flew off out to sea the next day, and one that crash-landed on a coast road in Sicily, where it was killed by a passing automobile. Yet even if they survive, such individuals are unlikely to return south because they cannot sustain flapping flight long enough to recross the doldrums.

Gliding and Soaring

Wandering albatrosses are a majestic sight as they glide and soar over the great waves produced by the winds that blow constantly around Antarctica. Their long, narrow wings are perfect for this style of flight, and in typically windy conditions an albatross can soar for days on end with scarcely a wingbeat. Its wings even have a mechanism at the shoulders for locking the humerus bone rigidly in place, so that the muscles and tendons do not tire of holding the wings outstretched.

An albatross will fly back and forth in a zigzag pattern, gliding down toward the surface before swooping into the trough between two waves, then wheeling around to climb above the wave face. As it clears the wave crest, facing into or across the wind, the air sweeping over its great wings produces lift that pushes it upward. After soaring to a maximum height of 50 feet (15 m) above the sea, it wheels around and turns downwind or crosswind to repeat the whole process.

Traveling at an average speed of 34 miles per hour (55 km/h), and reaching as much as 56 miles per hour (90 km/h) with the strongest winds, these champion flyers can cover as much as 310 miles (500 km) a day. One individual fitted with a lightweight radio transmitter was recorded covering the staggering distance of 20,500 miles (33,000 km) in just ten weeks!

Normally, albatrosses never beat their wings; but if the wind eases, they may need to flap occasionally between periods of gliding. If the wind dies completely, they are forced to sit on the sea, their bodies riding high in the water. When the breeze picks up, the birds must patter across the water for long distances to become airborne once again.

The long, narrow wings of the wandering albatross are adapted for soaring, but not for instant takeoff, so the birds must run for long distances to gain enough speed to become airborne. Slowing down to land can also be hard unless the birds can head into a stiff breeze, and a calm-weather approach often ends in an undignified crash-landing.

Wandering the World

Many accounts of wandering albatrosses refer to their habit of circumnavigating (traveling all the way around) the globe, spending a year soaring continually eastward on the prevailing winds in search of food before returning to their breeding colonies. It is a romantic idea, but it may turn out that only a few birds actually achieve this remarkable feat. Satellite tracking of albatrosses fitted with small, lightweight radio collars that cause the birds no harm has shown that, in two cases, birds from the breeding population on the Crozet Islands actually reached the islands by traveling westward from Australia, while a close relative, the Antipodes wandering albatross, doubled back after initially flying eastward.

Snatching a Meal

The wandering albatross feeds mainly on cephalopods—squid, cuttlefish, and their relatives. The most commonly taken is the large deep-sea squid *Kondokavia longimana*, which typically weighs over 6.6 pounds (3 kg), but they also eat over 60 other species. The birds may catch them while swooping low over the waves, snatching prey at or just beneath the surface, but they also land on the water to pick up prey. They often make shallow dives from the surface or midair to chase fish or squid. It is puzzling how the shallow-diving albatrosses manage to include various deep-sea species in

Wings outstretched, a pair of wandering albatrosses circle around each other in courtship near their nesting site in South Georgia. The display helps cement a pair-bond that will last the birds for life.

← Wandering albatrosses often trail fishing boats to feast on discarded fish offal and unwanted fish, such as the cookiecutter shark being enjoyed by this juvenile. Note the separate tubular nostrils, found on all albatrosses.

their diet, especially as some are far too large to have been killed by the birds. Some squid float to the surface after breeding, and the albatrosses may be taking advantage of these. They may also take fragments of the squid discarded by deep-diving sperm whales and other whales after they have eaten their fill.

Until recently, wandering albatrosses were thought to catch squid mainly at night, when the squid migrate to the surface. But recent research has shown that the birds feed almost entirely by day.

Wandering albatrosses also catch fish and jellyfish, including the venomous Portuguese man-of-war. They seem to eat more carrion than other albatrosses and have been seen eating the carcasses of penguins killed by leopard seals and devouring the fat from strips of skin torn from baby humpback whales by killer whales. They also follow ships for days on end to snatch any edible refuse thrown overboard. The birds are ever alert for signs of rich concentrations of food, such as gatherings of other seabirds, whales, and dolphins.

Like other seabirds, a wandering albatross has salt glands just above its eyes. These remove the excess salt that it ingests with its food or takes in if it drinks seawater. The glands filter the salt from the bird's blood, forming a highly concentrated salt solution. It passes down ducts and into the nasal chamber, then along special grooves between the bill plates to drip from the hooked tip of the bill.

Family Commitment

In nonbreeding years wandering albatrosses spend their time roaming the vast expanse of the southern oceans, but every other year they return to bleak, wet, windswept subantarctic islands to breed. For the next year they stay near the islands so they can feed their chicks, and each of the separate populations breeding on different islands has its own home range and migration patterns. The biggest populations occur on the two Prince Edward Islands, to the southeast of Africa—each with about 3,000

Courtship Rituals

Wandering albatrosses are known for their elaborate, repeated courtship displays. Facing each other, the two birds bow, wave their heads, and rattle the mandibles of their bills together like castanets. Then they circle around for half an hour or more without stopping, their great wings outstretched and tails fanned and raised. At the climax of this display they extend their necks and point their heads and bills skyward, giving loud, hoarse braying whistles. These displays are performed mainly by pairs that have only recently become acquainted; established pairs are usually less demonstrative.

breeding pairs—and on the Crozet Islands group further east as well as the island of South Georgia, east of the Falkland Islands—each with about 2,000 pairs. Moving further east, there are about 1,000 pairs on the Kerguelen Islands, just ten or so pairs on Macquarie Island, and a single pair on Heard Island.

A typical wandering albatross colony consists of scattered pairs nesting among grassy or boggy terrain. Most colonies are on sloping ground with no large obstructions, to give the birds scope for their long takeoff and landing runs. Where they need to nest in sheltered locations or among tall clumps of vegetation to avoid very strong winds, they may need to walk some distance to and from their "runways."

A nest may be used for several seasons, and then a new one may be built near the site of the old one. Each pair sets about gathering beakfuls of grass and soil and trampling the material with their great webbed feet to form a pile about 39 inches (1 m) across at the base and 18 inches (46 cm) high. The nest is shaped like a miniature volcano, with a hollow in the top where the female lays her egg.

Male and female take turns incubating the egg on the nest. While one sits, the other goes off to sea to feed. The first shift is taken by the female and usually lasts no more than an hour or two. Subsequent shifts are much longer, lasting up to five weeks, although the shifts shorten as incubation continues.

The newly hatched chick is covered in a wispy coat of white down. The parents brood it to keep it warm for three to six weeks in two- to three-day shifts. They feed it daily at first on a mixture of partly digested squid and fish mixed with their fat-rich stomach oil. This nutritious mixture enables it to put on weight very rapidly. After the initial daily feeding period the adults return to feed their offspring only once every few days, or longer if they are delayed by severe storms. By this time the chick can wander around, but it rarely goes far since

An incubating albatross may need to sit tight for up to a month while its mate forages for food over the ocean. Eventually, it is relieved by its returning mate and is able to set out on a fishing trip of its own.

its parents will feed it only on the nest. Its stored fat and thick coat of pale gray down feathers help it withstand the bitter cold of the dark southern winter, when both nest and chick are often covered in wind-driven snow.

About nine months or more after hatching, the youngster's down is replaced by its first true feathers. Eventually, after a period of flapping its wings and bouts of practice flying, the huge juvenile albatross flies off to explore the oceans for itself. Nearly all young birds eventually return to the islands where they were reared, mostly when aged five to seven, but some much later at ten or eleven years of age.

⇧ ***An albatross chick feeds on a mixture of half-digested seafood and concentrated oil—a rich diet that enables it to gain weight fast and survive days or even weeks without eating.***

Slow Breeders

Like all albatrosses, the great albatrosses are very slow breeders. No other birds take so long to reach maturity. They do not breed until eight to eleven years old, and some do not do so until they are aged 18 or more. Their breeding cycles are also very long, lasting over a year from nest building to the departure of the young bird. For this reason they can breed only once every two years.

Estimates suggest that the lifespan of a wandering albatross may average 30 to 40 years. One individual female was last observed breeding 55 years after she had been banded when already adult, and she presumably died at sea during the ensuing months. It is possible that some birds may even reach 80 years of age.

Dragged Under

With their great size and massive, powerful bills, adult wandering albatrosses are generally able to deal with natural predators. Even during the long periods when the chicks are left alone, few healthy youngsters seem to be at risk, although weak or sickly ones are sometimes overwhelmed by several skuas working together. The real enemies of the wandering albatross are not predators, but humans.

Commercial fishing in the southern oceans has greatly expanded over the past century or so. Although albatrosses have benefited from the increased availability of fish offal, fishing has brought new threats—chiefly the method called longlining that is used for catching tuna and other fish.

The lines may be 80 miles (130 km) long and carry up to 40,000 hooks baited with fish or squid. The birds snatch the bait as the lines are paid out from the boats and are hooked, dragged under, and drown. Tens of thousands of albatrosses die like this each year, including many wandering albatrosses. With a population estimated at no more than 28,000 mature adults and fewer than 8,500 breeding pairs, the species cannot sustain such losses for long before it is threatened with extinction.

The problem was at its worst between the 1970s and early 1990s. Recently some populations have shown increases, although others are still declining. Accordingly, the wandering albatross is classified as Vulnerable rather than Endangered. Various techniques have been devised to prevent albatrosses from becoming caught, such as weighting the lines so they sink quicker, feeding them down tubes so they emerge out of sight below the surface, and setting them at night when few birds feed. Some nations have also agreed to limit or even ban longlining where albatrosses feed, and it is to be hoped that these measures will help secure the future of these magnificent seabirds.

Brown Pelican

Pelecanus occidentalis

Common name Brown pelican

Scientific name *Pelecanus occidentalis*

Family Pelecanidae

Order Pelecaniformes

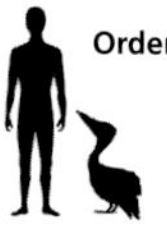

Size Length: 43–47 in (109–119 cm); wingspan: 75–85 in (190–216 cm); weight: 8–15 lb (3.6–6.8 kg)

Key features Typical huge pelican bill and throat pouch; mainly brown plumage; smaller and with less bright color on head and bill than similar Peruvian pelican

Habits Gregarious all year; plunges into sea from high in air to catch fish; young gather in crèches before fledging

Nesting Nests mainly in trees or shrubs; variable nest of sticks and grass; 2–3 chalky white eggs; incubation 28–31 days; young fledge after 63–78 days; 1 brood

Voice Adults make deep grunts, moans, and other sounds at breeding colonies; young utter higher-pitched noises, yelps, and screams

Diet Mainly fish; also carrion and crustaceans

Habitat Along coasts and islands, feeding in inshore waters, including estuaries; avoids open sea

Distribution Pacific coasts from British Columbia to Peru, including Galápagos; Atlantic coasts from New England through Caribbean to Guiana

Status Quite common; probably the second most numerous pelican after Peruvian pelican

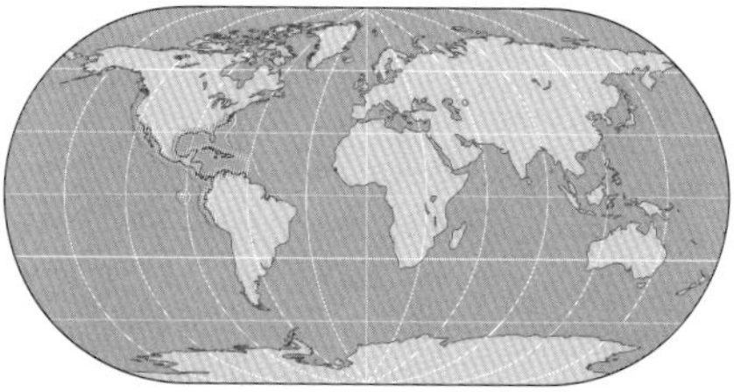

Ungainly and comical-looking on land, the brown pelican becomes elegant once airborne—gliding over the sea on its great, broad wings before plunging beneath the waves in search of fish.

THE SMALLEST OF ALL PELICANS, the brown pelican is one of only two species in its family that are truly marine, the other being its close relative the Peruvian pelican (*Pelecanus thagus*). These two species are also distinctive because of their fishing techniques. Unlike all other pelicans, which merely dip their heads or upend their bodies beneath the water to scoop up fish in their great pouches, they catch their food by spectacular plunge-dives from midair.

Versatile Bird

Like other pelicans, the brown pelican is essentially a bird of the tropics and subtropics. But it is a versatile species, able to tolerate the cooler climate of Maryland and Virginia as well as the tropical heat of the Caribbean.

Most pelicans have white plumage with areas of gray or black; but as its name suggests, the brown pelican is mainly pale brown with darker flight feathers and a chestnut nape in

Ⓓ *The brown pelican draws its head back onto its shoulders in flight. This allows it to support the weight of the huge bill by resting it on its neck, which is held in an S-shape.*

↑ ***When a brown pelican dives, it stretches its head and neck forward and angles its wings back to ease its passage into the water. As it strikes the water surface, it thrusts its wings and feet back to increase its speed.***

the breeding season. The very closely related Peruvian pelican is similar, but much bigger, with more white streaking below, more orange on the bill, and brighter areas of bare skin on the face when breeding. It was once considered to be just a race of the brown pelican, but is now generally regarded as a separate species.

Ocean Patrol

Brown pelicans can travel nonstop for great distances by using a flap-glide technique—a few powerful beats of their wings are followed by a long glide. They usually travel in V-formations or staggered lines, a habit that may save energy as each bird rides on the upwash of air from the wingtips of the bird in front. The birds generally fly very low over the water, with their wingtips almost touching it, taking advantage of updrafts created by waves by flying along the leading edge of the wave crests. At times, however, they soar high in the air.

Brown pelicans usually search for food in small groups, flying above the water in single file and watching for the slightest sign of a fish below. On sighting a single large fish or a shoal of smaller ones, one of the party peels off and plunges down, opening its great bill to trap the fish in its huge pouch.

The sound of the splash as a brown pelican hits the water can be heard from up to almost 0.6 mile (1 km) away. Yet the bird remains unharmed thanks to the air sacs beneath the skin of its chest that cushion the impact. They also make the pelican buoyant, so it bobs to the surface quickly if it has submerged. It always surfaces facing into the wind, to ensure an easy takeoff. However, it cannot rise until it has drained off the great volume of water trapped in its pouch—which can weigh more than the bird itself—and swallowed the fish.

Feeding Flocks

Brown pelicans feed mainly on fish, especially small schooling species. Large shoals of sardines or anchovies can attract big concentrations of the birds, and they may compete with human fishing interests, particularly along Pacific coasts. However, in other places, such as off the Atlantic coast of the U.S., most of the species taken by brown pelicans are fish such as menhaden that have little commercial value.

As well as fish, brown pelicans also catch some shrimp and other crustaceans. They

→ ***Immature brown pelicans are often targeted by pirates such as large gulls, which steal the pelicans' catch before they get the chance to swallow it. This juvenile is trying to swallow a fish.***

occasionally scavenge for animal remains, as well as any fish offal or dead fish they can glean from fishermen.

They feed almost entirely in the relatively shallow waters of estuaries and other sheltered inshore areas, within about 6 miles (10 km) of the coast. They are most active in the early morning or late afternoon, perhaps to avoid the glare of the Sun shining in their eyes, which makes it harder to dive accurately.

Brown pelicans often suffer from the attentions of other birds that make a habit of kleptoparasitism, or food piracy. In the Atlantic and Caribbean the most likely robbers are laughing gulls (*Larus atricilla*), which are bold enough to fly down and land on a pelican's head as it emerges from the sea with its catch, hoping to grab a free meal. In the subtropical and tropical parts of their range, from Mexico and Florida southward, the pelicans need to keep watch for another, more dedicated pirate—the very large magnificent frigatebird (*Fregata magnificens*).

When they are not feeding, brown pelicans spend a lot of time resting. Although they are powerful, buoyant swimmers, they cannot spend long periods on the water without their feathers becoming sodden, so they roost on sandbars or on trees or other perches. The birds also splash their feathers in the water before preening them, taking care to scratch their heads and necks thoroughly in an attempt to remove irritating parasitic feather lice.

Adapting to Humans

Of all pelicans, the brown pelican has adapted best to life alongside humans. Pelicans are generally shy and wary—and with good reason, since they have suffered much persecution at the hands of people. However, brown pelicans have managed to overcome this fear, particularly at fishing ports, tourist resorts, and other coastal settlements where they are regularly allowed to take discarded scraps of fish. At such places they are a common and much photographed sight as they glide in to take these offerings or digest them while resting on jetties, walls, posts, or moored boats.

Remote Refuges

If they can find them, brown pelicans nest in stands of mangroves or other trees to gain protection from ground predators and flooding. Otherwise, and especially in the Pacific region, they nest on the ground on small, remote flat islands and arid stretches of coast, often on steep, rocky slopes that are free from predatory mammals and human disturbance. Some of these colonies are maintained for many years, but others may be abandoned as a result of disturbance, heavy infection of the young with parasites, or a sudden drop in the food supply.

Whatever the site, the male chooses it and advertises for a mate with head-swaying displays and repeated bowing to show off the strip of rich chestnut feathers that runs up the back of the neck; he also jerks up his wingtips rhythmically about once a second.

If a male succeeds in winning over a female, he presents her with a gift of some twigs or grass, and she uses it to start building the nest. The male continues to gather nesting material and is not averse to stealing it from neighboring nests.

⊖ ***Brown pelican chicks beg for food by pecking at their parents' bills, trying to make them regurgitate a meal of half-digested fish. These pelicans have nested in mangrove trees in the Galápagos.***

Brown pelican nests built on the ground are merely hollows scraped out by the birds in the soil or even the birds' droppings, sparsely lined with a few feathers; the rim builds up to as much as 10 inches (25 cm) high as the pair add their droppings to the soil and debris. Nests constructed among trees or shrubs are much more substantial structures of twigs, grass, reeds, or other vegetation piled onto a platform of large sticks interwoven into the supporting branches.

Both parents share the task of incubating the eggs, placing them gently on top of the huge, warm webs of their feet. On hatching, the chicks look like miniature pterodactyls (prehistoric flying reptiles). The grotesqueness—at least to human eyes—is often increased by the sight of many parasitic ticks scuttling over their naked bodies.

At first their parents regurgitate half-digested food onto the floor of the nest for the chicks to pick up in their bills. After about ten days the chicks start growing coats of soft, white down and begin to take food directly from their parents' pouches. Unlike their generally silent parents, the chicks are very noisy, begging for food with piercing screams.

Before they are able to fly, young brown pelicans gather together in groups known as "pods." Each chick may need as much as 176 pounds (80 kg) of fish to survive to the fledging stage. If food is in short supply, the oldest is fed first, and one or both of the others may be left to starve, so that at least one survives. Older chicks may even eat younger ones.

Many chicks also die by being trampled underfoot when a hungry pod scrambles to obtain food from a returning adult, which often beats off or tosses aside chicks that are not its own. But if they survive these and other hazards to reach adulthood, brown pelicans may live to 25 years or more.

Problems with Pesticides

During the 1960s and 1970s brown pelican populations in the U.S. suffered massive declines as the birds accumulated the pesticides DDT and dieldrin in their bodies. These widely used poisons built up in the food chain and became concentrated in the fish that the birds ate. That affected the pelicans' eggs, thinning their shells so that they broke in the nests. In parts of their northern range brown pelican numbers slumped by as much as 90 percent in just 20 years, and the bird was declared an endangered U.S. species by 1973. Fortunately, the pesticides involved were then banned, allowing the pelicans to make a dramatic recovery, and in most areas populations had reached their former levels by the late 1980s.

Arctic Tern

Sterna paradisaea

Common name Arctic tern

Scientific name *Sterna paradisaea*

Family Sternidae

Order Charadriiformes

Size Length: 13–14 in (33–36 cm); wingspan: 30–33 in (76–84 cm); weight: 3–4.5 oz (85–128 g)

Key features Mainly gray, with black cap (white at front in nonbreeding season); white cheeks, rump, and tail; narrow black line on trailing edge of wingtips; translucent "window" on hind wing; very long tail streamers; bill and very short legs blood-red, turning black in fall

Habits Feeds at sea by plunge-diving from hovering flight; breeds in small, widely dispersed colonies; exceptionally long migrations

Nesting Nest a shallow scrape; 2–3 eggs; incubation 22–27 days; young fledge after 21–24 days; 1 brood

Voice Very noisy, with loud, high-pitched rasping and clear piping or whistling calls

Diet Mainly small fish; also crustaceans, insects, krill, earthworms, and fish offal

Habitat Breeds mainly along coasts and inshore islands, but also far inland; generally migrates and winters well offshore

Distribution Mainly Arctic, but south to northern Europe, northwest and northeast U.S; winters in Southern Ocean

Status Widespread and common, but many populations have suffered serious declines

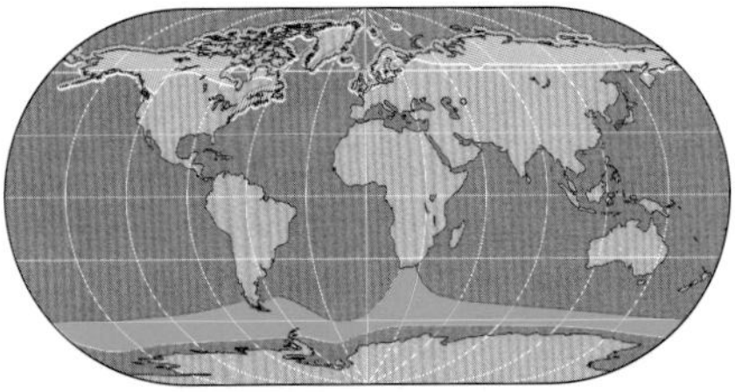

This elegant seabird travels farther than any other bird, flying halfway around the globe and back to migrate between its breeding and nonbreeding habitats near the North and South Poles.

WITH ITS LONG WINGS AND tail streamers, its sleek, streamlined body, and buoyant flight style, the Arctic tern is one of the most elegant of the seabirds. As its name suggests, it is the most northerly breeder of all the terns, nesting mainly north of the Arctic Circle, and it is the only member of the tern family that breeds in the high Arctic. Small Arctic tern colonies even survive the bitter cold of Cape Morris Jesup in extreme northern Greenland—the world's most northerly outpost of land, only 439 miles (707 km) from the North Pole.

↓ ***Although they spend much of their lives at sea, Arctic terns like to wash in fresh waters such as this pool in Iceland, sluicing away the salt and preening their feathers with their bills to restore their aerodynamic efficiency.***

The Greatest Migrants

After breeding, adult and young Arctic terns embark on a record-beating journey from their nesting grounds in and around the Arctic to the other end of the Earth, to spend the nonbreeding season in Antarctica.

Each year an Arctic tern may cover as much as 25,000 miles (40,235 km) on its round trip between the Arctic and Antarctica. If it flew there and back in a straight line, the distance would be only about 18,600 miles (29,935 km), but Arctic terns follow complex routes, hugging the irregular coastlines for much of the way. Some may travel overland surprisingly long distances for a seabird, and one was even found at an altitude of 6,500 feet (1,980 m) in the Colombian Andes. Others are forced to strike out over the open ocean.

Arctic terns that breed in Alaska travel south down the Pacific coasts of the Americas and then go around storm-battered Cape Horn to reach the Antarctic Ocean. Those that nest in eastern Canada and Greenland might be expected to follow the eastern coastlines of North America, the Caribbean, and South America; but instead, they cross the Atlantic, flying southeast toward Europe until they meet other migrant Arctic terns heading south from their breeding grounds in Europe and Siberia. After passing Spain and northwest Africa, some birds diverge to fly down the Atlantic coast of South America, while most continue to follow the African coast, past the Cape of Good Hope, and on to Antarctica.

When they reach Antarctica, the terns gather along the edge of the pack ice surrounding the Antarctic continent, where there is plenty of food. As the southern summer progresses and the ice retreats, the terns follow it southward. This takes them into a zone of westerly winds that help carry them east to a position to the south of the Atlantic, so they are ideally placed when they need to fly back north to breed again.

Some Arctic terns can reach an age of 25 or more (the record is 34). During their lifetimes these birds will have traveled a distance at least equivalent to flying to the Moon and back—over 620,000 miles (1 million km).

Since the Arctic tern spends its breeding season in the Arctic and much of the rest of each year in Antarctica, it enjoys the perpetual Sun of the polar summer in both regions and probably experiences more daylight each year than any other animal.

The stronghold of the species is in the subarctic zone, with by far the largest numbers breeding in Iceland. The Arctic tern population here fluctuates between about a quarter of a million and half a million breeding pairs, accounting for about 60 percent of the total population in Europe. The next largest concentration is in northern Britain, where almost 70 percent of the British breeding population of about 44,000 pairs is found on the island groups of Orkney and Shetland off northeast Scotland. In North America the greatest numbers occur in remote parts of Alaska and the Canadian Arctic.

Hover and Plunge

Throughout the year Arctic terns feed mainly on small fish, although they also include insects, crustaceans, and other animals in their diet. The proportions of these different foods vary from one area to another and throughout the year. In some breeding colonies, such as on the Arctic island of Spitsbergen, Arctic terns catch many krill to feed their young. In Antarctica they gorge themselves on the huge concentrations of these shrimplike crustaceans that build up in the southern summer. It is at this time that the terns molt and become flightless for a short period, but they can still feed because they can gather the krill from just beneath the surface as they swim around on the water with their small webbed feet.

An Arctic tern uses a variety of methods for obtaining its prey. Like other sea terns, it catches fish mainly by hovering against the wind until it spots a victim, then plunging down to enter the water with a splash and catch the fish just below the surface. However, its technique has some distinctive features. An Arctic tern typically descends in stages by hovering, then dropping down a few feet before hovering once more; it then either repeats the process or slips away to one side until it has a more precise fix on its target and makes its final dive.

On occasion an Arctic tern may also behave like its more distant relative the black tern (*Chlidonias niger*), dipping down low in flight to pick off insects and their larvae, taking crustaceans from the surface of the water, or even snatching caterpillars from low vegetation on land. It also alights to feed on earthworms.

Arctic terns sometimes steal food caught by other birds. In Iceland, for instance, they have been seen taking fish dropped by puffins being chased by jaegers; but they are far more likely to be victims themselves of these aerial pirates.

Fascinating Rituals

Most Arctic terns nest along coasts and on small, low, sparsely vegetated rocky or sandy inshore islands or sea stacks, around the fringes of the Arctic Ocean. The birds' favorite nesting sites are on rocky shores or on shingle or sandy beaches and among the sandy pockets that build up along ridges of gravel such as those that form beneath glaciers. There are also many breeding colonies far inland on tundra, heathland, rough pasture, sedge grassland, and islets in lakes or large rivers.

Arctic terns usually pair for life and return to the same nest site every spring. Their courtship and pair-bonding rituals are fascinating to watch.

Ⓓ *The Arctic tern is an exceptionally noisy seabird, especially at its northern breeding colonies; although when danger threatens, the whole colony can fall silent in a "dread."*

⊖ ***A remote, rocky, largely barren shore makes a perfect nesting site for Arctic terns, which are more than capable of defending their nests against ground predators such as foxes, weasels, and even people.***

Initially the male flies around higher and higher with a fish grasped in his bill, hotly pursued by his mate. Then both birds glide down with a curious, swaying flight action, to land close together on the ground. The female then begs for food like a chick, and the male feeds her with his trophy. This courtship feeding not only serves as an indication of the male's prowess at fishing, but also provides his mate with the nutrients she needs to produce her large, protein-rich eggs.

The beautifully camouflaged downy chicks leave the nest within a day or two, but they hide among vegetation or stones if danger threatens, prompted by alarm calls from their parents. At intervals the usual clamor of harsh calls from a busy colony abruptly ceases as almost all the birds suddenly take silently to the air and circle over the sea. After about half a minute they start calling again, return to their nests, and soon settle down. This odd behavior, known as a "dread," occurs most often in dense colonies where the nests are close together. Usually there seems to be no obvious reason for it, but researchers think that it may be linked to the presence of aerial predators, such as gulls, skuas, crows, ravens, or falcons.

Arctic terns also suffer from ground predators such as Arctic foxes, but they are extremely aggressive in defense of their eggs and young. Working together, the birds dive at any intruder, including a human one, rising into the air and then swooping down at the trespasser's head. They often strike with their sharp bills, which can easily draw blood from an unprotected scalp.

Delayed Molt

The Arctic tern delays the molt of its flight feathers until late in the year, after it has made its marathon migratory journey to Antarctica. It contrasts with most terns that breed in the north, including its close relative the common tern (*Sterna hirundo*), which has two partial molts in a year. It also helps birdwatchers distinguish these very similar-looking birds when they see them passing along coasts on their southward migrations—the Arctic tern's wings are neat and complete, while those of its cousin often show gaps where the primary flight feathers of the wings have been lost during molt.

⊖ ***While their parents are away fishing, Arctic tern chicks stay hidden, but they rush out to beg for food as soon as an adult bird appears. Sometimes the parent bird feeds its chicks from the air.***

Common Loon

Gavia immer

Common name Common loon (great northern diver)

Scientific name *Gavia immer*

Family Gaviidae

Order Gaviiformes

Size Length: 27–36 in (68.5–91 cm); wingspan: 50–57 in (127–147 cm); weight: 6.5–10 lb (3–4.5 kg); male slightly larger than female

Key features Heavily built, thick-necked bird; large head with big, pointed, blue-gray bill; sexes similar

Habits Almost totally aquatic; dives for food; pairs form lifelong bonds and nest well away from humans and other loons

Nesting Nest a heap of plant material close to water's edge; 1–3 eggs; incubation 24–25 days; young fledge after 63 days; 1 brood

Voice Yodeling and "tremelo" calls, and soft hoots

Diet Mainly fish, but also crustaceans, insects, mollusks, amphibians; also some vegetable matter

Habitat Large, deep freshwater lakes surrounded by conifer forests or tundra; flies south to winter on coasts and occasionally inland lakes—either alone, in pairs, or usually small flocks

Distribution Northern areas of the Northern Hemisphere and along coasts of North Atlantic and Pacific

Status Not globally threatened, but population has declined over the last 100 years, particularly as a result of human disturbance

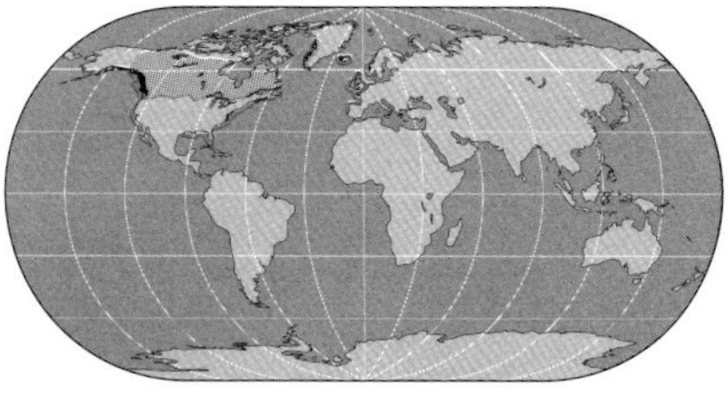

Few sounds are more evocative of the wild, lonely northern lakes and forests of the planet than the strange call of the common loon. Fiercely territorial, this bird is remarkably well suited to living in an often harsh environment.

THE SHAPE OF A COMMON loon in the water is quite distinctive. It has a long body—often sitting low in the water—a chunky neck, and a big head flattened on top, which drops from a peak to a thick bill, always held level. In the breeding season the head is black and bears stripes down both sides of the neck with white checkered upper parts and light underparts. In winter the upper parts become grayish, and the bill becomes much lighter in color. You might see the bird's big feet when it is in flight, but you would be lucky, for the common loon spends nearly all of its time in the water.

Fish-finders

Moving slowly on the surface of a lake, a loon is constantly searching for fish. Instead of simply looking from above, however, it regularly dips its head below the surface to get a clearer view. Loons hunt their live prey almost completely by sight, so they nest in clear waters and only hunt during the day. If the water is murky, they resort to feeling their way along the bottom of the lake, hoping to detect slow-moving crustaceans such as crawfish.

Unlike grebes and cormorants, which seem to leap from the surface and then dive under with a splash, loons prefer to lower their heads and slip under silently. Although they do not actually "dive" from the surface, they can easily reach depths of 33 feet (10 m). Loons have even been recorded at depths of 230 feet (70 m). Propelled at considerable speed by their feet and steering with their wings, loons usually find their food within a minute of diving.

A common loon in winter plumage. The common loon is considerably bigger than either the red-throated loon (Gavia stellata) *or the black-throated loon* (G. arctica).

A loon's food depends both on where it lives and the season. Fish make up the bulk of most loon diets, and some individuals eat nothing else. Trout and salmon are among the most common foods, although a variety of other fish are taken. Most are eaten whole underwater, but those that prove awkward or are too large to swallow in this way are taken to the surface and pulled apart. Crustaceans such as prawns and shrimp are also caught, as well as water snails, insects, occasionally frogs and other amphibians, seeds, and plant leaves.

Mating for Life

In spring, when the ice has melted from the lakes of the north, common loons return there to breed. For the next few months they lead a deliberately isolated existence; no pair will nest within sight of another loon, and if humans disturb them, they will abandon the lake.

The two birds that arrive on a large, deep, freshwater lake will probably have been there the year before and perhaps the year before that. Loons mate for life, and these strongly bonded birds return to the same site to nest year after year. The drab grays of the birds' winter plumage have been replaced by vivid black-and-white markings. And most remarkably, their irises turn red, giving the eyes a flaming intensity.

Loons always wait to form pairs on their breeding territory, even though these normally solitary birds gather in winter flocks. Usually a young male occupies a territory and waits for a female, making loud calls to attract one. Conversely, if the male of a pair has died during the fall or winter, the female can find a new mate within a matter of days. Birds that have remained silent all winter now begin to make an extraordinary range of calls that, on a still evening, can be heard for miles around.

The breeding colors of the common loon include bold black-and-white plumage markings, distinctive "necklaces," and vivid red eyes.

Their loudness is quite deliberate, for in most cases the wailing and yodeling calls are advertising ownership of a territory or warning away other loons. Each male has a yodeling call that studies have shown is unique to that particular bird. They also produce a rapid succession of notes described as a "tremelo" call. It can sound like manic laughter—hence the expressions "crazy as a loon" or "loony." Sometimes neighboring loons will begin a concert of calls, with both male and female responding to the calls of their neighbors—a contest between dusk and dawn that is often sustained over long periods of time.

The loons' courtship display before mating appears comical; the two birds face each other in the water, with their heads tipped forward, then begin dipping their bills in the water. The dipping grows faster, until eventually they dive past each other, turn, and begin the process all over again. Eventually the female draws her neck and head down and leads the male toward the shore. She leaps onto the land and often makes real or imaginary nest-building movements. It is enough to persuade the male loon to mate with her.

Fighting for Territory

When a pair of nesting birds occupies a fixed territory with only a relatively small amount of food available, it is essential that they defend the territory against intruders to ensure there will be enough food for the young. Given the harsh environment in which they live, it is not surprising that a male loon will fight for its territory.

Aggressive behavior begins with warning calls and a clear, threatening posture. The loon leans low and forward in the water, with its head and neck extended and its bill tipped upward. As an intruder approaches, one or both of the pair begins a ritual threat display. They will circle the intruder, dip bills in the water, jump or dive in front of it, then rush toward it and begin "fencing." The "homebird" and the intruder stand up in the water facing each other, wings stretched out, bobbing toward each other. The next stage is rarely reached; but if the loons begin to attack each other with their long, sharp bills, they can cause serious, even fatal, injuries.

Even when they nest, common loons try to minimize their contact with land. They build the rough mat of vegetation that passes for a nest as close to the water as possible—rarely more than a few feet away. They nest so close to water that heavy rains or storms can result in their nest being washed away or flooded. It appears that easy access to water makes the risk worthwhile. Besides, the female can lay a replacement clutch of eggs within a couple of weeks when necessary.

The female usually lays two eggs, two days apart. When hatched, the older, bigger chick stands a much better chance of survival because if food is short, it will be able to take most of it. It is not uncommon for the younger chick to starve within the first few days. The adults are kept busy finding food for their hungry young—a family of four will eat about a ton of fish during the breeding season.

Raising the Young

Young loons are on the water permanently within three days of hatching. To begin with, they ride on their parents' back. An eighteenth-century writer commented on a Faroe Island belief that the bird "is thought to hatch its young in a hole formed by nature under the wing for that purpose." On days when the water is calmer, the cheeping young learn to swim and dive. The adults guard the young against predators by rushing at intruders with their heads and necks outstretched. The family stays together, each hooting softly to the others to maintain contact.

It is no easy task for a young bird to learn how to fish. The parents encourage them to hunt for themselves by catching and disabling fish, bringing them to the surface, and then getting the baby birds to chase after them. Because of their rather inept first attempts, the

→ The nest is usually built on an islet close to the water's edge soon after the spring thaw. Human disturbance from recreation and vacation homes has increased on lakes in the southern parts of the bird's range, causing a decline in breeding.

young loons remain largely dependent on their parents for about seven weeks. But long after they have started to fish for themselves, they continue to take food from their parents—even when they have left the lake of their birth and flown south for the winter.

Mythical Birds

The behavior of loons has fascinated humans for thousands of years, encouraging many myths and legends. Many center around their unearthly calls. The Thompson River native Americans of British Columbia believed the sound would cause rain, and if humans imitated it, they could do likewise. In the early nineteenth century the famous U.S. ornithologist John James Audubon traveled with sailors who, when they heard the call of a loon, believed disaster would befall them. In medieval times the Scots considered the call a bad omen, and the Norwegians thought a loon call signified that a death was imminent. Much earlier human societies spanning the Northern Hemisphere, from the Inuit and native American peoples to the Scandinavians and Siberians, all had legends about the loon. Some linked its dive to the bottom of deep lakes with creation—they believed the bird brought up mud that formed the land.

Heading South

At the onset of fall the loons must leave the lake before it becomes frozen over. Most head south—usually toward the coast, although some winter on inland lakes. Their bulky, heavy bodies and narrow wings make takeoff difficult, and loons must first run across the water to get enough lift. Their slow-flapping, gooselike flight takes them to the sea, where they winter alone, in their breeding pairs, or in small, loose groups. Common loons can migrate considerable distances, for those that have nested on Canadian lakes may head to the coasts of California or Florida for the winter. The freshwater diet of the summer gives way to sea fish such as cod, herring, and haddock. However far they travel, one thing is certain—where there are loons, there is water.

Conservation Pressures

It is not surprising, given the loon's need for solitude during the breeding season, that human disturbance is the greatest threat to the bird today. Increasingly, lakes in the southern parts of its range are being opened up for recreation. Fishing and water sports cause

For the first two or three weeks after hatching, the tiny chicks of the common loon often ride on their parents' backs for safety.

An adult common loon offers a fish to its four-day-old chick on Bow Lake, New Hampshire. Food like this is presented whole and not regurgitated. The young are usually weaned by 11 weeks. Sexual maturity is reached after two years.

enough disturbance for a pair to abandon a lake, and even irregularly occupied lakefront cabins are sufficient to lead to desertion. As people use lakes more, so also do the gulls, crows, and mammals such as raccoons that live alongside humans. All of these predators may take the eggs and chicks of loons.

Loons are also affected by pollution, both on their breeding lakes and at sea. Heavy industries release sulfates into the atmosphere that gather moisture from the air and fall as acid rain. Not only does this damage lakeshore vegetation, it also has a major effect on food chains within the lakes themselves. As the quantity of algae, plankton, insects, and fish are reduced, the amount of food available to loons declines, too. Heavy metals from industry also cause problems for loons because they are high predators in the food chain. Elements such as mercury dissolve in water and accumulate in the gills of fish. Over time, as loons eat more fish, they build up lethal levels of mercury in their own bodies. By examining the feathers of loons, scientists can calculate the levels of mercury in lakes. And because the mercury remains in the feathers even after death, they are able to figure out how much mercury was in a lake decades ago.

At sea loons are more at risk from oil pollution than most birds. Their tendency to stay on the water close to the coast, diving continuously, makes them especially vulnerable. Once they are coated in oil, they are unable to use their feathers to regulate their body temperature, or they die from ingesting the oil when they try to preen their feathers. Loons are also prone to getting trapped and drowned in fishing nets—that is probably the biggest cause of death outside the breeding season.

A Popular Emblem

The common loon has featured in the everyday life of Canadians for a number of years. In the late 1980s the Canadian government decided to issue a dollar coin for the first time in more than 50 years. On one side it chose to depict a loon, one of the country's most distinctive birds. The coin soon became known affectionately as "the loonie." The loon is also the state bird of Minnesota, a lake-rich state with a big breeding population of loons.

American Bittern

Botauris lentiginosus

Common name American bittern

Scientific name *Botauris lentiginosus*

Family Ardeidae

Order Ciconiiformes

Size Length: 23.5–33.5 in (60–85 cm); wingspan: 41–49 in (105–125 cm); weight: 13–20 oz (0.4–0.6 kg)

Key features Thickset, medium-sized, streaky brown heron; small yellow bill; juvenile lacks the black line behind the eye broadening to a patch running down neck; sexes identical

Habits Solitary; normally secretive but occasionally seen stalking prey in open fields

Nesting Platform of vegetation in dense marsh cover; 3–5 eggs (exceptionally 2–7); incubation 28–29 days; young fledge after 14 days; 1 brood

Voice Male gives booming call in breeding season; alarm call is "kok-kok-kok"

Diet Very wide: fish, amphibians, snakes, small mammals, crawfish, mollusks, and insects

Habitat Marshes, bogs, open meadows; mangroves, and swamps outside breeding season

Distribution North and central U.S. states and southern Canada; also southern U.S., Central America, and Caribbean

Status Not globally threatened but declining throughout breeding range; declared as threatened or endangered in many U.S. states and Canadian provinces

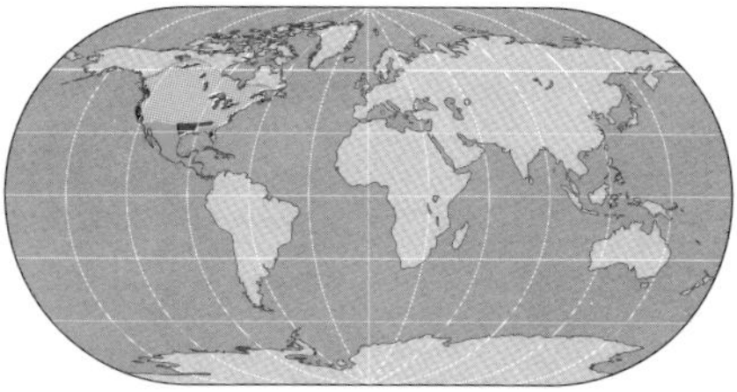

Bitterns are experts at concealment. Often hidden in the depths of a marsh, their camouflaged plumage makes them doubly difficult to see.

When it stands perfectly still among the rushes or cattails of a marsh, the American bittern blends in perfectly with its surroundings. Variable shades of brown on its upper parts contrast with heavy black streaks down its neck, becoming buff-colored on the belly. The brown-black mix can be indistinguishable from the surrounding dead vegetation. When the bittern flies on its broad but pointed wings, the dark flight feathers are conspicuous.

Active Hunter

The American bittern spends much of its time in marshes, although it is unique among the larger bitterns in looking for food in open meadows and dry grasslands, too. It stands in water or on a bank with its thin, pointed bill held low, waiting to strike at prey below. Now and then it takes very slow, measured steps forward. It usually hunts fish, but it will take anything that comes close enough. Sometimes it picks insects off plant stems or catches them in the air. The American bittern is undoubtedly more active in its feeding techniques than the other large bitterns—when hunting in tall grass on land, the bird often runs quickly after prey with its wings held up.

Booming Call

At the beginning of the breeding season the male produces an extraordinary booming call that advertises his territory and attracts a mate. Crouching on a perch, the male inflates his esophagus so that it acts like a giant wind pump, expelling a loud, booming belch. It has resulted in the bittern gaining such names as "thunder pumper," "bog bull," and "mire

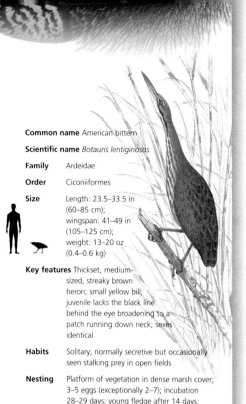

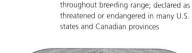

drum." He makes the sound several times at intervals of several seconds and utters it more and more often until the birds have mated.

Bitterns conceal their nests within dense cover, usually tucked into vegetation on a marsh, but occasionally in tall grasses on land. It is likely that the male chooses the nest site, and thereafter the female assumes all the duties. She shapes reeds, rushes, and other plants into a nest platform on which she lays her brownish eggs. After incubation she feeds the yellow chicks by regurgitating food she has brought back to the nest.

Birds in southern parts of the range remain largely where they are after breeding, but those from the northern U.S. and Canada prepare to migrate south for the winter, flying at night with fast wingbeats, on huge journeys into the Caribbean and Central America. Saltwater coastal marshes, mangrove, cattail, and sawgrass swamps are all favored winter habitats. Some lose their direction or get carried by winds, and American bitterns have been known to land as far away as Norway.

Bittern Numbers

The bittern's ability to remain hidden in tall vegetation can work against it. Although bitterns are widespread, conservationists are unable to ascertain exact numbers. But evidence suggests that since the Second World War the destruction of its wetland habitats has been catastrophic. Surveys estimate that throughout North America bittern numbers have more than halved. Many wetlands have been drained to make way for agriculture or development. Others have become polluted by chemicals from farm fields or have been damaged by uncontrolled grazing by livestock. Many more have simply silted up and become unsuitable. Conservationists are working to restore and recreate the bittern's habitat.

⇩ A solitary hunter, the American bittern feeds at dawn, dusk, and at night. This one, wading through the shallows on Long Island, New York, has caught a fish. Crawfish, salamanders, gophers, ground squirrels, and garter snakes are also items on the bittern's wide diet.

Greater Flamingo

Phoenicopterus ruber

The greater flamingo is the largest member of the flamingo family. Some observers have described them as grotesque, but to many they are graceful and attractive birds, with their long, elegant necks and legs, pink plumage, and crimson, black-edged wings.

Common name Greater flamingo

Scientific name *Phoenicopterus ruber* (Old World form *P. r. roseus*; New World form *P. r. ruber*)

Family Phoenicopteridae

Order Ciconiiformes

Size Length: 49–57 in (125–145 cm); wingspan: 55–65 in (140–165 cm); weight: 4.6–9 lb (2.1–4.1 kg)

Key features (*P. r. roseus*): Overall pale pink with pink legs and a red-pink, downcurved bill tipped with black; wing-coverts crimson; flight feathers black. (*P. r. ruber*): Much redder plumage; bill orange-pink and black, with a yellowish base

Habits Highly social species rarely, if ever, seen alone

Nesting Nest a low mound of mud or sand; 1 egg (rarely 2); incubation 28–31 days; young fledge after about 75 days; 1 brood

Voice Loud, gooselike honking call

Diet Feeds by filtering small invertebrates and plant matter from mud; food includes insects, mollusks, and crustaceans

Habitat Shallow lagoons, saltpans, and tidal mudflats

Distribution In Old World in parts of southern Europe, Africa, Middle East, and India; in New World in Galápagos, Central America, Caribbean islands, and northern South America

Status Not globally threatened

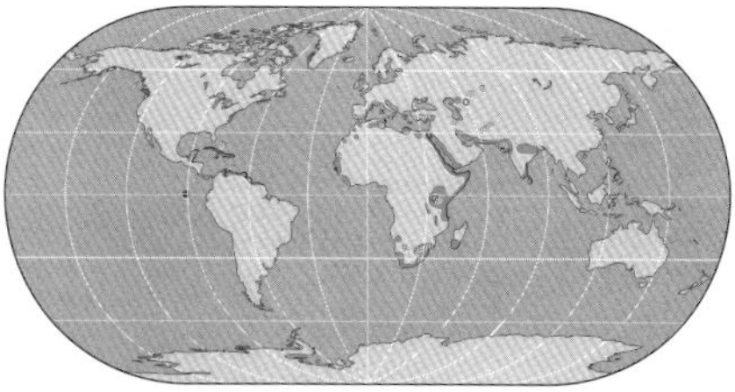

There are two geographically distinct forms of the greater flamingo: one occurring in the Old World (referred to as the greater flamingo) and the other found in the New World and known as the Caribbean flamingo. Together the two forms are the most widespread and the second most numerous of all the world's flamingos, with a population of between 500,000 and 600,000. (The most numerous flamingo is the lesser flamingo, *Phoeniconaias minor.*)

Inhospitable Habitats

The greater flamingo is found in tropical, subtropical, and mild temperate regions. In its Old World form it can be found in the southern parts of Europe, the Middle East, India, and Africa. The New World Caribbean flamingo can be found in a number of locations from the Galápagos to the Yucatán Peninsula, the north coast of South America, and in the Caribbean itself, with birds present on a number of islands (including the Bahamas and Cuba).

Across this wide range greater flamingos make their home in shallow lagoons, saltpans, and tidal mudflats. They can be found inland, but they are more commonly found on the coast and require saline or alkaline waters of less than 3 feet (1 m) in depth. They also need sufficient space to accommodate their large numbers, and ideally without too much interference from other species. The greater flamingos' unusual physiology, anatomy, and behavior enable them to make the most of these outwardly inhospitable places.

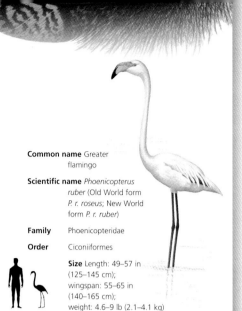

Upside-down Feeders

The flamingo's method of feeding and peculiar bill are among its many interesting features. Groups of birds pace the shallow water with heads held upside down. Then they move their bills in a scythelike motion, collecting water and silt. Occasionally they use their webbed feet to stir up the sediment. With their powerful tongue acting like a piston, they first draw water and silt into the beak and then force it out under pressure three or four times a second. As it is forced out, the water passes through special comblike filtering devices, called lamellae, that retain the small insects, mollusks, and crustaceans the bird eats.

To find suitable feeding spots, the birds might wander some distance from their roosting and breeding sites. In one Spanish colony flights of up to 100 miles (160 km) have been recorded.

Erratic Breeding

The breeding performance of the greater flamingo can be quite erratic. In some years the birds might not breed at all; in others they may do poorly and then have a "bumper" year. For instance, in a study in the Camargue, France, the birds bred every year from 1947 to 1963 then ceased for five years. Various reasons for this have been suggested, such as combinations of climate (particularly the apparent need for abundant rainfall prior to breeding), animal disturbance, and interference by humans.

The breeding season is signaled by an increase in intensity of the birds' fascinating social displays. During this special time groups of 15 to 30 simultaneously perform and repeat a series of stylized movements throughout the day. The series consists of a number of key movements. With neck held high and bills pointing skyward, the birds move their heads from side to side rhythmically while giving out short calls. This is commonly known as the head flag display. The dramatic wing salute display may follow, with the birds stretching their wings while raising their tails and extending their necks forward. Finally the birds may perform a twist preen, turning their heads toward their wings in a fake preening action.

The most intensive periods of display, which on average last from a few days up to a couple of weeks, coincide with male and

↓ ***Like all flamingos, the greater flamingo is highly social, with feeding, roosting, and nesting performed in large flocks numbering thousands or even tens of thousands of birds. This gathering on Lake Nakuru, Kenya, consists of both greater and lesser flamingos.***

female birds pairing together. Once pairs are chosen, the female flamingo leads the male away from the group and, with head forward and wings spread, signals for the male to mate.

Nest building is carried out by both sexes using the limited resources. The birds scoop together clay or sand—mixed with materials like stones if available—to form, layer by layer, a low mound. Those made of clay can reach up to 16 inches (40 cm) in height. In the hot sun they soon bake into a solid structure. Mounds made of less stable sand are lower, reaching only 6 inches (15 cm) in height. When they are nearly complete, the birds make a shallow basin on the top of the mound into which the egg is laid. During incubation the birds constantly add to their mound to keep it in prime condition.

Female flamingos normally lay only one egg. Occasionally they lay two, but it is rare for both to hatch. The eggs are oval in shape and slightly off-white, although they soon become discolored in the muddy nests. Sometimes eggs will accidentally roll out of the nests. When this

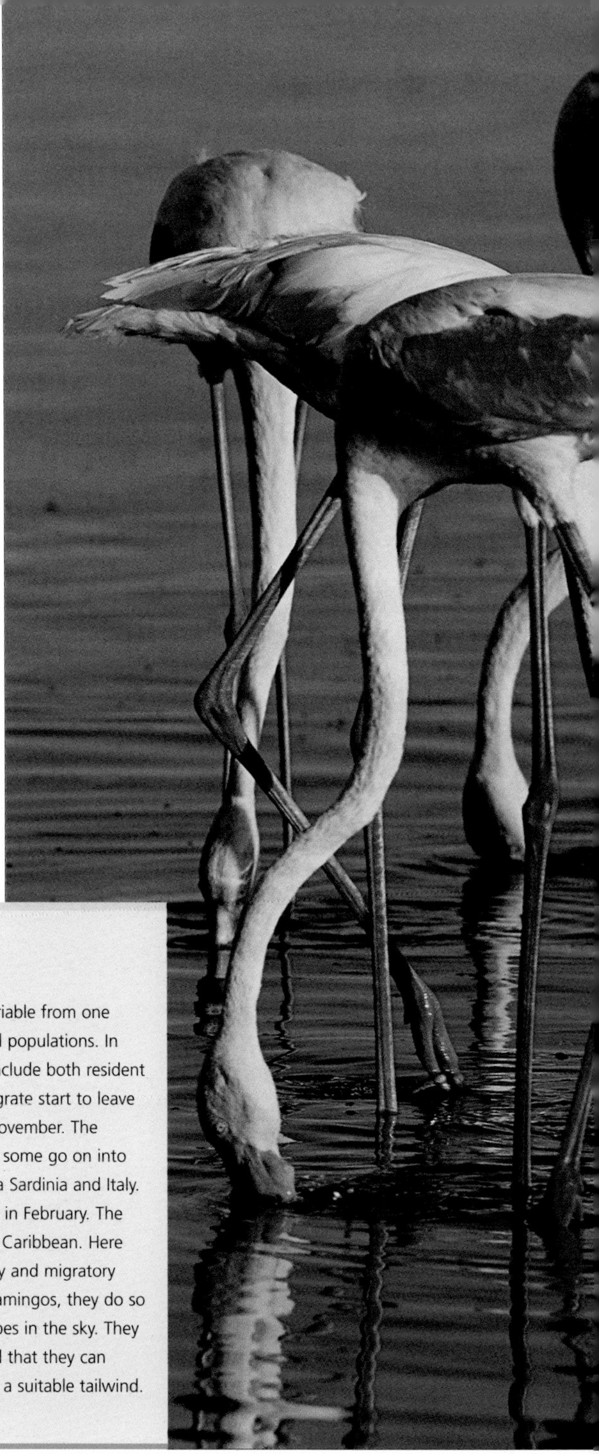

Feeding flamingos move through the water with their heads held upside down, sucking in water and filtering out tiny aquatic invertebrates to eat.

Flamingo Movements

The movements of flamingos are extremely variable from one location to the next and also within individual populations. In western Europe the flamingos of the Camargue include both resident birds as well as those that migrate. Those that migrate start to leave the area in September and continue through to November. The majority follow the coast southwest to Spain, and some go on into Algeria. Others winter in Tunisia, possibly flying via Sardinia and Italy. Here they remain until returning to the Camargue in February. The situation is similar thousands of miles away in the Caribbean. Here again, each population will contain both sedentary and migratory birds. When flying, like most activities involving flamingos, they do so in groups—in this instance forming distinct V-shapes in the sky. They move by day and night, and it has been estimated that they can travel at around 35 miles per hour (56 km/h) with a suitable tailwind.

happens, the birds make no attempt to rescue the egg. However, if the egg is lost early during incubation, the female may re-lay.

Once the egg is laid, both parents share the task of incubation. They occasionally turn the egg gently to ensure even heat distribution and to prevent the embryo sticking to the eggshell. When ready to hatch, the chick uses its egg tooth to chip its way out of the shell. Hatching can take between 24 and 36 hours. Once free from the shell, the chick is gently preened by its parents.

Flamingo chicks are gray-white in color and covered in soft down with straight beaks and short legs. They are not very mobile soon after hatching and are dependent on their parents. During their early weeks they are fed a special substance produced by their parents. It provides the chick with the necessary initial proteins and vitamins for growing feathers and bones, as well as carbohydrates and fat for energy.

Once the chick is out of the nest, the parents are extremely attentive toward it, guarding a space around it from unwelcome attention. After a week the chick will join a communal crèche with groups of other young birds. For a while its own parents, who recognize it by both sight and call, will tend to it. Later, parental attention wanes, and the young birds are increasingly left to fend for themselves. Amusingly, some young birds have been observed searching for their parents by nudging dozing adults in the hope of prompting a recognizable call in response. Typically, the birds will spend around 100 days in their crèche before becoming completely independent.

From independence to the age of two the birds are gray-white in color with hints of pink. From two years they develop adult plumage and can breed. Flamingos are quite long-lived birds and can survive three or more decades.

Stable yet Vulnerable

When seen in huge flocks, it is difficult to imagine that the greater flamingo might be a vulnerable species. Indeed, overall the population is currently stable and in some places actually increasing. However, while individual flocks may be huge, colonies are relatively few in number due to the bird's quite unusual habitat requirements. And any bird whose population is concentrated in a small number of sites is potentially vulnerable.

In some places the birds' preference for coastal locations can bring them into conflict with people. Here there is great pressure for tourist development, and with this development comes land drainage and direct disturbance. In other places the locations they choose are valuable economically due to their natural resources. The increasing demand for salt over the past hundred years (for the industrial use of sodium chloride and for spreading on roads in winter) has also led to pressure on birds that make homes in saltpans.

Pretty in Pink!

Birds obtain their color in two ways. First, the structure of their feathers scatters light and gives a variety of impressive iridescent effects. Starlings do this and look quite impressive in the breeding season. Second, they can manufacture the colors themselves chemically to create what are called pigmentary colors. The commonest pigment is melanin. It occurs in black, brown, red, brown, or even yellow and makes blackbirds black and yellow wagtails yellow, for example.

Another important set of color chemicals are called carotenoids (named after the chemicals in carrots). Carotenoids make the flamingo pink. They are entirely derived from the food the birds eat, especially blue-green algae and some aquatic invertebrates. Without access to carotenoid-rich food flamingos lose their color—a problem well known among those who have kept flamingos in captivity.

Until their own bills develop, young greater flamingo chicks are fed a special substance secreted by the parents' upper digestive tract. This substance resembles human milk.

Phoenix and Flamingo Tongue

Beautiful and at the same time bizarre, flamingos have long attracted human attention. Indeed, they were depicted in ancient cave paintings and among Christians became linked to the mythical Phoenix—the crimson-red, immortal bird born from its own ashes, a potent symbol of death and resurrection.

Flamingos have also been prized as a source of food. Thousands were killed by Romans, who valued their tongues as a delicacy. Both eggs and young birds have also been eaten throughout history. While this practice has now largely stopped in Europe, birds in India and North Africa still face pressure.

Flamingos are also prize exhibits in zoos. Initially birds were taken repeatedly from the wild to replace zoo stocks, since the captive birds would not breed. However, once it was discovered that the birds' natural diet was crucial to breeding success, zoos simply needed to feed the correct diet to ensure the birds would reproduce in captivity.

Not unsurprisingly, flamingos also found their way into art and popular culture with countless "Pink Flamingo" bars and nightclubs using the name and images of the bird to add some exotica to their surroundings. The flamingo even made an appearance as croquet sticks in Lewis Carroll's book *Alice's Adventures in Wonderland*!

However, with ingenuity and foresight problems can be overcome, and flamingos have been part of some pioneering conservation projects. In Bonaire in the Caribbean in the early 1960s salt production threatened the local Caribbean flamingo population. Local conservationists worked with the salt company, and after protracted negotiations it was agreed to set up a 138-acre (55-ha) nature reserve in the middle of the saltworks. Interestingly, while the reserve proved successful and attracted breeding birds, the loss of surrounding feeding areas means that the flamingos have to fly to nearby Venezuela for food!

Wood Duck

Aix sponsa

Common name Wood duck

Scientific name *Aix sponsa*

Family Anatidae

Order Anseriformes

Size Length: 17–20 in (43–51 cm); wingspan: 29.5 in (75 cm); weight: 1–2 lb (0.5–0.9 kg)

Key features Medium-sized, compact duck; male very colorful with blue-green head; patches of gold, reddish-brown, orange, and white on neck and body, generally separated by white lines; female dull brownish-gray, body spotted

Habits Forages on land and water; dabbles and upends in water

Nesting Nests in tree holes; 9–15 eggs; incubation 30 days; young fledge after 60 days; 1, sometimes 2, broods

Voice Soft, high-pitched squeals emitted by both sexes

Diet Seeds, nuts, fruits, and aquatic plants; also insects and other invertebrates

Habitat Rivers, lakes, pools, and swamps surrounded by dense forest

Distribution Found in southern Canada, U.S., Cuba, and Mexico

Status Conservation measures begun in early 20th century led to species becoming common and widespread once more

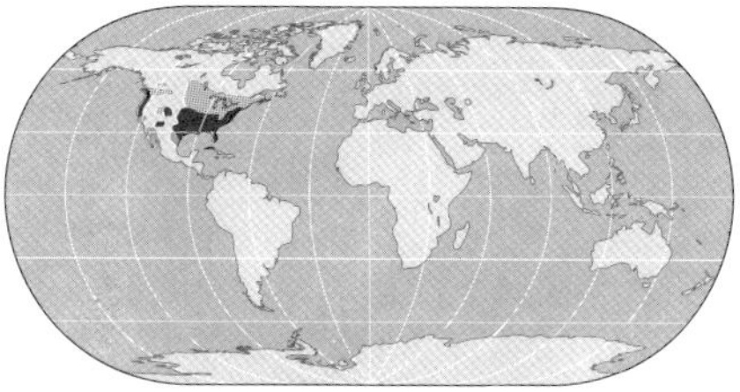

It is hard to believe that one of North America's most colorful and common ducks was once driven to the brink of extinction. Happily, conservationists have brought about an astonishing transformation in the fortunes of the wood duck.

THE WOOD DUCK'S SCIENTIFIC NAME *Aix sponsa* means "waterbird in bridal dress," and it is an apt description of the male's striking plumage! The sleek crest and neat white markings divide the bold patches of color on the head, neck, body, and wings of the male. The female is mostly grayish-brown, with spots on her breast and flanks, but she has a distinctive, teardrop-shaped, white eye patch. Wood ducks, and the closely related mandarin ducks, have claws on the toes of their webbed feet; both species are perching ducks, perfectly able to grip the branch of a tree.

Woodland Feeder

The wood duck is a bird of the forests, occupying beaver ponds, slow-moving river

backwaters, and other inland freshwater wetlands surrounded by deciduous trees. In fall and winter it regularly forages on land for acorns and the seeds of hickory, sweet gum, buttonbush, arrow-arum, bur reed, and wild rice. Wood ducks never venture far from water, however, and by the time spring arrives, they are dabbling in shallow water most of the time for insects and other invertebrates.

Tree Nesters

The birds pair and mate in early spring. The female selects a high tree hole—often one excavated by a woodpecker. In many habitats large trees with suitable holes are in short supply, and conservationists have long provided nestboxes on wildlife preserves for the birds.

Unlike most ducks, the male stays with the female while she nests but leaves once the eggs hatch. Not that the young stay in the nest for long. Within 24 hours the downy chicks use their tiny claws to climb out of the tree hole and drop to the ground to seek water, with their mother acting as protector and teacher. For their first few weeks the young feed mainly on insects and tiny fish, but by six weeks they begin to eat pondweed, algae, and other plants. Less than three weeks later the young ducklings are independent.

For more than 50 years human nestbox providers were baffled by the fact that the nestboxes were frequently used simultaneously by more than one duck! Other females would "dump nest"—lay their eggs in the same nest as the "official" occupant. Finding as many as 30 eggs in her nest, the rightful occupant would then usually desert. In the 1990s it was discovered that older ducks were being followed to highly visible nests by yearlings, which were simply imitating the older birds' actions. When the nestboxes were made harder to spot—as nest sites would be in the wild—dump nesting (also known as brood parasitism) fell dramatically, normal brooding behavior resumed, and chick numbers soared.

Wood ducks molt at the end of the breeding season—the male molts earlier, while the female waits until the arduous task of raising her young is over. Wood ducks breeding in Canada and northern U.S. states then usually migrate to the southern U.S. and Mexico to escape harsh winters. Birds in central states may not migrate at all in mild winters; those in states such as Georgia are resident all year long.

Hunting and forest clearance in the late nineteenth and early twentieth centuries led to the wood duck virtually disappearing from much of North America by the 1920s. However, restrictions on hunting and better management of forested wetlands saw numbers recover, and the population today is healthy at around 1.5 million birds. Below are a female (left) and a male (right).

Belted Kingfisher

Megaceryle alcyon

Common name Belted kingfisher

Scientific name *Megaceryle alcyon*

Family Alcedinidae

Order Coraciiformes

Size Length: 11–13 in (28–33 cm); wingspan: 20–27 in (51–68 cm); weight: 4–6.3 oz (113–178 g)

Key features Thickset with large head and ragged crest; huge, daggerlike beak; gray with white underparts; both sexes have gray chest belt, but female has red band on belly

Habits Spends most time perching, waiting for prey; dives into water for fish

Nesting Digs tunnel holes in banks; usually 6–7 eggs; incubation 24 days; young fledge after 42 days; 1 brood

Voice Loud, rattling calls given by both sexes

Diet Mainly fish, but also opportunistic—feeding on amphibians, insects, small mammals, and birds

Habitat Common around lakes, ponds, rivers, streams, and estuaries

Distribution Found throughout North America; also in Central America, Caribbean, and northern Colombia

Status Not globally threatened; widespread and common in many areas

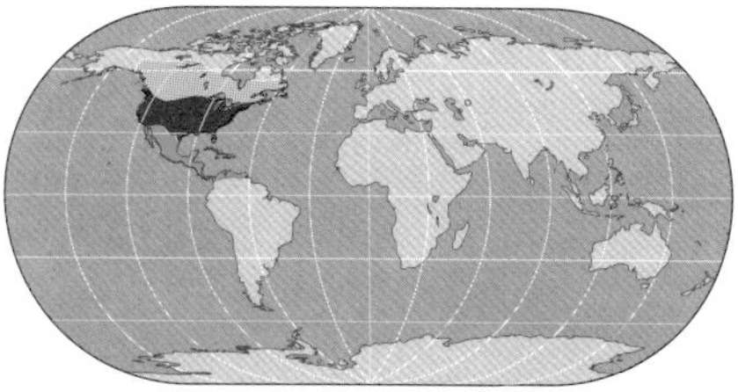

Perched almost motionless for hours at a time on a branch overhanging water, the belted kingfisher gets its reward with a quick and usually successful dive when a fish swims past. Its efficiency in hunting, coupled with an ability to colonize almost any fish-supporting water, mean that this bird is common throughout North America.

The belted kingfisher is definitely a heavyweight in the kingfisher world. Its big, shaggy crest gives it a somewhat disreputable appearance. The bird's large head is set on top of a thick neck, and the body is bulky, too. Its legs are short, but thick and fairly powerful. However, the tail is a surprise in a bird of this shape—it is relatively thin, barred, and pointed.

At rest the male and female are easy to tell apart. Both have a gray head and upper parts and a white collar and belly; but while the male has a gray band across the breast, the female has, in addition, a thin red band just below that runs down the flanks. This is one of the few bird species in which the female is more colorful

(→) A male belted kingfisher about to enter the nest hole. The breeding distribution of the bird seems to be limited only by the availability of nest sites. Birds become sexually mature in their first year.

(↓) A pair of belted kingfishers in customary pose over water. The female, on the left, is distinguished by the red band of plumage just below her breast.

than the male. It is possible to differentiate juvenile birds, too; young of both sexes have a tawny brown-spotted band instead of gray, but the female also has, on either side, the first signs of the red band underneath that will eventually meet in the middle.

Wide Choice of Habitats

Belted kingfishers can take advantage of most waters. They are found everywhere from sea level to 6,560 feet (2,500 m) up in the Rockies; they live in mangrove swamps, fast mountain streams, large, slow rivers—they even fish in backyard ponds! They can hunt up to 0.6 miles (1 km) off the shores of lakes or the sea. Such an ability enables belted kingfishers to occupy far more coastal waters than if they were restricted to hunting from a perch. And in the dry, sandy riverbeds of Arizona they are adept at catching lizards and spiders.

Fishy Offerings

In spring the male establishes his territory along a river or around a lake. At the sight or sound of an intruder he raises his crest, rocks his body, and gives a loud, rattling call of warning. He chases rivals away; and once he has formed a pair

with a female, she will join him in harrying away intruders, too.

Courtship of the female involves the presentation of a fishy gift. The female flies into the male's territory; and when the male returns to his perch with a fish, the female flies up to him and sits on the same branch. They shuffle toward each other until they are close enough for the male to offer the fish. She takes it unhesitatingly and promptly swallows it.

Once the birds have mated, they indulge in an aerial display, with the female flying close behind the male as he flies up into the sky. Even after the female has returned to her perch, the male continues his aerobatics, spiraling high, plummeting down, and then banking into a glide.

A well-drained earth bank beside a river is an ideal nest site, but belted kingfishers are remarkably unfussy. They willingly use human-excavated road cuttings, banks in gravel, or sandpits. Even a beaver mud slide will do. The male pecks at the "cliff face," and the female responds by calling from a perch nearby.

How to Catch Fish

Kingfishers rely on good eyesight to spot their prey. Belted kingfishers have good color vision and can see near-ultraviolet light. This probably enables them to avoid glare on the surface of the water. They also need clear water for good visibility. If the water is muddy or turbulent after rain, they may leave the area altogether.

The bird has two hunting strategies. It usually perches on a branch over water and remains there motionless but for slight movements as it turns its head to focus on any fish moving around. It can be a long wait. One study found that belted kingfishers spent 98 percent of their time perching. Alternatively, birds hover over water, sometimes as much as 50 feet (15 m) above, beating their wings rapidly to maintain position. At the moment the bird dives, it pulls the wings into the body, making it streamlined. When the kingfisher hits the water, the wings spread out to act as a brake. Most fish are caught near the surface. If the bird goes underwater, it pulls down a transparent third eyelid to protect the eyes and improve visibility.

The prey is held firmly in the beak, but not swallowed, as the kingfisher flies back to its perch. Usually, the fish is still alive, so the kingfisher juggles it until it is holding the tail, then it smashes the fish's head repeatedly against its perch. Not only does this stun or kill the fish, but it also breaks the bones and protective scales that might otherwise harm the kingfisher when it swallows the prey. Having done this, the kingfisher eats the fish headfirst.

A belted kingfisher and prey. The kingfisher aims to catch the fish about a third of the way down its body before returning to a perch to eat it.

Eventually she helps with the digging, although the male does about twice as much work. The bill is used like a pickax; and once they start excavating the tunnel, they use their feet to kick out the soil behind them. They dig a tunnel over 3 feet (1 m) long, with a lip in front of the egg chamber to keep the eggs from rolling out.

The nest is usually about 1 foot (0.3 m) from the top of the bank. That reduces the threat of flooding and lessens the risk of the young being taken by predators such as skunks. The pair take turns incubating the eggs, which are pure white, like those of all kingfishers. There is very little light in the nest chamber, and white eggs are easier to see and therefore less likely to get stepped on. The adults need to fish almost continuously once the eggs hatch, for in time the young will need up to ten fish a day.

After 20 days the young have developed all their adult feathers and reached their adult body weight. For the next three or four days their parents feed them less and less. Eventually the adults sit outside the nest with fish in their beaks, calling the young to leave the nest.

At first the adults teach them to catch food by dropping dead fish onto the surface of the water. Within a week the young have learned to catch their first fish, although their parents continue to feed them for a couple of weeks.

Heading for the sun

In the fall millions of kingfishers from Alaska, Canada, and the northern U.S. escape the freezing winter by flying south to the warmer lands of Texas, Florida, and other U.S. states, and further still to Central America and the West Indies. Migrating kingfishers move from wetland to wetland, so it is not unusual to see large numbers along the shores of big lakes and along the ocean seaboards. On Lake Michigan alone, 12 kingfishers per hour have been counted heading south in the fall.

Kingfishers and Humans

The modern world has treated the belted kingfisher comparatively well. The persecution the birds faced at fish farms in the early twentieth century has virtually disappeared, partly as a result of protective legislation and partly because scientific evidence has shown that the birds caused much smaller losses of fish than originally thought. The risks to kingfishers from water pollution are largely unknown, however. A study of industrial chemical pollution in Wisconsin found that kingfishers were building up high levels of toxins in their bodies, but the results were inconclusive as to whether the birds were adversely affected. The excavation of sand and gravel for the construction industry has affected kingfishers significantly, however. It has resulted in a proliferation of lakes that have boosted kingfishers in terms of both range and population.

As the kingfishers approach fledging, the parents leave food at the entrance hole. The young race down the tunnel to be first to the feast.

Osprey

Pandion haliaetus

The spectacular hunting style of the fish-catching osprey makes it one of the most recognizable of all birds of prey throughout its huge, almost global range.

Common name Osprey

Scientific name *Pandion haliaetus*

Family Pandionidae

Order Falconiformes

Size Length: 22–23 in (56–58.5 cm); wingspan: 57–67 in (145–170 cm); weight: 2.6–4.3 lb (1.2–2 kg); female slightly larger than male

Key features Long, narrow wings; dark-brown upper parts and mainly white underparts with dark-speckled breast band; white head with dark-brown stripe through yellow eye; black hooked bill; blue-gray legs; sexes identical; immature paler

Habits Hunts alone over shallow water; spends much time perched near water

Nesting Large, isolated nest of sticks and grasses, usually in top of tall tree near water; season varies with region; usually 2–3 eggs; incubation 35–43 days; young fledge after 44–59 days; 1 brood

Voice Loud yelping call; shrill "pyew-pyew-pyew" during territorial display

Diet Mainly live fish snatched from just below surface of water, plus a few frogs, snakes, and small birds

Habitat Coasts, estuaries, rivers, lakes, and swamps

Distribution Breeds virtually worldwide except South America, polar regions, deserts, and much of Africa; breeding birds from North America and northern Eurasia winter in warm-temperate and tropical zones

Status Badly affected by pesticide poisoning during 1960s and 1970s, but now flourishing throughout most of its range

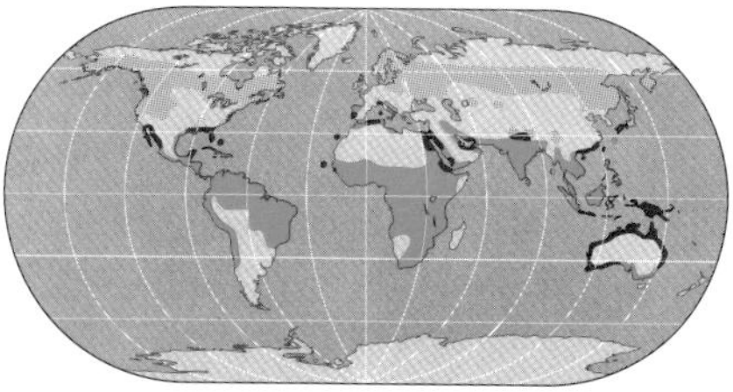

THE DISTINCTIVE BROWN-AND-WHITE osprey is a fish hunter. It is so highly specialized that it is classified in a family on its own. Other birds of prey catch fish, but the osprey has acquired a unique combination of adaptations that make it the most widespread and successful of its kind.

The osprey has oily, water-resistant plumage allowing it to plunge underwater to catch its prey, then surface and fly off without difficulty. It can close its nostrils as it dives to prevent water being forced into its lungs. The bird has extremely strong feet to absorb the impact of the dive, reversible outer toes, and long, curved talons. It also has a long, hooked bill as well as a variety of unusual internal features not seen in other birds of prey.

Adaptable Hunter

Ospreys may live in almost any habitat that offers regular supplies of medium-sized fish, from tropical swamps and coastal lagoons to the cold rivers and lakes of the northern forests. They are most numerous in rich, remote coastal habitats such as saltmarshes and mangrove swamps. However, they are unusually tolerant of human activity and are often seen fishing in suburban reservoirs and rivers flowing through

(↓) The osprey skewers its prey with long, curved talons. The soles of the feet are covered in sharp, spiny scales that help prevent the slippery prize from being dropped while being carried back to the feeding perch.

towns. They will even nest in such places, sometimes using man-made nesting platforms provided for the purpose. The willingness to exploit artificial habitats can cause conflicts with humans, however, for they may raid fish farms used for rearing trout or salmon.

Ospreys that breed in the tropics and around the coasts of Australia stay on or near their breeding grounds all year. During the northern winter the tropical residents are joined by birds that have migrated from North America, northern Europe, Scandinavia, Russia, and Siberia. The migrants breed in the north, mainly on the broad rivers and lakes of the great evergreen forests, and then fly south before their feeding waters freeze over. They fly strongly, covering distances of 2,500 to 6,000 miles (4,025–9,650 km). Unlike many birds of prey, they fly directly toward their destinations without making detours to avoid deserts or deep seas. Therefore, they do not gather in large numbers at favored crossing points like Panama, and it is unusual to see more than one or two ospreys together on migration.

Whether it is on its breeding territory, its wintering grounds, or on migration between the two, an osprey usually hunts in the same way. Cruising some 30–100 feet (9–30 m) above the water, it pauses to hover with its head bent down and legs dangling, searching for a fish just below the surface. If the bird sees a likely prey, it may descend to get a better view before diving headfirst with half-folded wings. Just before the osprey hits the water, it throws its feet forward with talons outspread to seize the fish. Its whole body may disappear

An osprey may take almost any medium-sized fish, depending on what is locally available, up to a weight of about 3 pounds (1.4 kg).

Display Flights

A male osprey usually returns to the breeding site before the female. As soon as he arrives, he stakes his claim with a spectacular switchback display flight, fluttering, wheeling, and diving high over the site, with shrill, whistling calls. When a female arrives, she is attracted by the display and joins him in the performance to strengthen the bond between them.

This type of display flight is common among birds of prey, particularly larger species such as eagles and harriers. In some cases the female flips onto her back in midair so the male can seize her by the talons. Locked together, the pair spiral slowly toward the ground before releasing their grip and flying up again.

underwater with a loud splash, leaving just the wings visible, but it soon struggles free, shakes the water from its feathers, and carries its struggling catch away in its talons, holding it headfirst to reduce wind resistance.

If the fish is too heavy to carry away, the osprey simply drops it, but sometimes the bird's talons are so deeply embedded that it cannot release its grip. Then the weight of the fish may drag its attacker back into the water, and ospreys have been drowned on such occasions.

Big Nests

A typical osprey nest is a big, broad pile of sticks and flotsam lined with soft grass and moss, securely wedged in the crown of a tall tree such as a fir, although the birds will also

nest on cliffs, ruined buildings, artificial platforms, aerials, and even poles supporting electricity lines.

The female usually carries out most of the five-week incubation, while the male keeps her supplied with fish. He also brings food for the chicks when they hatch and keeps the whole family fed until the chicks are fledged. As soon as they can fly, the young ospreys start fishing for themselves, but it takes them weeks, even months, to become as skilled as their parents. Most young ospreys breed in their fourth year.

Brighter Future

Since ospreys build such big, conspicuous nests, they make easy targets for hunters and egg thieves, and in the past they have suffered badly from persecution. As recently as the mid-nineteenth century they bred all over Europe, but within a century shooting and nest destruction had eliminated the breeding populations from nearly all of Europe west of the Black Sea. Then the survivors were hit by a new threat: poisoning by agricultural pesticides.

The worst effects of it were seen in the northeastern U.S., where chemicals draining into waterways and lakes contaminated the fish taken by ospreys as prey. The birds accumulated the poison in their bodies and either died or failed to breed. By the 1970s they were in serious decline; but when the offending chemicals were outlawed in North America and Europe, the situation began to improve. Today osprey populations are recovering strongly in the U.S., and they are also doing well in northern Europe, thanks partly to birds being reintroduced to regions where they were once common. In Scotland, for example, ospreys became extinct in 1902, but a reintroduction plan has now created a viable breeding population of more than 80 pairs.

Each pair of ospreys returns to the same site year after year, renovating the old nest and adding more material, so it grows bigger and bigger. Eventually the nest can become so huge that it collapses, and the birds have to begin again on a new site.

Mated for Life

Like many large birds of prey, ospreys often stay faithful to their partners for life. At the end of the breeding season the birds leave the nest and go their separate ways. When the time comes to mate again, the ospreys instinctively return to the same area. Unless one of the original pair has died, they both come back to the isolated nest, get reacquainted, and start another family.

However, some birds returning to the breeding area have never mated before. If one of a pair fails to arrive, the survivor may mate with one of the unattached birds and rear a brood of chicks in the old nest. If neither of the original breeders returns, a new pair may take over the nest, repair it, and use it themselves for the next few years. The same nest may be reoccupied every year for decades or even centuries.

A juvenile osprey calling. The pale undersides act as camouflage to help the bird conceal itself from prey as it swoops over the surface of the water.

Bald Eagle

Haliaeetus leucocephalus

Common name Bald eagle

Scientific name *Haliaeetus leucocephalus*

Family Accipitridae

Order Falconiformes

Size Length: 28–38 in (71–96.5 cm); wingspan: 66–96 in (168–244 cm); weight: 6.6–13.9 lb (3–6.3 kg); female larger than male; northern race *washingtoniensis* larger than southern race *leucocephalus*

Key features Large eagle with powerful yellow bill; yellow eyes and legs; white head and tail; dark-brown body and wings; sexes identical except for size; juvenile mottled white with dark bill and eye

Habits Normally seen singly or in pairs, but gathers in larger numbers to exploit rich food sources

Nesting Large stick nest, usually in a conifer tree or on a cliff 30–60 ft (9–18 m) above the ground; reused and added to each year; nests in summer in north, winter in south; usually 2 eggs; incubation 34–36 days; young fledge after 70–92 days; 1 brood

Voice A squeaky cackle

Diet Mainly fish; also ducks, rabbits, rodents, turtles, snakes, and carrion

Habitat Usually near open water in all kinds of terrain ranging from cold conifer forest to hot deserts

Distribution Most of North America from southern Alaska and Canada to northern Mexico, plus Aleutian Islands

Status Badly hit by persecution and pesticide poisoning in the past but now flourishing, especially in far northwest of range

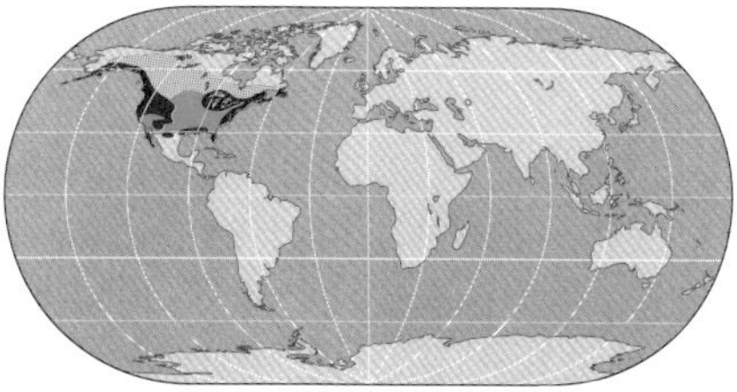

Despite being adopted as the national bird of the U.S. in 1782, the magnificent bald eagle has been lucky to survive extinction through the combined effects of shooting, poisoning, and habitat loss.

With its piercing yellow eye, big hooked bill, and fearsome talons, the bald eagle is one of the most imposing of all hunting birds. The name "bald" is misleading, because it suggests a head devoid of feathers like that of a vulture. In fact, the eagle has beautiful snowy white plumage on its head, matching its tail and contrasting with the rich, dark-chocolate plumage of the rest of its body.

The bald eagle is one of eight fish eagles of the genus *Haliaeetus* that includes the white-tailed sea eagle (*H. albicilla*) of Eurasia and the colossal Steller's sea eagle (*H. pelagicus)* of eastern Siberia and Japan. Many of these eagles hunt mainly at sea, but the bald eagle lives all over North America, often far from any ocean. It certainly likes fish, however, and away from coasts it is usually found near the shores of large lakes or by big rivers.

Two Races

There are two distinct races of the bald eagle: the northern and the southern. The northern birds are bigger, and in the summer they breed among the lakes and forests of Canada and

An adult (right) and three immature bald eagles scavenging from a garbage dump—the birds are adaptable and inventive feeders, exploiting a variety of food sources.

Alaska, as far north as the arctic tundra. When the northern rivers and lakes freeze over, many fly south as far as California, Arizona, or Florida. There they usually gather around rivers, lakes, and reservoirs. However, some may spend the winter far from water in dry sagebrush country or even desert, returning to their northern breeding grounds in spring.

Along the Pacific coasts and islands of Alaska and British Columbia the eagles can still feed in the sea even when lakes and rivers freeze, so they stay all year around. Most of the 100,000 or so bald eagles in North America live in this region, which is rich in fish and still largely wilderness.

The smaller, far less numerous southern race breeds in the winter in California, Texas, Louisiana, Florida, and the southern Atlantic states such as Georgia. Many young birds from the south move north toward Canada for the summer, but other individuals, mainly older adults, stay in the steamy south all summer.

Very Varied Tastes

Bald eagles eat a wide variety of food, dead or alive, depending on the season and availability. Many breeding pairs in the southern states feed their young almost entirely on roadkills—opossums being a favorite—while Alaskan birds scavenging on the seashore may make an outsized meal of a stranded whale.

Live prey is just as important, however, and bald eagles spend a lot of time hunting fish. The eagle is equipped for the task with a pair of massive, long-clawed feet. The toes are short and strong for maximum gripping power, and the hind toe has an extralong, supersharp claw that pierces the fish's body like a dagger and often kills it almost instantly. Often, the bald

When a bald eagle sees a big fish near the water surface, it swoops down, gaffs the fish with its talons, and flies off with it. Bald eagles hardly ever plunge into the water like ospreys, and they usually manage to lift their prey without getting anything other than their feet wet.

⊕ *Most of the 100,000 or so bald eagles in North America live along the Pacific coasts and islands of Alaska and British Columbia. The area is rich in fish and still largely an unspoiled wilderness.*

eagle watches from a perch such as a cliff ledge or a branch before swooping down to the water. Occasionally, bald eagles search for live fish in flight, but hunting from a perch saves energy. They also steal fish from other birds of prey such as ospreys (*Pandion haliaetus*), and a bald eagle may even snatch a meal from a sea otter as it floats on its back among the seaweed, gnawing at a fish held between its front paws.

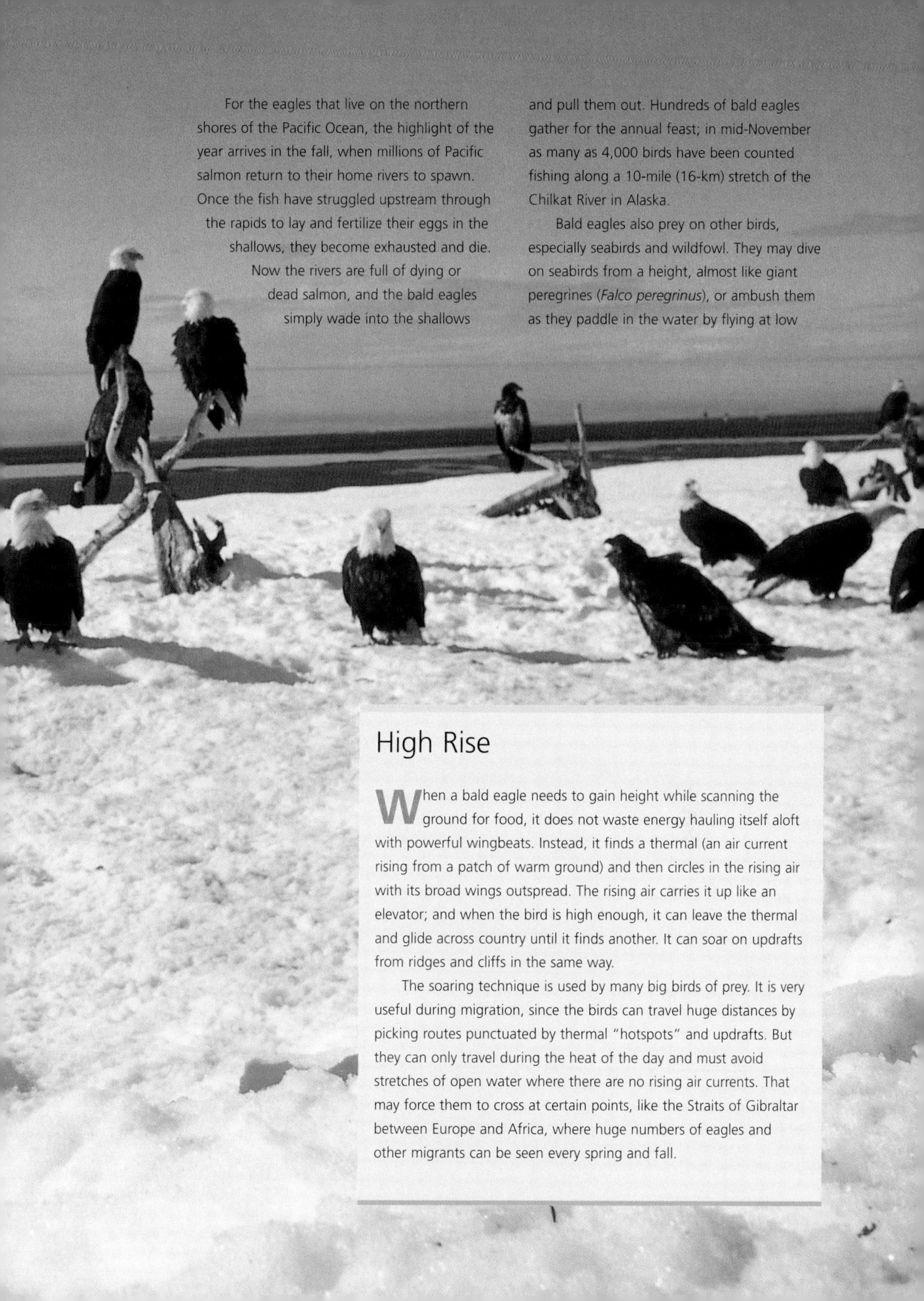

For the eagles that live on the northern shores of the Pacific Ocean, the highlight of the year arrives in the fall, when millions of Pacific salmon return to their home rivers to spawn. Once the fish have struggled upstream through the rapids to lay and fertilize their eggs in the shallows, they become exhausted and die. Now the rivers are full of dying or dead salmon, and the bald eagles simply wade into the shallows and pull them out. Hundreds of bald eagles gather for the annual feast; in mid-November as many as 4,000 birds have been counted fishing along a 10-mile (16-km) stretch of the Chilkat River in Alaska.

Bald eagles also prey on other birds, especially seabirds and wildfowl. They may dive on seabirds from a height, almost like giant peregrines (*Falco peregrinus*), or ambush them as they paddle in the water by flying at low

High Rise

When a bald eagle needs to gain height while scanning the ground for food, it does not waste energy hauling itself aloft with powerful wingbeats. Instead, it finds a thermal (an air current rising from a patch of warm ground) and then circles in the rising air with its broad wings outspread. The rising air carries it up like an elevator; and when the bird is high enough, it can leave the thermal and glide across country until it finds another. It can soar on updrafts from ridges and cliffs in the same way.

The soaring technique is used by many big birds of prey. It is very useful during migration, since the birds can travel huge distances by picking routes punctuated by thermal "hotspots" and updrafts. But they can only travel during the heat of the day and must avoid stretches of open water where there are no rising air currents. That may force them to cross at certain points, like the Straits of Gibraltar between Europe and Africa, where huge numbers of eagles and other migrants can be seen every spring and fall.

level through the troughs between waves. They use similar techniques to catch ducks, geese, and ptarmigan (genus *Lagopus*) on the treeless, hummocky subarctic tundra and may even cooperate to ensure a kill. Bald eagles also take voles, rats, rabbits, turtles, snakes, and even insects.

Paired for Life

At the beginning of the breeding season the mature males and females indulge in spectacular display flights, soaring high over their territory and tumbling out of the sky with their feet locked together. Pairs tend to stay together for life, but they still use display flights each breeding season prior to mating. The main reason pairs stay together is because both birds generally return to the same nest site every season and therefore meet up again with their partner from the previous year.

First the birds check out the nest to make sure it is still usable. Sometimes bald eagle nests become occupied by great horned owls (*Bubo virginianus*); and when this happens, the eagles must start a new nest elsewhere. Some pairs suffer from "nest squatting" quite frequently, so after three or four seasons the bald eagles may have several nests in their territory from which to choose.

Once they have chosen a nest, the birds repair it, adding more sticks and soft lining material such as grass or seaweed. When they are satisfied, the female lays her eggs, and both birds take turns incubating them. The eggs are laid at intervals of a few days and hatch at the same intervals. The last chick to hatch is smaller than the others, and competition for food in the nest often means that the youngest chick does not get enough and dies. Therefore, despite the best efforts of both parents, who share in bringing food to the nest, it is quite unusual for more than two chicks to survive to fledging time.

The young birds finally fly at about ten weeks old. At first they are dark all over; but as they grow, they become more mottled with white until they are four or five years old, when they grow their adult plumage and are ready to start families of their own. Most breed for the first time in their fifth year.

➔ Bald eagles usually add fresh sticks and other building materials to their nest each year. In time the nest can become an enormous structure weighing up to 2 tons (1.8 tonnes).

Prey Power

Before 1953 bald eagles in Alaska had a price on their heads. The state authorities believed that the eagles destroyed valuable stocks of Pacific salmon, threatening the economy, so they encouraged people to shoot them.

But they were wrong. Predators such as hunting birds very rarely destroy their own food supply. It requires a lot of fish to sustain just one family of bald eagles, so if the fish become scarce, the eagles disappear. That allows the numbers of prey to recover until there is enough to support the predators again. Therefore, the numbers of prey control the numbers of predators, and a big population of bald eagles is a sure sign that there are a lot of fish about.

Hacking Back

If nesting bald eagles lose their first clutch of eggs, the female simply lays some more. Wildlife conservators have made good use of this habit; they carefully remove eggs from bald eagle nests and put them in incubators to hatch. Meanwhile, the eagles incubate a second clutch, and the result is twice the number of chicks.

When they are about eight weeks old, the hand-reared chicks can be reintroduced to areas where bald eagles are scarce, using a technique called "hacking." Each young bald eagle is placed on a man-made nest protected by an enclosure and then fed by humans who stay out of sight. When the eagle is ready to fly, the enclosure is opened so that the bird is able to leave. Since food is still provided at the nest site, the young eagle rarely goes far. By the time it has learned to hunt for itself, it has settled into the area, and with luck the young bald eagle will breed and start a new population.

Back from the Brink

A few decades ago bald eagles were under threat for a variety of reasons. Their taste for valuable fish—particularly salmon—made them very unpopular. In Alaska in 1917 a reward of $2 was offered for every dead bald eagle. However, in 1940 Congress passed the Bald Eagle Protection Act, which made it illegal to kill or harass bald eagles throughout most of the U.S., though Alaska was excluded. The birds were not fully protected by law until 1953, and meanwhile, about 140,000 bald eagles had been shot—more than the entire population of the species alive today.

By the time shooting was outlawed, bald eagles were suffering from something even worse: pesticide poisoning. Like ospreys and many other birds of prey, bald eagles were eating prey contaminated with DDT and similar chemicals. The poisons accumulated in their bodies and had the effect of making their eggs so fragile that they broke in the nest. Eagle populations plummeted, and by the early 1960s there were only some 450 breeding pairs left in the U.S., excluding Alaska.

In 1967 the bald eagle was declared an endangered species south of the 40th parallel, and anyone found guilty of shooting one was liable to prosecution. But the real turning point came in 1972, with the virtual banning of DDT and related pesticides in the U.S. Since then eagle numbers have steadily increased. There are now some 4,500 breeding pairs south of the Canada–U.S. border.

Bald eagles are still suffering from loss of wild habitat and a shortage of natural prey, particularly in the southern part of their range. Many have also died from lead poisoning, caused by eating waterfowl that have swallowed lead shot from shotguns or from fishing lines. Lead shot has now been phased out, thanks to a five-year program instituted by the U.S. Fish and Wildlife Service. So despite these problems, bald eagle numbers are still increasing in most states, and in 1995 the eagle was taken off the endangered list and reclassified as Threatened.

Tawny Owl

Strix aluco

Common name Tawny owl

Scientific name *Strix aluco*

Family Strigidae

Order Strigiformes

Size Length: 14–15 in (35.5–38 cm); wingspan: 37–41 in (94–104 cm); weight: 12–21 oz (340–595 g); female bigger than male

Key features Big-headed; bulky, with broad, rounded wings and short tail; pale or rufous facial disk and dark eye; mottled red-brown to gray above, paler below with dark streaks; very variable; sexes identical; juvenile paler

Habits Roosts in trees by day; hunts from perch at night among trees

Nesting Nests in tree hole, rock or wall cavity, or old crow's nest in spring; usually 2–5 eggs, rarely up to 9; incubation 28–30 days; young fledge after 32–37 days; 1 brood

Voice Sharp "ke-wick"; long, multiple hoot

Diet Small mammals and small birds, plus frogs, insects, earthworms, and fish

Habitat Mainly mature woodland and forest; also farmland, parks, large gardens with trees, and even tree-lined city streets

Distribution Europe (except Ireland but including southern Scandinavia), North Africa, parts of western Asia, southern Asia from Nepal to China, and Korea

Status Generally common and widespread

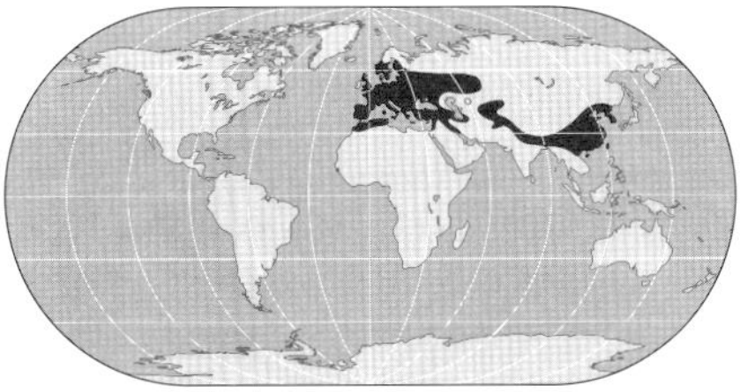

Although few people ever see the tawny owl, its hooting call is a familiar nocturnal sound throughout most of its range—from ancient oak forests to the leafy avenues of great cities.

THERE ARE MANY KINDS OF OWL, but the tawny owl is certainly one of most commonly depicted. Plump, round-faced, with big eyes and beautiful soft, mottled brown plumage, it is like an owl from a storybook. It also behaves in a typically owl-like manner: It flies only by night and proclaims its presence with the classic owl call—a long, quavering ghostly hoot.

The tawny owl is essentially a bird of the forests. It has comparatively short, rounded wings for maneuvering easily through the trees. Despite its apparent bulk, it flies slowly and buoyantly and with barely a sound from its soft-edged flight feathers. It has exceptionally good night vision even for an owl, so it can find its way through the dark forest even on moonless, starless nights that, to a human eye, seem pitch black.

Ⓣ ***Tawny owls often nest in tree holes, particularly ones that were originally made by smaller birds but have enlarged through decay.***

Familiar Territory

A tawny owl occupies the same territory all year around, so it is able to learn every detail of its hunting range. It knows all the best places to find prey; so instead of using precious energy flying back and forth in search of a meal, it usually selects a perch overlooking a likely spot.

The owl then sits and waits, watching for any movement and listening for the slightest noise that might indicate prey on the ground below. It might be a wood mouse searching for seeds or a mole surfacing from its burrow. The owl swivels its head to pinpoint the source of the sound, locks onto its target, glides down, and strikes. The victim is often killed outright by the long, sharp talons; but if not, the owl despatches it with a quick bite to the neck after carrying it back to its perch. Then, with a toss of its head, it swallows the prey whole.

In its natural forest habitat the tawny owl eats mainly voles, mice, and similar small mammals, but it is an adaptable bird that has learned to live in some surprising places. In England some 50 pairs breed in the parks and gardens of London, where they prey mainly on small birds such as sparrows that the owls beat from their night roosts with their wings. They have also been known to snatch fish from ornamental garden ponds!

Tawny owls retire to their own roosts at dawn, perching motionless on branches, in tree holes, or amid dense ivy. Sometimes they are betrayed by small birds that harass them from a safe distance, but usually their superb camouflage makes them very difficult to see. They change their roosts regularly but nearly always stay within their territory.

Night Caller

In spring single males advertise for mates with a penetrating "hooo-hoooo" call. A female may reply with similar hoots, but more often with the sharp "ke-wick" contact call. When the pair come face to face, the male displays on the perch with swaying wing-raising movements and by ruffling his feathers and grunting.

Once formed, tawny owl pairs usually stay together for life. They nest in simple tree holes and cavities, but defend them fiercely against intruders. Tawny owls nesting in town parks have been known to swoop down on people walking too close, often without knowing it, and slash at them with their sharp talons.

The female has the task of incubating the eggs and caring for the chicks, while the male hunts for food. Most young tawny owls breed for the first time in their second year.

The birds are adaptable, and their success at colonizing towns and other unlikely habitats suggests they are less vulnerable to man-made changes than many other owl species.

A tawny owl arriving at its nest hole with a mouse. Small mammals form a large part of the bird's prey, but it is a versatile feeder, eating whatever is available.

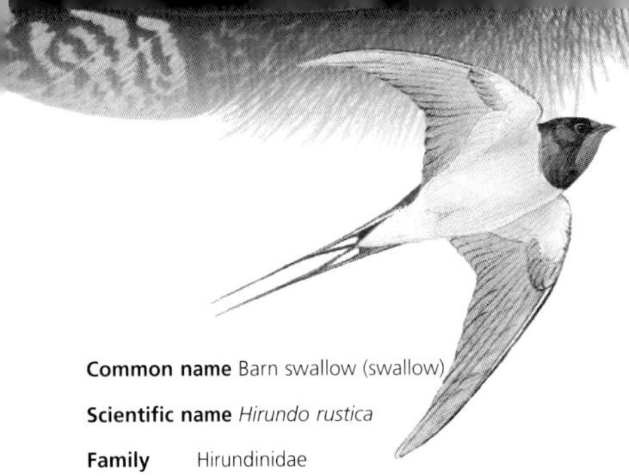

Common name Barn swallow (swallow)

Scientific name *Hirundo rustica*

Family Hirundinidae

Order Passeriformes

Size Length: 6.7–7.5 in (17–19 cm); wingspan: 12.5–13.7 in (32–35 cm); weight: 0.6–0.8 oz (17–23 g)

Key features Slim, medium-sized swallow; small bill; long wings and forked tail, with outer tail feathers elongated into streamers; shiny metallic blue-black above, pale to reddish buff below with blue-black chest band and chestnut forehead and throat; sexes similar; female has shorter tail streamers; juvenile duller, with paler forehead and throat, and short tail streamers

Habits Hunts in the air by day, mostly at low level, often over water, with graceful swooping flight; often perches on overhead wires

Nesting Open, featherlined cup of mud and dry grass on ledge, usually in outbuilding or beneath bridge, sometimes in cave or tree; 4–6 eggs; incubation 11–19 days; chicks fledge in 18–23 days; 2–3 broods

Voice Song a melodious, twittering warble; call a sharp "tswit tswit"

Diet Flying insects, particularly large flies such as blowflies, horseflies, and hoverflies

Habitat Open country, especially grassland, pasture, and marsh grazed by large animals, with suitable buildings for nesting

Distribution Temperate Eurasia and North America, Africa, Central and South America

Status Common but declining in north due to loss of breeding sites, feeding habitat, and prey

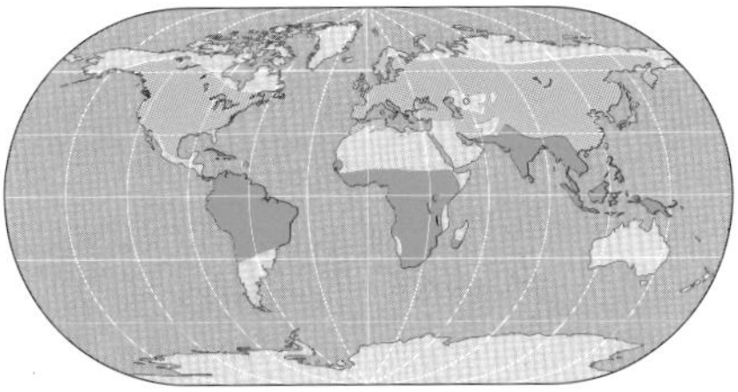

Barn Swallow

Hirundo rustica

Throughout the northern lands of the world, the annual appearance of the forktailed barn swallow is an eagerly awaited sign that the warm days of summer have finally arrived.

Fast, graceful, and supremely agile in the air, with long wings and tail streamers, the barn swallow is one of the most elegant of all hunting birds. It is also one of the most successful, with a range that extends virtually worldwide apart from Australasia, the icebound polar regions, and a few oceanic islands.

Insect Diet

The barn swallow feeds almost entirely on flying insects, and like other insect-hunters, it retreats to the tropics to find prey in winter. Barn swallows from northern Europe fly 6,000 miles (9,656 km) or more to southern Africa, while North American birds make similar journeys to Latin America. In spring they return north to breed and take advantage of the seasonal flush of hatching insects to rear their young.

In the tropics the barn swallow eats a wide variety of small insects, including flying ants and aphids, but in the north the bird prefers big, burly flies such as blowflies, dung flies, and bloodsucking horseflies. These insects are particularly common on open grassland, where they feed on grazing animals and their dung, so the felling of forests and expansion of farming and ranching over the past 2,000 years or so have suited the barn swallow very well.

The barn swallow is often to be seen hunting at low level over pastures and stockyards, swooping among the cattle and sheep with a relaxed, fluid flight action, using its long tail to steer as it pursues its insect prey. Lakes and rivers are also good places to find prey, especially when bad weather drives most insects from the skies. At such times the barn swallow frequently hunts low over the water and even hovers over marginal plants looking

→ *The barn swallow thrives in climates ranging from the dusty prairies of North America to the damp Atlantic coasts of Europe and from the southern fringes of the arctic tundra to the plains of Africa.*

Broad-front Flyers

Many migrant birds follow well-defined routes as they travel from their breeding grounds to their winter quarters and back again. Birds of prey, in particular, often soar on thermal upcurrents to gain height for gliding, so they follow routes where such updrafts are common and avoid broad stretches of cool water. They are "narrow-front" migrants, all passing through the same air corridors.

By contrast, barn swallows migrate on a broad front. In Europe, for example, they work their way south in the early fall until they gather all along the northern shores of the Mediterranean. Then they set off across the water to north Africa in a great wave. After a break they carry on across the Sahara Desert without attempting to skirt the vast expanse of inhospitable sand. Swallows from Central Asia fly straight across the wastes of Arabia in the same way. Eventually they all arrive on the savanna grassland, where they can rest before carrying on south of the equator.

for flies and beetles that have settled on the leaves. When it needs a drink, the barn swallow darts across the surface of a pool and skims a mouthful of water from the surface with its lower bill. In early summer it also forages along woodland edges looking for caterpillars dangling from the trees on silken threads and seizes them on the wing.

It takes a week to build a new nest, and over 1,000 mud pellets like the ones this barn swallow has gathered in its beak are used in the construction.

Many Nest Sites

Barn swallows breed in early summer, and the caterpillars provide vital protein for nesting birds and their young. The birds pair up as soon as they return from the tropics, and any that have bred before usually return to the same site and renew their pair-bond. The male arrives first, checks out the old nest, and may start repairing or rebuilding it. When the female arrives, she often takes over most of the task of nest building, while the male defends the site against rival swallows.

Originally barn swallows nested in tree cavities and rock crevices, but for centuries they have favored ledges and beams in outbuildings and roof spaces or under bridges and culverts. An ideal site is among the roof beams of an open-fronted cattle shelter in a traditional farmyard, offering protection from the weather, easy access, and a plentiful supply of flies. But barn swallows will also often nest in garages, porches, verandas, and other such places.

The nest is built from pellets of mud gathered by the birds in their bills, reinforced with dried grasses or straw, and lined with feathers. When the eggs hatch, the parent birds feed the hungry chicks on insects that they carry to the nest in their throats, like swifts. Swallows often raise a second or even third brood, although they may get some assistance

Barn swallows are well adapted to a life in the air and even feed each other on the wing.

Fine Feathers

To humans one of the most attractive features of the dashing barn swallow is its forked tail, in which each of the outer feathers is extended into a long, tapering streamer. It appears that humans are not the only ones to appreciate the tail. Males have longer streamers than females, and there is evidence that the males with the longest tail streamers get the opportunity to mate earlier and enjoy more breeding success. The females clearly prefer their mates with fine feathers and compete for the favors of the most eligible long-tailed suitors. Long streamers may indicate health, strength, and strong genes.

from one of the first brood, which stays on at the nest to help out with the food supply. Barn swallows can breed in their second year.

Heading South

At the end of the breeding season barn swallows leave their nests to perch in restless, noisy groups on overhead wires and to form mass night roosts as they prepare for migration. They often roost in reed beds, along with related species of swallows and martins. Such gatherings are frequently targeted by birds of prey such as the hobby, a fast-flying falcon that specializes in hunting swifts and swallows.

Older birds migrate first, blazing a trail for the younger birds that follow afterward. Swallows take long breaks as they move south, usually roosting in reed beds, and the young birds may stop off in an area for up to two weeks before resuming a journey that may last two months or more.

Decreasing Insect Prey

Barn swallows are still widespread, but they are less common than they once were, especially in regions where traditional mixed farming has been abandoned in favor of intensive, chemically assisted agriculture. Chemical pesticides kill off the birds' insect prey, and flies in particular have become harder to find. Many flies breed in animal dung, and it has become less common as farmers have turned to artificial fertilizers and plowed up their pasture to grow crops. Suitable nesting sites are also becoming scarce as outbuildings are demolished and roof spaces are sealed up. So while the barn swallow will probably never disappear from northern skies, its appearance every spring will no longer be something that can be taken for granted.

Each nestling may eat more than 150,000 insects between hatching and fledging, so a pair with a brood of five chicks is kept very busy indeed.

Mourning Dove

Zenaida macroura

Common name Mourning dove

Scientific name *Zenaida macroura*

Family Columbidae

Order Columbiformes

Size Length: 12 in (30 cm); wingspan: 18 in (46 cm); weight: 4.2 oz (120 g)

Key features Small, slim dove with long, graduated tail; mostly soft brown, grayer toward head, with large button-shaped black spots on the wing; some tail feathers tipped black-and-white; red legs; sexes alike

Habits Perches on wires, aerials, trees, and bushes; feeds mostly on ground; forms flocks in winter; male has spiraling aerial display

Nesting February–October; flimsy-looking cup nest of sticks in a tree fork; 2 white eggs; incubation 14–15 days; young fledge after 12–14 days; regularly 3 broods, occasionally up to 6

Voice A low mournful "oo-AAH coo coo coo"

Diet Mostly seeds

Habitat Highly adaptable, anywhere from cities and towns to dry scrub and semidesert

Distribution North America as far north as southern Canada, and ranging south to Central America

Status Widespread and often very common, despite large-scale hunting

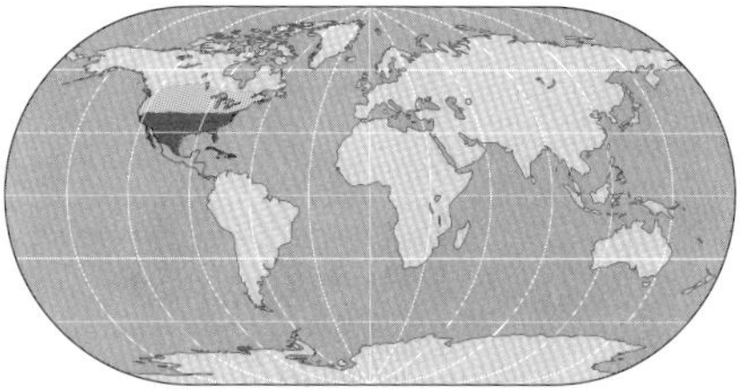

Fed by some, hunted by others, the mourning dove is one of North America's commonest birds. Originally from wild, arid places, it has adapted to all kinds of artificial habitats from farms to city centers.

THE AMERICAN MOURNING DOVE IS NAMED after its sad-sounding song: a series of gentle coos with a wistful, regretful tone. Its lamentations are a familiar sound throughout the farmlands and settlements of North America. It is an attractive bird, with the slender, slightly fragile look typical of small doves. Its plumage is unremarkably brownish-pink, with a few button-shaped black spots on its wings, but its tail is distinctive and unusual: long with a very sharp tip. The shape is described as graduated—broad at the base but gradually getting narrower toward the end. The edge of the tail is decorated with white spots, so that when the tail is spread, it looks like a necklace of pearls.

The mourning dove is so common in many North American cities that it is hard to believe that it was originally a bird of dry savanna and semidesert. It still occurs there and shows typical desert toughness. Mourning doves have been known to survive without water for four days and have been found incubating eggs in outside temperatures of 110° F (43° C). Birds that still live in the desert often nest in large cacti, using the plants' imposing thorns as protection for the nest. Although some need to commute long distances to find water at the beginning and end of the day, that does not prevent them thriving in such a harsh habitat.

Seed Specialists

Mourning doves are typical seed-eating members of the pigeon family. In fact, they have been recorded feeding on no fewer than 200 species of seeds even in one small area. Most of these seeds come from grasses that the doves can pluck from the stems while they are feeding on the ground, as is their custom.

The seed-eating habits of mourning doves have caused problems ever since people began growing crops in North America. These adaptable doves can devour all sorts of wild and cultivated grain, including corn and wheat. In some areas they are a serious pest and are shot in enormous numbers. In fact, it has been estimated that in the course of any one year in the U.S. no fewer than 45 million mourning doves are shot for pest control or recreational hunting. The populations of many species would buckle under the strain of such a slaughter, yet the ever-resilient mourning dove somehow manages to survive and thrive.

Multiple Broods

One reason for the mourning dove's resilience lies in its high breeding potential. Although the female lays the characteristic pigeon clutch of two eggs, mourning doves have a very long breeding season. They often attempt at least three successive broods and occasionally up to six. The high brood rate is more than any other North American bird, giving the mourning dove the ability to recover quickly from any setback.

The nest consists of a bare minimum of sticks interwoven to form a fragile-looking platform. The young are quickly "weaned," so although they depend on the adults' crop milk for their first three days of life, they are feeding entirely on seeds by the time they are a week or so old. With nest building typically taking just a single day, incubation taking 15 days, and the hatched young taking just 30 more days to achieve independence, the mourning dove "production line" is fast and efficient.

It seems, therefore, that the population of mourning doves is balanced, and those that are shot are quickly replaced. Yet there is no room for complacency, as the case of the passenger pigeon (*Ectopistes migratorius*) shows. Once North America's most abundant bird, with a population of up to 3 billion, the passenger pigeon was eliminated in fewer than 100 years, mainly by hunting. So no bird, not even the mourning dove, is ever completely safe.

The mourning dove's nest is a slapdash affair, little more than a few sticks loosely woven into a flimsy platform; but in desert habitats it is often sited in a large cactus such as a saguaro, where the brood is protected by the plant's formidable defensive spines.

Budgerigar

Melopsittacus undulatus

Most of us know the budgerigar as an affectionate, colorful pet, but it is also a wild bird that lives in the arid heart of Australia and gathers in vast flocks to drink at water holes or feed on the ground.

Common name Budgerigar

Scientific name *Melopsittacus undulatus*

Family Psittacidae

Order Psittaciformes

Size Length: 7 in (18 cm); wingspan: 10 in (25 cm); weight: 1 oz (28 g)

Key features Small, slender, sparrow-sized parrot with long wings and tail; small, hooked bill; mostly apple-green with bluish tail, yellow on head; wings and head patterned with scales; domestic birds include blue and yellow varieties; sexes similar, but male has blue skin above the bill (blue-gray in breeding season), while female has brown skin (brownish-pink in breeding season)

Habits Roams in nomadic, noisy cohesive flocks, usually of about 100 birds

Nesting Builds nest in tree hollow, often in loose colony; 4–6 white eggs, occasionally up to 8; incubation 18–20 days, by female only; young fledge after 35 days; often several clutches laid in quick succession

Voice Chirruping call

Diet Seeds and grain

Habitat A wide variety of open habitats, including savanna and farmland

Distribution Inland Australia

Status Abundant

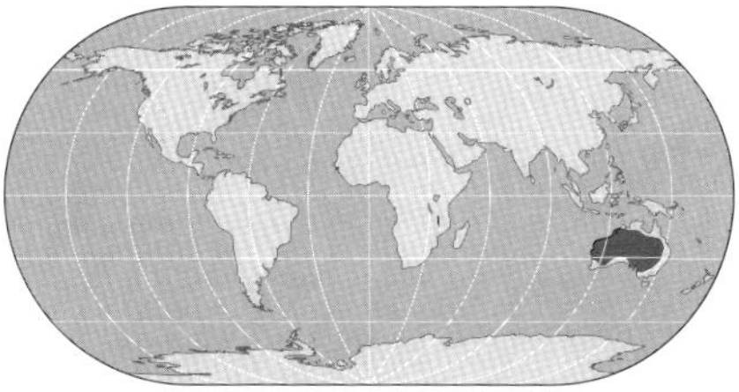

UNTIL 1840 THE BUDGERIGAR WAS known only to the Aboriginal people who had shared its Australian outback home for centuries and to a few European settlers. But in that year the English naturalist John Gould brought a few living specimens back on the long sea voyage from Australia to Europe. He called them "warbling grass parakeets" and wrote: "They are the most animated, cheerful little creatures you can possibly imagine."

The rest of the world agreed, and within a few years many thousands were finding their way to the bird markets of Europe, to be sold as pets. Today the budgerigar is still one of the world's most popular cage birds. It is found so widely that many people are quite unaware of its origin in the heartland of Australia.

Miniature Parrot

The budgerigar is small by comparison with most parrots—not much bigger than a sparrow. It has a long, pointed tail, which can be spread like a fan in flight. Its wings are also long and pointed, providing the aerial maneuverability that is a necessity when flying in dense flocks. The plumage is green and yellow, and scalloped with black in such a way that one of its old names was "shell parakeet." Males and females look much alike, except in the breeding season, when the cere of the female (the skin at the base of her bill) turns brownish-pink, in contrast with the blue-gray cere of the male.

It was the Aborigines of Liverpool Plains, near Sydney, that stopped the bird being called a "warbling grass parakeet." Their name for the bird was "betcherrygah," of which a rough translation is "good food," although it is also a rough approximation of the bird's main call.

Although familiar as a cage bird, in the wild the budgerigar is an agile, highly sociable seed-eating parrot of the arid Australian outback—a harsh environment where it still thrives in great numbers.

There is no doubt that the Aborigines would have been very familiar with the voice of the budgerigar, as well as its taste. The birds are very noisy, although their vocabulary consists of only eight vocalizations, a small number for a member of the parrot family. They have a flight call, which keeps flocks together; a preflight call, which is used as an intention to move on; and an alarm call. Both the female and young also make begging calls to the male.

Grass Parakeet

The budgerigar is still common in its native land, where it lives in open forest, light woodland, farmland, and even the more arid habitats of desert scrubland and mulga. As suggested by Gould's name, it belongs to a group known as "grass parakeets" because the seeds of grasses are its main food. It also feeds on the seeds of another group of plants known variously as goosefoots, oraches, or chenopods, which also grow close to the ground. Most of the seeds that the bird takes are very small.

A feeding flock of budgerigars moves across the ground on a broad front, like a mass invasion. Groups of birds can be seen climbing nimbly up and down the plant stems, busily running the seed heads through their bills to squeeze out the seeds. Any seeds that they dislodge and drop are picked up from the ground before the birds move on.

Budgerigars are very much inland birds, and in the continental interior the climate is

The male budgerigar feeds his mate during courtship to demonstrate his food-gathering abilities. This is important, because when she lays her eggs, he must keep her supplied with food so she can devote all her time to incubation.

harsh and unpredictable. An area of desert may not get any rain for years, then be struck by a rainstorm that makes it burst into bloom. The resulting abundance of seeds attracts the budgerigars, which follow the rains in search of food. When they have eaten their fill, they move on and will not return until the rains come again; one year there may be a great influx of birds to a particular area, the next year none.

In some places people have slightly modified the budgerigar's habitat, sinking wells and providing permanent sources of water where once there was none. That has allowed the local budgerigar population to increase and adopt a less nomadic way of life.

Vast Flocks

Normally budgerigars travel in flocks of up to 100 birds; but when resources are scarce, the flocks may join up to make enormous gatherings. At least a million birds have been seen concentrated into a small area, the sky filled with swirling, perfectly coordinated flocks and ringing with their chattering calls. When they settle on trees, such crowds of budgerigars have caused branches 1.5 inches (4 cm) in diameter to break by sheer weight of numbers.

A wild budgerigar's day begins just after dawn, when the birds in a roosting flock begin to call softly and preen their plumage. Moments later they leave their chosen trees and disperse to feed. Most foraging activity occurs during the morning, before the sun becomes hot, and the animals of the outback retreat into the shade. There is another peak of activity before dusk, when there are some delightful and spirited aerobatics. Birds gathering at a roost site wheel around the sky in close formation, passing with dizzying speed over the treetops, calling all the while before the whole flock settles down for the night.

Sociable Breeders

Budgerigars lose none of their sociability when breeding. It is common for pairs to nest in close

Budgerigars in Captivity

There is no doubt that budgerigars take readily to captivity, soon becoming tame and at ease in human company. They are easy to breed, too, which is a sure sign of their adaptability to confinement. If they are well looked after, they regularly live to seven to ten years of age, and there are many well-documented cases of birds living for twenty years or so.

One of the many delights of the budgerigar is its ability to talk, a talent that far exceeds that of similar small parakeets. Males are usually far better talkers than females; and if a bird is taught from a young age, it can accumulate a vocabulary of three hundred words or more.

Wild budgerigars are mostly green, but color variants do occur naturally. The green coloration results from the combination of a yellow pigment with a blue effect caused by reflections from the internal structure of the feathers. With a little selective breeding the pigment can be removed, making both blue and gray varieties. Other colors have also been bred, including both yellow and white.

Interestingly, despite coming from an environment given to extreme heat, budgerigars can soon become acclimatized to life outdoors even in the cooler parts of North America. This proves the adaptability and toughness of this indomitable bird.

proximity to each other, in the same tree or even along the same branch, as long as there are enough suitable holes. The birds also search for food together during the breeding season. Only the immediate vicinity of the nest is treated as exclusive territory; and if any of the neighbors get too close, the female in particular reacts aggressively to drive away the trespasser.

Breeding is stimulated by rain. Where conditions allow, a pair will produce several broods in succession or may breed twice at different times of year. As a rule, however, the populations in the north of Australia breed between June and September, while those in the south breed in the Australian spring and summer, between August and January.

The nest site is in a hole, usually in a tree, but a fence post or fallen branch may also be used. The female tends it carefully. If necessary, she removes any unwanted debris in order to ensure that the base of the hole is flat and covered in wood dust.

The male, meanwhile, is merely a visitor to the nest hole, since the female incubates the eggs alone. However, he does keep her fed throughout the incubation period, bringing food and regurgitating it straight into her mouth. Being provided for in such a manner means that the female can sit tight no matter what, and during this period she sets about her task with great dedication. There are records of females remaining on their eggs even when the nesting branch has been cut down.

↑ The natural nesting site of a budgerigar is a tree hole tidied up by the female to provide a comfortable, secure nursery. If there are enough holes, several pairs may nest together in close proximity.

Budgerigar Courtship

It is a common sight to see a pair of captive budgerigars huddled close together on a perch, apparently conversing with each other, and every so often preening each other's feathers. That is standard pair-bonding and pair-reinforcing behavior. By coming close and nibbling the other bird's face feathers, a budgerigar can clearly see the color of the bare skin above the bill, which is blue-gray in the male and brownish-pink in the female.

Courtship also involves a great deal of chasing, especially in the wild. After racing around for some time, the male and female alight on a perch side by side. The male feeds the female by regurgitation and then mounts her, keeping his balance by placing one wing and then the other alternately around her shoulder. After this the male feeds his mate once again. Shortly afterward the two fly off to resume their day's activities.

Bouncing Back

Budgerigars mature quickly. The young become independent almost at the time they are fledged, and they can breed from the age of about six months. Such a speedy cycle enables budgerigars to reproduce very quickly, to

In the desert interior of Australia a water hole may attract large flocks of thirsty budgerigars. Sometimes the birds are so eager to drink that they splash down into the water itself, pushing each other beneath the surface.

counteract any reductions in populations that may be caused by severe food shortages. Consequently, their numbers may fluctuate wildly from year to year, but budgerigars always seem able to bounce back from adversity. Such abilities have enabled the budgerigar to become the most successful parrot of Australia's arid, hot interior.

Although the trade in captive birds has affected wild populations in some areas, the budgerigar is such a numerous and resilient species, and lives in such a remote habitat, that it continues to prosper. Since the Australian government has banned the trade in wild-caught Australian parrots, the wild budgie's future seems more secure.

The Problem of Water

Like many birds of arid regions, budgerigars are tolerant of temperature extremes and can go for long periods without water. At such times they obtain their moisture from their diet instead, since water is a by-product of digestion. In addition, water loss is minimized by the fact that birds do not sweat.

However, budgerigars are seldom found far from a water source. Many visit water at least once a day; and if the temperature should rise above 104° F (40° C), a daily intake of water becomes necessary for their survival.

The birds usually visit in flocks, which gather nervously in the trees around a water hole. A few bold individuals settle on the ground and tiptoe to the water's edge. They drink for just a few seconds, then they fly away, their thirst satisfied.

If the site remains undisturbed, large numbers will fly down to the water, crowding the shore and virtually forming lines to get at the vital liquid. At times impatient budgerigars will even drink on the wing, splashing down to the surface and taking gulps while briefly floating. Occasionally this can go disastrously wrong as the birds land on top of each other, causing death by drowning—a strange fate in the heat of the otherwise parched desert.

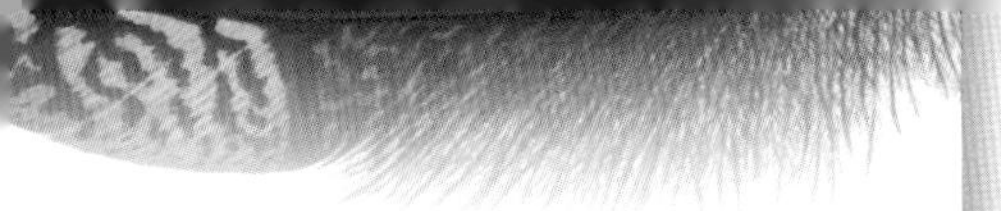

Ruby-throated Hummingbird

Archilochus colubris

Common name Ruby-throated hummingbird

Scientific name *Archilochus colubris*

Family Trochilidae

Order Apodiformes

Size Length: 3.75 in (9.5 cm); wingspan: 4.5 in (11.5 cm); weight: 0.1 oz (2.8 g)

Key features Minute, with long, pointed wings typical of hummingbirds and making soft hum; short, forked tail with spiky tip; long, slender needlelike bill; small head and thin neck; plumage mainly iridescent green, with whitish underparts; male has glittering red throat

Habits Active and pugnacious, usually seen hovering at flowers

Nesting Cup nest of bud scales and lichen, bound with spider silk, usually on horizontal or downward inclining branch of deciduous tree; 2 white eggs; incubation 16 days by female; young fledge after 15–28 days; 1 brood

Voice Male's song is high-pitched rattle; also "tsip" call during chases

Diet Nectar and insects

Habitat Deciduous and mixed woodland and gardens

Distribution Eastern North America and Central America

Status Common, but may be in decline

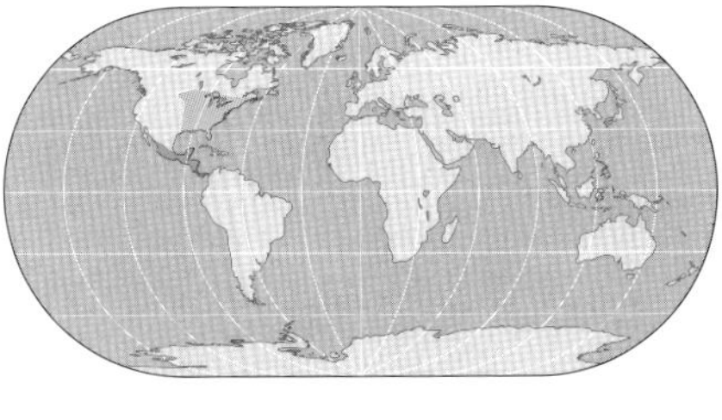

Perhaps the best-known hummingbird in North America, the tiny ruby-throat is remarkable for its long-distance migration, often traveling 1,000 miles (1,610 km) or more to reach its winter quarters.

AT CERTAIN TIMES THE RUBY-THROATED hummingbird can look completely out of place on its northern breeding grounds, especially if caught by a late flurry of snow when it arrives in spring. But this pioneer among hummingbirds is a tough and resilient bird. It is one of the few hummingbird species to have ventured out of the tropics or subtropics to breed, and it is the only one that has conquered most of the eastern half of North America. By doing so, it has found a new opportunity unnoticed by its competitors and made the most of it. The ruby-throated hummingbird has a wide distribution and is probably one of the most numerous of all the hummingbirds.

The ruby-throated hummingbird is a small hummingbird, and by the standards of its relatives it is not very brightly colored. But the male does have a brilliant scarlet throat, which he shows off to advantage during display. The bird's tail is short and forked, and each tail feather has a spiky tip. Its bill is long, straight, and needle-thin for sipping nectar from inside narrow-throated flowers.

Possessive Owner

The ruby-throated hummingbird is a territorial species, defending a concentrated patch of nectar sources against competitors, including insects and other birds. When another hummingbird intrudes on its territory, a male ruby-throat attacks it unhesitatingly, driving it off using its claws and bill. Sometimes birds in combat hold onto each other and may even fall to the ground still locked together. Such fights

Only the male ruby-throated hummingbird has the glittering red throat, which he shows off to a succession of females in a stylized aerial "pendulum" display.

Taking a Break

When hummingbirds are feeding, they do not satisfy their hunger in one burst. Instead, they hover and feed in front of flowers for short bursts, then return to a perch for a "rest" before hovering again. Each feeding burst lasts less than a minute, and a hummingbird can manage about 15 bursts every hour. For the rest of the time it perches motionless.

Researchers have found the reason for this unusual feeding pattern. When hummingbirds drink nectar, the liquid passes immediately into a storage organ called the crop, from where it is transferred to the rest of the digestive system. But the crop only has a limited capacity. When a hummingbird feeds, its crop takes less than a minute to fill, but rather longer to empty. So a point is reached when the hummingbird cannot take in any more food until the crop has emptied some of its store of already-eaten food. That is when the hummingbird takes its rest. In fact, hummingbirds resume foraging when their crops are half-empty, not completely empty. This stage is reached after about four minutes into the resting period.

between rival birds look vicious, but they rarely result in any injury.

Red and orange flowers are the food sources most favored by the ruby-throat. They include the red blooms of columbine, trumpet creeper, and bee balm, and orange touch-me-not flowers. The bird also visits members of the horse chestnut tree family, especially the dwarf buckeye. The importance of a particular species in the diet varies from place to place. Studies have also shown that the ruby-throat exploits comparatively few native plants (only about 30) throughout North America. The bird visits more varieties in gardens, but for its general welfare it requires a comparatively small number of plants growing in abundance in the wild.

When the birds migrate north in spring, they are sometimes faced with a lack of available blossoms. It is then that they look for a most unusual resource for a hummingbird: tree sap. Rich in sugar, sap is nutritious enough to nourish them until things improve. To find it, they search the trees for holes drilled by a species of woodpecker: the yellow-bellied sapsucker (*Sphyrapicus varius*). It is likely that the northern distribution of the ruby-throated hummingbird is directly related to the activities and distribution of the yellow-bellied sapsucker.

⊖ ***Wings whirring, a ruby-throated hummingbird sips a meal of energy-rich nectar from a red columbine flower. Such red tubular flowers have evolved especially to attract hummingbirds, since the pollinating insects cannot see the color red.***

Insects form yet another part of the ruby-throated hummingbird's diet. It captures most of them during short aerial chases, but it may also glean some from flowers. The importance of insects as food items varies, but it has been reported that they can account for up to 70 percent of a ruby-throated hummingbird's diet during the winter, apparently while suitable nectar is still available.

Aerial Displays

The males form the vanguard of the spring migration, arriving on the breeding grounds a week or so before any females. During this time the males settle disputes among themselves and set up territories. By the time the females arrive, the males have spread out and are ready to perform their impressive aerial display routines, each starting from his own set of perches.

When a male has attracted a female's attention, he displays before her in a swinging, side-to-side flight, whose course mimics the motion of a pendulum. At its height the male's flight arc takes him 10 feet (3 m) above the female and 6 feet (2 m) to the side of her. If this considerable effort pays off, more intimate displays follow, involving the male and female flying face-to-face. The birds eventually drop to the ground and mate.

Separate Roles

Once he has mated with a female, the male plays little further part in any of the breeding tasks except a little nest building. Having invested so much effort in obtaining a territory and refining his display, he puts most of his skills to use by trying to attract further females.

Meanwhile, the female sets about finding the materials to build a nest, including bud scales and other items for the main structure, lichens for the outside, and plant down for the

The Incredible Journey

It seems amazing that a bird as small as a hummingbird could make a journey of 1,000 miles (1,610 km) or more, but that is what ruby-throats routinely do on their migration between eastern North America and Central America every spring and fall. Even more surprising is the fact that, according to available evidence, at least some make a 620-mile (1,000-km) nonstop crossing of the Gulf of Mexico to get there. There are well-authenticated records of birds seen flying some 25 feet (7.6 m) above these waters far from land.

A ruby-throated hummingbird has to double its body weight before attempting to cross the gulf, or it will not have enough reserves to make the flight. Once it sets off, it must continue at a speed of some 25 miles per hour (40 km/h) to make the crossing in about 25 hours. It is an extraordinary feat.

nest lining. The nest is bound with cobwebs to ensure strength and flexibility.

The female follows the typical hummingbird pattern by laying two white eggs, one a day. She incubates them for a standard 16-day period, but the young may leave the nest any time between 15 and 28 days after hatching. The considerable variation is probably caused by fluctuating weather and food supplies. The female also feeds the young after they leave the nest, but for how long is uncertain. Much is still to be learned about this part of the ruby-throat's breeding cycle.

Very occasionally a female will attempt to nest twice, extending the breeding season until July or even August. But that is a gamble, since it will not be long before these tiny birds must embark on their long migration southward. The males, unfettered by the tasks of parenthood, take no such chances and leave early on their travels, well before the females and their young.

In recent years the ruby-throat appeared to be declining in many areas, leading to it being placed on the Blue List of birds of conservation concern. Yet the latest breeding surveys show no clear national change in population between 1966 and 1994. That is good news because it suggests that the future of one of the toughest and most resilient of hummingbirds is secure.

Nectar-rich feeding territories are vital to the survival of ruby-throated hummingbirds, and males in particular regularly fight each other for possession of suitable flowers.

While a male ruby-throat concentrates on mating with as many females as possible, the female tries to maximize her breeding success by ensuring the survival of her young. She takes on most of the job alone, from building the nest to feeding the nestlings.

Common name Hawfinch

Scientific name *Coccothraustes coccothraustes*

Family Fringillidae

Order Passeriformes

Size Length: 7 in (18 cm); wingspan: 11–13 in (28–33 cm); weight: 1.8–2.1 oz (51–60 g)

Key features Small to medium-sized songbird; plump body; short tail; enormous conical bill; largely pink-brown, with black chin and gray nape; wings and tail black-and-white; both sexes, but especially male, have club-ended inner primaries; female has gray secondary bar

Habits Very shy, often elusive finch that tends to forage in the treetops but sometimes feeds on the ground; found in groups of pairs in breeding season, larger flocks in winter; powerful, bounding flight

Nesting Cup nest of twigs, plus roots, grass, lichen, and moss on horizontal tree branch; 4–5 eggs, whitish with a few spots; incubation 11–13 days by female; young fledge after 12–13 days; usually 1 brood

Voice Typically, explosive "pix" and "seep" calls; song is slow sequence of call notes

Diet Seeds, fruits, and insects

Habitat Broadleaved and mixed woodland; parks and gardens

Distribution Europe and Central Asia east to Japan and Kamchatka; also North Africa

Status Not threatened but declining in some areas; uncommon, but has large range

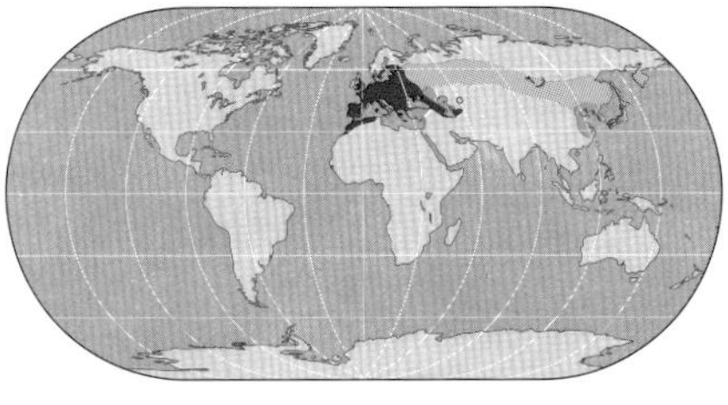

Hawfinch *Coccothraustes coccothraustes*

Almost overbalanced by its outsized bill, the hawfinch is a specialized feeder on the toughest nuts and fruits. Despite this, it can also deal with insects, gleaning them from leaves in its treetop home.

Some finches have delicate bills that they use as precision tools. The hawfinch, however, has a bill that is built for strength. No other finch can match its size and power. Together with its massive head and thick neck, packed with strong muscles, this gives the hawfinch a decidedly top-heavy look. When the bird flies, it moves with powerful bursts of rapid wingbeats that give the impression of compensating for the front-heavy load; when it perches, the posture is upright.

The hawfinch's exceptionally big, heavy bill is a special tool adapted to break open the toughest seeds and fruit stones—foods that are far beyond the capacity of most other finches. In addition to the family trait of having grooves on its palate, the hawfinch has two furrowed knobs at the base of each mandible that clench the seed in a tight grip. The powerful skull muscles can exert sufficient force to even split cherry stones and, if put to such a use, could even sever a human finger. This enormous strength enables the hawfinch to exploit its very own seed-eating niche.

Orchard Raider

Most of the seeds that the hawfinch eats are produced by large deciduous trees, so it is primarily a bird of open woodland, especially of mixed oak and hornbeam. It also has a great fondness for wild and cultivated fruit trees, including apples, pears, and various types of cherry. Not surprisingly, orchards are popular places for them to visit, and very occasionally the hawfinch can become an economic pest.

Despite its unusual ability to crack the hardest of nuts, the hawfinch is nevertheless a versatile feeder. It feeds both on the ground

Hawfinch courtship is a quiet, private affair, in which the birds may appear to "kiss" each other on the bill.

and high in tree crowns, using its bill to bite off fruits and buds at the stalk. In addition, perhaps surprisingly for such a specialized bird, it also captures insects. Caterpillars, especially those that hide away in rolled-up leaves, form an important part of its summer diet, and it also feeds them to its nestlings. On the forest floor the hawfinch also comes across beetles with hard wingcases, which soon succumb to that nutcracker bill. In fall this all-rounder feeds on berries and fruits; indeed, it gets its name from taking the berries of the hawthorn bush, which are called haws.

Throughout its extensive range from Europe east to Japan the hawfinch has a well-deserved reputation for being shy and unobtrusive. When feeding on the woodland floor in company with other birds, it is usually the first to fly up to the treetops at any sign of danger and the last to return.

Bowing Courtship

Hawfinches live in small flocks during the winter, and pairs form within these flocks. Courtship involves a certain amount of bowing and wing spreading; sometimes the birds touch bills and appear to prod each other. It is an intimate, subtle display. Male hawfinches do sing, but the song is soft and jerky; it has no territorial function but serves as an embellishment to the courtship routine.

Despite a low population density, it is common for several pairs of hawfinches to nest close together, sometimes even in the same tree. Such "neighborhood groups" often forage for food together. Each pair looks for a nest site with quite specific requirements; it must be well lit and with easy access—perhaps because hawfinches are not especially skilled at flying in tight spaces. The chosen site is usually along a horizontal branch. Although hawfinches are birds of the treetops, their nests are rarely more than 30 feet (9 m) above ground.

There are no signs that the hawfinch is under any major threat despite its core habitat being extensive open woodland with mature trees. Its range of feeding options and surprising adaptability to artificial environments should ensure its continuing survival.

Despite its outsized bill, the hawfinch is adept at catching insects, especially caterpillars, which it both eats and feeds to its hungry nestlings to give them the protein they need to develop properly.

Black-capped Chickadee

Parus atricapillus

Often tame and confident around people, this small, lively, neat bird of woodlands, parks, and gardens is the most widely distributed tit in North America and one of the most familiar of all backyard birds.

Common name Black-capped chickadee

Scientific name *Parus atricapillus*

Family Paridae

Order Passeriformes

Size Length: 5 in (12.7 cm); wingspan: 7–8 in (18–20 cm); weight: 0.4 oz (11 g)

Key features Black crown and nape, chin, and throat; broad white cheek patch; upper parts gray-brown with paler panel along closed wing; underside rusty-buff; short black bill and gray-black legs; sexes alike

Habits Active, acrobatic, often in mixed flocks; frequently visits garden feeders

Nesting Nests in hole in tree; 6–8 eggs; incubation 12–13 days by female; young fledge after 16 days; 1 brood

Voice Typically a buzzy, gurgling "chick-a-dee-dee-dee"; also "day-day-day" and high, clear whistled "phe-be" or "phe-be-be"

Diet Insects, seeds, berries, spiders, and snails

Habitat Mixed woods, thickets, woodland edges, and suburban gardens

Distribution North America from Alaska to California and east to Newfoundland

Status Widespread and common, stable or increasing

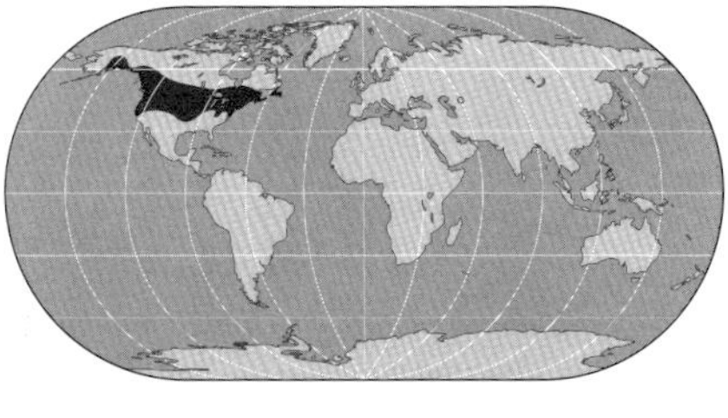

In winter small parties of black-capped chickadees descend on gardens throughout much of North America to exploit the food that people leave out for them. As a result, this adaptable, acrobatic little tit is one the most recognizable of all suburban songbirds. It gets its name from the black cap that, together with the wide black bib over its chin and throat, outlines its strikingly white cheeks. The lower edge of the black bib is slightly ragged in fresh plumage, compared with the sharper edge on the very similar Carolina chickadee (*Parus carolinensis*). Apart from this it is mainly gray-brown above, with pale edges to some of the wing feathers that create a band of pale gray along the closed wing. That is less obvious in late summer, when the feathers are worn, and the pale feather edges are much reduced. Its underside is a quite rich, bright tawny-buff, whiter beneath the bib.

Winter Survivor

The black-capped chickadee is a common bird across a broad band of North America from western Alaska and the southern half of Canada south to extreme northern California in the west and eastward in a narrowing belt to the Atlantic coast. In the north it is found across southern Manitoba, Ontario, and Quebec, and through Nova Scotia to Virginia. The southern limit of its range runs through Kansas, Missouri, Indiana, and Ohio, with a southward spur along the Appalachians. The bird is a resident within this area, able to survive severe winter weather, but occasional food shortages sometimes force it south in winter. Its breeding range may then be extended south for a season or two.

The bird lives in a variety of mixed and deciduous wooded habitats in and around the edges of forest and in open woodland and parkland. It also feeds in gardens and in thickets and scrub. Its frequency in gardens depends largely on the food supply in winter and the availability of nest sites in summer. The black-capped chickadee is commonest in open birch and alder woodland, often close to clearings, and avoids pure stands of conifers.

Where other chickadees occur, reducing its feeding options, the bird is mostly found in clumps of deciduous trees. In the Appalachians, where both black-capped and Carolina chickadees live, black-caps prefer higher areas, and Carolinas favor valleys and low foothills.

Broad Diet

Although mostly insectivorous, the chickadee eats a wide range of food, taking whatever is available. In summer it eats mostly caterpillars and other small insects, spiders, and various other invertebrates. Vegetable food then forms only about ten percent of its diet. But in winter seeds, fruits, and berries may make up as much as half its diet, and it also eats more insect eggs and pupae.

It searches for food among small twigs and branches and their foliage, picking prey from the bark and often hanging underneath to scour the whole surface. A chickadee has specially developed leg muscles that enable it to take food from the undersides of branches that is missed by many other birds. Its feet and toes are short, but strong, with an excellent grip. Its feeding technique involves careful examination of the bark, with much pecking and probing. It may also hover occasionally to reach particularly difficult places, and it can catch flying insects in midair like a flycatcher.

(↑) Throughout much of North America the black-capped chickadee is a familiar visitor to garden bird feeders in winter, when food may be hard to find elsewhere. In spring they disappear into the forests to breed, reappearing when the weather deteriorates again in the fall.

Courtship Feeding

Beginning in late winter, the male chickadee starts to feed the female—an activity called courtship feeding. It is seen in many species of birds, including warblers, chats, and tits, and has two obvious functions. One is to reinforce the pair-bond. It is essential in birds that spend most of their lives repelling others but that must now work together to mate, nest, and rear a brood of young. Courtship feeding helps break down the birds' desire to "keep their distance," allowing close contact and trust between the pair. The female must also produce a clutch of eggs, laying one egg a day. It is a huge drain on her body resources, and any extra high-nutrition food supplied by the male helps the female greatly at this time.

In winter a chickadee must spend around 80 percent of its day searching for food. It is typical of the many small birds that must maintain a continual intake of energy in the short daylight hours of winter if it is to survive the low temperatures and the long, dark nights when it is unable to feed. Studies in England of the very similar willow tit (*Parus montanus*)—once regarded as the same species—revealed that each bird must find one average-sized insect every 2.5 seconds to ensure its winter survival. To achieve this goal, it might have to examine more than 1,000 trees in a day.

The black-capped chickadee visits feeders in gardens especially in winter, where it seeks out food items such as seeds and suet in particular. It eats any kind of fatty material such as bacon rind or pork fat, as well as split squash or pumpkin seeds and sunflower seeds.

Food Stores

When feeding, a black-capped chickadee may take a big food item up to a large branch and then clamp it securely with the front toes of one or both feet, while it pecks it to pieces. The use of the feet when feeding is limited to this activity, however. Food is always located with and then grabbed by the bill. Indeed, only one family of passerines, the drongos, are known to catch and lift food using their feet.

Chickadees store food in bark crevices or similar places and usually recover it later in the course of normal foraging. They store insects as well as seeds, usually killing them first, but sometimes squeezing them into a tight space while still alive. Related European species may store up to 4,700 items per day in spring, but only 200 or so per day in winter. A single bird may store up to half a million items in a year.

↑ Chickadees often spend most of the daylight hours searching for food, especially in winter, when they need extra energy to keep warm during the long, dark, cold nights. At this time they eat a lot of seeds, but in summer they take mainly insects.

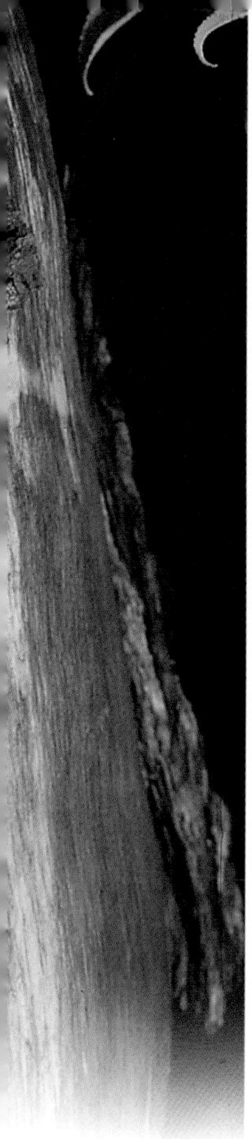

Winter Flocks

Black-capped chickadees are active and lively birds, always adding life and movement to the winter woods when they join the small mixed bands of nomadic birds that roam in search of food. They call frequently with the contact note that gives them their name, and that allows them to be picked out from the various nuthatches, kinglets, and other birds with which they associate. At this time many woods seem empty until one of these feeding flocks appears, and the chickadee's call is often the first clue to the flock's approach.

Sociable feeding in winter appears to be a way of maximizing feeding efficiency, since concentrations of food are more likely to be found by a wandering group moving through on a broad front than by single birds. When one bird stops to feed, the others notice and concentrate on the area, too, moving on only when the food is exhausted.

Furthermore, many pairs of eyes are better than one pair at spotting potential predators, and chickadees are quick to raise the alarm at the approach of a predator. They may also feel more secure in a flock: A single bird is the sole target of a predator, but in a flock the chances of being singled out for attack are reduced.

Despite their generally sociable nature, these little birds are aggressive in close encounters and very possessive when it comes to food or nest sites. In confrontations with other chickadees they try to avoid actual fighting when possible. Instead, they stretch upward, ruffle their body feathers, or raise their head feathers in display—all in an attempt to appear bigger and more threatening. That may be enough to discourage an intruder, but sometimes an open bill or even a quick peck has to reinforce the meaning of such postures.

The black-capped chickadee is no great songster, but its frequent, familiar calls are welcome in the winter woodland. It shares a basic pattern of vocabulary with several other tits, such as the European willow tit and marsh tit (*Parus palustris*). Chickadees respond to imitations of their calls or even to squeaking sounds. They seem to be confident when approaching people and may come to within arm's length of someone keeping still.

A chickadee often bathes, and it preens regularly to keep its plumage in top condition. It will sunbathe, too, pressing itself flat with its wings extended, and the feathers of its back and rump raised to allow the heat of the sun to warm its exposed skin.

A cavity in a birch tree makes an ideal nest site for a pair of black-capped chickadees. The pair works together to enlarge it with their bills and shape it to their requirements, but the female alone is responsible for building the hair-lined nest inside the hole.

Pairing Up

Chickadee pairs form in the fall and remain together within the winter flocks. Their courtship is simple and does not involve complex postures or displays. In spring the paired birds begin to feed on their own on nice days but may return to the flock if the weather deteriorates. Eventually the flock splits up, and each pair defends a territory together. The male calls with sweet "phe-be" or "phe-be-be," the first note longer and higher than the others.

The pair finds a suitable site, usually a natural cavity in rotten wood that can be enlarged or reshaped with their bills. Old woodpecker holes are sometimes used, as are artificial nestboxes. Sometimes a shallow cavity made by a woodpecker digging for larvae under the bark is chipped away to make a larger nest hole. They never excavate holes in sound wood. The hole is usually 6 to 20 feet

Ⓓ When other birds fly south for the winter, the black-capped chickadee stays on. It is partly sustained by the food that it has stored in crevices scattered over its home range, but it also joins other birds in winter feeding flocks.

Varied Chickadees

In the southeastern states the black-capped chickadee is replaced by the similar Carolina chickadee, which sometimes learns to imitate the black-cap's song and occasionally interbreeds with it. They look alike and occupy similar habitats, but the Carolina chickadee, living in milder areas, is less likely to visit garden feeders. In the west it is also found with the mountain chickadee (*P. gambeli*), a mountain conifer forest specialist, and locally the chestnut-backed chickadee (*P. rufescens*); in the north it overlaps with the browner boreal chickadee (*P. hudsonicus*), also a conifer forest species.

(1.8–6 m) above the ground. Both sexes enlarge the nest hole if necessary, but the nest itself is built only by the female, using moss or other soft vegetable matter with a lining of hair.

Like other tits, the female black-capped chickadee covers her eggs with nest material when she leaves an incomplete clutch. She incubates the eggs herself, with the male often bringing her food. When the chicks have just hatched, the male brings food while the female remains with them in the nest; but as they grow and become more demanding, both parents find food. The chicks typically leave the nest early in the morning and need constant attention, calling greedily to be fed. Many are taken by predators, or starve if food (especially caterpillars) is scarce, or succumb to cold, wet weather in poor springs. But populations are able to recover quickly from such setbacks in warm, dry seasons with plentiful caterpillars.

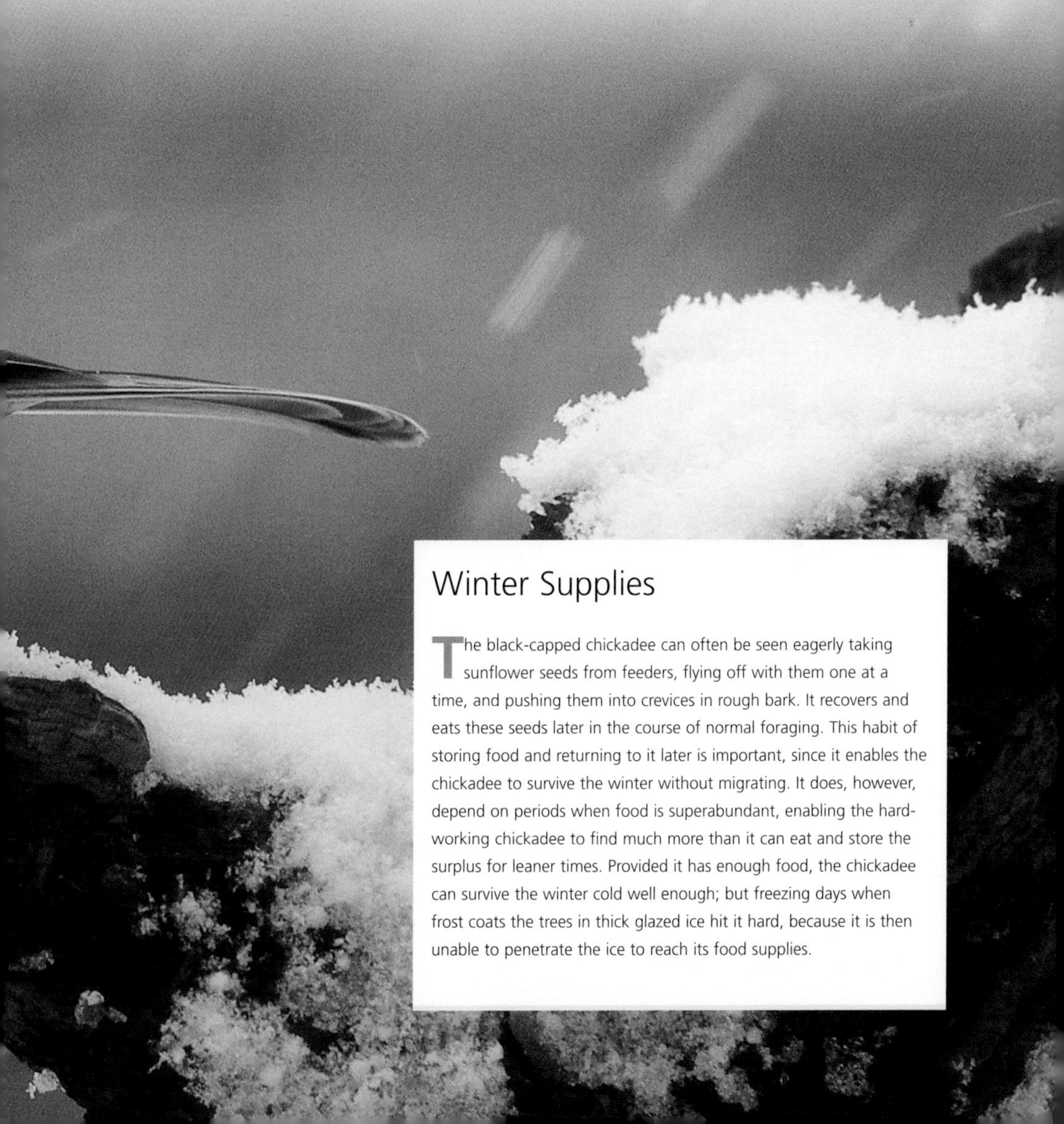

Winter Supplies

The black-capped chickadee can often be seen eagerly taking sunflower seeds from feeders, flying off with them one at a time, and pushing them into crevices in rough bark. It recovers and eats these seeds later in the course of normal foraging. This habit of storing food and returning to it later is important, since it enables the chickadee to survive the winter without migrating. It does, however, depend on periods when food is superabundant, enabling the hard-working chickadee to find much more than it can eat and store the surplus for leaner times. Provided it has enough food, the chickadee can survive the winter cold well enough; but freezing days when frost coats the trees in thick glazed ice hit it hard, because it is then unable to penetrate the ice to reach its food supplies.

Pileated Woodpecker

Dryocopus pileatus

One of the biggest and most spectacular of its family, the pileated woodpecker is a much admired, successful bird that has extended its habitat from its stronghold in mature old-growth forests to parks and even suburban gardens.

Common name Pileated woodpecker

Scientific name *Dryocopus pileatus*

Family Picidae

Order Piciformes

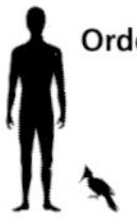

Size Length: 16–19 in (41–48 cm); wingspan: 16.5–18 in (42–46 cm); weight: 8.8–12 oz (249–340 g)

Key features Big, long-billed woodpecker; black plumage with white streaks along head and neck; red crown with crest; female has black forehead, male has red forehead and red "mustache" stripe; juvenile browner, with paler crown

Habits Largely solitary; feeds both in trees and on ground; not particularly shy around people

Nesting Excavates hole in large tree at a height of 20–40 ft (6–12 m); 2–4 eggs; incubation 18 days; young fledge after 26–28 days; 1 brood

Voice Loud "wuk" or "cac," either singly or repeated; drums with two-second rolls once or twice a minute

Diet Invertebrates, especially ants; also nuts, fruits, and berries

Habitat Old-growth forests and woodlands with large, old trees; also some secondary woodlands and town parks with older trees

Distribution From British Columbia across southern Canada and through eastern U.S. to Florida

Status Increasing in east of range

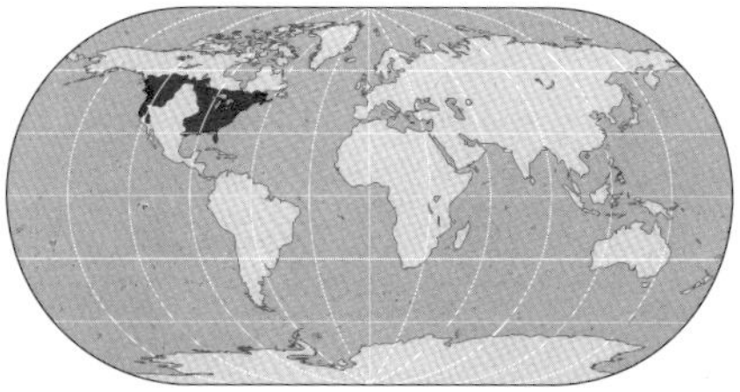

INSTANTLY RECOGNIZABLE BOTH BY ITS size and its bold black, red, and white coloration, the pileated woodpecker makes a dramatic sight. Both sexes have a crest of red feathers that can be erected to a point ("pileated" simply means "crested"), but a male can be distinguished from a female by his red "mustache." Young birds are browner than adults and have a hint of orange in their crest. The adult's call is a distinctive, loud staccato note, often repeated. It carefully selects a resonant piece of dead timber to hammer with its bill, producing rolls of drumming that carry a long way across the forest. Sadly, the only species with which the pileated woodpecker could be confused was the ivory-billed woodpecker (*Campephilus principalis*), which is now feared extinct.

Although well equipped for hacking wood-boring insect grubs from their tunnels, the pileated woodpecker also takes a lot of its prey from the ground, especially ants such as the big, heavy-jawed carpenter ant.

Essential Trees

The pileated woodpecker has a large range across southern Canada and down through the eastern U.S. Throughout this range the woodpeckers mainly inhabit old-growth forests and woodlands where large old trees provide a great many opportunities for roosting and nesting. They may nest in "second growth" woodlands or even in town parks, but older trees are essential. Within these places the birds often favor areas near rivers or other bodies of water.

Like all the larger woodpeckers, the pileated woodpecker uses its feet, legs, and tail to support itself on the trunks of trees as it hammers at the timber. In one of the various woodpecker "design variations" all four of its toes can point forward; that allows the lower part of its leg—the tarsus—to sit on the timber and help grip the surface. In smaller woodpeckers one or two toes point backward, preventing the bird from using the tarsus to provide grip. The bird uses its tail for extra support, wedging its strengthened tail feathers into the bark when it is at rest.

Chiseling for a Meal

Like many of its relatives, the pileated woodpecker eats a lot of ants. It is particularly fond of carpenter ants. It also preys on the larvae of wood-boring beetles, exposing them by persistently chiseling away at the timber. It eats caterpillars and termites when available. When invertebrates are less plentiful during the

cold winter months, the woodpecker increases the proportion of nuts, berries, and seeds in its diet. And like its relatives in other parts of the world, it may be attracted to gardens by bird foods containing suet.

A Great Excavator

Pairs hold territory year-round; but as the nesting season approaches in mid to late winter, the territorial and pair displays begin in earnest. Each pair indicates the boundaries of their territory by calling and drumming. Meanwhile, they display to each other with ritualized movements, including mutual head swinging, bobbing, and raising their red crests. They accompany these displays with exaggerated flights that show off their white wing patches. All of this helps establish a strong pair-bond.

Work on nest construction begins once the pair are established. In most cases a new nest is constructed each year, probably because the construction process is integral to maintaining the pair-bond. In over half the cases the chosen tree will be dead or dying. Obviously, the timber of a dead tree is weakened and easier to hack away, so the birds save energy in excavation. Even when an apparently healthy tree is chosen, it may have been weakened internally through the action of fungi. There has been speculation that with many woodpecker species abortive excavation attempts in hard live wood actually initiate attacks by fungus that are later utilized by other woodpeckers.

The nest hole itself is often at some height above the forest floor. Both sexes share the work of excavation, but the male does more work than the female. The job itself starts with the birds chiseling a conical entrance hole running horizontally into the tree trunk. Chiseling can last for several minutes without a break, apart from pauses while the birds fling wood shavings away from the nest site. As the

The bright red crest of the pileated woodpecker forms part of a colorful pair-bonding display in the breeding season. This bird's red "mustache" stripe indicates that it is a male.

Woody Woodpecker

Perhaps the most famous woodpecker—and one that shares the pileated woodpecker's proud red crest—is the mischievous cartoon character Woody Woodpecker. A hit for Universal, Woody was created by Walter Lantz in the early 1940s and first appeared in an Andy Panda cartoon called *Knock, Knock*. Lantz declared that the inspiration for Woody came to him when on honeymoon. He and his new wife were both irritated and amused by a woodpecker that regularly visited and drummed on the wooden cabin in which they were staying. But amusement and irritation turned to frustration when, after a storm, they discovered rain pouring in through the freshly excavated holes in the walls!

hole gets deeper, the birds start to dig down to create a vertical nest chamber.

At first, the birds perch outside while excavating; but as the job progresses, they disappear inside the tree. The only signs of their presence are occasional puffs of shavings from the entrance hole. When completed, the nest cavity can measure up to 26 inches (66 cm) deep and 6.5 inches (16.5 cm) across. The last of the shavings are left to line the base of the nest chamber. Here they provide a soft surface for nesting and a suitable medium to soak up waste material from the chicks. The whole construction process takes around 25 days.

As the woodpeckers excavate their nest chamber, they toss the wood chippings out of the entrance hole.

Buzzing Youngsters

Once the nest is complete, the female lays her clutch of white, almost translucent eggs. One egg is laid each day until the clutch is complete, but incubation may start before the final egg is produced. Both sexes share incubation duties; but as with nest construction, the male is in attendance more than the female and always incubates at night. During this sensitive period at least one bird attends 99 percent of the time. As is the case with other woodpeckers, the incubation period is relatively short, and the young appear after some 18 days. At first, they are blind, naked, and completely helpless.

For the first seven to ten days both parents brood the offspring, the male again doing more work than the female. Indeed, the male's role is vital. In a couple of observed cases the death of the male led to the female abandoning the nest, while on the death of a female the male continued to raise his offspring.

When in the nest, the young are fed a diet consisting mainly of insects and other small

Best Foot Forward

Nearly all birds have four toes, but they are arranged in a variety of ways and have evolved into numerous shapes to help the bird make the most of its habitat and lifestyle.

By far the most common layout is three toes to the front and one—the "hallux"—to the rear. This standard arrangement is called "anisodactyl." In many waterbirds the three forward-pointing toes have developed webbing or lobes to help movement in water. Birds of prey have developed sharp, powerful talons, and the feet of the osprey (*Pandion haliaetus*) have evolved special barbed nodes to help grip slippery fish. In the passerines, or "perching birds," the arrangement of tendons in the feet provides an automatic grip when the bird perches on a branch.

A slight variation on the anisodactyl arrangement has two of the forward toes fused together. It is called "syndactyl" and is typical of the rollers and their allies in the order Coraciiformes.

A different arrangement has two toes to the front and two to the rear. Called "zygodactyl," this layout has developed independently in birds such as the cuckoos, parrots, and in some woodpeckers. In the trogons the position of the fourth toe is slightly different and is called "heterodactyl."

Last, some groups, such as the African mousebirds, have "pamprodactyl" feet in which the hallux and fourth toe can be placed either forward or backward.

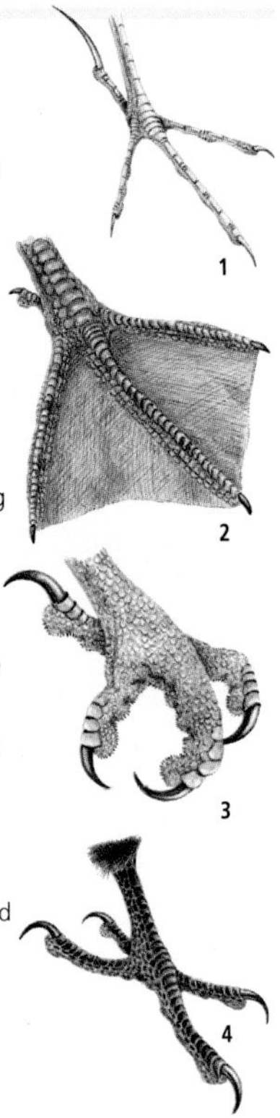

Different types of bird feet: anisodactyl foot of a perching bird (1); webbed foot of a typical waterbird (2); powerful, strong-clawed talon of a bird of prey (3); zygodactyl foot of a small woodpecker (4).

invertebrates. Food is regurgitated on demand, the young birds taking turns to receive the food directly from their parents' bills. Initially food is brought at least hourly; but as the chicks grow, the parents visit once every two hours.

At first, the newly hatched chicks can do very little apart from call for their food. These calls have been described as sounding like a "buzzing beehive." As the young grow, their confidence develops, and they begin to scale the walls of their nest chamber. By 15 to 18 days they are able to reach the nest entrance, where they wait for their parents to return.

Between 24 and 30 days they leave their nests, but their first flights are short and rather speculative. Initially, they remain within easy reach of their natal home, only gradually exploring new areas. As their confidence develops, they accompany their parents around the forest on feeding flights and remain together in family flocks. But with the onset of winter the family group splits up. By the following spring the first-year birds are able to nest themselves and begin to set up territories.

Doing Well

Pileated woodpeckers suffered quite a range contraction in the face of extensive logging in the nineteenth and early twentieth centuries. However, they have recovered and are not of global conservation concern. In the east of their range their population is actually increasing.

When they are old enough to climb up to the nest entrance, the young woodpeckers perch there and wait for their parents to return with food.

Bohemian Waxwing

Bombycilla garrulus

Bohemian waxwings are handsome nomads, best known to most people from their wintering areas rather than their more northerly breeding grounds, which form an almost complete ring around the Arctic.

Common name Bohemian waxwing (waxwing)

Scientific name *Bombycilla garrulus*

Family Bombycillidae

Order Passeriformes

Size Length: 7 in (18 cm); wingspan: 12.5–14 in (32–36 cm); weight: 1.75–2.6 oz (50–75 g)

Key features Plump bird with back-swept crest; pink-brown with gray rump; black chin; thin, black mask; white wing bars; yellow-and-white edges to primary tips; waxy, red extensions on secondaries (in some birds); yellow tail tip

Habits Appears in flocks in winter to eat berries

Nesting Nest is a bowl of twigs, moss, and grasses in tree, with lining of grasses and lichens; 5–6 gray-blue to blue eggs, spotted with gray and black; incubation 14–15 days by female; young fledge after 14–15 days; 1 brood

Voice Call is a thin, trilling "sirrrr"; song similar; rattles wings when taking off and landing

Diet Insects in breeding season; berries in winter

Habitat Breeds in northern forests, especially in old, lichen-covered conifers; may winter in temperate zones wherever there are suitable berries, including city centers and backyards

Distribution Northern Eurasia and northwest North America, in taiga zone surrounding Arctic, ranging south to more temperate latitudes

Status Probably reasonably secure

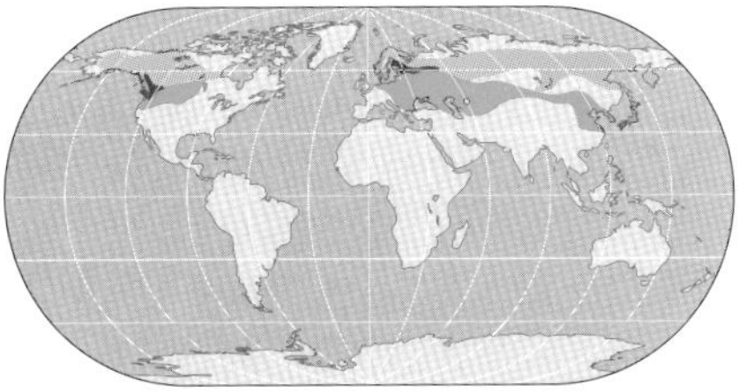

SEEN IN A PICTURE ON A PAGE in a book, the Bohemian waxwing looks unmistakable. Its pinkish plumage, flamboyant crest, odd feather ornaments, and generally exotic appearance are virtually unique among northern birds. But it is similar in size and shape to the European starling (*Sturnus vulgaris*), and in some lights its highly distinctive plumage can appear all dark, making confusion with starlings even more likely. It also has a habit of forming similar tight flocks, although waxwing flocks are seldom as large as starling flocks and rarely contain more than a few hundred birds.

When the bird is seen well, it is unmistakably a waxwing, although in North America it can be confused with the cedar waxwing (*Bombycilla cedrorum*), which is browner, has much plainer wings, and is white rather than red-brown under its tail. Males and females look more or less alike, though the female's black chin may be smaller and with a less well-defined lower edge. Females may also have fewer, smaller red waxy extensions on their wings. Juveniles look like washed-out adults, with whitish eyebrows and a white stripe behind each eye.

The Bohemian waxwing has gone by many names in the past, including silk tail, Bohemian chatterer, waxen chatterer, and the chatterer of Carolina. The "chattering" refers to the bird's habit of rattling its wings, rather than its trilling call. Currently, three races are recognized, all of which are similar in appearance. One of these races, *Bombycilla garrulus pallidiceps*, lives only in North America; the others are found in Europe, Siberia, and Asia.

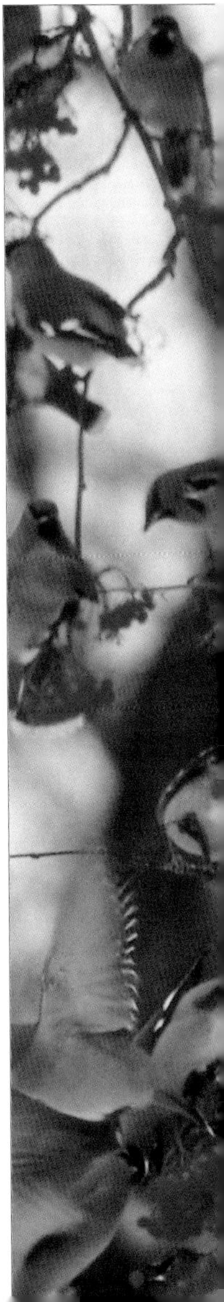

Waxwings feasting on berries feed mainly in the trees, but sometimes they gather fallen fruit from the ground. Sometimes they hang upside down and attack berries from below; at other times they hover briefly to feed.

Long-distance Wanderers

Some Bohemian waxwings choose to stay on their breeding grounds through the winter, but others go south. Individual waxwings often return to breed in widely separated areas from one year to the next and winter in very different places in successive years too. One Bohemian waxwing was banded as a wintering bird in Poland and found the following winter in eastern Siberia, 3,200 miles (5,150 km) away.

Birds that breed in Scandinavia normally move to more southerly and westerly parts of Europe. But their wanderings can take them much further, to Iceland and Greenland. North American birds that breed in northwest Canada and Alaska winter in southern Canada, all the way east to Nova Scotia. Those breeding in western Canada fly to southern California, Arizona, New Mexico, and Texas. Others go to Ohio, Indiana, and New England.

Irruptive Species

A typical bird migrant makes a predictable journey between its breeding grounds and wintering area. It breeds in the same area every year and winters in the same area every year. It migrates over a well-defined route and has well-developed homing skills.

Irruptive species like the Bohemian waxwing are different. The numbers that head south in the fall and the distance they travel vary from year to year. Individuals may breed in widely separated areas and winter in widely separated areas. They do not follow predictable migration routes and may fly off in a different direction every year.

Irruptive species often depend on one or two types of food. If there is not enough, they are forced to look elsewhere and normally travel only as far as the first appropriate food. Many are birds of high latitudes where fluctuations in food supply are common.

The spruces of southern Sweden produce a good crop every 3–4 years, providing food for the red crossbill (*Loxia curvirostra*). In any one area all of the spruce trees are likely to be cropping at the same time. A good crop results in a higher winter survival rate and, therefore, a larger crossbill population. But good crops do not normally happen two years in a row, so the large population has a poor food supply. The result is an "irruption year," when large numbers of crossbills go farther than normal to find food in winter.

Meat-eating birds may do the same. In the boreal forests of North America northern goshawks (*Accipiter gentilis*) are among the bird species that eat snowshoe hares. But the hare populations fluctuate on a ten-year cycle, causing the goshawks to irrupt south every ten years or so.

Waxwings must choose between spending the winter on their breeding grounds or heading south and looking for food in more temperate regions. In irruption years large numbers may fly south and turn up wherever they can find the right berries. Their diet is varied and includes rowan, hawthorn, cotoneaster, currants, apples, pears, firethorns, holly, and ivy. A waxwing can eat three times its body weight in berries in a day. A well-fed bird can look lazy and easy to approach until you get just a little too close, and the waxwing's crest goes up in alarm.

Yet the waxwing's winter diet is not confined to berries. It also eats buds and flowers, including those of crocus, fuschia, birch, and aspen. Waxwings have also been seen taking maple sap, snails, and beetles. Between berry meals they take on lots of water and can even be seen flycatching snowflakes!

Wedding Gifts

Bohemian waxwings are monogamous. Their courtship includes a very deliberate gift-passing ceremony, which is conducted in silence. The male stretches out his neck and puts a gift—which may or may not be edible—into the female's expectant and open bill. The gift may be offered to the female more than once and

Summer Flycatchers

In the summer Bohemian waxwings eat mostly insects. Mosquitoes and midges are favorites, but they also eat mayflies, caddisflies, and stoneflies. They catch insects by flying out from perches to seize them in flight, like flycatchers.

In the fall their diet switches to berries. It is a gradual change rather than a sudden one, the rate of change depending on the weather and the availability of insects. The change back to insects in the spring is likely to be gradual, too—waxwings have been seen taking insects when the sun shines, and switching to fruit when it becomes cloudy.

Waxwings swallow smaller berries whole with a toss of the head. When they tackle larger berries, they eat only the flesh and seeds and leave the skin.

Bohemian or Cedar?

There are two waxwing species in North America: the Bohemian waxwing and the cedar waxwing. How do you tell them apart? Bohemian waxwings breed in much of the western half of Canada and up into Alaska. In the winter their range extends as far south as Utah and Colorado in the western U.S. and sometimes farther. In some years they are found in the northeast, too. Cedar waxwings breed in southern Canada and the northern U.S. in both the east and the west. They winter farther south, right down into Mexico.

The adult cedar waxwing is smaller. Its belly is yellowish, whereas the Bohemian waxwing is gray underneath. The cedar waxwing's undertail is white, but the Bohemian's is red-brown. The Bohemian waxwing has a white wingbar and yellow markings on its wings; the cedar waxwing has neither of these. The juveniles of both species are like washed-out adults with streaked underparts, but juvenile Bohemians have white wing patches; juvenile cedars do not.

Look through flocks of cedar waxwings carefully—occasionally there is a Bohemian waxwing in there.

↑ Bohemian waxwing pairs normally build their nest 10–50 feet (3–15 m) above the ground in a conifer tree, typically a spruce or pine—although they may also use a smaller bush or stunted pine.

may go back and forth between the two birds many times. After a successful gift passing, the birds move apart, stay still for a few seconds, then move back together and try again.

Where waxwings are numerous, pairs may nest quite close to each other with little territorial dispute between the birds. While the female incubates, males gather together to feed. Things change when the eggs hatch, and both sexes do their bit in feeding the young. The family stays together as a unit until late summer or early fall, and at this point the families merge into flocks.

Boreal forests are relatively remote and cover vast areas, so barring large-scale changes to their quality or quantity, the Bohemian waxwing probably has a secure future.

Common name Blue jay

Scientific name *Cyanocitta cristata*

Family Corvidae

Order Passeriformes

Size Length: 9.5–12 in (24–30 cm); wingspan: 15–16 in (38–41 cm); weight: 2.3–3.8 oz (65–108 g)

Key features Medium-sized, colorful crow, with small crest; blue wings and tail barred with black and white; underparts whitish apart from black "necklace"; black bill and legs

Habits Very bold and noisy; hops rapidly from branch to branch

Nesting Nests made of twigs, moss, grass, and even string in fork or horizontal branch; usually 4–5 eggs; incubation 17–18 days; young fledge after 17–21 days; 1–2 broods

Voice Wide variety of calls, including piercing "jay jay" call and wheedling musical sounds

Diet Fruits, seeds, insects and other invertebrates, small mammals, lizards, nestling birds and eggs, and carrion

Habitat Wooded areas, including forests and parks

Distribution Eastern and central North America

Status Widespread and common; range expanding westward

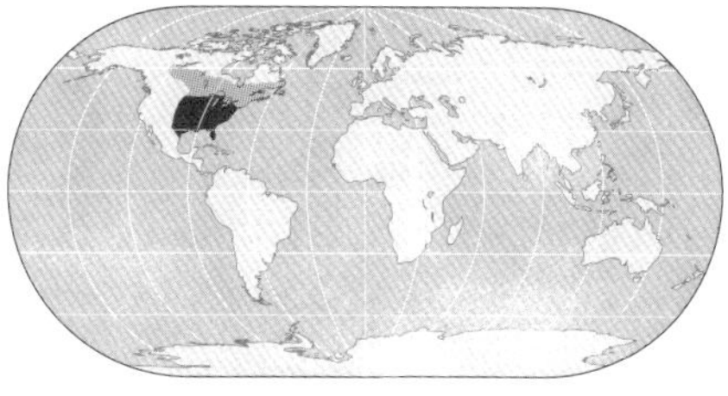

Blue Jay

Cyanocitta cristata

It is hard to ignore a noisy, confident neighbor, and the vociferous character and audacious habits of the blue jay have earned it an almost iconic status in its native North America.

EVEN THOUGH IT IS ABSENT from the western side of the continent, the blue jay is known throughout North America. Its appearance is certainly memorable. It is strikingly light blue on the top of its head, its wings, back, and tail, with a blue crest at the back of its head. A black eyeline runs into a thick "necklace" that loops around its upper breast. There are fine black bars on its wings, as well as white patches that are highly visible in flight, and it has a long, black-barred tail. It has a voice to match its vivid colors, with an extensive vocabulary ranging from piercing calls to musical whistles.

Essentially, it is a bird of the woodland edge rather than deep forest. In Illinois, for example, its population is higher in towns than in the forests outside. Human settlements offer an attractive alternative to the forests, provided there are enough nut-producing trees available.

In winter blue jays rely heavily on nuts and seeds, and they are quick to visit garden bird feeders to gather what they can. Out in the forests they survive by making food caches to see them through the winter.

In late summer and fall the annual berry crop provides a feast for blue jays intent on building up their energy reserves before winter closes in.

There are a wide variety of backyard microhabitats in town, with many offering bird feeders, potential nesting material, and open areas for hiding supplies of food. Blue jays have learned to thrive in close proximity to humans.

Only a very small proportion of blue jays migrate, and those that do tend to be birds spending the summer in northern states of the U.S. and Canada. Many jays are resident even in northernmost areas. The travelers seek company, with day-flying flocks of 20–30 birds flying in a southerly or southwesterly direction.

Exaggerated Notoriety

A painting by the famous nineteenth-century naturalist Audubon shows three jays stealing the eggs from another bird's nest. In reality its reputation as a nest raider is greatly exaggerated, for the eggs and young of other birds make up only a tiny part of its diet. Fruit, insects, and other invertebrates are much more important, and the birds regularly take rodents and carrion, as well as scavenging scraps. But the blue jay is primarily a seed-eater, favoring the nuts of oak, beech, chestnut, hickory, and

The jaunty crest, colorful plumage, and bold character of the blue jay have made it a backyard favorite over much of its range, although it also has an ill-deserved reputation for raiding the nests of other songbirds.

hazel. In every month of the year, apart from July and August, these nuts alone make up nearly half of its diet.

Like the Eurasian jay (*Garrulus glandarius*), the blue jay is a prodigious collector of acorns, with each individual collecting between 3,000 and 5,000 acorns each fall. By choice the jay plucks them from the tree, although it will also take nuts from the ground as long as they are not infested with weevils or other insects. Unlike its transatlantic cousin, the blue jay does not travel far for its acorns: 2.5 miles (4 km) is about as far as it will go. It also carries fewer in its bill, with no more than five acorns at a time. It returns to an open patch of land, perhaps a plowed field or a recently mowed meadow, and

Go West, Young Jay

Historically, North America has been divided between two species of blue jay, with the Great Plains acting as a huge wild frontier. To the east the blue jay has occupied the land as far as the Atlantic coast. On the other side of the Plains Steller's jay (*Cyanocitta stelleri*) has traditionally had western North America to itself. Since the late 1940s scientists have noticed a westward expansion of the blue jay's range. It continues today, with nesting recorded in British Columbia, Oregon, Montana, Wyoming, and New Mexico among others.

Why should this have happened? The most likely reasons have to do with how humans have altered the Great Plains. Until comparatively recently, the open, treeless prairies would have offered little for a tree-dwelling species, and so this area remained jayless. But modern settlement has brought more tree cover to these areas. Farm shelter belts have been planted, and new residential areas have brought new woodland and a plethora of backyard bird feeders. The opportunistic blue jay has taken advantage.

As the blue jay has spread, it has moved into areas that are already occupied by Steller's jays. These very closely related species share a number of physical and behavioral characteristics. For example, they both feed primarily on nuts and seeds, take food readily from humans, and nest in trees. In some places they have even begun to breed with each other, although at the moment such hybridization is rare. It is too early to know whether North America's two blue jay species will become competitors in the future, but ornithologists are watching very closely.

makes a pile of acorns. Once it has a sizable collection, it buries the acorns close together, topping off each cache with a stone or a leaf.

Studies of captive blue jays suggest that they have a good memory for hidden food supplies. Once a jay has retrieved an acorn, it holds it against a branch or other hard object with one foot and batters it open with its bill. Like other New World jays, it has a specially strengthened lower jaw to cope with the twists and stresses of repeated battering.

Many blue jays stay on their breeding ranges all year despite freezing winter temperatures. They can fluff up their plumage to keep out the cold, and their caches of stored food ensure they never go hungry.

Another Bluer Bird

People from the western states and provinces of North America are often puzzled when they first learn to identify birds. They see an almost completely blue bird with a black crest that should be a blue jay. Except that it is not. The settlers on the eastern side of the continent had already named the bird now called the blue jay by the time eighteenth-century ornithologist Georg Steller discovered another, slightly bigger blue jay in Alaska. The much bluer bird that he found was named Steller's jay. Today, the blue and Steller's jay are recognized as the only species within the genus *Cyanocitta*. So, in one respect, they do share the same name, albeit a scientific one.

Highly Adaptable

During the winter months blue jays are especially dependent on acorns for food. One difficulty they face is that acorns are high in tannin, a chemical that interferes with the digestion of protein. If jays ate nothing but acorns during this period, they would probably die, but the birds are able to supplement their diet by searching out small numbers of spiders and insects. Invertebrate food seems to counteract the protein-inhibiting properties of tannin, ensuring that the jays survive.

In spring and summer insects and other invertebrates become a significant source of food for this highly adaptable species. It hunts both in trees and on the ground for creatures such as caterpillars, grasshoppers, cicadas, and ground beetles, and occasionally takes to the air to snatch a dragonfly in flight. On finding a wasp's nest, it may break the nest off from where it is attached and carry it to a perch before deftly tearing it open with its bill and pulling out the larvae one by one.

Bobbing Blue Jays

In early spring blue jays get unusually and loudly sociable. Small flocks, which can number more than 20 birds, work their way through a woodland, calling loudly and engaging in a conspicuous bobbing action. The "bob" involves the bird sinking onto a branch, then extending its legs quickly, pointing its bill skyward, and raising its crest at the same time. At tense moments a bobbing bird may bob up so fast that it loses its footing on the branch and springs into the air.

Ornithologists used to think that this bobbing display formed part of courtship, but close observation suggests that the apparently random groups consist of several pairs of mated birds and a few unattached individuals. Blue jays are thought to mate for life; but although most pairs stay roughly within the same area all year around, they are not really territorial. It is likely that these loose gatherings evolve so that individual pairs can establish their own breeding space, as the groups patrol a larger area.

When the birds do engage in courtship behavior, their display has a touching quality. The birds nudge each other on a branch, pass twigs, and even "kiss" bills. The male cements the pair-bond by bringing food to the female shortly before nesting. Such offerings are a prelude to more serious feeding once the female is incubating eggs.

Enterprising Nesters

Once the birds find a suitable nesting tree, the sexes tend to fall into specific roles. The male collects most of the material, while the female builds the nest. Gathering up the twigs that the male has thrust at her, she constructs an outer shell and then begins to slot in other materials. In wild areas they use bark, moss, grasses, and leaves, but around human settlements blue jays are quick to use paper, string, wool, and pieces of plastic. The nest is then lined with roots and fallen leaves, which are often held together with mud. In North America the use of mud in nest construction is unique to both the blue jay and the Steller's jay.

Some nests are never finished. Scientists once thought that the abandonment of "false nests" was part of courtship behavior. It is more likely that disturbance by a human or a predator is the main cause.

During incubation, and for the first few days after hatching, the male provides all the food for his growing family, while the female broods the young. After about 12 days the chicks have gained their first feathers and opened their eyes, and the female begins to forage, too. By the time the chicks are ready to fledge, they have already made sorties into the outside world, perching on the edge of the nest or venturing just beyond. Within two days of fledging they are able to fly erratically between trees and climb up them to relative safety.

Some young blue jays leave their parents in midsummer. Others stay with their parents for the rest of the summer, fall, and part of the winter. Their parents, meanwhile, begin their molt. By the end of the summer they are restored to full plumage, ready for the winter.

Nesting blue jays take advantage of any building materials they can find, including artificial ones such as paper, string, plastic, and other garbage. Yet despite this, the nest itself is very well built.

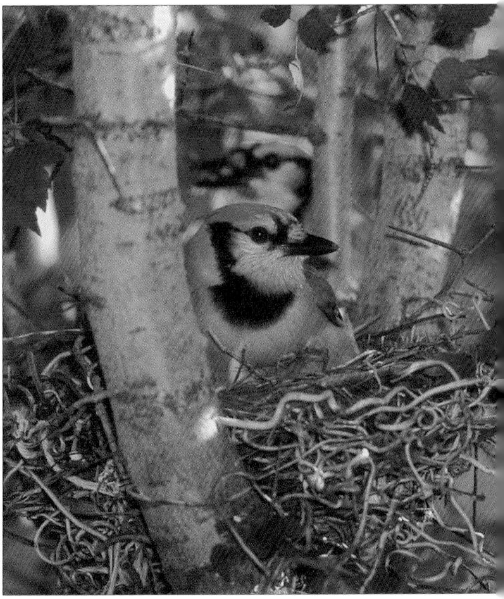

Early Warning System

The blue jay's vocal skills are legendary. Not only does it have a range of loud, instantly recognizable calls, it also has a huge talent for mimicry.

The specific function of each of the jay's calls is not well understood, partly because individual jays defy categorization. Birds will give forth a random selection of calls in different situations; and since a bird's syrinx—its voicebox—can make two sounds at once, it is quite possible for a bird to produce elements of two different calls at the same time. Yet some of the jay's calls are distinctive. Its harsh, so-called jeering call carries far and seems to be used most when danger threatens or when the birds want to keep in touch. More melodious is the bell-like musical whistle that sounds from cover. We tend to hear this call a lot—perhaps because it is an early warning alarm call that says "humans are approaching."

The blue jay can imitate the calls of a number of raptors, including the red-tailed hawk (*Buteo jamaicensis*) and red-shouldered hawk (*B. lineatus*), as well as crows, cats, and fragments of human speech. Yet the reason why the blue jay mimics other species is something of a mystery. By imitating a predator, it may be warning other birds that danger is present. Or it may simply gather interesting sounds to add to its musical repertoire.

Common name Scarlet macaw

Scientific name *Ara macao*

Family Psittacidae

Order Psittaciformes

Size Length: 33–35 in (84–89 cm); wingspan: 55 in (140 cm); weight: 2–3 lb (0.9–1.5 kg)

Key features Very large parrot with outsize bill, long wings, and very long tail; mainly scarlet with blue-and-yellow wings; light-blue rump and undertail; upper mandible pale yellow, lower mandible black; bare cheek with white skin; gray feet; juveniles have shorter tail

Habits Flies with slow, measured wingbeats, often quite high over forest; often in small groups

Nesting No nest; uses large tree hole, often high above ground; 1–4 eggs; incubation 24–28 days; young fledge after 14 weeks; 1 brood

Voice Very loud croaking screech; also squawks and growling sounds

Diet Wide variety of plant parts, including seeds, flowers, leaves, fruit, and even bark

Habitat Lowland forest and savanna, often near rivers

Distribution Local in Central America, from eastern Honduras and Nicaragua to Colombia; much commoner and more widespread in lowland Amazonia

Status Central American race threatened by habitat destruction and trapping for cage-bird trade; South American race still common

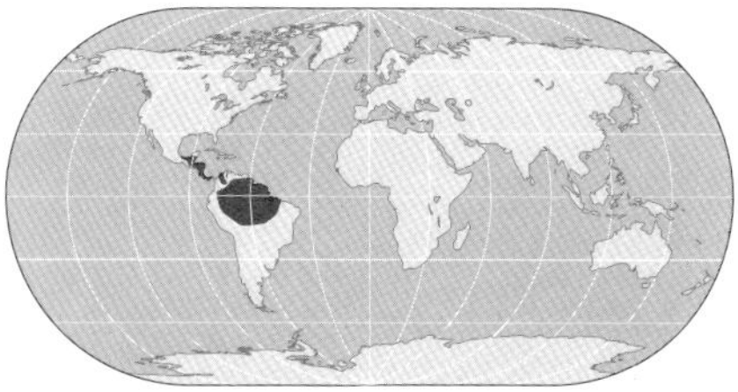

Scarlet Macaw

Ara macao

Everyone's idea of a tropical bird, the scarlet macaw is regularly featured in vacation brochures and jungle movies. Yet despite its familiarity and popularity, it thrives in the wild only in remote areas, far from human disturbance.

THERE CAN BE FEW BIRDS as evocative of the tropical forest as the scarlet macaw. With its large size, unusual shape, and gaudy plumage it seems to epitomize the strangeness and lavishness of the jungle. Its image is familiar to us from tropical bird gardens to Hollywood movies, and from children's animal books to travel brochures. It is an icon of the exotic.

The reality is not disappointing. The wild scarlet macaw is indeed a bird of tropical forests, especially those of the lowlands. It is spectacularly colorful and profoundly impressive, especially in the wild. It makes the classic parrot croak, but adds a level of volume, and feeds in the tops of large trees surrounded by the richness of its lush home.

The scarlet macaw is one of several species of macaw found in Central and South America. They are all very large parrots with long, pointed wings and even longer, graduated tails. Such a shape is characteristic of a bird that needs to travel long distances, and all macaws fly dozens of miles from their feeding to their roosting sites each day. They often fly in flocks, one after the other, moving with surprising speed in view of their deliberate but shallow wingbeats. When flying in a flock, pairs keep close together, their wings virtually touching as they move through the air.

Extraordinary Plumage

The scarlet macaw is perhaps the most extravagantly colored of the macaws. Its body, including its crown, back, breast, belly, tail, and shoulders, is clad in a vivid shade of crimson, neatly offset by bright blue on the flight feathers and rump. Its "shoulders" are mustard-

The red-and-green macaw (Ara chloroptera) occurs in much the same habitat, and eats much the same food, as the scarlet macaw. The two species are often found close together. Notice, however, the green—not yellow—color in the center of the wings of this slightly larger species.

yellow, tipped with either green or blue. Its face is adorned with an area of bare white skin that can turn pink when the bird blushes in excitement, and its huge bill is pale yellow and black. It is an arresting combination.

Although it is usually considered a bird of deep forest, the scarlet macaw is surprisingly versatile. It is probably most common in lowland rain forest—a census in Manu National Park, Peru, revealed one pair every 0.4 square miles (1 sq km)—but it also occurs in strips of river valley forest penetrating deep into savanna. It can be found in deciduous woodland in Costa Rica and even among pine trees in Honduras. It will enter forest that has been partially cleared, and it can even live in open areas with scattered stands of tall trees. Although mainly found below 1,640 feet (500 m), it has been recorded as high as 4,920 feet (1,500 m). Throughout its range it seems to be fond of rivers, often breeding in tall trees along their banks.

Very Varied Diet

One of the keys to this versatility is the scarlet macaw's varied diet. It will eat almost any part of a plant, including seeds, flowers, leaves, pulp, fruit, nectar, and even bark. Items on its menu include the mature leaves of palm trees, the fruits of trees such as figs, the seeds of jacaranda trees, the bark of the ceiba tree, the sap of the clarisia plant, and the flowers, fruits, and seeds of the tabebuia. Its enormous bill enables it to crush the hardest nuts, including Brazil nuts, and yet it can also be delicate and dexterous when eating small berries and flowers. It seems to prefer the seeds of plants that are dispersed by wind or water, including the winged seeds of the mahogany tree, but it is not a specialist. It will eat almost anything.

Scarlet macaws usually feed high in the canopy and, in contrast to most scarlet macaw activities, in silence—perhaps to avoid giving away potential feeding sites to competitors. Yet once they have finished feeding, their noisy habits reassert themselves. Relaxed birds utter conversational sounds resembling the creaking of a door, punctuated by continual loud screeches, squawks, and growls. When flocks are flying, or birds are settling into their roosting trees, their raucous calls can be almost deafening. As befits such sociable birds, they have a wide, loud vocabulary.

Secure on their perch high in a palm tree, a pair of scarlet macaws indulge in mutual preening. Such behavior has more than practical value because it also helps reinforce their pair-bond.

A Memorable Sight

It is unusual to see a scarlet macaw on its own. The basic unit of society is the pair; the pairs tend to form groups, and groups form feeding flocks of up to 30 or so. At a favored roost site

In the Treetops

Appropriately enough for a big, impressive bird, the scarlet macaw has a particular liking for large forest trees. Without them, in fact, it cannot survive in the wild. The bird needs them for all its basics in life: for feeding, breeding, and roosting; and it will also simply loaf on the topmost branches of trees, watching the world go by. Macaws need never descend from their favored treetops to find food, for the rain-forest canopy contains an abundance of possibilities, especially for a bird with a broad diet such as a macaw. The birds occasionally descend to drink from forest pools, but the succulent fruits in their diet normally provide them with adequate water, so they can remain aloft.

Roosting is another treetop activity, this time for safety reasons. A bird high up is well placed to hear and locate any danger, or it may also feel the approach of a predator from below. The macaws' habit of roosting in large groups simply magnifies their vigilance. When disturbed, they call loudly, eventually flying off with a deafening chorus of irritated squawks. Scarlet macaws also select tall trees for their nest sites. Although holes used by macaws have been recorded as low as 23 feet (7 m) above the ground, most are above 66 feet (20 m), and they may even be as high as 131 feet (40 m) up. Again, there appears to be greater security at these heights and perhaps less disturbance. Few other birds nest so high in the trees.

Cliffs of Clay

As part of their diet, macaws take large quantities of unripe fruits. They do so in order to gain a competitive advantage over the many other herbivores that share their habitat, but that have a more delicate constitution. Many rain-forest fruits, ripe or otherwise, contain toxins that can cause severe intestinal complaints, but the macaws appear immune to them.

Part of their strategy for coping with unpalatable fruits appears to be their regular daily visits to cliffs of clay. Such cliffs are usually found along the banks of large rivers and may be 100 feet (30 m) high in places. Here the birds settle in large numbers, often in company with other parrot species, and gnaw away at the clay, ingesting large amounts of it. They spend a lot of time at these exposed sites, potentially vulnerable to attack by predators. It seems that the clay absorbs the toxins in their diet, leaving the most nutritious parts of the fruits for the birds to digest. The substance called kaolin that people take for stomach upsets works in a similar way. Observers have also noticed that the birds may arrive in a very excited state but become calmer as they ingest the clay.

it is not unusual to see 50 birds together. There are few more memorable sights than a large, noisy flock of macaws flying in formation over the treetops on their way to roost.

Scarlet macaws do not just associate with their own kind. A regular companion and rival is the red-and-green macaw (*Ara chloroptera*), which is slightly larger and bulkier. The two species are closely related and live in similar habitats, even feeding in the same trees, and it is unclear how they differ ecologically at all. All the macaws will also share fruiting or flowering trees with smaller parrots, especially the blue-headed parrot (*Pionus menstruus*) and various species of amazon (genus *Amazona*). But the macaws are the more dominant birds and can easily drive off these smaller competitors.

Limiting Factor

For breeding purposes everything depends on a pair's ability to find a large hole in a tall tree for their nest. So important is this asset that suitable holes may be claimed months in advance of actual occupation, often by aggressive exchanges, because there are not enough for all the breeding pairs. This single factor limits the scarlet macaw population as much as any other natural factor.

Females lay between one and four eggs, but the immediate prospects of the resulting chicks differ wildly. The oldest chick in the clutch has the best prospects, with second, third, and fourth chicks having a higher mortality rate. It is possible that the oldest chick claims most of the food brought by the parents on their infrequent visits, but it is not certain. In any case, overall productivity is good; in one study nine out of 14 pairs that were observed fledged at least one chick, and of the 21 chicks hatched, ten survived to leave the nest.

Although a high proportion of nesting scarlet macaws are successful, the number breeding in any one year is remarkably small. Observations of postbreeding flocks in Amazonia indicate that only about 20 percent of pairs have young accompanying them after each breeding season. This low number no

Fast Disappearing

Macaws and people simply do not mix. These large birds are often the first casualties of human settlement, even in remote areas. The effect of settlement is greatest in Central America, where the distinct race *cyanoptera* (whose yellow wing coverts are tipped with blue rather than green) is now under threat of extinction. It once ranged all the way from Mexico to Nicaragua, but there are only about 4,000 left. The main threat is the destruction of the birds' habitat. Although the birds show quite a wide ecological tolerance, they always need ample stands of tall trees for feeding and nesting: something which rarely survives conversion of the land to agriculture. Second after habitat loss is trapping for the bird trade, of both adults and especially nestlings. Trapping is a particular problem when numbers are already low, and for a bird that reproduces slowly it can lead to the extinction of a local population. A third threat comes from hunting, not just of the birds themselves but also for their bright plumage. Once worshiped in Central America as an oracle of the sun, these macaws can also suffer for their finery.

Although the scarlet macaw has a broad range, it would be foolish to consider that it is not at all threatened in the longer term. Whenever people arrive, this species tends to disappear very quickly, and of course the human population is always expanding. Alarmingly, several field workers have noticed that where scarlet macaws were common only five to ten years before, they can completely vanish from a local area. This shows just how vulnerable they are, and how urgent is the need to protect both the birds themselves and their natural rain-forest habitat.

doubt reflects the lack of nesting holes available to these macaws, but it may also suggest that as a matter of course, certain pairs may only breed once every few years. If so, the overall productivity of the scarlet macaw is very low.

A Worrying Future?

Since macaws are long-lived birds, their naturally sluggish reproductive rate would not be a problem in natural conditions. Each individual would have several chances to breed during its lifetime. However, where people intervene and trap actively breeding adults, it is not difficult to predict the dire effects on the overall population.

⇧ An ideal nest hole is both large and high above the ground. Relatively soft-wooded trees are preferred because the owners like to modify the shape and size of the cavity. Dead trees are used more often than live ones for the same reason.

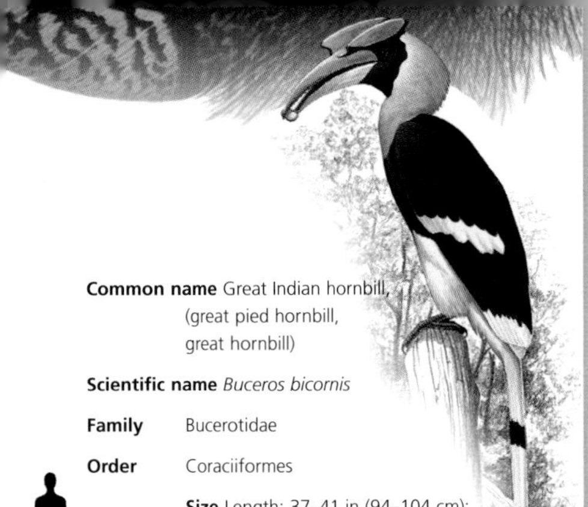

Great Indian Hornbill

Buceros bicornis

Common name Great Indian hornbill, (great pied hornbill, great hornbill)

Scientific name *Buceros bicornis*

Family Bucerotidae

Order Coraciiformes

Size Length: 37–41 in (94–104 cm); wingspan: 58–64 in (145–163 cm); weight: males 5.7–7.5 lb (2.6–3.4 kg), females 4.6–7.3 lb (2.1–3.3 kg)

Key features Large bird with huge yellow-and-black downcurved bill and large concave-topped casque; black face, back, underparts, and wings, with double white wing bar; white neck, upper breast, thighs, and undertail; tail white with broad black band; male has red eyes with black rims; female has smaller bill and casque, and white eyes with red rims

Habits Monogamous; territorial; usually seen in pairs or small groups

Nesting Natural tree hole, female sealed inside it for 4 months; 1–4 (usually 2) white eggs; incubation 38–40 days; young fledge after 72–96 days; 1 brood

Voice Hoarse barks, roars, and grunting sounds; distinctive, reverberating, repeated "tok"

Diet Mainly fruit; also large insects and other invertebrates, small reptiles, birds, and mammals, especially for feeding young

Habitat Mainly primary evergreen and deciduous rain forest, but will cross open areas to travel between forest patches

Distribution Southwestern India, southern Himalayas, northern Burma, southern China, Vietnam, south to Malay Peninsula and Sumatra

Status Near-threatened; declining in many areas

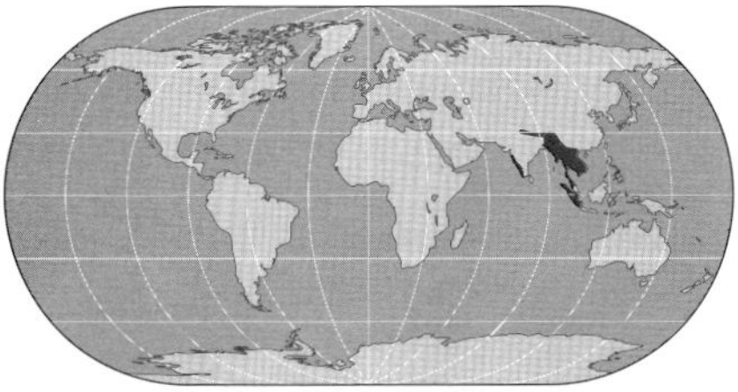

One of the largest of the world's hornbills, this magnificent bird is declining in many parts of its wide range in southern Asia. But for the present at least it can still be regularly seen in its native forests.

THE GREAT INDIAN HORNBILL IS AN IMPOSING sight as it flies high above the forest canopy in search of food on broad wings that may span over 5 feet (1.5 m). Adult males may grow to the size of a turkey; and like other large hornbills, they are equipped with one of the biggest and most impressive bills possessed by any bird—up to 13 inches (33 cm) long. Furthermore, the bill is topped by a great horny casque with a concave top; in the male the casque is slightly larger, U-shaped, and more elaborately sculpted. Despite its size, the casque is not a hindrance, since (like its great bill) it is of lightweight construction, being hollow inside apart from narrow supporting struts of bone.

The strong yellow tinge that usually colors the bill and casque and the white feathers of the rear of the head, neck, and wing bars is due not to pigments but to the bird smearing its yellow preen oil on them while it preens its feathers, typically in several bouts during the morning. The hornbill collects the oil from the preen gland at the base of its tail, like other birds, and the opening of the gland is often visible as a yellowish patch.

Canopy Lifestyle

The great Indian hornbill spends much of its time high in the forest canopy, searching for fruit and animal food. Despite its great size, it moves easily among the branches with a series of rapid and rather ungainly sideways hops. Sometimes it descends to the forest floor to take advantage of fruits that have fallen from the trees, when it may rest on its "knees" while feeding on them, or to search for animal prey.

A magnificent male great Indian hornbill—recognizable by his red eyes and U-shaped casque—stakes a claim to a breeding territory with loud, resonant calls that echo through the tropical forest.

When it flies, its great rounded wings make an extraordinary, loud whooshing sound similar to that of a puffing steam locomotive. Audible to humans for over 0.6 miles (1 km), the noise is caused by the wind rushing through the bases of the hornbill's flight feathers (which lack underwing coverts) and the two stiff outer flight feathers. Its flight is buoyant, consisting of a few flaps alternating with short glides.

Great Indian hornbills are usually seen in pairs or small family groups. Sometimes, however, large groups can gather outside the breeding season: For example, flocks of up to 70 birds have been seen in the magnificent tropical rain forest of the Khao Yai National Park in south-central Thailand.

Challenging Calls

The hornbills are very noisy at the start of the breeding season, each pair proclaiming ownership of their territory by repeatedly uttering very loud "kok" calls that reverberate through the forest. The birds stretch their necks upright and thrust their giant bills skyward as they roar out these challenging calls, which carry up to half a mile (0.8 km). They signal aggression by bouncing up and down on their perches and also communicate by striking their bills against branches.

For a long time before they mate, and especially just before the female is ready to lay her eggs, the male frequently presents his partner with a gift of food. The gifts help maintain their pair-bond as well as providing for the female. During this ritual courtship feeding, the two great birds sometimes grapple each other with their bills.

Despite their great size, great Indian hornbills nest in tree cavities at heights of about 25 to 80 feet (7.6–24 m) above the forest floor, preferring a tall, narrow vertical entrance that is easy to seal. They choose holes that have a chimneylike space above the nest chamber so that if danger threatens, the female can wriggle up and hide away out of sight. Both sexes share the job of sealing the nest entrance with a mixture of mud and the female's feces.

⊖ *The male (on the right) has sharp points at the front of his casque. The female's casque is less elaborate, but still very impressive.*

Threatened Species

Great Indian hornbills are still hunted by humans in many parts of their extensive range. The meat of the adults and young is highly prized by local people, and the casques are sold as trophies. Hunters find it relatively easy to open up the nest holes or even cut down the nesting trees at the right time to take females and their offspring. Together, they provide enough meat for a large family. The species is also used in traditional medicine, while in Kerala, India, the blood of the female and chicks is believed to comfort the souls of the dead. In addition, some of the chicks are kept alive and reared locally as pets or for sale to zoos and aviculturalists.

Trade in wild birds is controlled by the Convention on International Trade in Endangered Species (CITES), with this species being accorded the highest status—CITES 1. However, the main cause of the species' decline is the destruction and degradation of its habitat, especially since a single family group of these great birds may need a home range of as much as 230 square miles (596 sq km). The population of great Indian hornbills in the Western Ghats (low mountain ranges) of southwestern India is isolated far from the rest of the species' range, and here declines are particularly severe. A recent estimate put the total number there at only 3,500 birds, now confined to just 100 patches of forest. The populations living in Vietnam, Cambodia, Sumatra, and other areas are also greatly reduced. Conservationists have officially classified the species as Near-threatened.

The Indian great hornbill was bred in captivity for the first time in 1953. Some captive individuals live for a long time: The record is held by a 41-year-old female that did not lay her first egg until she was 39 years old.

⊖ ***Having selected a suitable nesting hole, a female hornbill waits for her partner to return so they can begin the job of cementing up the entrance.***

Mixed Diet

Great Indian hornbills eat a wide range of different fruits. They follow a regular routine, visiting favored fruiting trees at the same time each day; they are particularly fond of various kinds of fig and nutmeg. The huge birds generally dominate, intimidate, and chase away other birds and even small monkeys that also visit the trees to harvest their crop of fruit.

The hornbills are also always on the alert for animal prey and eagerly hunt down a great variety of creatures. Their recorded victims include beetles, cockroaches, stick insects, centipedes, giant scorpions, snails, frogs, crabs, flying lizards, snakes, birds (even small owls), and squirrels.

Walled In

Once the female has walled herself into her nest cavity, she may spend four months or even longer in her self-imposed prison—covering the whole period of egg-laying, incubation, hatching, and development of the young almost to fledging. During this time the male is kept extremely busy finding enough food for the female and young. Males have been seen bringing up to 185 separate food items to the nest to maintain the fast-growing chicks. They include both fruits and animals transferred through the narrow slit of the walled-up entrance by the male regurgitating them from his crop or, in the case of animal prey, holding them in the tip of his bill.

To keep the nest hole clean, the female and older young stick their rear ends out of the entrance to defecate with impressive force, and the female also throws out any food remains. The female usually molts all her flight feathers in both wings and tail while she is inside and grows new ones during her long task of incubating the eggs and brooding the chicks. When the nestlings are a few weeks old, their mother breaks open the seal at the nest entrance and emerges to help the male feed them. The young close up the hole again until they are fully fledged. Then it is time for them to break the hole open once more and venture into the unfamiliar world outside.

Raggiana Bird of Paradise

Paradisaea raggiana

Common name Raggiana bird of paradise

Scientific name *Paradisaea raggiana*

Family Paradisaeidae

Order Passeriformes

Size Length: male 13.5 in (34 cm), plus 14–21 in (36–53 cm) elongated flank plumes and central tail feathers in breeding plumage, female 13 in (33 cm); wingspan: 19–25 in (48–63.5 cm); weight: male 8.3–10.5 oz (235–298 g), female 4.8–7.8 oz (136–221 g)

Key features Male's forehead and throat iridescent green surrounded by a yellow shawl; body and wings mainly reddish-brown; breeding plumage has long, lacy, crimson or orange-red flank plumes and a long, wirelike, central pair of tail feathers; female mainly brown, darker beneath, with yellow shawl

Habits Males display communally in trees

Nesting Cup-shaped nest of plant fibers, rootlets, or vines interwoven with leaves in fork of a tree lined with softer plant material; 1–2 eggs; incubation 18–20 days; young fledge after 18–20 days; 1 brood

Voice Male song loud, harsh cawing notes; calls at lek include high-pitched wails and bill clicking; female occasionally gives quiet calls

Diet Mainly fruit; also insects and spiders

Habitat Primary and second-growth forest and other wooded habitats

Distribution Southern and eastern Papua New Guinea

Status Common and widespread

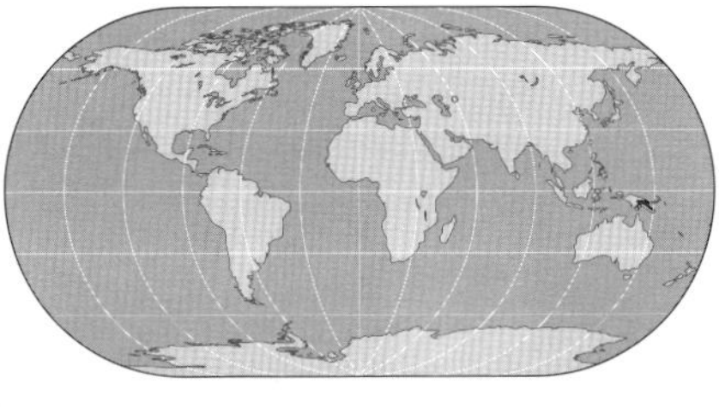

Among the most spectacular members of their family, male Raggiana birds of paradise perform a dazzling communal courtship display high in the trees, shivering flame-colored plumes twice the length of their bodies to attract watching females.

THE RAGGIANA BIRD OF PARADISE is one of the commonest of all birds of paradise. Its range still includes almost two-thirds of mainland Papua New Guinea (the country occupying the eastern half of the island of New Guinea), and it inhabits a wide range of forest types ranging from sea level to around 4,900 feet (1,495 m). As a result, its overall numbers are little affected by the hunting that still continues for the males' spectacular plumes.

Although it prefers undisturbed areas of rain forest, it is an adaptable bird that will forage for fruit in plantations and on other cultivated land, including gardens and fields near houses or other buildings. In some places females nest in isolated trees near villages.

Raggiana birds of paradise spend most of their time high in the tree canopy, where they find most of their food. Often, one or more will join mixed foraging flocks of other birds, including other species of birds of paradise.

Dramatic Display

The breeding season begins in April. From dawn onward groups of up to ten males gather at their communal display ground, or "lek," high in the tree canopy. Each bird has his own display perch from which he removes the foliage so that females and rival males can see every detail of his display. Major leks are usually at traditional sites that may be used every year for over ten or even twenty years.

First, the males proclaim their arrival with a cacophony of wild, raucous songs that may resound through the forest for more than

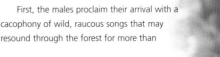

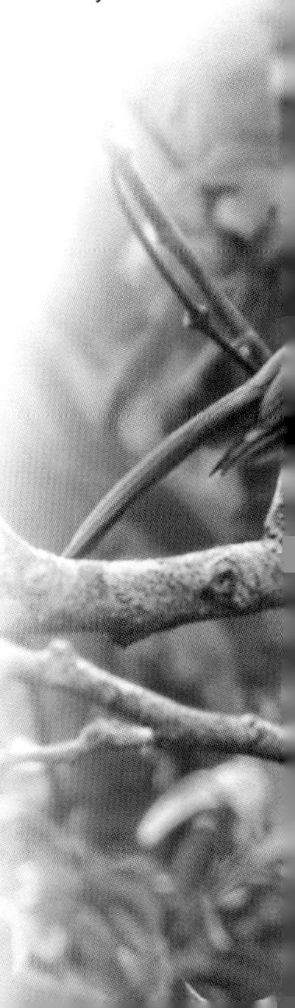

Mesmerized by the glorious plumage of a displaying male (right), a female approaches and prepares to mate. Once mated, she will build her nest, incubate her clutch of streaked, pinkish eggs, and rear her chicks entirely alone.

0.6 miles (1 km). As the females start to arrive, the males work themselves up into a frenzy, calling loudly and charging around from perch to perch. After clapping his wings over his head with a loud thud, a male leans forward and erects his long flank plumes. He then calls loudly as he bobs his head and chest up and down so that the lacelike flank plumes tremble around him in a dazzling cascade of color. A female beguiled by this performance may approach so near that her head is briefly buried in the plumes. At most leks just one dominant male accounts for most of the matings. After the courtship season is over, the males molt their display plumes, growing a new set of the beautiful feathers for the next season.

Devoted Mother

The female hides her nest so well among the foliage that it is very difficult to find. At first she feeds her nestlings on insects, adding increasing amounts of fruit to their diet as they grow. When a predator searching for a meal of eggs or young birds approaches, a female returning with a cropful of food for her offspring may "freeze," remaining absolutely motionless on her perch for up to nine minutes or more.

The youngsters develop fast and soon leave the nest, by which time they are about three-quarters of their mother's size. However, young males do not attain their full complement of magnificent plumes until they are about six or seven years old.

Common name Secretary bird

Scientific name *Sagittarius serpentarius*

Family Sagittariidae

Order Falconiformes

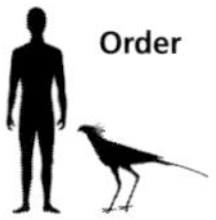

Size Length: 49–59 in (125–150 cm); wingspan: 83 in (211 cm); weight: 5–9.4 lb (2.3–4.3 kg)

Key features Very large, with a unique shape: long, almost cranelike legs, half feathered in black, plus long, pointed wings and long, graduated tail; bare, red face; typical raptor's bill; long, wispy crest, largely ash-gray plumage, but black crest, wings, tail tip, belly, and leg tops

Habits Terrestrial, usually seen walking on ground with measured steps; roosts in tree; sometimes flies, even soars; usually in pairs

Nesting Any time of year; large nest a platform of sticks in a thorn-tree canopy and lined with grass; usually 2 eggs; incubation 42–46 days; young fledge after 65–106 days; sometimes several broods in succession under good conditions

Voice Silent except at nest, where it makes a hoarse growling, deeper than most birds of prey

Diet Mainly insects, especially grasshoppers and beetles; also small vertebrates such as snakes, small mammals, and birds

Habitat Steppe and savanna, with short grass and thorn trees

Distribution Sub-Saharan Africa, except west-central Africa and the Horn of Africa

Status Not threatened

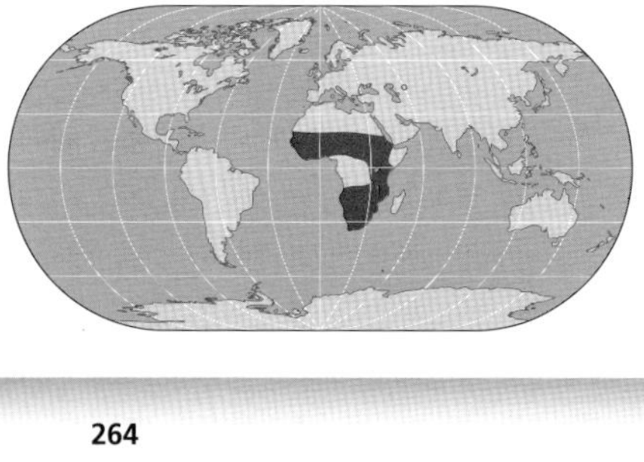

Secretary Bird

Sagittarius serpentarius

Unique in appearance with its amazingly long legs, thin body, and long tail, the secretary bird also has an unusual lifestyle, spending its days striding over grassland and running after its terrestrial prey.

IT ONLY TAKES A GLANCE to see that the secretary bird is a very strange creature indeed. No other bird looks remotely like it. It seems to have the bill of a hawk, the body and wings of a heron, the crest of a peacock, the tail of a pheasant, and the long legs of a crane. It also has unique skeletal features and adaptations to its way of life. So it is not surprising that it has been classified in a family of its own. Its closest relatives are probably eagles, but it must have diverged from them long ago in the evolutionary history of predatory birds.

The name is thought to derive from its unusual crest feathers, which are long, plume-like, and jet-black as if dipped in ink. They look like the long quill pens once used by clerks or secretaries, set behind the ear ready for use. An alternative suggestion is that the bird's name comes from the Arabic *saqr et-tair* ("hunter-bird"), although that name could refer to any number of species that live on the African plains.

↓ The long reach of the secretary bird's strong, well-protected legs allow it to deal with the most dangerous of all prey—venomous snakes. By punching down with its small, sharp-clawed feet, it can trample them to death.

Foot Patrol

Although its crest is unusual and its tail feathers are spectacular, it is its legs and feet that really make the secretary bird special. The legs are quite extraordinarily long, resembling those of an ostrich (*Struthio camelus*), but much slimmer. A secretary bird stands 4 feet (1.2 m) tall, and the legs account for at least half of this. Up to the bird's "knees" the legs are bare and covered with heavy protective scaling, but from the knees up they are densely feathered in black, making it look as though the bird is wearing short trousers.

The secretary bird puts its long legs to good use, since it is forever walking, its preferred method of locomotion; it seldom flies. Each day it marches over a part of its territory in search of food, walking this way and that, and not normally following a set route. As it goes along with measured steps, its head and neck move back and forth in time with each stride, in the manner of a chicken. When foraging, a secretary bird walks at around 120 paces per minute at a speed of 1.5–1.8 miles per hour (2..4–2.9 km/h)—an impressively rapid rate of progress. It is common for a single bird to cover 12 miles (19.3 km) in a single day.

When it sees prey, however, or if it is intentionally trying to flush something into view, its pace quickens. Then it can take 180 strides a minute, with a more stamping style. During a chase it can also raise its wings to help its balance and maneuverability. A secretary bird on the march is a formidable enemy to a small, ground-living creature.

Feetfirst

If it discovers a small animal, it usually chases it and grabs it in its bill; but when faced by a more challenging target—such as a mammal

The ragged crest feathers of the secretary bird are said to resemble the ink-stained quill pens of old-fashioned clerks. This one is eating a mouse that it has caught after a short chase on the ground.

Fast and Furious

A secretary bird will eat almost anything that it can catch on the ground, either by running after it or taking it by surprise. Its most frequent victims are insects, especially grasshoppers, locusts, and beetles, which present little challenge to the secretary bird's fast run and long reach. Fast-moving rodents, frogs, and lizards are also easily outrun. More surprisingly, it often catches other birds—not just helpless chicks and eggs in nests, but also free-flying adults of several species, notably ground-nesting plovers, game birds, and larks. Most of them are probably caught by surprise when a secretary bird stumbles across them, leaving no time for escape.

Larger prey include mongooses, small cats, small hares, and even poisonous snakes. The snakes include big, deadly species such as cobras and puff adders, but the secretary bird has no trouble killing them with deft, powerful blows of its long, well-protected legs and feet. Small antelopes, including the steenbok and the mountain reedbuck, flee at the sight of a secretary bird. Such animals are probably too big to be killed, but they do not wait to find out.

Perched on a flat-topped tree that could make a perfect breeding site, a pair of secretary birds cement their relationship with necks entwined.

armed with sharp teeth—the secretary bird puts its other speciality, its unusual feet, to good use. The feet are quite small, but they have stout toes and are armed with sharp, curved claws, a dangerous combination of force and cutting edge. To disable an animal, the secretary bird simply kicks at it, raining heavy, incredibly fast downward blows on its victim. Being tall and spindly, it can keep its head and other areas of its body well out of reach of any striking animal, while still performing its bizarre murderous dance—jumping, running, and kicking until its prey succumbs.

Such an unusual method of killing has enabled the secretary bird to become one of the few predators to take on venomous snakes, an ability celebrated in its scientific name *serpentarius*. Keeping well out of striking range and aiming well-directed kicks, the secretary bird can easily breach the defenses of even large snakes, and across its range grateful farmers greatly admire this unusual gift. But ironically it also occasionally kills and eats those other snake-killers, the mongooses.

The feet are ideal for kicking prey to death, but they are not so good for grasping

or carrying food. Most birds of prey carry their kills to a perch in their talons before eating them or delivering them to the nest, but a secretary bird simply cannot lift cargo in flight. Instead, it swallows its food whole, making use of its unusually wide gape. It is a strange sight to see snakes and other animals disappearing down the bird's throat, but it is the only way.

Two Essentials

In order for their ground-dwelling lifestyle to be effective, secretary birds must live in open country without too much forest cover. However, the ground must not be too open, like a desert, because any potential prey can spot the birds coming from far away. The ideal habitat is grassland, with vegetation cover no more than 3 feet (1 m) tall and preferably half that. Each bird patrols a varying amount of such habitat, depending on the amount of food it yields. In rich savanna grassland a pair will defend a territory covering about 7.7 square miles (20 sq km), whereas in dry grassland it will be double the area, and in mountain grassland over treble.

Other than grassland there is one other essential for every secretary bird territory—a suitable tree for nesting. Although terrestrial, these birds do not build nests on the ground, for that is far too dangerous. Instead, they choose the densest thorn tree they can find, trample down the canopy, and place a platform of sticks on top. In East Africa they often use bushes that have been "pruned" by browsing

Nesting in a thorn tree such as an acacia provides protection against ground predators that might steal eggs or nestlings, but the parents have to keep a wary eye open for other birds.

giraffes and have thickened up as a result; they provide a good defense against enemies that otherwise can climb up and raid the nest. The height above ground is not important, ranging from 8 to 43 feet (2.4–13 m), depending on the tree chosen.

A secretary bird nest is easily recognizable, not so much from its structure or size but by what is left on the platform. Many raptors leave parts of dismembered bodies, but secretary birds, which feed their young on regurgitated food, leave behind castings or food pellets, many containing the remains of insects.

Both sexes build the nest, first hauling sticks up in their bills to create the main platform, then bringing tufts of grass, either picked up or tugged out from the ground, for the lining. Occasionally the nest is built well before any eggs are laid, especially if adverse weather conditions hamper its construction. Pairs are known to wait six months between

Defending Their Patch

The hunting ground of a pair of secretary birds is very much their own private territory. They do not tolerate the presence of intruders. If another secretary bird sets foot inside their borders, there will be a skirmish, beginning with a chase. As soon as a resident bird spots the trespasser, it begins to run fast toward it, with wings held above the back to demonstrate its annoyance. Intruders usually flee at this point, but if not, the chase will turn into a fight.

The fight starts when the resident bird catches up with its unwelcome visitor, jumping above it and striking powerfully down with its strong feet, like a kind of kick boxing. A single strike may force the stranger to flee, but occasionally much longer fights develop, the birds exchanging blows until one or both are exhausted. Sometimes both members of a pair gang up on the intruder until it is repelled. Once the dispute is settled, the winners—usually the resident birds, but not always—circle around each other in triumph.

completing the nest and laying the first egg, depending on the weather, for hatching is timed to coincide with the rainy season. If it is too dry, breeding is delayed; but if it remains wet for a long time, several broods may be raised in rapid succession—sometimes with only a three-week break between seeing off one family and starting the next.

Shared Parental Duties

There is a very even division of labor among secretary bird parents. Building the nest is a combined effort, and so are the duties of incubating the eggs, brooding the chicks, and feeding the young. The adults work shifts—one bird sitting, the other searching for food—and when there is a changeover, the event is marked by a gentle bowing display.

Feeding the chicks is something of a rare event, happening just three times a day: late morning, midafternoon, and finally in the early evening. The loads brought are often large, since they are the result of long foraging trips: One was recorded with ten lizards, a mouse, and a young hare. The gap in visits also allows the adult bird to feed itself as well as foraging for the family, but finding enough food for either is not necessarily a formality. Both adults and young are at the mercy of the conditions, and young that have thrived for several weeks can still die of starvation. In a normal brood there are two chicks; while one may prosper and fledge as early as 65 days after hatching, the other may lag way behind and often dies. There are reliable records of chicks finally leaving the nest no fewer than 106 days after they first chipped out of the egg, all because of an unpredictable food supply.

The parents provide water as well as food. When a parent feeds a youngster, liquid can trickle into the chick's bill along with food; often the last act of a returning adult before flying up to the nest is to take a drink. On hot, sunny days a chick may refuse to take any food before being given something to quench its thirst. Providing water along with food is a very unusual piece of behavior for a bird of prey.

Water provision, nourishing the young on regurgitated food, and performing greeting ceremonies at the nest when changing shift are all behaviors that differ from the routines of most day-flying birds of prey. But all of them are performed by another family of large birds that walk along the ground to feed—the storks.

Recent DNA studies have shown that the storks and New World vultures are closely related, so the secretary bird may also be part of this group. Such an interesting idea merits further study. But whether the secretary bird is related to storks or not, that does not detract from the unique nature of this strange, long-legged killer that strides the African grasslands.

Flights of Fancy

Although the secretary bird lives on the ground most of the time, it is an excellent flyer. With its long, broad wings it can soar high above the plains, using thermal air currents, and has been recorded by aircraft at a height of 12,500 feet (3,800 m).

Many soaring flights, usually those below 1,640 feet (500 m), are associated with display. Both members of a courting pair rise together above the nesting area, calling in a croaking voice. Once at a good height, they perform aerobatics, closing their wings and plummeting toward the ground, only to swoop upward again using their momentum. These "pendulum flights" may be embellished by more spectacular maneuvers, with both birds flying toward each other and locking their feet in midair.

With their broad, fingered wings and long, trailing legs secretary birds in flight look very much like storks. Recent research suggests that the resemblance may be more than a coincidence.

Greater Roadrunner *Geococcyx californianus*

Perhaps best known as a cartoon character, the roadrunner lives in the deserts of the southern U.S. and Mexico. True to its name, it really does run along roads, but it is also famous as a fearless predator that kills and eats small rattlesnakes.

Common name Greater roadrunner

Scientific name *Geococcyx californianus*

Family Cuculidae

Order Cuculiformes

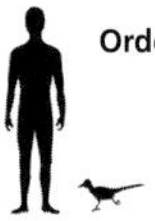

Size Length: 23 in (58 cm); wingspan: 22 in (56 cm); weight: 13 oz (369 g)

Key features Very long tail; long, powerful legs; long, thick bill; short, ragged crest that can be raised; blue-and-red patch of bare skin behind eye; plumage mostly streaky brown, straw-colored, with fewer streaks on belly

Habits Forages on ground; prefers to walk and run, rarely flies

Nesting Any time of year, depending on rains and range; nest of sticks in low tree, bush, or cactus, lined with leaves, feathers, dung, and snake skins; 2–6 eggs; incubation 17–18 days; young fledge after 17–25 days; 1–2 broods

Voice Series of low pitched "coo" notes descending in scale; also bill rattling

Diet Wide range of animal foods, from insects to small mammals and birds; a few seeds and fruits, such as prickly pear

Habitat Arid, open country

Distribution Southwestern U.S. and northern Mexico

Status Not threatened

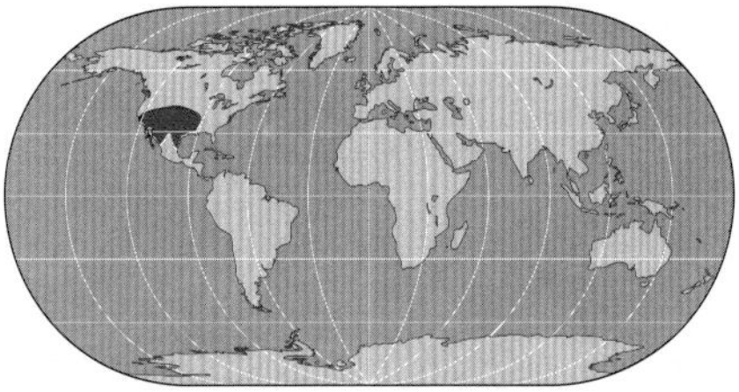

THERE IS NOT A SMALL creature in the deserts of the southwestern U.S. and Mexico that does not cower at the approach of a greater roadrunner. This highly modified cuckoo lives up to its name with its athletic behavior, and it is equipped with specially adapted long legs for speed. Using its long tail to help it steer, the roadrunner careers across the desert floor, a match for anything that tries to flee from its multipurpose bill. Nothing, not even the most fleet-footed lizards, can outrun it.

Its prey may fear the roadrunner, but many people see it differently, recognizing the perky creature immortalized in children's cartoons. It is relatively big and tame, and is popular among humans who share its desert home.

The deserts of the Southwest are not the easiest places to make a living, but the greater roadrunner is adapted to make the best of its harsh habitat.

Desert Survivor

There is no doubt that the roadrunner is a highly effective survivor. It could not thrive in the desert without a range of adaptations, both behavioral and physiological, to the unique stresses of its environment: extreme heat by day, extreme cold by night, and constant aridity. It has several solutions to these problems.

Its adaptations to a lack of water include an ability to reabsorb liquid from its lower intestine and a system for removing water-sapping salt through its nasal glands. The bird rarely needs to drink because it obtains most of its liquid requirements from the body fluids of its prey. To combat extreme heat, it can cool itself down by evaporating water from its skin. It can pant like a dog, and it can expose the pale feathers below its wings to reflect heat.

It can also lose heat through the blood vessels in the head. To combat the cold desert nights, the bird can reduce its body temperature to use less energy, then warm itself up again in the morning sun. It is the definitive, resourceful desert dweller.

Morning Patrol

A typical day starts when the birds bask in the morning sun. Having lowered their temperature overnight, they work to raise it again by ruffling their back feathers and drooping their wings to expose their black dorsal skin directly to the sun. The sun warms the skin like a solar panel, and the birds are soon ready to be active. By using the sun like this, roadrunners can save up to 60 percent of the energy they would need to heat themselves internally.

The morning is the best time to go on patrol in search of food before it becomes too hot. The roadrunner walks to a suitable hunting area, stopping to look around and maybe running after something that it has spotted before looking around again. It is also proficient at flushing out prey: Sometimes it will simply brush past an herb or bush and disturb something; at other times it will jump around and flap its wings.

When a roadrunner is running flat out, it can attain a speed of 18 miles per hour (29 km/h)—almost as fast as a human—but its stamina is far greater. When running fast, the

⬇ ***Although the greater roadrunner gets most of the water it needs from its food, it drinks when it can. Roadrunners are opportunists and always make the most of the available resources.***

roadrunner holds its head and tail in a straight line, horizontal to the ground to improve its streamlining. To cope with the uneven surface of the desert, its toes are mobile and flexible, so they can change in shape as the bird runs. It can also fly, although it seldom does.

A Varied Diet

The roadrunner eats an enormous variety of different animals, including venomous tarantulas, scorpions, and snakes. It regularly takes lizards, frogs, toads, small mammals (including young ground squirrels and rabbits), and all kinds of insects. Roadrunners even catch birds, snatching them in midair as they sweep low over a dry riverbed or visit favorite feeding sites on or near the ground. Hummingbirds drinking nectar from low-growing flowers are particular favorites. Adventurous roadrunners may also visit caves to pick up bats that have fallen from the ceiling. Ten percent of its diet also consists of fruit, such as prickly pear.

From time to time pairs of roadrunners cooperate in hunting, especially when faced with large snakes and other potentially dangerous animals. One bird distracts the prey, while the other strikes at the back of its head with its long, sharp bill. Once the victim is subdued, they beat it to death.

Snake Dance

A rattlesnake is a formidable creature, but it is just another item on the roadrunner's menu. When a roadrunner encounters a rattler, it is an absorbing contest. If the roadrunner makes a mistake, the result will be fatal, so it has to move with extreme caution. The bird crouches, watching the snake intently, then it begins to circle around it. The snake follows it with its gaze. The roadrunner feigns a strike, then retreats, still circling. During the next few minutes the combatants follow each other's moves in a kind of gruesome dance—a dance to the death. But the battle is an uneven one, and before long the far more mobile roadrunner gets the chance it needs.

It dashes in and catches the snake by the back of its neck, effectively finishing the spectacle apart from the writhing of its victim. The rattlesnake now suffers the indignity of a slow death, being beaten against a hard surface for up to 15 minutes until it is unconscious. The beating breaks many of the bones in its body, making it easier for the roadrunner to swallow the snake whole.

The ability of the roadrunner to kill snakes has made it greatly respected among desert people, and several legends have grown up concerning its almost supernatural powers. One folklore tale suggests an alternative snake-catching scenario. Instead of killing it directly, the roadrunner finds a sleeping serpent and stealthily builds a ring of cactus around it. Woken up by a cactus thrown at it by the bird, the snake angrily begins crawling toward its tormentor, spearing itself to death on the corral of spines.

The roadrunner's long, sharp bill is a multipurpose tool, able to deal effectively with a wide range of prey from insects and mice to venomous rattlesnakes.

Mating for Life

Pairs of greater roadrunners live together in their own territory and probably mate for life. The male defends his borders each breeding season, using a low-pitched cooing like that of a dove or an owl, which carries for a great distance. If an intruder crosses into his territory, the male approaches with his head lowered, the bare red skin on his face fully exposed, his tail raised and wagging feverishly. This display is usually enough to drive away the stranger.

Nesting depends on the prevailing temperature and, especially, on the amount of recent rainfall. Stimulated by suitable conditions, the male begins to bring substantial food items—mainly mice, lizards, snakes, or small birds—as offerings for the female, helping her get into condition.

The pair begin building, but they are fickle househunters, happy with a site at one moment and uncertain the next; they have been known to abandon work just minutes after starting. It may be several days before they finally begin to put a few thorny twigs together. The male finds the materials, and the female assembles the nest, piling up sticks to make an open platform about 12 inches (30 cm) in diameter and up to 4 inches (10 cm) deep. The site is usually 3–10 feet (1–3 m) above ground in a bush or cactus clump, preferably in the shade. The nest is often lined with leaves, feathers, dung, and appropriately for a roadrunner, snake skins. Fussy as ever, they may continue adding bits to the nest even when the female is incubating.

In common with many species of birds adapted to a habitat with an unpredictable food supply, greater roadrunners leave several days between laying each egg, but start the incubation with the first. The result is that chicks hatch on different days, and some nestlings are as much as seven days older than others. Better at begging for food, the older chicks have the best chance of survival. The survival of younger chicks is a bonus. Sometimes the issue is settled by the nestlings themselves, the older chicks evicting the younger ones in an eerie reminder of their cuckoo heritage.

Growing Up

Nestling roadrunners are feisty survivors, like their parents. Their skin is black, so they can warm themselves effectively in the sun. If they are disturbed on the nest, they can expel a disgusting, smelly black liquid at any intruder. The adults also defend their offspring by performing several distraction techniques, such as making themselves obvious by running around and fanning their tails or pretending to have broken wings.

This male has caught a lizard as a wedding gift for the female, but he will not present it to her until after they have mated.

Sometimes a disturbance can lead to young roadrunners leaving the nest early, although they usually fledge between 17 and 24 days. When they leave, the youngsters are only half as heavy as their parents and still greatly dependent on a constant provision of food.

Roadrunner Courtship

Roadrunners form long-term pair-bonds and live in a territory all year around, but that does not stop them from performing some entertaining courtship displays prior to breeding. The first sign of mating is a series of chases around the territory. Either bird can lead, and they may rush around in this way for hours. At intervals each bird may jump toward the other, spreading its wings and tail, then calling. The courtship becomes more serious when the stick presentation begins. In this display either bird will collect a stick and place it at the other's feet. It is an obvious prelude to nest building.

The "prance display" leads to copulation. At this time the two sexes have definite roles to play. The male approaches the female with a food offering in his bill. Wagging his tail, he runs back and forth, toward and away from the female, every so often lifting his wings. He may also wag his tail from side to side. After doing this for some time, he calls and jumps on the female's back, still holding the food offering, which she takes from the male following mating.

Over the next few days the young move further from the nest site, following their parents toward the best feeding areas. They learn how to catch food for themselves, and by 40 days old they are more or less independent.

If the weather has been good, the female parent is less generous with her time toward her fledglings because she is preparing to lay a second clutch of eggs. Then the male will take over the whole task of looking after the first brood. It is a demanding time for him because besides feeding his young he also has to provide for the female on the nest. Yet making two or even three nesting attempts is well worth the effort since ideal conditions are always at a premium in the desert.

Although losses from nests are high—73 percent in some cases—the greater roadrunner has a built-in capacity to withstand difficult circumstances. It has a stable population throughout most of its range, although in California it has been shown to disappear when its habitat is fragmented. For now this tough bird is doing well enough to be under no risk.

A roadrunner uses its long tail like a rudder to help it steer as it hurtles over the desert on its powerful legs. The bird rarely flies, although it can do so perfectly well if it needs to escape danger.

Sitting in Partnership

There is a very definite division of labor to be seen among parent roadrunners when they are incubating their clutch of eggs. The male takes the night shift, while the female incubates for two long sessions during the day.

There is a good reason for this arrangement. Once she has reached the incubation stage, a female roadrunner's energy reserves are depleted by the effort required to produce the eggs and build the nest. In contrast, the less stretched male should be in peak condition. When it comes to incubation, the night shift is by far the harder task, since the sitting bird must expend much energy in keeping the eggs adequately warm, but the fit male should be able to cope well.

Freed from this task, the female can get a proper rest at night. She can lower her body temperature and metabolic rate, and save some 36 percent of the energy she would normally use up. What food she has eaten can then be used in getting her body back into good condition and in better readiness for the tasks ahead.

Axolotl

Ambystoma mexicanum

Common name Axolotl (Mexican mole salamander, Mexican walking fish)

Scientific name *Ambystoma mexicanum*

Family Ambystomatidae

Order Caudata (Urodela)

Size 8 in (20 cm) but exceptionally to 12 in (30 cm)

Key features 4 limbs; 3 pairs of feathery external gills; high dorsal and caudal fins; head broad and flat; mouth has a wide gape; eyes small; wild-type axolotls are dark gray in color with scattered, small black spots; laboratory strains may be white or different colors produced by selective breeding

Habits Totally aquatic; more active at night

Breeding Females lay up to 1,000 eggs attached singly or in small clumps to twigs or aquatic plants; eggs hatch after about 2 weeks

Diet Aquatic invertebrates, including insect larvae and worms; fish and tadpoles

Habitat High-altitude lakes

Distribution Lake Xochimilco and Lake Chalco on the central Mexican plateau

Status Protected (CITES); Vulnerable IUCN

Similar species 4 other Mexican *Ambystoma* species (3 from central Mexico and 1 from Puebla) are axolotls and therefore similar in appearance

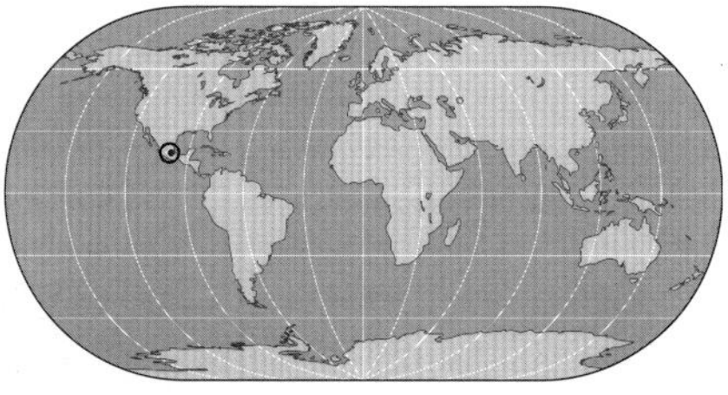

The axolotl is, in effect, an enormous tadpole. Adults retain many of their larval characteristics and can even reproduce as larvae.

THE AXOLOTL IS THE LARVAL FORM of the Mexican mole salamander, *Ambystoma mexicanum*. Its metamorphosis is incomplete: Although it develops small lungs and a reproductive system, it does not lose its external gills or the fins around its tail and along its back, and its skin does not take on characteristics of adult salamanders. Nor can it survive out of water.

Grown-up Axolotls

Metamorphosed axolotls are almost unheard of in the wild or in captivity. Although some sources maintain that an axolotl will metamorphose if the water level in its aquarium is lowered slowly, this is not so. Neoteny is a genetic trait in the axolotl, caused by low levels of iodine. Iodine is an essential component of hormones belonging to the thyroxin group, which are necessary for growth and development. Only by injecting axolotls with hormones of this type will they metamorphose (except in very rare cases, where they metamorphose spontaneously). Grown-up axolotls are very similar to adult tiger salamanders from Mexico, being dark gray with lighter mottling, and are closely related to them.

The axolotl's natural habitat is the montane lakes of central Mexico: Lake Xochimilco and Lake Chalco. Unfortunately, Lake Chalco exists no more, having been built over as Mexico City expanded southward. Lake Xochimilco survives as a network of canals and lagoons. It is under pressure from the growing human population nearby, but it is still rich in plants and animals.

Research Animals

The plight of wild populations of axolotls has led to the species being protected under CITES regulations and listed as Vulnerable by the

Aztec Connections

The axolotl's name has Aztec origins. It derives from two words: *atl,* meaning "water," and *xolotl,* meaning "monster." In Aztec mythology the god Xolotl was the twin brother of Quetzalcóatl, the plumed serpent god, but was disfigured and regarded as a monster. The local name for the species is *ajolote*, which has the same origins (bearing in mind that in Spanish the *x* and the *j* are pronounced as an *h*). *Ajolote* is also used for a completely different species, the amphisbaenian, *Bipes biporus* (a type of worm lizard), that lives in the Baja California region of Mexico. In pre-Hispanic Mexico the axolotl was a delicacy and was said to taste like an eel. Its fat was used as a medicine in the same way that cod liver oil is used nowadays.

IUCN. What is strange is that axolotls are bred in huge numbers by laboratories and amateur enthusiasts around the world. Axolotls were first bred in laboratories to provide material for teaching and research, especially in the field of embryology. They were suitable because they could be persuaded to lay fertile eggs at any time of the year and on demand. The jelly layer surrounding the eggs is also easy to remove, allowing cell division to be observed. Because of their wide availability scientists in other disciplines began to use them too.

Nearly everything we know about axolotls has been learned from captives. Wild populations, apart from being rare, are also difficult to observe. The first reference to them is in a book published in the early 17th century, but they were not named until 1789, as *Gyrinus mexicanus*. In 1830 the first reference to their local name and their eventual common name was made when they were renamed *Axolotus pisciformis*. In Paris in 1863 they were bred in captivity for the first time, and their strange life history was revealed.

The white form of axolotl,* Ambystoma mexicanum, *is the most common. It is not a true albino because, although its skin lacks pigment, its eyes are black.

Axolotls in Captivity

The most common axolotl is the white form, and there are probably more in captivity than in the wild. It is a genetic mutation in which pigment is lacking from cells in the skin but not from the eyes (known as leucisitic). There is an albino strain with pink eyes, but it has not been bred for as long as the white form and is seen less often. There are other, less distinctive varieties.

Axolotls need a spacious tank, but it does not have to be filled to the top—the most important factor is surface area. Axolotls eat earthworms, strips of lean meat, and other animal food. The young eat bloodworms, *Daphnia*, and pieces of each other; but the more often they are fed, the less they will mutilate each other. The tank bottom should be filled with large pebbles that the axolotls cannot ingest accidentally. They will use hiding places (broken crocks or drainpipes), but it is best to avoid building elaborate rock caves, because they are easily dislodged—sometimes with fatal results.

In the wild axolotls experience water temperatures of 41 to 68°F (5–20°C). Animals kept warmer than this will develop larger, more feathery gills but will also be prone to fungus and bacterial infections. A small filter helps keep the water clean, but axolotls dislike strong currents, so power filters should be avoided. The best way to keep them clean is to change about 20 percent of the water every week or so, using a siphon tube to take the water from the bottom of the tank. Rainwater is best; but if tapwater is used, it should be left to stand overnight before using it so that chlorine and other additives can disperse. If the replacement water is much colder than the water in the tank, the sudden temperature drop may stimulate breeding activity.

Breeding

Axolotls will breed at any time of the year, although a sudden drop in water temperature usually triggers courtship activity in males. Courtship includes nudging of the female by the male, after which she follows him until he deposits his spermatophore. Females start spawning a few hours later, laying their eggs singly or in small clusters, and attaching them to aquatic plants, twigs, or rocks. Larger females produce more eggs, and the clutch size can vary between 100 and 1,000 eggs. The eggs hatch after about two weeks, although the exact time varies with temperature. The young larvae are small at hatching and feed on very small aquatic creatures at first, such as young water fleas, *Daphnia*.

Axolotls have a characteristic method of feeding in which they remain motionless until a

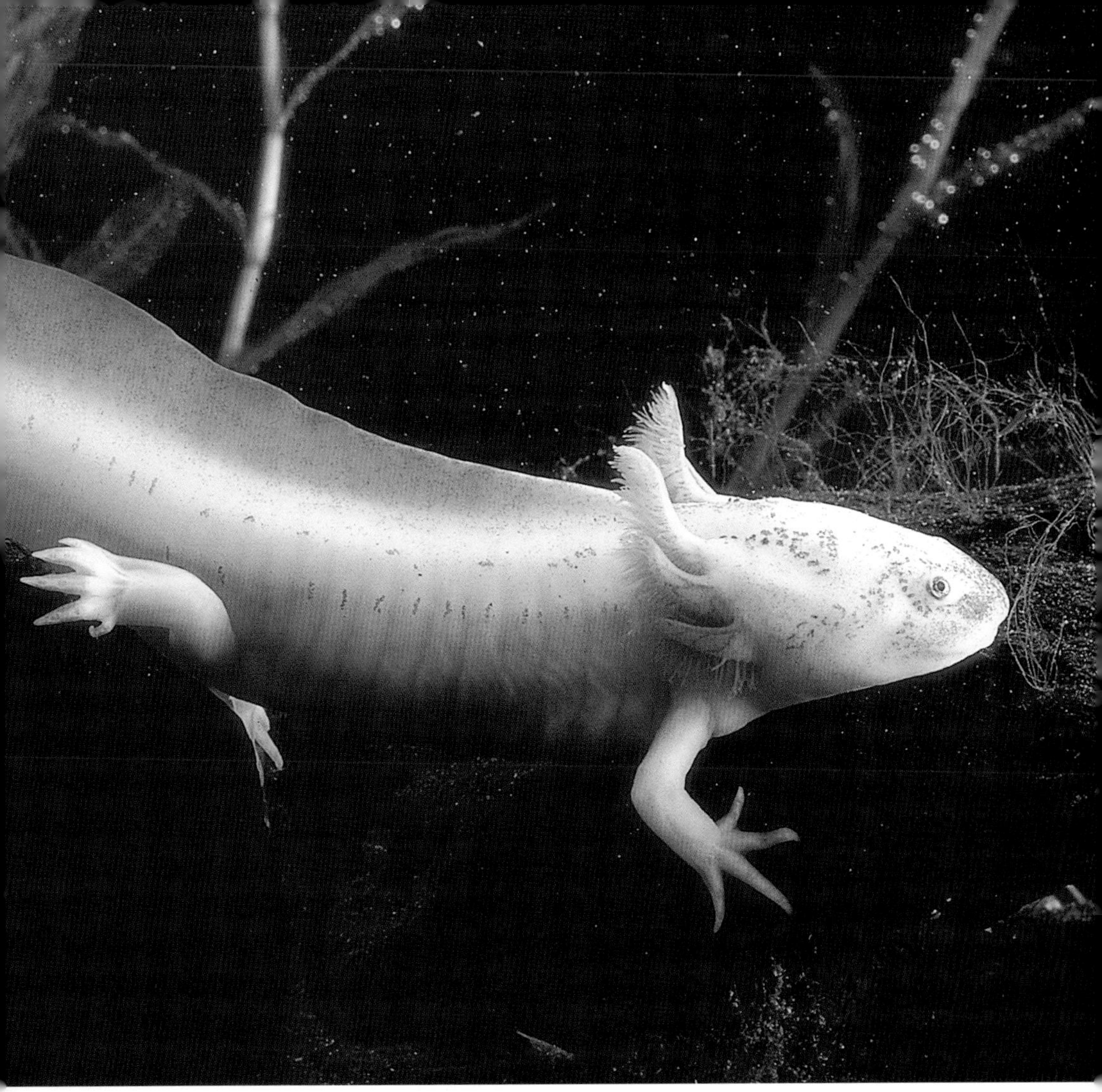

suitable prey animal comes within range. Then they open their mouth so that water rushes in. At the same time, they move forward and upward slightly before sinking back to the bottom. As they grow, they become more voracious and often bite limbs and pieces of external gills from each other, especially during feeding frenzies. Under extreme circumstances a young axolotl can lose all four of its limbs. Far from being fatal, the loss does not seem to bother them, and the limbs eventually regrow.

Endangered Relatives

The axolotl is part of the tiger salamander group, but its closest relatives are the other four neotenic species that live in Mexican lakes. At least two of them are endangered—the Lake Pátzcuaro salamander, *A. dumerilii*, is listed in Appendix II of CITES, while the Lake Lerma salamander, *A. lermaense*, is listed by the IUCN as Critically Endangered. Shrinking habitats and pollution are the main reasons for the decline of these species.

Axolotls are easy to keep in captivity, but their status in the wild is under threat. Today there are many more living in fish tanks than there are in Mexican lakes.

Midwife Toad

Alytes obstetricans

Common name Midwife toad (common midwife toad, bell toad)

Scientific name *Alytes obstetricans*

Family Discoglossidae

Order Anura

Size From 1.5 in (3.8 cm) to 2 in (5 cm)

Key features Body plump and rounded; limbs short; eyes prominent with vertical pupils; a row of small wartlike glands runs down each side of its back, and there is a larger gland behind each eye; body color pale gray, brown, or olive with randomly scattered small, dark markings; warts may be pinkish or yellow in color

Habits Nocturnal and terrestrial; usually hides under stones, logs, or in crevices by day; may dig a short burrow with its front limbs

Breeding Takes place in springtime and on land; male carries the eggs until they hatch after 3–8 weeks

Diet Small invertebrates

Habitat Varied, including open woods, fields, parks, old quarries, and drystone walls

Distribution Europe from the northern half of Spain and Portugal through France and Belgium and into southern Netherlands and parts of Germany and Switzerland; several well-established, introduced colonies in England

Status Common in suitable habitats but disappearing rapidly in the north of their range through habit disturbance and possibly climate change

Similar species There are 3 other midwife toads in the genus; 1 is confined to the island of Majorca, but the others could be mistaken for this one where their ranges overlap

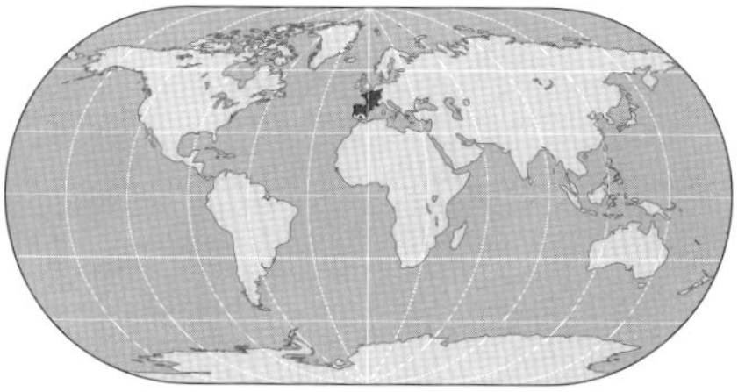

The midwife toad gets its name from its breeding habits. The males carry one or more strings of eggs wrapped around their hind legs and nurture them until they are ready to hatch.

Males of the midwife toad call at night or on rainy or cloudy days, often from a hidden place away from water. The call is a melodious "poo...poo...poo" repeated many times, with different individuals answering each other. Females also call during courtship. A chorus of calls can sound like the peal of church bells and has given them the alternative name of bell toad. Females are attracted to larger males, which they identify by the deeper calls.

Amplexus is inguinal at first, and after about half an hour the female lays a string of eggs. At that point the male moves to an axillary position so that he can fertilize the eggs and wind them around his hind legs. After spawning, the male may continue to call on subsequent nights and may end up carrying two to four strings of eggs at the same time.

Nurturing Male

He keeps the eggs from drying out by selecting a moist microenvironment, such as a burrow, in which to hide. If the weather becomes dry, he may enter a small pool or puddle to dunk them occasionally. By carrying the eggs in this way, he is providing some protection from predators. He also secretes substances from his skin that protect the eggs from fungal infections.

After three to eight weeks the eggs develop to the point of hatching, and the male takes them to a pond, the backwater of a stream, or the edges of a lake to release the tadpoles. There they continue to develop in the normal way and often overwinter before metamorphosing into toadlets when they are about 1 inch (2.5 cm) long.

Midwife toads are popular among naturalists because of their pleasant call and

The Mystery of the Inky Pads

A book published in 1971 by the author Arthur Koestler, *The Case of the Midwife Toad*, described how a midwife toad led to the downfall and eventual suicide of the Austrian scientist Paul Kammerer in 1926. Kammerer claimed to have caused the formation of nuptial pads in midwife toads by forcing them to breed in water. (Because they normally breed on land, midwife toads have no need to develop the pads.) His findings seem to contradict those of Darwin and support a theory called "the inheritance of acquired characteristics," originally proposed by a scientist called Lamarck.

The toad specimen showing the pads was the subject of much controversy in the 1920s, but it was eventually shown that the pads contained Indian ink. Had they been doctored from the beginning, or had the ink been injected by an assistant to "restore" a specimen that was in poor shape? Koestler's very readable book looks into the scandal and the scientific background leading up to it, but mystery still surrounds the origins of the doctored specimen.

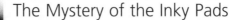

← A male midwife toad carrying eggs on its back seeks shelter in a garden in England where the species has been introduced.

interesting breeding behavior. For this reason they have been encouraged in gardens and parks, and introduced to places outside their natural range.

At the end of the 19th century some tadpoles were accidentally introduced to a garden in Bedford, England, along with some pond plants, and they became established. In 1922 the site was destroyed, but some of the toads were moved to another site in Bedford. Toads still occur in and around the town today. In 1947 a group of toads from the Bedford stock was moved to a garden in Nottinghamshire, England. When the owner of that garden moved to another county in 1965, she took some of them with her. Other small colonies thrive in counties much farther north and south. The midwife toad also lives in northern France, right up to the English Channel, and it is thought that if the British Isles had not been cut off from the rest of Europe following the Ice Age, the toads would probably have spread north naturally.

Agalychnis callidryas

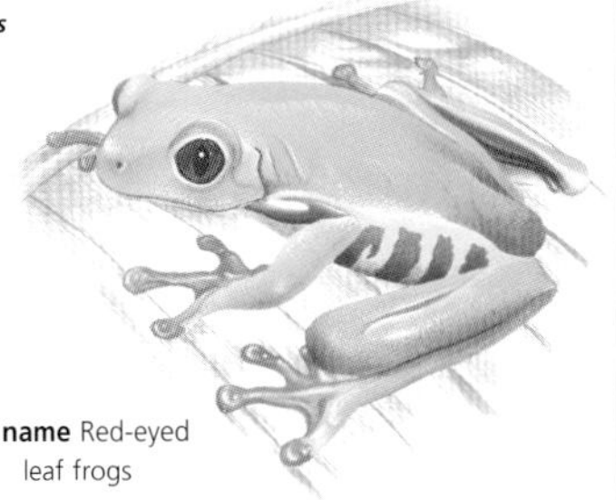

Red-Eyed Leaf Frogs

Agalychnis callidryas and *A. saltator*

No other frogs characterize the exotic fauna of the rain forests, or "jungles," of South America as well as the red-eyed frogs. Their distinctive image is often used to represent the countries where they live.

Common name Red-eyed leaf frogs

Scientific names *Agalychnis callidryas* and *A. saltator*

Subfamily Phyllomedusinae

Family Hylidae

Order Anura

Size *A. callidryas* 2.8 in (7 cm); *A. saltator* 2.4 in (6 cm)

Key features Body slender; waist narrow; legs long and spindly; feet webbed; toes have expanded sticky pads; eyes very large with brilliant-red irises; pupils vertical, separating them from all other treefrogs except other members of the Phyllomedusinae; *A. callidryas* has blue-and-cream markings on its flanks, varying according to location

Habits Highly arboreal; mostly nocturnal

Breeding Eggs laid on leaves overhanging small pools; on average female lays 29–51 eggs, possibly in several clutches; eggs hatch after 5 days (*A. callidryas*); 21–72 eggs that hatch after about 6 days (*A. saltator*)

Diet Invertebrates

Habitat Lowland rain forests

Distribution Central America from southern Veracruz and the Yucatán Peninsula, Mexico, to the Canal Zone, Panama (*A. callidryas*); *A. saltator* has a more restricted range from northeastern Nicaragua to northeastern Costa Rica

Status Common in suitable habitat but declining

Similar species Several other *Agalychnis* species occur in the region but none with bright red eyes

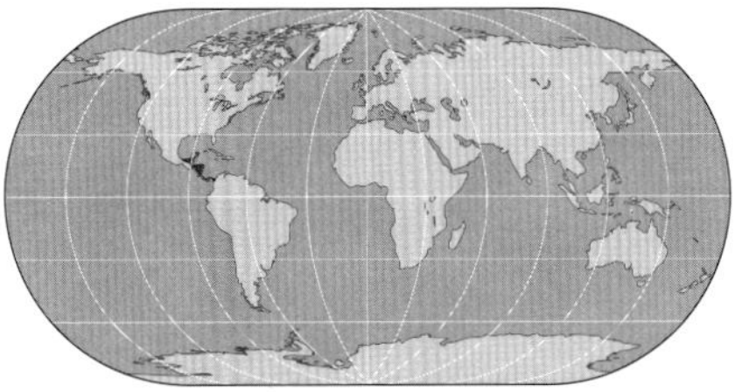

INSTANTLY RECOGNIZABLE, the more common species of red-eyed leaf frog, *A. callidryas*, appears on posters, postage stamps, and in numerous books and magazines throughout the world. The smaller species, *A. saltator*, sometimes called the lesser red-eyed leaf frog, is only found where *A. callidryas* also lives but has a more restricted range. Both species are limited to primary rain forests, living in the canopies of tall forest trees such as palms or in bromeliads and other epiphytic plants (plants that live on other plants). They rest by day and become active at dusk, often descending to lower levels, especially in the breeding season.

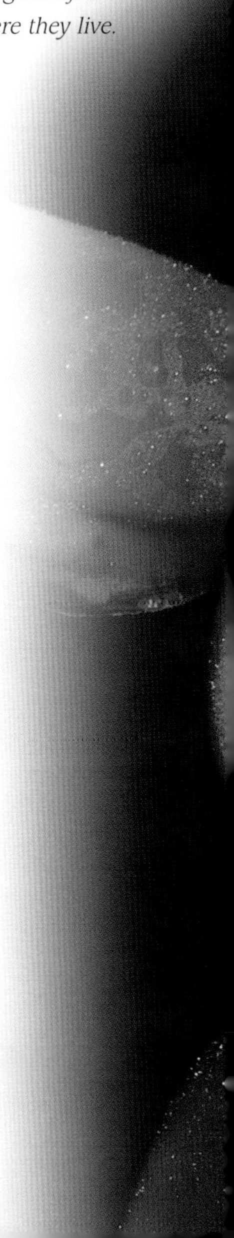

Calling Positions

Agalychnis callidryas breeds during the rainy season in small forest pools, including temporary ones. As soon as the sun sets, males call from high up in the branches where they have spent the day. These preliminary calls are sometimes called "rain calls." As they descend, they stop calling until they take up positions near the breeding sites. Once they have arrived there, their calls are different from the rain calls and consist of single- or double-note "chock" or "chock-chock," with a pause of anything from eight seconds to one minute between calls. Calling males usually position themselves on the stems of shrubs, sitting across the stem at right angles. Sites are typically 3 to 9 feet (0.9–2.7 m) above small ponds. Unless the population is very dense, the frogs are usually well spaced out.

Females in breeding condition approach, attracted by the males' calls. When a female is

Agalychnis saltator in Costa Rica. Like many red-eyed animals, the red-eyed leaf frogs hunt at night.

a few inches from a male, he stops calling, moves toward her, and climbs on her back. If the female approaches from behind where the male cannot see her, she places a hand on his back. Once they are in amplexus, the female descends to the water, where she fills her bladder. She uses the water to produce the jelly that will surround her eggs. Then she climbs back into the bush or tree and walks around until she finds a suitable egg-laying site.

While this is going on, the male (which is substantially smaller than the female) simply

Red Eyes

Red eyes are associated with nocturnal species. Apart from the species described here, there are several treefrogs, *Hyla* species, with red eyes as well as a large Australian red-eyed frog, *Litoria chloris*. On Madagascar a number of frogs belonging to the genus *Boophis* also have red or pink eyes.

Perched on a Heliconia *bract, a red-eyed leaf frog,* Agalychnis callidryas, *perfectly matches the colors of the plant.*

hangs on and may close his eyes. Eventually, the female walks along a stem until she arrives at a leaf that is hanging over the water. She crawls to the tip of the leaf and turns so that she is facing upward. As she lays her eggs, she moves slowly up the leaf so that the egg mass is elongated. The male fertilizes the eggs while this is happening.

Clutch size seems to vary according to locality: In Veracruz, Mexico, females lay an average of 51 eggs, while in Guatemala the average is 29. It is likely that they lay several clutches, because dissected females contain significantly more eggs than these figures suggest, although it is not known if they are laid during a single breeding session.

⇦ ***Moving along a leaf in a Costa Rican rain forest, a female*** **Agalychnis calcarifer** ***lays her eggs in an elongated shape. The male, still attached, fertilizes them as they are laid.***

⇩ ***In Costa Rica a pair of flap-heeled leaf frogs,*** **Agalychnis calcarifer,** ***mate while an overenthusiastic male of a different species tries to get in on the act.***

If the leaf is shaken, however, as it may be if a snake is approaching the nest, the tadpoles are likely to hatch whether it is raining or not. A human can also trigger hatching by shaking the leaf. This is not thought to be a defense mechanism, simply reaction to a movement similar to that caused by heavy rain.

Assuming they do not get eaten, the tadpoles hang with their tail pointing downward in the water near the surface, often in a patch of sunshine. They metamorphose after about 60 to 80 days. The newly changed young are green but have yellow eyes at first; the red pigment appears after about two weeks, starting at the outer edges of the irises and spreading inward until the eyes are completely red.

Taking to the Water

The eggs take about five days to hatch. At the time of hatching the jelly mass begins to liquefy so the tadpoles can move around in their nest. Hatching is usually triggered by rain, and the tadpoles wriggle until they slide down the leaf and drip off the end into the pond below. When they hit the surface, they swim to the bottom and remain there for a minute or two before reappearing at the surface.

Sometimes things go slightly wrong, and the tadpoles miss the water. If the distance is only an inch or two, they can usually flip themselves into it. If they hatch during dry weather, they stay in the nest to avoid the possibility of dripping onto mud or into a shrinking pool.

The purpose of laying eggs on leaves rather than in the water is to avoid predation by fish, other tadpoles, and aquatic invertebrates and their larvae. The strategy is only partially successful, however. At least two species of snakes, the plain blunt-headed snake, *Imantodes inornatus*, and one of the cat-eyed snakes, *Leptodeira septentrionalis*, have learned to search for the eggs among the leaves of pond-side shrubs. The snakes, which also eat adult frogs as well as lizards, swallow mouthfuls of the jelly as they pull the eggs off the leaf.

↑ A juvenile red-eyed leaf frog,* A. callidryas, *emerges from the water in Belize. Its eyes will turn red after about two weeks.

Breeding Differences

All the *Agalychnis* have a similar breeding system, but the details vary slightly. The smaller red-eyed leaf frog, *A. saltator,* for instance, is an explosive breeder (meaning that the breeding season is very short, and large numbers of the frogs all mate simultaneously). On suitable nights, usually immediately after torrential rain, several hundreds may congregate on vines hanging over ponds. The females plaster their egg masses to clumps of moss surrounding epiphytic plants or to their roots. Although each clump is separate at the time of laying, the vigorous activity of the frogs (both single males and breeding pairs) tends to mix the clutches together into a single mass. This species lays its

Origins of the Names

Agalychnis is derived from two Latin words, *aga,* meaning "very," and *Lychnis*, the name of a genus of plants containing several species with bright red flowers. The reference is presumably to the red eyes of the two species. *Saltator* is a straightforward translation from Latin, meaning "the jumper," and *callidryas* comes from two words: the Greek *kallos,* meaning "beautiful," and dryad (from Greek origins), meaning a tree or wood nymph.

eggs in the early morning, and some pairs are still around the laying sites at noon the following day. They lay between 21 and 72 eggs that hatch after about six days. Apart from the snakes mentioned above, their eggs are eaten by ants, warblers, and capuchin monkeys.

The flap-heeled leaf frog, *Agalychnis calcarifer*, is a large, spectacular, and rarely seen species. It breeds throughout the year, not just in the rainy season. It does not use forest ponds but lays its eggs on leaves above water-filled cavities in fallen tree trunks. Males call from standing trees nearby; once a female has appeared, the pair make their way to a suitable site while in amplexus. Egg laying usually takes place the next morning.

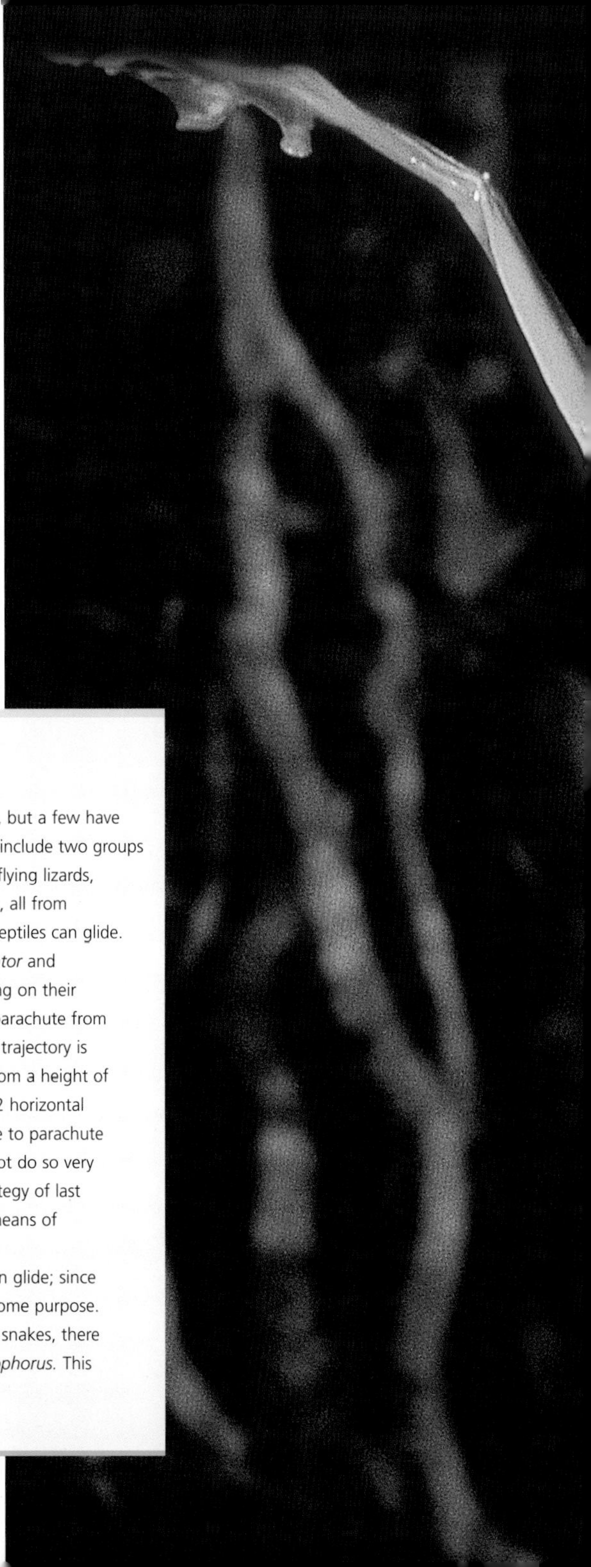

⊖ *Not a flying frog but, more accurately, a gliding frog.* Agalychnis spurrelli *uses the enormous areas of webbing between its fingers and toes as a parachute.*

Flying Frogs

No reptiles or amphibians have mastered flight, but a few have evolved the shape and ability to glide. They include two groups of lizards, the flying geckos, *Ptychozoon*, and the flying lizards, *Draco*, and the so-called flying snake, *Chrysopelea*, all from Southeast Asia. As far as we know, no American reptiles can glide.

Some leaf frogs, for example, *Agalychnis saltator* and *A. spurrelli*, also glide. They have extensive webbing on their front and hind feet, which they spread widely to parachute from high branches. It is not controlled flight, and their trajectory is less than 45 degrees: A frog that launches itself from a height of about 15 feet (4.6 m) would at best land about 12 horizontal feet (3.6 m) away. *Agalychnis callidryas* is also able to parachute and can perform as well as *A. spurrelli* but does not do so very often. In any case, parachuting seems to be a strategy of last resort in response to danger rather than a quick means of moving from treetop to ground level.

It is likely that most members of the genus can glide; since they do not swim, their webbed feet must serve some purpose. In Southeast Asia, the home of gliding lizards and snakes, there is also a group of gliding frogs in the genus *Rhacophorus*. This genus and *Agalychnis* parallel each other closely.

Common name American bullfrog

Scientific name *Rana catesbeiana*

Subfamily Raninae

Family Ranidae

Order Anura

Size From 3.5 in (9 cm) to 8 in (20 cm); when stretched out, they can measure 36 in (91 cm)

Key features A large frog (the largest in North America) with long, powerful hind legs and heavily webbed feet; eardrum prominent and larger in males than in females; color mottled olive, brown, or green above and lighter green on the head; legs are banded or spotted with dark brown or black; chin and throat also have dark markings; its bellowing call is loud and distinctive

Habits Semiaquatic, rarely seen far from water

Breeding Female lays masses of spawn in water in spring and summer; eggs hatch after 4 days

Diet Large invertebrates and small vertebrates, including other frogs

Habitat Large ponds and lakes; usually stays near the water's edge or rests among floating vegetation

Distribution Eastern and central North America; introduced to western United States and other regions

Status Common

Similar species Adults are distinctive on account of their size; juveniles could be confused with several other medium-sized ranids from the region

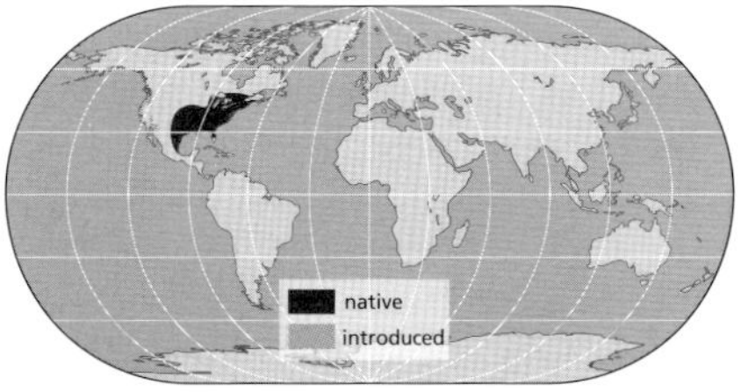

American Bullfrog

Rana catesbeiana

Large, powerful hind legs launch the bullfrog on a long, arching trajectory when it makes its enormous leaps. They also propel it through the water at great speed when it swims.

THE BULLFROG IS THOROUGHLY AQUATIC, with heavily webbed hind feet. It is often seen basking at the water's edge, facing the water or floating just below the surface with only the top of its head and its eyes visible. It is wary, however; if disturbed on land, it jumps into the water, making a considerable splash, and swims away rapidly. With one or two kicks it covers several feet and can dive to the bottom. Equally, it can jump into nearby vegetation on land.

Bellowing Calls

Bullfrogs come ashore at night to hunt for food, and males also come ashore in spring and summer to call. The breeding season varies with locality: In the north it is during May, June, and July, but in the south it is extended and can last from February to October. Males produce their famous bellowing calls and defend territories from other males, fighting if necessary to drive them away.

Males have much larger tympana than females, but nobody knows why. Both sexes apparently hear equally well. Territory holders puff up their bodies and raise themselves out of the water. The males with the best territories have higher success rates in terms of breeding. Females are attracted to males with "good" territories even though they often swim off to another part of the pond to lay their eggs after they have paired up.

Females lay huge masses of spawn averaging over 11,000 eggs that float near the surface in a foamy film. The record is 47,840

eggs, more than any other frog or toad. Females usually produce just one clutch of eggs in their first breeding year, but they produce two or more in subsequent years. The frequency depends on the local climatic conditions, and in places where the summer is short, they may only lay one clutch regardless of their age. An average female probably produces over 80,000 eggs in her lifetime.

The eggs take about four days to hatch. The tadpoles' development depends on climate. In the north they can take three or more years to grow, but they metamorphose at a larger size than in the south. Northern frogs grow more slowly after metamorphosis, however. It is not uncommon for bullfrogs to become mature within a year of metamorphosing, but females can take an extra year. They can spend more time as tadpoles than as growing juveniles.

Huge Tadpoles

The tadpoles are spotted and grow very large, with bodies as big as golf balls. In northern regions they may overwinter for two successive

Bullfrogs often spend two years in the tadpole stage and are very large. This tadpole already has well-developed legs.

Adult bullfrogs are very large and robust with big golden eyes. Both sexes have a pronounced tympanum ("eardrum") just behind and below the eye.

years, living beneath the ice in frozen ponds. Compared with other frogs, tadpole survival rates are good—about 15 percent. Considering the number of eggs laid, subsequent mortality must be high, or bullfrogs would have overrun the world by now.

Metamorphosed juveniles from the center of their range (for example, Illinois) grow quickly for the first two years until they weigh about 7 ounces (200 g). Then they slow down and take two more years to reach just under 9 ounces (250 g).

Bullfrogs are the largest frogs in North America. Taking the measurement from the tip of the snout to the tip of their toes with the feet held straight out behind them, they are the longest in the world, measuring 36 inches (91 cm). A frog this size was recorded as weighing 7.25 pounds (3.3 kg). Although it has shorter limbs, the Goliath frog, *Conraua goliath* from West Africa, is much bulkier: The largest one weighed 8.1 pounds (3.7 kg).

Unwelcome Visitors

Bullfrog tadpoles have been imported into Britain in large numbers since the 1980s and sold in garden centers and pet stores. They were often released into garden ponds either as tadpoles or young frogs. They prefer larger bodies of water, however, and mostly migrated to lakes and flooded gravel pits where, because they are shy, they often went unnoticed for a while.

Since they grew slowly, the effects were not immediately apparent, but some began to terrorize local amphibians. Calling males have been heard in various localities, and breeding was first reported in 1999 on the border of Surrey and Kent in the southeast of England, where thousands of young dispersed. The bullfrogs have also bred in the Netherlands and northern Italy.

Temperature Control

The bullfrog experiences a wide range of temperatures throughout its large north-south distribution. Although other species of frogs and toads have evolved different temperature preferences according to where they live, the bullfrog appears not to have adapted in that way. It prefers the same temperatures whether it lives in Florida or Nova Scotia.

Always ready to take on a challenge, a voracious bullfrog attempts to eat a ribbon snake.

It regulates its temperature by basking. In cold places it basks as long and as often as possible, exposing the greatest part of its body to the sun. But in warmer spots it may seek shade or reduce the amount of heat it absorbs by changing the shape and orientation of its body. In particular, it can tolerate very high temperatures by sitting in water. As water evaporates, it cools the frog's body. The frog replaces the water by absorbing more through its skin, so there is a continual movement of water into the frog through its underside and out again through its upper surfaces.

Competing for Food

Bullfrogs are voracious predators, taking small mammals, lizards, snakes, and other frogs, including smaller members of their own species. In places where they have been introduced (California and several other western states, Mexico, Cuba, Puerto Rico, Hispaniola, and Jamaica in the Americas; the Netherlands, France, Spain, and Italy in Europe; and Java, Japan, Thailand, and Taiwan in Asia) they are often implicated in the disappearance or reduction in numbers of native species living in similar habitats. In California, for instance, they are one of the causes of the decline of the red-legged frog, *Rana aurora*.

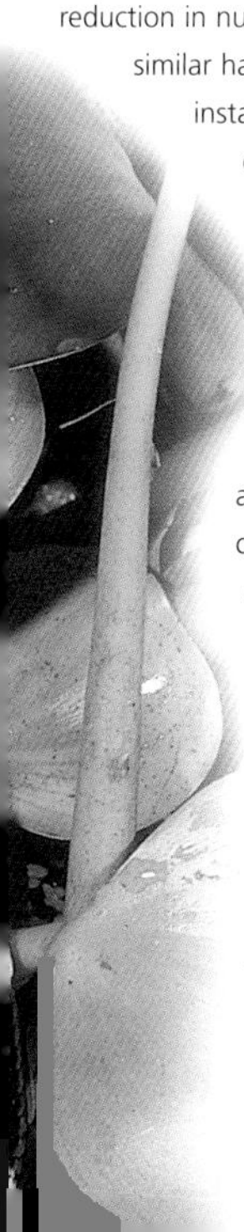

Their method of feeding is to sit and wait for prey to come within range, but there is some evidence that they are attracted to the distress calls of other frogs, including those of other bullfrogs (presumably in the hope of getting an easy meal). Food is taken with a lunge, and the frog may use its short front legs to help stuff the food into its mouth.

Similar Species

There are two other large green frogs from eastern North America. The pig frog, *Rana grylio*, named for its call (as is the bullfrog, of course) has a more limited range mainly in Florida and neighboring states. It is even more aquatic than the bullfrog and lives in weedy places such as lakes, swamps, and ditches. It is hunted for its legs, which are edible. It grows to over 6 inches (15 cm) and, confusingly, is also known as the bullfrog in places.

The green frog, *Rana clamitans*, is smaller, growing to about 4 inches (10 cm). Its range coincides almost exactly with that of the bullfrog, but it prefers shallower water. Whereas the bullfrog and the pig frog both have smooth backs, the green frog has a pair of fleshy ridges running down either side of its back.

The frog-jumping contest held annually in Jubilee, California, dates back to 1928. Today thousands of contestants from all over the world give the unique event international acclaim.

"The Celebrated Jumping Frog of Calaveras County"

In the 1860s the author Mark Twain visited Calaveras County, California, as a struggling journalist and heard a tale about a frog-jumping contest. In 1865 he turned it into a short story that became his first success and put him on the road to fame. The story is celebrated every year in the small town of Jubilee with a bullfrog-jumping competition in which participants catch bullfrogs and persuade them to compete with each other in the long jump. More than 2,000 frogs take part every year, and after the event they are returned to the ponds from which they were taken.

Each frog makes three consecutive jumps, and the winner is the frog that covers the greatest combined distance. The event attracts 40,000 tourists during May, and past champions, such as "Splashdown," "Ripple," and "Wet Bet," are commemorated on bronze plaques displayed along some of the town's sidewalks. Pride of place goes to the current world record holder, "Rosie the Ribiter," who leaped 21.48 feet (6.5 m) in May 1986.

Ironically, the bullfrog probably did not occur in Calaveras County in Twain's day, although it does today. Much controversy surrounds the origin of the story: Does it refer to the local red-legged frog, *Rana aurora*, or is it simply a fiction? Either way, the frogs used nowadays in the competition are descendants of the bullfrogs that were introduced into the Sierra Nevada in the late 19th century and are now gradually replacing the native species.

Jackson's Chameleon

Chamaeleo jacksonii

Common name Jackson's chameleon

Scientific name *Chamaeleo jacksonii*

Family Chamaeleonidae

Suborder Sauria

Order Squamata

Size 12 in (30 cm) long

Key features 3 horns present on the head—2 at eye level (orbital), the 3rd located on the tip of the snout (rostral) and curving upward; dorsal crest of prominent tubercles gives the impression of a saw blade; female's horns much reduced or absent; basic coloration green; small crest to the rear of the head is outlined by conical scales

Habits Solitary, each with its own territory; individuals from middle elevations hold their body perpendicular to sun's rays to warm up in the morning; color changes to yellow when it becomes too warm; moves into deep foliage for shade and to begin feeding

Breeding Live-bearer; female produces 1 or 2 clutches each year; each clutch contains up to 35 young; gestation period about 6–9 months

Diet Insects, particularly grasshoppers, butterflies, katydids, spiders, and flies

Habitat High altitudes; found at elevations of 8,000 ft (2,440 m) that have high rainfall and distinct wet and dry seasons leading to fluctuations in temperature and humidity; common in primary and secondary forest

Distribution Mountains of Kenya and Tanzania (East Africa); introduced to Hawaii

Status Common

Similar species *Chamaeleo johnstonii* (although this species is an egg layer)

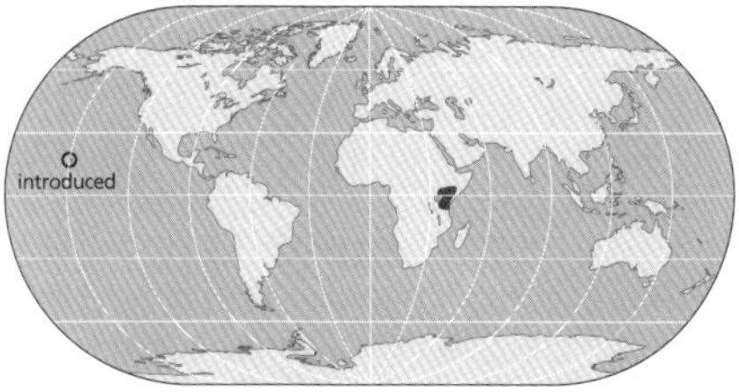

Jackson's chameleons are found on the African continent, predominantly on the highlands of Kenya and Tanzania. The three-horned males look like miniature Triceratops.

OF ALL THE THREE-HORNED CHAMELEONS, Jackson's is the best known. There are three subspecies—*C. j. jacksonii*, *C. j. merumantana*, and *C. j. xantholophus*. The main differences between the subspecies relate to size, with *C. j. xantholophus* being the largest and *C. j. merumantana* the smallest. There is also variation in the females' horns (or lack of them) depending on subspecies. *Chamaeleo j. xantholophus* is often described as the most attractive of the three forms. It has a yellow crest and yellow on the ridge at the back of its head. In the past Jackson's chameleon has been confused with Johnston's chameleon, *Chamaeleo johnstonii*, an egg layer from the mountains of Burundi, Rwanda, and Zaire.

Jackson's chameleon's habitat in the mountains of East Africa is moderately cool with high humidity. Although rainfall exceeds 50 inches (127 cm) per year, there are distinct wet and dry seasons. Daytime temperatures reach 80°F (27°C), and an average nighttime temperature is 59°F (15°C), although it can drop to as low as 42°F (5°C). Human population explosion in Kenya and Tanzania has led to the felling of considerable tracts of primary forest; as a result, Jackson's chameleon has adapted to living in secondary forest and plantations, the latter being particularly rich in insect life. In fact, plantations have the highest population density of Jackson's chameleons.

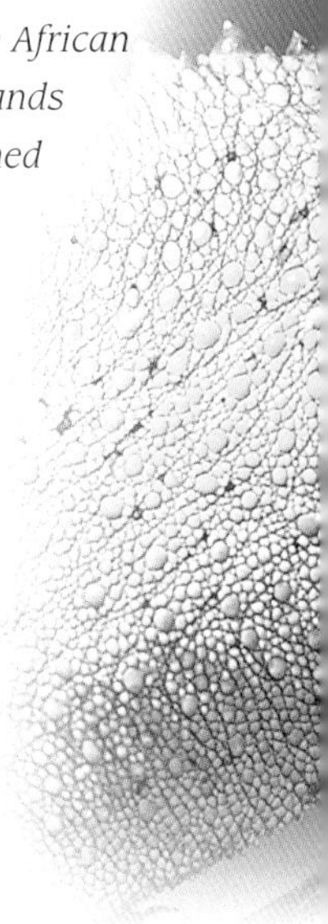

The horns on male Jackson's chameleons are not just ornamental. These two males have locked horns in a ritualized shoving contest over a mating territory.

Color and Defense

The basic coloration of Jackson's chameleon is a uniform green to yellow-brown with pale blotches forming a faint lateral line. This lichenlike coloring provides excellent camouflage among foliage. Juveniles are dark green, almost black, with white triangular markings on either side of the dorsal crest that serve to break up their outline.

When a threat from a bird is perceived, the chameleon moves deeper into the foliage where the bird cannot follow. An alternative defense strategy is to relax its grip on the branch, fall to the ground, and move to the base of a shrub. If it detects a threat from other predators, such as venomous and nonvenomous tree snakes, it responds by flattening the sides of its body and darkening its color. The mouth gapes, and the chameleon swings its head around in an attempt to bite.

Breeding

While breeding males intensify their colors, those of receptive females become lighter. Following a successful mating, the female gains weight. She tends to stop feeding for several weeks prior to giving birth as the developing young take up more room. The gestation period

varies depending on temperature. Gravid females spend more time basking, angling their body so that the underneath of the body gets the sun's rays. They give birth to live young, usually in the morning. The young emerge from the female's cloaca, each encased in a membrane that is deposited on a branch and from which the baby breaks free. They disperse among the foliage and catch their own food within hours.

Horns

The horns of Jackson's chameleons are not collected for use in traditional medicine, but many East Africans regard cutting off a chameleon's horn as an act of great courage.

Male Jackson's chameleons engage in combat, locking horns and using them to try to force their opponent off the branch. Larger horns are obviously an advantage, since an individual can inflict damage on its opponent without receiving any.

Hawaiian Habitat

In 1981 the Kenyan government halted the previous widescale export of Jackson's chameleons, but the owner of a pet store on the Hawaiian island of Oahu obtained a permit to import a few specimens. Because they arrived in poor condition, they were released into a garden to try to improve them. They found the climate similar to that of their native habitat in East Africa, and from this initial group scattered populations of Jackson's chameleon have become established on the islands of Oahu and Maui.

Marine Iguana *Amblyrhynchus cristatus*

Common name Marine iguana

Scientific name *Amblyrhynchus cristatus*

Subfamily Iguaninae

Family Iguanidae

Suborder Sauria

Order Squamata

Size From 30 in (75 cm) to 4.1 ft (1.3 m)

Key features Heavy bodied with muscular limbs and a powerful tail; a crest of elongated, toothlike scales runs along the center of the back and tail; top of the head covered with horny, conical scales of varying sizes; color usually gray, although some subspecies are more colorful with patches of red or turquoise

Habits Diurnal, basking by day on rocks and entering the sea to feed

Breeding Egg layer; female lays 1–6 eggs in tunnels on shore; eggs hatch after about 95 days

Diet Marine algae (seaweed)

Habitat Rocky seashores

Distribution Galápagos Islands

Status Protected under national legislation but possibly at risk in the long term from human pressures

Similar species The marine iguana is unmistakable; the only other iguanas on the islands are the Galápagos land iguanas, *Conolophus subcristatus*, and the much smaller lava lizards, *Microlophus* sp.

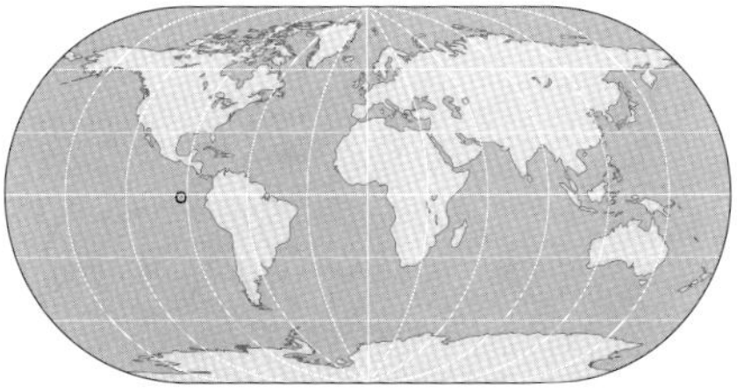

Marine iguanas are unique. They are the only seagoing lizards and the only lizards that feed on seaweed—a lifestyle that has resulted in many special adaptations.

After visiting the Galápagos Islands, the English naturalist Charles Darwin wrote, "The rocks on the coast are abounded with great black lizards between three and four feet long; it is a hideous-looking creature, of a dirty black colour, stupid and sluggish in its movements." We have no idea what they thought of him!

The Galápagos Islands straddle the equator and are about 600 miles (1,550 km) off the coast of Ecuador. The ocean there is very cold, but the Humboldt Current drives up the west coast of South America and brings with it the waters of the Antarctic, rich in nutrients and fish. Much of the land, on the other hand, is barren, formed by lava that resulted from the volcanic eruptions to which the Galápagos owe their existence.

Marine iguanas arrived on the Galápagos from South or Central America many thousands of generations ago and adapted to an environment in which food was readily available in the sea but not on the land. Their ancestors would have been one of the larger iguanas, possibly something like the spiny-tailed iguanas, *Ctenosaura*, that live on the mainland today. A few individuals (or a single gravid female) were swept out to sea on a raft of vegetation and drifted west until they washed up on one of the islands. Later they spread to all the larger islands as well as many smaller islets in the archipelago. Some populations, particularly on far-flung islands, evolved distinct sizes and coloration, and scientists recognize seven separate races, or subspecies.

Ⓓ *Marine iguanas are just as at home beneath the water as on land. Large adults can graze among rocks in shallows for up to an hour.*

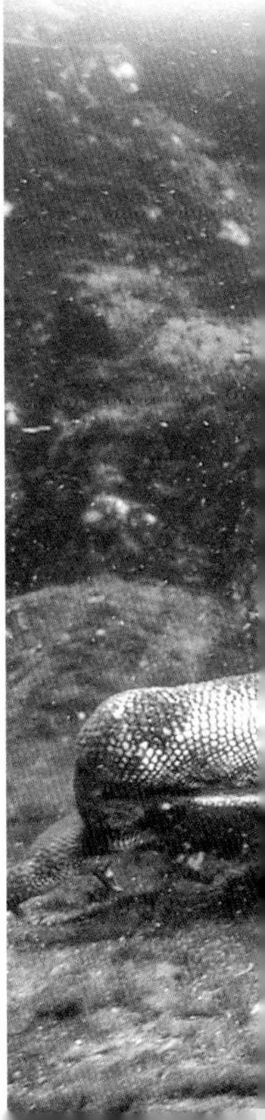

Diving and Feeding

The iguanas' most remarkable talent is for diving, which is how they find the seaweed on which they feed. Although a typical dive lasts only for a few minutes, large iguanas can stay underwater for up to an hour and reach depths of 40 feet (12 m). The amount of time they can spend in the water is limited by temperature. The water is only a few degrees above freezing; being ectotherms, the iguanas lose mobility if their body temperature falls too low. Larger individuals (mostly males) can store heat in the core of their bodies, but females, young males, and juveniles get cold quickly. As a result, there are two different groups: divers and nondivers.

The feeding patterns of large males depend on temperature. They bask on the lava rocks during the morning until their core body temperature has reached the preferred level—about 100 to 104°F (38–40°C). Then they make their way down to the water regardless of the state of the tide and swim several hundred yards out to sea before diving down to the beds of sea lettuce that grow below the low-tide mark. Between dives they can crawl out onto emergent reefs or return to the shore to bask and top up their temperature. They swim by holding their limbs close to their body and swinging their tail from side to side to propel them through the waves and surf.

By late afternoon their body temperature is falling to the point where they can hardly

On the Galápagos Islands marine iguanas bask to raise their body temperature before plunging into the cold sea to feed.

move, so they make their way back to shore and crawl slowly up the beach and rocks until they reach a place where they will spend the night. They prefer the company of hundreds of other large iguanas and form great heaps that help limit heat loss from their bodies.

Females and smaller males have a completely different routine. They do not dive but feed on the algae that is exposed at low tide. Females and subadult males may have to swim across short channels of water to reach it, but juveniles never take to the water. They lose heat too quickly and are vulnerable to predation in open water. An average-sized adult can survive on about 1 ounce (28 g) of algae each day partly because its metabolism is slow but also because red and green seaweeds are very nutritious. Brown algae, however, is poor in nutrients, and the iguanas refuse it unless they are desperate.

Island Races

There is little or no gene exchange between the iguana populations on different islands because they are not able to swim large distances. Many of the more remote islands were probably only colonized once many thousands of years ago, perhaps by a handful of waifs after storms in the region. Other islands (those that are closer to their neighbors) may have had several "invasions." Scientists have recognized some of the differences and have divided the marine iguana into seven races, or subspecies. The first three subspecies, which appear to be closely related, come from the westernmost islands where the seas are richer. Consequently, they grow slightly larger than the other subspecies.

Amblyrhynchus cristatus cristatus—large, dark gray form from Fernandina Island
A. c. albemarlensis—largest form, also gray, from Isabela
A. c. hassi—large gray form from Santa Cruz
A. c. mertensi—medium form from Santiago and San Cristóbal
A. c. nanus—very small, black in color, from the remote northern island of Genovesa
A. c. sielmanni—medium-sized form from Pinta
A. c. venustissimus—a large, spectacular form from Española with deep red patches on its body

↑ ***Head-butting matches between rival males can last for hours or even days. This pair of males belongs to the subspecies* A. c. mertensi *from Santiago Island.***

← ***Males of the subspecies* A. c. venustissimus *from Española Island develop striking patches of brilliant red and green during the breeding season as a result of eating species of seaweed that occur only during the summer.***

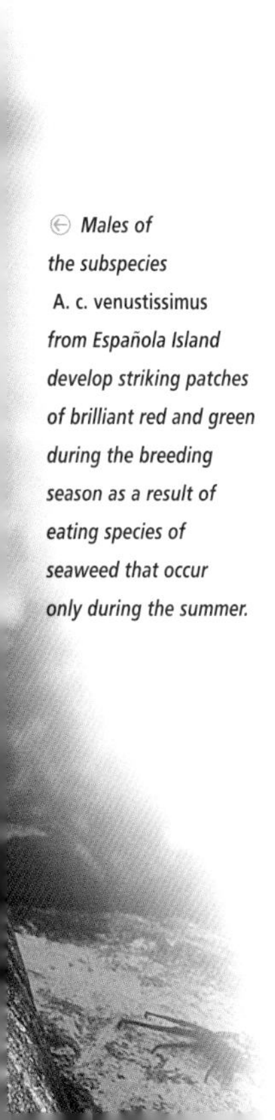

The iguanas' snouts are very short, and their mouths are bordered by tough scales so that they can crop the algae closely. Feeding iguanas are often pounded by large waves and seem as though they must be washed off the rocks and out to sea. However, they cling to the lava with very long claws like grappling hooks and remain in the same position until the surf subsides before continuing to graze.

Because they spend so much time in the sea and because they eat seaweed, marine iguanas accumulate a lot of excess salt in their system. To counteract this, they have salt glands just above their nostrils where the excess salt accumulates. While they bask, they eliminate it by snorting fine sprays of concentrated salt water from their nostrils at regular intervals.

Breeding

Mating takes place from November through to January or February but varies a little from one island to another. The large males defend territories containing many females; at this time the males become more colorful, often reddish or greenish depending on locality. They posture with much head bobbing and strutting. Rivals are chased away. If they persist, a fight breaks out. The head butting and shoving can last for several hours with short breaks between bouts. When two males are well matched, the bouts can continue on successive days with both males becoming bruised and bloody.

During mating the male mounts the female and grasps her neck in his jaws while he forces the rear part of his body under hers so that copulation can take place. Mating can last for several minutes. Small males, however, can "steal" matings lasting only a few seconds; to increase their chances of fertilizing the female, they transfer sperm into their hemipenal sacs before mating. Males probably take about 10 years to reach a dominant position in the colony, and each male controls a territory that can contain several dozen females.

A few weeks after mating, females look for suitable egg-laying sites. They are often several hundred yards back from the shore in sand or shingle. The eggs, numbering one to six, are laid at the end of a short tunnel and then covered over. Good sites are in short supply, and females often stay near their eggs to chase away other gravid females that may dig up the nest while excavating a tunnel of their own. During this time they look emaciated and in poor shape.

The eggs hatch after about 95 days, and the young iguanas dig their way out of the ground and make their way to the shore. They are very vulnerable to predation, especially by Galápagos hawks, snakes, and gulls. Hatchlings and juveniles live a secretive life hidden in crevices in the lava and only emerge for short periods to feed. They never go to sea; instead, they graze on algae in the spray zone. Nor do they bask, but close contact with the dark lava causes heat to transfer to their bodies.

Future Prospects

Marine iguanas have few predators once they are adult. Juveniles are eaten by the few snakes on the islands and by birds of prey. Gulls take a few of the hatchlings. On many islands humans have introduced feral populations of rats, cats, dogs, and pigs, which destroy nests and eat hatchlings. Up to 60 percent of juveniles may die during their first year.

Tourism may have some negative effects because of increased disturbance and pollution. On balance, however, it is probably beneficial, because it brings much-needed income to the islands and in particular to the Galápagos

National Park, which accounts for nearly all the area covered by the archipelago. Programs to eliminate feral goats and other pest species are funded by tourist dollars.

Marine iguanas are not found anywhere else in the world. They must be considered vulnerable to any serious environmental disaster along the lines of the oil tanker that sank off the islands a few years ago. Such events could wipe out whole populations. In addition, the human population of the Galápagos has swollen from 4,000 to 12,000 at the end of the 20th century, mainly through migrants from the mainland who are attracted by work in the tourism and fishing industries. Unless the influx of people is carefully managed, it is bound to put pressure on the environment.

⊖ ***Marine iguanas are protected by national legislation, but they are vulnerable to marine pollution and the effects of human development.***

El Niño

The El Niño phenomenon has serious implications for the marine iguanas. During El Niño years the warm waters of the western Pacific push farther east than usual and prevent the cold, rich waters of the Humboldt Current from welling up to the surface. The result is more cloud and heavier rainfall in the Galápagos, killing much of the algae on which the iguanas feed. Up to 90 percent of the lizards may die during those years.

El Niño years used to occur roughly every seven years; but for reasons that are not fully understood, they now occur more often—sometimes every second year—and the frequency prevents populations from recovering. The hundreds of iguanas that used to be seen basking on Punta Espinosa on Fernandina, for instance, may soon be a thing of the past. Individual iguanas in good condition may be able to draw on stored food reserves, and there is evidence that they may also be able to shrink themselves by up to 2 percent to limit the damage.

The effects of El Niño are also significant for the other animals for which the Galápagos Islands are famous. The seabirds, including endemic gulls, boobies, albatrosses, and frigate birds, all rely on fish for their food, and the warmer water drives away fish stocks. Many seabirds fail to raise a family during El Niño years.

Gila Monster

Heloderma suspectum

Common name Gila monster (Aztec lizard)

Scientific name *Heloderma suspectum*

Family Helodermatidae

Suborder Sauria

Order Squamata

Size From 13 in (33 cm) to 22 in (56 cm)

Key features Head rounded and bears a patch of light-colored scales; nose blunt; neck short; body heavy with short, powerful limbs and long claws; tail short and fat; scales beadlike; eyelids movable; camouflage colors of black, orange, yellow, and pink on the body; has 2 elongated cloacal scales

Habits Active by day, at dusk, or at night depending on season and temperatures; spends much of the time in burrows or in shaded areas

Breeding Female lays 1 clutch of up to 12 eggs in late summer; eggs hatch 10 months later

Diet Small mammals, eggs of birds and reptiles, insects

Habitat Dry grassland, deserts, and foothills of mountains

Distribution Southwestern United States and northwestern Mexico

Status Vulnerable (IUCN); listed in CITES Appendix II

Similar species *Heloderma horridum*

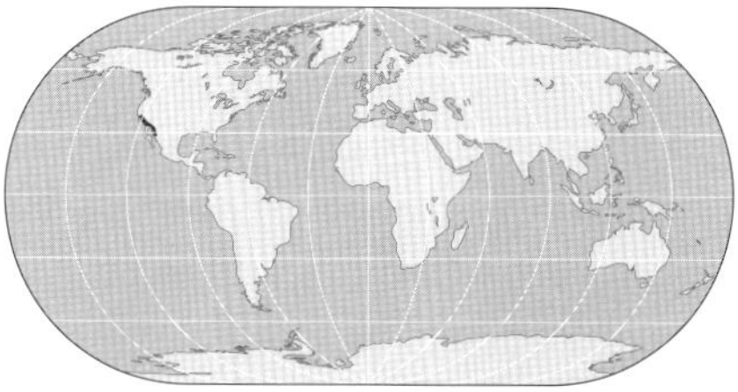

Surrounded by myths and superstitions, the Gila monster is one of just two venomous lizards. Although potent, its venom has hardly ever been known to kill a human.

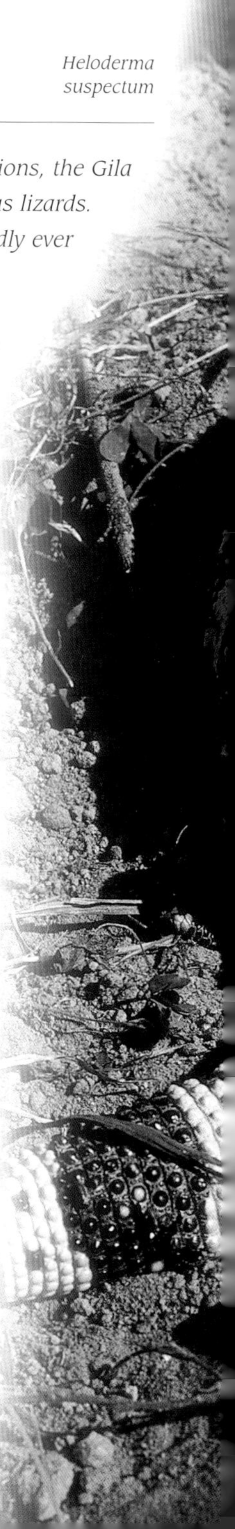

THE GILA MONSTER is named after the Gila basin in Arizona where numbers of the lizard are plentiful. It is sometimes referred to as the Aztec lizard, since it has featured in paintings by the Aztecs. Although it has a wide distribution in southern Nevada, southeastern California, southwestern New Mexico, and Arizona, numbers are concentrated in small pockets. There are two subspecies: *Heloderma suspectum suspectum*, the Gila monster, and *H. s. cinctum*, the banded Gila monster, which is slightly smaller and whose coloration contains lighter-colored bands. Its range includes southwest Utah and southern Nevada.

The habitat of Gila monsters varies from desert grassland, Mohave and Sonoran desert scrub, to Sonoran thorn scrub. They can be found on lower mountain slopes in arid and semiarid areas and also on adjacent plains and occasionally irrigated areas. They inhabit canyon bottoms—deep ravines with streams that may dry up for part of the year. In parts of Arizona the Gila monster's range extends into oak woodland and in Sonora onto beaches.

Seeking Shade

Within its habitat it seeks shelter under rocks, in dense thickets, and in wood-rat nests. It also digs burrows as well as making use of those belonging to other animals. Although Gila monsters are adapted to an extremely dry habitat, their optimum temperature is only about 86°F (30°C), which is considerably lower than other desert lizards. To avoid the high daytime temperatures during the summer, Gila monsters tend to be active at dawn and dusk. They spend the rest of the day in burrows, often dug using their powerful limbs and long

claws, or under rocks and shrubs. In Arizona Gila monsters spend 98 percent of their active season underground, and in Utah they live for 95 percent of the time in burrows.

During winter when temperatures fall below 50°F (10°C), they hibernate in burrows that have a south-facing entrance. On sunny days they wake and emerge to bask at the entrance. During the rainy season they become active at dusk and nocturnal; but after emerging from hibernation when temperatures are still relatively low, they are diurnal.

The Gila monster has a more rounded head, a shorter tail, and is a smaller species overall than its close relative the Mexican beaded lizard, *H. horridum*. Its long claws are useful when climbing trees, which it frequently does in the rainy season to escape the threat of torrential rain flooding its burrows. In spring it eats insects, but in June and July it changes to small mammals and birds. It can live for several months without food, although loss of weight shows mainly in the tail, which can lose 20 percent of its girth in one month without food.

Distinctively patterned in colors of light yellow, orange, pink, and black, the Gila monster is hard to spot against a dark background or in dappled shade.

Camouflage and Warning Coloration

Coloration of Gila monsters consists of irregular bands and blotches of black, orange, yellow, and pink. Younger specimens have more extensive lighter areas. Unusually for lizards these colors act both as camouflage and as a warning to enemies. Since the Gila monster is active primarily at dawn and dusk, the bands of color are difficult to see in the dappled shade when it moves or shelters beneath creosote bushes and other shrubs. Against a dark background the black markings blend in, and the light markings resemble gravel. Its nose is black, providing excellent camouflage when peering from burrows.

When it moves away from vegetation, its bright body markings become warning coloration, advertising its toxicity. In response to a threat the Gila monster will hiss and gape, revealing the pink venom glands that contrast with the dark lining of the mouth—yet another warning signal.

Beaded Lizard Venom

Venom in reptiles is usually associated with snakes. However, the two species of beaded lizard (the Gila monster and the Mexican beaded lizard) are the only venomous lizards. At first scientists debated whether or not they were venomous and gave the Gila monster the name *Heloderma suspectum*, since at the time it was only suspected to be venomous.

Beaded lizards have 10 teeth in each jaw. When compared with snakes, their venom-delivery mechanism is rather primitive. There is a gland on each side of the jaw with ducts next to the points where the teeth emerge from the jaw. When the animal bites, venom is expelled from the glands some distance from the teeth. The venom flows along a mucous fold between the lip and the lower jaw before reaching the front surface of the teeth. This is an inefficient method compared with the stabbing or biting stroke of vipers and cobras. Instead, Gila monsters must grip the prey or enemy tightly with both jaws and hang on to allow time for the venom to flow into the wound. Its jaws are very strong and difficult to disengage.

The poison produced is a neurotoxin that causes swelling, dizziness, drowsiness, vomiting, palpitations, swollen tongue, paralysis, labored breathing, and a fall in blood pressure. Some people unfortunate enough to have been bitten may experience just one or two symptoms. The swelling and pain that accompany a bite are due to the way in which the venom is injected. The lizard uses its vicelike grip to hold on, and chews with a sideways action of the teeth. It is possible for the elongated, inwardly curved, sharp teeth to break off and remain embedded in the victim. Teeth lost in this way are difficult to detect even using X-rays. Tissue destruction at the site of bites indicates that the venom also contains certain enzymes that play a role in digestion.

Gila venom is classified as sublethal, since there have been relatively few human deaths from it. Exhaustive studies have concluded that only eight to 10 people have ever died from beaded lizard bites. (It is interesting to note that all of them had consumed varying quantities of alcohol.) In the mid 1990s, as a result of studies on beaded lizard venom, pharmaceutical companies began experimenting with new treatments for diabetics based on elements of the venom. Even more recently the venom was found to have memory-enhancing properties, but more research will need to be done on this. Had the Gila monsters not been given protection, such medical advances would not have been possible.

A flaccid tail is an indication of poor condition in a Gila monster. As with other desert creatures, most of the moisture it needs is obtained from its food.

Reproduction

In the mating season Gila monsters have a structured social system in which dominance is established by male-to-male combat. Having spent much of the cooler months hibernating in burrows, they feed voraciously to regain body weight as soon as they emerge. Males become highly territorial in April, and wrestling matches take place. They frequently bite each other but are immune to the venom. Mating occurs in late spring and early summer. In late summer

females lay three to 12 elongated, leathery eggs, which they bury in a sunny spot near a stream at a depth of about 5 to 6 inches (13–15 cm). The eggs overwinter and hatch out about 10 months later.

Endangered Gila Monsters

Gila monsters live in small groups each with a home range of several acres. Although slow moving, they can travel several hundred yards a day. Much of their habitat has been reduced by human encroachment or destroyed by agriculture and industry. Deliberate killing through fear, superstition, or ignorance has depleted numbers further. Many Gila monsters have been collected for the reptile trade, and some have gone to institutions and serious herpetologists for captive breeding programs.

These lizards have enlarged lungs, which means that they need extra biotin (part of the vitamin B complex) to turn oxygen into carbon dioxide. In the wild this presents no problems, since fertilized eggs containing biotin form part of their diet; but in captivity many have been fed solely on unfertilized hens' eggs that lack biotin, with disastrous results.

Gila monster enjoy a degree of protection. In Arizona it is forbidden to keep them, but the law is not always enforced. They are listed in CITES Appendix II, and pressure is being applied to upgrade the listing to CITES Appendix I to restrict the trade in them still further.

Gila monsters grip their prey very tightly in their jaws. Since most of their prey is small and defenseless, venom is not usually needed. Here a Gila monster feeds on a young rodent.

Common name Komodo dragon

Scientific name *Varanus komodoensis*

Family Varanidae

Suborder Sauria

Order Squamata

Size Up to a maximum of 10.3 ft (3.1 m)

Key features Body very large; head relatively small; ear openings visible; teeth sharp and serrated; tail powerful; strong limbs and claws for digging; scales small, uniform, and rough; color varies from brown to brownish or grayish red; juveniles are green with yellow-and-black bands

Habits Spends much of the time foraging for food; digs burrows to which it retreats at night and during hot weather

Breeding Female lays clutch of up to 30 eggs (depending on size of female); eggs buried in earth and hatch after 7.5–8 months

Diet Insects, reptiles, eggs, small mammals, deer, goats, wild boar, pigs

Habitat Lowland areas ranging from arid forest to savanna, including dry riverbeds

Distribution Islands of Komodo, Rinca, Padar, and Western Flores in Indonesia

Status Vulnerable (IUCN); listed in CITES Appendix I; protected locally

Similar species None

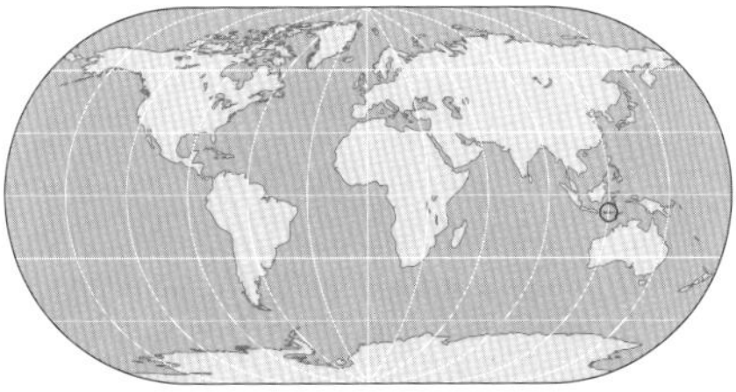

Komodo Dragon

Varanus komodoensis

Growing to just over 10 feet (3 m) long, the Komodo dragon is the largest lizard in the world. Up to 5,000 Komodos are restricted to a few small islands in Indonesia, where they reign supreme.

THE KOMODO DRAGON IS KNOWN LOCALLY as the *ora* or *buaja daret*, meaning land crocodile, and is named after a mystical dragon famed for its size and ferocity. The total area occupied by these monitors is about 390 square miles (1,000 sq. km). It is found on the Lesser Sunda Islands of Rinca, Komodo, and Flores and the smaller islands of Gili, Montang, and Padar, although the latter does not have a permanent population. All the islands except Flores are now part of the Komodo National Park.

The native habitat of Komodo dragons consists of arid, volcanic islands with steep slopes. At certain times of the year water is limited, but during the monsoon season there may be some flooding of the area. Average daytime temperatures are 80°F (27°C). Komodos are abundant in the lower arid forests, savanna, and thick monsoon forest near watercourses. Adults prefer the more open areas of savanna with tall grasses and bushes. Hatchlings and juveniles are more arboreal and tend to stay in forested regions, where they spend much of the time on branches away from would-be predators.

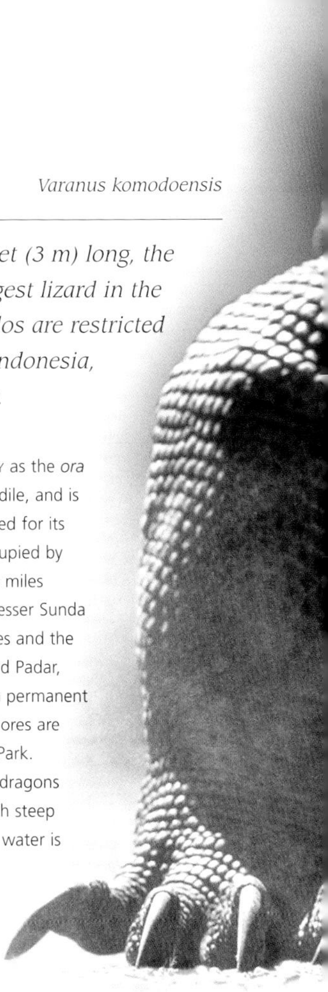

Despite their enormous size and weight, Komodo dragons are quite fast runners and can swim well. Young Komodos are also adept at climbing.

Largest Lizard

Although the Crocodile tree monitor, *Varanus salvadorii* from New Guinea may be slightly longer (due to its long, slender tail) and weighs up to 200 pounds (90 kg), the Komodo dragon is classed as the world's largest living lizard. It weighs up to 330 pounds (150 kg). Its head is relatively small when compared with its large,

stout body. Unlike in many other monitor species, the nose is somewhat rounded and blunt. External ear openings are visible. The strong jaws, which are capable of crushing bones, contain 60 laterally compressed teeth with serrated edges (similar to those of flesh-eating sharks), which can be replaced many times. The highly flexible skull allows the monitor to swallow large pieces of food, and the muscular, powerful legs end with clawlike talons that are ideal for ripping open carcasses. A heavy, muscular tail makes an additional weapon to help overcome prey and is capable of delivering a crushing blow.

The body of a juvenile Komodo is more sinuous and, together with its sharp claws, enables it to pursue an arboreal lifestyle. Green background coloration with pale yellow-and-black bands provide effective camouflage against the foliage. Juveniles lead secretive lives,

Discovering the Dragons

Although there had been tales of "monsters" on Indonesian islands, it was only early in the 20th century that serious consideration was given to mounting an expedition to search for them. This was after a Dutch pilot had crashed in the area and taken back to the West information from tribes in the Lesser Sunda Islands about "huge monsters—land crocodiles more than 20 feet [6.1 m] in length." An expedition led by Major P. A. Ouwens, director of the Zoological Museum in Buitenzorg, Java, produced the first scientific description of the dragons; shortly after, in 1912, the Indonesian government closed the area. Hunting of the dragons was outlawed, and the numbers sent to zoos were restricted. However, myths of enormous 20-foot (6.1-m) dragons persisted.

After an exhaustive study of the creatures in the wild, in 1981 the American paleontologist Walter Auffenberg recorded the largest specimen encountered as 9.8 feet (3 m) long. To date the largest authenticated Komodo dragon is a 10.3-foot (3.1-m) male. It died in 1933 and is on display at the Tilden Regional Park in Berkeley.

Despite the existence of the dragons, dangerous felons were once exiled on Komodo Island. The survivors built Komodo village, which makes most of its money today from tourism and fishing.

spending most of their time foraging in trees, avoiding predation by adults. As they grow and become too heavy to live in trees, their diet alters, and they become more terrestrial.

Adult Komodos lose the juvenile sinuousness to become robust creatures. The rough scales give the skin a beaded appearance, and coloration changes to brown or reddish gray. Some individuals may have darker limbs and a patch of peach color around the eyes. Both adults and juveniles have a yellow tongue. Despite their size and weight, Komodos can move surprisingly quickly and are excellent swimmers. Some of the populations on the smaller islands are transient, swimming from island to island in search of food.

Top Predator

Much of the Komodo dragon's day is spent patrolling its territory. The core range containing burrows may cover an area of 1.2 square miles

Attacking and Scavenging

The Komodo dragon obtains food both by attacking and by scavenging. Using ambush techniques, it hides in the long grass along well-used mammal trails. To be successful, the monitor needs to be within 3 to 5 feet (1–1.5 m) of its prey. Rushing from its hiding place, it seizes a leg, and its sharp teeth sever the tendons to disable the prey. The dragon then kills its victim by a bite to the throat or by using its sharp claws to rip out its intestines. Should a victim escape after the first bite, it may still die. Initially, Komodo dragons were thought to be venomous. However, it is now known that their saliva (of which they produce copious amounts) contains 57 types of bacteria (seven of which are extremely infective) and an anticoagulant—all acquired as a result of eating carrion.

Eventually the prey succumbs either from shock, blood loss, or infection. The smell of its rotting body can easily be detected by other dragons from as far away as 5 miles (8 km). When several Komodos find carrion, a complex social structure is observed. Using their serrated teeth to rip off large chunks, large males eat their fill first, followed by smaller males and females. Any juveniles in the area wait until the larger dragons leave before descending from the trees to scavenge on any leftovers. A Komodo dragon can eat up to 80 percent of its body weight in one meal. It has been estimated that only 13 percent of a corpse is left by Komodos—the intestines, fur, and horns are the only parts not eaten.

A keen sense of smell enables Komodo dragons to seek out carrion from several miles away. Tearing at a carcass with their sharp teeth, the feast is soon over.

Komodo dragons are now the focus of a growing tourist industry. In some areas of Komodo Island the dragons are so well fed that they just lie around waiting for tourists to bring the next meal of goat or sheep. However, their future surivival is threatened by habitat destruction.

(2 sq. km), but feeding ranges, which may be shared, extend farther. It is not unusual for a dragon to cover 6.3 miles (10 km) in a day. Burrows are used to regulate body temperature. They enable the dragon to cool down during the hottest part of the day and serve as retreats for shelter and warmth at night, since they retain some of the daytime heat.

Komodo monitors are formidable predators at the top of the food chain. Juveniles feed on grasshoppers, beetles, small geckos, eggs, and birds, and move up to small mammals as they grow. Adults consume a variety of large prey, all of which has been introduced to their islands by humans, including goats, pigs, deer, wild boar, horses, and water buffalo. Smaller, weaker dragons make up about 10 percent of an adult's diet. Eye witness accounts tell of an adult Komodo eating a 90-pound (41-kg) pig in 20 minutes; on another occasion one ate a 66-pound (30-kg) boar in 17 minutes!

Courtship and Monogamy

Courtship rituals have been observed in most months of the year, but mating activity peaks in July and August. When they are ready to mate, female Komodos give off a scent in their feces that is detected by a male when patrolling his territory. He follows the scent until he locates the female and then sniffs all over her body. He rubs his chin on her head, scratches her back, and licks her body—tongue-licking gives him clues to her degree of receptivity. The female communicates that she is ready to mate by licking the male. Grasping her with jaws and claws, he lifts her tail with his, which allows him to mate. An unreceptive female hisses, inflates her neck, bites, and lashes with the tail to drive away the male.

Up to 30 eggs are laid either in a specially dug nest chamber and covered with earth and leaves or in a burrow. Female Komodos have been seen to use the nest mounds of the male brush turkey. By adding or removing material, the male bird keeps the mound in which his mate's eggs are laid at a constant temperature, making an ideal incubator for Komodo eggs. The hatchlings emerge about 8 months later and measure 15 inches (38 cm). Mortality rates are high, with many falling prey to larger Komodos, predatory birds, snakes, and feral dogs. As soon as possible, the hatchlings try to make for the trees and comparative safety.

It is interesting to note that monogamy (having only one mate) and courtship displays have been observed in many Komodo dragons. These large monitors are capable of inflicting fatal wounds and readily eat members of their own species. Therefore it would seem that pair bonding in this way enables them to recognize certain individuals and ensures the continuation of the species.

Dragons in Danger

There are estimated to be between 3,000 and 5,000 Komodo dragons in the wild, and males outnumber females 3 to 1. They have been placed on CITES Appendix I to control trade in them, but occasionally specimens are smuggled out illegally. The Indonesian government has also given them the highest level of protection, and they are regarded as "national treasures." They are classed as Vulnerable by IUCN. The threat to their survival comes from habitat destruction and poaching of their prey: Volcanic activity and natural fires can have a serious effect on their already restricted distribution, and the poaching of their prey by humans may also have serious consequences for the dragons.

Leatherback Turtle

Dermochelys coriacea

The leatherback turtles are true giants. They are the largest of all marine turtles and the heaviest reptiles in the world. Their very distinctive shells have a leathery appearance.

Common name Leatherback turtle

Scientific name *Dermochelys coriacea*

Family Dermochelyidae

Suborder Cryptodira

Order Testudines

Size Carapace can be up to 8 ft (2.4 m) in length

Weight Up to 1,650 lb (750 kg)

Key features Carapace very distinctive with 7 ridges running down its length; surface of the carapace is effectively a rubbery skin rather than made up of scales; skin strengthened with very small bony plates; color dark with whitish markings; plastron bears about 5 ridges and varies in color from a whitish shade to black; flippers lack claws; front flippers extremely long; carapace of hatchlings has rows of white scales

Habits Often favors open sea, swimming widely through the world's oceans

Breeding Clutches consist of about 80 viable eggs; female typically produces 6–9 clutches per season; egg-laying interval typically 2–3 years; youngsters emerge after about 65 days

Diet Almost exclusively jellyfish

Habitat Temperate and tropical waters

Distribution Has the largest range of any marine turtle; found in all the world's oceans from Alaska to New Zealand

Status Critically Endangered (IUCN); listed on CITES Appendix I

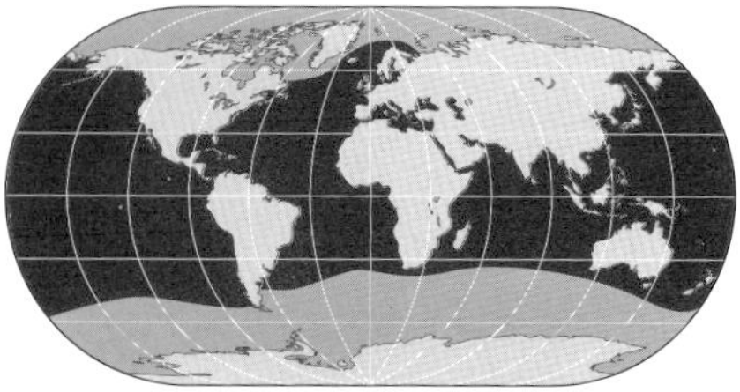

AT ABOUT 8 FEET (2.4 M) LONG and weighing up to 1,650 pounds (750 kg), the leatherback's bulk probably enables it to maintain a sufficiently high core body temperature that allows it to venture farther into temperate waters than any other species of marine turtle. Leatherbacks are apparently unaffected by sea temperatures even below 41°F (5°C), and they range as far north as the seas around Alaska. Their body is actually slightly warmer than that of their surroundings in these cold waters, which suggests that they have a basic mechanism to regulate their body temperature.

These turtles are also found in the oceans below the southern tip of Africa and off the Chilean coast as well as close to New Zealand. In fact, the largest leatherback recorded was not found in the tropics but was discovered stranded on a beach on the coast of Wales in the British Isles in 1988. It is possible that global warming and its effects on sea temperature are affecting the range of these turtles.

Remote Nesting Sites

Leatherbacks return to the tropics to breed. They often choose remote areas for this purpose, although there are about 50 nests recorded along the Florida coastline each year. They traditionally use beaches onto which they can haul themselves up without difficulty, and where they can come directly out of deep sea rather than swimming across reefs. This is possibly to protect their vulnerable underparts from injury and may explain why they tend to nest more commonly on mainland areas rather than islands. Unfortunately, these beaches can

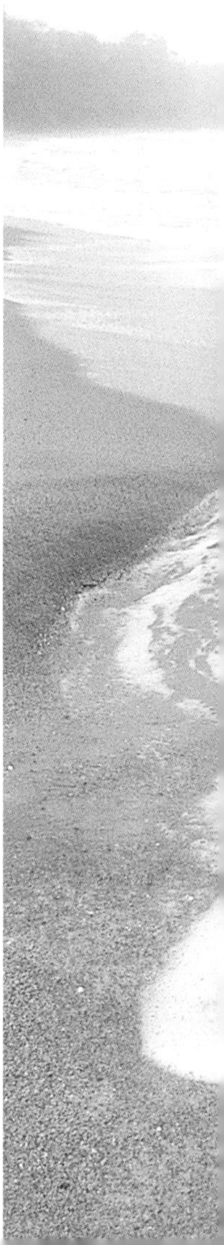

be badly eroded in storms, leaving the leatherback's developing eggs at greater risk of being lost than those of other marine turtles.

Egg stealing has been a threat in some areas in the past, but improved protective measures mean that it is less of a problem today. The oil in the leatherback's body was also used for the manufacture of many products, including cosmetics and medicines, but the introduction of synthetic substitutes has ended this trade. Leatherbacks are not hunted for their meat, which is regarded as unpalatable.

Although leatherbacks often lay eggs on their own, they sometimes nest in small groups. Their breeding range extends almost all the way around the world—from the Caribbean region across to the western coast of South Africa to India, Sri Lanka, Thailand, and Australia right across the Pacific to the shores of Mexico. Clutch sizes laid by leatherbacks in the eastern Pacific region tend to be smaller than those produced in other parts of their range.

What is suspected to be the largest breeding colony of leatherbacks in the world was only discovered as

Female leatherbacks, such as this one in Trinidad, come ashore to nest every two to three years on the warm sands of remote tropical beaches.

Long Journeys

Tagging studies have revealed the remarkable distances that leatherbacks can cover in the world's oceans—one individual tagged on its nesting ground in Surinam, northern South America, was rediscovered on the eastern side of the Atlantic over 4,226 miles (6,800 km) from the original tagging site. Unfortunately, leatherbacks have tended to lose their tags more readily than other turtles, so fewer data are available, but it certainly appears that those encountered along the northern coast of South America regularly undertake journeys of over 3,125 miles (5,028 km). Switching the tag site on the leatherback's body from the front flipper to the inner side of the back flipper has helped, however, since the tags are exposed to less physical force in this area of the body. This should ensure that more information about their movements can be obtained.

recently as 1976 thanks to the confiscation of a large number of leatherback eggs that were on their way to Mexico City. The trail led to an area known as Tierra Colorado on the Pacific coast.

Studies have since revealed that up to 500 leatherback females may come ashore to lay eggs there every night during the nesting period, mainly in December and January each year. It appears that, at least in this area, female leatherbacks return on their own with no males congregating offshore in search of mates.

An unusual phenomenon is the presence of small, apparently immature eggs found in the nests of leatherback turtles. Their presence may be linked in some way to the interval of time between the laying of the clutches, which is much shorter than in other marine species. It is often no more than seven to 10 days, and some eggs do not develop fully in this time. It takes about 65 days for the young leatherbacks to hatch and emerge at the surface, by which stage they are about 2.5 inches (6.3 cm) long. The hatchlings are unmistakable: The longitudinal ridges are well defined, and there are rows of white scales that appear as stripes along the length of the flippers.

It is quite straightforward to determine the sex of leatherback turtles, since males have much longer tails than females and, as in many other chelonians, a slightly concave plastron.

Imprinting Behavior

One strange phenomenon that has been repeatedly documented is the way in which, after she has completed the task of egg laying, a female leatherback circles the nest site, just as the young do once they hatch. It may be that this behavior somehow imprints onto the memories of the youngsters, aiding their return to the same place in due course. Current estimates suggest that there could be between 100,000 and 115,000 breeding female leatherbacks in the world's oceans today.

Predators

Leatherbacks tend to dive deeper than other turtles, which may give them some protection against being attacked. They are also well equipped to swim fast out of harm's way thanks to the propulsive power of their front flippers. They are longer than those of any other marine turtle and can extend to nearly 9 feet (2.7 m) in length.

Even once they are fully grown, however, these turtles still face a number of predators. Various sharks, including the notorious great

Death at the Hands of Humans

The leatherback's wide range means that it is very difficult to build up an accurate population estimate, but there are signs that the species is in trouble. This is not essentially because of hunting pressure but largely as a result of its feeding habits. Its rather slender jaws with their scissorlike action are used to capture jellyfish, which form the basis of its diet. Unfortunately, these turtles find it hard to distinguish between jellyfish and plastic detritus such as plastic bags and other similar waste floating on the surface of the sea. When seized and swallowed, these items are likely to get stuck in the turtle's gut, resulting in a slow and painful death. Controlling losses of leatherback turtles is exceptionally difficult, and there is no easy way of solving this problem.

There has been progress, however, in addressing some of the other threats facing leatherback populations. It was estimated that about 640 of these turtles were being accidentally captured in nets in U.S. waters annually. Many of them died through drowning or injuries sustained during their capture. Devices to keep turtles out of the nets were developed, and the law was changed to make their use mandatory in U.S. waters. Elsewhere, however (often in international waters), problems remain, with the turtles being caught in fishing nets or becoming entangled in ropes or lines. Even if the leatherback can free itself, the resulting injury can prove fatal. The leatherback's urge to swim, together with its specialized feeding habits, mean that nursing it back to health in captivity is often a difficult task too.

A leatherback turtle hatching on the Virgin Islands in the Caribbean. Hatchlings use a sharp tooth called an "egg tooth" to break through the eggshell.

In French Guiana a group of young hatchlings have just emerged from their eggs. They must make their way to the ocean quickly to avoid predatory seabirds.

white shark, *Carcharodon carcharias* from Australian waters, represent a hazard; killer whales, *Orcinus orca*, are also known to prey on leatherback turtles, the reptile's size being of little use against such fearsome predators.

Virtually nothing is known about the potential life span of these turtles, but for individuals that escape being hunted, it is thought to be measured in decades, as in the case of other sea turtles. While it is generally assumed that the leatherback turtle is solitary by nature, there have been accounts of sightings at sea of groups numbering as many as 100 individuals. Whether or not the groups are drawn together for mating purposes is unclear; it could simply be that they tend to congregate in areas where food is plentiful.

Common name Galápagos giant tortoise

Scientific name *Geochelone nigra*

Family Testudinidae

Suborder Cryptodira

Order Testudines

Size Carapace from 29 in (74 cm) to over 4 ft (1.2 m) in length depending on subspecies

Weight Approximately 500 lb (227 kg)

Key features Large, bulky tortoise; shell shape varies depending on subspecies; neck often long; carapace and plastron are a uniform dull shade of brown; males have longer, thicker tails than females and often have a more yellowish area on the lower jaw and throat

Habits Seeks out sun in the morning, basking before setting off to feed; usually inactive in the latter part of the afternoon, sometimes wallowing in a muddy hollow; quite agile despite its large size

Breeding Female lays clutch of 2–10 eggs, occasionally up to 16; eggs hatch usually after 3–4 months

Diet A wide range of vegetation and fruit; can even eat the spiny shoots of the prickly pear cactus

Habitat Generally prefers upland areas

Distribution Restricted to the Galápagos Islands

Status Endangered, critically in some cases (IUCN)

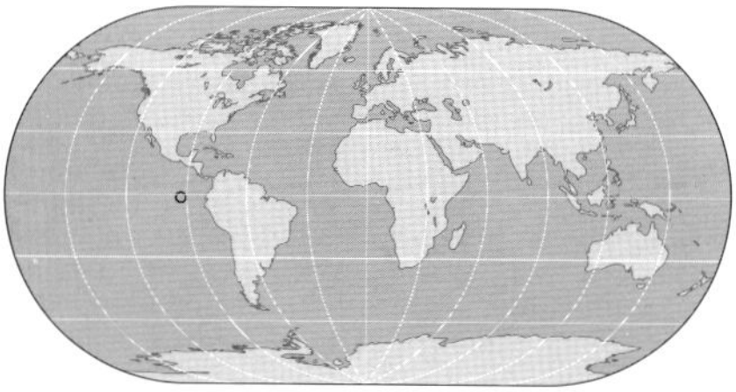

Galápagos Giant Tortoise

Geochelone nigra

The giant tortoises of the Galápagos Islands have played an important part in the field of biological science. They provided one of the pieces of evidence used by Charles Darwin to support his theory of evolution, which stunned the world in the 19th century.

THE BRITISH NATURALIST AND EXPLORER Charles Darwin visited the Galápagos Islands as the zoologist aboard *H.M.S. Beagle* in 1835. The population of giant tortoises, *Geochelone nigra*, on these volcanic islands had already been known to European whaling ships for many years. Crews regularly used to take the giant tortoises on board, and the creatures were able to survive for up to 14 months without food before being butchered and eaten.

Ships' Mutton

The numbers removed are quite staggering. Ships' logs reveal that a total of 115,000 were taken off the islands between 1811 and 1844, and the trade was well established by the time Darwin visited. The meat of the tortoises was even named "Galápagos mutton." They were not just used for food, however—their fat was distilled into oil along with their eggs. This plundering had a damaging effect on the tortoise populations, not all of which survived.

It is thought that there were 14 distinct races, or subspecies, on the islands. Only 11 are still there today—one of them, *Geochelone nigra abingdoni,* is facing imminent extinction and has been reduced to a single individual.

After such heavy persecution it is remarkable that it was not until 1876 that the first of these tortoises died out. It used to live on Charles Island and was flat backed with a very shiny shell. The next to disappear was the undescribed Barrington Island race, which was certainly extinct by 1890. Subsequently,

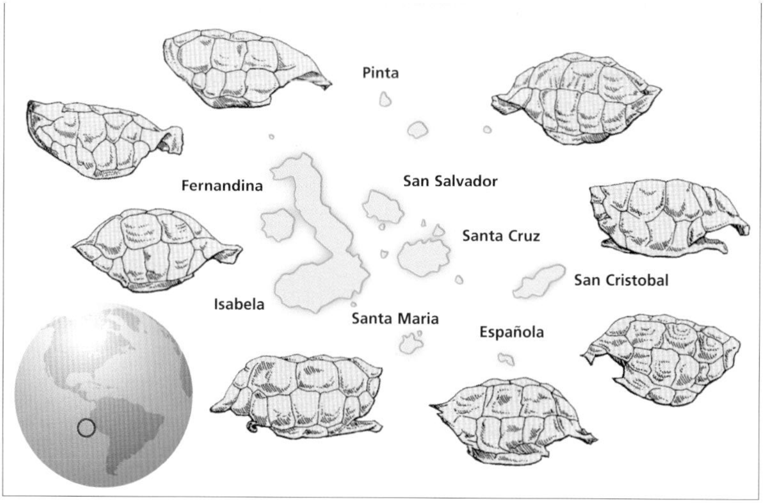

Several races of the Galápagos giant tortoise live isolated from each other on different islands in the Galápagos. The correlation between the different conditions on each island and the marked divergence in shell shape helped Charles Darwin formulate his ideas on evolution.

the Narborough Island tortoise with its characteristically flared marginal shields located at the back of the carapace had also disappeared by 1906.

Where Did They Come From?

The Galápagos Islands themselves consist of a group of 20 islands located approximately 600 miles (1,000 km) off the coast of Ecuador in northern South America. They are volcanic in origin, which means that there was no indigenous wildlife on the islands.

It is thought that the ancestors of the giant tortoises drifted south from Central America through the Pacific Ocean and were ultimately washed up on the beaches. They managed to colonize and spread

The Galápagos giant tortoise is the largest and heaviest living tortoise. This old male roams across the landscape at a speed of just 0.16 miles per hour (0.3 km/h).

Lonesome George

The population of giant tortoises on Abingdon Island, *Geochelone nigra abingdoni*, was particularly vulnerable to trade in tortoise meat in the 18th and 19th centuries because of its location—it was the first island in the archipelago to be encountered by whalers heading down toward Antarctic waters. Surprisingly, the population just managed to survive this era until the introduction of three goats in 1958. They stripped the tortoises' habitat, and by 1971 there was thought to be only one surviving male on the island. Named "Lonesome George" by staff at the Charles Darwin Scientific Research Station on Santa Cruz Island where he now resides, this individual is estimated to be between 50 and 80 years old.

Sadly, in spite of intensive searching on Abingdon Island for more than 30 years, it has proven impossible to find George a mate, and he shows no interest in breeding with females of any other subspecies. He is likely to be the last of his line, although he is only middle-aged at present. With a potential life expectancy approaching 200 years, there is the possibility that some of today's oldest tortoises on the islands were already resident there as hatchlings at the time of Charles Darwin's visit in 1835.

across the islands, or (more probably) there were several such strandings. Recent studies involving mitochondrial DNA, which is used for tracking ancestries, have revealed that the oldest group of tortoises can be found on Española. A second wave of colonization established populations on southern Isabela, Volcan Darwin, and Volcan Alcedo, followed by a third on other islands within the group.

It may seem unlikely that tortoises could drift through the ocean and end up being washed onto such tiny specks of land. Yet they are not the only reptilian colonists from the American mainland on these islands. Marine iguanas, *Amblyrhynchus cristatus*, thought to be descended from the green iguana, *Iguana iguana*, also live there. It is not uncommon even today for tortoises to be carried out to sea on floodwaters—they are, in fact, well equipped to

survive in these surroundings, remaining afloat with little effort and bobbing along on the waves. They do not need to eat, since their body stores fat that can be metabolized. It is possible that the early reptiles made the crossing not in the sea itself but by floating on debris, a process known as rafting.

What is particularly significant is that there would not necessarily have been any need for more than one tortoise to have reached the Galápagos Islands in the first instance to begin the colonization process. A mature female that had bred previously would not have needed to mate again in these new surroundings in order to lay fertile eggs, since she could still have been carrying viable sperm in her reproductive tract. Based on studies of modern chelonians, we know that a female may well be able to lay regularly for as long as four years without a male, producing many tens of offspring during this period. The young would have hatched in a relatively safe environment, so the population probably started to increase in number quite rapidly.

As night falls over the Alcedo Volcano on Isabela Island, a group of giant tortoises wallow in a pool to cool down and gain relief from ticks and mosquitoes.

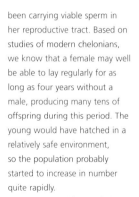

Food and water can be scarce. The Galápagos giant tortoise eats prickly pear cacti and fruits, bromeliads, water ferns, leaves, and grass. It can store large amounts of water, enabling it to survive the long dry season.

It is impossible to calculate how many of these island giants there were, but some people suggest there could have been hundreds of thousands of them at one stage. The biggest problem they would have faced would have been the ability to find enough food in a limited range. As a result, they evolved physical adaptations to reflect their environment, a fact that excited Darwin during his visit.

Three Types of Tortoise

Zoologists now tend to classify the different races of Galápagos giant tortoises in three separate categories based on these physical adaptations. First, there are those known as saddlebacks, a reference to the way in which the shell at the front of the carapace is raised above the neck. These individuals tend to be found on islands where conditions are relatively arid. This adaptation enables them to browse on taller plants that are less affected by periods of drought than vegetation growing at ground level. Their neck is long as well, and their limbs are elongated, so they can use their height to maximum effect.

Remarkably, the plants on the islands have responded to the browsing behavior of the tortoises. Where saddleback populations occurred—for example, on Abingdon Island—the prickly pear cactus, *Opuntia*, which is one of the tortoise's main foods, altered its shape too. It developed a tougher outer casing and adopted a more treelike growth pattern, making it harder for the tortoises to feed on it.

On islands where saddlebacks are not present, the prickly pear's shape is unaffected.

Second, there are Galápagos giant tortoises with a more typically dome-shaped appearance and a short neck. They tend to be encountered on upland areas of the islands where grazing conditions are generally good. The third group consists of tortoises that display intermediate characteristics between these two extremes.

The legacy of the seafarers' visits to the islands is still apparent today and represents an ongoing threat to the survival of various populations, in spite of the fact that hunting has ceased and the tortoises are fully protected. Today's problems revolve largely around the other creatures that were brought on the ships and were frequently abandoned on the islands. They too have thrived, often to the detriment of the tortoises. In order to supplement their rations, sailors often left goats on remote outposts, quite oblivious to the environmental problems they would cause. On the Galápagos Islands goats have competed with the tortoises for food and can destroy their nests as well. Pigs are also a hazard, since they will actively seek out nests using their keen sense of smell.

Saving the Tortoises

A number of different programs are being undertaken to conserve and increase the populations of giant tortoises, not least by controlling the introduction of mammals, including black rats, which are another legacy of sailing ships that visited the islands. Intensive captive-breeding programs are also underway both in the Galápagos and abroad. Zoological collections around the world are cooperating for this purpose.

The success achieved can be remarkable, as shown by the work of the Darwin Foundation, which has hatched over 2,500 young tortoises in barely 40 years. This has provided a major boost to a population estimated at no more than 10,000 individuals in total. The tortoises are kept safely in pens until they are three years old and large enough to be no longer at risk of predation by endemic birds of prey. It may take a quarter of a century for these tortoises to become sexually mature.

Even today, however, unexpected hazards can occur and threaten populations of the tortoises, as in October 1998, when lava from the erupting Cerro Azul volcano started to flow toward a group of tortoises. An airlift was organized, but in spite of these efforts, a small number of tortoises died from being trapped in the lava or the resulting fires nearby. They included a member of the critically endangered subspecies *G. n. guntheri,* whose total population is at most about 100 individuals. Shifting the gigantic tortoises is a difficult and costly exercise. Helicopters were used to ferry them to the coast from 5 miles (8 km) or so inland, from where they could be taken in boats to the safety of the breeding center.

Reproduction

Male Galápagos giant tortoises often make a roaring sound when mating. Courtship itself is a fairly brutal process, with the larger males battering at the shells

The sailors have gone, but today tourists still flock to see the wildlife on the islands, including the giant tortoises on Santa Cruz.

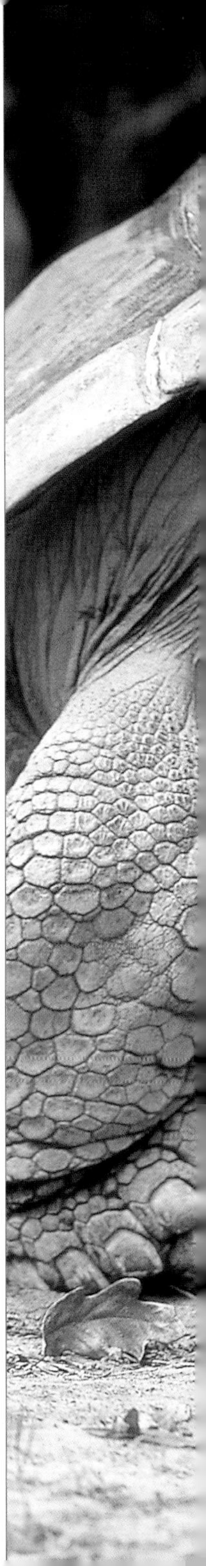

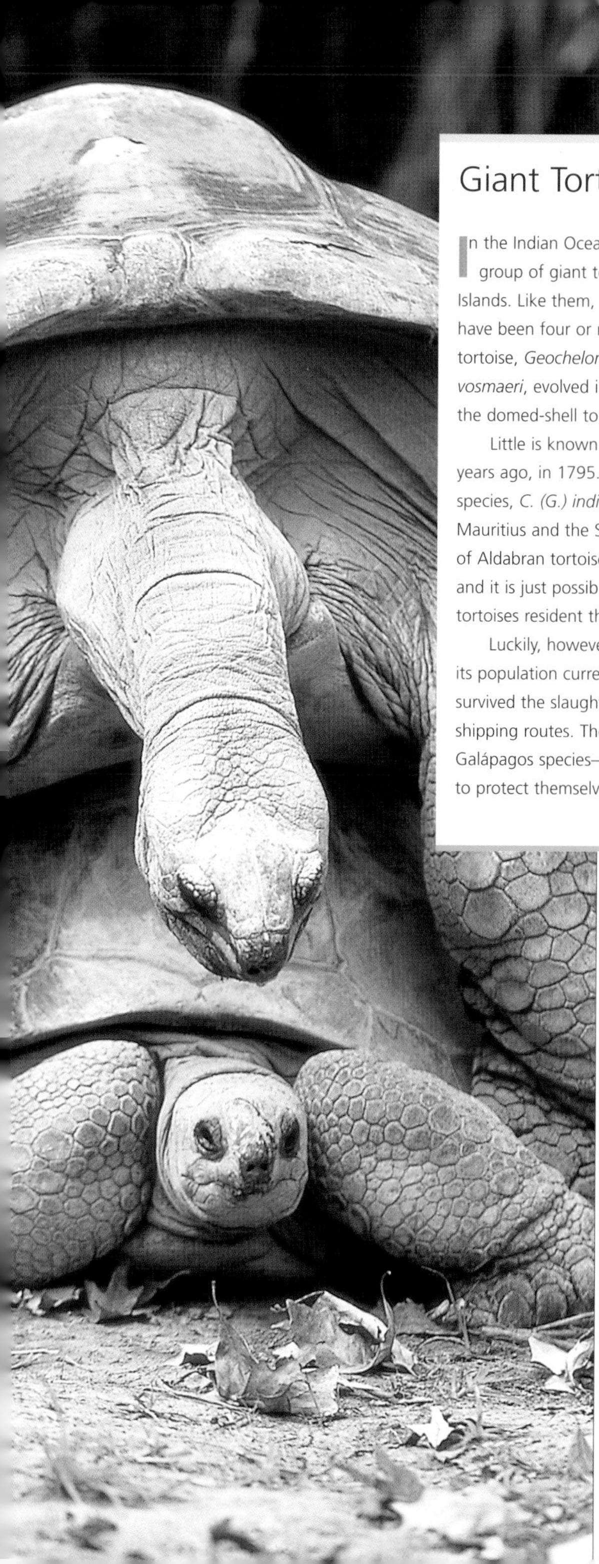

Giant Tortoises Elsewhere

In the Indian Ocean off the southeast coast of Africa a completely separate group of giant tortoises suffered a fate similar to those on the Galápagos Islands. Like them, they were captured in large numbers by mariners. There may have been four or more species, of which only one survives today—the Aldabran tortoise, *Geochelone gigantea*. Interestingly, a saddleback form, *Cylindraspis (G.) vosmaeri*, evolved in the region—on the island of Rodriguez—and was larger than the domed-shell tortoises, *C. (G.) peltastes*, which were also found there.

Little is known about these two species, which became extinct about 200 years ago, in 1795. Just prior to this the last surviving example of the Reunion species, *C. (G.) indica,* had died out as well. Native populations also existed on Mauritius and the Seychelles, but information about them is sketchy. A number of Aldabran tortoises were taken to the Seychelles and Mauritius in the 1800s, and it is just possible that they might have interbred with any surviving native tortoises resident there.

Luckily, however, the future of the Aldabran species itself seems secure, with its population currently consisting of over 100,000 individuals. Its ancestors survived the slaughter essentially because of their remote location away from shipping routes. Their behavior is similar in some respects to that of the Galápagos species—like them, they wallow in mud to cool their bodies and to protect themselves against mosquito bites.

Mating in large reptiles can be a dangerous business. This is a mating pair of captive Aldabran tortoises, **Geochelone gigantea,** ***in the Seychelles.***

of the females and pinning them down by clambering on top.

Females lay their eggs between July and December, but this varies on different islands. Although clutches contain relatively few eggs—usually from just two to 10 but occasionally up to 16—females may lay more than once during this period. The eggs themselves have hard shells and are spherical in shape. The incubation period lasts on average between three and four months but can extend up to seven months. The young tortoises emerge during the wet season when there is fresh grass and other vegetation available for them to eat. The carapace of a newly hatched individual measures about 2.4 inches (6 cm) in length.

Common name American alligator

Scientific name *Alligator mississippiensis*

Subfamily Alligatorinae

Family Crocodylidae

Order Crocodylia

Size Large specimens measure up to 13 ft (4 m); reports of individuals up to 20 ft (6 m) long are unsubstantiated

Weight Can exceed 550 lb (249 kg)

Key features Body almost black; snout relatively long, wide, and rounded; front feet have 5 toes on each; hind feet have 4; when the mouth is closed, only upper teeth visible (which distinguishes alligators from crocodiles)

Habits Active during the summer; may hibernate during the winter, especially in northern areas; semiaquatic, emerging to bask on land; can move quite fast on land and will search for new habitat when pools dry up

Breeding Female lays clutches of 30–70 eggs; hatchlings emerge after about 2 months

Diet Carnivorous; feeds on prey ranging from crustaceans to much larger aquatic life, including fish, turtles, and wading birds, as well as mammals

Habitat Rivers, marshland, and swamps; sometimes in brackish water; rarely seen at sea

Distribution Southeastern United States from Texas to Florida and north through the Carolinas

Status Delisted from being an endangered species in 1985, having been the subject of a successful recovery program; listed on CITES Appendix II

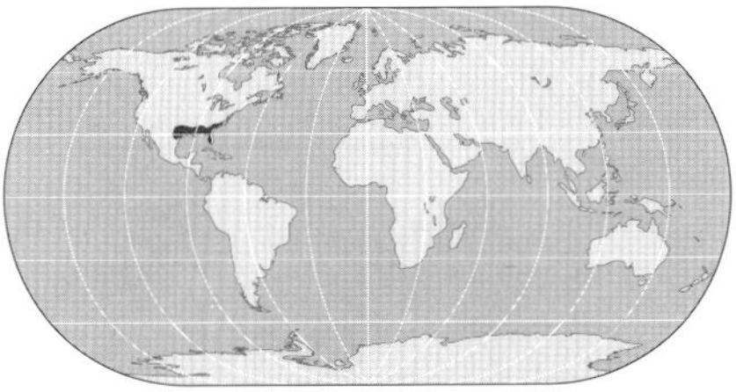

American Alligator

Alligator mississippiensis

Once on the verge of extinction, the American alligator has made a real comeback. Trade in its skin and meat is now strictly controlled, and the alligator has been reinstated as a vital part of the entire ecosystem.

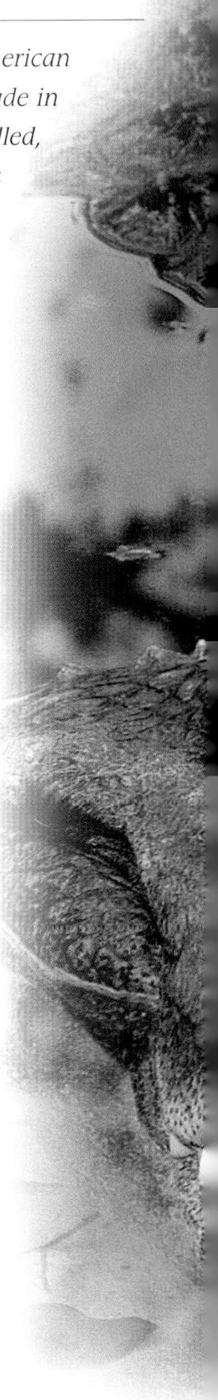

The American alligator used to range over a much wider area. About half a million years ago it reached as far north as the present-day state of Maryland. Then climatic changes occurred, and its range started to contract. However, when European settlers reached the southeastern area of the country, they found that these reptiles were still very common. Habitat modifications and hunting pressures subsequently reduced their range even more, and American alligators disappeared from the southeastern parts of Virginia and Oklahoma. Today their range includes Mississippi, Arkansas, eastern Texas, the Carolinas, and Alabama, although the species' main strongholds are southern Georgia, Louisiana, and Florida.

The relatively large size of these reptiles has given them a critical role in maintaining the entire ecosystem in which they occur because they dig so-called "gator holes" using their tail and snout. These provide temporary reservoirs of water and therefore maintain suitable aquatic habitats for various other animal and plant life. Vegetation around "gator holes" always tends to be lush thanks to the silt that the alligators deposit on the banks. The movements of alligators on regular paths can also create additional channels that enable water to run into marshlands more easily during periods of heavy rain.

Disguised as Logs

These reptiles often spend long periods floating motionless on the surface of the water, where they resemble partially submerged logs. They lie

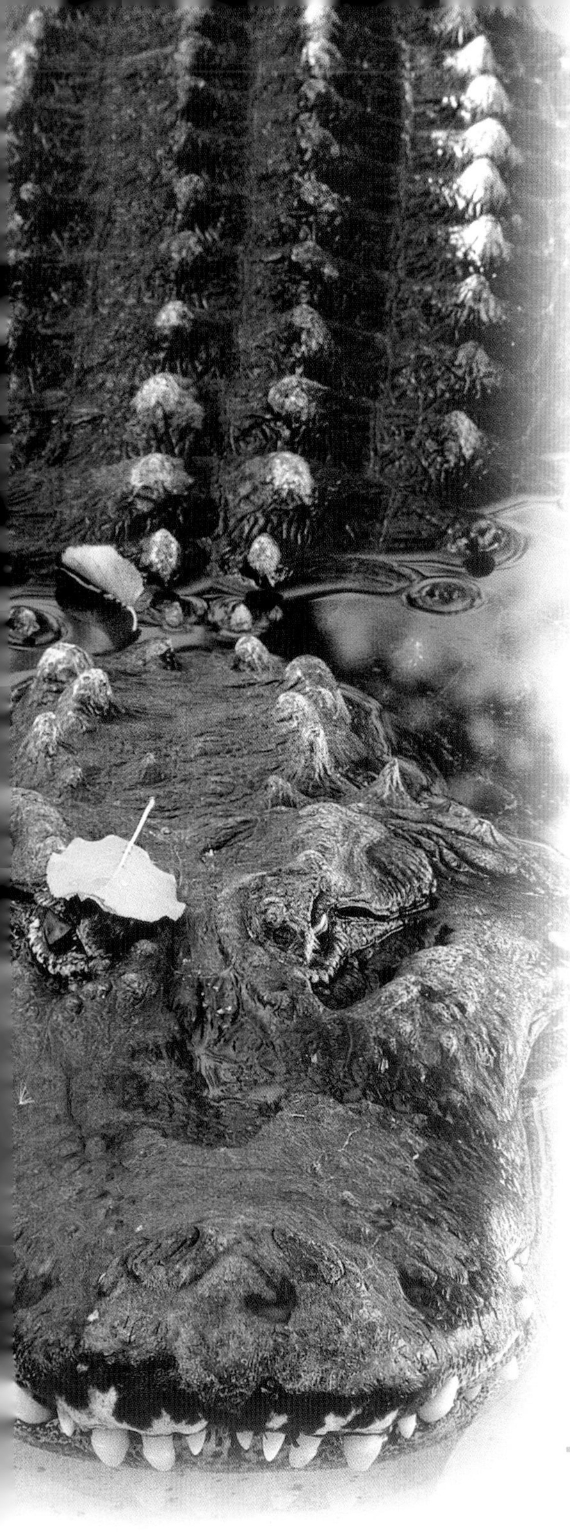

with their nostrils above the water's surface so that they can breathe easily. This behavior allows them to spot and ambush prey and also helps them maintain their body temperature, since they can warm themselves up from the sun without leaving the water. This is achieved by means of the osteoderms, or bone swellings, along the back that are linked with blood vessels. Heat is absorbed into the body there, helped by the alligators' dark coloration, and then circulated through the bloodstream.

A similar method is used by many other crocodilians, but it is especially important in this species because of the relatively temperate areas in which the alligators are found. During the winter they become sluggish. They retreat to the bottom of the waterway or burrow into a riverbank below the waterline and only emerge when the weather is warm. At this time their heart rate can reduce to just one beat per minute. The heart has a complex four-chambered structure more like that of a mammal than a reptile. American alligators can also survive being trapped in ice, provided that their nostrils are not submerged. It has even

Almost black in color, the American alligator has prominent eyes and nostrils and coarse scales all over its body. Its upper teeth are visible along the top jaw.

It Just Takes Two

The only other species of alligator is the smaller Chinese alligator, *A. sinensis*, which reaches a maximum size of approximately 7 feet (2.13 m). It has a very limited area of distribution today in China's Yangtze Valley and is highly endangered, with an overall population of only about 300 individuals. Captive-breeding programs in China and overseas, particularly in the United States, are underway with the aim of creating a more viable population. In terms of its habits this species appears to have a lifestyle similar to that of the American alligator, hibernating in burrows over the winter. The young mature slightly earlier, however, typically at about four years old.

been known for them to recover after over eight hours frozen beneath the water's surface without breathing thanks to their low oxygen requirement under these conditions. Alligators lose their appetite dramatically in the winter, and they are likely to stop eating altogether simply because their slow metabolism does not allow them to digest food at this stage.

Their relatively wide snout allows them to tackle a variety of prey, and the mouth itself contains about 80 teeth. They are constantly replaced throughout the alligator's life as they become worn or even broken, but the rate of growth slows markedly in old age. As a result, older alligators may have difficulty catching prey to the point of facing starvation. Older individuals are more likely to resort to attacking people for this reason, since they often represent a relatively easy target.

Encounters with Humans

With the ability to swim and run over very short distances at speeds of up to 30 mph (48 kph)—significantly faster than a human—American alligators will take a wide variety of prey. Generally they do not pose a major threat to humans. But as they have increased in numbers again over recent years and development has encroached farther into the swamps of Florida, for example, greater conflicts have arisen. They often take the form of an alligator emerging onto the green of a golf course or roaming into a backyard area rather than actual attacks. Unfortunately, chain-link fencing is not an effective barrier, since these alligators can climb fences up to 6 feet (1.8 m) tall without a problem. Those that threaten or harm the public are caught under a nuisance alligator program and may be moved elsewhere.

When attacks on people occur, they are often the result of the reptile being threatened or caught unawares. Feeding alligators is

Mutant Alligators

Two very rare color mutations of the American alligator have been documented. There is a pure albino form, characterized by its reddish eyes and white body. There is also a separate leucistic variant, in which the alligators have an attractive pale yellow body color. They can be further distinguished from the albino form by their blue eyes.

There are an estimated 70 albinos, and many of them are exhibited in zoological collections or breeding farms that are open to the public. This is because their coloration makes them so conspicuous that they would be extremely vulnerable to predators in the wild. Leucistic alligators are even rarer, known from a clutch of just 17 individuals that were discovered in Savoy, Louisiana, in 1987. A single female was then found at a site 100 miles (160 km) away in 1994. Both these mutant forms are also vulnerable to skin cancer because of the lack of protective melanin pigment in their bodies, and so they need to be kept in shaded surroundings.

(↑) Albino American alligators are quite rare. Most of them, including this individual from Los Angeles, are kept in captivity because they would be unable to survive in the wild.

(→) American alligators will eat anything they can catch. In the Florida Everglades a raccoon is this alligator's next meal.

especially dangerous, since they soon come to associate people with being a source of food. Children are more vulnerable to attack than adults because of their smaller size, but dogs are especially at risk. Alligators appear to have a particular dislike for them, possibly because they regard their barking as a threat.

American alligators communicate with each other by letting out a roar that can be heard over 1 mile (1.6 km) away. They also make a noise by slapping down their jaw on the water's surface. In addition, they keep in touch with each other by means of vibrations transmitted through the water using their throat and stomach. These sounds are made more frequently in the spring—males call to attract females in their territories, which may extend over an area of up to 10 square miles (26 sq km). They also track each other by means of special scent glands located in the cloaca and on each side of the jaw.

Dry Nesting Sites

The mating period is influenced by locality but typically lasts from March to May, with egg laying occurring a month later. The female will seek out a spot that is unlikely to flood but that is nevertheless located close to the water and often partially concealed among trees and other vegetation. The eggs will not survive in flooded ground and will be ruined if they are immersed for more than 12 hours. The female constructs a nest for her eggs by piling plant matter up to a height of 36 inches (90 cm). As the vegetation rots, it emits heat and warms the eggs, which measure about 3 inches (7.5 cm).

The incubation temperature is critical in determining the gender of the hatchlings. At temperatures below 85°F (29.5°C) the majority of hatchlings will be female, whereas above that figure males will predominate. It will be about two months before the young

↑ ***Although as adults they are among the largest reptiles and can grow up to 13 feet (4 m) long, American alligators are only about 9 inches (23 cm) in length when they hatch.***

alligators emerge from the nest. Their mother hears them uttering their distinctive "yipping" calls and helps them out. She carries them to the water in her mouth, with her tongue serving as a pouch.

The young alligators measure about 9 inches (23 cm) long when they hatch and are much more brightly colored than the adults, with a black-and-yellow banded patterning on their body. They stay together as a group (known as a pod) in close proximity to the female until they are two years old. During this time the mother will try to protect them. A number will be lost, however, sometimes even to large males. Other potential predators include wading birds, gars, and other large fish. By the time they are six years old, the young alligators are likely to have reached about 6.8 feet (2.1 m) in length, after which their growth rate slows significantly.

Alligator Recovery Programs

In the first half of the 20th century American alligators were killed in large numbers. Some estimates suggest that more than 10 million of these reptiles were hunted and killed for their skins between 1870 and 1970. Since that time, however, their numbers have increased dramatically thanks to effective conservation measures based partly on an acknowledgement of the commercial value of the alligators.

There are now over 150 alligator farms in various states, including Louisiana, Florida, and Texas. In the early days especially they helped restore wild populations. Farmers were permitted to remove a percentage of eggs from the nests of wild alligators, which they could hatch artificially, but a significant percentage of the resulting offspring had to be returned to the wild to repopulate areas where the species had disappeared or become very scarce.

An incidental but important benefit of these recovery programs has been our increased knowledge of the biology of the alligators. In turn this has helped develop effective management plans for wild populations. In Florida, for example, it has been shown that the alligators' reproductive potential is such that eggs could be taken from half of all nests with no adverse effects on the overall population.

Because of better habitat management larger areas are available to alligators and the other creatures living alongside them. There are some new concerns, however, notably about the rising level of mercury in certain alligator populations as a result of industrial pollution. Since the alligators are at the top of the food chain, this contaminant accumulates in their bodies from their prey. Its long-term effects are as yet unclear because, once they have survived the vulnerable stage as hatchlings, alligators can live for at least 50 years and possibly closer to a century in some cases.

This eight-week old hatchling in the Florida Everglades is vulnerable to predation by larger aquatic animals. Juveniles usually stay in small groups close to their mother for the first two years.

Skin Tagging

Careful monitoring by means of tagging ensures that skins of illegally killed alligators cannot be traded. The success of this program has been shown by the fact that the alligator population in Louisiana has grown today to just below that of a century ago in spite of the massive development that has occurred during this period.

Although the skins are the most valuable items and are exported worldwide (especially to markets in Europe, such as Italy, as well as to Japan), alligator meat has also acquired something of a gourmet reputation and can be found on the menus of fashionable restaurants in many cities. Even the teeth of these reptiles are in demand and are made into jewelry or simply sold as curios.

American alligators often live in close proximity to humans and are an important attraction on the itinerary of many tourists visiting the southeastern states.

Emerald Tree Boa

Corallus caninus

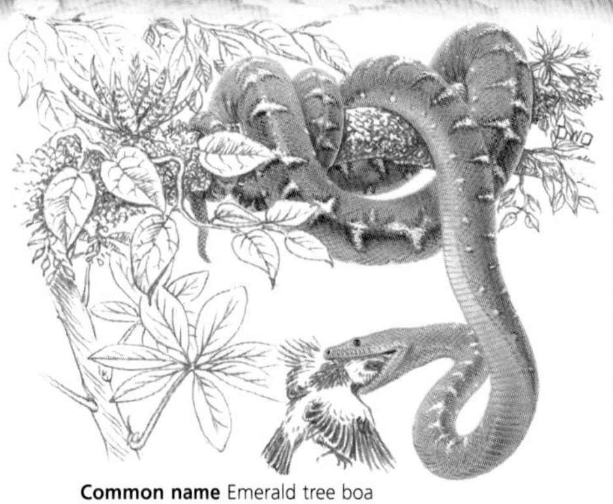

Common name Emerald tree boa

Scientific name *Corallus caninus*

Family Boidae

Suborder Serpentes

Order Squamata

Length From 5 ft (1.5 m) to 6.5 ft (2 m)

Key features Adults bright green with narrow white crossbars; sometimes yellow underneath; newborn young are bright yellow or red; scales covering the head are small and granular; lips bear prominent heat pits; eyes have vertical pupils

Habits Completely arboreal; rarely, if ever, comes down to the ground; when resting during the day, it drapes its coils over horizontal boughs in a characteristic way

Breeding Bears live young, with up to 15 in a litter

Diet Birds and small mammals, which it catches at night

Habitat Lowland rain forests up to 3,000 ft (900 m)

Distribution South America (mainly within the Amazon Basin)

Status Common but hard to find; habitat destruction is its biggest threat

Similar species Green tree python, *Morelia viridis*, in Australasia; within its range it could possibly be confused with several green pit vipers

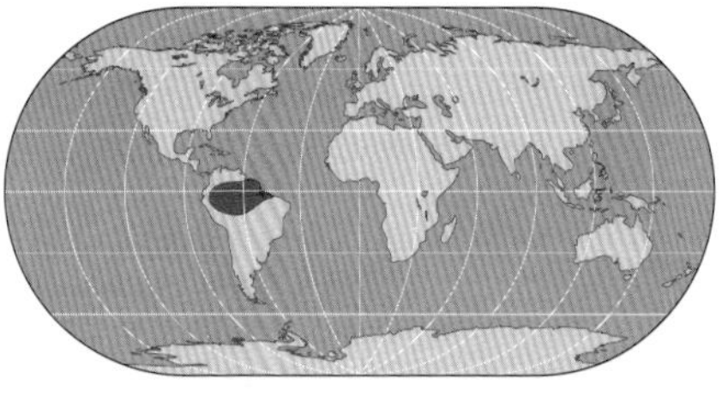

This beautiful snake lives only in the humid tropical forests in the high rainfall areas of the Amazonian lowlands. It is highly specialized for life in the canopy and rarely, if ever, comes down to the ground.

The emerald tree boas are undoubtedly some of the most distinctive and colorful members of the family Boidae. As their common name suggests, they are bright green. They have widely spaced, narrow white bars across their back. Sometimes the bars are continuous from one flank to the other, but usually they are broken or staggered along the center of the back. They may be gray near the head, and individuals from some regions have black borders to the white crossbars.

The head is wide and covered in numerous small scales. Two large bulges on the back of the head behind the eyes are muscles that help in catching prey. The teeth are long and curved backward. The snakes have a formidable bite; and once the prey has been grasped, there is little chance of it escaping. All these features relate to the snakes' lifestyle and diet.

Lazy Days

Emerald tree boas live in tall rain-forest trees mainly in the Amazon Basin, where the high temperatures and year-round humidity are essential for their survival. They spend the day motionless, their coils draped over a branch. At night they may move around to find a good hunting place, or they may stay where they are and unwind a couple of coils, allowing their head to hang down, with one or two bends in the neck. They can remain in this position for hours on end—all night if necessary.

If a suitable prey animal moves into range, the snake strikes by straightening its neck and

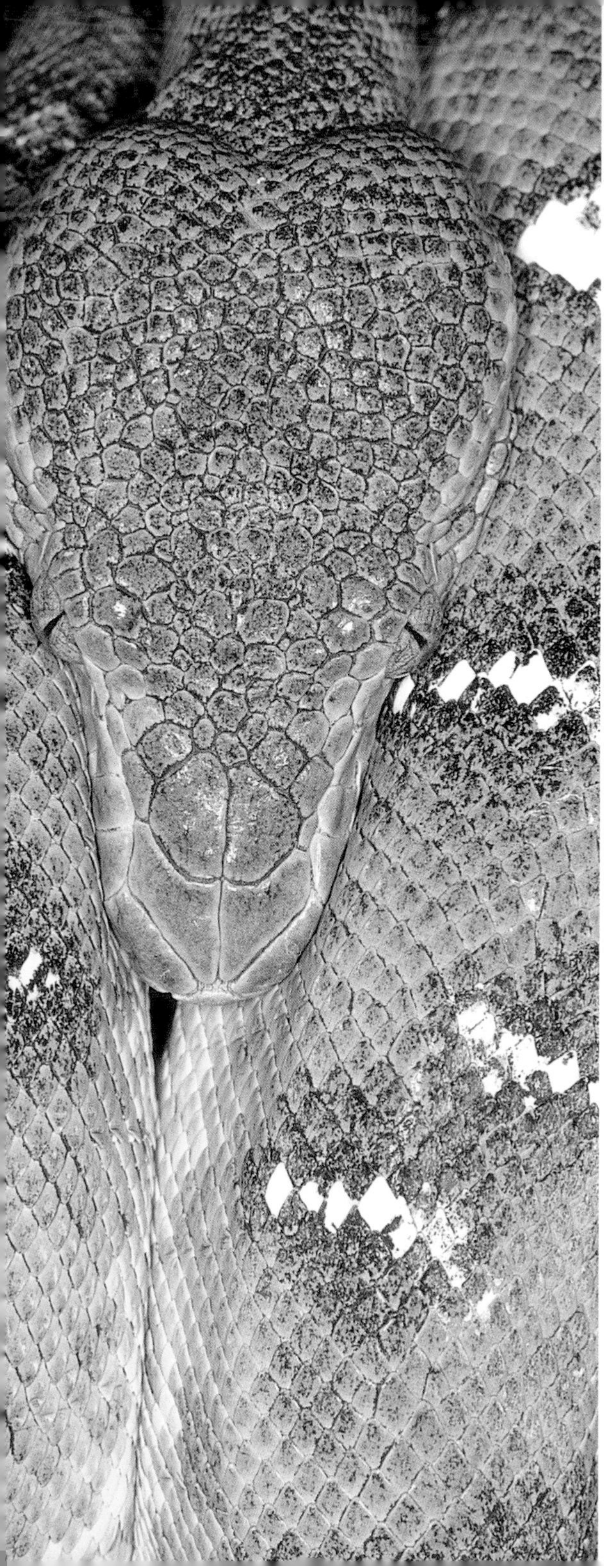

grasping the animal in its wide mouth. The massive muscles on top of the head help the snake clamp the prey firmly in its mouth while—still hanging from a branch—it throws a coil or two of its body around it. The extremely long, backward-pointing teeth enable it to get a good grip on mammals with thick fur or on the plumage of birds.

Because the snake hunts in trees, it only gets one chance to capture its prey. Once the prey has stopped struggling, the snake begins to swallow, still with its head hanging down. This is a very specialized method of feeding, and the emerald tree boas seem incapable of swallowing while in any other position.

Sensing Prey

As in all members of the genus *Corallus*, the emerald boas have very deep, prominent heat-sensitive pits. They are situated between the scales bordering the mouth (the labial scales) on both the upper and lower jaws. The snakes seem to rely almost exclusively on these sense organs when locating and striking at prey. If there are other heat sources in their cage, captive snakes are often confused, and their heat pits do not function well—having sensed the proximity of food by smell, they strike at the heater instead. Their eyes are small and probably play little part in the hunting process.

In common with the other tree boas, their body shape is long and slender, quite unlike that of ground-dwelling boas. It is also flattened from side to side and is girder shaped in cross-section, allowing the snakes to stretch out the front part of their body to span the gap between branches when they are moving through the forest canopy. The tail is relatively long and prehensile. The ventral scales are narrow and join the scales on the flanks at a sharp angle, forming a ridge along both sides.

Heat pits for locating prey line the upper and lower lips of the emerald tree boa and are more numerous in this snake than in other boids. After a large meal it does not feed for a long time and rests for weeks.

These features help them grip irregular surfaces, especially bark, and can also be seen in other climbing snakes such as some of the North American ratsnakes, *Elaphe*. When climbing stout branches, they move slowly with a concertina type of locomotion. When they come to rest, they slowly arrange their coils over a horizontal bough, hanging down on each side with their head in the center. They will remain like this for hours, or even days, on end. The green tree pythons, *Morelia viridis* from New Guinea and Australia, which are similar in appearance, also rest in this position.

Reproduction

Like other boas, this species gives birth to live young. Mating takes place in response to a slight temperature drop, perhaps triggered by the beginning of the rainy season. Details of courtship and mating in the wild are lacking. In captivity, however, the mating couple coil together and allow their tails to hang down during copulation. The gestation period lasts about six to eight months, during which time the female will actively seek out warm basking positions to maintain her body temperature at about 86°F (30°C). Litter size ranges from two in young females to 15 in older, larger ones.

The young measure about 8 to 12 inches (20 to 30 cm) long and come in a variety of colors. The most common color is orange, but they may also be bright coral red, yellow, green, or brown. Young of different colors may be present in a single litter, and nobody knows why the juveniles' colors should differ so much from that of the adults. In each case the white markings along the back are present at birth.

As the youngster grows, its color changes slowly, so that by the time the snake is about one year old, it is green, like the adult. Males probably reach breeding size in three to four years, while females take a year longer.

Looking at this group of juvenile brown emerald tree boas shortly after birth, it is hard to believe they are related to the green adults.

Convergent Evolution

When unrelated organisms look and behave like one another, they may be showing signs of a phenomenon known as "convergent evolution." There are many examples throughout the plant and animal kingdoms (such as agave and aloe plants in North America and southern Africa, and bats and birds), but none are such close counterparts as the emerald boa and the green tree python (*Morelia viridis*).

These two species live on opposite sides of the world—South America and Australasia—but resemble each other so closely that they are almost identical to the untrained eye. Both grow to about the same size, and both are flattened from side to side. Both species are green with white dorsal markings, and both coil characteristically over horizontal branches. Even more remarkably, both species produce young that are different in color than the adults—orange, red, or yellow in the case of the emerald boa, and yellow or red in the case of the green tree python.

Evolution converges when two species develop parallel adaptations due to similar lifestyles and habitats. The emerald tree boa and the green tree python both live in trees in humid tropical forests and feed on birds and tree-dwelling mammals. Both have developed similar physical adaptations relating to climbing, feeding behavior, and camouflage.

Other examples of convergent evolution in snakes include the sidewinder of North America, *Crotalus cerastes* (a small species of rattlesnake), and the horned adder of southern Africa, *Bitis caudalis*, (a true viper). In lizards the plumed basilisk, *Basiliscus plumifrons* from Central and South America, closely resembles the Asian water dragon, *Physignathus cocincinus*.

Sidewinder

Crotalus cerastes

The common name for the sidewinder refers to its method of locomotion. It moves quickly over loose sand with a characteristic sideways looping technique.

Common name Sidewinder (horned rattlesnake)

Scientific name *Crotalus cerastes*

Subfamily Crotalinae

Family Viperidae

Suborder Serpentes

Order Squamata

Length From 24 in (61 cm) to 30 in (76 cm)

Key features Body smaller and more slender than other rattlesnakes; head flat with raised scales over the eyes, giving the appearance of horns; pattern consists of large blotches of various colors interspersed with dark speckles; background coloration varies with the soil type and may be yellow, beige, pink, or gray

Habits Terrestrial; semiburrowing by shuffling its body down into loose sand; active at night; moves in a sideways looping motion

Breeding Live-bearer with litters of 5–18; gestation period 150 days or more

Diet Mainly lizards, especially whiptails; also small rodents

Habitat Deserts, especially where there are extensive dunes of loose, wind-blown sand

Distribution Southwestern North America

Status Common

Similar species The speckled rattlesnake, *Crotalus mitchelli*, has a larger rattle, but it lives mostly among rocks and does not sidewind

Venom Not very potent, causing pain and swelling around the site of the wound

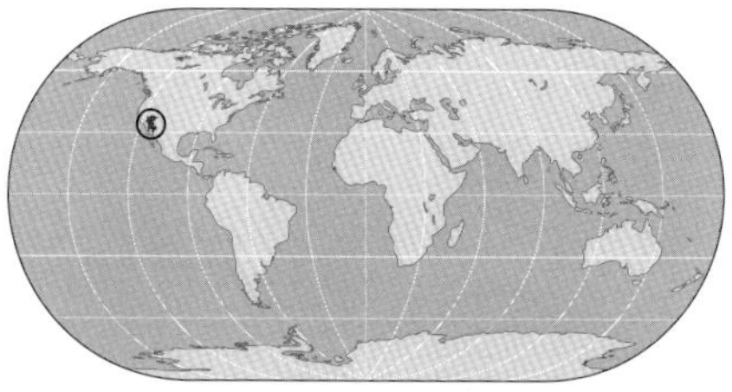

When snakes are placed on a very smooth or a yielding surface such as sand on which it is difficult to gain a hold, many of them use a sidewinding locomotion in their attempts to move. This is also true of the sidewinder, which has developed it into an efficient and rapid way of covering loose ground.

Other desert species that sidewind include the carpet, or saw-scaled, vipers, *Echis* species from Africa and Asia, Peringuey's adder, *Bitis peringueyi* from southern Africa, the Sahara horned viper, *Cerastes cerastes* from North Africa, and the Patagonian lancehead, *Bothrops ammodytoides*. Another type of sidewinder is the bockadam or dog-faced water snake, *Cerberus rynchops*, from Southeast Asia and northern Australia, which sidewinds across the tidal mudflats on which it lives.

Desert Nomads

Sidewinders are unusual among snakes (especially rattlesnakes) in having no home range. They appear to wander randomly across the desert, covering several hundred yards each night in search of prey, probably looking for sleeping lizards in their burrows. In the morning the sidewinders' distinctive tracks often indicate the route they have taken. By daybreak they shuffle down into the sand to escape the heat, often choosing a patch at the base of a shrub where the sand is cooler. The next evening they emerge to continue their wanderings.

If the opportunity arises, they will ambush prey from their daytime resting position, striking up out of the thin layer of sand that covers them and holding on until their venom takes effect. This avoids the need to venture out in order to locate their dead prey later. If they had to leave their cover and move onto an open patch of sand, they would be very conspicuous.

The sidewinder,* Crotalus cerastes*, has horn-shaped scales bulging out above the eyes, earning it the nickname of "horned rattlesnake" in some places.

Diet of Lizards

They mainly eat desert lizards, especially whiptails, *Cnemidophorus*, which are almost unbelievably fast moving during the day when they are warm but easy to catch at night when they are cold and therefore not very energetic. Other prey species include side-blotched lizards, *Uta stansburiana*, and fringe-toed lizards, *Uma notata*. One captive sidewinder was seen eating a desert horned lizard, *Phrynosoma platyrhinos*, without any apparent ill effects; but on the other hand, a wild one was found dead with one of these spiky lizards lodged in its throat. Immature sidewinders apparently use their tails as lures for small lizards, moving them slowly across the ground so that the segments look like those of a crawling insect.

Apart from lizards sidewinders occasionally eat small desert rodents and birds, although opportunities to eat the latter must be very limited since they are hard to catch. Sidewinders have been found swallowing small rodents, apparently killed by traffic in which rigor mortis had set in. Vipers in general, including many rattlesnakes, will take advantage of food that they did not kill themselves.

Some Like It Hot—but Not the Sidewinder

Sidewinders come from the hottest parts of the American Southwest, including Death Valley, California, which has the highest-ever recorded temperature on earth. You might think that would make them more tolerant of higher temperatures than other snakes, but that is not so.

Sidewinders avoid the extremes of heat by being strictly nocturnal. If they are exposed to daytime temperatures, they soon die. Their somewhat flattened body shape enables them to gain and lose heat quickly from the soil or other surface because more of their body is in contact with the surface. As the temperature falls at night, they form a flattened coil on a warm surface (for example, on tarred roads) to absorb heat quickly and remain active. During the day they shuffle down into cool sand and lose the heat.

A sidewinder moves across the sand in the Anza-Borrego Desert, California. The sideways looping technique keeps much of its body off the ground, enabling it to move efficiently across shifting surfaces.

Hammerheads Carcharhinidae

Unmistakable and awe-inspiring, hammerheads are among the most intriguing of all sharks. The scientific name for eight of the nine species, Sphyrna, *means "hammer" and is a reference to the fact that the sharks have rather unusual heads.*

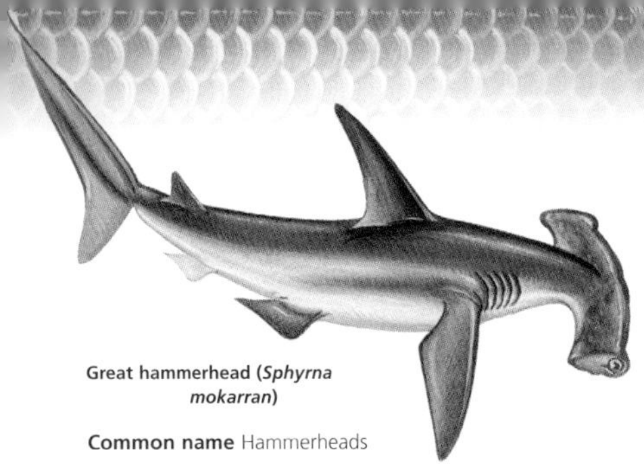

Great hammerhead (*Sphyrna mokarran*)

Common name Hammerheads

Family Carcharhinidae (sometimes placed in their own family, Sphyrnidae)

Order Carcharhiniformes

Number of species 8 or 9

Size Smallest: scalloped bonnethead—3 feet (90 cm); largest: great hammerhead—around 19.7 ft (6 m)

Key features Characteristic and variable lateral lobes on head (the "hammer"); eyes at ends of "hammer"; nostrils widely spaced near outer front extremities of "hammer"; body powerfully muscled; first dorsal fin high and prominent, second very small; pectoral fins small; caudal fin with long, pointed upper lobe bearing a distinct notch, lower lobe small and pointed

Breeding Internal fertilization: nourishment initially supplied by egg yolk; subsequent nourishment via placenta; gestation around 8 months; litter sizes from 6 to over 40 pups, depending on species and size of female

Diet Wide range of prey from open-water and bottom-dwelling bony fish to skates, rays, other sharks (including hammerheads), squid, crustaceans, and sea snakes

Habitat Open and shallow waters, ranging in depth from inshore reefs and near-shore shallows down to around 1,000 ft (300 m) in scalloped hammerhead; most species stay in upper 260 ft (80 m) of the water column

Distribution Widespread in many tropical and warm-temperate regions

World population No species currently threatened with extinction (some are very abundant), but some, for example, scalloped hammerhead, heavily fished following discovery of schooling sites; such populations have declined due to uncontrolled fishing

↑ ***The great hammerhead* (Sphyrna mokarran) *has been known to attack humans.***

THERE ARE EIGHT OR NINE species of hammerhead known, and all have the characteristic head shape that makes this group of sharks immediately recognizable. The head has traditionally been referred to as being hammerlike, but in fact the head shape more closely resembles a "T" than a hammer—although even this is not equally applicable across all species.

Winglike Heads

One feature all species have in common is that they possess lateral extensions on either side of the head. The positioning of the nostrils and eyes, at the edge of these fleshy extensions, is also similar in all species. A third common factor

↓ ***One of the eyes, each of which is situated at the end of the lateral lobes of the head, can be seen clearly in this scalloped hammerhead being cleaned by two king angelfish* (Holacanthus passer)*.***

is that in cross-section the extensions are thin and winglike, with a slightly curved top surface, a flat under surface, and a tapering back edge. They are definitely not hammerlike in cross-section. Indeed, the extensions are so slim that they are hard to make out when viewed end on.

The shape of the "hammer" differs from species to species, a fact that is partly reflected in some of their names. The winghead shark (*Eusphyra blochii*) has long, winglike extensions that can be almost half as long as the body. Then there are the similarly descriptive scoophead (*S. media*) and the mallethead or scalloped bonnethead (*S. corona*).

In the scalloped hammerhead (*S. lewini*) the front edge of the "hammer" has a pronounced indentation in the center. In contrast, as its name implies, the smooth hammerhead (*S. zygaena*) lacks the indentation. In both these "hammers" the front edge is convex, a feature that distinguishes them from the great hammerhead (*S. mokarran*) in which it is almost straight. The smalleye hammerhead (*S. tudes*) has a wide "hammer" with a central indentation similar to that found in the scalloped hammerhead. The back edge is, however, almost straight, and its eyes, as indicated by the name, are relatively small when compared with those of other hammerheads. In the uncommon whitefin hammerhead (*S. couardi*) the head is similar to that of the scalloped hammerhead. In fact, many taxonomists regard the whitefin simply as a variant of the scalloped hammerhead.

Enigmatic Hammers

As long as hammerheads have been known, one question has repeatedly been asked: What is the function of the "hammer"? Four factors may throw some light on the possible roles of the "hammer," although conclusive proof has not yet been provided for any of them.

Sharks have small, jelly-filled pits known as the ampullae of Lorenzini on their snouts. The ampullae are very sensitive at picking up the weak electrical discharges that living creatures emit. As a result, sharks can detect prey even when it is buried under sand or gravel.

In hammerheads the front edge and front part of the underside of the "hammer" are richly supplied with ampullae of Lorenzini. This suggests it is used in prey location, which in hammerheads often consists of animals that live close to the bottom or buried beneath it.

The widely separated nostrils, one at each end of the front edge of the "hammer," may

Costs and Benefits

Natural selection often produces distinct advantages or benefits in one direction, but may be accompanied by a loss of ability in another. For example, if a fish develops very large, powerful jaw muscles during the course of evolution, they will occupy more space than smaller, less powerful muscles. The larger muscles must be fitted within the skeleton of the head. The question is, where? It can be done by increasing the overall size of the head or creating suitable spaces through the reduction in size of other structures. Either way there are consequences. A larger head results in loss of overall body power despite the increased power of the jaw itself or a loss of streamlining and, consequently, speed through the water.

The body design of a hammerhead presents an excellent example of the balance between costs and benefits. On the one hand, the tall first dorsal and small pectoral fins help the fish hunt for food along the bottom. However, the arrangement provides relatively little lift for the fish as it swims—an important factor for sharks that spend much of their time in open water. This required lift may be provided by the hammer itself because it is winglike in cross-section. It is also believed that the back or trailing edge of the hammer can be adjusted by special muscles located within the hammerhead's jaw, thus giving the fish greater control over its movements.

Within the "hammer" the separation of the nostrils and ampullae of Lorenzini may provide benefits in terms of prey location. Equally, the eyes, located at the ends of the "hammer," may also cover a wider field of vision. However, the cost of this arrangement is that a hammerhead cannot see what lies directly ahead of it unless it swings its head from side to side.

also help in prey location by providing the shark with a wide field over which it can smell potential food items. The field may be widened even further by the side-to-side movement of the head that a hammerhead makes when scanning the bottom in search of prey.

While the ampullae of Lorenzini may enhance a hammerhead's ability to home in on its targets by their electrical discharges, the capability is only brought into play once the shark is relatively close to its victim—about 12 inches (30 cm). However, the nostrils can smell prey at much larger distances, and this, allied to the enhanced visual field provided by the widely separated eyes, may help make hammerheads such efficient hunters.

A shiver of scalloped hammerheads, the most abundant hammerhead, at a seamount in the Pacific. Such gatherings may number more than 200 individuals. The reason for these mass congregations is unclear.

It is also suggested that the winglike shape of the "hammer" provides lift and therefore helps hammerheads stay afloat.

Hammerhead Shivers

If an individual hammerhead is impressive, imagine what 200 or more gathered together looks like, for this is precisely what happens above isolated seamounts in the eastern Pacific. Elsewhere, as off the Natal coast of South Africa, the schools (more correctly known as shivers) tend to consist of around 20–30 individuals—still impressive, but not as dramatic as the much larger Pacific congregations.

Shivers equaling or surpassing the eastern Pacific ones were once also known from the Gulf of California in Mexico, but they were decimated by commercial fishing. Much information regarding hammerheads has been obtained from studies carried out on shivers. They also raised many questions.

Why, for example, should the Mexican shivers contain six times more females than males? Why should they form only during the day and disperse in the evening? Why should they tend to form near the surface? What is the main purpose of these daytime schools?

Mating is probably one reason; but since it is not the main activity observed, and since communal hunting behavior is absent, could there be other, more fundamental purposes, such as safety in numbers? In other words, could the hammerheads be using this type of behavior more as a means of protection against predators like killer whales?

As far as we know, the only species that forms shivers is the scalloped hammerhead, but what natural selection pressures led to the evolution of schooling just in this species?

Head-butting Shark

At least one species of hammerhead, the great hammerhead, has been reported as using its "hammer" in a most unusual way to immobilize bottom-dwelling prey like skates and rays. The great hammerhead has evolved the technique of using its hammer to butt and then pin down its prey to the bottom. Having achieved the feat, the shark can then spin around and bite out pieces of the victim's "wings," thus preventing it from escaping and making it considerably easier to devour.

While this behavior has not been documented in any other species of hammerhead, and only rarely in the great hammerhead, the possibility exists that it may be more widespread than our current level of knowledge reveals.

Some Schooling Clues

Although we do not possess conclusive proof of their purpose, we do have evidence of some of the advantages that schooling provides. We know, for example, that the largest females control the center of the schools, and that they are very dominant over smaller females. Bouts of aggression displays toward the subordinate individuals are therefore common (they can also be directed at other large females as a means of maintaining a "respectful" distance). The displays can include a range of behaviors, from head shaking and sideways body thrusts (shimmying) to upside-down swimming and spiraling through 360° (corkscrewing).

If such displays do not persuade a subordinate female to swim away from the immediate vicinity of a dominant female toward a less central (and hence less favored) location, the larger female may actually hit the smaller one with her chin. There is thus a movement that helps ensure that the fish at or near the center of the shiver are the largest and, consequently, the most "desirable" females; in other words, they are capable of producing more offspring than their smaller competitors.

Mature males also visit a school from time to time, often in search of a female. When this happens, the male will swim straight for the center of the school where the most desirable females are waiting. On approaching a potential mate, the male is usually challenged as an intruder and will respond by tilting his underbelly toward the female. This may be a way of showing the dominant female that he is not an intruding rival but a suitor.

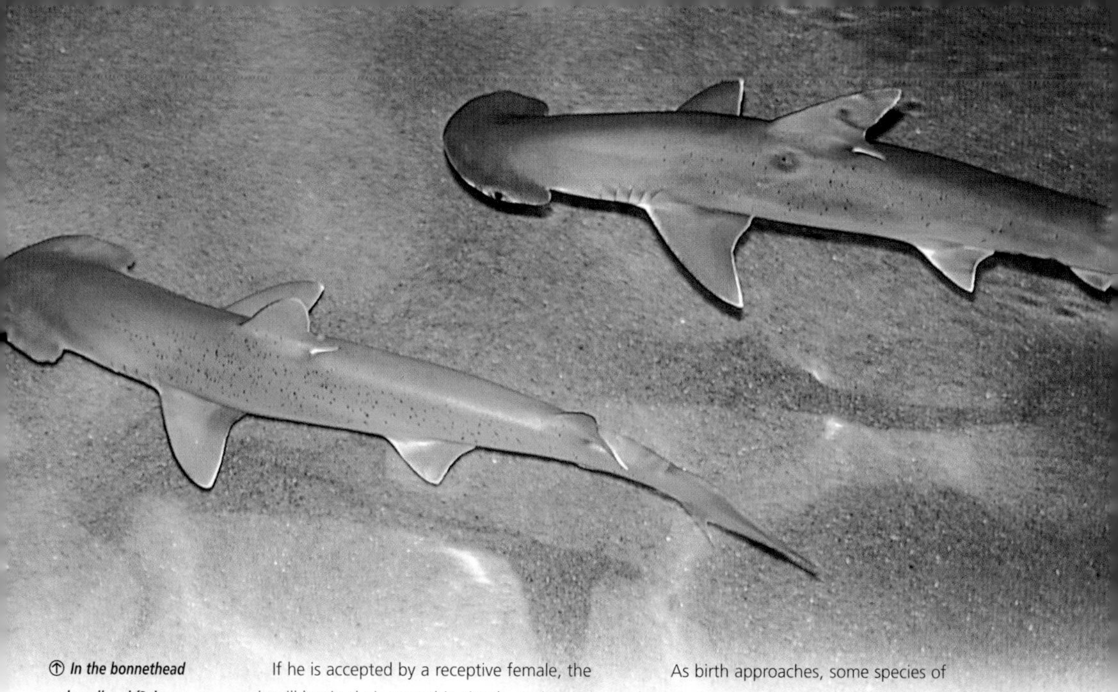

↑ ***In the bonnethead or shovelhead* (Sphyrna tiburo) *the head profile is rounded at the front, resembling a spade, shovel, or bonnet.***

If he is accepted by a receptive female, the pair will begin their courtship rituals. As in most other sharks, it involves the male chasing and biting the female. Actual mating does not occur within the school itself but in open water or as the pair sinks toward the bottom. Again as in other sharks, the male will bite the female on one of her pectoral fins, thus partially immobilizing her and helping him achieve an appropriate position from which he can insert one of his claspers in her cloaca and transfer his sperm into her reproductory tract.

After mating has been completed, the male plays no further part in the reproductive cycle. The females, though, will return to the school.

"Caring" Parents

Hammerheads have a pregnancy period lasting around eight months. During this time the embryos initially obtain nourishment from their yolk sac. However, once it has been used up, the yolk sac attaches itself to the uterine (womb) wall of the mother and develops into what is termed a "yolk-sac placenta." From now on, each embryo obtains nourishment from its mother via the placenta, as a result of which it develops into a well-formed, self-sufficient pup by the time of its birth.

As birth approaches, some species of hammerhead shark move into relatively shallow water where they may release as few as six or over 40 pups depending both on the size of the female and of the species. Baby hammerheads are born with their "hammers" folded back against the side of the body, thus making the birth process easier.

After birth the young of some species—notably the scalloped hammerhead—will form schools in shallow-water bays, dispersing at dusk to hunt in the surrounding reefs and returning at daylight. Over a period of several months, from spring to early fall, the number of young may gradually grow until there could be as many as 10,000 young sharks.

There are some intriguing reports from the Red Sea that indicate that the scalloped hammerhead may exhibit parental behavior to an unexpectedly sophisticated level for a shark. In these instances it was noted that schools of young sharks were surrounded by adults in what appeared to be some form of protective "shield." Should this unusual behavior be confirmed as constituting parental care, it would represent an aspect of shark reproductive biology that no one could have predicted from studies undertaken so far.

Common name Great white shark (white pointer, blue pointer, maneater, Tommy, death shark, uptail, white death)

Scientific name *Carcharodon carcharias*

Family Lamnidae

Order Lamniformes

Size Specimens in excess of 36 ft (11 m) reported, but confirmed data indicates a maximum size of 18–20 ft (5.5–6.0m)

Key features Torpedo-shaped body with conical, pointed snout; teeth of upper and lower jaws very similar and saw-edged—upper teeth slightly broader; top half of body slate-gray to brownish; irregular line separates top half from pure-white lower half of body; lobes of caudal fin more similar to each other than in most other species, but upper lobe a little larger than lower; underside of pectoral fins have blackish tips

Breeding Livebearing species that gives birth to 5–14 young (probably more) after gestation period of up to a year; scars predominantly on pectoral fins of mature great white females suggest males bite females during mating, as in other sharks

Diet Mainly bony fish; also cartilaginous fish (including other sharks), turtles, seabirds, and marine mammals, including dolphins, seals, and sea lions

Habitat Wide range of habitats from surfline to offshore (but rarely midocean) and from surface down to around depths exceeding 820 ft (250 m)—although it has been reported to dive to a depth of over 4,000 ft (over 1,200 m)

Distribution Predominantly in warm-temperate and subtropical waters, but also warmer areas

World population Sometimes quoted at around 10,000, but true numbers unknown

Status Listed by IUCN as Vulnerable; not listed by CITES

Great White Shark

Carcharodon carcharias

The huge great white shark is the perfect hunting machine. It is also many people's worst nightmare. Yet, for all its awesome reputation, this shark has more to fear from us than we have to fear from it.

THE GREAT WHITE IS A SUPREME hunter. It frequents a wide array of habitats and is found at various depths. In terms of dominance and predatory behavior the great white shark is probably rivaled only by the orca or killer whale—a voracious marine mammal.

Long-distance Hunter

The great white is magnificently adapted for its way of life. The shark has a streamlined, torpedo-shaped body and jaws armed with huge teeth that can be replaced by a "conveyor belt" system when lost. Furthermore, a battery of sensors that almost defy human comprehension enable it to detect prey from distances exceeding a mile (1.6 km).

A great white can thus detect the presence of a prey animal like a seal or sea lion and home in undetected—until it may be too late for the selected victim to avoid an attack. When the shark strikes, the first bite can take less than one second. However, in that brief period the following actions occur:

- the snout is lifted
- the lower jaw is dropped
- the upper jaw is pushed forward
- the upper jaw teeth are exposed
- the lower jaw is pushed forward
- the lower jaw is pushed upward
- the lower jaw teeth puncture the prey
- the upper jaw snaps shut.

The hunting technique, involving long-distance detection followed by homing in on the prey, a final burst of speed, and a lightning-fast biting action, has proved exceedingly successful for great whites in their pursuit of

⊖ Attracted by bait from a boat, a great white shark rears its head out of the water, baring a fearsome, tooth-lined gape to those on board.

seals and sea lions. It is estimated that about 45 percent of all such attacks are successful, with experienced individuals probably enjoying a success rate as high as 80 percent.

Another technique employed by great whites is called sky hopping. The method consists of the fish raising its head above the water to search around for a suitable victim and is often observed near seal colonies. Around Seal Island in South Africa, and at some other locations, great whites are also known to breach, in other words, jump out of the water during attacks on seals (see box "Breaching Great Whites," page 88).

Poorly Known Breeding Habits

Carrying out field observations on the breeding habits of a generally wide-ranging and potentially dangerous species like the great white presents scientists with a monumental challenge. Even in those cases in which individuals or groups are known to remain within a relatively restricted home range, such observations have, to date, remained elusive.

The upper jaw teeth of a great white shark caught off the coast of South Africa. The teeth have sawtoothed edges that help the shark cut large pieces of flesh from its prey.

We know that fully mature females are larger than males (the largest specimens caught tend to be females), and we know that many females attain sexual maturity when they are approximately 15 feet (4.6 m) in length, with males maturing at around 12 feet (3.6 m). Their age at maturity is estimated to be between 10 and 12 years. We also believe that some "populations" (exactly what constitutes a population of great whites is open to debate)

Wide-ranging Tastes

Although the great white includes pinnipeds like seals and sea lions in its diet, they are generally reserved for colder periods when the shark's preferred food items—mainly large fish—have migrated to warmer regions.

Irrespective of season, the great white shark feeds on a very wide range of prey and carrion. In the Mediterranean, for example, it is reported to include the swordfish (*Xiphias gladius*) in its menu. Quite how a relatively slow-moving species like the great white shark manages to catch such fast-swimming prey, however, is not clear.

Cetaceans (whales and dolphins) also form a regular part of the diet of the great white. They include both slower-swimming species, like some of the larger whales (taken alive or scavenged), as well as fast movers like dolphins and porpoises.

A wide range of bony and cartilaginous fish (including rays, skates, and other sharks) will also be taken, along with turtles, large squid, seabirds, and a whole host of other animals.

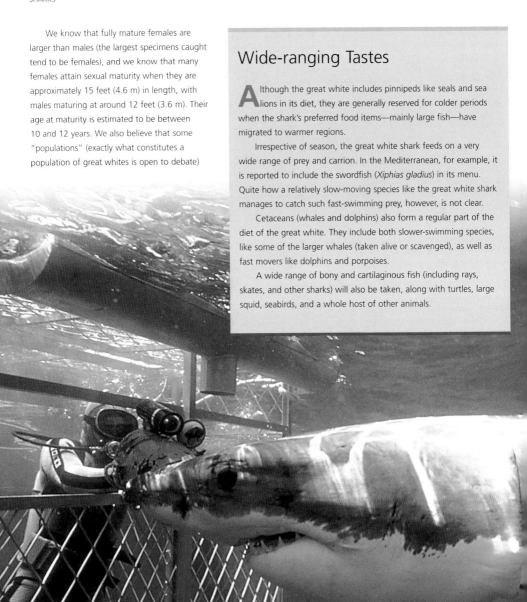

The sheer size of a great white shark can be judged from this specimen, investigating a diver in a safety cage. Although much photographed and even captured, a great deal of the great white's biology is still not known.

may congregate at traditional breeding sites. Evidence indicates that mating probably occurs during spring and summer, and that internal fertilization is followed by a gestation lasting up to one year. Males probably bite females during mating; this behavior is well documented in other species.

Following fertilization, the early embryos are released into a chamber that functions as a womb or uterus. There they develop and grow on a diet consisting largely of egg yolk released by the mother into the uterine chamber.

Nourished in this way, embryos grow to a substantial size and may measure around 5 feet (1.5 m) at birth. The total number of young in a single brood varies, with estimates ranging between five and 14.

Survival Threats

Human exploitation has led to a large decline in great white shark numbers. Direct killing by rod and line, harpooning, or chain-line fishing (using long lines baited with numerous hooks) —all primarily to provide sport for anglers and shark products for the curio and other trades— have inflicted significant damage on great white populations. Passive killing, with great whites being accidentally caught in nets and lines set out for other target species, has exerted its own pressure on populations, as have shark nets installed along shark-threatened coastlines to protect bathers.

All such human activities are particularly significant because the great white shark has a 10 to 12-year preadult phase, the female produces only small numbers of pups, and she may produce as few as four to six litters of pups in total during her life.

The extent of the decline and the total number of great whites remaining in the wild are very difficult to quantify. There are several reasons for this, including the diversity of nomadic/homing habits exhibited by the species. Some specimens, for instance, frequent relatively localized home "territories," while others are known to roam over large distances. A further complicating factor is that worldwide the species is relatively scarce.

As a result, although a figure of 10,000 has been cited as an approximate global total, we really do not know how many great whites remain. However, we do know that there are worryingly few, and that they are therefore in desperate need of protection.

Concerned at the decline, several countries and states have, since the 1990s, implemented protection programs based on the so-called

Precautionary Principle. In other words, where doubt exists, it is always better to take steps to protect a species and then modify the action as more data becomes available. The measures range from the banning for sale of all great white shark products to the prohibiting of other directed targeting activities, such as sport fishing or even the active attraction of great whites so that tourists can view them under water.

Further action is, nevertheless, being urged by some conservation bodies that fear the current listing by the World Conservation Union (IUCN) as Vulnerable may not be correct, and that the species may, in fact, already be in the Endangered category.

Breaching Great Whites

Like all open-water shark species, the great white shark tends to launch its attacks either from below or when swimming horizontally just under the surface, often with just its dorsal fin projecting above the water. Prior to or during some of its attacks the great white will also "sky hop." In other words, it frequently raises its head above the water to check on the whereabouts of likely prey.

In addition to these more "conventional" strategies great whites exhibit a third hunting technique known as breaching. Breaching—in which the body is flung partly or completely out of the water—is a behavior more commonly seen in whales and dolphins, and is generally not associated with feeding. In the great white, though, breaching has only been observed during attacks on pinnipeds (seals and sea lions). It is known to occur in several shark populations, but appears to be more closely associated with those found around Seal Island, a small rocky outcrop 8 miles (13 km) off Cape Town in South Africa. It seems that breaching attacks occur more frequently off the western and southern sides of the island where there is sufficient water depth close to the steep rocky shore for vertical attacks to be mounted by the shark.

↑ A breaching great white. During a breaching attack both the shark and its victim are carried clear of the water.

As the shark launches into the attack, it thuds into its victim with such force that its momentum carries both prey and predator clear of the water surface. Once the prey has received the first major incapacitating bite, it is often released. It is then subjected to further attacks while still in the traumatized state produced by the first bite.

Attacks on Humans

Attacks by great white sharks on humans make the headlines worldwide, but the actual number of attacks is extremely low. Of the 50 or so attacks by all shark species that are officially reported each year, only a small proportion of them can be attributed to great whites. Where they happen, it is more likely that the shark mistakes the human for a seal or other prey, rather than identifying the human as a threat or an intruder into its territory. Experiments carried out off Seal Island show that when variously shaped dummies are floated on the surface, great white sharks will go for a seal-shaped dummy more frequently than for, say, one shaped like a square of wood. However, when the dummies are presented as moving targets, the distinction disappears.

A surfer, paddling while waiting for a wave, could therefore be easily confused with a pinniped because from below the overall silhouette against the sky could look, to a shark, like a seal, sea lion, or turtle. Once riding a wave, the surfer could also—irrespective of silhouette—be regarded as a prey animal, since the shape of the moving target will not be quite so important to a great white.

Although predominantly found in warm-temperate and subtropical waters, the great white may also be found in warmer areas. It is only infrequently encountered in cold boreal regions.

Common Stingray

Dasyatis pastinaca

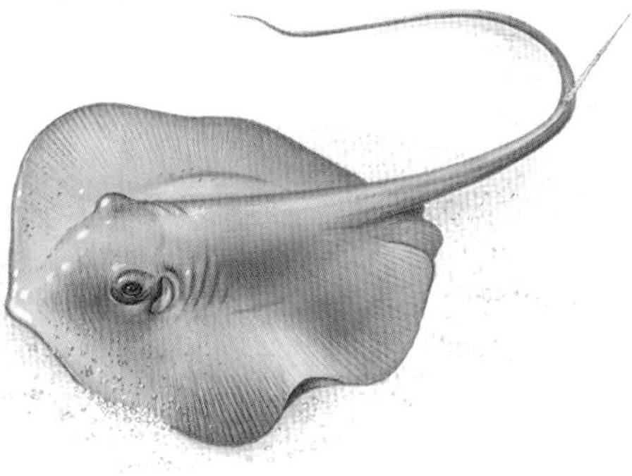

Common name Common stingray

Scientific name *Dasyatis pastinaca*

Family Dasyatidae

Order Rajiformes

Size 2 ft (60 cm)

Key features Relatively broad, triangular front to body; long, narrow tail twice as long as distance between snout and vent; dark color on upper surface, light below; prominent spiracles adjacent to eyes

Breeding Females give birth to 6–9 young

Diet Invertebrates and fish

Habitat Open areas of seabed close to shore; stays close to sandy bottom

Distribution Northeastern Atlantic down to Mediterranean, most common in the west; recorded as far south as coast of Zaire

Status Still relatively common but potentially vulnerable, especially where heavily fished

Common stingrays are equipped with a sharp sting. It resembles a dagger extending back as a projection near the base of their long tails and can measure up to 14 inches (35 cm) in length.

THE STING IS ACTUALLY A DENTICLE that has become modified into a venomous, barbed spine. Sometimes it is shed naturally or breaks off and then regrows, although during this period the ray is less able to protect itself. These stingrays occur in shallow coastal waters, typically not below depths of 200 feet (60 m). They may also be found in estuaries, surviving well in brackish water and coastal lagoons, especially where the bottom is either sandy or muddy.

The common stingray's spine is used entirely for defensive purposes rather than for capturing prey. For example, the spine becomes impaled in the flesh of a pursuing shark, driving its sharp point into the body as a result of external pressure. The barbs along the edge of the spine then help anchor it firmly in place, delivering the venom through two parallel channels present on the underside of the sting. The venom itself is a neurotoxin that attacks the nervous system; the stings are very painful from the outset. Typical symptoms include temporary paralysis as well as breathing difficulties and sickness. It is rare that people die directly as a result of being stung by common stingrays.

The barbed, poisonous spine of the common stingray can measure up to 14 inches (35 cm) in length. The spine is used for defensive purposes and can be dangerous for bathers and divers. Occasionally this stingray will shed and replace the spine.

Hazard to Swimmers and Divers

There is also a risk that the spine can penetrate vital organs, and sometimes these fish will stab repeatedly, using this weapon if cornered and inflicting more serious damage. If the spine becomes broken off and pieces remain embedded in the wound, they can trigger an infection even after the effects of the venom itself wear off. The best emergency treatment usually recommended to combat the effects of

a sting is to bathe the affected area with hot water, which will denature the protein present in the venom and neutralize its effects.

Since these rays often come close inshore and frequent sandy areas, they can represent a significant hazard to swimmers who may come into contact with them simply by stepping on them unexpectedly with bare feet. Common stingrays are actually hard to spot on the seabed—a hazard for divers too since they remain largely buried out of sight. The spiracles through which they breathe are located behind the eyes and are left uncovered; they can be confused with the eyes themselves, which are actually hidden in these surroundings.

Stingrays are usually found near shellfish colonies where they will prey on crustaceans, crunching up the shells with powerful, sharp teeth. Present in both jaws, the teeth also help the rays grab and overpower small fish. Electroreceptors—organs that detect weak electrical impulses emitted by other animals—help these rays find prey even if the water is murky. Like that of related species, the nose of the common stingray is very flexible, helping it dig in the substrate and grab food more easily.

Live Offspring

Females retain their eggs within their bodies, ultimately giving birth to between six and nine offspring. Their gestation period lasts for approximately four months, during which the young are nourished by outgrowths from the female's uterus.

Scientists once thought these outgrowths actually grew through the spiracles located behind the eyes and then connected down into the gut of the embryonic fish, but in fact they simply envelop the body. The spine itself is already developed in the young at birth.

In common with many other rays the rate of reproduction in this species is low. Scientists estimate that it is likely to take at least 15 years, even under ideal conditions, for any population of common stingrays to double in size. Out of the water these rays are still a dangerous proposition, since they will thrash about and can impale anyone close by. In spite of the danger inherent in handling them, common stingrays are caught commercially, with the wings often sold for food, frequently smoked, while the remainder of their bodies is often processed into fishmeal.

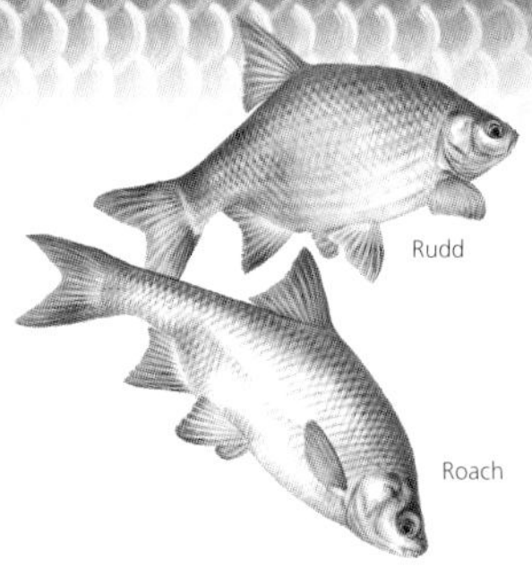

Common name Rudd and roach

Scientific names *Scardinius erythrophthalmus* (rudd), *Rutilus rutilus* (roach)

Family Cyprinidae

Subfamily Leuciscinae

Order Cypriniformes

Size Rudd: up to 20 in (50 cm) long and a weight of around 4.4 lb (2 kg) but often smaller; roach: up to 21 in (53 cm) long and a weight of around 4 lb (1.8 kg) but usually 13.8 in (35 cm) long

Key features Rudd: relatively deep body; smallish, scaleless head; mouth slanted upward; all fins well developed; adipose fin absent; dorsal fin toward rear; iris of eye golden/orange-red; scale keel along belly; coloration: greenish-brown on back, bronze along sides, and creamy along belly; reddish fins; roach: slimmer than rudd; smallish, scaleless head; mouth terminal; all fins well developed; adipose fin absent; dorsal fin central; iris of eye red; coloration: bluish- or greenish-brown on back with silvery sides; dusky dorsal and caudal fins; pelvics and anal orange to red; reddish pectorals

Breeding Both species breed between April and June; both egg scatterers; rudd eggs take 8—15 days to hatch; roach eggs take 9—12 days; rudd females may lay up to 200,000 eggs (usually fewer); roach females produce around 15,000 eggs, maximum 100,000

Diet Both species feed on insects, small crustaceans, and plant matter

Habitat Rudd: slow-flowing or still waters; also found in lowland rivers and lakes; roach: generally similar and also faster-flowing waters

Distribution Rudd: widespread across Europe north of the Pyrenees and eastward to middle Asia; roach: widely distributed in Europe as far east as the Urals

Ⓣ ***The rudd* (Scardinius erythrophthalmus) *and roach* (Rutilus rutilus) *require close examination to tell them apart.***

Rudd and Roach

Leuciscinae

Although they belong to different genera, the rudd and the roach are similar species both in appearance and in general lifestyle, and are therefore often confused.

The Rudd (*Scardinius erythrophthalmus*) is also known as the red-eye ("erythrophthalmus" means "red eye") and the pearl roach. It also has at least 34 other common names in over 20 languages. The roach (*Rutilus rutilus*) has one other English-language name: Siberian roach (used for the Mongolian populations) and around 36 non-English names in over 20 languages.

Both are predominantly European species, with the rudd more widely distributed in Asia than the roach. Although the rudd has been reported from Siberia, it is now known that the reports were the result of confusion between roach populations that occur in Siberia and the very similar-looking rudd.

From their natural ranges both species have been introduced into a number of countries where they do not normally occur. The rudd, for example, has been introduced into Ireland, Spain, Morocco, Tunisia, Madagascar, New Zealand, Canada, and the U.S. The roach has also been introduced into Ireland, Spain, Morocco, and Madagascar. In addition, it has also been introduced into Cyprus, Italy, and Australia, but not into New Zealand, Canada, or the U.S. The first introduction of the rudd (into Ireland) occurred during the earliest years of the 18th century; roach introductions began (also into Ireland) nearly 200 years later in 1889.

In most cases populations have become established in the new locations, except in Madagascar. Although it is known that some of the introductions have affected the natural balance in the rivers concerned, this has not always been the case.

Neither species is predatory, in the sense of

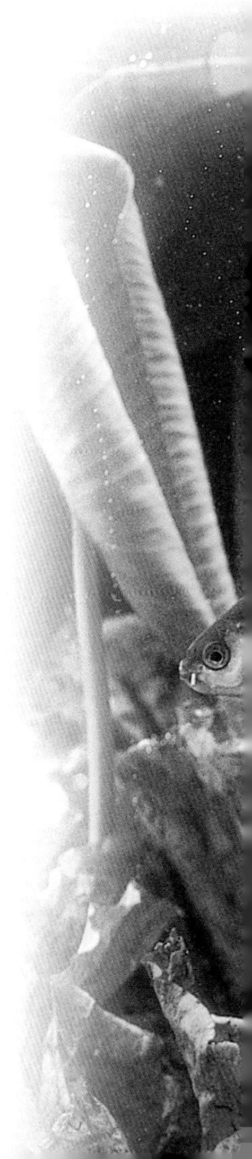

Like many other freshwater fish species, roach (Rutilus rutilus) *tend to shoal in groups containing individuals of about the same size.*

feeding on other fish, although they both feed on invertebrates. They also eat plants. In some countries into which the roach has been introduced, most notably Australia, it is regarded as a pest, not just because it churns up the bottom sediments in its search for food, but also because it competes for food with another introduced species, the trout (*Salmo* species). It also competes with some native species.

The rudd is more of a surface feeder, so it does not tend to cause water turbidity. However, it is a species that can hybridize with other species in the family Cyprinidae. In Canada and the U.S. there are concerns that the rudd's ability to interbreed with the golden shiner (*Notemigonus crysoleucas*), which it resembles quite closely in coloration and other features (although the rudd is larger), could pose a threat to the genetic purity of the shiner.

Other Rudds

Both the rudd and the roach have become so well known that many people believe them to

⬆ *Two rudd* (Scardinius erythrophthalmus) *courting. Rudd are typically surface-dwelling fish of the reed-fringed margins of still waters.*

Rudd and Roach Compared

Although rudd and roach are similar to each other in many respects—to the extent that they are often confused—they can be told apart on closer examination. The most distinctive features relate to body color, body shape, fin positions, positioning of the mouth, and eye color.

In the rudd the dorsal fin is set farther back along the body than the pelvic fins; in the roach these fins are in line with each other.

In terms of body color the rudd is a less silvery fish (more bronze colored) than the roach; the body is also deeper in the rudd than in the roach. The mouth slopes upward in the rudd, indicating that it is predominantly a surface and midwater feeder; in the roach the mouth is more terminal.

The color of the fins, particularly the pelvic and anal fins, is redder in the rudd than in the roach. However, despite one of its common names, the red-eye, the rudd has orange-red eyes, while the roach has genuinely red eyes.

Note: A golden variety of the rudd is very popular among ornamental pondkeepers, particularly in parts of Europe. This is a commercially produced color form that is not found in the wild.

be the only representatives of their respective genera. However, this is not the case.

There are, in fact, four rudds (though not all of them are known as rudds). By far the most widespread species of rudd is *Scardinius erythrophthalmus*. It is so widely distributed that since its first scientific description in 1758 it has been redescribed under 14 different names (other than *S. erythrophthalmus*). One Romanian population, in particular, was considered so different that it was long believed to be either a distinct subspecies or a new species (*S. e. racovitzai* or *S. racovitzae*). Its main difference is that it is found in waters whose temperature ranges from 82 to 93° F (28 to 34° C); in fact, these rudds are said to die if the temperature drops below 68° F (20° C). However, the fish is now regarded as no more than a localized variety of the rudd.

Scardinius graecus is, quite appropriately,

found in Greece. It is a slimmer species than the rudd and has larger scales. Like the rudd, it is fished commercially, but quite unlike the rudd, it is officially listed by the World Conservation Union as being Vulnerable. The main threats to its long-term survival are pollution, draining of water for agricultural and other purposes, and destruction of its habitat.

Scardinius scardafa occurs in several lakes in Italy, Albania, and Dalmatia. Few details relating to this species are available. It is not, however, believed to be under threat in the wild. The same goes for *S. acarnanicus,* which occurs in the Acheleoos basin in Greece.

Other Roaches

In addition to the roach there are 12 other, less well-known species. Most, in fact, do not have common names.

One that does have a common name is the Danube roach (*R. pigus*). Two populations of this species are known, one from northern Italy and the other from the Danube River basin. It is a slimmer species than the roach and is notable because of the spawning "rash" of breeding tubercles that males develop not just on their head but also on the back and sides of the body, as well as the fins.

Scardinius erythrophthalmus ***is the most common rudd, found widely in Europe, Russia, and Central Asia in ponds, lakes, and slow streams. It grows to about 10 inches (25 cm).***

The Kutum, or Black Sea, roach (*R. frisii*) is one of the largest of the roaches, attaining a length of around 27.5 in (70 cm) and a weight of some 11 pounds (5 kg). It is also exceptional in that large specimens may feed on small fish. Some populations are known from brackish water habitats, and—unlike their totally freshwater counterparts—they migrate twice a year for spawning. The "fall" populations spend the winter in the lower reaches of rivers, migrating upstream and spawning in early spring. The spring populations only enter the lower reaches of these rivers once the ice begins to melt, thus allowing them to move upriver to their spring spawning grounds.

A few roach species are under threat in the wild. Some, like *R. arcasii* and *R. alburnoides* from Spain and Portugal, are affected by pollution but are not yet considered to be under immediate threat of extinction. However, *R. meidingerii,* which occurs in alpine lakes and the upper reaches of the Danube River in Austria, Germany, and Slovakia, and was once thought to be a subspecies of the Black Sea roach, is now officially listed as Endangered by the World Conservation Union.

Rudd/Roach Hybrids

Although the rudd and the roach belong to separate genera, *Scardinius* and *Rutilus*, respectively, they are nevertheless sufficiently close to each other in biological terms for them to interbreed in the wild. The resulting hybrids tend to have eyes that are similar to the rudd's in color and fins that are redder than those found in the roach.

The rudd is also known to be able to hybridize with the bream (*Abramis brama*), the white bream (*Blicca bjoerkna*), and the bleak, or alburn (*Alburnus alburnus*). The roach can interbreed (in addition to the rudd) with at least the bream. In most cases hybrids are infertile and are produced when mixed species spawnings occur in the wild. In captivity, of course, different rules apply, since the whole reproductive process can be controlled. In the early 1990s rudd were crossed with golden shiners (*Nometigonus crysoleucas*) in the U.S. The resulting hybrids did not, themselves, breed, leading to the belief that they were probably infertile.

Marine Hatchetfish

Sternoptychidae

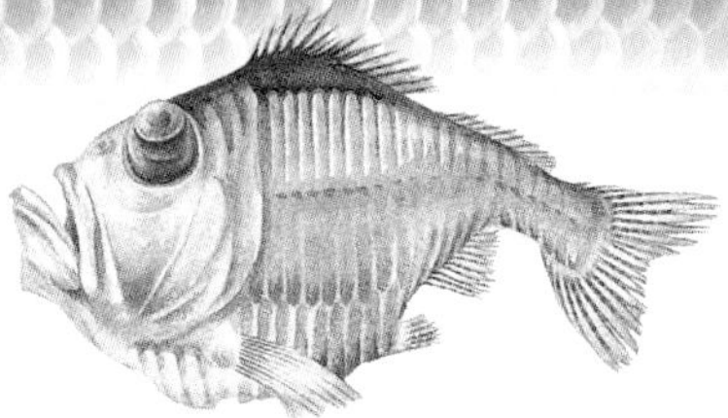

Pacific hatchetfish (*Argyropelecus affinis*)

Common name Marine hatchetfish (pearlsides, constellationfish, and allies)

Family Sternoptychidae

Subfamilies Maurolicinae (pearlsides and constellationfish); Sternoptychinae (marine hatchetfish)

Order Stomiiformes

Number of species About 71 in 10 genera

Size From around 0.8 in (2 cm) to 5.5 in (14 cm)

Key features Maurolicinae: elongated body, never compressed; mouth directed at upward angle; eyes almost central on head in normal direction, or above center and directed upward; Sternoptychinae: deep, extremely compressed body; mouth directed nearly vertically; eyes in top half of head, directed upward, telescopic in some species; keel-like chest; bladelike structure formed from pterygiophores in front of dorsal fin; rear of body slim (i.e., the "handle" of the hatchet); photophores (light-producing organs) present in all species, some inside mouth

Breeding Unknown for most species, but eggs and larvae planktonic; pearlsides mature in 1 year, spawn March to September, producing 200–500 eggs; constellationfish may only live for 1 year but spawn many times, producing 100–360 eggs each time

Diet Predominantly invertebrates, including copepods; some species also eat small fish

Habitat Most are deepwater species though not living on the bottom; depth ranges from the surface down to more than 12,000 ft (3,660 m); many hatchetfish never rise above 650 ft (200 m), some remain in deeper water at 1,300 ft (400 m)

Distribution Atlantic, Indian, and Pacific Oceans

The 3.3-inch (8.4-cm) Pacific hatchetfish (*Argyropelecus affinis*) occurs in the Atlantic from the Gulf of Mexico east to the Gulf of Guinea, as well as the Indian and Pacific Oceans. Mainly it is found between 985 and 2,130 feet (300–650 m), but it can go as deep as 12,700 feet (3,870 m).

Some 43 species of deepwater hunters mimic the tiny hatchets. The slim back leading to the tail is the "handle," and the sharp-edged belly is the "blade." However, these fish do not cut anything at all, not even with their teeth, but swallow their food whole.

Hatchetfish, as these tiny "short-handled axes" are called, form the subfamily Sternoptychinae, one of two in the family Sternoptychidae. The remaining 28 or so species do not look anything like hatchets; more streamlined and elongated, they form the subfamily Maurolicinae.

Linking Factors

Members of the Maurolicinae—like pearlsides (*Maurolicus muelleri*) and constellationfish (*Valenciennellus tripunctulatus*)—show greater color variations than hatchetfish but retain some of the latter's silvery scales. Also, pearlsides have greenish-blue shades along the back, while constellationfish have two rows of spots along the body and photophores (light-producing organs) on the tail. The latter also change color between day and night, and become much darker as nighttime approaches.

Deep-diving Hatchets

Hatchetfish are well adapted to living in deep water, as their color and light organs show. Found near the surface at night, pearlsides can go down to around 5,000 feet (1,524 m) during the day. This lower limit is well into the depth zone for typical hatchetfish, exceeding that of the best-known species—"the" 5-inch (12.7-cm) hatchetfish (*Argyropelecus gigas*).

Pearlsides and their relatives occur closer to the surface than hatchetfish, some of which never rise above 650 feet (200 m). They can dive to and live in much greater depths, like the diaphanous hatchetfish (*Sternoptyx diaphana*), which has been found at 12,000 feet (3,660 m).

Hatchetfish, such as this Pacific hatchetfish (Argyropelecus affinis), contain photophores. Two are quite large and are located on the roof of the mouth—some of the light generated by these oral photophores reach reflective strips of cells, or "striae," found on the lower half of the iris of each eye.

The remaining photophores, located on the lower part of the body, work independently of the oral ones; they have a silvery reflector that directs part of the light downward. Scientists believe that hatchetfish use oral photophores to attract prey, as well as to control the rest of the light by matching its intensity with the light in the surrounding water and from above—so that they "disappear" in the partial or total darkness, to protect themselves against predators.

Armored stickleback (*Indostomus paradoxus*)

Common name Sea horses, pipefish, and allies

Families Syngnathidae (sea horses, pipefish, pipehorses, seadragons), Solenostomidae (ghost pipefish), Indostomidae (armored sticklebacks)

Subfamilies Syngnathidae: Syngnathinae (pipefish, pipehorses, seadragons); Hippocampinae (sea horses)

Order Gasterosteiformes

Number of species Syngnathidae: around 270 in 52 genera; Solenostomidae: 4 in 1 genus; Indostomidae: 3 in 1 genus

Size From 0.95 in (2.4 cm) to 37.4 in (95 cm)

Key features Elongated body (encased in bony rings or star-shaped plates): held upright (sea horses), or horizontal (pipefish, seadragons); long snout (short in armored sticklebacks), small mouth; 1 to 2 dorsal fins, some with spines and soft rays; some species lack pelvic, caudal, anal fins; long, slim caudal peduncle (armored sticklebacks); varied coloration: muted browns to bright colors; sometimes patterned body or dark bars on fins

Breeding Male carries eggs in belly pouch or mass of spongy tissue (sea horses); female carries eggs in pouch formed by pelvic fin (ghost pipefish)

Diet Invertebrates, worms, and other bottom-dwellers

Habitat Shallow coral reefs, seagrass meadows above 165 ft (50 m) depth or to 310 ft (95 m); some in brackish estuaries; armored sticklebacks in still or slow-moving fresh water, leaf litter on bottom

Distribution Widely distributed in tropical, subtropical, and warm temperate regions of Atlantic, Indian, and Pacific Oceans, and Indo-West Pacific; also Myanmar, Cambodia, Thailand, Mekong Basin

Status World Conservation Union lists 45 sea horse and pipefish species as under threat; sea horse species: 19 Vulnerable, 1 Endangered; pipefish species: 5 Vulnerable, 1 Critically Endangered

This 1.2-inch (3-cm) long armored stickleback (*Indostomus paradoxus*) can leap out of the water.

Sea Horses, Pipefish, and Allies

Syngnathidae, Solenostomidae, Indostomidae

We call sea horses quaint and delightful and often do not even think of them as fish. Yet they are beautiful examples of evolution, resulting in creatures ideally adapted to their environment.

Sea horses do not look like fish at all. They stand upright in water, their head at the top and tail at the bottom. In the closely related pipefish the head is at the front and the tail at the back. In sea horses the head points forward, as in normal fish, so that it sits at right angles on top of the body rather than in line with it.

Like all sea horses, this colorful slender sea horse (*Hippocampus reidi*) has the typical pronounced snout, small mouth, and upright position in the water. Sea horses acquired their name from the horselike appearance of the snout.

Unfishlike Fish

These are not the only unfishlike characteristics that these remarkable creatures have. The tail, for example, does not have a fin but is a long, rounded extension of the body (the caudal peduncle), used to hold on to plants, just like monkeys on land. Sea horses do not have pelvic fins, and their small pectoral fins look like ears; their long snout makes them look horselike, hence their name. The single dorsal fin has flexible rays and is located halfway down the body, pointing backward (not upward as with other fish). They use this fin for swimming; it acts like a caudal fin in more conventional fish.

Sea horses have bony plates, not scales, on their bodies—a protective body armor that makes sea horses hard-to-swallow prey. In atypical fashion it is the male sea horses that become pregnant and give birth, not the females. Sea horses are truly unfishlike fish.

Not-so-faithful Breeders

It was thought sea horses paired for life, but loyalty only exists between some pairs depending on species and other factors; in the pot-bellied sea horse (*Hippocampus abdominalis*) there is little loyalty, for example.

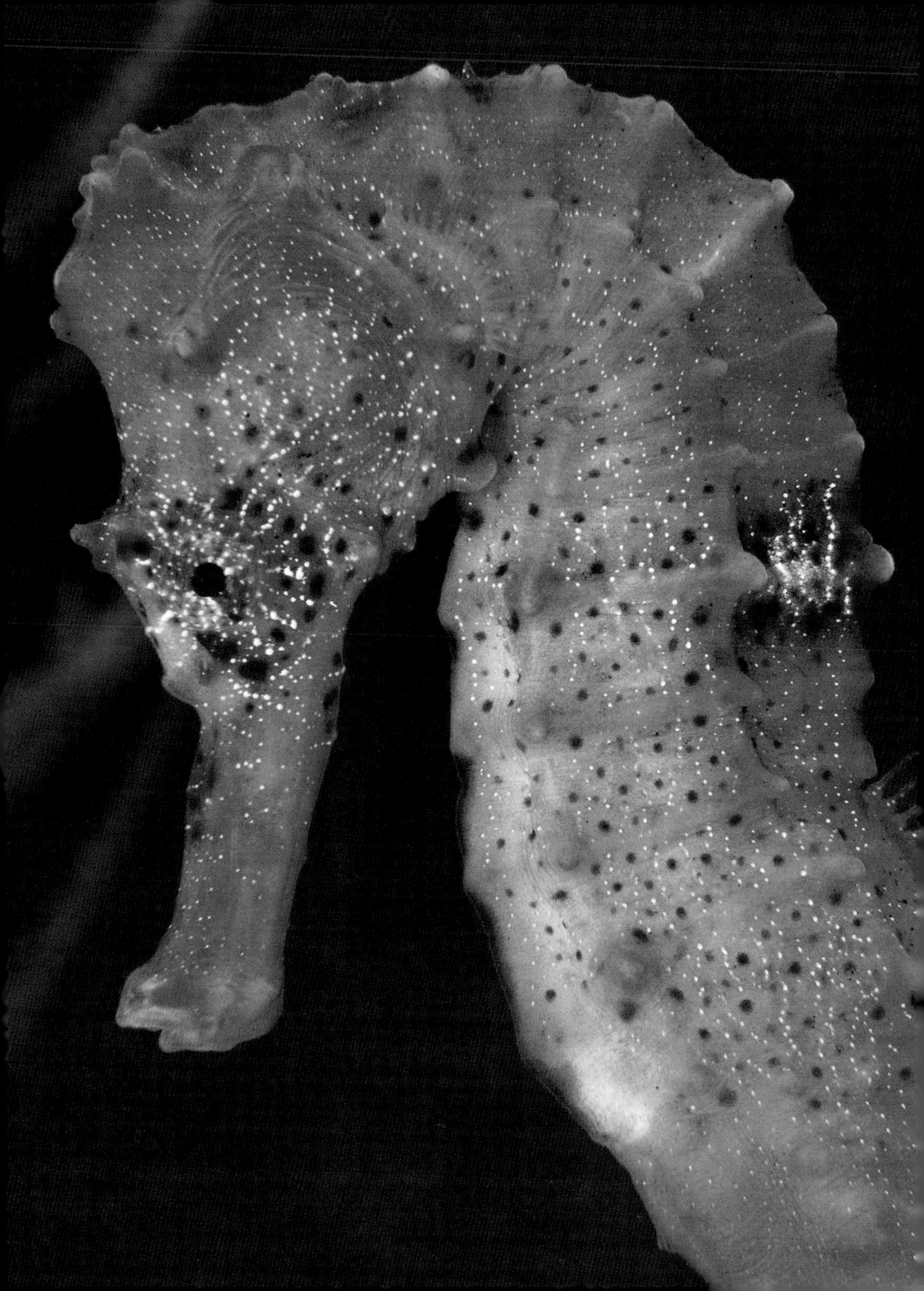

Record-breaking Discovery

Depending on which classification or book is consulted, there are as few as 32 species of sea horse—or as many as 120. To them must now be added a new one that was described in 2003.

It is Denise's pygmy sea horse (*Hippocampus denise*)—a record-breaker in that it is the smallest sea horse species known to science. Fully grown males measure just 0.9 inches (2.2 cm), with females being only slightly larger, about 0.95 inches (2.4 cm). Sexual maturity can be reached when the fish are only 0.6 inches (1.6 cm) in length.

According to its discoverer, zoologist Sara Lourie (who also codescribed the species with J.E. Randall), this tiny species lives deeper within coral heads than most other species, which could help its survival in the wild. It is also a more active species than other small sea horses, which makes its name "Denise" most appropriate, since it is derived from the Greek and means "wild or frenzied."

*The World Conservation Union has classified the Knysna sea horse (*Hippocampus capensis*) as Endangered. It occurs in the Knysna Lagoon west of Port Elizabeth, South Africa.*

When courting begins between a potential breeding pair, the female looks fuller than the male—he then develops a swollen belly pouch to show his readiness to mate. After a graceful display of "dancing" and entwining of tails, the pair face each other and bring their bellies close together. As the male opens the top of his abdominal pouch, the female transfers some eggs into it, and then he fertilizes them. Depending on age, size, and species, a female can produce up to 1,570 eggs (usually considerably fewer, often less than 100), which the male incubates. Two to four weeks later he gives birth, a process that can last up to 12 hours or more.

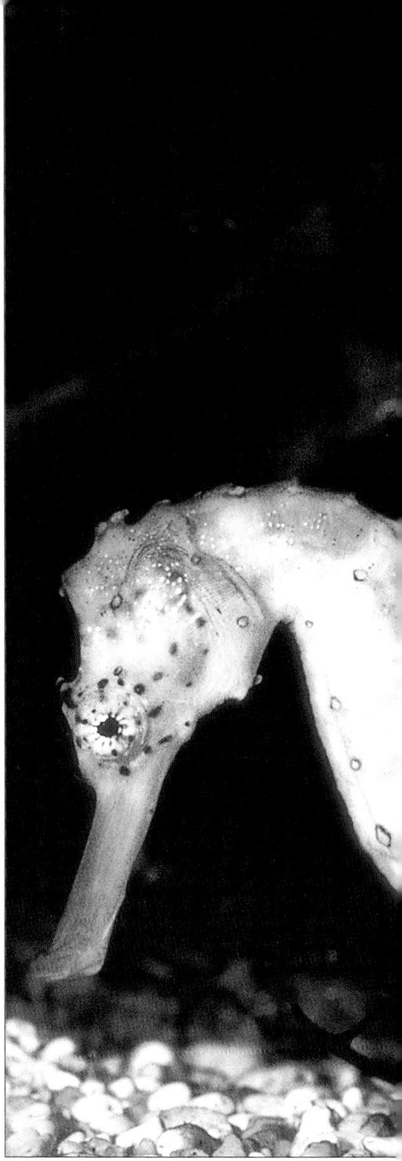

Newborn sea horses look like miniature adults. They are totally ignored by their father, so they have to fend for themselves from the start.

Similar, but Different

In their closest relatives—pipefish, pipehorses, and seadragons—the males also brood their eggs in special belly pouches, or spongy tissue under the tail, eventually giving birth.

However, in the pipefish the body is aligned in the more conventional way, with the head and snout directed forward, the tail directed backward, and the dorsal fin directed upward. In the seadragons (such as *Pycodorus* and *Phyllopteryx*) and the pipehorses (such as *Solegnathus* species) frequently the head and tail are held at an angle that lies somewhere between a sea horse and a pipefish.

Both the seadragons and pipefish have the same sort of snout that sea horses have. They also lack pelvic fins, and their pectoral fins lie close to the head and, in many species, have the appearance of ears. Along with other features, such as body casing, this means that currently pipefish, pipehorses, seadragons, and sea horses are all regarded as members of a single family (Syngnathidae) but belonging to

Ⓣ ***A pair of long-snouted sea horses*** **(Hippocampus guttulatus)** ***perform their graceful courtship display by "dancing" and entwining their tails.***

Seaweed-imitating Dragons

There are three members of the pipefish that bear no resemblance to their other relatives. In fact, one looks so much like a clump of floating seaweed that it is frequently impossible to clarify that it is a fish at all. Indeed, the camouflage of the leafy seadragon (*Phycodurus eques*) is so effective that neither its predators nor its prey are even aware of its presence. Therefore predators miss a possible meal, while prey do not know that they are being hunted until it is too late.

The weedy seadragon (*Phyllopteryx taeniolatus*) also gives a good impression of a seaweed, but perhaps not quite so effectively—although its young are next to impossible to spot among bottom vegetation. The ribboned seadragon (*Haliichthys taeniophorus*) looks a little like a very slim, nonupright sea horse with tufts of seaweed growing out of its body. Of the three seadragon species it is the least developed (in terms of leafy growths) and, at 12 inches (30 cm) in length, probably looks more like a single, long frond of seaweed than a clump.

Like all members of the family Syngathidae, the seadragons are male brooders. The eggs are embedded in soft, spongy tissue that runs from just below the belly along the lower edge of the caudal peduncle. A large male can carry up to 300 eggs for up to eight weeks. When the young hatch, they look more or less like miniature replicas of their parents, and they are able to fend for themselves after the first few hours. Both the leafy and weedy seadragons have been bred in captivity.

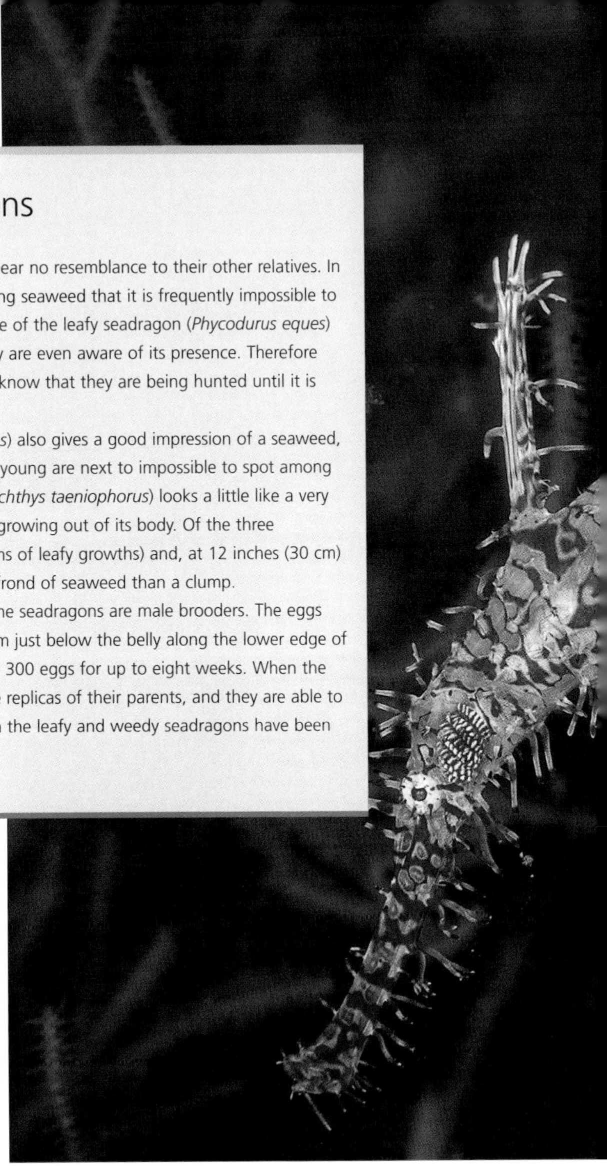

two separate subfamilies—Syngnathinae (pipefish, pipehorses, and seadragons) and Hippocampinae (sea horses). However, this situation may change after further study.

Ghostly Relatives

Closely related to both the sea horses and the pipefish are the ghost pipefish, which make up the family Solenostomidae. There are only five species in the family, ranging in size from about 2.4 inches (6 cm) in the armored pipefish (*Solenostomus armatus*) to 6.7 inches (17 cm) in "the" ghost pipefish (*S. cyanopterus*).

Like their namesakes, the pipefish, *Solenostomus* species, hold their bodies in the normal way—that is, horizontal, with their head pointing forward and their tail back. However, they can be easily separated from the other pipefish because they have two dorsal fins, a large tail, and large pelvic fins. As a result, they are better swimmers than their relatives. Their body armor, too, is different and consists of large, star-shaped bony plates.

The pelvic fins (totally lacking in sea horses and pipefish) serve a very important purpose in the ghost pipefish. In females they form a pouch in which she carries her eggs until they hatch. However, in the sea horses and pipefish the developing eggs are carried in the belly pouches of the males.

Controversial Sticklebacks

In the world of family relationships fish are no different than other animals or even humans. Sometimes scientists argue about how different species are related. The armored stickleback (*Indostomus paradoxus*) is an excellent example of such a debate.

Until 1999 it was the only known member of its family (Indostomidae)—of this fact there

Ⓣ ***At 6.7 inches (17 cm) long the ornate ghost pipefish (*****Solenostomus paradoxus*****) is the largest species in the family Solenostomidae. It inhabits the shallow coral reefs in Indonesia.***

was no dispute. The actual relationship of this family to other armored fish families has been hotly contested for years, however. Even its scientific name reflects this—"paradoxus"—a paradox being something that is contradictory or apparently absurd, but that may be true.

The discovery and subsequent naming of two further species in 1999 did little to resolve the situation. And so the controversy carries on to this day. Most scientists take the view that the three armored sticklebacks belong within the same order as the sticklebacks, along with sea horses, pipefish, seadragons, and ghost pipefish, but in a group of their own—the infraorder Indostomoida.

These elongated, slender fish only measure around 1.2 inches (3 cm) in length; but unlike their relatives, which are all marine, they are restricted to fresh water. They are shy, retiring fish that inhabit still or slowly flowing waters. They spend most of their time hiding and hunting in the thick layers of leaf litter that line the bottom of streams, lakes, ditches, canals, and swamps, where they feed on small, slow-moving invertebrates such as worms.

One species—"the" armored stickleback—is known primarily from Lake Indawgyi in Myanmar (formerly Burma) but may also extend into Cambodia. *Indostomus crocodilus* (no common name) is known only from a blackwater stream in Narathiwat Province, Thailand, while *I. spinosus* (no common name) has a wider distribution in the Mekong Basin.

Very little is known about the biology and, particularly, the breeding habits of these intriguing little fish, although the armored stickleback occasionally is available for home aquariums. Thanks to this some important information has emerged over the years. We know, for example, that this species is among the very few fish that can actually raise and lower its head. We also know that it frequently rests on the bottom with its body aligned at a steep, upward angle, and that it creeps up on worms—using its pectoral fins to move forward and then turning at very fast speed to snap up its prey.

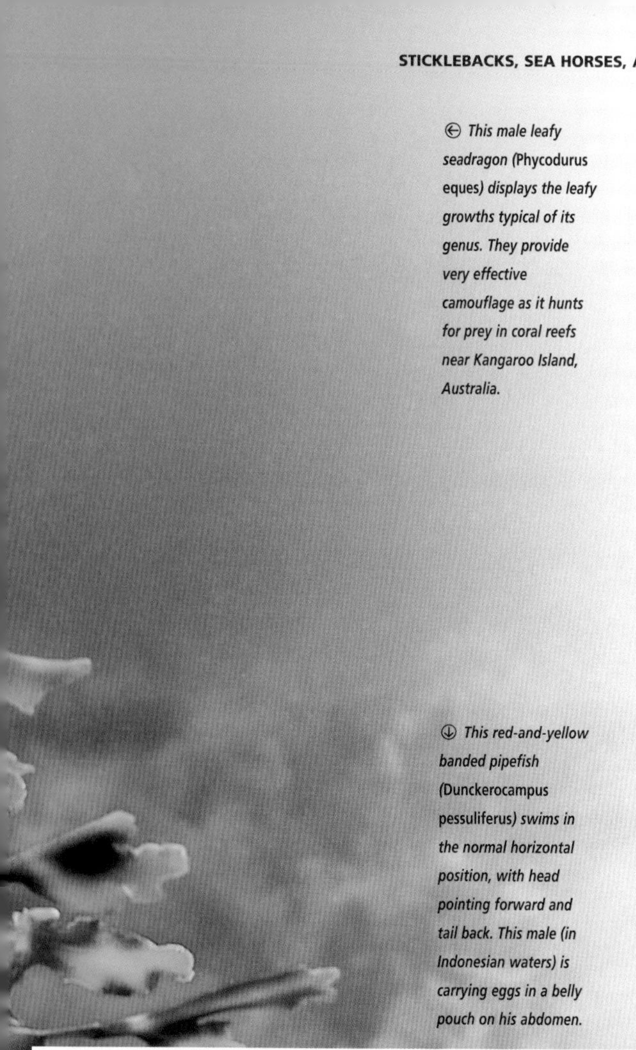

This male leafy seadragon (Phycodurus eques) displays the leafy growths typical of its genus. They provide very effective camouflage as it hunts for prey in coral reefs near Kangaroo Island, Australia.

The Sea-horse Trade

Although it is difficult, perhaps impossible, to state accurately just how many sea horses are caught and traded worldwide, it is safe to say that the figure is over 15 million each year. Sea horses are fished, both as targeted species (that is, they are specifically sought out and collected) or as bycatch (that is, they are caught accidentally in nets set out for other fish). Either way, for many years now there has been mounting concern for the continued survival of at least some species of sea horses, pipefish, and pipehorses in the wild.

There are three main markets for sea horses—traditional Chinese medicine (TCM), ornaments (or curios), and home aquaria. Of them the TCM market is the largest by far, with dried sea horses being sold either whole or in powdered form. Whole sea horses are generally used in tonics and other health-associated drinks, while powdered sea horses are used in a wide variety of medicines designed to treat numerous ailments and illnesses—from asthma to thickening of the arteries or even for broken bones.

These popular remedies have spread around the world, and they now are sold outside China in countries such as the Philippines, Indonesia, India, the U.S., U.K., and other countries that have an Asian expatriate community. It has been estimated that across Asia some 45 tons (40.8 tonnes) of dried sea

This red-and-yellow banded pipefish (Dunckerocampus pessuliferus) swims in the normal horizontal position, with head pointing forward and tail back. This male (in Indonesian waters) is carrying eggs in a belly pouch on his abdomen.

Sea Horses Under Threat

Together the 45 or so countries that trade in sea horses account for between 3 and 15 tons (2.7–13.6 tonnes) of fish every year. This translates into many millions of individual specimens and has led to concern about their status in the wild. No fewer than 19 are now officially listed as Vulnerable by the World Conservation Union, and one—the Knysna, or Cape, sea horse (*Hippocampus capensis*)—is considered Endangered. (Below are sea horses (*Hippocampus* species) for sale for traditional Chinese medicine use in Sabah, Malaysia.)

Among the pipefish five species of *Solegnathus* are also listed as Vulnerable, while the river pipefish (*Syngnathus watermeyeri*) is Critically Endangered.

In the case of the Knysna sea horse, which is found west of Port Elizabeth in Cape Province, South Africa, tourism and pollution have put the species at risk. Tourism is responsible for creating pressure on the estuary around Knysna Lagoon, where freshwater floods have caused heavy die-offs among the resident sea-horse population (these sea horses cannot tolerate low salinity). Increasing levels of pollution also mean that even captive-bred specimens cannot be released into the waters, so restocking is not possible. However, if attempts to control conditions in the natural habitat are successful, the release of captive-bred specimens may be possible in the future.

The situation facing the river pipefish is even worse. This species is restricted to tidal areas of just three South African rivers: Kariega, Kasouga, and Bushman's. This extremely small distribution means that the species is at high risk from external influences like pollution, flooding, loss of its seagrass-bed habitat, or disease. Furthermore, this pipefish appears to have a very short breeding season. Therefore anything that upsets weather or water conditions during this time could pose a threat to the survival of the species.

horses are imported annually. In terms of actual numbers of specimens this probably represents over 15 million individual sea horses.

Large numbers are also sold as curios or ornaments, mainly (but not exclusively) in vacation areas near the sea. Sea horses of all sizes are used and sold—incorporated into anything from a keyring to a lamp base.

In contrast, live sea horses are mainly destined for home aquaria. Past estimates suggest that many hundreds of thousands were caught specifically for this purpose. However, studies carried out in recent years indicate that the numbers are more likely to be a few tens of thousands; this does not mean that only these numbers are caught alive. Many more may be collected and subsequently sold for TCM and curio purposes.

In a global attempt to protect all species of sea horse the Convention in International Trade in Endangered Species of Fauna and Flora—known as CITES—agreed in the fall of 2002 to put all *Hippocampus* species on their Appendix II list. This agreement came into effect on May 15, 2004, which means that special permits have been required to sell and buy sea horses since this date. It is not a ban on trade, but it does mean that trade in these species is now monitored and controlled.

A further and important development in recent years is the considerable increase in the numbers of sea horses being bred in captivity especially for the marine hobbyist. Many thousands of these captive-bred sea horses (consisting of several species) are now being produced in a number of countries, including Australia, Ireland, and the U.K., for sale worldwide. Therefore the future of sea horses now appears to be more promising, although the problem of large numbers being caught accidentally still continues.

Here in waters off southeast Australia a "pregnant" male short-snouted sea horse* (Hippocampus breviceps)*, carries his eggs in a belly pouch. In two to four weeks' time he will give birth to live young, a process that lasts up to 12 hours or more.

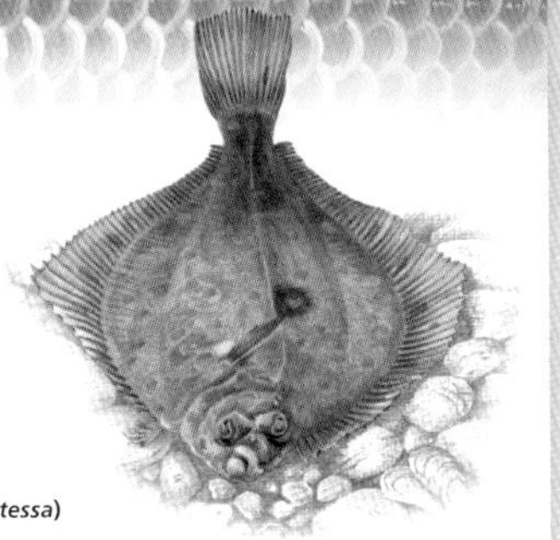

European plaice
(*Pleuronectes platessa*)

Common name Flounders

Families Bothidae (lefteye flounders), Pleuronectidae (righteye flounders)

Subfamilies Bothidae: Bothinae and Taeniopsettinae; Pleuronectidae: Pleuronectinae, Rhombosoleinae, Poecilopsettinae, and Paralichthodinae

Order Pleuronectiformes

Number of species Bothidae: about 157 in 20 genera; Pleuronectidae: nearly 120 in about 44 genera

Size From 1.4 in (3.5 cm) to 8.5 ft (2.6 m)

Key features Asymmetrical, oval-shaped bodies; head with both eyes on same (top) side; front edge of dorsal fin located above or in front of eyes; all fins separate from each other; pelvic fins asymmetrical in lefteyes, symmetrical in righteyes; coloration: top side heavily patterned in many species; capable of rapid color changes

Breeding About 2 million eggs released

Diet Invertebrates; larger species also take fish

Habitat Nearly always marine; Bothidae: tropical and temperate zones; usually over fine-grained bottoms; shallow or relatively shallow waters, normally above 330 ft (100 m); Pleuronectidae: tropical, subtropical, temperate, and (almost) arctic zones; usually over fine-grained bottoms; depths above 660 ft (200 m); some species may enter brackish water

Distribution Atlantic, Indian, and Pacific Oceans; Pleuronectidae: also Arctic Ocean

Status World Conservation Union lists Atlantic halibut (*Hippoglossus hippoglossus*) as Endangered and yellowtail flounder (*Limanda ferriginea*) as Vulnerable

*The bony ridge of this 40-inch (1-m) European plaice (*Pleuronectes platessa*) is visible behind its eyes. Lying flat on the rocky bottom of very shallow brackish or marine waters, it hunts for its favorite mollusks at night.*

Flounders

Bothidae, Pleuronectidae

The righteye flounders, with few exceptions, have both eyes on the right side of the head and are most familiar to us on our plates. Of course, the reverse is true of the aptly named lefteye flounders.

TOGETHER THE LEFTEYE FLOUNDERS (FAMILY Bothidae) and their right-eyed counterparts (family Pleuronectidae) account for nearly 280 of the 690 or so species that make up the order of flatfish (Pleuronectiformes). At around 157 species the lefteye flounders are the largest of the families. The righteye flounders, with 120 species, rank third, being slightly outnumbered by the tonguefish family (Cynoglossidae), at around 135 species in just three genera.

Fish on the Menu

Most of the best-known species that are fished commercially for food are righteye flounders, but there are also some familiar types not just among the lefteye flounders but also members of other families (see box).

Usually flatfish are caught in trawl nets over fine-grained bottoms at varying depths depending on species and time of year. Some, such as the Atlantic halibut (*Hippoglossus hippoglossus*), can be found at great depths—from around 165 feet (50 m) down to around 6,560 feet (2,000 m). The Pacific halibut

*The eyed flounder (*Bothus ocellatus*) is found in the Indian and West Pacific Oceans.*

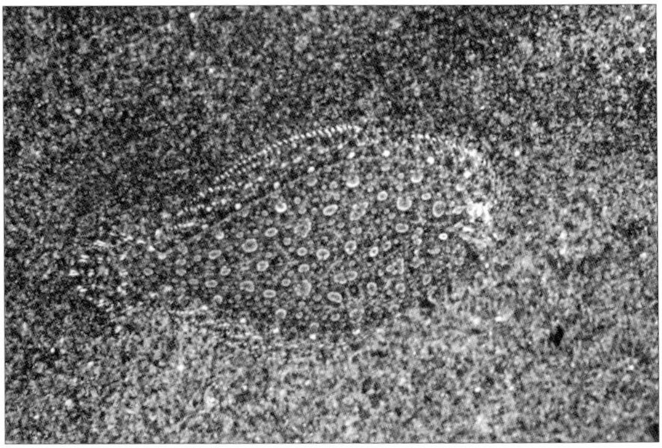

(*H. stenolepis*) does not extend to such great depths but can still be found at around 3,610 feet (1,100 m). Both fish are highly commercial and are usually caught at considerably shallower depths than their maximum.

In the past the Atlantic halibut has been fished very heavily, to such an extent that now the World Conservation Union officially lists it as Endangered. With dwindling stocks and the continuing high demand for this excellent food fish, several experimental projects aimed at rearing the species under controlled conditions have met with some success.

The commercial breeding of European plaice (*Pleuronectes platessa*) is far better established, and important quantities of farmed stocks are now available. It is not endangered, and demand has led to captive rearing.

Soles are also popular food fish, with the lemon sole (*Microstomus kitt*) and Dover sole being particularly highly regarded in international cuisine. However, the Dover sole enjoyed by European diners is quite distinct from that consumed in the U.S. The European Dover sole is *Solea solea*, which can grow to 24 inches (60 cm). It is not a member of the Pleuronectidae or Bothidae (the two families discussed here) but of the Soleidae (discussed under "Soles"). In the U.S. the American Dover sole is *M. pacificus*, a larger fish at around 30 inches (76 cm); it is a member of the Pleuronectidae along with the lemon sole, itself a sizable fish at 26 inches (65 cm) long.

Undoubtedly, the leading species is the European plaice, a northeastern Atlantic species that can grow to around 40 inches (100 cm), weighs around 15.5 pounds (7 kg), and can live for up to 50 years. Few people, though, ever get to see any specimens even closely approaching this size, weight, and age.

↑ ***The European plaice* (Pleuronectes platessa) *is distinguished by the orange spots on one side of its body, while the other side is characteristically pale. Plaice tend to move from relatively shallow water to deeper water as they grow older.***

The vast majority seen in food markets are less than half this size and are nowhere near the age limit for the species. This species is the most important flatfish in Europe and is sold both fresh and frozen in large quantities.

Adult European plaice can be found in waters as deep as 650 feet (200 m). Although adults can also be found in very shallow water, most of the specimens encountered in such habitats are small. Few, if any, small individuals are ever encountered at depth.

Other Popular Flounders and Friends

While the species mentioned above are among the best-known and most popular flatfish that are eaten in many countries, numerous other species (belonging to several families) are also consumed, some in large quantities. In fact, there are probably more members of this order that are regarded as food fish than of most others. The brill (*Scophthalmus rhombus*), for example, is a 30-inch (75-cm), 16-pound (7.2-kg) European, Mediterranean, and Black Sea member of the family Scophthalmidae, with a broad body and delicate flesh that is popular mainly (but not exclusively) in the more northern European regions.

Another member of this family, the topknot (*Zeugopterus punctatus*), is even more northern in its distribution and is popular in Britain and parts of Scandinavia.

The dab (*Limanda limanda*) is also a predominantly northern Atlantic species. It can grow to 17 inches (42 cm) and weighs around 2.8 pounds (1.3 kg). The flounder (*Pleuronectes flesus*) is longer and heavier, and extends further south to the Moroccan coast and into the Mediterranean and Baltic Seas. Both are members of the family Pleuronectidae that enjoy considerable popularity.

Along the Pacific Coast of the U.S. many species of flatfish are taken both as game and food fish. They include the Pacific sanddab (*Cithraichthys sordidus*) and the California flounder (*Paralichthys californicus*) from the large-tooth flounder family (Paralichthyidae)—plus several members of the righteye flounder family, including the rex sole (*Glyptocephalus zachirus*) and the petrale sole (*Eopsetta jordani*). In the more northern regions the rock sole (*Lepidopsetta bilineata*) is fished in large numbers, while the English sole (*Parophrys*

The Fishing Flatfish

All flatfish are predators and tend to ambush their prey. However, the angler flatfish (*Asterorhombus fijiensis*) in the family Bothidae takes matters a significant step further and actually fishes for its food. It has a form of built-in fishing rod with a bait or lure that, through the remarkable process of "parallel" evolution, closely resembles the "rod and lure" arrangement found in the angler fish (order Lophiiformes).

This 6-inch (15-cm) Indo-Pacific species is found in shallow tropical waters, often on coral sandy bottoms at depths of less than 100 feet (30 m). There it lies motionless, partly covered or camouflaged and thus invisible to its potential prey. One part of the body, though, is very visible—the rodlike first spine of the dorsal fin and its modified tip that looks like a small shrimp. The angler flatfish waves this rod and lure (called the "ilicium" and "esca," respectively) in the water until an unsuspecting victim becomes attracted by the "shrimp." However, this "shrimp" is no meal, as the would-be predator dramatically discovers when the flatfish sucks it into its large mouth in a lightning-fast move.

vetulus) is similarly fished from British Columbia down to California.

Among the Asian species the pelican flounder (*Chascanopsetta lugubris*) of the family Bothidae is one of the more unusual-looking food species. It grows to nearly 16 inches (40 cm) and occurs at depths of between 200 and 3,300 feet (60–1,000 m). It has a large mouth with a saclike throat, hence the name pelican. This huge gape allows it to feed on large prey.

The above is a small selection of the many species of flatfish that are consumed in various regions. Though markets and demands may vary, the vast majority of these fish are sold either fresh or frozen. Some, though, are dried, salted, or ground into fishmeal, while a few, such as the butter sole (*Isopsetta isolepis*) and the American Dover sole, are also sold for feeding to captive-reared mink on fur farms.

Lefteyes and Righteyes Compared

Apart from the fact that the lefteye and righteye flounders can, with few exceptions, be told apart—depending on which side of the head the eyes are located—there appear to be few other easily observed differences between the members of these families. Indeed, some scientists think that the righteye flounders of the subfamily Pleuronectinae resemble the lefteye flounders more closely than they do the members of the other subfamilies within their own family.

The fact is that at first sight, members of both the lefteye and righteye families look remarkably similar and share similar lifestyles. For example, the dorsal fin in both starts far forward on the body, above or in front of the eyes. They also both have their dorsal and anal fins quite separate from the tail, and so on.

Indeed, it is only when we start looking at smaller details, like the presence or absence of oil globules in the eggs and relative lengths of the pelvic fins, that distinct differences begin to appear. It is not surprising, therefore, that opinions differ among scientists on how these families should be identified, or if the subfamily of righteye flounders, which contains the European plaice, the halibuts, and around 40 other species, are really righteye flounders or special types of lefteye flounder.

↓ *The dab (*Limanda limanda*) feeds largely on crustaceans and small fish, and can be found at depths down to 490 feet (150 m). It is native to the northeast Atlantic and the Baltic Sea.*

Green sunfish (*Lepomis cyanellus*)

Common name Sunfish

Families Centrarchidae (sunfish), Elassomatidae or Elassomidae (pygmy sunfish)

Order Perciformes

Number of species Centrarchidae: about 30 in 8 genera; Elassomatidae: 6 in 1 genus

Size From about 1.3 in (3.2 cm) to 38 in (97 cm)

Key features Body ranging from relatively elongated to oval shaped; snout pointed in Centrarchidae, rounded in Elassomatidae with mouth at tip; lower jaw longer than upper in more predatory species; eyes relatively large; lateral line usually extends from behind gills to caudal peduncle but absent in pygmy sunfish; all fins well formed; dorsal and anal fin have hard unbranched spines at front, followed by soft branched rays; caudal fin usually forked but rounded in pygmy sunfish; coloration extremely varied

Breeding All Centrarchidae except Sacramento perch are nest builders; some Elassomatidae scatter eggs and abandon them; others deposit eggs in vegetation, and male guards them until they hatch

Diet Small invertebrates in pygmy sunfish and smaller centrarchids; fish and amphibians in larger species

Habitat Ponds, lakes, creeks, and large rivers, often with overhanging vegetation and overgrown banks; pygmy sunfish favor quiet waters, including swamps and sluggish streams, usually heavily vegetated and with muddy bottoms

Distribution Sunfish widely distributed in North America; some species, notably pumpkinseed and largemouth bass, introduced to numerous locations outside home ranges, including Europe, Africa, Asia, and Caribbean; pygmy sunfish restricted to eastern U.S.

Status Two species of pygmy sunfish considered under threat in the wild

Ⓣ ***The green sunfish* (Lepomis cyanellus) *is a native of east and central North America, although it has been introduced elsewhere. Growing to about 12 inches (30 cm), it is a drought-tolerant species found in warm, shallow fresh waters.***

Sunfish

Centrarchidae, Elassomatidae

The sunfish are known for the bright, even dazzling colors often acquired by breeding males. But some males have a more subtle strategy—pretending to be females so they can slip past powerful rivals and mate with the females they are guarding.

THE FAMILY CENTRARCHIDAE CONSISTS OF SOME 30 species variously known as sunfish, basses, crappies, and perches. However, the last-mentioned group should not be confused with the Eurasian perch, *Perca fluviatilis,* or the American yellow perch, *P. flavescens*, both of which are members of the family Percidae.

Sizes vary widely within the family Centrarchidae. Among the smallest are species such as the bluespotted sunfish (*Enneacanthus gloriosus*) from some eastern zones of the U.S., which grows to just 3.7 inches (9.5 cm). At the other end of the spectrum the largemouth bass (*Micropterus salmoides*) can attain a length of about 38 inches (97 cm).

All species are hunters. The largemouth bass and its nearest relatives in the genus *Micropterus*, the allied *Ambloplites* species (for example, the 14.5-inch/36-cm Roanoke bass, *A. cavifrons*) and the 28.8-inch/73-cm Sacramento perch (*Archoplites interruptus*) are particularly voracious predators that are sought after by anglers owing to their sporting qualities.

Other species also feed primarily on animal matter but hunt much smaller prey, including aquatic insects and invertebrates. The group contains some of the best-known sunfish, like the pumpkinseed (*Lepomis gibbosus*), the longear sunfish (*L. megalotis*), and the bluespotted sunfish. The pumpkinseed, in particular, is well known outside its U.S. home range, owing to its importation as an aquarium fish into Europe as far back as 1877. Since then it has remained popular with aquarists.

Species of both *Enneacanthus* and *Lepomis* are frequently colorful, with the body often liberally "dusted" with pearl-like scales. In

Ⓓ ***The bluegill sunfish* (Lepomis macrochirus) *is one of the largest of the species in the genus, growing to a length of about 16 inches (41 cm). The spots and bands that characterize the bodies of many sunfish become more intense in males when breeding.***

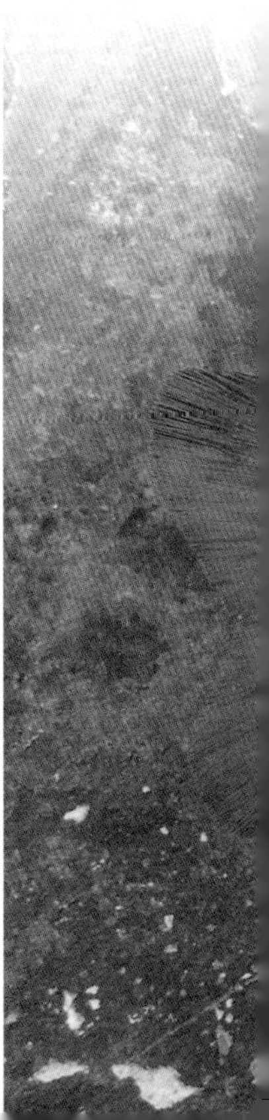

Lepomis males the back edge of the gill cover often has an elongated flap or "ear" that is colored differently from the body and is especially long in the appropriately named longear sunfish.

Satellites and Sneakers

Some sunfish have evolved an unusual breeding strategy. For example, in the bluegill (*Lepomis macrochirus*) there are three different types of male. First, there are "normal" males. These individuals form the bulk of the male members in any population. They set up territories and spawn with a number of females. Such males develop intense coloration during the breeding season. They spend most of their time displaying toward rival males in an attempt to ward them off and then showing their colors and fins to females in an attempt to entice them to enter their territories and mate.

The other males are called satellites and sneakers. They look like females rather than breeding males and do not display their colors

Unwelcome Introductions

The pumpkinseed and largemouth bass are among the most widely traveled of spiny-finned fish. Since the 19th century the pumpkinseed has been introduced to locations across the U.S. and to at least 31 other countries, including much of Europe from Britain to the Black Sea states, the Congo, Chile, and Morocco. Adaptable and opportunistic, it has established viable, self-sustaining populations from the Baltic to the equator.

Unfortunately, the introduced pumpkinseeds have had negative effects on many native species of fish and other aquatic creatures, as well as their habitats. The problem is even more pronounced in the case of the largemouth bass, which is even more predatory than the pumpkinseed and has been introduced into more than 70 countries as a sport and food fish. This large sunfish preys on young native fish and competes so successfully with larger native predators that they become scarce. The largemouth bass has also brought at least two North American fish parasites with it, and they have become established among native species.

or engage in bouts of display behavior. Satellites and sneakers look similar to each other, but they behave in quite different ways.

Satellites—as their name implies—tend to hover around the edges of a dominant male's territory. However, because they look like females, dominant males do not appear to be able to identify satellites as males and therefore do not attack them. Consequently, satellite males are sometimes able to enter a dominant male's territory and mate with one of the females without, apparently, being detected. Even if they are detected, they often manage to shed their sperm among the female's eggs before making their getaway.

Sneakers, on the other hand, dash, or sneak, in and mate rapidly with a female while the dominant male is engrossed in his own mating activities. They then make their escape, often before the dominant male realizes what has happened.

Satellites and sneakers are perfect examples of how different solutions to a problem or challenge—in this instance how to get to mate with a female—arise in the course of evolution. However, exactly what advantages such males bring to the overall survival of the species is unclear at present.

In all centrarchid sunfish the eggs are usually laid in a nest dug by the male. The nest is a circular depression on the bottom, often lined with plants. The male defends the eggs until they hatch several days later

Varied Pygmies

Sunfish range in size from about 3.5 inches (9.5 cm) to 38 inches (97 cm). The pygmy sunfish, in marked contrast, are at most 1.9 inches (4.7 cm) long. Pygmy sunfish can also be distinguished from the larger sunfish by the lack of a lateral line on the body and a rounded tail. The other sunfish have a lateral line and, usually, a forked tail.

Although there are only six species of pygmy sunfish, they show some variability in breeding strategies. The Everglades pygmy sunfish (*Elassoma evergladei*), the blue-barred

It is clear to see how the largemouth bass (*Micropterus salmoides*) gets its common name. A voracious hunter found throughout the U.S., it is an important game fish as well as a food fish.

Same Name, Different Fish

At one time the six species of pygmy sunfish were thought to be so closely related to the sunfish that the two groups were classified as subfamilies of the family Centrarchidae: the Centrarchinae and Elassomatinae. Today, however, the pygmy sunfish are considered quite different, so they have been allocated a family of their own: the Elassomatidae (sometimes called the Elassomidae).

Yet while the split into two families is now generally accepted, there is still a lot of debate about how closely related the two types of sunfish really are. Most scientists see them as near relatives, but some believe that the pygmy sunfish are considerably more like the sticklebacks of the family Gasterosteidae or even swamp eels of the family Synbranchidae. Such debates may run for many decades, but recently developed techniques for comparing the DNA of different families may eventually resolve them beyond all doubt.

pygmy sunfish (*E. okatie*), and the Okefenokee pygmy sunfish (*E. okefenokee*), for example, scatter their eggs in open water, among vegetation, or over the bottom and abandon them. In the spring pygmy sunfish (*E. alabamae*) and the banded pygmy sunfish (*E. zonatum*), however, the eggs are protected by the male until they hatch a few days later.

All species are rather secretive and usually occur in standing waters with heavy vegetation and a mud bottom. There they feed on small invertebrates, primarily worms and tiny crustaceans, such as shrimp.

Yet despite their small size and rather timid nature, all species are territorial when it comes to breeding. At such times the males, like the larger sunfish, develop intense colors and establish their own patch, which they defend against all comers.

*With its reflective blue speckling the pumpkinseed (*Lepomis gibbosus*) is an attractive species that is usually peaceful except during breeding. In pumpkinseeds and relatives the back edge of the gill cover has a flap that is a different color than the body and head.*

Multiple Threats

Some pygmy sunfish populations are currently facing a number of threats to their survival, none more so than the blue-barred and Alabama pygmy sunfish.

The spring pygmy sunfish (*Elassoma alabamae*), for example, disappeared and was presumed extinct some years after its discovery in 1937. It was not until 1973 that it was rediscovered in Moss Spring, Limestone County, Alabama. One important factor affecting its apparent disappearance was the introduction of nonnative species of plants that smothered the springs in which the species originally occurred. Others included the filling of reservoirs that ended up flooding a number of important habitats, river channeling, pollution, dredging to create waterholes for cattle, and so on. In the few places where the species occurs, it is quite plentiful. The problem is that there are very few such locations. However, releasing captive-bred stocks, plus a number of rescue projects in the wild, seem to be proving successful.

For the blue-barred pygmy sunfish the situation is worse. It is officially listed by the IUCN as being Vulnerable and therefore at high risk of becoming Endangered or Extinct if appropriate steps are not taken.

Sponges

Porifera

Sponges are found in large numbers in all the seas of the world. The best-known forms are probably the bath sponges, which have been used by humans for thousands of years.

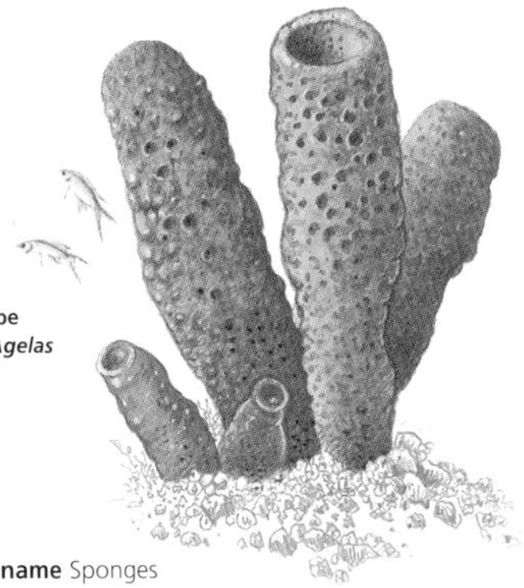

Brown tube sponge *(Agelas conifera)*

Common name Sponges

Phylum Porifera

Number of species About 5,000

Size Variable, from 0.1 in (2.5 mm) to 40 in (100 cm) or more in height; occasionally over 10 ft (3 m) across

Key features Simple, radially symmetrical but irregularly shaped animals; made up of largely undifferentiated (nonspecialized) tissues around a system of channels and chambers through which water can flow; mostly colorful, in shades of red, orange, purple, yellow, and green; occasionally dull and inconspicuous

Habits Nonmoving, usually attached to hard substratum

Breeding Asexual by budding or production of gemmules (cell packets), or sexual with internal fertilization and direct development into small adults

Diet Small bacteria, protists, and particles of organic material

Habitat Mostly marine at all depths; some freshwater species exist

Distribution Worldwide

Ⓣ Columns of the brown tube sponge,* Agelas conifera, *rise from the seabed like smokestacks. This sponge is found in seas around the Bahamas, the Caribbean, and Florida. Growing up to 36 inches (90 cm) tall, brown tube sponges are sometimes home to small fish that live inside their hollow core.

SPONGES ARE GENERALLY accepted to be the most primitive multicellular animals, separated from metazoans (animals with tissues and organs) by their lack of fully specialized tissues. Early natural historians classified them as plants because of their sedentary nature. Their various encrusting, erect, branching, and vaselike forms of growth are similar to lichens, but usually on a bigger scale. Sponges range in size from a fraction of an inch to over 10 feet (3 m) wide and 4 feet (1.2 m) tall. All sponges are aquatic, and the vast majority are marine.

Sponges have an extensive fossil record dating back to the Precambrian period (which began more than 540 million years ago). Even then the three classes known today—Calcarea, Demospongia, and Hexactinella—were quite distinct. The earliest sponges belong to the genus *Palaeophragmodictya*, discovered in 1996 in ancient rocks in Australia. The group had its heyday in the Cretaceous period (140 to 65 million years ago); and although diversity and abundance have declined somewhat since then, the sponges are still a successful group today.

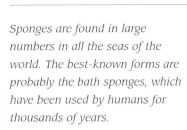

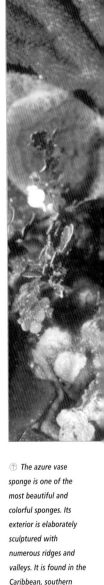

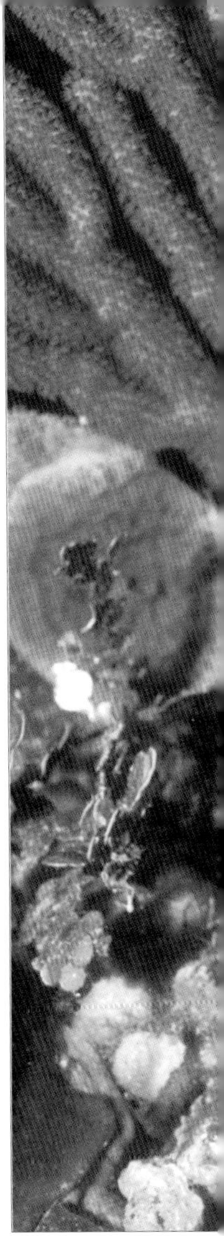

Ⓣ The azure vase sponge is one of the most beautiful and colorful sponges. Its exterior is elaborately sculptured with numerous ridges and valleys. It is found in the Caribbean, southern Florida, and the Bahamas.

Body Forms

There are three basic sponge body forms. In order of increasing complexity they are the asconoid, syconoid, and leuconoid sponges. They should not be confused with taxonomic groups, which may include sponges of one or more different structural types. Asconoid sponges are basically tube shaped and rarely more than 4 inches (10 cm) long. Their outer surface is covered in a layer of cells called pinacocytes and is pitted with many tiny pores

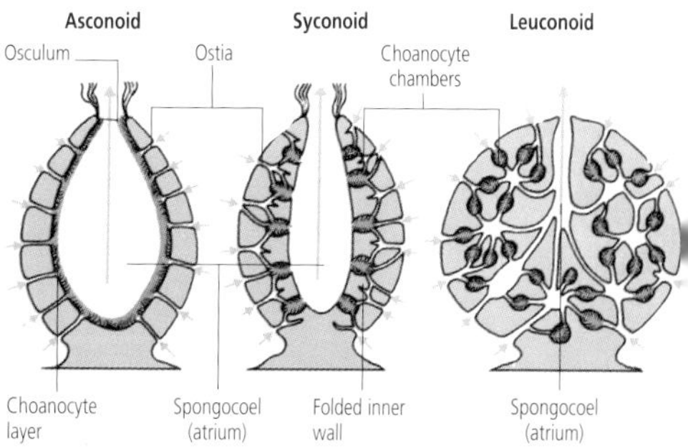

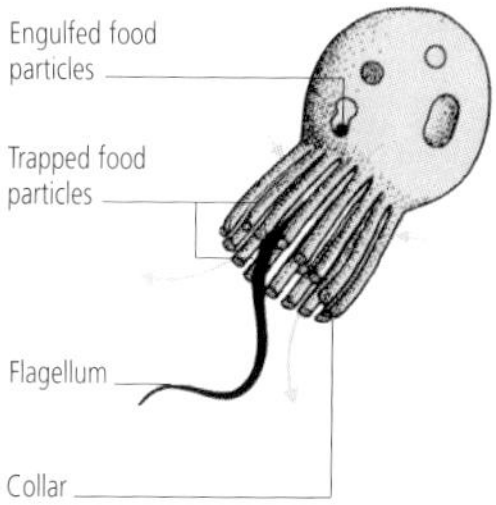

The three sponge body forms (above) and a single choanocyte (below). In the asconoid sponges choanocytes line the body cavity, while in the more complex forms the wall is folded so the cells line the many chambers. The blue arrows show water flow.

known as ostia. The pores allow water to move through the body wall into the central cavity (the spongocoel, or atrium). The atrium is lined with special cells known as choanocytes (derived from choanoflagellates, the protozoans thought to be the ancestors of sponges and possibly of all multicellular animal life). Each choanocyte has a single long flagellum encircled by a collar of tiny projections called microvilli.

The beating of thousands of choanocyte flagellae inside the sponge generates a flow of water through the sponge. Water is drawn in through the ostia and out through a single large opening at the top of the tube called the osculum. This water current is the sponge's life-support system. It brings oxygenated water and food within reach of individual cells and carries away carbon dioxide and other waste products.

The efficiency with which a sponge can pump water relates to the surface area of flagellated cells and therefore the overall volume of the atrium. This imposes a strict size limit on the asconoid body plan. For sponges to grow bigger than about 4 inches (10 cm), they must become more complex. Syconoid sponges such as *Scypha ciliata* have

Resembling large baked cheeses, these orange puffball sponges, Tethya aurantia, ***are solidly attached to the rocky substratum on a California coast.***

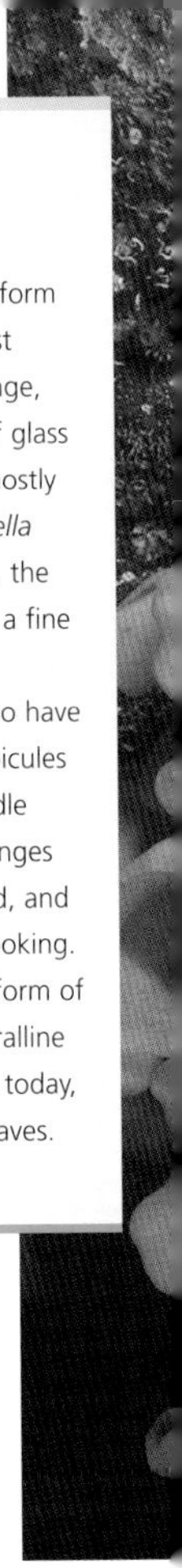

The Sponge Skeleton

Between the inner and outer surfaces of the sponge body is a mass of supporting material known as mesohyl. In most sponges the mesohyl is a gelatinous mass containing skeletal materials such as protein fibers (collagen and spongin), mineral spicules (supporting structures), and wandering amebalike cells. These so-called amebocytes are undifferentiated (nonspecialized), but they are able to develop into any other kind of sponge cell. When more of a particular cell type is required for growth, repair, or maintenance of the body, the versatile amebocytes are recruited to the cause. The mesohyl forms the bulk of the sponge's mass, and its composition is one of the major characteristics used in the classification of different sponges.

Members of the class Hexactinella are known as glass sponges because their skeleton is made of the mineral silicate. Specialized amebocyte cells in the mesohyl, known as sclerocytes, produce highly distinctive six-spined spicules that fuse together and form an intricate scaffold that supports some of the largest known sponge species—for example, the cloud sponge, *Aphrocallistes vastus*. There are about 600 species of glass sponge, and the majority live in silicate-rich water, mostly at great depths. The best-known example is *Euplectella aspergillum*, sometimes called Venus's flower basket, the skeleton of which forms a long brittle tube made of a fine lattice as delicate as lace.

The calcareous sponges of the class Calcarea also have a mineralized skeleton; but instead of silicate, the spicules are made of calcium carbonate. They are either needle shaped or have three or four spines. Calcareous sponges come in all three structural types (asconoid, syconoid, and leuconoid), but are generally quite small and drab looking. In a few calcareous sponges the skeleton takes the form of a solid external wall—such species are known as coralline sponges. They were more common in the past than today, and the few surviving examples tend to live in sea caves.

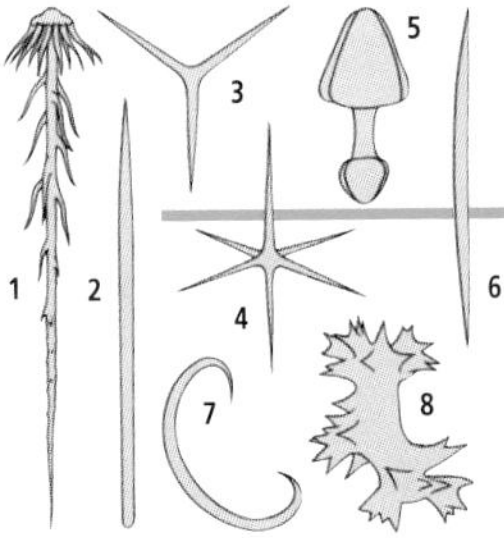

The various shapes of sponge spicules can help identify sponge types. Spicules have various forms—with barbs (1), straight (2),(6), with terminal processes (5), and with recurved ends (7). Other notable shapes are triaxon spicule (3), hexaxon spicule (4), and polyaxon spicule (8).

a folded internal structure that increases the surface area of flagellated cells. In the most complex sponges, the leuconoids, the atrium is reduced to a network of narrow channels and minute chambers containing a few dozen to several hundred choanoctyes. The leuconoid plan is so efficient that some species can process up to 20,000 times their own volume of water in a single day.

Complex Skeletons

By far the largest sponge class is the Demospongia, with over 4,000 species. They include all the typical "spongy" species such as *Spongia* and the 150 or so freshwater species of the family Spongillidae. All members of the Demospongia conform to the complex leuconoid structural type, but they display a bewildering variety of sizes, shapes, and vibrant colors. Demospongid skeletons can be made of one- and four-spined silicate spicules (supporting structures) or the collagenlike protein spongin, or both.

Microscopic Meals

Sponges generally feed on microscopic particles including bacteria, algae, and organic particles ranging from 1 to 500 microns in size. The glass sponges (class Hexactinella) specialize in trapping particles so tiny that no other metazoan animals are equipped to make use of them. The quantity more than makes up for the tiny size, however, and the sponges often have this particular food resource all to themselves.

Sponges are remarkably efficient feeders, especially those with a leuconoid body structure. Food particles entering the atrium are snared on the microvilli that encircle the flagellum of each choanocyte cell. Once in contact with the cell, the particle is engulfed and stored inside a food vacuole. A small proportion of food may be digested within the choanocyte that caught it, but most is passed on to digestive cells within the mesohyl (supporting material of the sponge body wall).

reproduce, releasing small quantities of nutrition into the sponge cell. In the gold sponge, *Verongia aerophora*, symbiotic algae make up 30 percent of the body's volume.

Living in Harmony

Algae are not the only organisms with which sponges have cultivated mutually beneficial relationships. Several species of Venus's flower basket (*Euplectella*) are home to much larger commensals, including spider crabs, isopods (such as sea slaters), and *Spongicola* shrimps. The crustaceans enter as juveniles and soon become too large to leave. In Japan and the Philippines dried *Euplectella* preserved along with their little lodgers are sometimes presented to newlywed couples as a symbol of a successful lifelong partnership.

Sponge commensals benefit from the association, gaining a safe place in which to live. However, they do nothing for the sponge in return. A more mutually beneficial relationship is the one between *Suberites domuncula* and various species of hermit crab. The crabs use the sponges as a substitute for a shell, thereby allowing the sponge to occupy soft-bottomed habitats where it would not normally be able to grow. However, the strategy is not completely risk free. If the sponge is discarded in favor of a real shell, it may be buried in sediment or cast up onto a beach where it is in danger of drying out.

Killer Sponges

One group of sponges is effectively carnivorous. Members of the family Cladorhizidae (class Demospongia) have a silicate skeleton whose spicules pierce the surface layer, creating a surface as snaggy as Velcro™. Small animals, mainly planktonic crustaceans, become caught on the spicules. Specialized amebocytes then converge on the trapped "prey" and secrete enzymes that begin to digest it.

Some sponges can supplement their diet with carbohydrates produced by symbiotic algae and cyanobacteria living in the sponge's own body. The organisms are taken in by choanocytes but not digested. Instead, they are passed to amebocytes where they live and

↑ **Aphrocallistes vastus** ***cloud sponges are deepwater glass sponges with silica spicules that can penetrate human skin.***

→ ***Sponges can provide homes for small crustaceans. In the Pacific waters of the Philippines a decorator crab crawls over a vivid red sponge.***

Reproduction in Sponges

Sponges reproduce both sexually and asexually. Asexual reproduction can occur by budding, but is usually the result of gemmule formation. Gemmules

are packets of cells released from the parent. They can survive for prolonged periods apparently dormant before settling and developing directly into an adult.

When it comes to sexual reproduction, most sponges are nonsimultaneous hermaphrodites, which means that individuals can produce both male and female sex cells, but not at the same time. Clouds of sperm released into the water by functionally male sponges find their way into the spongocoel of females. Here they are taken in by choanocytes in the same way as food particles; but instead of being digested, they are transported by amebocytes to eggs developing in the mesohyl. The eggs are fertilized and then released into the water or brooded. Zygotes that settle on a suitable substratum develop into new sponges.

Reproduction provides sponges with a once-in-a-lifetime opportunity for dispersal. Once settled, most sponges are committed for life. Some aquarium specimens have been observed creeping along the substratum at the almost imperceptible rate of about 0.1 to 0.2 inches (2–4 mm) a day, but they are to all intents and purposes sessile (fixed).

Sponges have colonized almost every available corner of the world's oceans. Relatively few have made the adaptations necessary to survive in fresh water; but one family, the Spongillidae (class Demospongia), has some common freshwater species.

Bath Sponges

Sponges have long been harvested by humans, mostly for use at bath time. The springy protein skeleton of traditional sponges (family Spongidae) is soft enough to be used on delicate skin, and the intricate structure that once supported the complex system of channels and chambers makes it very absorbent but easy to squeeze dry. Most bath sponges are now manufactured from synthetic materials, but the genuine article remains popular and often sells at a premium price. Large sponge fisheries still exist in the Mediterranean, the Caribbean, and the Gulf of Mexico.

Reef Builders and Borers

One group of sponges that is less abundant now than in the past is the coralline sponges (belonging to the sublass Sclerospongiae within the class Demospongia). Instead of a fine lattice of spicules, they secrete a hard calcium carbonate skeleton. In the Devonian period 370 million years ago the earth's atmosphere contained about 12 times as much carbon dioxide as it does today. The sponges of the day were able to use some of it to create massive reef systems similar to those built by modern corals. Sponge reefs today are more likely to be built by glass sponges. They are rather rare and grow slowly—for example, the sponge reefs off British Columbia, Canada, are at least 9,000 years old.

Another group of sponges is more likely to be involved in dismantling reefs than building them. Several species belonging to the family Clionidae are able to bore into reefs (and other carbonate substrates such as large mollusk shells) by secreting chemicals that etch away the underlying minerals. Over a prolonged period the sponge sinks into its own custom-made pit in the substratum.

⊖ ***In Bali a functionally male barrel sponge,* Xestospongia testudinaria, *releases sperm into the water. They will be taken up by a female to fertilize her eggs.***

⊖ ***In the waters of the Caribbean a yellow tube sponge lives alongside brain coral, adding to the structural diversity as well as to the color of the reef.***

Jellyfish

Scyphozoa and Cubozoa

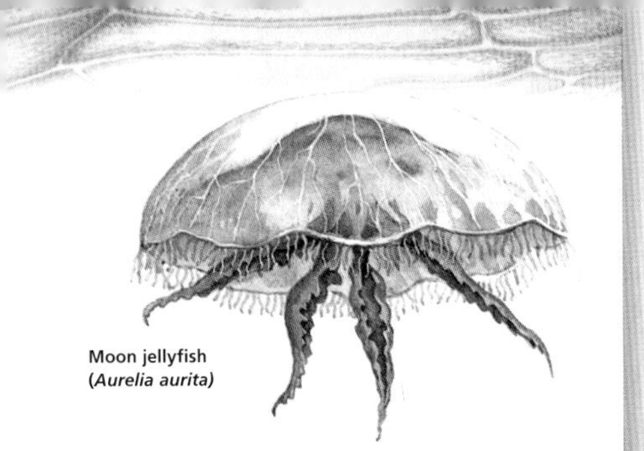

Moon jellyfish
(*Aurelia aurita*)

Common name Jellyfish (sea jellies)

Class Scyphozoa and Cubozoa

Phylum Cnidaria

Number of species About 200

Size Mature medusae measure 0.5 in (13 mm) to 6.5 ft (2 m) in diameter

Key features In most species the predominant form is a saucer-, bell-, or helmet-shaped medusa with fringe of tentacles around the edge or elaborate arms trailing from mouth in center of underside

Habits Most swim freely in open seas by means of pulsating bell; may migrate vertically to feed in shallower water at night

Breeding Medusae shed gametes via mouth; fertilization takes place in the water; embryos develop via 2 larval stages: The swimming planula larva develops into fixed polyplike scyphistoma larva, from which miniature medusae are produced asexually

Diet A wide variety of invertebrate prey and some fish killed by stinging cells on tentacles or oral arms

Habitat Marine, mostly open seas, occasionally bottom dwellers

Distribution Worldwide

↑ *The adult medusa of the moon jellyfish,* Aurelia aurita. *The moon jellyfish has global distribution and can survive a wide range of sea temperatures. Its sting causes an itchy rash. Diameter 10 inches (25 cm).*

An accidental encounter with a jellyfish while swimming in the sea can be an unpleasant, even life-threatening, experience. Yet these ancient creatures have a mysterious charm of their own.

↑ *The lion's mane jellyfish,* Cyanea capillata, *is one of the largest species of scyphozoan, readily exceeding 6 feet (1.8 m) in diameter. The largest specimens are found in the Arctic Ocean.*

WITH THEIR ELEGANT MOVEMENTS and translucent bell-shaped body fringed with frills and fine tentacles, jellyfish, or sea jellies, are undoubtedly among the most graceful and beautiful animals in the sea. But like the Sirens of Greek mythology, these ethereal creatures are also potentially deadly, and concern over their venomous stings colors our opinion of the whole group to such an extent that they rarely get the admiration they deserve. In fact, only about one-third of the 200 or so known jellyfish species are harmful to humans, and many of these "stingers" cause little more than an irritating rash.

Turned to Stone

Being entirely soft bodied, jellyfish tend to decompose quickly when they die, and their remains are so easily obliterated that fossils only form under very special circumstances. The chances of these unusual fossils ever coming to light are even more remote—most will remain hidden forever in the rocks beneath our feet. Every once in a while, however, paleontologists

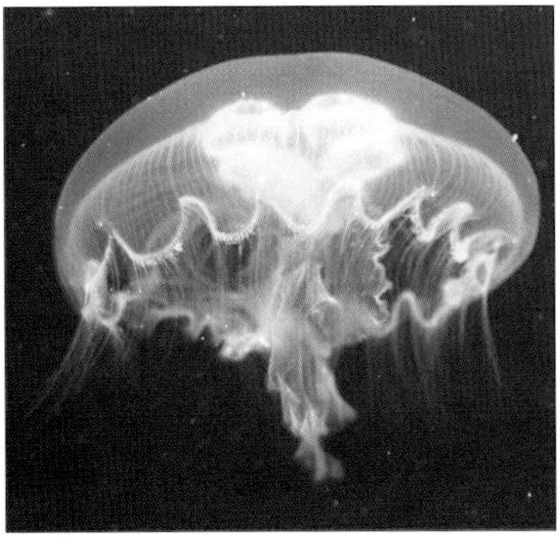

← *The moon jellyfish,* Aurelia aurita, *snares food in its fine tentacles. Its venom is not dangerous to humans, but is fatal to small planktonic organisms such as copepods and protozoans.*

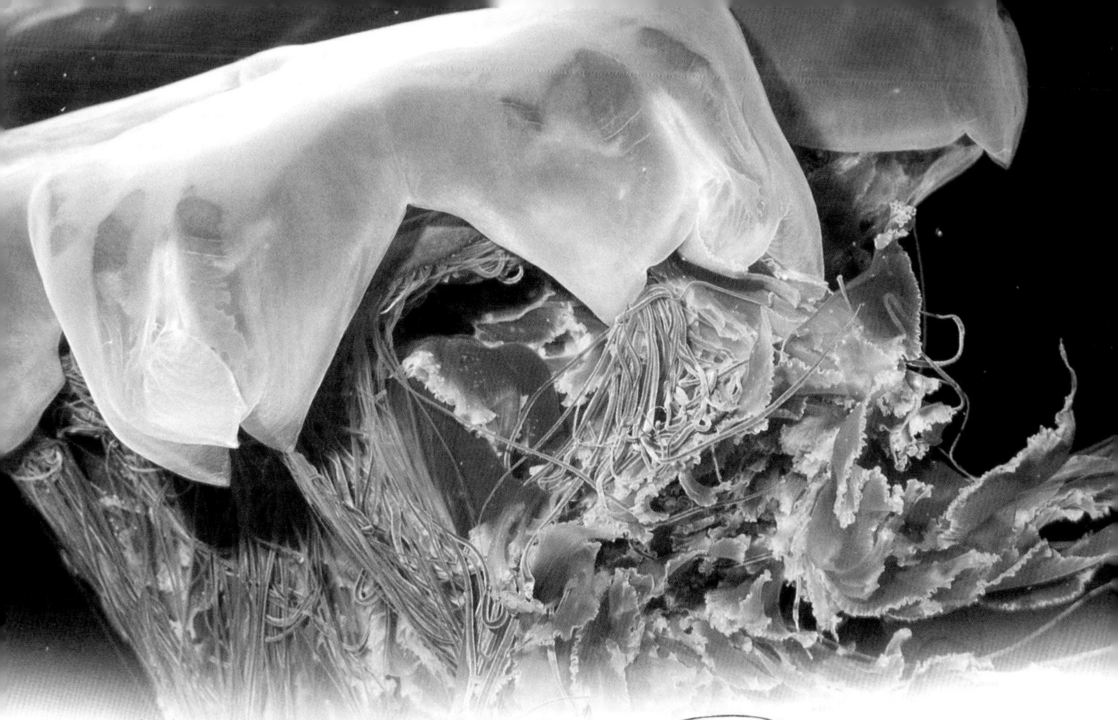

are presented with a treasure trove of fossil evidence. One such source was discovered in a limestone quarry at Solhofen in the mountainous German province of Bavaria. The rocks here date from the late Jurassic period, about 150 million years ago, and they contain exquisitely detailed jellyfish fossils in which even fine tentacles and internal structures such as gonads and gastric pouches can clearly be seen.

Less perfect fossils still recognizable as jellyfish are found in some of the oldest rocks on earth, dating back as far as the late Precambrian era, 550 million years ago. By adopting a simple but effective body plan, this much maligned group of animals has already survived twice as long as the class Mammalia and about 300 times longer than humankind.

Jellyfish Structure

In most jellyfish species the predominant stage in the life cycle is the free-swimming "medusa." It can be anything from 0.5 inches (13 mm) to 6.5 feet (2 m) in diameter—in the case of the magnificent lion's mane jellyfish, *Cyanea capillata*. The shape of the bell varies from a shallow saucer as in the moon jellyfish, *Aurelia aurita*, to the highly domed helmet characteristic of the cannonball jelly, *Stromolophus melagris*. The overall structure, however, is similar in all species. Most medusae exhibit clear four- or eight-fold symmetry, reflected in the number and arrangement of organs, including tentacles, oral arms, and reproductive, digestive, and sensory structures. The edge of the bell is frequently scalloped, with lobes (known as lappets) always numbering some multiple of four. Nowhere is this symmetry more obvious than in the cubozoan or box jellyfish, in which the bell has four distinct sides. Until quite recently the cubozoans were regarded as a subgroup of the Scyphozoa. But differences in their life cycle and

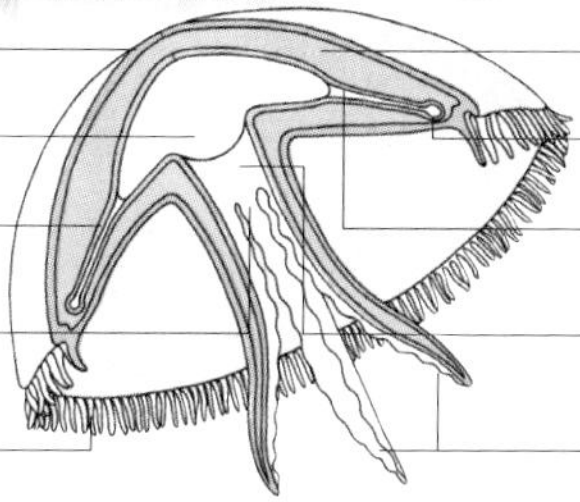

This diagram of the medusa stage of a jellyfish clearly shows the dome-shaped bell and the masses of tentacles arranged in a fringe around it.

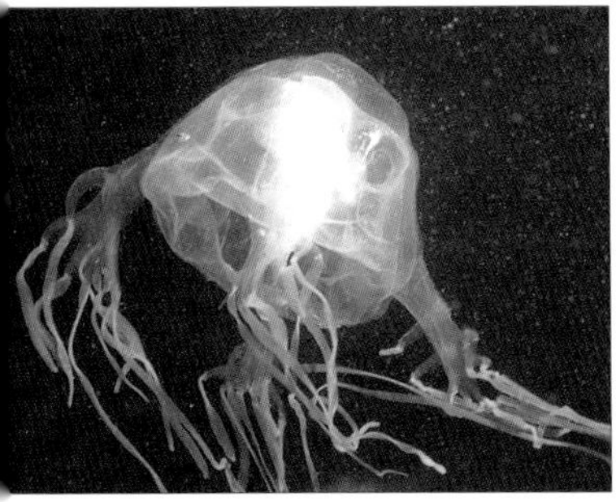

↑ ***An Australian box jellyfish (or sea wasp),* Chironex fleckeri, *devours a fish, which can just be seen inside the bell. This jellyfish is one of the deadliest animals in the world—its sting can kill a human in 20 minutes.***

the structure of the scyphistomal larval stage and medusa mean that they are now recognized as a separate class.

In most scyphozoan species there may be anything up to several hundred tentacles fringing the bell. In the moon jelly they are little more than a short fringe less than 1 inch (2.5 cm) long. In a large specimen of the Artic jelly, *Cyanea arctica*, the tentacles can trail an astounding 230 feet (70 m). Members of the order Rhizostoma lack peripheral tentacles. Instead, they develop an elaborate set of oral arms with several mouthlike openings though which food can be ingested.

Jellyfish have no brain and no centralized nervous system. However, they do have rudimentary sense organs. They include gravity sensors called statocycsts, chemosensory pits for "tasting" the water, and small eyespots that allow them to tell light from dark. In some cubozoans the eyes can be quite well developed, allowing the animal to determine the direction of a source of light and orient itself accordingly. In most jellyfish these sensory structures are located on small, club-shaped organs called rhopalia that are distributed

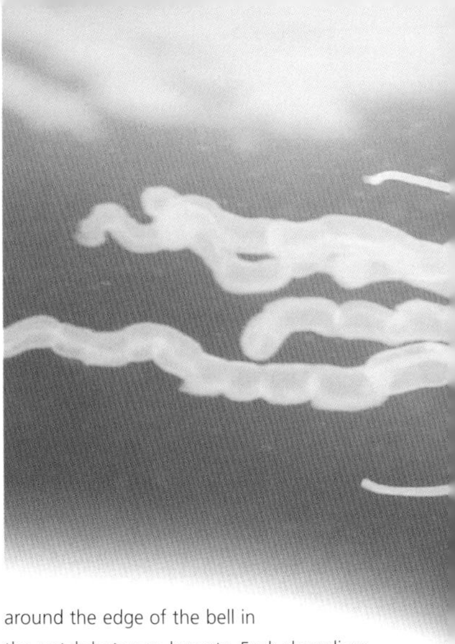

around the edge of the bell in the notch between lappets. Each rhopalium also contains a concentration of nerve cells that in all but cubozoans and the Coronatae help coordinate swimming movements.

Jellyfish Jelly

The "jelly" that gives the jellyfish their name is a clear, gelatinous substance called mesoglea (meaning "middle glue.") It fills the place between the inner and outer walls of the animal's body—the endoderm and the ectoderm. The mesoglea is very elastic thanks to a matrix of stretchy collagen fibers. Unlike the mesoglea of hydrozoans, the "stuffing" of jellyfish contains some living cells. These so-called amebocytes originate in the ectoderm and migrate into the jelly matrix. The mesoglea of jellyfish is so similar to that of other cnidarians that living amebocytes from various species of sea anemone transplanted into jellyfish jelly will attach and migrate into it as normal.

Although mesoglea appears simple, cold, and colorless, it is not as inert as it may seem. In some jellyfish species it has been shown to actively accumulate and store or expel certain heavy chemical compounds in order to maintain buoyancy.

How Jellyfish Swim

Swimming in jellyfish is brought about by a circlet of musclelike fibers running around the underside, close to the edge of the bell. When the muscle band contracts, the bell closes in on itself, and an amount of water is expelled, generating propulsion. Swimming is most efficient in species with a deep bell and especially in the box jellyfish, which have a membrane called the velarium (similar to the velum of hydrozoans) that partially blocks the opening to the underside. Water is therefore ejected much more forcefully, allowing the animal to show real speed.

Jellyfish live in all the oceans of the world from the equator to the polar seas and from shallow coastal waters to great depths. One of the commonest species, the moon jellyfish, has a global distribution and can survive sea temperatures ranging from 21 to 86°F (-6 to 30°C). Most jellyfish are wholly marine, but several tolerate the reduced salinity of estuaries. The sea nettle, *Chrysaora quinquecirrha*, thrives in water about one-third as salty as the sea and sometimes forms huge swarms that cause problems to local fisheries and wildlife.

Ⓣ *Jellyfish swim by contracting the muscle fibers around the bell, creating propulsion. The most efficient swimmers are therefore species with a deep bell.*

Ⓓ *The upside-down jellyfish,* Cassiopeia frondosa, *in the seas off Dominica in the West Indies.*

Sea nettles are just one of several species that sometimes occur in plague numbers. Jellyfish are not naturally gregarious—large swarms are usually brought together by good feeding conditions and converging currents rather than any desire for company.

Swimmers and Settlers

The majority of jellyfish species are pelagic, meaning that they swim in midwater. However, there is one group, members of the order Stauromedusae, that forsakes the free-swimming lifestyle in favor of a more permanent arrangement, living attached to the substrate by an elongated stalk that develops from the upper surface of the bell.

Another exception to the pelagic rule are the upside-down jellyfish, *Cassiopeia* species, which, as their common name suggests, live upside down on the seabed in relatively shallow water. The mouth and oral tentacles face upward and collect some food particles, but a large part of the animal's nutritional needs is met by colonies of algae, mostly dinoflagellates, living within the jellyfish's own tissues. Excess carbohydrates and other nutrients produced by the algae help sustain their host.

Few other jellyfish have such a passive approach to feeding as *Cassiopeia*. For the most part they are active, well-armed predators. In most species prey is snared by the long trailing tentacles and stung when it comes into contact with stinging cells (cnidocytes). Usually they are concentrated in the oral arms around the mouth. Inside, the pharynx and stomach are lined with yet more stinging cells and numerous gland cells that secrete enzymes. The enzymes begin the process of digestion as soon as the prey is ingested.

In so-called septate species the pharynx opens out onto four chambers called gastric pouches separated by partitions known as septa. The pouches are connected to each other by small side openings and by the network of radial canals that carry water, nutrients, and respiratory gases out toward the ring canal at the edge of the bell. Members of the order Semaeostoma have just one central stomach but no pouches or septa.

Reproduction

Most jellyfish have separate sexes, and eggs and sperm are produced in gonads located in the lining of the central stomach or gastric pouches. Ripe eggs are shed first into the stomach, then passed out through the mouth to be fertilized by sperm released by male medusae close by. The resulting embryo develops into a tiny larva called the planula. Most species are prolific breeders. For example, a 4-inch (10-cm) diameter Atlantic sea nettle, *Chrysaora quinquecirrha*, is capable of producing over 40,000 eggs a day.

To give their larvae a slightly better chance of survival, many jellyfish shelter their offspring among their oral tentacles. Some pelagic species, including the lion's mane jellyfish, *Cyanea capillata*, take brooding behavior yet a

step further and allow their larvae to develop into polyps (scyphistomae) while still attached to the parent.

Second Stage

Jellyfish medusae are fascinating animals, but they are only half the story. Most jellyfish species have a much less conspicuous phase—the asexually reproducing polyplike stage called the scyphistoma. Scyphistomae look something like small hydras or miniature anemones. They form in two ways: either by budding from other scyphistomae or developing from planula larvae, which are the result of sexual reproduction by mature medusae.

Scyphistoma larvae can live anything from one to several years depending on species. At certain times of year they begin producing miniature medusae in a process called strobilation. This is another form of asexual reproduction. Instead of budding a smaller version of itself from one side, the scyphistoma splits across the middle; and the top part, bearing a mouth and tiny tentacles, becomes a tiny jellyfish medusa. These "minimedusae," known as ephyra larvae, may be produced and shed one at a time, or the scyphistoma may undergo several splits within a short period of time, resulting in a stack of would-be medusae that are released altogether. Once free of their parent, the ephyra larvae then grow into sexually mature medusae, a process that can take anything up to two years.

The scyphistoma larva of a freshwater jellyfish devours another species of jellyfish in a lake in Borneo.

Jellyfish and Humans

Large groups of jellyfish can create a problem for fishermen by clogging their nets. They are even more unpopular when they turn up close to shore around bathing beaches. There have been numerous attempts in different parts of the world to control jellyfish and create safe, pleasant bathing conditions, but few have met with great success. Nets strung across the approach to beaches work for a while but soon become clogged, and often the jellyfish break up or shed tentacles that get through and still cause unpleasant stings.

In places where stinging jellyfish are common prominent signs usually warn of the danger at certain times of year and offer advice on how to treat stings. The arrival of swarms is often governed by the tides and is therefore predictable. For example, in Hawaii the potentially dangerous cubozoan *Carybdea alata* turns up on wind-sheltered shores between eight and 10 days after a full moon.

The sea nettle species* Chrysaora fuscescens *moves with grace, but its venomous trailing tentacles cause a painful rash in humans and are fatal to fish.

Just When You Thought It Was Safe!

The tropical beaches of Australia's northeastern coast look like paradise for bathers, but from November to April every year they are strangely empty. This is jellyfish season, when swarms of Australian box jellyfish, *Chironex fleckeri*, gather offshore. This cubozoan species is one of the deadliest animals on earth. A moderate sting can kill a human in a matter of minutes, and a lone swimmer has virtually no chance of survival. Most fatalities are by respiratory failure or drowning because toxins from the sting paralyze the lungs and other parts of the body. Even if the victim is helped to shore, he or she is unlikely to survive more than 20 minutes without receiving medical attention, including the administering of an antivenom. Box jellyfish have caused at least 70 fatalities in Australia, and it is only thanks to intensive public information campaigns that the death toll is not much higher.

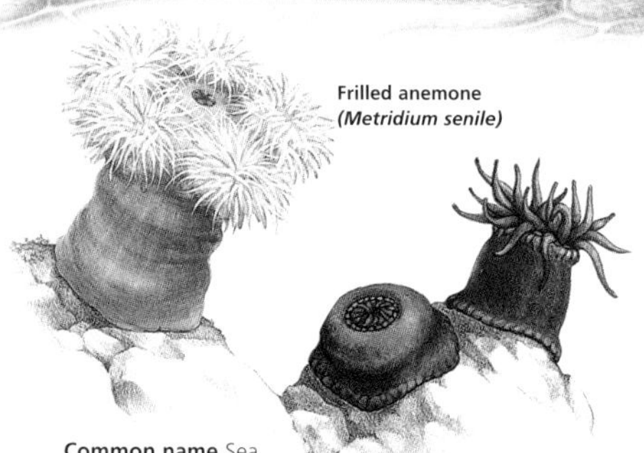

Common name	Sea anemones
Order	Actinaria
Class	Anthozoa (part)
Phylum	Cnidaria
Number of species	About 1,000
Size	Up to 40 in (100 cm) in diameter
Key features	Solitary polyps with predominantly 6-fold symmetry; often very colorful
Habits	Mostly slow moving with long periods attached to a single spot; may creep, climb, burrow, or swim; solitary
Breeding	Sexual reproduction results in planula larva that settles and metamorphoses into miniature polyp; most species also reproduce asexually by binary fission or regeneration from small fragments of tissue
Diet	Various invertebrate prey, occasionally snare fish with stinging tentacles; many species receive proportion of nutritional requirements from symbiotic algae
Habitat	Marine, from coastal zones to deep oceans
Distribution	In all oceans and adjoining seas worldwide

⇧ **Metridium senile,** ***the frilled anemone, is found from the Arctic to southern California. Large specimens can have 1,000 tentacles. Height up to 18 inches (46 cm).*** **Actinia equina,** ***the beadlet anemone, is from the Atlantic and Mediterranean. It is the most common anemone found on northern European rocky shores. Height about 3 inches (7 cm).***

Sea Anemones

Actinaria

Sea anemones look more like exotic underwater plants than real animals. However, these graceful-looking creatures hunt and kill prey, move, and communicate. They are very definitely animals!

THE WORD ANEMONE MEANS "wind flower." It was first used in biology to describe a certain kind of plant whose delicate buttercuplike flower heads dance on slender stems even in a very light breeze. The sea anemones that live in seas and oceans around the world are equally decorative. They come in a kaleidoscopic range of colors—red and green, orange and purple, or pink and white—and their tentacles wave in the water as though riffled by the wind.

However, there is one major difference between sea anemones and their terrestrial namesakes: Sea anemones are not plants but animals. They are surprisingly animated, able to move independently, to hunt and kill prey including fast-moving fish, and to defend themselves from attack by other animals, not least other anemones.

⇩ **Tealia lofotensis** ***on the seafloor in the Canadian Pacific. Although anemones spend most of their time attached to the substrate, they do move from time to time.***

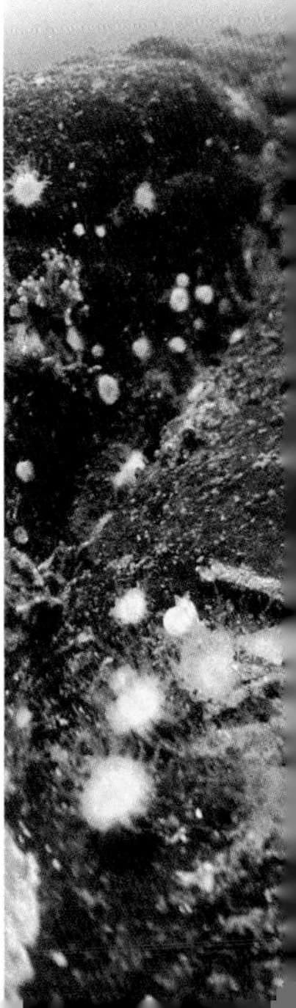

"Flower" Animals

Anemones belong to the same class of cnidarians as corals, namely, the Anthozoa, or "flower animals." However, unlike corals, anemones are not colonial. Each individual lives independently, and most are quite small. Some would fit comfortably in a thimble, others in a coffee cup, while a few would fill a gallon pail. The world's largest species belong to the Australian genus *Stichodactyla* and the northwestern Pacific *Tealia*, both of which can grow 40 inches (100 cm) across.

Like all cnidarians, anemones have a long history. Animals very similar to modern anemones were probably among the earliest multicellular life forms to take shape in the late Precambrian era over 540 million years ago, and they have probably changed very little since. Proving this is difficult, however, since anemones do not fossilize under normal circumstances.

Anemone polyps have many tentacles. The total is usually some multiple of six, reflecting an overall six-fold body symmetry. Some species have adhesive growths called papillae on the trunk, which they use to decorate themselves with shell fragments or gravel for camouflage.

Anemones have no supportive hard skeleton and rely on muscles and water pressure to maintain their body posture. The main body cavity is full of seawater, which goes in and out as required through grooves called siphonoglyphs on either side of the mouth. The main cavity is usually divided into six connected chambers by vertical tissue partitions called mesenteries.

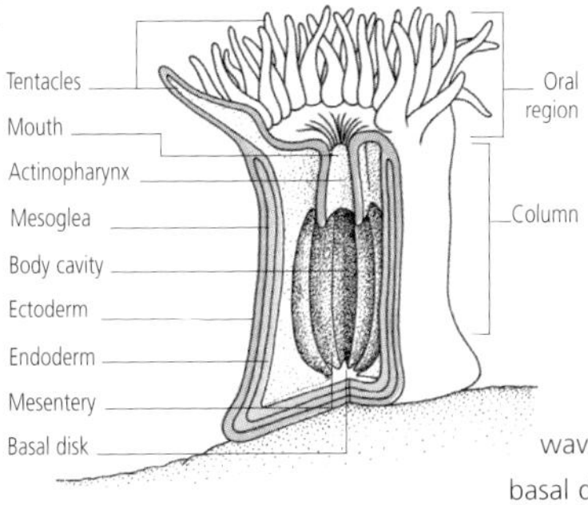

Body structure of a sea anemone. The main body cavity is divided into six connected chambers, reflecting the six-fold body symmetry.

Creeping and Looping

Anemones spend most of their adult lives attached firmly to the seabed or some other object by a specialized basal disk, but they are not rooted to the spot in the same way as truly sessile animals such as barnacles or keelworms.

Anemones can and do move around from time to time, and they achieve these movements in a variety of ways. Some remain upright and creep along, propelled by wavelike contractions of muscles on their basal disk. Others topple sideways, attach their sticky tentacles to the substratum, release the basal disk, and pull themselves forward. By alternately attaching and detaching their disk and tentacles, they achieve a looping movement like that of a leech or caterpillar.

Some anemone species can even swim short distances, using vigorous strokes of their tentacles or by thrashing the whole body from side to side. This is a good way of getting out of trouble fast.

Anemone tissues are nutritious, especially the fat- and protein-rich gonads. Being slow

The fireworks anemone, **Pachycerianthus multiplicatus,** ***off Connemara, Ireland, its tentacles bent in a strong water current.***

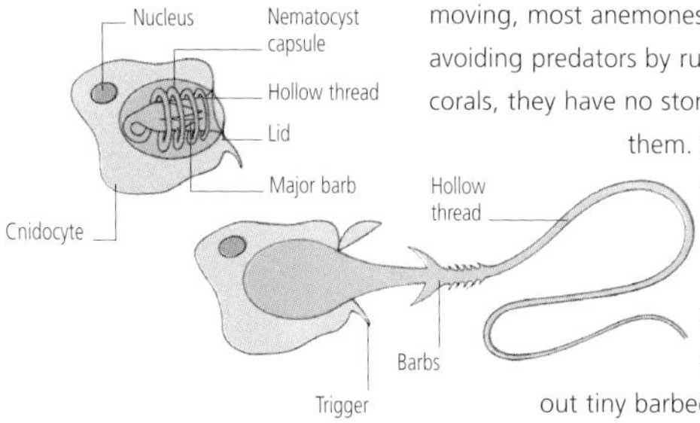

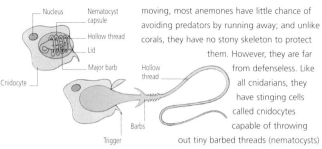

The stinging cell (cnidocyte) of a sea anemone before discharge of the nematocyst (above) and after the stinging thread has been expelled.

moving, most anemones have little chance of avoiding predators by running away; and unlike corals, they have no stony skeleton to protect them. However, they are far from defenseless. Like all cnidarians, they have stinging cells called cnidocytes capable of throwing out tiny barbed threads (nematocysts) that catch in the skin of prey or unwanted visitors and deliver toxins into the flesh.

Poison Threads

Anemones produce several different kinds of toxin. There are neurotoxins that disable prey by inhibiting the nerves that control muscles, and proteins called cytolysins that eat into tissues, rupturing cells and destroying their contents. Such substances can kill a small animal and cause severe pain in larger ones, including humans. Very occasionally a sting can lead to liver damage or renal failure; but such complications are rare, and sea anemones are not generally regarded as dangerous animals.

Two other kinds of thread-producing capsules—ptychocysts and spirocysts—occur in

***Alicia mirabilis** lives in the Mediterranean Sea. This rather rare anemone with stinging tentacles only comes out at night.*

Burrowing Anemones

Anemones are less common in soft sediments such as mud or sand, but various species have adapted to such conditions in different ways. Some seek out hard objects on which to attach themselves, while others use a broad basal disk to gather up a ball of sediment that acts as an anchor. Several species, including the Pacific *Pachycerianthus fimbriatus*, opt to live partially buried in the substratum. Most burrowing anemones are rather long and thin, and cannot stand up straight unless they are supported by a burrow. The basal disk is modified into a bulbous knob, called the physa. The anemone uses rhythmic muscular contractions to alternately expand and contract the knobby base, thereby loosening the sediment bit by bit and sinking into the seabed.

Fighting for Space

Despite their gentle appearance, sea anemones are far from passive organisms. In fact, they are highly aggressive. Encounters between neighboring animals are rarely friendly, since individuals are usually in direct competition for precious resources such as food, daylight, and living space.

Neighboring animals sense one another's presence by "tasting" chemicals in the water and will reach out with tentacles to touch one another. Sometimes they appear to tussle quite violently until one backs down. Such territorial disputes appear to happen between anemones both within the same species and of different species.

Ⓣ ***A beadlet anemone,*** Actinia equina ***(right), attacks another anemone. Surprisingly, anemones are highly aggressive creatures.***

some specialized species. Ptychocysts form a dense tangle of threads around the body, protecting the animals from attack or creating a burrow lining in species that live in soft sediment. Spirocysts produce long, sticky threads that help the anemone cling to fast-moving prey or enable it to get a grip on rocks when climbing.

Feeding Apparatus

Most anemones are not fussy eaters. They will eat almost anything of suitable size that comes within reach of their tentacles. A number of species specialize in collecting microscopic organisms such as protozoa and algae. These tiny organisms are trapped in a layer of sticky mucus covering the anemone's body. They are then carried to the tips of the tentacles by the beating of thousands of tiny cilia covering the tentacles. The tentacles bend toward the mouth and allow the food to drop right in. This was probably the method used by the earliest anemones—primitive species have cilia all over their body so that food can be collected from wherever it first makes contact.

Large anemones use their tentacles to more deadly effect, snaring, stinging, and transporting a wide variety of larger prey, including crustaceans, worms, and even fish. Carrion and fragments of organic material drifting down from above are just as acceptable. The slightest touch from a passing prey animal triggers the nematocysts to fire their tiny toxic threads into the victim, which is paralyzed in seconds and bundled toward the mouth. The mouth is pulled open by special retractor muscles to accept the meal.

Digestive enzymes break down the body of the prey into a nutrient-rich soup that can be easily absorbed. Any indigestible material is pushed back out through the mouth.

Following a large meal, the tentacles become temporarily desensitized and may not respond when touched. Very hungry anemones, however, are hypersensitive to touch and will swallow just about anything—even shells and pebbles. It takes a very long time for a sea anemone to starve. Their low-energy lifestyle means they can sit out long periods of food shortage, shrinking gradually as they begin to metabolize their own tissues to survive.

Anemone Habitat

Anemones live in all kinds of marine habitats, but they are most diverse and abundant in shallow waters of the tropics. Most coastal species can tolerate short periods of exposure to the air when the tide is low. They tend to settle in crevices or under overhangs where they are shaded from direct sunlight.

The body of an exposed anemone looks like a rubbery blob closed by a ring of muscle at the top like a drawstring bag. Seawater trapped inside the body helps stave off dehydration and overheating.

Phlyctenanthus australis ***feeds on a prawn. The flexible body of the anemone will expand to accept even large prey like this.***

Anemones in Partnership

Not all interaction between anemones and other species is predatory or aggressive. Many species also cultivate cooperative relationships with other organisms that benefit both partners. Several species of hermit crab seek out anemones and encourage them to attach to the shell in which they live. The anemone provides an additional level of defense for the crab against predators. In return, it receives morsels of food dropped by the crab as it eats. Boxer crabs (genus *Lybia*) carry a stinging anemone in their front claws and brandish it at any other animal they perceive to be a threat.

A Calliactis parasitica ***sea anemone, tentacles retracted, hitches a ride on the snail shell being used by a hermit crab.***

Like corals, most sea anemones play host to colonies of single-celled algae known as zooxanthellae. Like all plants, zooxanthellae produce carbohydrates to live on using energy from sunlight. Some of it is allowed to leak from the cells and provides an extra source of carbohydrate to the anemone host. In some tropical anemones the zooxanthellae are contained in special "pseudotentacles" around the top of the trunk. They are extended during the day, exposing the algae to as much sunlight as possible to aid photosynthesis.

Anemones are attacked by some predators: Certain fish nibble off tentacles, and several sea slugs are apparently immune to the stings. However, in most cases the damaged anemone manages to regenerate lost parts. The process is so effective that a whole body can be regrown from a very small piece of tissue. In fact, this process forms the basis for the commonest method of reproduction. Anemones can reproduce themselves exactly either by splitting

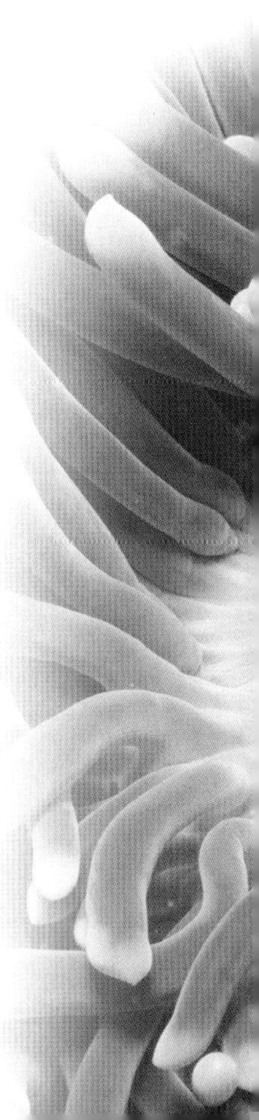

down the middle to create two individuals or by shedding tiny fragments of the basal disk, which then develop into new animals.

When it comes to sexual reproduction, most anemones are protandrous hermaphrodites, meaning individuals begin adult life as functional males producing sperm then switch later on to become egg-producing females. Fertilization is external in most species, and embryos develop into feeding, swimming larvae called planulae. After a few days or weeks the larva becomes a minute adult. In brooding species fertilization and early development take place inside the body cavity of the parent or in brood pouches. Anemones are slow growing—some individuals may be 70 or 80 years old.

Bring in the Clowns

One of the best-known mutualistic relationships is that between sea anemones and clownfish (genus *Amphiprion*). The fish hides amid the anemone's tentacles, safe from most predators. It avoids being stung itself by secreting a slime that lacks the chemical cues the anemone uses to detect other animals. The clownfish is highly territorial and will fiercely defend its anemone from other animals that might try to eat it. It may also share food with its host. The relationship is extremely effective. If a fish is separated from its anemone, both will be attacked and killed within a day or two.

A false clownfish hides among the tentacles of a magnificent sea anemone,* Heteractis magnifica*, in the seas off Papua New Guinea. A single large anemone may be home to several kinds of fish as well as small shrimps and crabs.

Corals

Anthozoa

Coral reefs are among the most diverse natural environments in the world, with many marine species finding a home within the coral's chalklike skeleton. However, the reefs face many environmental threats.

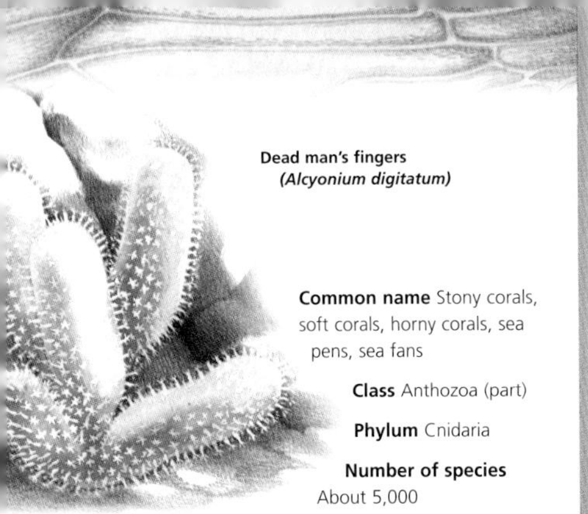

Dead man's fingers *(Alcyonium digitatum)*

Common name Stony corals, soft corals, horny corals, sea pens, sea fans

Class Anthozoa (part)

Phylum Cnidaria

Number of species About 5,000

Size Solitary forms up to 20 in (50 cm) in diameter; polyps of colonial forms usually less than 0.2 in (5 mm) in diameter; colonies up to several feet across, entire reefs can extend for miles

Key features Mostly colonial polyps, either soft bodied or overlying a stony skeleton of secreted calcium carbonate; colony may be encrusting or erect, making antler, feather, fan, plate, slipper, or boulder shape; colors include vibrant shades of red, purple, orange, green, and blue or brown and black

Habits Sessile (attached by the substratum); colonial, but compete aggressively for growing space

Breeding Colonies grow by asexual budding; sexual reproduction involves simultaneous shedding of gametes into the water; fertilization leads to development of free-swimming planula larvae that disperse and settle to found new colonies elsewhere

Diet Reef-building (hermatypic) corals gain most of their nutrients from symbiotic algae living inside each polyp; other food, mainly plankton and bacteria, is captured from water by tentacles

Habitat Marine, mostly shallow tropical seas; some specialized corals live in deeper and colder water

Distribution Worldwide, mainly in the tropics

Colonies of the soft coral* Alcyonium digitatum*, or dead man's fingers, can be found around the coasts of Western Europe. Colonies can grow up to 8 inches (20 cm) in height.

CORALS ARE CLOSE COUSINS of the sea anemones, belonging to the same class, the Anthozoa, or "flower animals." Like anemones, their adult form is a polyp, which can reproduce either sexually by releasing gametes (eggs and sperm) to be fertilized in the water or asexually by budding. However, for most corals newly budded individuals do not separate from their parent polyp but remain attached and share a common gastrovascular cavity. This kind of reproduction leads to the development of a coral colony. In the so-called hard or stony corals (order Scleractinia) each polyp in the colony secretes a supporting skeleton of calcium carbonate (limestone). Limestone deposits build gradually; and as the colony spreads, the living tissues withdraw from old skeletal structures, leaving behind a dense lattice of stone. A cross-section through a large colony will show a massive mineral center surrounded by a thin veneer of living polyps.

Wreck fish* (Anthias *species) swim over lettuce coral in the Red Sea, Egypt. The deep crevices between the coral plates create a complex system of channels and holes, within which countless other small animals may hide.

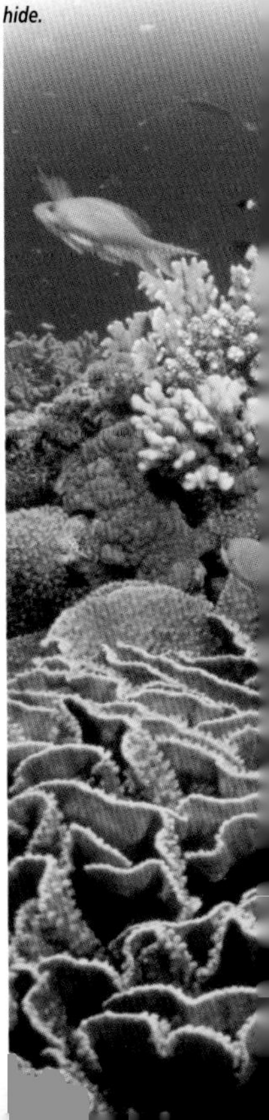

Coral Shapes

Coral colonies possess a wide variety of shapes, often suggestive of other structures. They give rise to various common names—staghorn coral, sea fan, brain coral, plate coral, or lettuce coral. However, the eventual shape of a colony is not entirely predetermined by its genes, and in some species growth can be influenced by environmental conditions. For example, the Australian species *Turbinaria mesenterina* has two growth forms determined by depth. In shallow water, 6 feet (2 m) or less deep, it is a lettuce coral, with a highly complex shape that allows it to grow in a confined space alongside many competitors. In 20 feet (6 m) of water it forms a flat, platelike colony. Because less light

Ⓣ ***Closeup of sunflower or tube coral,* Tubastrea faulkneri. *The tall polyps elevate the feeding tentacles into the water current where they can collect food.***

penetrates deep water, the colonies here attempt to maximize their share of the light by spreading wide. Over a period of years a colony transferred from one environment to another will change the way it grows. The existing skeleton does not change, but new growth will develop an appropriate form.

Not all corals are colonial. Some solitary polyps grow very large and secrete an individual skeleton rivaling some entire colonies in size. Mushroom corals such as *Fungia scutaria* are single polyps with a skeleton that looks like the gills of a large upturned mushroom with the stalk removed. The same corals can also take on an oblong or "slipper" form, with the mouth as an elongated central slit.

The basic structure of a coral polyp is very similar to that of an anemone—a tubelike body fused at the base to the substratum, with an opening at the top (the mouth) surrounded by a ring of tentacles. While anemones and most corals generally conform to six-fold radial symmetry, there are

Ⓓ ***Cross-section of a colonial soft coral polyp. Soft corals protect themselves against predators by forming sharp spicules in the body wall.***

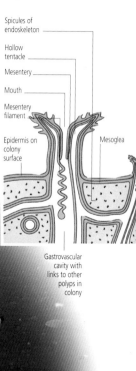

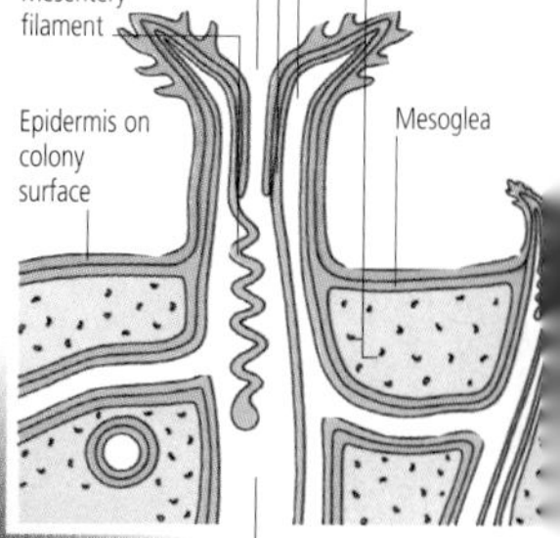

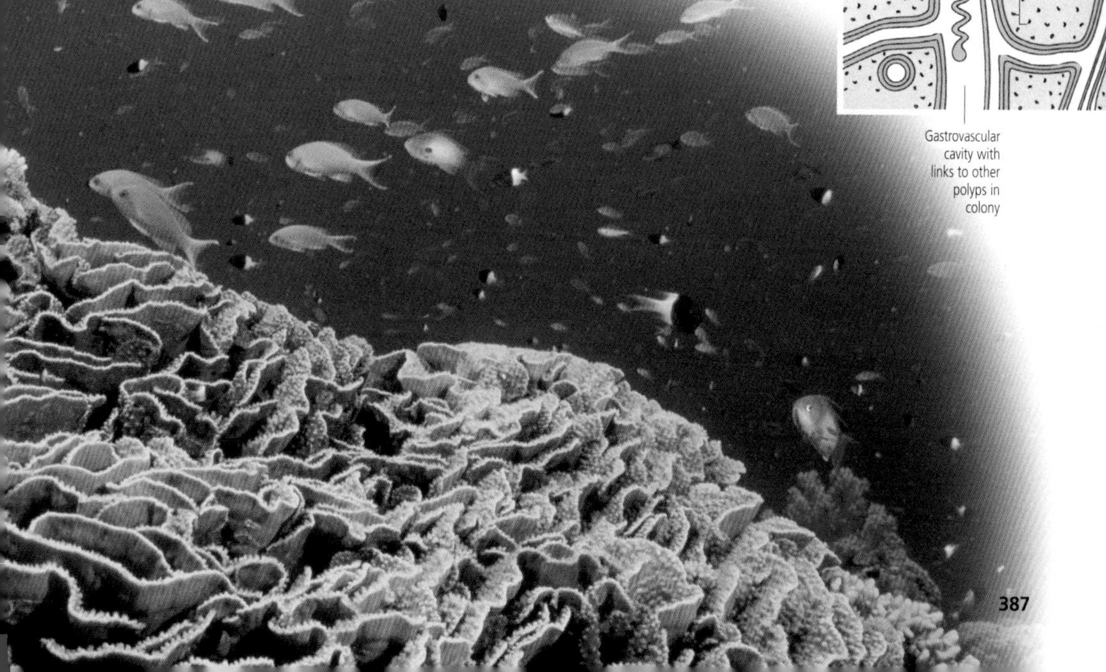

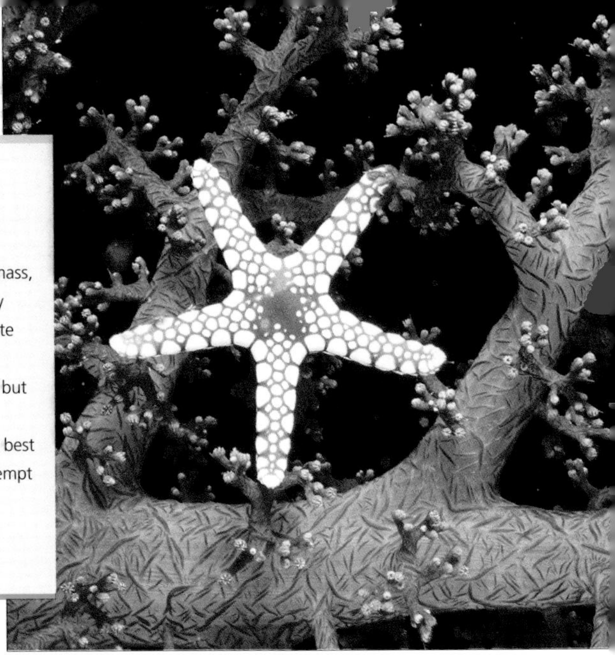

Soft Corals

Soft corals (order Alcyonacea) do not produce a limestone skeleton. Instead, their polyps grow from a rubbery basal mass, sometimes several feet in diameter. Instead of secreting a stony fortress to protect them from predators, some soft corals secrete sharp thornlike spikes called spicules. The majority, including *Sarcophyton* and *Alcyonium* species, have no hard parts at all, but protect themselves from predators by producing chemical deterrents, mostly compounds called terpenes. Terpenes are at best highly distasteful, at worst toxic, and very few animals will attempt to ingest them. Many plants also use the same chemicals to protect against insects and plant-eating animals on land.

several coral orders, known collectively as the octocorals, for which eight is the norm. Eight internal mesenteries (partitions) and eight tentacles surround each polyp mouth.

The tentacles are armed with stinging cnidocytes, few of which are toxic enough to be dangerous to humans, although many will cause an unpleasant rash. The tentacles are generally extended at night, when they trap small plankton organisms and pass them to the mouth. This kind of feeding is particularly important in the few coral species that live in deep water, such as the black coral *Antipathes*. However, for the vast majority it is merely a supplement. Most reef-building corals acquire about 97 percent of their food from symbiotic algae living within the polyps.

A candy cane starfish on an alcyonarian soft coral in the Red Sea, Egypt.

The dependence of most corals on well-lit warm waters means that competition for space in shallow waters of the warm tropics is intense and sometimes violent. Neighboring corals will attack each other by turning out the silky linings of their gut and secreting digestive enzymes that kill off the tissues of rival polyps growing too close.

Diverse Environment

The varied shapes adopted by different species of coral to maximize their share of space and precious sunlight mean that reefs are immensely complex three-dimensional structures with myriad channels, crevices, and secret chambers. The huge surface area of the reef means there is room here for many more times the number of encrusting organisms than can grow on a flat seabed. Some of these organisms, including colonial hydrozoans, coralline algae, and certain sponges, contribute their own limestone skeletons to the reef infrastructure. Coral reefs attract more different animals per unit area than any other environment on earth, with the

A juvenile octopus provides a meal for a **Tubastrea** ***species cup coral in the Red Sea, Egypt.***

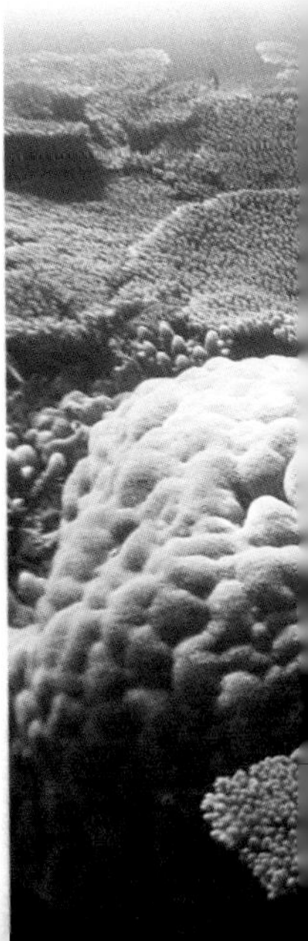

possible exception of some tropical rain forests. Many of them are permanent residents, including worms, mollusks, crustaceans, echinoderms, and fish. Others are occasional visitors, for example, turtles, sharks, and other fish. They are attracted by opportunities to feed or perhaps to enjoy a personal valet at one of the many "cleaning stations" operated by various shrimps and cleaner fish.

Types of Coral Reef

Fringing coral reefs develop in the shallow water close to shore. They are usually quite narrow. Atoll reefs develop around the rim of ancient volcanoes and usually surround a central lagoon, which may in time get silted up and become an island.

Barrier reefs, also known as ribbon reefs, develop offshore and run parallel to the coastline, separated from the shore by a large lagoon, which is usually calm because the reef absorbs most of the energy from waves breaking over it. The Great Barrier Reef in Australia—said to be the world's largest living structure—is in fact a series of about 2,500 smaller reefs. Platform reefs form on shallow patches of ocean and sometimes develop into coral cays (or keys)—small islands made of coral. Shallow reefs are prone to weathering by the effect of waves and to erosion by the actions of feeding fish. The product of erosion is a white coral sand that gradually accumulates to form a low-lying island, which will be colonized by land organsims.

Coral reefs are the only living structures visible from space. And yet each one began as a tiny swimming planula larva that, having drifted for days in the vastness of the ocean,

Perfect Partnership

The relationship between corals and their symbiotic algae, known as zooxanthellae, is not only mutually beneficial—it is crucial to the survival of both partners. The algae are dinoflagellates of the phylum Sarcomastigophora. They are provided with safe growing space inside the coral colony. In return for such hospitality the corals reap a regular harvest of sugars, which the dinoflagellates produce by photosynthesis.

Corals take in single dinoflagellates while they are still larvae or soon after they settle and metamorphose into a polyp. The dinoflagellate cells are incorporated into the lining of the coral's gastrovascular cavity, where they live and reproduce. The host corals ensure that their internal garden of algae gets just the right amount of light that they need by growing in bright shallow waters but producing chemical sunscreens to filter out excessive ultraviolet rays that can be damaging to the algae.

A landscape of the Great Barrier Reef, Australia, shows a selection of diverse coral forms—brain, staghorn, and plate corals all compete for space.

just happened to find a suitable spot in which to settle and found a colony. The planula larva is the product of sexual reproduction, which in most corals is seasonal. Different coral species may have male and female individuals, or they may be hermaphrodite; but fertilization usually takes place in the water and depends on eggs and sperm being released more or less simultaneously by neighboring coral colonies. The synchronized spawning of corals on large reefs is one of the great wonders of the natural world. In order to ensure the best chances of fertilization, coral polyps use reliable celestial cues to time their spawning to the minute. For example, the earth's position in its orbit around the sun determines the correct season, the phases of the moon dictate a particular day, and the turning of the earth on its axis allows the polyps to pinpoint a precise time of day—usually an hour or two after sunset.

Within minutes of the first tiny round egg emerging from a polyp mouth, the reef is engulfed in a snowstorm of eggs and sperm. Usually more than one species is involved—mass spawning creates a glut of food that attracts egg eaters and larger filter feeders, but the sheer quantity produced means that the chances for any one egg are better as part of a mass spawning than if it was released alone.

Enemies of the Reef

Despite their admirable fortifications, corals have a number of enemies. Like any sessile animal, they suffer from being unable to move away from predators or unfavorable conditions. Several animals eat coral, including the notorious crown-of-thorns starfish and a variety of reef fish.

As if these natural threats were not enough, coral reefs are facing a number of man-made challenges. Deforestation on land means that many reef systems are becoming choked with silt. With the forests gone, erosion of the land increases, and large quantities of sediment are washed down rivers and out to sea. Silty, turbid water blocks out the sunlight needed by the coral's symbiotic algae. Reefs suffer physical damage caused by shipping and recreational use. Collisions and careless anchoring break off large chunks of coral, while clumsy snorkelers and scuba divers can easily snap off smaller pieces with their flippers.

Some damage is deliberate. The precious and beautiful pink coral used to produce jewelry and carvings is a species of horny coral called *Corallium*. Its skeleton can be polished to a luxuriant shine. Other corals are sold simply as tourist souvenirs.

Coral Bleaching

One of the more insidious threats to coral reefs is climate change, especially global warming. The most serious effect of increased temperatures is coral bleaching. It is a phenomenon that affects reef-building corals that gain most of their nutrients from symbiotic algae. Consistently high water temperatures (above 86°F or 30°C) actually hinder photosynthesis and cause a harmful oxidation reaction in the algal cells. The dying cells begin to poison their coral host, and so they are expelled from the polyps. Without its algal symbionts the coral becomes very pale (hence the term bleaching). Colonies can recover from mild bleaching events, but prolonged periods of warming such as those predicted by scientists studying global climate change will be fatal to many.

Bleached staghorn coral in the Caribbean Sea shows the effects of global warming.

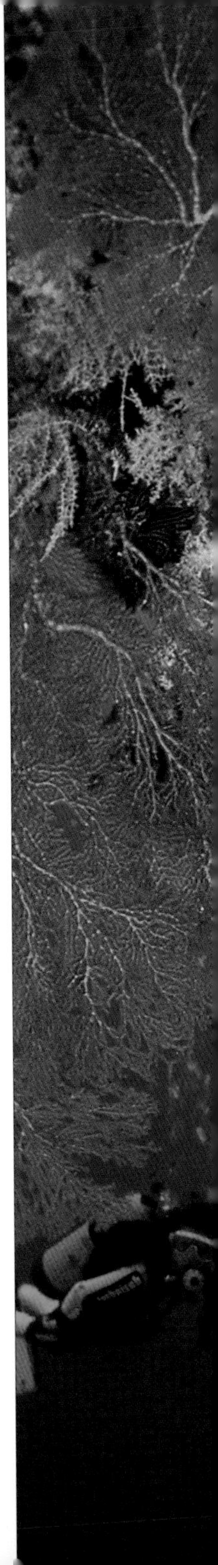

A cave entrance off Papua New Guinea surrounded with many coral species, including sea fans.

Millipedes

Diplopoda

In terms of their body shapes and sizes the millipedes are the most variable of the Myriapoda. They range from long and cylindrical, through medium length and flattened, to short and humped, to name but a few.

Giant millipede (order Spirostreptida)

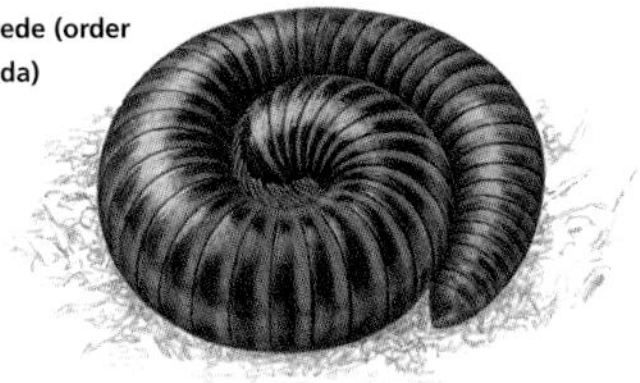

Common name Millipedes

Class Diplopoda

Subphylum Myriapoda

Number of species About 10,000 (2,167 U.S.)

Size From about 0.16 in (4 mm) to 12 in (30 cm)

Key features Head with 1 pair of very short antennae, 1 pair of eyes, and chewing mouthparts; body shape very variable, from long and cylindrical to short and humped or long and flattened; all have many segments with 2 pairs of legs per segment; some species can roll up into a ball when threatened

Breeding Courtship rituals are quite common; some males use sound communication to attract the female; female usually makes some form of nest in which eggs are laid and then left

Diet Plant material, especially that which is dead and decaying

Habitat Forests, grassland, desert and semidesert, mountains, and gardens

Distribution Worldwide, but commoner in tropical regions

↑ A giant millipede, order Spirostreptida, curled up in a defensive coil. The Spirostreptida are subtropical and tropical millipedes. Length 0.5 inches (13 cm) to 11 inches (28 cm).

All the different millipede body forms share a common characteristic: The apparent individual body segments are in fact two segments joined together so that they appear to be one. They are called "diplosegments," and each of them has two pairs of legs, one pair for each segment. The exception is the first segment, which is legless, as are one or more of the segments at the tail end of the body. The body segments vary in their profile according to the order to which the animal belongs. The snake millipedes (orders Julida, Spirobolida, and Spirostreptida) have segments that are almost circular in outline. The pill millipedes—the ones that can roll up into a ball—(orders Glomerida and Sphaerotheriida) have arch-shaped segments flattened on the underside. The flat-backed or plated millipedes (order Polydesmida) have rounded segments, but each has a flat extension on either side that looks rather like an airplane wing.

Hard Exoskeleton

All the orders mentioned so far have the exoskeleton strengthened by the addition of calcium salts, a feature they share with the crustaceans. One order, the bristly millipedes (Polyxenida), are tiny, soft-bodied millipedes that do not have calcium in the exoskeleton.

The head bears a pair of short antennae, which have a right-angled turn in them so that they can be pointed forward and down. The antennae can therefore reach downward to "test" the surface on which the animal is walking. With the exception of the flat-backed millipedes and a few species in other orders, the head bears a pair of "eyes." They are not eyes in the strict sense of the word but a group of

↓ A closeup of the head of one of the larger millipedes showing the rather short antennae and an eye. The eye consists of a number of single units in a neatly arranged group, but it is not a true compound eye.

The two pairs of legs to each segment are clearly visible in the flat-backed millipede, *Pararhacistus potosinus*, climbing a tree in a mountain forest in Mexico.

light-sensitive ocelli situated on either side of the head. The number of ocelli per eye varies from four to 90, depending on the species. Since virtually all millipedes are nocturnal or live beneath leaf litter or in the soil, sight is not really a necessity. The jaws are made up of a pair of cutting mandibles and

The Millipede "Wave"

Millipede legs are similar to those of insects except that they have two extra sections—the prefemur between the trochanter and the femur, and the postfemur between the femur and the tibia. Anyone who has watched closely as a millipede walks will know that the legs appear to move in waves. The legs actually move in pairs, the left- and right-hand legs of the same pair moving together. A split second after one pair of legs has started to move, the pair in front of it begins to move, then the pair in front of that and so on all along the body, each pair of legs being slightly out of phase with the pair in front and the pair behind.

With such a large number of legs on some of the longer millipedes, many movement waves can be seen running along the body at the same time. As in insects, the legs have claws at the tip, allowing them to grip the surface and move vertically or even upside down on rough surfaces such as tree bark or rocks.

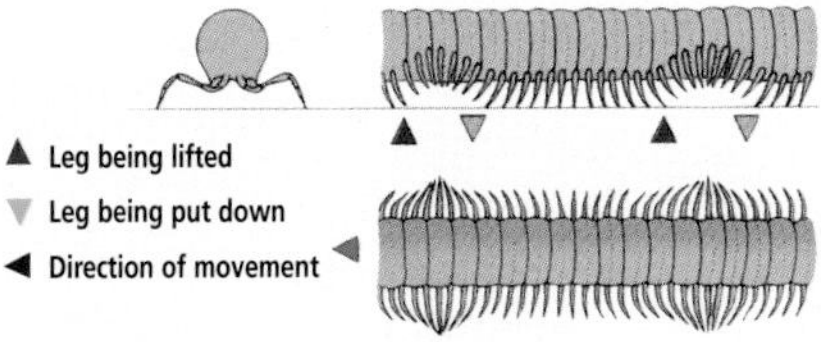

In a typical slow-moving, burrowing cylindrical millipede (order Julida) most of the legs at any one time are in contact with the substrate.

a pair of shredding maxillae that are used to nibble off and chew up the food, mainly decaying vegetable matter.

During the few investigations that have been made into feeding in millipedes, it was found that they seem to prefer plant material that is fairly rich in calcium, which they use to strengthen the exoskeleton. The South American millipede *Myrmecodesmus adisi* feeds on algae on tree trunks. What is unusual about this habit is that for several months of the year these trunks are covered by floodwater, and the millipede is able to live and feed beneath it.

Millipede Life Cycle

Millipedes employ a variety of different strategies to attract a partner, to conduct courtship, and to mate. It is likely that pheromones play quite an important part in bringing together male and female millipedes, and in keeping them together. As the distance between the two sexes decreases, sound becomes an important attractant in some species. Quite a number of males stridulate, for example, by rubbing their legs together.

The stridulatory sound made by some of the large African *Sphaerotherium* species is actually audible to the human ear. Males of the European *Lobogomeris pyrenaica* stridulate while holding onto the female. Stridulation seems quite important in preventing males of the species from attempting to mate with females of *L. rugifera,* which live in the same habitat. If the wrong male does make contact with the wrong female, then his incorrect stridulatory message is immediately recognized by the female, and she coils up and rejects him.

Members of one of the faster-moving millipede species, *Chordeuma silvestre* from Europe, normally rush off at high speed in the opposite direction the moment they encounter one another. So, to keep any female he meets interested in him, the male tremulates by bashing his head against the ground or whatever he is sitting on. Any interested female then approaches him and begins to lick at special glands on his trunk. This releases

pheromones that persuade the female to adopt a position in which mating can take place.

Before they mate, the male has to prepare a spermatophore to pass to the female. He produces it from his reproductive opening, and it is then sent forward to a special pair of legs at the front of his trunk. They are known as the gonopods and are used to insert the spermatophore into the female. Transfer of the spermatophore is normally carried out when courtship has been successful and the couple are head to head, with their undersides in contact with each other. The male of the African giant pill millipede, *Sphaerotherium dorsale*, lacks gonopods. He grips the female tightly, releases the spermatophore from near the rear end of his body, moves it forward from one pair of legs to the next, and then gives it to the female as it reaches her reproductive opening.

↑ *With large numbers of males around looking for mates, there is bound to be some degree of competition for females. Here two giant millipede males,* Epibolus pulchripes, *are competing for the attentions of a single female in Kenya.*

Methods of Sperm Transfer

Some *Glomeris* species males behave even more unusually. The male picks up something in his front legs, usually one of his own droppings, and shapes it with his jaws until it is roughly globular. He then releases the spermatophore onto this "tool," moves it along his legs, and uses it to give his sperm to his mate.

The male of the bristle millipede, *Polyxenus lagurus* from Europe, does not transfer his spermatophore directly to the female. Instead, he makes a zigzag web of his silk over a small hollow on the bark of a tree. He then deposits his sperm onto the web and walks off, drawing two strands of silk out behind him as he goes. They are covered in the male's pheromones and are used by the female to find her way to the sperm he has left for her.

← *A pair of giant millipedes,* Epibolus pulchripes, *with their front ends in close contact as they mate in a Kenyan tropical dry forest. The male is using his gonopods to insert his spermatophore into the female.*

Male millipedes may get more than they bargained for in the pursuit of an unresponsive partner: The females of a number of different species have been observed to direct a squirt of defensive chemicals straight into the face of a male that is being too persistent.

The females usually build a nest under the ground in which to lay their eggs. It is made from their droppings and is shaped using special folds on the end of the body. Females of the order Chordeumatida construct their nests from silk. The number of eggs laid depends on the species as well as the female's size and state of health. Numbers are normally in the hundreds, but up to 2,000 may be laid at one time by some of the large species.

In some species the eggs are laid all in one nest, while in others a smaller number of eggs are placed in separate nests. Rather than covering a whole batch of eggs in a protective nest, the European pill millipede, *Glomeris marginata,* coats each egg individually with the nest-building material. Some of the longer-lived millipedes may lay several egg batches during their life. Others die after laying just one batch.

Extra Legs

Millipede eggs begin to develop as soon as they have been laid irrespective of the time of year. Each of the developmental stages of the millipedes is called a "stadium" (plural stadia), equivalent to the nymphs or larvae of insects. From the egg an immobile pupoid hatches. The pupoid then molts to the first true stadium, which has four diplosegments with three pairs of legs. Behind the leg-bearing segments are two or three segments without legs. This stadium goes through further stages, with the number of diplosegments and pairs of legs increasing each time.

The total number of stadia before the adult stage varies from six to 15. Development in some millipedes is slightly complicated by the fact that despite reaching the full leg count, they are not yet fully mature. They may then go through further molts to maturity without increasing the number of diplosegments.

Beware All Predators

All millipedes are good at defending themselves from attack by predators large and small. The calcium salts present in the exoskeleton make it much tougher. Most of the long-bodied millipedes have the ability to roll up into a spiral so that the more delicate undersides are on the inside, and the tough dorsal plates are on the outside. This is taken to extremes in the pill millipedes: They can roll up into a complete ball so that their whole body is surrounded by a layer of armor plating.

An interesting form of physical defense has been noted in one of the bristly millipedes, *Polyxenus fasciculatus* from North America (indeed it could well apply to the whole order Polyxenida). On the rear end are two tufts of bristles. When the millipede is attacked by ants, it wipes the tufts against the ants' bodies. That causes the bristles—which have hooks at the tips—to lock onto hairs on the ants. The bristles also have barbs along the shaft that interlock with the barbs on other bristles embedded in the ant to form a mass in which the ant gets completely entangled. As the ant struggles to free itself, it gets even more tangled up and eventually reaches the state where it cannot move, and it dies.

Millipedes have a second type of defense that involves the use of chemicals. In most of the body diplosegments they have a pair of stink glands with small openings outside the body. The secretions that they produce vary in nature; but they can have a horrible taste, they can be poisonous or corrosive, or they can even act as a sedative if swallowed. The flat-backed millipedes release the extremely deadly substance hydrogen cyanide. Care should be taken when handling millipedes because the secretions produced by some can irritate the skin and can cause blindness if wiped into the eye. Some jungle tribes have used millipede poison on their arrowheads for hunting.

⊖ *All neatly rolled or rolling up into armored balls is a group of the European pill millipede,* Glomeris marginata. *They are in a defensive pose.*

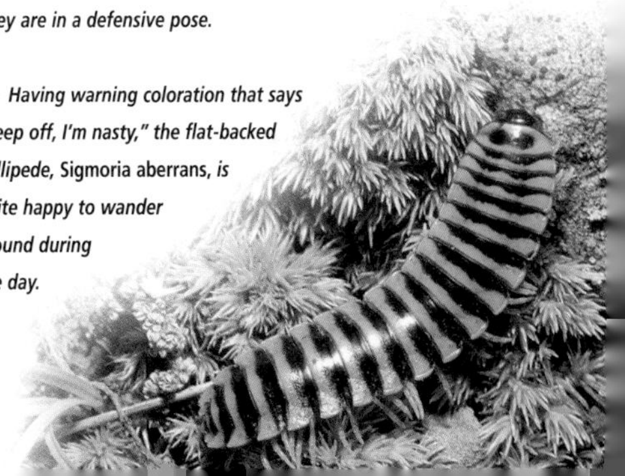

⊕ *Having warning coloration that says "keep off, I'm nasty," the flat-backed millipede,* Sigmoria aberrans, *is quite happy to wander around during the day.*

/ Southern hawker (*Aeshna cyanea*)

Common name Dragonflies, damselflies

Order Odonata

Class Insecta

Subphylum Hexapoda

Number of species About 6,500 (438 U.S.)

Size From about 0.7 in (19 mm) to 5 in (13 cm)

Key features Head with large compound eyes and well-developed jaws; antennae very short; 2 pairs of transparent wings almost equal in size; abdomen long and slim in most species; dragonflies hold their wings out to the side, damselflies fold their wings over and along the body; jaws in nymphs can be extended for grabbing prey; damselfly nymphs have 3 external gills, dragonfly nymphs have gills inside the rectum

Habits Damselflies normally found hunting for prey close to water; stronger-flying dragonflies may often be found hunting a long way from water; nymphs mostly aquatic

Breeding Males may grab females in midair or pounce on sitting females; some species have complex courtship routines; eggs laid in or near water

Diet Both adults and nymphs are predators

Habitat Any habitat with suitable still or running water, the latter not too fast; some species can inhabit deserts provided water is available at least for a short time

Distribution Found all over the world except for the North and South Poles

A female southern hawker,* Aeshna cyanea, *lays her eggs in a soft, water-logged tree stump. (*Aeshna *means ugly or misshapen and* cyanea *means dark blue, although there is no blue color present in the female of the species.) The southern hawker is widespread throughout Europe. Wingspan up to 3.5 inches (9 cm) and body length up to 2.8 inches (7 cm).

Dragonflies and Damselflies

Odonata

With their large size and often bright colors the dragonflies and damselflies must rank among the most easily recognized insects. Although their size may make some of them seem rather frightening, they are in no way harmful to humans.

In the gloom of an approaching thunderstorm a flame skimmer dragonfly,* Libellula saturata, *sits on vegetation close to a pool in Utah. Typical of the dragonflies, it sits with its wings held at roughly 90 degrees from the body.

THE ODONATA IS SUBDIVIDED into three suborders: the dragonflies in the Anisoptera, the damselflies in the Zygoptera, and finally a very small group (which is almost extinct) called the Anisozygoptera. The latter is known by just two living species from Asia. Dragonflies are heavily built insects and, at rest, can be recognized by the position of their wings—they can only hold them out sideways at roughly right angles to the body. The damselflies have a long, slim body and can both fold the wings up over the body and bring them together vertically, rather like a butterfly.

All-Round Vision

Adult Odonata are normally found close to water. They are predators, mainly catching other insects in flight. The fact that they are skillful fliers helps, but there is another important feature: The dragonflies in particular have very large compound eyes almost meeting on top of the head and giving them excellent all-round vision. The eyes of some dragonflies are made up of as many as 28,000 single units (the ommatidia), each with its own individual lens. In order to help them look around for prey, their neck is very flexible, and their head can be turned from side to side and moved up and down. Some other hunting insects, such as mantids and robber flies, have the same ability.

Dragonflies prey on faster-flying insects such as flies. They can take larger prey—for

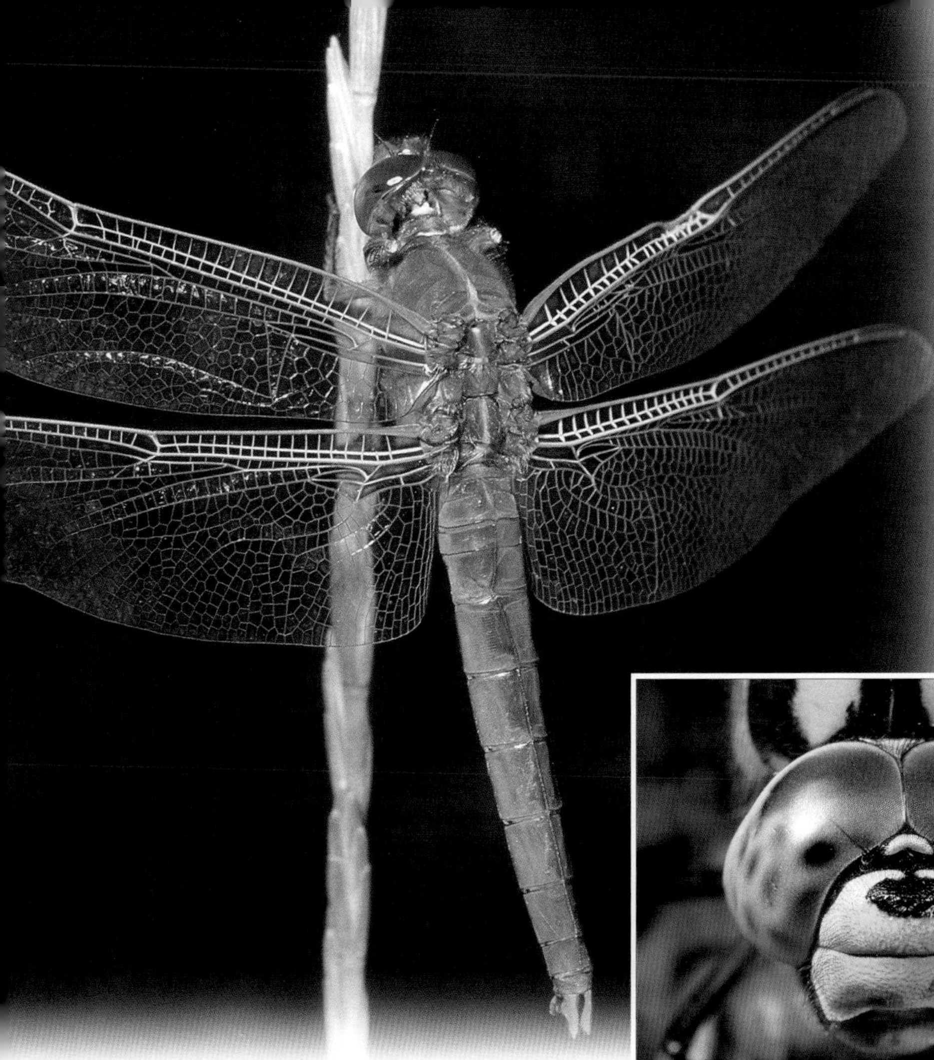

example, wasps—and have even been observed to be accidental cannibals, eating members of their own species. Despite their large eyes and strong flying capabilities, they often miss their prey, which can be equally agile in escaping from them. Damselflies, on the other hand, have smaller eyes and a weaker flight, and tend to go after weak-flying, fluttery insects such as small moths.

The legs of both dragonflies and damselflies are poorly adapted for walking, but they are extremely useful for keeping hold of prey items while they are being eaten. Dragonflies in particular can often be found hunting miles away from the nearest stretch of water.

Spider Hunters

A more unusual type of prey is sought by two genera of damselflies from South and Central America. *Megaloprepus* and *Mecistogaster* species include the world's largest damselflies, and *Megaloprepus coerulatus* has the largest wingspan of any of the Odonata. It can sometimes reach 7.5 inches (19 cm). Adults of both genera specialize in spiders as prey, taking them either as they sit at the center of their orb

In this face-on view of the southern hawker dragonfly,* Aeshna cyanea *from Europe, the huge compound eyes are very obvious. They are used by the dragonfly in aerial pursuit of prey.

webs or as they sit around on vegetation. Hovering like a helicopter, its transparent wings a blur and its long slim body pointing behind it, the damselfly remains undetected by the spider as it approaches. It then makes a final dart at the spider, grabs it, and with its mandibles cuts off the abdomen from the spider's body. It then lets the rest of the body fall to the ground while it feasts on the juicy abdomen.

Life as a Nymph

In a few families the developmental stages of the Odonata—the nymphs, or stadia—bear some resemblance to wingless adults, but in others there are few similarities. Damselfly nymphs are very slim, while dragonfly nymphs are more heavily built. Some have an abdomen almost as wide as it is long. Apart from the fact that they have a lighter build, damselfly nymphs can be recognized by their three external gills. They are often leaf-shaped structures protruding back from the end of the abdomen.

Masked Killers

Dragonfly and damselfly nymphs, like the adults, are voracious carnivores. They are mostly aquatic and feed on almost any kind of prey that is small enough for them to handle. That includes water insects and their larvae, tadpoles, small frogs, and small fish. The nymphs hunt by stealth, creeping around very slowly on the bottom of the mass of water in which they live or on water vegetation. Just a few species have larvae that live and hunt in marshes, and there is also a handful of species whose nymphs do not live in water at all.

The water dwellers bury themselves beneath loose gravel, mud, vegetation, or other material on the bottom of a lake or pond, effectively concealing themselves from passing prey. When a suitable item of prey comes within range, they employ their killer "mask." The mask is in fact the modified lower lip of the nymph's mouthparts; it gets its name because, when at rest, it covers the other mouthparts like a mask. The labium is long and hinged, with two inward-pointing claws on the end. To catch prey, blood is forced into the labium at high pressure, making it shoot forward very rapidly. The nymph then uses its claws to dig into and trap the prey, which is then pulled to the front of the nymph's face. There it is dealt with by the biting and chewing jaws. Research scientists have found that the mask can be shot out in as little as 25 milliseconds (25 thousandths of a second).

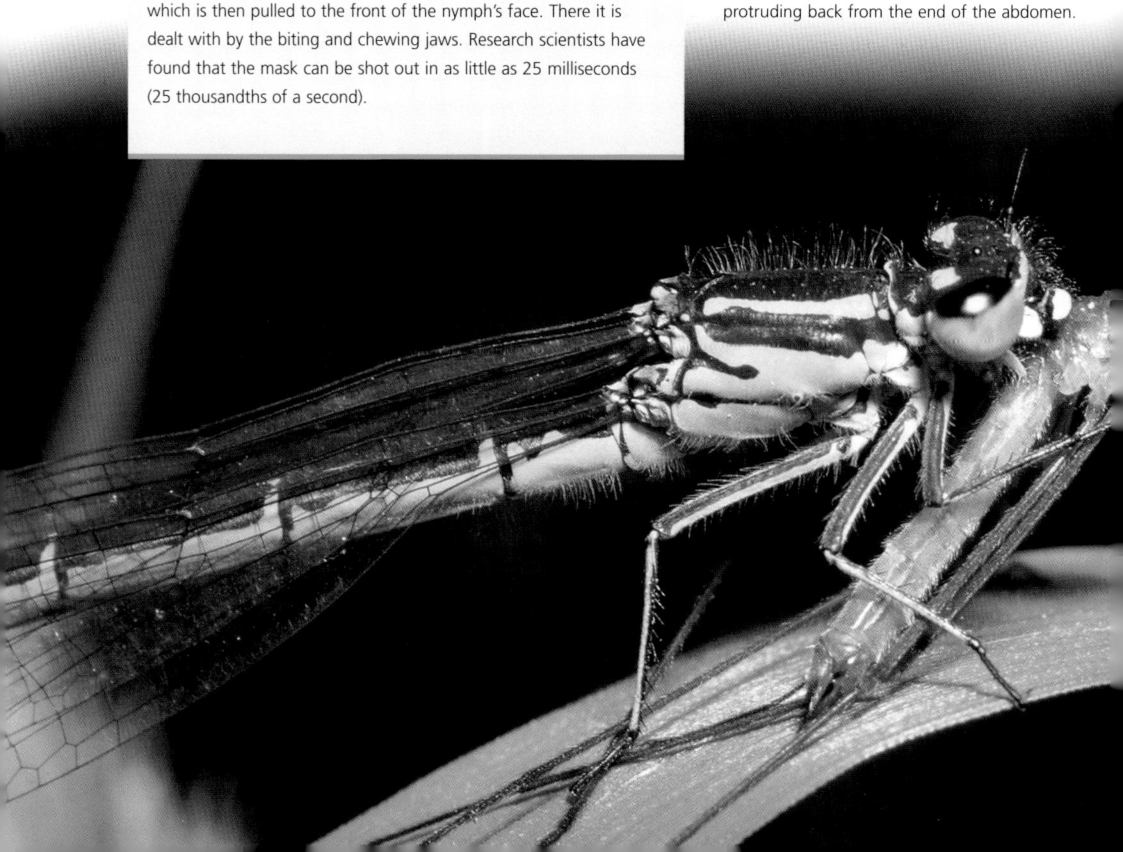

The gills take up oxygen from the water. The oxygen moves from the gills into the nymph's body. Dragonfly nymphs lack these external gills: Instead, they have gills in the rectum, in the rear end of their gut. Water is pumped in and out of the rectum to ventilate the gills.

Although they are proficient killers, the nymphs (especially when they are small) are themselves likely to fall prey to larger predators. They do, however, have one trick that helps them escape. If they are grabbed by a leg, it can break at a weak point at the base of the femur, leaving the predator with just a leg in its mouth and giving the nymph a chance to escape. Dragonfly nymphs have an alternative means of escape. They are able to squirt water under high pressure from the gill chamber in the rectum out of the end of the abdomen. The action shoots them forward in the water and away from possible danger.

Damselflies, unlike dragonflies, have the ability to fold the wings back over the body. Feeding on a small crane fly is an azure damselfly, **Coenagrion puella*****, while sitting on vegetation beside an English pond.***

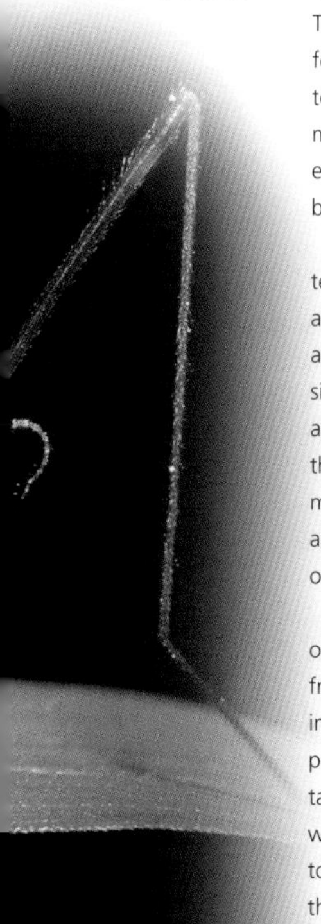

Territorial Skirmishes

The main aim of male Odonata is to find a female and mate with her. That of the female is to find a mate and then lay her eggs. Since the majority of dragonflies and damselflies lay their eggs in water, courtship and mating take place by ponds, lakes, streams, and rivers.

Most male Odonata set up and defend a territory that is suitable as an egg-laying site for a mate. This behavior is often most noticeable around a small pond. It is common to find a single male dragonfly patrolling back and forth across the water, investigating any flying insect that comes near. If it turns out to be another male of his own species, a skirmish may ensue, and the intruder is often chased off. A number of different species often patrol the same pond.

At intervals the defending male may land on a favorite spot and continue his surveillance from there, flying off to investigate any likely intruders. Quite often the male will leave the pond after an hour or so, and his place will be taken by another male, which will stay for a while before he too leaves. They may be leaving to hunt, or they may be moving off to check the availability of a neighboring pond. If a receptive female turns up during these patrols, they mate, and the female lays her eggs.

A male banded demoiselle damselfly, **Calopteryx splendens*****, claps his wings at another male who is trying to invade his territory. The owner is perched on a yellow water lily.***

Other species, however, maintain a patrol over their territory during all the hours of daylight throughout their entire short lives, only deserting it if they are driven off by a stronger male. Defending a territory does not guarantee that a male will be the only one to mate with any females that arrive, because the females may have mated before they got there. The females hunt away from water, where they are likely to come across males that are not strong enough to hold a territory but will mate with a passing female.

Males Miss Out

Some dragonflies and damselflies are nonterritorial, in which case there is just a free-for-all. The first male to reach the female is the one that mates with her. Near suitable egg-laying sites males will always outnumber females. The result is that some males never get a chance to mate—perhaps 50 percent, or fewer, succeed. By contrast, all females will mate, some several times.

While courtship in many dragonflies is brief or nonexistent, in damselflies it can be quite complex. A good example is that of the banded

Wheels and Tandems

Members of the Odonata mate in a very unusual way. The structure and position of the sex organs in male Odonata are unique in the insect world. One set of reproductive structures, called the primary genitalia, is in the normal insect position toward the end of the abdomen. There is, however, a set of secondary genitalia on the underside of the second abdominal segment. In addition to that unusual arrangement the males also have a set of special hooks at the tip of the abdomen. Before he is ready to mate, the male releases a spermatophore from the primary genitalia and curves his abdomen around to transfer it into the secondary genitalia. He then looks for a mate.

Having found a female that is happy to receive his advances, he flies above her and grasps her in his legs. He then curves his abdomen forward and holds onto her with the hooks on the tip of his abdomen. In dragonflies the hooks grasp the female by the top of the head, while in damselflies the female is held by the top of the thorax (the pronotum). The arrangement and size of the male's hooks and the shape of the head or thorax of the female vary from species to species, but they are the same for all members within an individual species. Only the hooks of a male from the correct species will fit the shape of the head or thorax of a female of the same species, so cross-mating between different species is avoided. Both insects are able to fly while the male is holding onto the female—this is known as the "tandem" position.

A pair of golden-ringed dragonflies, Cordulegaster boltonii, *sit in the wheel position as they mate. The female is the lower of the two.*

The next stage in the courtship is for the female to bring her abdomen around beneath her body until her reproductive openings make contact with and lock onto the male's secondary genitalia. In this position their bodies form a rough circle, the so-called "wheel" position. The male is then able to pass the spermatophore to the female. The length of time that they remain in the wheel position varies from just a few seconds in some dragonflies to several hours in many damselflies. It is not unusual to find dozens of pairs of damselflies in the wheel position sitting on plants in and around a favored egg-laying pond.

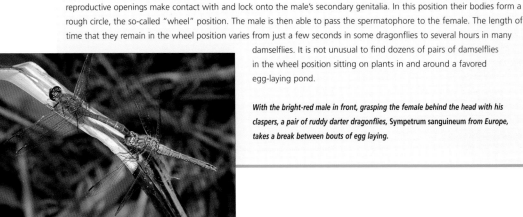

With the bright-red male in front, grasping the female behind the head with his claspers, a pair of ruddy darter dragonflies, Sympetrum sanguineum *from Europe, takes a break between bouts of egg laying.*

demoiselle, *Calopteryx splendens*, a European species. This handsome species, which has closely related species in North America, is found beside canals and slow-moving streams and rivers, especially where there are water lilies on the surface and reeds and rushes growing beside the water. As the female enters the male's territory, she flies in a manner that indicates to him her interest in mating. As he catches sight of her, the male, perched on his favorite water lily leaf, belly-flops into the water. This tells her that he would like to mate with her and that this is a very good place to lay her eggs. The female's response is to fly in a zigzag path over him. Her flight shows that she accepts his invitation to mate and also allows her to memorize exactly where she is to oviposit.

The female then flies to a nearby rush or reed stem and sits there in a manner that indicates to the male that she has accepted him. He performs a short courtship flight, hovering beside her, before they finally mate. If she does not immediately fly to his chosen egg-laying site, he will lead her to it. He shows her the way by using a special wing-whirring flight low over the water. He will also land and float on the water at the chosen place, waggling his tail to encourage her to follow.

Aerial "Dogfights"

In order to lay, she has to make her way beneath the water. During that time she is vulnerable to the attentions of other males. The resident male therefore stands guard close by, chasing off any intruders. If there are too many, he will sit on the female's back to keep them off until she disappears beneath the water. Males defending a territory often have to spend hours at a time defending it against rival males. This involves aerial "dogfights," with one male trying to force his opponent to crash into the water. In years when the area becomes overpopulated with males, the whole courtship system can break down and is replaced by a complete free-for-all. This is not good for the females, however: They can easily get drowned by the crush of males trying to mate with them.

North American demoiselles also have fairly complex courtships of this kind, but the behavior of one of them—*Hetaerina vulnerata*, the canyon rubyspot—has puzzled scientists. The males normally select and defend a suitable egg-laying site on a fast-flowing stream. Here they mate with visiting females as expected. However, in about one-third of the cases studied, instead of staying to lay, the female somehow persuades the male to leave and go with her, attached in the "tandem" position, to a site of her choice. Most sites are already occupied by other resident males; but if she finds one that is not and she likes it, she stops suddenly in midair. She persuades the male to land with her and to let go of her while she backs into the water to lay her eggs.

Sperm Chambers

The males of some Odonata (both damselflies and dragonflies) have the ability to ensure that most of the eggs laid by the female are fertilized by their own sperm and not by some male with which she has previously mated. That is because the sperm from the spermatophore is stored in a special chamber, the spermatheca, inside the female's body before it is used to

↑ Dragonflies are often found some distance from water, which they only need to visit for breeding purposes. This eastern amberwing dragonfly, Perithemis tenera *from North America, is hunting in a cemetery some distance from the nearest stretch of water.*

fertilize her eggs. For example, in some damselflies of the family Coenagrionidae the male uses a special structure called a sperm scoop to remove from the female's spermatheca any sperm that have been placed there by another male. Only then will he pass over his spermatophore to the female. A slightly different method is used by some dragonflies of the family Libellulidae. Instead of scraping the sperm out, the male pushes aside any sperm that is already in the spermatheca and places his own sperm on top of it. The result is that most of the eggs will be fertilized by his sperm. This behavior is known as "sperm competition."

Egg-Laying Variations

Dragonflies and damselflies use a number of distinct methods of egg laying (oviposition), although as is so often the case with living things, there are exceptions to the rules. In general, however, most species oviposit in one of the following ways:

One method involves the female making her way into the water until she is completely submerged and then inserting her eggs into the stems of water plants. This method is used by damselflies of the genus *Enallagma* in both North America and Europe. The female, in tandem with her mate, lands on a suitable plant stem sticking up out of the water. The female then backs down the stem and into the water, and the male lets go of her as she becomes completely submerged. She lays her eggs and then rises up to the surface again using air bubbles trapped on her body. Meanwhile the male usually waits for her to reappear and then couples up with her again.

Another common way involves the female sitting and laying her eggs directly into the water or sitting at the surface and laying them into plant tissues below the water. This method is used by many different species of dragonflies and damselflies. A good example occurs in *Aeshna juncea*, known in North America as the sedge darner dragonfly and in Europe as the common hawker dragonfly. Dragonflies that oviposit in this way often accompany the egg laying with a loud rustling of their wings.

In a third method the female oviposits into mud or dead wood, plant debris, or mosses along the water's edge. This is a method favored by some of the *Aeshna* species darner dragonflies from North America and Europe.

Inventive Egg Laying

The females of the giant damselflies of the genus *Mecistogaster* from South and Central America choose an unusual place in which to oviposit—in the water that collects in the rosettes of leaves of members of the plant family Bromeliaceae, such as the pineapple. The water is fairly deep among the leaf bases, which may be why these damselflies have a long, slim body. The nymphs feed on the larvae of other insects living in the so-called "bromeliad tanks." There is evidence from the examination of stomach contents that the larger nymphs eat the smaller ones.

Insects always seem prepared to make use of anything that humans can provide for them in the way of new habitats. That seems to be the case with these damselflies. Sugarcane is grown in large quantities in the region. After the sugarcane has been cut, the remaining hollow stems fill up with water before they eventually decompose. The damselflies have taken to using these stems as alternative egg-laying sites.

↓ *A female southern hawker dragonfly,* Aeshna cyanea, *pushes the tip of her abdomen into a rotten log to lay her eggs.*

Again, egg laying is often accompanied by a very loud rustling of the wings.

In yet another method the female oviposits directly into sand or mud along the water's edge while in flight. This occurs commonly in the *Sympetrum* species dragonflies, known as meadowhawks in North America.

Alternatively, as she skims over the water, the female lays her eggs directly into it, either among vegetation or straight into deeper water. Again, some *Sympetrum* species dragonflies favor this method. The male may even help in some instances: For example, in the European ruddy darter dragonfly, *S. sanguineum*, the two sexes fly in tandem. The male leads and holds the female behind her head with the claspers at the end of his abdomen. She releases the eggs in batches onto the end of her abdomen, and he then swings her downward so that the eggs enter the water. There they are washed from the female's abdomen and fall among submerged water plants. In a slight variation the female of the European keeled skimmer dragonfly, *Orthetrum coerulescens*, dips toward the water and flips a droplet of the water, where the eggs have fallen, up onto the bank

With the males standing above them to keep other males away, two azure damselfly females,* Coenagrion puella *from Europe, lay their eggs among pond vegetation.

or onto the leaves of water plants so that the eggs stick to the plants. A more simple strategy is for the female to drop her eggs into the water as she flies over it without making contact with the water surface.

Some variations in these egg-laying methods occur. Females of the setwing dragonfly, *Dythemis cannacrioides* from Mexico, perch for a while before egg laying commences. During that time they produce a large mass of eggs, like a bunch of grapes, on the end of the abdomen. They then seek out a place where a cluster of plant roots hangs from the bank into a stream or river. They drop the mass of sticky eggs into the cluster of roots.

Runaway Eggs

A dragonfly species whose females seem to adopt different methods of laying is *Zygonyx natalensis* from Africa. They are found along streams and rivers with frequent waterfalls and rapids, and which contain mats of vegetation washed over by currents. When she is ready to oviposit, the female sits on one of the mats and releases her eggs into the water. They swell up and become sticky as they are washed away by the current, and they become glued to the first thing with which they come into contact. Sometimes, however, the female will sit by shallow water and lay her eggs directly onto the bottom of the stream or river. Alternatively, she will dip her abdomen into the water during flight and drop her eggs directly into it.

The ovipositing behavior of the dragonfly *Tetrathmis polleni* from southern Africa has been seen to involve males as well as females. The males set up a territory of their own on the single leaf of a waterside plant, and they defend it from other males that attempt to take it from them. Following successful mating, the male takes his mate back to his chosen leaf, where she lays a batch of eggs on the underside. As she does so, the male flutters excitedly around the leaf, landing on it every now and again close to the ovipositing female. Within a couple of days the eggs hatch out, and the tiny nymphs fall into the water below.

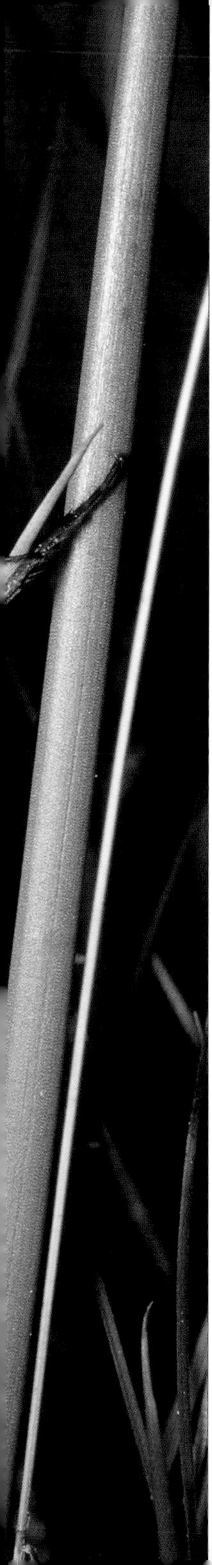

Egg to Adult

Eggs are of two types, depending on how they are laid. Those laid straight into the water are roughly spherical, while those laid into plant tissues are more elongate. Being inside the plant helps protect the eggs, but those laid in water are covered in a layer of sticky jelly. This not only means that they stick to objects, such as plants, in the water but also makes it difficult for predators to eat them. While in some species the eggs may hatch within a few weeks, in colder climes the eggs may overwinter, hatching the next spring.

When the young hatch from the eggs, they do so as a prolarva, which is covered in a membrane. If the egg has hatched under water, the membrane immediately splits, and the first instar nymph emerges. Quite a number of species of dragonfly lay their eggs out of water but fairly close to it. In this instance the prolarva is able to leap, by bending and straightening its body, to carry it to the main body of water in which it will spend its nymphal life. Once in the water, the membrane again splits to release the first instar nymph.

Varied Development

Development time is mainly dependent on the temperature of the water in which the nymphs live, as long as adequate food is available. In warmer regions nymphs develop more quickly than those in colder areas. There can even be differences in rate of development over quite a short distance. In Britain, for example, nymphs of the blue-tailed damselfly, *Ischnura elegans*, take one year from egg to adult in the south but two years in the north. A few hundred miles farther south in France, and there may be two or even three generations per year.

Once the final instar nymph is fully grown, it leaves the water and climbs up onto a suitable piece of vegetation, either doing so directly from the water or by crawling out onto waterside plants. Emergence in Aeshnidae, which go by the common name darners in the United States, takes place during darkness so that they are ready to fly as soon as it gets light, a useful way of escaping predation by birds. Most of the other damselflies and dragonflies start emerging at dawn so that they are fully emerged and drying off as the sun rises.

Emergence itself is much as in other insects. The last instar nymph must sit head up, as near vertical as possible. The top of the head and thorax then splits, and the adult forces itself out, using gravity to help it fall back and pull itself free from the old skin. Once out of the skin, it sits head up, inflates its wings, dries off, and then makes its first flight. When newly emerged, the young adults are called tenerals, differing from the mature adult in having very shiny wings and drab colors, the full adult color taking up to a week to appear.

⊖ ***A newly emerged 4-spotted skimmer dragonfly,* Libellula quadrimaculata, *hangs from the old nymphal skin as it dries off its freshly inflated wings.***

⊖ ***A new adult* Aeshna juncea, *known as the sedge darner in North America, emerges from its old nymphal skin.***

Tawny earwig
(Labidura riparia)

Common name Earwigs

Order Dermaptera

Class Insecta

Subphylum Hexapoda

Number of species About 1,800 (20 U.S.)

Size From about 0.2 in (5 mm) to 1 in (2.5 cm)

Key features Relatively elongate, rather flattened body; head with large or small compound eyes (or lacking eyes) and biting and chewing jaws; winged or wingless; forewings only very small; hind wings semicircular in shape, folding up neatly to fit beneath the forewing covers; cerci highly modified to form "pincers"; nymphs resemble adults

Habits Most are nocturnal; some live in burrows, a few unusual species live on mammals

Breeding Males of some species use the pincers to hold the female; parental care by females not uncommon

Diet Feed as scavengers on a variety of dead and decaying organic matter; some eat flowers; a few are semiparasitic

Habitat Grassland, forests, deserts, and gardens

Distribution Worldwide

↑ ***The tawny earwig,* Labidura riparia, *sometimes flies to lights at night and can emit an unpleasant smell when captured. It is found across the southern United States. Length up to 1 inch (2.5 cm).***

Earwigs Dermaptera

In days gone by people believed that earwigs had the habit of crawling into human ears as the victim slept. Whether that is the true origin of their common name, however, is unknown.

WITH THEIR WELL-DEVELOPED, often pincerlike cerci at the end of the abdomen, earwigs are instantly recognizable insects. Most earwigs are nocturnal, feeding mainly on dead and decaying vegetable matter, with just a few predaceous species. The common European earwig, *Forficula auricularia*, which has now been spread to other parts of the world by humans, is one of the few species that can be a pest. It is very common in gardens, where it has the habit of living in the heads of flowers such as dahlias and can cause considerable damage by feeding on them.

On the other hand, earwigs may also prove to be beneficial. Researchers are looking into the possibility of using some of the predaceous species as biological controls for some caterpillar pests.

Storing the Wings

Although earwigs have wings and can fly quite well, they do not seem to use them very often. The large hind wings are around 20 times the area of the forewings. The hind wings are stored beneath the forewings when not in use. To see how the earwig folds the hind wings up to fit neatly beneath the forewings, with just a tiny bit protruding at the back, is a fascinating experience. Earwigs of the suborders Arixeniina and Hemimerina that live in association with bats or rodents (as parasites or semiparasites) lack wings.

Earwigs can use their cerci as a form of defense: Anyone who has picked an earwig up carelessly knows that they can deliver quite a sharp pinch, probably enough to frighten off a

↑ ***A female European earwig,* Forficula auricularia, *feeds on a buttercup flower in an English meadow. Accidentally introduced to North America, the earwig is now widespread and something of a pest.***

Ⓣ *Although mainly nocturnal, the linear earwig,* Doru lineare, *sometimes comes out to feed during the day. It is widespread over much of the New World.*

Weird Earwigs

Two suborders of Dermaptera—the Arixeniina and Hemimerina—live as ectoparasites on mammals.

The Arixeniina has just one family, the Arixeniidae, consisting of five species in two genera. These atypical earwigs are completely wingless, hairy, and flattened. Their eyes are strongly reduced or even absent, probably because they live in the dark. They are known from a few caves and hollow trees in the Malaysian region, where they feed on the bodily fluids and skin debris of free-tailed bats of the family Molossidae. They also eat bat fecal matter and dead insects, although usually only when threatened with starvation. The arixeniids give birth to live young that, unlike typical earwigs, have only four instars.

The Hemimerina are restricted to sub-Saharan Africa, where they are found on pouched rats. There is again one family, containing two genera and 11 species. They look more like cockroaches than earwigs and are blind and wingless. They are smooth and flattened in shape, with strongly developed tarsi for gripping the hairs of their hosts, enabling them to move rapidly through their fur. Unlike the arixeniids, the hemimerines never leave their hosts, feeding exclusively on skin fragments and bodily secretions. It is possible that the insects may even be of benefit to the rats, since they are thought to help clean the rats and thus reduce the risk of skin infections.

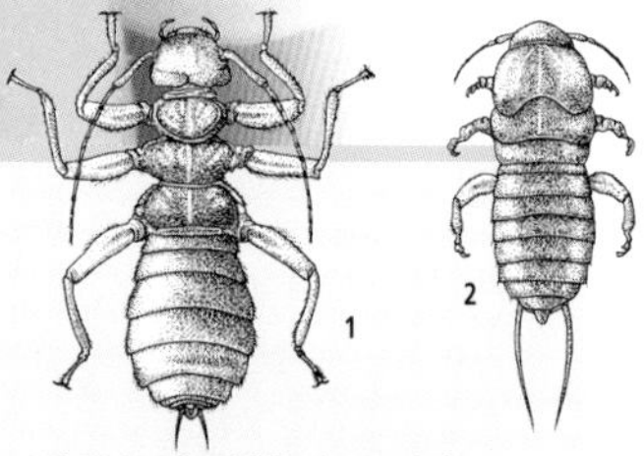

The Arixeniina (1) live in association with free-tailed bats; the Hemimerina (2) have a possibly mutually beneficial relationship with pouched rats.

Another species that lives in close association with bats is *Chelisoches bimammatus.* These earwigs live in bat caves in Thailand and Malaysia, and feed on the guano of the fruit-eating lesser dawn bat, *Eonycteris spelaea.*

small predator. The earwig *Doru taeniatum* from the Americas has a different method of defense. This species has a pair of glands on the abdomen from which it shoots out an unpleasant spray when disturbed. It aims the spray by swinging its abdomen toward the attacker and can also bring its pincers into action at the same time.

Studies of the European earwig have revealed that the cerci are not only used for defense but are also important in courtship and mating. The males use the pincers in fights over females. Males without pincers are unable to mate. Mating takes place tail to tail. In harsh climate conditions the spermatophore that the male passes to the female may, in some species, be retained for several months before the sperm contained is used for fertilization.

Earwig Family Life

It has long been known that female earwigs care, at least to some extent, for their eggs and offspring, although only a few species have been examined in detail. The amount of care can vary from very little to a great deal, depending on the species: Females of *Hemimerus talpoides* (one of the species of Hemimerina that live on pouched rats) do little other than help the nymphs escape from their eggshells when they are ready to hatch.

At the other extreme the much-researched European earwig female is a very attentive mother. She first digs a tunnel beneath a stone, at the end of which is a chamber where she will lay her eggs. She uses her jaws to dig the tunnel, carrying the loose earth to the surface to dispose of it. Sometimes she will allow her mate to help her in this task; but as soon as she is ready to lay her eggs, he is driven off. She seals the tunnel with earth before standing guard over her eggs until they hatch. During that time she does not feed but carries out other parental duties. In the early part of the day she carries the eggs up the tunnel to just below the surface, where it is beginning to warm up from the sun's rays. As

The striped or sand earwig,* Labidura riparia, *seen here in Arizona, is a very widespread species occurring over much of the warmer areas of the world.

Ⓣ ***A group of baby European earwigs,*** **Forficula auricularia,** ***beneath a stone in an English garden. Their mother is presumably off searching for food.***

Ⓣ ***A pair of European earwigs,*** **Forficula auricularia,** ***mating in an unusual position. Mating is normally tail to tail, but here the larger female is reversing direction by walking over the smaller male as she comes to the end of this rather narrow perch.***

the stone warms up in the heat of the day, she moves the eggs farther down so that they do not overheat. She also cleans the eggs regularly with her mouthparts, presumably to remove fungal spores that might otherwise hatch and infect the eggs. In fact, if the eggs are not cleaned, they soon become infected with fungi and die. Although such care is necessary for the survival of the eggs of a number of different species of earwig, in others the eggs hatch perfectly well without being cleaned.

Guarding the Eggs

The female earwig defends her eggs against all comers, driving off even predatory ground beetles that get into the nest tunnel. She seems to be able to detect when the eggs are ready to hatch, because she spreads them out so that each nymph has space in which to emerge. The nymphs are like miniature adults and go through a number of instars before reaching adulthood. Once they have hatched, she gathers them together and places them beneath her body, bringing back any stragglers in her mouth in much the same way that a mother cat brings back a straying kitten.

At first she brings food, which can be all manner of dead or decaying material, to her young nymphs. She also regurgitates liquid food for them from her own mouth. Soon, however, they begin to leave the nest to find their own food, returning to the nest to shelter after a period of feeding. When they eventually leave the nest for good, however, their mother fails to recognize them; and in some predaceous species nymphs can end up being eaten by their own mother.

Queen Alexandra's birdwing *(Ornithoptera alexandrae)*

Common name Swallowtail butterflies (apollos, swordtails, birdwings)

Family Papilionidae

Order Lepidoptera

Number of species About 550 (27 U.S.)

Wingspan From about 1.2 in (3 cm) to about 11 in (28 cm)

Key features Mainly large butterflies (including the world's largest), often with hind-wing tails; colors varied, often consisting of just 2 colors, such as black and yellow or black and green, sometimes with red or blue spots; some species (apollos) have semitransparent wings; antennae knobbed but never with hooked tips; all 6 adult legs of equal size; caterpillars often with "Y"-shaped defensive osmeterium

Habits Adults feed on flowers or on salty ground, where they may form large aggregations; caterpillars mainly feed singly

Breeding Male and female of most species look very similar; many males use pheromones from androconial scales during courtship; eggs spherical, usually laid singly; caterpillars with smooth skins, often with knobby projections; pupa suspended upright from silken girdle

Diet Adults feed on flowers, damp ground, or dung; caterpillars eat leaves belonging to plants of many families, including poisonous *Aristolochia* vines

Habitat Commonest in tropical rain forest, but found in many temperate habitats such as swamps, parks, and gardens; some species found only on high mountains or open tundra in the far north

Distribution Worldwide, occurring as far north as northernmost Alaska

↑ *Queen Alexandra's birdwing,* Ornithoptera alexandrae, *is found to the east of the Owen Stanley Ranges in southeast New Guinea. It is one of seven protected butterfly species on the island. Wingspan 6.6–11 inches (17–28 cm).*

Swallowtail Butterflies

Papilionidae

Papilionid butterflies are mainly large, and include the biggest butterfly in the world—the Queen Alexandra's birdwing, Ornithoptera alexandrae, *from New Guinea. Females can have a wingspan of over 11 inches (28 cm).*

The males of some of the birdwing butterflies from tropical islands such as New Guinea and parts of Indonesia are among the most spectacular of all butterflies. They are highly prized by collectors, and special butterfly farms now exist to breed the choicest species to satisfy the market for perfect unmarked specimens. That helps take the collecting pressure off the remaining wild populations.

In common with other true swallowtails, the birdwings constantly flutter their wings while feeding on flowers, a characteristic unique to the Papilionidae. The reason for the behavior is unknown. The suggestion that it supports the heavy butterfly's weight on a flimsy flower seems unlikely, since some species also vibrate their wings while sitting on the ground puddling. During active flight the wings in many species are only flapped a few times a second, although some tropical swallowtails are among the fastest and most acrobatic fliers of all butterflies. Not all swallowtails have tails on the hind wings. Many species are tailless; in others tails are present in males but not in females of the same species, while in the subfamily Parnasiinae tails are largely absent.

↑ *The artemisia swallowtail,* Papilio machaon, *seen here in France, is unusual in being found on both sides of the Atlantic. It has the fairly short tails typical of* Papilio *species swallowtails.*

The Three Subfamilies

The family Papilionidae is divided into three subfamilies, all with very different habits and appearance. The smallest subfamily is the "primitive" Baroniinae, containing just a single species, *Baronia brevicornis* from southern Mexico. The forked hairs on the head and body

→ *Puddling on a riverbank in a rain forest in Thailand, this fivebar swordtail,* Graphium antiphates, *displays the long tails typical of the genus* Graphium.

of the larva are unusual, while the arrangement of veins on the adult's wings is unique.

The biggest subfamily with the widest distribution is the Papilioninae (although the vast majority of species are tropical). It contains the most familiar and "typical" of swallowtails, represented in North America and Europe by *Papilio*, the largest "true" swallowtails. The 27 North American species are mainly found in the south, although one species—the artemisia swallowtail, *Papilio machaon*—ranges north into Alaska. It is also unusual in being the only swallowtail (and one of the few butterflies) found both in North America and Europe. Some species share communal roosts, which in the African citrus swallowtail, *P. demodocus*, contain from three to 12 (or more) individuals. Most return to the same spot night after night.

In *Eurytides* and *Graphium*, often called kite swallowtails, the hind-wing tails (where present) are much longer and more pointed than in *Papilio*. *Graphium* are known as swordtails in Africa and Asia. *Eurytides* is found in the tropics of Central and South America, with just a single species resident in the southeastern corner of the United States. The butterflies are seldom found feeding on flowers and often congregate in large numbers on damp, salty riverbanks and springs. They pass so much liquid through their systems that a jet of water is squirted from their rear ends every minute or so. In the poison eaters, such as *Parides* and *Troides*, the caterpillars can feed unharmed on poisonous *Aristolochia* pipevines. The most familiar species in North America is the pipevine swallowtail, *Battus philenor*, one of the few species found outside the tropics. The birdwings of the genus *Ornithoptera* also belong in the Papilioninae.

The subfamily Parnasiinae, with about 50 species, is unusual in being mainly found in the coolest parts of the northern temperate zones. Most species are restricted to mountainsides up to the snow line, while two of the three species found in North America are also found far to the north on the tundras of Alaska. A small selection of much more colorful species called festoons are found in warmer areas, such as around the Mediterranean Sea. Most of the high-mountain and tundra species are white, with two or more red eyespots, and are called apollos. In some species the scales on large areas of the wings are soon shed, leaving them semitransparent. Both larvae and adults are poisonous to vertebrates such as birds and are generally left alone. The tough, densely hairy body of the adults is well able to withstand the kind of brief attacks mounted by inexperienced enemies before they learn better.

Ⓣ ***Crawling around on the desert floor in Arizona in search of a fresh food plant, pipevine swallowtail caterpillars,* Battus philenor, *are protected by their distinctive "warning" uniform.***

Ⓓ **Eurytides agesilaus *is often seen in large numbers drinking on damp sand beside rivers running through rain forest, as here in Peru.***

Eggs, Larvae, and Pupae

In most species the eggs are more or less globular and are usually pale green and lacking any surface sculpture. In some species the egg is coated with a waxy substance that is eaten along with the eggshell by the newly hatched caterpillar. Such eggs are usually laid away from the host plant or on tiny seedlings unable to support the caterpillar's appetite. Therefore the caterpillar probably needs the additional eggshell meal in order to fuel its search for a suitable source of food. In most species the eggs are laid singly on the food plant. The pipevine swallowtail is one of a number of species that lays eggs in clusters, and the young caterpillars feed shoulder to shoulder in ostentatious squads along the edge of a single leaf. The red-spotted swallowtail, *Papilio anchisiades*, found from Texas to Brazil, lays its yellow eggs in clusters of up to 40. The caterpillars always stay close together and feed and molt in unison. During the day they form densely packed

Ⓡ ***Caterpillars of the orchard swallowtail,* Papilio aegeus *from Australia, start out as bird-dropping mimics but change to this form as they grow. Here the red osmeterium is just being extruded.***

throngs on the trunks of their host trees. Food plants vary, but some species can be pests on cultivated plants. The caterpillar of the giant swallowtail, *Papilio cresphontes*, is known popularly as the "orange dog" and can be a pest in citrus orchards in the United States. In some species the caterpillars feed openly; in others they make a shelter by curling a leaf over and fastening it with silk.

The papilionid pupa is attached in an upright position by the cremaster at the rear end and usually supported by a silken girdle around the middle. The pupa may take on different colors such as green or brown to correspond with its background. In some species the pupa is attached to a tree trunk where in shape, texture, and color it bears an extraordinary resemblance to the stump of a small snapped-off twig or branch, even to the extent of being decorated with splashes of green, resembling lichens.

Mimicry in Swallowtails

Mimicry occurs both between different members of the Papilionidae and between papilionids and members of various other

The Osmeterium and Other Deterrents

Swallowtail caterpillars are generally smooth bodied. In most species a "Y"-shaped defensive organ called an osmeterium can be suddenly protruded from just behind the head—like the forked tongue of a snake—when the caterpillar is prodded or otherwise molested. The osmeterium is red or orange in most species, and its protrusion is accompanied by an unpleasant smell (emanating from isobutyric acids) that presumably deters predators. If so, it is strange that birds generally seem to be resolutely undeterred. Parasitic (ichneumon) wasps may also walk around on the caterpillar while the osmeterium is in use. It could be that its main function is to scare away ants by emitting a copy of their alarm pheromones. The visual effect alone can be quite startling, for example, when a dense knot of *Papilio anchisiades* caterpillars sitting on a tree trunk simultaneously extend their brilliant scarlet osmeteria, producing a sudden and quite unexpected eruption of color.

The habit of feeding on toxic *Aristolochia* plants renders poison eaters such as the pipevine swallowtail poisonous to vertebrate predators such as birds. Pipevine swallowtail caterpillars wear a conspicuous warningly colored uniform of bright reddish-brown. They are often found crawling around on the ground in a life-or-death quest for fresh food plants, having exhausted their supply of some of the smaller *Aristolochia* species.

In a number of species, such as the North American spicebush swallowtail, *Papilio troilus*, the caterpillar bears a pair of prominent eyelike spots above the head, giving it the appearance of a small snake. The deception is reinforced when the tonguelike osmeterium is suddenly flicked out. A quite different ploy used by the caterpillars of a large number of species is to mimic bird droppings. The caterpillars make no attempt to conceal themselves but sit motionless all day in full view on a leaf of their food plant, killing time until night falls, when they can resume feeding in safety. In some examples the resemblance to a bird dropping is only found in the smaller larvae, being lost in the later and much larger instars, which may be green or some other color. In the American tropics the commonest species of bird-dropping caterpillar is the king swallowtail, *P. thoas*. The species is one that maintains its deception throughout its larval life.

The female mocker swallowtail of the family Papilionidae (top) bears a remarkable resemblance to the common tiger butterfly, Danaus chrysippus (family Danaidae), its mimicry model.

families of butterflies, and even a few moths. In some cases only the females are mimics, the males retaining a normal appearance. In North America the somber hues of the pipevine swallowtail, whose adults are rejected on sight by most birds, are mimicked by both sexes of the spicebush swallowtail and by the females only of the tiger swallowtail, *Papilio glaucus*. Male tiger swallowtails are always mainly yellow with black markings, and some females have the same colors. Nonmimetic females are generally found in areas such as Florida, where the nasty-tasting pipevine swallowtail is rare or absent. Females that resemble the mainly yellow males seem more attractive to them and mate more often. That means that dark-colored mimetic females only thrive in areas where their mimicry of the pipevine swallowtail gives a clear boost to their survival rates, outweighing any reduced sexual success. The pipevine swallowtail is also mimicked by the red-spotted purple, *Limenitis arthemis* (a member of the Nymphalidae). However, the mimicry only occurs over parts of North America within the exact geographic range of the pipevine swallowtail. To the north the red-spotted purple is differently colored and nonmimetic.

Harmless Copycats

In Central and South America the numerous species of *Parides* cattle-hearts feed on poisonous host plants as caterpillars, giving rise to adults that provide the central models for many mimics. As with *Battus*, the adult's body is very tough and can withstand attacks from inexperienced birds that have not learned to avoid butterflies of a certain color and pattern. Most female *Parides* look very similar, being black with red spots. The males are more distinctive, usually having green spots as well as red. Both sexes may lack hind-wing tails. The females, being unpalatable themselves, are Müllerian mimics of each other. They form core role models for a wide range of Batesian mimics—harmless species that copy their warning coloration. They include species of true swallowtails (*Papilio*) and kite swallowtails (*Eurytides*).

The most complex and downright bewildering examples of mimicry occur in the African mocker swallowtail, *Papilio dardanus*. The males are pale yellow with black

Perched in the open on a citrus leaf in Madagascar, a Papilio caterpillar extrudes its orange osmeterium as a response to being gently prodded.

The female tiger swallowtail, **Papilio glaucus,** *is a perfectly palatable mimic of the pipevine swallowtail. The males, being nonmimetic, look quite different.*

Shivering its dark wings continuously in the manner typical of many swallowtails, the pipevine swallowtail, **Battus philenor,** *feeds on flowers in the United States. The distinctively colored and highly unpalatable species is the model for several mimics.*

markings, have conventional hind-wing tails, and are not mimetic. In Madagascar, where no suitable unpalatable models exist, the females resemble the males. Over much of Africa, where unpalatable models are legion, the females lack tails and mimic various species of disgustingly inedible butterflies, including *Amauris* (Danaidae) and *Bematistes* (Acraeidae). Several other species of African *Papilio*, as well as some *Graphium* species, also mimic various members of these two families of very unpalatable butterflies.

Hilltopping and Chastity Belts

In common with insects as varied as flies and wasps, various swallowtails resort to "hilltopping" behavior in which the males wait on some prominent feature until females arrive. This form of sexual rendezvous is particularly common in species inhabiting flattish deserts, where a hill protruding from the landscape will be very noticeable and provide a distinctive landmark visible for miles around. Hilltopping is very important in many species of North American *Papilio*. Once the virgin females have visited their hilltop, selected a suitable partner from the assembled males, and mated, they no longer show any particular interest in areas of high ground. Instead, they devote their time to flying around looking for host plants on which to lay their eggs. Choosing the best mate from the selection assembled on the hill is made easy for the females by the males themselves, who compete for the highest point on the hill. It ends up being monopolized by the dominant male, making him easy to find by any female wanting the pick of the bunch to father her offspring. She just heads straight for the highest point and is sure to find a winner in residence. The males compete for "top spot" by engaging in "spiral contests" up into the sky for a considerable distance, during which the loser will suddenly peel away and leave possession of the area to the victor. In many tropical papilionids the males establish territories on a perch high up in the canopy of some rain-forest tree. The opposite strategy, seen in many common species, is for the males to patrol over a wide area, searching for females on flowers and other likely places.

After losing her virginity, there is usually no barrier to the female if she wants to take another mate in the future. But in *Parides* and some members of the Parnassiinae the females are prevented from mating again for some time by the presence of a genital plug called a sphragis. It consists of a hard, brown, horny material that is applied in liquid form by the male at the time of mating. It closes off the fermale's genital pore, preventing her from engaging in any further acts of copulation until she has laid her eggs. Eventually the sphragis falls apart, leaving the female free to mate again. In *Cressida cressida* from Australia the sphragis can be half as long as the female's abdomen, projecting well out from her rear end. It is so big that it persuades males that it is not worth trying to make contact with her, and saves her from wasting valuable time and effort staving off unwelcome mating attempts.

The act of copulation in swallowtails is quite lengthy; and if the pair is disturbed, they will usually (except in Parnassiinae) fly strongly, the female doing all the work and carrying the male drooping from her rear end.

Fire ant (*Solenopsis geminata*)

Common name Ants

Family Formicidae

Suborder Apocrita

Order Hymenoptera

Number of species About 15,000 (about 600 U.S.)

Size From about 0.04 in (1 mm) to about 1.4 in (3.5 cm)

Key features Body usually black, brown, reddish, or yellowish; eyes small; antennae elbowed; waist (known as a pedicel) with one or two beadlike or scalelike segments; stinger may be present; wings absent in workers—usually present in sexual forms, but discarded later

Habits All ants are fully social, often constructing very large nests containing thousands of individuals; some species live in the nests of others or take other species as slaves

Breeding Most species release large numbers of winged males and females, which form nuptial swarms; after mating, queens break off their wings and establish new nest, usually without help of male, who normally dies (unlike in termites, where male becomes "king" alongside his "queen"); queen ant stores all sperm needed for fertilizing many eggs over a long period

Diet Adults feed mainly on nectar and honeydew or on fungus; larvae eat food of animal (mainly insect) or plant (mainly seed) origin; sole diet for some species is a fungus that they cultivate in special "gardens"

Habitat Found in all terrestrial habitats, where they are often dominant; no aquatic species

Distribution Worldwide; commonest in the tropics, absent from very dry or cold areas

↑ Solenopsis geminata, *the North American fire ant, is a serious crop pest. The common name derives from the burning sensation caused by the ants' venomous bites. Body length 0.03–0.2 inches (1–6 mm).*

Ants

Formicidae

Ants live in fascinatingly complex societies of often many millions of individuals that each know their place in the hierarchy. It has helped them become the dominant insect in many areas where they are found.

THE ANTS ARE THE MOST completely social members of the Hymenoptera. Unlike in bees and wasps, in which some species are solitary, some social, and some a mixture of both, all ants live in highly organized societies within a communal nest. Not all ant societies are equally well organized, and some rely on the press-ganged labor of other species for services such as the harvesting of food and rearing of young.

→ *These* Oecophylla longinoda *weaver ants from Africa are about to carry their entire brood to a new nest. Note how the pupae are naked, not enclosed in a cocoon.*

Dominant Insects

Wherever ants are found, whether in sun-baked desert or rain-shrouded cloud forest, they are almost always the dominant form of insect life. In terms of numbers and impact on their environment ants are rivaled only by the exclusively vegetarian termites. Most ants are considered beneficial to humans on account of their preying on insect pests. However, some ants are pests themselves. *Atta* leaf-cutting ants can damage orchards and plantations of trees; *Camponotus* carpenter ants may destroy wooden structures. *Solenopsis* fire ants damage plants and sting readily, while the Pharaoh ant, *Monomorium pharaonis*, is now a widespread pest in hospital and restaurant buildings.

All the hard labor in ant societies is carried out by the worker caste. They are sterile, wingless females that are not able to reproduce,

↓ *The various castes of* Messor *species harvester ants, showing all members of the colony.*

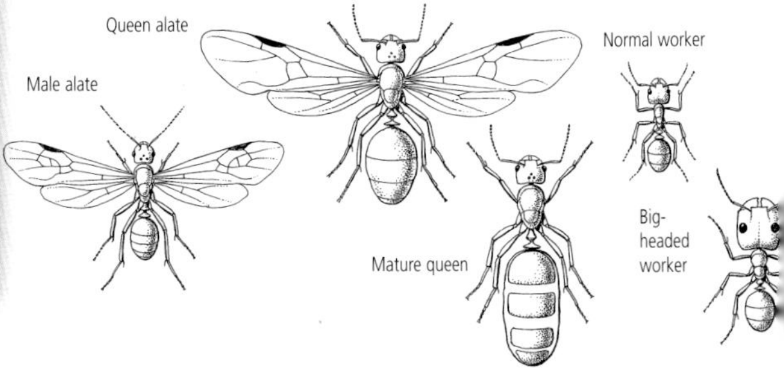

but devote their lives to the service of their mother, the queen. The queen's sole duty is to churn out an endless succession of eggs. In termite societies the workers consist of both males and females. Ant workers carry out all the daily tasks of housekeeping within the nest. They keep the nest interior tidy, help extend its tunnels, and may rush to build earth ramparts around the entrance if heavy rain is on the way. One of their main duties is the gathering of food and care of the young, which is undertaken with close attention to detail. If the weather is too hot, the workers will carry the developing brood down to lower, cooler regions of the nest. If it is too cold, they will set out the larvae and pupae near the surface to warm in the sun. There is scrupulous attention to hygiene, and the young are kept constantly groomed. If threatened by flood waters, the workers will make an emergency evacuation of the brood to a safer spot on higher ground or in the branches of a tree.

Note the antennae with their right-angled elbows and the typical narrow waist of the giant **Paraponera clavata** ***bullet ant from the rain forests of the American tropics.***

Caring for the Queen

It is also the job of the workers to groom and feed their queen, who never leaves the nest. In some species the workers produce sterile so-called trophic eggs, which act as an additional source of food for the larvae and the queen.

Trophic eggs are much smaller and softer than the eggs produced by the queen.

In most species the workers can adapt to carry out any given task both inside and outside the nest, but in some species the bodies of some workers are specially adapted into a tool for performing certain tasks. In *Pheidole* some workers have outsize heads on which extralarge jaws capable of crushing seeds can be comfortably mounted. In other ants large heads and jaws are fitted to so-called soldiers whose job is to defend the nest and its workers, although they may also help in other tasks as needed. In *Paracryptocerus* and *Zacryptocerus* turtle ants disk-headed workers hurry to the nest entrance (in a hollow twig or branch) whenever the alarm is raised and use their smooth, armored heads as plugs to deny access to intruders.

Workers of* Camponotus detritus *forage for food in the Namib Desert situated on the coast of southwest Africa. Gathering food is one of the main tasks for worker ants.

In a forest in Thailand a weaver ant worker* Oecophylla smaragdina *drinks a droplet of liquid from the jaws of a nestmate, a process known as trophallaxis.

Chemical Defense

Many species also use chemicals to defend themselves and their nests against attack. Some can sting; others spray an irritant chemical (usually formic acid) at an aggressor. The sting of some of the enormous bullet ants from South America is very painful and may be fatal even to humans. In smaller species the sheer number of stings from a massed attack can have a serious effect, and an onslaught by hordes of southern fire ants, *Solenopsis xyloni* from the United States, is believed to have been responsible for the death of a baby.

Defense of the nest is usually carried out with total disregard for individual safety and survival. That strategy is taken to its extreme conclusion in certain *Camponotus* workers from the United States. The workers are able to self-destruct in the face of an enemy, exploding with a force that disables an adversary beneath a shower of chemical debris.

Language of Touch

Ant workers use the language of touch to communicate with each other. When one ant worker meets another, one of them will often beg for food by using its antennae to stroke its nest mate's face and antennae. The donor will usually respond by serving up a droplet of liquid and holding it on its jaws so that the recipient can feed on it. Such mutual feeding is known as trophallaxis.

The touch code that leads up to it, along with the "nest-scent" code, has been "broken" by a number of beetles and other so-called ant guests that spend their lives as spongers in ants' nests. The liquid donated during trophallaxis is often honeydew, a sugary secretion that the ants harvest from aphids, treehoppers, and other bugs in the order Hemiptera. Ants also glean nectar from plants, partly from flowers and partly from so-called extrafloral nectaries situated on the stems or leaves.

↓ ***With a soldier termite held in its jaws, a*** **Pachycondyla commutata** ***worker hurries back to its nest. This South American ant preys exclusively on termites.***

Termite-Slaying Ants

Many ants are among the most omnivorous of all insects and will eat just about anything, whether of plant or animal origin. Yet some species are not only exclusively predaceous but will only attack a specific kind of prey. A number of them will only feed on termites. Termites are highly social insects with well-organized defensive capabilities involving specialized soldier castes. A successful raid against such formidable opposition needs to be mounted with care. In *Pheidole titanis* from the southwestern United States and Mexico raids are made against large parties of foraging *Nasutitermes* worker termites, which are guarded by a much smaller squad of soldiers. If the group of termites is not too large, the ants will try to encircle it and then rush in and attempt to overwhelm the soldiers by force of numbers before picking off the workers one at a time. In South America *Termitopone* scout ants wander randomly around on the rain-forest floor until one of them chances on a foraging party of *Syntermes* termites. The scout rushes back to the nest by the most direct route, laying down a "trail pheromone" along which it returns accompanied by a band of helpers. The group then launches a mass attack on the termites and returns to the nest in a column, each holding a termite in its jaws.

Some ants prey exclusively on other ants. An Australian species of *Cerapachys* that preys on *Pheidole* is so heavily armored that it can attack the adult workers without needing to bother about retaliation from its victim's powerful sting. Adult *Pheidole* are stung and killed, but larvae are only lightly anesthetized and remain in a torpid state for up to eight weeks, providing a long-lasting supply of fresh food for the conquering *Cerapachys*.

Predatory ants seize their prey in their jaws, which in some species are highly adapted for the purpose. In *Odontomachus* and other so-called "trap-jawed" ants the large, pincerlike jaws project prominently outward at either side of the ant's face. Between the open jaws there is usually one or two pairs of long, forward-pointing sensory hairs. When touched, these hairs trigger an instant snapping shut of the jaws, which in the larger species is accompanied by an audible click.

Swarms of Ants

Worker ants are both wingless and sexually inactive. One of their jobs is to rear more sisters like themselves to act as workers and maintain the life of the nest. At a specific time of the year, usually in late summer in cooler climates or at the start of the rains in the seasonally dry

Queen ants are fully winged, enabling them to leave the nest on a brief nuptial flight that ends in mating. This is the large queen of *Atta cephalotes*, a leaf-cutter ant from Costa Rica.

Some ants' nests are only small. This is the fully formed nest of a *Dolichoderus* species ant from Trinidad, affixed to the leaf of a bush in the rain forest.

tropics, the workers start to rear larvae that are destined to be future queens, as well as the first male larvae. They are larger than the workers, especially the queens, with a fully functioning sexual apparatus. They also have a complete set of wings. These sexually functioning ants are known as alates.

Maiden Flights

At the appropriate time the workers herd these future colonists together near the nest entrance. When conditions are right, usually when the weather is warm and calm or shortly before a rainstorm that will soften the ground, every nest over a huge area will suddenly begin shepherding its alates to the entrance and spurring them into the air. Millions may emerge simultaneously so that the air and ground are suddenly swarming with winged ants. A nest does not usually commit its entire stock of alates on the first release. Some are usually held in reserve for departure on subsequent days.

With such huge numbers involved, males and females have no problems finding one another and mate on the ground or in the air. The males then die off, their sole reason for life having been fulfilled.

For the female the prospect of becoming a future queen by founding her own nest is bleak—only a tiny proportion will be successful. Stored within her body is a supply of sperm derived from her single mating that is sufficient to fertilize all the eggs she is ever likely to produce. Her task now is to lay the groundwork for her future reproductive career, usually by digging a small initial nest either in the ground or in wood, depending on species. Before starting work, she sheds her wings, since their only function, to carry her on her nuptial flight, is now complete.

Varied Nests

Most ants' nests are in the ground, where many of the smaller species nest beneath stones or logs. Other species nest in dead wood or inside branches and twigs. *Camponotus* carpenter ants excavate extensive nesting galleries in dead wood, such as old tree stumps or dead standing trees. Unfortunately, they also use the old wood in houses, where they can become a pest, weakening the structure. They are not as destructive as termites, but may have to be

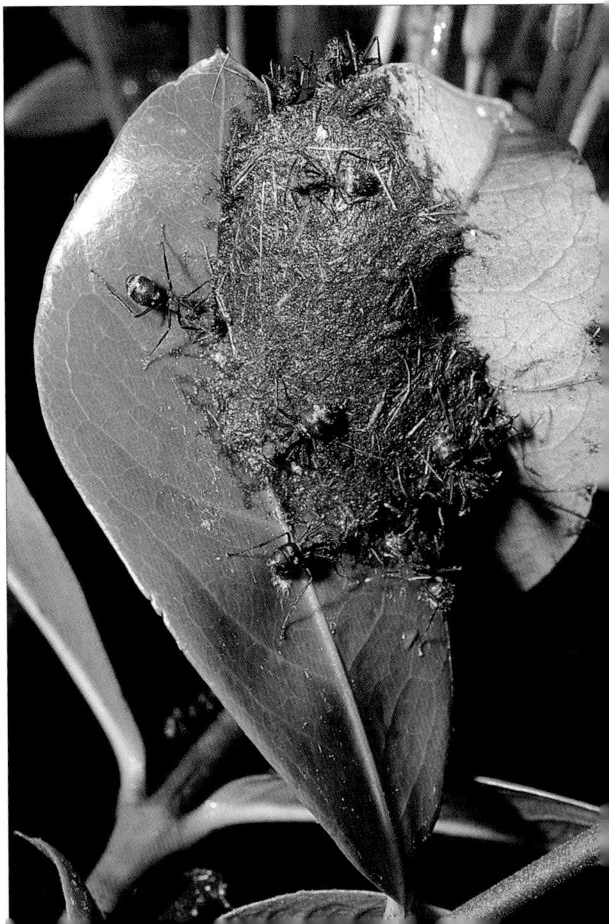

The large carton nests of Azteca ants are a conspicuous sight in many South American forests. This nest, about 2 feet (60 cm) long, is attached to a tree trunk.

controlled with chemicals. In the tropics many ants build packagelike carton nests attached to trees, using chewed-up wood mixed with bodily secretions. In Central and South America the carton nests of *Azteca* are a frequent sight on tree trunks and can reach a width of around 40 inches (100 cm) and a depth of more than 6 feet (2 m). Some tropical ants build nests of carton, earth, or detritus beneath leaves, which keep the rain off. Weaver ants build their nests from living leaves.

Founding a New Nest

Having established herself in a small breeding cell, the female lays her first eggs. She is usually alone, but in some species several queens club together to found a nest jointly. During that first stage the queen does not take any food. She feeds her brood on products derived from

Scent Trails

When away from the nest, ants navigate in a number of ways. Lone scouts, especially in desert-dwelling species, use the sun, which in more arid habitats is visible on most days. A scout that locates a good source of food navigates back to the nest by sight, where it recruits a single nest mate to accompany it back to the food source, a process known as "tandem running." When they return, they recruit two more, doubling up each time they return so that eventually quite large numbers may be trotting back and forth with food. In more sophisticated species the route between nest and food source will be precisely marked out with a trail pheromone. The pheromone can easily be followed by any number of workers, although in some species the actual numbers required can be defined by the strength of the pheromone laid down. The use of scent trails explains how hordes of ants crossing a road all follow the same narrow path even when they belong to species whose workers are blind. If a car crosses and disturbs the scent trail, the ants all mill around in confusion for a while until they relocate it.

Pheromones are also used by ants for communicating danger. These "alarm pheromones" are given off by the first ant to be disturbed, which causes its near neighbors to react likewise. That triggers a snowballing effect that very rapidly spreads the message to every ant in the vicinity. The pheromones differ not only from species to species but also within species, so that every ant belonging to a particular nest is "coded" with a scent specific to that nest. The ants' sensory apparatus is so finely tuned that they use the so-called nest scent to distinguish between members of their own nest and strangers from another one, which may even be attacked and killed simply because they do not belong. In ants there is no concept of acting for the good of the species—only for the good of the nest.

Scurrying back to their nest carrying their booty from a recent raid, worker Dorylus nigricans driver ants follow a trail pheromone that guides them across a track in Uganda.

One Good Turn

Special relationships have arisen between ants and plants whereby a certain type of plant provides the ants with food and a home. In return the ants constitute a private army always at the ready to defend their host from leaf-eating animals with total disregard for self-preservation.

In Central America it is the hollow, grossly swollen bases of the thorns of various acacias that provide the *Pseudomyrmex* foot soldiers with secure living quarters. The ants only need to forage a short way from home to find all the food they need, which is laid on specially for them by their leafy host. Energy to fuel the ant colony is provided in the form of nectar secreted from the leaves.

Protein for rearing the ant brood is provided in the form of special egg-shaped modifications to the leaf tips called Beltian bodies. The worker ants harvest them, chop them up, and feed them to the larvae. In return for such hospitality the ants descend in furious cohorts on any animals—humans included—that dare so much as brush lightly against their acacia home. Despite the small size of the individual ants, a combined assault by a large squad is so painful that most intruders instantly retreat. As a result of employing their private armies, swollen-thorn acacias usually manage to keep all their leaves intact, while other acacias around them are stripped bare.

In Africa the whistling-thorn acacia, *Acacia drepanolobium*, provides even more spacious accommodation in its enormous bulbous thorn bases. Protein is provided from small outgrowths on the anthers inside the flowers. Back in Central America, the tree *Ocotea pedalifolia* provides a home for its ant guardians but no food. However, it does make feeding sites for two species of *Dysmicoccus* mealy bugs (Pseudococcidae) that supply the ants with honeydew. There are dozens of such relationships between ants and plants. Some plants "bribe" ants into dispersing their seeds, whose coats are equipped with special edible appendages (elaiosomes). The ants carry off the seeds, strip away the elaiosome for food, and dump the seeds on their garbage heaps, where germination is likely to occur far away from the parent plant.

The grossly swollen thorns of various acacia trees provide secure waterproof lodgings for their ant guardians. The entry holes are clearly visible. These* Pseudomyrmex ferruginea *ants are from Costa Rica.

breaking down her now functionless and quite substantial flight muscles, along with other energy reserves stored within her body. Her first brood of larvae are small and puny compared with what will come later, but their efforts will pave the way for future prosperity. In most ants the fully grown larvae spin a cocoon of silk in which to pupate; but in some, such as weaver ants, the pupa is naked.

The newly emerged pioneers of the first brood break free of the cell and begin foraging, bringing back enough food to rear a second brood of larger workers. They begin supplying the queen with her first food since her mating flight. She can now dedicate the rest of her life to being a committed egg-laying machine, permanently released from her initial brood-care duties. From now on the rapidly increasing force of workers will carry out all necessary tasks in the growing nest.

Once the nest has reached a certain size, the queen starts producing two types of eggs. Diploid (fertilized) eggs will eventually develop into queens after being afforded special treatment, including a richer diet. Haploid (unfertilized) eggs will become males.

Going Back Home

Sometimes a queen will return to her old nest rather than make a new one by herself. Her parent nest may eventually end up containing several queens, all of which are fertile and turn out eggs. When conditions get too crowded, some of these resident queens may leave home, accompanied by a retinue of workers, to found a new nest. This therefore presents an alternative and perhaps more reliable way of getting a new nest started without the hazards of life as a "single mother" during the early stages. In some ants in the primitive subfamily Ponerinae there is no queen at all. In *Pachycondyla sublaevis* from Australia egg laying is undertaken by the most highly ranked of the workers within the nests, which are usually small, sometimes with fewer than 10 members. If the top-ranked egg layer dies or is removed, another worker can quickly be

The swarms of fully winged jet-black ants, **Lasius fuliginousus,** ***gathering at the entrance to their nest in a rotten stump, are queens ready for their maiden flight.***

"promoted" to take her place, since most of the workers within the colony are capable of laying productive eggs. In *Ophthalmophone berthoudi* from Africa up to 100 workers in each nest are inseminated and produce fertile eggs, although on a very slow and infrequent basis. They do not compete with one another or emerge above ground to forage.

Ant colonies are usually much longer lived than colonies of bees or wasps, especially in temperate regions where the latter die off during winter and have to start over again the following spring. Ant colonies survive the winter intact by going into hibernation, usually migrating deeper into the ground, after which the workers cluster closely around the brood throughout the coldest period.

Parasites and Slave Takers

As in most forms of life, the ants have their fair share of freeloaders who take things easy and profit from the industry of others. In the complex world of ants various versions of such a lifestyle exist, some more work shy than others. In one version there is a queen who does not attempt to establish her own nest but instead takes over the nest of a different species by killing the queen and taking her place. The queen's assassination is not necessarily accomplished in open combat or through the invader's superior fighting ability—in fact, the opposite may be true.

Off with Her Head!

Queens of *Bothriomyrmex decapitans* from North Africa gain entry to the nest of *Tapinoma nigerrimum* by allowing themselves to be treated like food and carried into the nest by the workers. Once safely within the nest, the invading queen sneaks up onto the back of the host queen and sets about the rather lengthy task of gnawing her head off. By the time this is done, the upstart queen has acquired enough of the vital nest odor to ensure her future acceptance, enabling her to foist her eggs on her adopted workforce. They dutifully rear the "cuckoo" eggs, producing large numbers of replacement workers belonging to the invading species. Eventually the new workers are left in sole charge of the nest, once the original workers have all died off.

In *Labauchena*, a tiny species from South America, several queens invade the nest of the *Solenopsis* host. The queens form an

Hooked on Honeydew

One of the most sought-after foods for many ants is a sugary liquid called honeydew. It is a waste product excreted mainly by various bugs, especially aphids and some kinds of hoppers such as treehoppers in the family Membracidae. Colonies of these bugs are tended by ants that "milk" them for their honeydew. In return, the ants will drive away many predators that threaten their precious food source. Some bugs become remarkably reliant on having a "police force" of ants on hand to deter undesirable intruders. Females of many treehoppers have a long-term commitment to their eggs and young. Yet *Entylia bactriana* stays for only a short time before handing over the job of guarding her family to the ants that have been hanging around from the start. The ants are so efficient at enforcing a "keep clear" zone around the mother and her family that she will desert her eggs if no ants are available.

In some species, such as the Texas shed-building ant, *Crematogaster lineolata*, the ants reduce the risk of losing their honeydew suppliers to enemies by constructing bowers around them made of chewed vegetable matter. They can then be milked under cover in relative safety. Some ants will pick up aphids and move them to plants nearer the nest, so that the honeydew supplies can be harvested more easily. *Dolichoderus cuspidatus* from Malaysia lives in temporary bivouacs that contain not only the adult ants, along with their eggs, larvae, and pupae, but also herds of their mealy bug "cattle," *Malaicoccus formicarii*. The ants cart the bugs off and pasture them on fresh sappy growth near the nest. When fresh growth near the bivouac has been exhausted, the ants break camp and move to a better area, carrying their domestic "cattle" along with them.

assassination squad and work together to bite the head off the vastly larger host queen, a process that can take several weeks.

In some species the eggs laid by the replacement queen and reared by the host workers all turn into winged males and females. They leave the nest to invade other nests, leading to the eventual decline and extinction of the host colony once all the original workers have perished. The premature collapse of the colony is sometimes avoided when the invading queen spares the life of the host queen, enabling two production lines of offspring to be run side by side. The continued output of workers by the original queen is sufficient to keep the nest running smoothly.

Slave Labor

In slave-making ants the queens found new nests as normal, producing workers that at first perform their regular domestic duties around the nest. Once the colony has reached a certain size, the workers change from placid home helps into warlike raiders that set off to plunder the nest of a different species of ant, robbing the colony of its pupae. They are carried back to the raiders' nest to hatch into a lifetime of slavery.

From now on the slaves carry out all the daily tasks of the nest, leaving the workers free to go out in search of fresh conquests. In some species the original workers simply become degenerate parasites with no useful role in the nest. In other species, such as *Anergates atratulus* from Europe, there is no worker caste—only slaves—and the queen produces only males or queens. She cannot even feed herself without the help of her slave workers and becomes hugely swollen with eggs, turning out as many offspring as possible before her slaves die off, and the colony becomes extinct.

In most slave-making ants the mandibles are slender and sickle shaped, adapted for raiding, not for the day-to-day chores within a nest. In *Strongylognathus huberi* the muscles for the formidable-looking jaws are too weak to be of much use, so most of the fighting on

Many ants have close relationships with lycaenid butterfly caterpillars. These green tree ants, **Oecophylla smaragdina** *from Australia, are defending a* **Narathura** *species larva.*

In temperate regions aphids are often closely attended by swarms of ants. These red ants, **Formica rufa** *in Europe, are "milking" aphids for their honeydew.*

slave-making forays is done by existing slaves, which accompany their "owners" on raids.

Leaf-cutting Ants

Trails of leaf-cutting ants winding their way across the rain-forest floor are a familiar sight in the tropical regions of the Americas, although a single species, the Texas leaf-cutter, *Atta texana*, reaches as far north as Texas and Louisiana. Leaf-cutting ants have become farmers, cultivating a fungus that is their sole source of food. It is only found inside their nests. In order to thrive, the fungus needs a suitable compost. The ants manufacture it by harvesting large quantities of plant material, often stripping huge forest trees of their leaves in the process.

By using its jaws to cut in a semicircle, each worker quite rapidly snips away a small section of leaf, although sometimes fruits or flower petals are used instead. The ant then hoists the leaf section up in its jaws and carries it back to the nest. Hundreds of thousands of ants may be simultaneously hurrying back to the nest with their little green "parasols," often forming processions over 12 inches (30 cm) wide and more than 100 yards (100 m) long. Both normal-sized workers and large-headed, pincer-jawed soldiers engage in cutting and carrying the leaves, some of which bear an additional cargo of tiny "minim" workers. Their task is to ride shotgun on the leaf fragments and deny their use to parasitic flies (Phoridae), which will try to use the leaf as a foothold in order to lay their eggs on the carrying ant's head capsule.

As the plant supplies pour into the nest in a continuous stream, the process of turning them into compost begins. Processing work is carried out by more minims that never leave the nest. First, they carefully cleanse and scrape the surface of each leaf, probably to remove the spores of undesirable fungi and bacteria. Each segment is then chewed up and anointed with saliva and feces to form a sticky pulp. It can now be added to the "garden" and "planted" with a few tufts of fungal material (mycelium). The warm, humid hothouse interior of the nest is ideal for fungal growth. Development is so rapid that swellings are soon produced that the

Holding their sections of leaf above their heads like parasols, a column of **Atta cephalotes** ***leaf-cutting ants heads back to the nest in a South American rain forest.***

ants cut off and feed to the larvae. It is vital that the fungus beds are not contaminated with other fungi or bacteria that could act as weeds and spoil the garden. Leaf-cutters are remarkably adept at maintaining their fungus cultures in a pure state, possibly because they constantly apply salivary secretions that may be active against bacteria and foreign fungi.

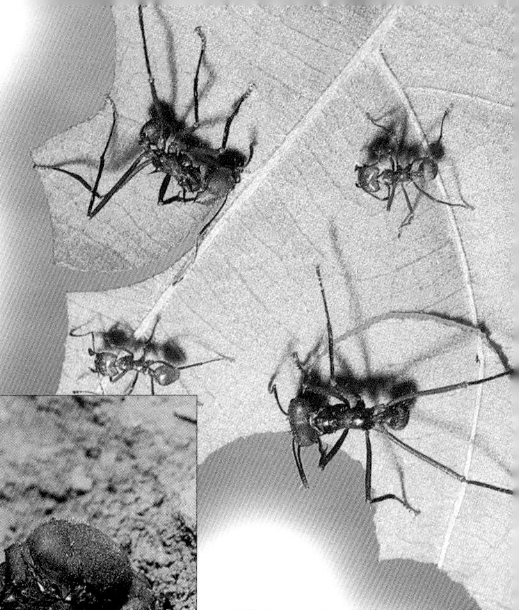

Working around in a semicircle, a quartet of Atta *species leaf-cutting ants quickly and efficiently snip away sections of a leaf in a rain forest in Trinidad.*

Cultivating a Garden

A queen leaving the nest on her nuptial flight will always carry with her, stored in a special pouch within her body, a fragment of the fungus mycelium to act as "seed corn" in her new nest. Having mated several times high in the air on her single nuptial flight, the queen lands and breaks off her wings. She pushes them back one at a time at right angles so that they snap at predetermined zones of weakness. She then starts to dig a new nest, scooping out the soil with her mandibles and bulldozing it up to the surface with her head. She next ejects the pellet of fungal material from her mouth and manures it with her own eggs and droplets of fecal material. Once the garden is starting to prosper, she will lay fertilized eggs and raise her first brood of workers. For the next four to five weeks she tends her miniature garden, neither feeding nor drinking, waiting for her first batch of workers to mature. If the garden fails now, she will die, since she cannot secure new supplies of fungus to make a fresh start.

Once she has shed her wings, the first task for this newly mated queen 2-lobed leaf-cutter ant, Atta bisphearica *in Brazil, is to start digging a new nest in the ground.*

Once the first workers emerge, they take on all the routine chores within the nest, cleaning their mother and tending to the garden. Once there are enough workers, some of them will start to forage for fresh leaves to develop the garden. After four to five years the colony will be as large as the mature one that the queen originally left. After a further three to four years it will probably decline and fade away after the death of its queen. However, some colonies have been known to last for at least 20 years. *Atta* nests in tropical rain forests can be extremely large, up to 50 yards (46 m) across and with dozens of entry tunnels. They

In the warm spring sun of the Arizona desert western harvester ants, Pogonomyrmex occidentalis, *plod along carrying seeds back to their nest in the desert floor.*

are easy to spot because the surface is usually an open, bare, well-worn expanse of earth. Few plants are present, since the ants diligently remove most of them. The fungus gardens are deep undergound. The whole nest may contain as many as 5 million ants.

Harvester and Honeypot Ants

Pogonomyrmex harvester ants are found widely in the United States and Mexico, especially in the arid lands of the Southwest. They harvest seeds and grains (and sometimes other insects) and are active during the heat of the day even in the hottest desert regions. Their mating swarms are unique among ants, since they use the same meeting place year after year. The rendezvous point can be a hilltop, the crowns of tall trees, or even a piece of flat desert with no obviously distinctive features. Despite that, each generation of males and females knows just where to head after leaving their nests.

The males normally arrive first, and every female that appears is quickly deluged with suitors, all competing to be first to mate with her. The male has large, clamplike mandibles designed to grasp the female firmly around her thorax. Even so, males sometimes get hauled off their mounts by pressure of numbers and may accidentally snip off the female's abdomen.

Honeypot ants are found in arid regions of Australia and North America. *Myrmecocystus* is the main genus, although ants of several other genera have "honeypot" habits. During times of plenty they collect large quantities of nectar from plants or honeydew from aphids and other bugs. They then store it in a special worker caste called repletes, which use their bodies as living casks. Each replete accepts food regurgitated by incoming workers until its abdomen becomes so swollen that even small movements are virtually impossible. The repletes must devote their entire lives (which may last several months or even years) to being store pots, hanging head-upward from the ceiling by their claws. When food runs low outside the nest, the workers begin tapping the supply stored in the repletes, which regurgitate droplets of food on request.

Weaver Ants

There are two species of weaver ants, *Oecophylla longinoda* from Africa and *O. smaragdina* from Asia and Australia. In Asia *O. smaragdina* is reddish-brown and is known locally as the red tree ant, while in Australasia the same species is green. Both species use the living leaves of trees and shrubs to form a pouchlike nest. Sometimes a single large leaf is folded over on itself to form a pouch; in other cases several leaves may be fastened together. Large nests made up of over 20 leaves can measure over 12 inches (30 cm).

During nest construction rows of workers position themselves neatly along the edge of one leaf and use their jaws like a row of staples to hold the edge of the opposing leaf in the correct position. Squads of workers hurry to their required places like well-trained artisans. Yet scientists have no idea how they know where to go or which leaves to hold, where to hold them, or even how they know that nest

Forming a highly disciplined team, these Oecophylla smaragdina *weaver ants in Thailand are holding together the edges of two leaves until they can be set in place with silk.*

building is about to start. Once in position, they will stick tight, often for many hours or even days, until the two edges of the leaves have been securely fastened together with silk. That is mainly accomplished from within the nest. Since adult ants cannot produce silk, larvae are used instead. In the last instar larva of weaver ants the silk glands are disproportionately well developed for the task of nest construction. Unlike in most ants, there is no silken cocoon for the pupae, which lie naked within the nest.

Sewing Kit

Holding a larva in her jaws like a tube of glue against the edges of the two leaves to be joined, the worker ant uses her antennae to drum on the larva's body. That is an instruction for the larva to start squirting out silk into the required spot. By weaving its head from side to side as the silk is emitted, the worker ensures that gaps of varying widths can be fully sealed.

Being fashioned from living leaves, the finished nest is very durable and will last for many months, although eventually the leaves begin to wither and die. Scout ants then establish a site for a new nest. Once it is completed, the entire contents of their old home—consisting of eggs, larvae, and pupae, plus the queen—are assembled on the outside of the old nest in preparation for a mass exodus to the new living quarters.

Weaver ants cannot sting, but will bite fiercely and hang on with their jaws when molested. Much of the weaver ants' food consists of dead insects scavenged from the forest floor. Living insects are also killed. They are gradually torn apart by a ring of ants pulling in opposite directions.

Army Ants

Ants with army-style habits are mostly found in the tropics. One of the main characteristics they all share in common is their nomadic lifestyle. Nests, if they are made at all, are only temporary. Many species merely establish short-lived bivouacs that are soon abandoned as the army breaks camp and moves on. Army ant colonies are also usually extremely large, containing many thousands or even millions of individuals, all generated by just a single queen. All species are predaceous.

By far the largest raids are mounted by the tropical American species *Eciton burchelli,* during which entire areas of forest may be picked clean of every speck of animal life, large or small, that cannot either escape or buy immunity to attack through using chemical defenses. Certain insects are so distasteful that they can be surrounded by thousands of ants and remain completely untouched. Yet being armed with a formidable sting, usually a reliable way of avoiding trouble, is of scant help against such massed onslaughts. Paper wasps that are avoided by most other creatures in the forest can only hover helplessly nearby and watch their nests being stripped bare of their entire stock of larvae and pupae. Like an audience at a disaster movie, the wasps are powerless to intervene and protect their property.

Stashing the Booty

The victorious ants carry much of their booty back to their living quarters in one piece, often employing several ants like pallbearers to carry larger items. Especially bulky prey is usually cut to pieces and transported in parts. It will join a continuous column of workers and soldiers moving back and forth between the nest site and the assault front, returning one way laden with plunder and hurrying back empty-handed in the other direction to rejoin the fray. In such a

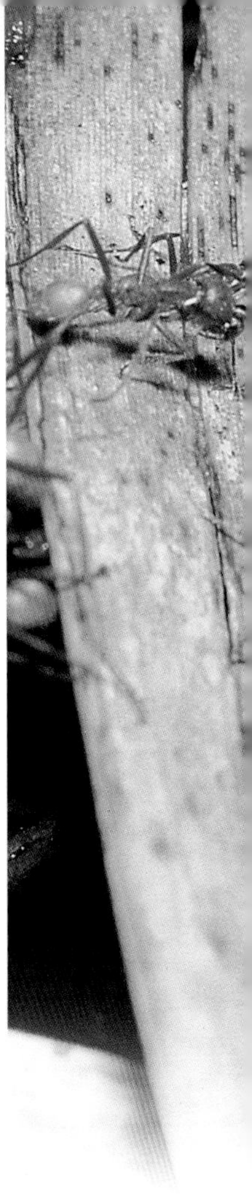

Working under cover of darkness, an **Oecophylla smaragdina** ***weaver ant in India seals up a gap in the nest using silk secreted from a larva held in her jaws.***

"bombardment" style of warfare speed to and from the battlefield is essential. To make travel as smooth as possible, any tiny gaps in the roadway are crossed using the bodies of living workers to form bridges. When the amount of loot coming onstream is too great to handle, it will go into temporary storage in protected caches along the trail until labor is available to shift it. When a new source of food is discovered, a fresh gang of attackers can be recruited from the marching columns in about one minute, the fastest-known recruitment time in any social insect.

The most notorious of these massed raiders are the *Dorylus* driver or legionary ants from Africa and the *Eciton* army ants from Central and South America. Both are credited with attacking large animals such as snakes, chickens, pigs, and monkeys when they are confined in cages and cannot escape. Although unable to sting, army ant soldiers have large heads and long, curved jaws, which can inflict a painful bite. Once their jaws have sunk into yielding flesh, the ants will often die rather than let go. They rush to the attack as soon as they sense a threat to the column of hurrying workers. They use vibrations as their cue rather than sight, since they, like the workers, are blind. The whole complex battle scenario is arranged using scent trails to mark out the routes, which are initially laid down by scouts.

For several weeks at a time the ants roam through the forest, spending each night in a different temporary bivouac. They then settle

Hurrying back to their temporary bivouac, a column of* Eciton burchelli *army ants in Trinidad crosses a living bridge made of interlocked workers clinging to one another.

With its large, curved sicklelike jaws bared in readiness for attack, an Eciton burchelli *soldier in Trinidad prepares to defend its nest mates. Like the workers, it is blind.*

down for about three weeks in a more permanent bivouac in which the queen can begin replacing the colony's losses. For the first week her body swells at an enormous rate as it fills with tens of thousands of eggs. Then over a period of a few days she suddenly slims down by disgorging her cargo of 300,000 or more eggs. They have developed into larvae by the time the colony breaks camp and resumes its nomadic lifestyle. The workers carry and feed the developing larvae and cluster around them each night in the temporary bivouac.

In the *Dorylus* driver ants from Africa the bivouacs are more stable than in *Eciton* and are established deep within the soil. In some areas chimpanzees "fish" for the ants by dipping a stick into the nest entrance. As soon as a few ants have leaped to the defense of their nest by running up the stick, the chimp lifts it out and uses its lips in a rapid swiping action to sweep the ants off into its mouth.

In the North American legionary ant, *Labidus coecus*, temporary nest sites are established under stones or in logs or tree stumps. Every two to three weeks the workers fashion tunnels made from leaf fragments leading from the nest to a new locality nearby. Using such a covered walkway, the colony is free to move either by day or night, taking their larvae with them.

Bullet Ants

The largest ants in the world all belong to the subfamily Ponerinae. Some of the largest Central and South American species are called bullet ants. A single sting from some species is said to be fatal in humans. The sting is extremely painful and accompanied by considerable swelling. The shiny coal-black *Paraponera clavata* is one of the biggest ants in the American tropics. The heavily built workers reach up to 0.8 in (20 mm) long. They are a common sight over a wide area from Nicaragua to the Amazon Basin roaming around in the rain-forest understory. They may sometimes kill their own insect prey, but most food is probably picked up already dead.

Bullet ants are loners, and each ant forages singly. If a rich source of food is discovered, there is no rush to communicate the fact to other workers, and the finder exploits its discovery alone. Nectar is also an important source of food, and the ants are often seen trekking back to the nest with nothing more than a shiny droplet of nectar held in the mandibles. If two workers from the same nest meet, they temporarily abandon their solitary habits and may engage in an exchange of food through trophallaxis. If two workers from different nests bump into one another, they will fight to the death.

Foaming and Stinging

In the rain forests of Malaysia two slightly smaller species of ponerines, *Pachycondyla tridentata* and *P. insularis*, employ an unusual method of self-defense. They can spray out foamy threads from the venom gland to a distance of up to 4 inches (10 cm). It is particularly effective against swarms of smaller ants, which are instantly swamped by the foam and take some time to exctricate themselves. As well as foaming, the ants can also defend themselves by inflicting a painful sting.

Bullet ants are solitary and tend to forage alone, as in this Paraponera clavata *from the American tropics, seeking nectar on a* Heliconia *flower.*

Honeybees and Relatives

Apidae

The diverse members of the Apidae are united by a single outstanding feature—the presence of "pollen baskets" on the hind legs. They are used to transport food and building materials to the nest.

Apis mellifera

Common name Honeybees, stingless bees, bumblebees, orchid bees

Family Apidae

Suborder Apocrita

Order Hymenoptera

Number of species About 1,000 (60 U.S.)

Size From about 0.08 in (2 mm) to about 1.1 in (2.7 cm)

Key features Small, hairless, mainly brown or black body (stingless bees); medium-sized, slim-waisted, brown body (honeybees); stout and densely hairy rusty brown or black body, often with red or yellow bands (bumblebees); brilliant metallic-blue or green body, sometimes hairy like bumblebees (orchid bees); tongue long; pollen baskets generally present on hind legs

Habits Most species common on flowers and are important pollinators of many crops; honeybee often domesticated in hives

Breeding Most species often highly social, living in large nests containing thousands of workers (nonbreeding females); social species eventually rear males and females who leave nest for mating purposes; mated queens then found new nest, usually in following spring after winter hibernation; some species are cuckoos in nests of others

Diet Adults feed mainly on nectar; in tropics orchid bees and stingless bees often feed on dung or urine-soaked ground; larvae eat pollen and nectar; larvae of some stingless bees eat carrion

Habitat In all terrestrial habitats from sea level to the limits of vegetation on high mountains; many species common in urban gardens

Distribution Worldwide in areas that are not too arid or permanently cold; honeybee introduced into the Americas, Australia, and New Zealand

The honeybee *Apis mellifera* is found worldwide thanks to commercial beekeeping. It plays an important role in plant reproduction, transferring pollen from plant to plant. Body length (of worker) 0.5 inches (13 mm).

It is difficult to believe that the tiny, naked-bodied stingless bees or brilliant metallic *Euglossa* orchid bees belong to the same family as the massive, stout-bodied, densely furry bumblebees. Even the familiar honeybee, *Apis mellifera*, seems to have little in common with any of them. The only shared feature—the "pollen baskets," or corbicula, on the back legs—consist of the smooth, slightly convex outer surface of the tibia fringed by a stockade of long, stiff hairs. The pollen basket is used to transport pollen, resin, or other materials to the nest. It has been lost in cuckoo species.

Most members of the Apidae are social, although the orchid bees are generally solitary. A few species of orchid bees and bumblebees are cuckoos in the nests of other bees. Unlike in other bees, female Apidae do not construct nest burrows but always nest inside existing cavities or build external nests.

Orchid Bees

The orchid bees are some of the most brilliantly colored of all bees. Many species of *Euglossa* are jewel-like green or blue, gleaming with a metallic splendor as they dart around in the tops of rain-forest trees. By contrast, *Eulaema* are more like bumblebees, with attractively banded furry bodies. Most species of orchid bees have long tongues, and all are restricted to tropical Central and South America.

Orchid bee females construct their nests underground or as free-standing structures in the open. They use mud or resin as building materials, sometimes blended with animal

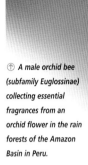

A male orchid bee (subfamily Euglossinae) collecting essential fragrances from an orchid flower in the rain forests of the Amazon Basin in Peru.

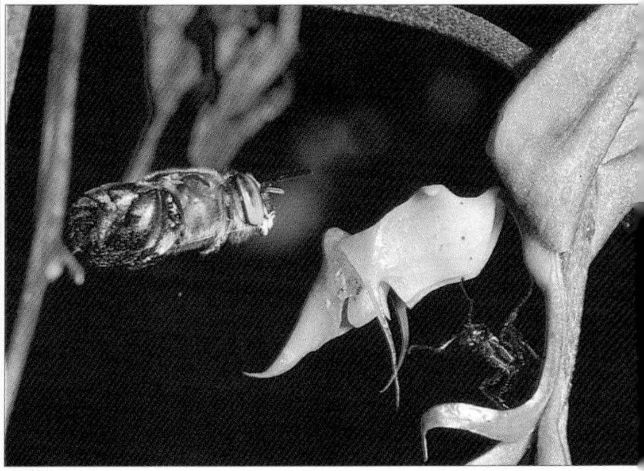

Euglossa orchid bees are brilliant metallic insects with a fast, darting kind of flight. This male in Costa Rica is about to land on an orchid flower.

dung or chips of wood. A number of species, especially in *Eulaema*, are communal or even bordering on the social, with several females building and stocking a single nest.

Male *Euglossa* have a relationship with certain species of orchids for which they may be the sole pollinators. The orchids do not offer either nectar or pollen as a reward, but instead provide the male bees with special perfumes contained in oily droplets on the flowers. The males brush the drops off with special pads on their front feet and pass them back to storage organs on the rear legs while in hovering flight. *Eulaema* males are not associated with orchids but collect aromatic substances from rotting logs. Despite many experiments and observations, scientists are still uncertain what the role of the perfumes could be. Males sit and "display" on trees around light gaps in the forest, and it is possible that the perfumes are used to mark the display sites.

Bumblebees

Bumblebees are among the most familiar and well loved of insects. Although they are armed with a stinger—which, unlike honeybees, they can use over and over again—they seldom resort to stinging. They are only likely to sting if provoked, for instance, when roughly handled.

Bumblebees belong to the single genus *Bombus*. They are spread throughout the world except in Australia and Africa south of the Sahara Desert. In New Zealand they have been introduced by humans. Bumblebees are more common in cool, temperate areas than in the warm tropics, where they mainly occur on mountains. However, they are also present in permanently warm, humid areas such as the Amazon Basin in Brazil.

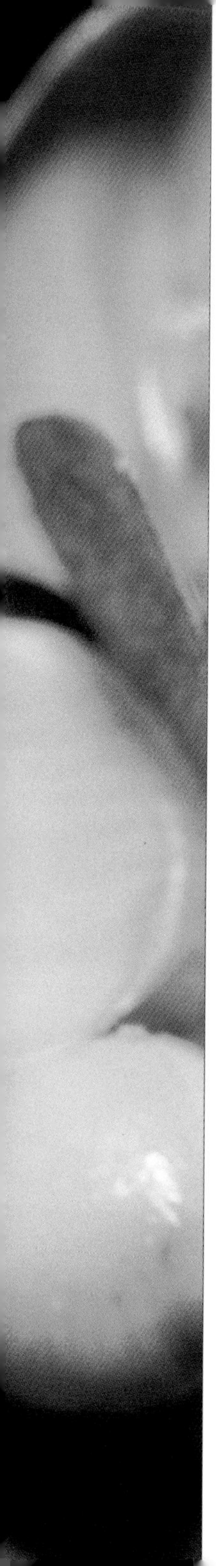

Bees and Flowers

Bees and flowers have a close relationship that is normally beneficial to both parties. The bees are rewarded with the pollen and nectar, without which they could not survive and reproduce; the flowers are rewarded by a pollination service that is both reliable and adaptable. Worldwide the value of crops pollinated by bees runs to more than $1.5 billion annually. Honeybees are the main providers of this vital activity, although with their short tongues they are unsuited to pollinating certain valuable crops such as red clover, *Trifolium pratense*. For this the longer tongues of bumblebees are needed.

We are familiar with the bright colors flowers use to attract insects such as bees. Unlike humans, bees can see into the ultraviolet end of the spectrum and can see colors and patterns on flowers that are invisible to the human eye. Yet bees cannot see red, which appears black to them. While visiting flowers, the dense clothing of branched or feathery hairs on the bodies of most pollen-collecting bees becomes dusted with pollen grains. The bee uses its front and middle pairs of legs to comb the pollen off its body and onto the pollen-storing apparatus, usually situated on the hind legs. Bumblebees often hang by their jaws while combing pollen, leaving all their legs free.

Many flowers are specialized for visits by bees. The powerful hinge on antirrhinum flowers can only be depressed by large, powerful insects such as bumblebees. They are therefore the only insects that can reach the pollen and nectar inside. However, the bees do not always play fair in their relationship with flowers. Short-tongued bumblebees often rob certain kinds of tubular flowers of their nectar by biting a hole at the base of the flower tube. Since the bee no longer enters by the legitimate route, it does not come into contact with the pollen-bearing anthers or the stigma. So while the bee gets the nectar, the flowers remain unpollinated.

Founding the Nest

In cool temperate regions a bumblebee nest gets underway in early spring. It is founded by a queen who mated the previous fall and spent the winter in hibernation under moss, in a crevice, beneath bark, or in some other protected site. With the first warm days of springtime the queen begins to spend most of the daylight hours on flowers. She sips nectar for energy and eats pollen to build up the bodily reserves she needs to produce her first batch of eggs. She also devotes a great deal of time to searching for a suitable nest site. In the

← ***The pollen baskets on the back legs of this buff-tailed bumblebee,* Bombus terrestris *from Europe, are well filled with pollen.***

↑ ***Following the spotted guidemarks, a common carder bumblebee,* Bombus pascuorum, *enters a foxglove (*Digitalis purpurea*) flower in England.***

many species that nest underground the queens fly along inspecting anything that resembles an old mouse hole or similar cavity. A number of species place the nest on the ground and cover it with a thatch of dry grass and moss.

First-Time Mother

The queen's first brood cell is made from wax secreted from glands in her own body and is stocked with a clump of up to a dozen eggs. The queen spends much of her time perched on top of the cell, keeping it warm and accelerating the development of her first brood. She also devotes some time to foraging for nectar, regurgitating the honey into a little storage pot that she builds of wax.

As the larvae grow, she builds a wax cell around each one. It will be removed to use elsewhere once the larvae have pupated and emerged as adults. The first workers are always tiny, sometimes too small even to leave the nest. However, they can help with domestic chores while the queen goes out foraging for food. She soon produces a further brood; and once the first batch of workers leaves the nest to take over the task of collecting food, she can stay and concentrate on laying eggs. The size of workers emerging from the brood cells gradually gets larger as they receive more generous food supplies as larvae. Nevertheless, they always remain smaller than the queen and are all females. They occasionally lay eggs, but these are quickly eaten by the queen, who reserves sole right to produce offspring.

The colony grows as the output of new workers exceeds the death of the old ones. The clumps of brood and storage cells are gradually extended in a haphazard arrangement typical of bumblebees. As well as storing nectar in wax pots, some species also store pollen in old, disused larval cells. In these species the food supply for each larva is regurgitated through a hole in the cell wall bitten by a worker, who seals it up afterward. In other species the workers place food as and when it is needed in a pouch that they construct to one side of the larval cell. Bumblebee nests never attain the size seen in honeybees and rarely contain more than 400 workers at any one time, with around 100 being the usual figure.

Having spent the winter months in hibernation, a queen early bumblebee, **Bombus pratorum** *from Europe, stokes up with nectar from a springtime wildflower.*

↑ ***The small garden bumblebee,* Bombus hortorum *from Europe, builds its nest in dense grass tussocks. Note the typically haphazard brood cells (occupied by larvae or pupae) and the storage cells containing honey.***

As the nest size increases in late summer, the queen is no longer able to eat all the eggs laid by the workers, and some of them develop into adults. They are all males, since the workers have never mated and so lay only haploid eggs. The queen goes on producing daughters, some of which will be treated to a special diet that will result in the emergence of new queens. Along with the males, they leave the nest to seek a mate. After mating, the males die, and the queens find a hibernation site, ready to start the process again in spring.

Sexual Roundabout

Sexual behavior in male bumblebees varies from species to species. In *Bombus nevadensis* from the United States the male has enlarged eyes. He uses them to constantly scan his territory, a conspicuous perch on an open mountain slope. He chases off rival males, sometimes engaging in aerial clashes that can injure the assailants. Females only rarely show up; but when they do, mating takes place on the wing.

In most species the males patrol a regular beat or circuit, stopping at distinct points to deposit a sweet scent from a gland in the mouthparts. The scents are specific for each species, which helps avoid confusion when several species are using the same circuit, as often happens. In such cases all the males move around the circuit in the same direction to avoid meeting. There is also a broad degree of height separation between species, and different species use the circuits at different times of the day. When virgin queens encounter the circuits, they investigate the scent-marked patches and mate with the first male to arrive.

Cuckoos in the Nest

Some species of bumblebees do not found their own nests but enter the nests of other species and act as cuckoos. Each species of cuckoo targets a specific host. For instance, in Europe *Bombus bohemicus* lays its eggs only in the nests of the common *B. lucorum*. Some cuckoo queens creep stealthily into the host nest and spend a day or two quietly absorbing its specific odor. This lulls the suspicions of the workers when the cuckoo finally emerges from cover and begins to lay eggs in cells that are about to be stocked with food. She does not kill the rightful queen, but eats her eggs whenever she comes across them, so that gradually more and more cuckoo males and females are produced.

The opposite tactic is used by certain other cuckoos. They rely on their powerful sting and thick skin to batter their way past any workers that get in the way, killing any that resist. The cuckoo's goal is to find and execute the rightful queen and take over the nest, leaving the

remaining workers no option but to rear male and female cuckoos until the nest finally expires through lack of a workforce. The cuckoo lifestyle is common in bees, being found in nearly one-fifth of all species.

Stingless Bees

The 300 or so species of stingless bees belonging to the subfamily Meliponinae are the smallest members of the Apidae. The smallest species is only 0.08 in (2 mm) long, and the largest only slightly exceeds the size of a honeybee. Most are black or reddish-brown, although some are yellow. All are restricted to the tropical zones, especially South America. The nests are organized on a highly social basis and last for many years unless destroyed by predators, of which there are many. However, unlike most nests made by tropical wasps, the nests of stingless bees are usually immune to mass invasion by that scourge of the rain forest, the army ants. That is because their nests are usually situated deep inside hollow trees or termite nests. However, some attach a free-standing nest to branches. The sole entrance is formed by a narrow projecting tube that is smeared with a sticky coating of resin. The resin traps most insects on contact. If that fails, the bees plaster any intruders with a gluelike secretion that quickly gums up their legs. The

↑ ***A battalion of*** **Plebeia** ***species stingless bee workers forms a defensive throng on the tubelike entrance to their nest sited deep within a hollow tree in Brazil.***

→ ***Several*** **Trigona fulviventris** ***stingless bees harvest sweet honeydew secreted by a cluster of adults and nymphs of the bug*** **Aethalion reticulatum** ***in Peru.***

nest itself is made of resin that is transported on the pollen baskets of the workers. Supplies are often harvested from resin oozing from the borings of beetle larvae in tree trunks. Back at the nest, the workers mix the resin with wax to form cerumen. The substance is used for making larval cells as well as slightly larger cells for storing pollen and honey. The nest's outer envelope consists of a durable substance called batumen, a blend of resin, wax, and other materials such as mud or animal droppings.

Some of the large species of stingless bees maintain an "exclusion zone" around the nest and attack anything that comes too close. In humans it is the head that is usually the focus of a massed attack by the enraged bees, which although unable to sting, have sharp jaws that can pierce human skin. Some species follow this up by dripping an irritant secretion from their head glands into the wound, causing burning blisters that have earned the insects the name of "firebees." Most people just run when under attack, but it can be difficult to tear the bees out of one's hair since they will die rather than let go with their jaws. Some colonies are well able to expend a few workers in defense of their nest. In *Trigona* the nest may contain as many as 180,000 individuals, although a few hundred is more common in many species.

Raising the Brood

Stingless bees are unusual among highly social bees in using mass provisioning for their larval cells, much as in most solitary bees (and wasps). In the nurse bees that are in charge of feeding the larvae, the head gland is greatly enlarged and can produce large amounts of a jellylike substance similar to the royal jelly of honeybees. Several workers gather around a completed cell. They squirt it full of food, attracting the attention of the queen. She eats some of the food, along with an egg that is always laid by a worker. It is in that way that the queen gets much of her food, although she also feeds directly from the workers' mouths. She responds to her meal by laying her own egg in the open cell. The workers then seal the cell, enclosing the egg with the food that the larva needs to complete its development.

Production of males and new queens in most stingless bees is similar to the process in honeybees, except in *Melipona*, in which queens, workers, and males are reared in cells of the same size. Whether or not a larva will turn into a queen or a worker is probably determined genetically. New nests in stingless bees are founded by workers using supplies of cerumen and honey from the old nest. Once the group of pioneer workers has built a few brood cells and honey pots, a young virgin queen, along with a few workers, will forsake the old nest for the new. When the new queen has mated with one of a number of males (they hail from other nests and hover expectantly around the entrance of the new nest), she goes back inside and never emerges again.

Honeybees

There are seven species of honeybees, all included in the single genus *Apis*. Six of them are restricted to Asia, including the largest species, the giant oriental honeybee, *Apis dorsata*. The most widespread species is the western honeybee, often called just the honeybee, *Apis mellifera*. It is one of the most familiar of all insects, although *Eristalis* hover flies are often mistaken for it. The honeybee has been domesticated in hives for thousands of years and, although native only to Africa, the Middle East, and Europe, has in more recent times been introduced to the Americas, Australia, and New Zealand to act as a pollinator of crops and to provide honey. The honey produced in their nests (and also in smaller quantities in stingless bee nests) has been valued by humans since time immemorial. In some parts of the world people will take amazing risks in order to rob the bees of their supplies of the prized commodity.

The Economy of the Honeybee Nest

Native sites for honeybee nests are inside hollow trees and rock clefts. The giant oriental honeybee nests in a single, large, exposed comb attached high above the ground on the limbs of forest trees. Most common honeybees now nest inside artificial hives provided by beekeepers. Within the nest clusters of cells are used both to rear larvae and store honey. They are hung back to back on either side of a central plate of wax to form a comb, which is suspended from the nest roof. Each cell is hexagonal, since it is the most economic shape to use in an enclosed space. The cells are built of wax secreted by glands in the adult bee's abdomen.

All the labor within the nest is carried out by the workers, of which the nest may contain as many as 80,000. The sole duty for the queen, who is bigger than the workers, is to lay eggs. She does so with machinelike regularity, producing as many as 2,000 per day. During her six weeks of life every worker is capable of carrying out all the various tasks within the nest. In practice, jobs are allocated according to age. While she is still young (during the first three weeks), glands in the worker's abdomen that secrete wax and those in her head that produce royal jelly (a special food given to the larvae) are functioning in top gear. She therefore remains in the nest as a house bee, using her wax to build cells and doling out supplies of royal jelly to the larvae. She also receives nectar from incoming foragers. She "ripens" it by holding it in her jaws and exposing it to the air. It thickens via evaporation and can now be placed in a storage cell. Here the ripening process—which eventually produces honey—will continue, aided by other house bees who fan their wings to accelerate the evaporation process. Another duty for the young house bee is to feed the larvae in their open-fronted cells. During its life each larva will receive some 140 meals, after which it spins its silken cocoon. That stimulates the house bees to perform yet another task—capping the pupal cell with wax. New cells will also be needed to extend the size of the comb, while old cells require cleaning out. Sometimes they will be used again for rearing larvae, but more often for storing honey or

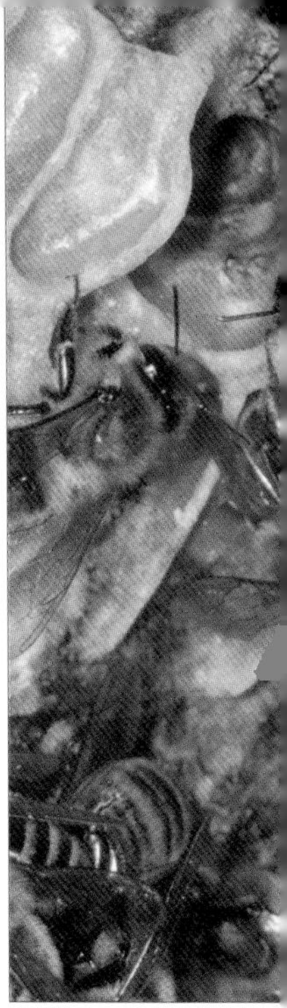

Worker honeybees throng on their comb, which, being built against a glass panel, reveals the larvae inside their wax cells.

A beekeeper, wearing protective clothing, checks the condition of the honeycomb in the hive. Most honeybees now nest in artificial hives provided by beekeepers.

A worker bee on a honeycomb—note the regular hexagonal shape of the open cells. All labor in the nest is carried out by workers.

supplies of pollen brought in by foragers. After about three weeks the house bee herself will become a forager, although in an emergency she is still capable of carrying out her duties in the nest.

Swarming in Honeybees

When a honeybee colony becomes too large, the queen starts to lose control over it. In the normal way she exerts her influence via a powerful pheromone, which is distributed among the workers. When the colony gets too

A still shot from the 1978 movie* The Swarm. *However, in reality killer bees do not roam around looking for victims to attack.

The Menace of "Killer Bees"

Killer bees are Africanized honeybees, *Apis mellifera scutellata*. They are a subspecies of honeybee that is the result of a crossbreeding experiment gone wrong.

In 1956 scientists in Brazil imported colonies of African honeybees with the intention of crossbreeding them with resident European honeybee populations to improve honey production. However, a number of queens—along with their workers—escaped. They have since spread northward, interbreeding with the local populations along the way, through South America into Mexico and the southern states of the United States. They first arrived in Texas in October 1990 and have since colonized New Mexico, Arizona, Nevada, and California.

The problem with Africanized honeybees is that they are far more aggressive than their European honeybee counterparts. Although their venom is no more potent than that of European honeybees, they are highly defensive and will attack perceived intruders much more readily and in far greater numbers. They react to disturbance much more quickly and will give chase over longer distances. Their alternative name of "killer bees" is deserved: Between 1988 and 1995 there were 175 reported fatalities from killer bee attacks in Mexico. The first reported death in the United States occurred in Harlingen, Texas, in July 1993. However, Africanized bees do not roam in swarms looking for victims to attack; the bees simply act in self-defense. Also, most serious attacks occur when the person is unable to get away quickly. Pets and livestock have most often been killed when they have been tied up and unable to escape.

The queen honeybee* (Apis mellifera) *is larger than the drones (males). The drones are themselves slightly larger than the workers, the queen's daughters.

big for every worker to receive its daily pheromone ration, the workers prepare to split up the colony by initiating a swarm.

The first move must be to rear a number of new queens, and some of the workers start building special outsize queen cells. When the first of the virgin queens emerges, she stings all her sister queens to death in their cells. She then leaves the nest in order to mate. Shortly after her return the old queen flies out of the nest along with a large swarm of workers, leaving the young queen in charge of her old home. The old queen and her retinue then start a new nest in a fresh site.

Royal Diet

Larvae destined to be queens are fed a pure diet of royal jelly, more appropriately known as bee milk, since it is also fed to the workers. Bee milk is a highly nutritious food, being a mixture of secretions produced by two glands in the head. Larvae committed to developing into workers receive a weak mixture for the first few days, then just the thinner of the two secretions mixed with pollen for the rest of their development. The queen larvae get only the richest milk. Males (called drones) are reared simultaneously in cells with wider mouths than normal. The queen perceives the shape of the cell and lays an unfertilized (haploid) egg.

Somewhere in the middle of this swarm of honeybee workers* (Apis mellifera) *is the queen. She will found a new colony if a suitable nesting site can be located.

The Bee Dance

Worker honeybees that are allocated the job of foraging for nectar and pollen on flowers do not just leave the nest each morning and see what they can find. Instead, they wait in the nest until scout bees return from an exploratory trip to find the best sources of food that day. The scouts can communicate the exact location of the food (usually a patch of flowers or a flowering tree) using a remarkable "dance." It is performed on the vertical face of the comb and is a reenactment in mime of the trip that the scout has just made.

In the common honeybee, *Apis mellifera*, the dance is performed in the dark interior of the nest. A number of workers closely surround the performer and monitor her every move with their antennae. It is in *A. mellifera* that the "language" of dance is most advanced and informative. The performer is able to communicate not just the route to the food source and its exact position but also how good it is.

If the food lies within 80 feet (25 m) of the nest, the scout performs the "round dance," running several times in a circle with many changes of direction. The higher the concentration of sugar in the food, the higher the number of switches in direction. If the food source lies more than 330 feet (100 m) away, the bee performs a "waggle dance." She runs in two semicircles to form a figure eight, waggling her abdomen as she runs down the straight line that links the two halves of the figure. Distance is defined by the duration of the straight run and the frequency of waggles. A bee may also perform a mixture of the two "dances" for food lying in between the two distances. The direction and angle of the bee's dance represent the position of the food source in relation to the sun. The performer knows what the angle of the sun is at any one time during her dance, even within the darkness of the nest. Her internal clock compensates for the movement of the sun that takes place during her performance, which can last 30 minutes or so—enough time for the sun to move considerably from the position she memorized when she entered the nest. Food quality is probably communicated by the intensity of waggles and buzzes.

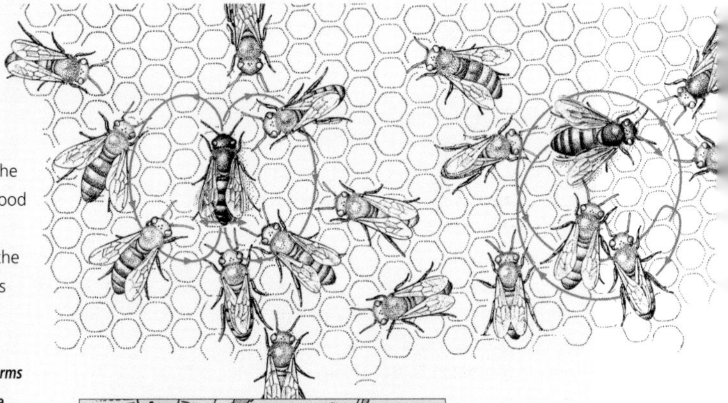

➚ The two general forms of honeybee dance: the "waggle dance" (left) and "round dance" (right).

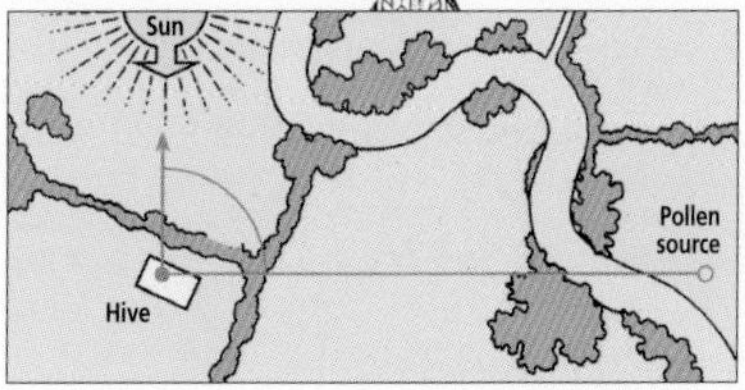

➔ The position of the food source as described in the waggle dance, viewed from the hive entrance.

Picture Credits

Front Cover: Photos.com

Ardea: Hans & Judy Beste 150-151, Jean-Paul Ferrero 147t, Ferrero-Labat 68-69, 91, 92-93, Kenneth W. Fink 134, Francois Grohier 54-55, 122-123, Nick Gordon 94-95, Clem Haggner 121, Chris Harvey 120-121, Ralf Keifner 340, Ken Lucas-Photo 369, 374-375, J.M. la Roque 98-99, Pat Morris 342, D & E Parer-Cook 56, 296, 298-299, Ron & Valerie Taylor 376, Adrian Warren 64, 142, 284l, 284b, 305, Chris Martin Bahr 261, Ferrero-Labat 267, Francoise Gohier 174, 202, 257, S. Roberts 232-233, William Stribling 245, John E. Swedberg 240, Donald & Molly Trounson 219, M. Watson 254-255; Auscape: Jeff Foott 271t; **Bruce Coleman Collection:** Franco Banfi391, Bruce Coleman Ltd. 222-223, Fred Bruemmer 154-155, 158, Jane Burton 130-131, Alain Compost 260, Janos Jurka 112-113, Wayne Lankinen 226, Luiz Claudio Marigo 124-125, Joe McDonald 205, 206-207, Bruce Montagne 184, Dr. Scott Nielsen 198, Jens Rydell 140-141, Kim Taylor 203, Rinie Van Meurs 168-169: **Chris Mattison:** 276-277, 283t, 297, 316, 324-325; Corbis: 31, James L. Amos 117, Yann Arthus-Bertrand 65, Anthony Bannister/Gallo Images 392-393, Bettmann 116, B. Borrell Casals/Frank Lane Picture Agency 444-445, Tom Brakefield 132-133, Brandon D. Cole 370-371, 376-377, Treat Davidson/Frank Lane Picture Agency 444r, Paul Edmondson 379, Michael & Patricia Fogden 436-437, Stephen Frink 368-369, 390, Gallo Images 148-149, Hulton Deutsch Collection 106, Amos Nachoum 374, 386-387, Lynda Richardson 444l, Jeffrey L. Rotman 384-385, Ted Streshinsky 291, Jim Zuckerman; **Dave Watts:** 152-153, FLPA: D. Maslowski 366-367, Minden Pictures 295b, 313, 314, Mark Newman 315, Silvestris 136-137; **Frank Lane Picture Agency:** T. Andrewartha 208-209, Ron Austing 197, F. Bavendam/Minden Pictures 372, Dembinsky 372-373, S. & D. & K. Maslowski 231, Minden Pictures 52053, 56-57, 106-107, Mark Newman 50-51, P.Perry 269, Fritz Polking 70t, Jurgen & Christine Sohns 173, Terry Whittaker 105, 258-259, Winifred Wisniewski 170; **ICCE Photolibrary:** C. & R. Aveling 66-67, Andy Purcell 114-115; J.W. Wilkinson: 142-143; **Nature Picture Library:** Doug Allan 161, T. Andrewartha 201, 228-229, 244, Ingo Arndt 98, 99, 100-101, 293, Miles Barton 70b, Peter Blackwell 118-119, John Cancalosi 320, Adrian Davies 178, Georgette Douwma 388-399, John Downer 81, 96-97, Richard Du Toit 77, Jeff Foott 76-77, 139, Jurgen Freund 307, 352-353, 358, 371, 380-381, 382-383, 387, Florian Graner 361, David Hall 377, Tony Heald 156-157, 295c, Martha Holmes 160-161, Paul Johnson 280-281, David Kjaer 209, 210, Avi Klapfer/Jeff Rotman 330-331, 332-333, Thomas D. Mangelsen 242-243, Barry Mansell 321t, Conrad Maufe 337b, George McCarthy 322b, Lawrence Michael 234-235, Stephen David Miller 323t, 323b, Vincent Munier 159, Pete Oxford 164-165, 309, Constantinos Petrinos 354-355, Michael Pitts 306, Jeff Rotman 337c, 338-339, 388t, 388b, Phil Savoie 262-263, 283, Peter Scoones 356-357, Anup Shah 72-73, Martin H. Smith 345, David Tipling 178-179, Tom Vezo 172, 186-187, 246-247, 248-249, 317, Doug Wechsler 288-289, Dave Welling 271b, 272, 274-275, 319, Doc White 58-59, 60, Solvin Zankl 311r; **NHPA:** G.I. Bernard 90b, Stephen Dalton 116-117, 212, 253, Daniel Heuclin 301, 302-303, 329-330, Robert Erwin 194-195, Martin Harvey 62-63, 190-191, Hellio & Van Ingen 193, E.A. Jones 78-79, T. kitchen & V. Hurst 104, Stephen J. Krasemann 204, Mike Lane 80-81, Trevor McDonald 335, Haroldo Palo Jr. 138-139, Rod Planck 250, Andy Rouse 266-267, Jany Sauvent 311t, 326-327, Kevin Schafer 18-19, 134-135, Jonathan Scott 14-15, John Shaw 87, B. & M. Shimlock Jones, Eric Soder 125, Mirko Stelzner 256, Ann & Steve Toon 265, Roy Waller 362-363, Dave Watts 152, 220, 221, Alan Williams 211, 181, Norbert Wu 52, 349, 378; **Oxford Scientific Films:** 88-89, 128-129, 129, 233, 273, 384t, Andrew Anderson/Survival Anglia 185, Kathie Atkinson 384b, Anthony Bannister/ABPL 28-29, Rafi Ben-Shahar 48-49, Niall Benvie 126-127, G.I. Bernard 85, David W. Breed 28b, Clive Bromhall 71, 359, Alan & Sandy Carey 22, 30-31, 37, 110-111, David Cayless 188-189, Martyn Colbeck 84-85, 86, Daniel J. Cox 20-21, 23, 32, 38-39, 74-75, 180-181, Kenneth Day192, Richard Day 196-197, Daybreak Imagery 227, 246, 251, Tui De Roy 60-61, 162-163, 175, John Downer 27, Carol Farneti Foster 285, Michael Fogden 82-83, 286-287, Nick Gordon 6-7, Jon A. Green/Animals Animals 41, Mark Hamblin 36, 113, Mike Hill 21, 26-27, Rodger Jackman 383, Mark Jones 168, Paul Kay 381, Breck P. Kent 289, Zig Leszczynski 290, Ted Levin/Animals Animals 241, David Macdonald 8-9, 10, 10-11, 11, 12-13, Marty Stouffer Productions/Animals Animals 34-35, Joe Macdonald/Animals Animals 34-35, Milkins Colin 346, Ben Osborne 166-167, 171, Richard Packwood 176-177, Purdy & Matthews/Survival Anglia 17, Norbert Rosing 42-43, Frank Schneidermeyer 16, 24-25, 237, A. & M. Shah/Animals Animals 28t, Claude Steelman/Survival Anglia 40, Keren Su 44-45, 46, 47, David Tipling 15, Tom Ulrich 102, 103, 225, Konrad Wothe 32-33, 163, Zebra Films Ltd./SAL 90t; **Photomax:** Max Gibbs 347, 351, 352, 360, 365, 367b; Premaphotos: Dr. Rod Preston-Mafham 403, 417, Jean Preston-Mafham 398-399, 409, 416-417, Ken Preston-Mafham 393, 394-395, 396, 397, 399, 400-401, 401, 402l, 402r, 404, 404-405, 406-407, 407, 408-409, 410, 410-411, 411, 412-413, 413, 414t, 414b, 415, 416, 419t, 419b, 420-421, 420, 421, 422t, 422b, 423t, 423b, 424-425, 425, 426-427, 428-429, 429t, 429c, 430-431, 430, 432-433, 432, 434, 435, 437, 438-439, 440-441, 440, 442-443, 446-447; **Jeff Rotman:** 341; Steve Parish Publishing: 147b; **Still Pictures:** Roland Seitre 124; The Kobal Collection: Warner Bros. 445; **Windrush Photos:** Arthur Morris 238-239